ENCOUNTERS

ESSAYS FOR EXPLORATION AND INQUIRY

SECOND EDITION

ENCOUNTERS

ESSAYS FOR EXPLORATION AND INQUIRY

PAT C. HOY II

New York University

ROBERT DIYANNI

Pace University

Boston   Burr Ridge, IL   Dubuque, IA   Madison, WI
New York   San Francisco   St. Louis
Bangkok   Bogotá   Caracas   Lisbon   London   Madrid   Mexico City
Milan   New Delhi   Seoul   Singapore   Sydney   Taipei   Toronto

McGraw-Hill Higher Education

A Division of The **McGraw-Hill** *Companies*

ENCOUNTERS: ESSAYS FOR EXPLORATION AND INQUIRY

 This book is printed on acid-free paper.

2 3 4 5 6 7 8 9 0 9 FGR/FGR 0 9 8 7 6 5 4 3 2 1 0

ISBN 0-07-229045-5

Editorial director: *Phillip A. Butcher*
Senior sponsoring editor: *Lisa Moore*
Developmental editor: *Laura Barthule*
Project manager: *Pat Frederickson*
Senior production supervisor: *Lori Koetters*
Coordinator freelance design: *Mary L. Christianson*
Freelance cover design: *The Visual*
Cover image: *Copyright © Keith Carter*
Photo research coordinator: *Sharon Miller*
Senior supplement coordinator: *Marc Mattson*
Compositor: *Precision Graphics*
Typeface: *10/12 Berkeley Book*
Printer: *Quebecor Printing Book Group/Fairfield*

Library of Congress Cataloging-in-Publication Data

Hoy, Pat C.
    Encounters: essays for exploration and inquiry / Pat C. Hoy II, Robert DiYanni.
      p. cm.
    Includes bibliographical references and index.
    ISBN 0-07-229045-5 (acid-free paper)
    1. College readers. 2. English language --Rhetoric--Problems, exercises, etc. 3. Report writing--Problems, exercise, etc.   I. Title.   II. DiYanni, Robert.

PE1417 .H69 2000
808'.0427 21--dc21   99-043521

http://www.mhhe.com

ABOUT THE AUTHORS

Pat C. Hoy II, director of the Expository Writing Program and Professor of English at New York University, has also held appointments as Professor of English, U.S. Military Academy, as senior preceptor in the Expository Writing Program, and as director of the Summer Writing Program, Harvard University. He received his B.A. from the U.S. Military Academy and his Ph.D. from the University of Pennsylvania.

Professor Hoy is the author of *Reading and Writing Essays: The Imaginative Tasks* (McGraw-Hill) and *Instinct for Survival: Essays by Pat C. Hoy II* (U. of Georgia Press). He is coeditor of *Prose Pieces: Essays and Stories* and *Women's Voices: Visions and Perspectives*. He is coauthor with Robert DiYanna of *The Scribner Handbook for Writers*.

His essays on pedagogy appear in *Literary Nonfiction: Theory, Criticism, Pedagogy* (Southern Illinois University Press), *How Writers Teach Writing* (Prentice-Hall), and *What Do I Know?: Reading, Writing, and Teaching the Essay* (Boynton). He has also published essays in *Sewanee Review, Virginia Quarterly Review, Agni, Twentieth Century Literature*, and *South Atlantic Review*. Five of his essays have been selected as "Notables" in *Best American Essays*.

Professor Hoy regularly teaches freshman composition.

Robert DiYanni is Professor of English at Pace University, Pleasantville, New York, where he teaches courses in literature, writing, and humanities. He also taught at Queens College of the City University of New York, at New York University in the Graduate Rhetoric Program, and most recently in the Expository Writing Program at Harvard University. He received his B.A. from Rutgers University (1968) and his Ph.D. from the City University of New York (1976).

Professor DiYanni has written articles and reviews on various aspects of literature, composition, and pedagogy. His books include *The McGraw-Hill Book of*

Poetry; Women's Voices; Reading Poetry; Like Season'd Timber: New Essays on George Herbert; and *Modern American Poets: Their Voices and Visions* (a text to accompany the Public Broadcasting Television series that aired in 1988). With Pat C. Hoy II he wrote *The Scribner Handbook for Writers,* and with Janetta Bauton, *Arts and Culture: An Introduction to the Humanities.*

TABLE OF CONTENTS WITH
LIST OF ARTWORKS

A SPECTRUM OF STUDENT WRITING

A SPECTRUM OF PROFESSIONAL WRITING

STUDENTS RESPOND TO THREE PROFESSIONAL WRITERS IN DEPTH

THINKING AND WRITING ABOUT PAINTINGS AND PHOTOGRAPHS

ANNOTATED TABLE
OF CONTENTS

What high-speed air travel has done to the idea of place, the Internet
is, in its way, doing to the idea of individuality and isolated selfhood. It
is injecting a new range of possibility into our conception of relation—
among other things.

Since Keith Carter is a notably modest man, it seems very much in
keeping with his personality that he does not force into his
photographs much acknowledgment of his presence. He doesn't stalk
his subjects, nor does he ask them to represent themselves as they'd
like to be seen . . . .His photographs give us the sense that he has either
stumbled upon a peculiar moment accidentally—a smiling dog!—or
has waited patiently for a defining image to emerge out of a life almost
the way the photographic image clarifies under the surface of the
developing solution, deepening as we watch for it.

A doctor may as well have gone house to house down Common,
Haverhill, and Jackson streets, so numerous were the cases. Often his
knock would go unanswered, since it wasn't the family who had
sought him out. More likely the sickness had been reported by their
landlord or neighbor—afraid that the influenza would spread—so the
doctor heard a sudden silence within and a face at the window disappearing into shadow.

The picture is a happy interpretation of family life but not a very
searching one, even for a pre-Freudian age. Families are more complicated than this. Family relationships produce frictions and irritations
as minor evils, agonizing psychological conflicts as major ones.

Having come from a house designed for a single family back in Puerto
Rico—my mother's extended-family home—it was curious to know
that strangers lived under our floor and above our heads, and that the
heater pipe went through everyone's apartments.

Any woman might be a man. The fact of it clanged through the chambers of my brain. In broad day, in the midst of traffic, with my parents

I'd smile. Shyly I'd smile, never betraying my sense of the irony: I was not proud of my mother and father. I was embarrassed by their lack of education. It was not that I ever thought they were stupid, though stupidly I took for granted their enormous native intelligence. Simply, what mattered to me was that they were not like my teachers.

For most of its brief life, San Francisco has entertained an idea of itself as heaven on earth, whether as Gold Town or City Beautiful or Treasure Island or Haight-Ashbury. San Francisco can support both comic and tragic conclusions because the city is geographically *in extremis*, a metaphor for the farthest-flung possibility, a metaphor for the end of the line. Land's end.

The secret of torture, like the secret of French cuisine, is that nothing is unthinkable. The human body is like a foodstuff, to be grilled, pounded, filleted. Every opening exists to be stuffed, all flesh to be carved off the bone.

In any discussion of homebirth, ideas of safety—"Aren't you afraid?"— usually come up. In New Mexico, the statistics of midwives and their homebirths are consistently better or similar to hospital births. Indeed, studies across the country and across the world confirm the reasonableness of having a baby at home. . . . Safety is a priority. It is not, necessarily, the heart of the matter.

Since we give labels to all that puzzles us, as we name every bland space on the map, I could say that what I stumbled into in Wayland were the mysteries of death, life, beasts, food, mind, sex, and God.

It is ten o'clock at night as we drive up to the Copacabana, a dilapidated brothel on the rue Dessalines in the red-light district of Port-au-Prince. My guide is a young Haitian, Jean-Bernard. Ten years before, J-B tells me, at the age of fourteen, "like every good Haitian boy" he had been brought here by his older cousins for his *rite de passage*.

THEMATIC TABLE
OF CONTENTS

Within the configurations described below, many essays are listed more than once. Such listing speaks of the richness of the essays themselves. They are not about just one issue, one topic. Placing essays in several categories allows us to see how they bear up under multiple readings, yielding insight and evoking new questions every time we look into them.

FAMILY AND COMMUNITY

These essays explore and examine issues related to family and community—life at home as well as life in the larger community beyond the hearth: the extended family, the hometown, the nation, the world. Inherent in these explorations are inquiries into parenting and the power of home, ethnicity and language, identity and growth, race and racism, disease and trauma, shelter and conflict within the state.

GENDER AND SEXUALITY

These essays, many of them listed under several configurations in this alternative table of contents, remind us how complex and interesting issues of gender and sexuality can be, how difficult they are to understand.

IDENTITY

Reading these essays, we begin to see that searches for identity—an individual's move toward independence and wholeness—almost always take the searchers back to their beginnings, no matter how long the journey, how arduous the pilgrimage. Perhaps identity must be viewed, always in relationship to gender and sexuality as well as family and community. These matters are not discrete.

WRITING AND LANGUAGE

Although these essays are about much more than writing and the use of language, they bring to our attention the very nature of composing—the act of using language to confirm ourselves, to construct a sense of what we think the world is like, to give voice to a writer's vision of how things are, or were, or could be.

RACE

These essays point toward diversity, tolerance, and complication, but they do not offer tidy solutions to the thorny issues associated with race and ethnicity. Instead they raise questions about the difficulty of resolution, the importance of sovereignty, and the wisdom of difference.

COURAGE

These essays suggests a variety of ways in which we might revalue the notion of courage—courage in the face of opposition, disease, the unknown, physical pain, torture, death, loss, and sport.

THE MYSTERIES

These essays dare to reach out toward what we cannot always see, cannot quantify precisely, cannot easily pin down. Yet what these writers reach out for—what's there just beyond seeing—they manage, somehow, to make palpable, momentarily accessible to us: truth, connectedness, things of the spirit, animal secrets, beauty, creation, imagination, time's complexity, tribal wisdom, aging, the nature of dying. We are reminded, indirectly, of the power of language to recover what has been lost, what, over time, we have learned to leave out of our rational investigations, and perhaps, out of our lives as well.

LOOKING AT PAINTINGS AND PHOTOGRAPHS

In these essays we get to see writers using art objects to help them develop their ideas, but we see as well how writers can become artists, creating art out of the ordinary, the commonplace—a race car, an island, a battlefield, a drawing in the earth, a wound to the eye, a death. We gain access to the writer's transfiguring imagination, get to see that imagination at work.

SCIENCE AND THE NATURAL WORLD

These essays explore aspects of science and nature, including human nature. They invite consideration of the relationship between civilization and the so-called natural world.

ASPECTS OF POPULAR CULTURE

These essays identify central figures, features, and events of postmodern American culture. These writers are preoccupied with relationships among aspects of contemporary culture and the shifting values that animate them.

RHETORICAL TABLE
OF CONTENTS

Within the configurations described below, many essays are listed more than once. Such listing speaks of the richness of the essays themselves. Placing essays in several categories allows us to see how they bear up under multiple readings, yielding insight and evoking new questions every time we look into them.

ESSAYS THAT ALTERNATE BETWEEN PRESENTING
EXPERIENCE AND EXPLORING AN IDEA

These essays introduce personal experience as the basis—or rather one of the bases—for exploring an idea or a series of related ideas. Some, like Dillard's "Living Like Weasels" and Gordon's "Mary Cassatt," develop an idea based on the story of the writer's experience. Others, like White's "The Ring of Time," work back and forth between description and exploration of an idea.

ESSAYS THAT SNEAK THE IDEA IN THROUGH
IMAGE OR METAPHOR

The essays in this group work largely by implication. The writers of these essays do not state their claims about an idea explicitly. Instead they work by suggestion, using details and images to convey their attitudes and perspectives. Some like Ehrlich's "Looking for a Lost Dog," talk about one thing (the symbolic meaning) in terms of another (the literal action described in the essay). Others like Kincaid's "On Seeing England for the First Time," let readers determine the author's implied point from the selection of detail.

ESSAYS THAT MOVE SYSTEMATICALLY
BETWEEN EVIDENCE AND IDEA, ARGUING

The essays in the following group typically present their ideas in a direct and straightforward manner. The writers of these essays state their claims and then support them with evidence. Some, like Bowman's "Gender Switching" and Son's "Men at the Mercy of Women," are analytical and thus use details of the texts analyzed as evidence to support the writer's interpretation. Others, like Cronon's "The Trouble with Wilderness" and Sontag's "AIDS and Its Metaphors," argue their cases by bringing logic and analysis to bear on ideas and evidence not contained in a single text or place.

ESSAYS THAT USE HUMOR AND IRONY

These essays use humor to engage their readers and to convey the writers' attitudes toward their subjects. Some, like Abbot's "The True Story of Why I Do What I Do," employ a humorous narrative voice that is fun to hear. Others, like Fussell's "Indy" use irony to create a satiric tone. Still others, such as White's "The Geese" and Hughes's "Salvation," blend humor with sadness.

ESSAYS THAT CELEBRATE

These essays celebrate their authors' subjects. The writers of these pieces convey a sense of excitement about their subjects, carrying readers along on a wave of energy and enthusiasm. They write from a desire to share perspectives and to convey their admiration or love, as Grice does about the black widow spider; Gordon, about the paintings of Mary Cassatt; and Neffinger, about his uncle, a master builder of houses of cards.

ESSAYS THAT LAMENT OR CONDEMN

These essays express dismay, anger, disgust, as well as other critical perspectives. Some, like West's "Race Matters," and Shilts's "Talking AIDS to Death," propose solutions for serious social problems. Others, including White's "The Geese" and Jordan's "Many Rivers to Cross," lament life's pain.

ESSAYS THAT DESCRIBE SCENES AND SITUATIONS

These essays contain sharply described scenes and clearly identified situations. The writers use the scenes and situations to establish what is important to them. Through carefully arranged, precise details, these writers bring their scenes and situations vividly before their readers, allowing descriptive detail and action to express attitude and convey meaning.

ESSAYS THAT SPECULATE ON THE UNKNOWN

These essays wonder and wander. The writers do not argue points or explain their ideas succinctly and clearly from the start. Instead, they choose to explore an idea's implications and ramifications. They invite readers to share their wondering and also their amazement at what they have discovered through their reading and their experience.

ESSAYS THAT PERSUADE, EXPLAIN, URGE

The following essays are passionate in their convictions. They aim to convince readers of something that the writers hold dear. Their tone sometimes becomes urgent and insistent, in keeping with the intensity of the writers' feelings. Some of the essays, like Brent Staples's "Just Walk On By," express indignation. Others, like Nancy Mairs's "On Being a Cripple," express dissatisfaction. Still others, like Richard Selzer's "A Mask on the Face of Death," express a kind of quiet desperation.

ESSAYS THAT ANALYZE SOCIAL AND CULTURAL ISSUES

This group of essays centers on issues of race, gender, class, and ethnicity. Toni Morrison and James Baldwin analyze what being black means in America today, while Nadine Gordimer analyzes the place of whites in South Africa. Other writers, including Gloria Anzaldúa and Richard Rodriguez, address issues of cultural difference for Hispanic and Latino/Latina Americans, analyzing, as well, issues of gender and sexual disposition. Still others in this group, including N. Scott Momaday and Leslie Marmon Silko, consider issues faced by Native Americans.

ESSAYS THAT MOVE ACROSS THE SPECTRUM

These essays use experiential evidence and evidence gleaned from a host of other sources, such as history, nature, art. They work toward a marriage of the exploratory and the argumentative, raising questions, analyzing, and offering provisional resolutions. They retain something of the conversational tone of the exploratory essay while veering toward an academic voice. In these essays the persuasive impulse emerges from the exploratory frame of mind.

PREFACE FOR THE INSTRUCTOR

If writing is thinking and discovery and selection and order and meaning, it is also awe and reverence and mystery and magic.

TONI MORRISON

Different kinds of essays affect readers in different ways. Some readers respond enthusiastically to informal, familiar essays that explore, searching as they go along for the elusive answer to a nagging question; other readers respond more readily to essays that get right to the main idea, arguing or defending in some reasonable way a point of view. The first kind of essay lets readers in on the writer's thinking, so they can participate in the exploration or inquiry; the second type concerns itself more with presenting the fruits of thinking, making a claim, and justifying it.

Good essays, however, are rarely so tidy, and they often defy easy classification. Truly satisfying essays often manage to do both these things at once—to give us a sense of writers' thinking even as they manage to make their claims, working in an exploratory way, while moving forward, methodically, to persuade us.

Looking into these various forms of the essay—the exploratory, the argumentative, the combined—seeing how they work, what they have to say, student writers can gain a clearer sense of what they might be able to do in their own essays. Reading and studying these essays, they can learn something about possibilities; they learn about writing as well as about the ideas in the essays.

We have selected the essays in this book with care and with the help of astute readers so that students can begin to glimpse new possibilities as writers, new opportunities in life. Opening up such possibilities is the overarching aim of this collection.

New to This Edition

We have based this new edition of *Encounters* on the same writing practices and pedagogical principles that informed the book's initial edition. Users of the first edition, however, will notice the following improvements:

- A new subtitle that better reflects the book's inclinations toward exploration and inquiry.
- A clearer explanation of the idea of the spectrum of essays from exploratory to argumentative.

- Inclusion of a greater number and percentage of essays on the argumentative end of the essay spectrum.
- More student essays—18 in all.
- A section on interpreting and writing about painting and photographs.
- A new section of black and white photographs included in the art insert at the back of the text.
- Additional rhetorical and thematic categories.
- A freshening of the anthology of professional essays (72 in all), including the following:

James Baldwin	"The Discovery of What It Means to Be An American"
Roland Barthes	"Toys"
Sven Birkerts	"The Idea of the Internet"
Rosellen Brown	"Mojo"
Jane Brox	"Influenza 1918"
John Canaday	"The Peale and Bellelli Families"
Bernard Cooper	"Burl's"
William Cronon	"The Trouble with Wilderness"
Joan Didion	"On Self-Respect"
Gerald Early	"Life with Daughters: Watching the Miss America Pageant"
Gretel Ehrlich	"Spring"
E. M. Forster	"Not Looking at Pictures"
Jaclyn Geller	"The Celebrity Bride as Cultural Icon"
Gordon Grice	"The Black Widow"
Bernd Heinrich	"Sex in Trees"
Pat C. Hoy II	"War Elegy"
Sue Hubbell	"Passionate Science"
George Orwell	"Shooting an Elephant"
Lewis Thomas	"The Lives of a Cell"
Richard Rodriguez	"Late Victorians"
Margaret Talbot	"Les Très Riches Heures de Martha Stewart"
Jeanette Winterson	"The Semiotics of Sex"

- The addition of a third essayist, Richard Selzer, to the two other multiply-represented writers, Maxine Hong Kingston and E. B. White.

Tables of Contents

We have arranged the essays alphabetically by author so that we do not limit the way students can see them. The essays sit there in the collection and in the first table of contents, waiting for the sampling; in the annotated table of contents, each listing is accompanied by an inviting quotation that points toward the essay's richness. The thematic table of contents suggests ways to group the essays according to many of our culture's most compelling preoccupations: family and community; identity; writing and language; race; courage; the mysteries; and art. Moreover, for each of the thematic configurations, we have provided a brief explanation that highlights social and thematic implications. These thematic headings, however, are suggestive rather than definitive. Within the collection, there are many more ways to group the essays.

We have provided still another way of looking at these essays. The rhetorical table of contents suggests *how* the essays make meaning, rather than *what* they might mean. That table points toward writerly concerns rather than cultural or personal ones. Our rhetorical categories are not entirely traditional; they seek to move beyond established boundaries, suggesting unique ways for students to think about the way writers write. The categories highlight techniques and call attention to the various ways writers create meaning.

Headnotes and Questions

We have kept the author headnotes brief so as not to distract readers from the essays themselves and to avoid preempting students' responses to them. Our suggestions for thinking, connecting, and writing that follow each essay point across the collection and outside it to related ideas, corresponding essays, complementary poems, and interesting writing techniques. These suggestions help students discover things to write about; they provide clues about how to write, how to develop their ideas. Taken together, the suggestions reflect our strong sense of the many ways that reading, thinking, and writing intertwine to enrich our classrooms and our lives.

The Spectrum of Student Writing

Perhaps the most compelling aspect of this collection is the spectrum of student writing that complements the spectrum of essays by the professionals. The student essays point the way for other students, giving them a chance to see just how some of these essays were developed, what the writing leading up to the final essays looked like. The student essays, like the ones written by professionals, represent the spectrum of essays we mentioned at the outset.

At one end of the spectrum are exploratory essays based largely on writers' lived experiences; at the other end are essays more traditionally academic, argumentative. Essays of the first type, exemplified by Michael Cohen's "You Can Shave the Beast, but Will the Fur Grow Back?," China Forbes's "Naked," and Gian Neffinger's "House of Cards," charm as they amble from story to story, their implicit complexity masked by narrative seduction and a playful intimacy. Beneath the surface of these experience-based essays, and in and around the stories included within them, the writers explore in ways that point to the more assertive mode of the analytical and argumentative essay. But they persuade in a more casual, some might say more hospitable, way.

The more argumentative essays usually make a more explicit claim to complexity, but they are intellectually playful as well. Anna Norris's argument about "reading" photographs, and David Reich's argument about Amy Tan's "Mother Tongue," exemplify this more analytical and objective mode. The idea in each of these essays emerges quickly, and the essays are efficiently organized. Yet you will find in both the twists and turns of the essayist's mind playing over rich material, entertaining doubt, making concessions while also making a point.

All the student essays, wherever they fall on the spectrum, have much in common—a basic three-part structure (beginning, middle, and ending), an interest in ideas, a concern for clarity, an inherent coherence. But each is different in its own right, in the way it moves from the beginning through the middle to the end, in the particular writer's way of thinking about a chosen subject, in the many ways each writer tells stories or amasses evidence gleaned from reading, in the way each causes us to see ourselves or the world in which we live. The collection of student essays overall invites us to see their obvious differences while encouraging us to search for their more intriguing similarities: the rigor, complexity, and subtle analysis that underlie the more apparent surface differences.

Instead of focusing primarily on the ends of the spectrum, we have included some student essays that combine the best features of the exploratory and the argumentative—the ambling, personal nature of the one with the more distanced, analytical rigor of the other. Mid-spectrum student essays that accomplish this combining feat in compelling ways are Kristen E. Hughes's "I Will Be My Own Hero," which begins with the writer's encounter with Picasso's *Guernica* and leads to an exploration of an idea about heroism and gender; Elizabeth MacDonald's "Odalisque," which combines her interest in beauty and suffering with her interest in paintings by Ingres and de Chirico; and Han N. Pham's essay "Down the Unwritten Path," which focuses on cultural continuities and discontinuities and draws on the experience of her Vietnam-born parents and grandparents while reflecting on the evidence gleaned from her reading of Frances Fitzgerald's *Fire in the Lake*.

To some extent, all the student essays, even those we have identified as closer to one end of the spectrum than the other, resist easy classification. They do not want to be pigeonholed. These three student pieces—"I Will Be My Own Hero," "Odalisque," "Down the Unwritten Path"—along with the two essays explored in detail in the student introduction, provide elegant yet varied examples of how student writers can effectively negotiate the spectrum.

Two Student Writers at Work

For the two student essays in the introduction, we have provided a detailed explanation of how they came to be written. We give the assignments that led to the essays and show you how the students responded to those assignments—their preliminary exercises and their initial drafts. For Maile Meloy's "The Voice of the Looking-Glass," we supply the two brief exercises that she developed into the first full draft of her essay. We present her preliminary writing clean, without a reader's comments; we then show the first draft with the instructor's marginal comments and intertextual annotations. Following this draft, we include a portion (about half) of Maile's second draft, along with comments about changes and additions she made. Then we print the final version of her essay without annotations or comments to allow students to see for themselves what additional revisions Maile made. This snapshot of her work allows students to see as well how Maile's reading and thinking, along with instructor conferences and collaboration with classmates, helped her revise and develop her essay.

In addition to Maile Meloy's exploratory essay, which weaves in analysis and interpretation of texts as she pursues an idea, we have provided a second student essay, Robynn Stacy Maines's analysis of Gretel Ehrlich's "Looking for a Lost Dog." For Robynn's essay, too, we present exercises and drafts as well as her finished piece. As with Maile's essay, we give students the assignments that led Robynn to her essay. For her exercises and drafts, we have included student responses to her work in progress, their questions and comments, along with her instructor's annotations. For Robynn's second draft, which we present in excerpt, we include her own editing and revising without further annotations and comments.

We have presented these two different types of student essays in detail, with the assignments and excerpted drafts, to show students how to build up a strong and fully developed piece of writing that evolves over time from a number of smaller pieces. We show the writing process in all its messy complexity and recursiveness. We want students to see that regardless of the type of essay being written, they can build toward strong essays over time when they rethink what they are doing and attend to others' comments about their writing.

Spectrum of Professional Writing

The student essays develop out of a broad spectrum of professional writing in the rest of the collection. The professional essays also touch both ends of the exploratory-argumentative spectrum, but most of them rest comfortably in between. A highly personal piece such as Zora Neale Hurston's "How It Feels to Be Colored Me" is complemented by Cornel West's "Race Matters," a more rigorously analytical piece. While some essays situate themselves at the ends of the spectrum (Scott Russell Sanders's "Wayland" and Lee K. Abbott's "The True Story of Why I Do What I Do," for example, on the personal side and Jaclyn Geller's "The Celebrity Bride as Cultural Icon" and Susan Sontag's "AIDS and Its Metaphors" on the argumentative side), the vast majority of essays in the book move across the middle of the spectrum.

An essay such as Barry Lopez's "The Stone Horse," for example, yokes Lopez's love of animals with his fascination about historical, archeological detail. Arthur Danto's "Gettysburg" combines Danto's firsthand knowledge of the historic battlefield with his propensity to cross the boundary lines of traditional academic disciplines (in this case, art and philosophy and military history). Both writers give us pleasurable insight into just how malleable the form of the essay can be. Neither essay loses any of its academic force or credibility as a result of the writers' deep personal attachments to their subjects.

Indeed, these essays are more persuasive and, we can guess, more rigorous, because of Lopez's and Danto's personal attachments. Reading the essays, we have the distinct feeling that we are reading about important subjects that have to do with their lives and with the lives we ourselves are trying to live. Lopez is deeply curious about animals and has spent long periods of time in the wilderness studying them. His published study of wolves—*Of Wolves and Men*—is as thorough as the work of the most detached scientist, but his concern about the wolf is anything but detached. He nudges us always in the direction of mystery rather than the direction of certainty, and when, in his essay, he brings us upon the stone horse, it is to cause us, finally, to contemplate the horse's heritage, and ours.

Danto peers into the history of warfare, but he looks at history through the particular details of the Gettysburg battlefield, especially the statue of an infantry soldier—his uniform, his weapon, his vulnerability at a moment in history when technology was drastically changing the nature and consequence of organized fighting. Danto's interest in art and his background as a philosopher enable him to see there on that battlefield what others could not see—about the soldier, about the battlefield itself, about war, about us. Lopez and Danto take us close to their subjects, but their investigations are rigorous and, at the same time, personal, sometimes moving; these essayists seem to be inviting us, personally, into conversations regarding the broader implications of their ideas about destruction and preservation.

Three Writers in Depth Accompanied by Student Essays About the Writers' Work

In addition to supplying a range of professional writing for students to read, study, learn from, and work with, we have included three writers whose work is represented with multiple selections. We reprint three selections by Maxine Hong Kingston, E. B. White, and Richard Selzer, and we include extensive headnotes that provide biographical information while offering rhetorical perspectives on their work.

Along with the multiple selections by Kingston, White, and Selzer, we have included student essays based on those writers' works. Kingston's brief "On Discovery" is complemented by three student essays that analyze and interpret it. Two of the essays are by women, one young and of Asian descent, the other an older student of European descent. The third piece was written by a third-year male, who was pursuing a degree in engineering. You will not be surprised that the three essayists read Kingston's piece in very different ways.

The student writing based on the work of E. B. White does something different. Instead of analyzing a single essay by White, Christian D'Andrea, in "The Human Atlas: Locating E. B. White," refers to half a dozen of White's essays as he attempts to define the mind of the writer as reflected in the essays. Although not a formal research essay, D'Andrea's piece includes parenthetical citations for each of his references to White's essays.

Radhika A. Jones's research essay on White represents the more familiar and traditional type of researched piece. Like D'Andrea's essay on White, Jones's contains an idea, a thesis she presents early and develops throughout her argument. Unlike D'Andrea's essay, Jones's looks beyond White's essays, and includes references to his letters and his famous children's books, especially *Charlotte's Web*. As a research essay, it also includes references to secondary sources, a list of works cited, and parenthetical in-text citations, which follow MLA formatting guidelines.

We have included two student essays on Selzer: one an analysis of the sexual imagery in a single essay—"The Knife"—the other a more far-reaching investigation of the qualities and ideas that animate a number of Selzer's essays. Students can see from these examples how to write two very different kinds of argumentative essays, each of which requires extensive analysis, a thorough understanding of the form and characteristics of essays, and a deep interest in their subjects. Each, based on imaginative reading of Selzer's work, encourages intellectual risk taking.

Selzer's own essays in this collection inspire such risk taking. Each shows Selzer crafting his experiences as a surgeon to evoke ethical and philosophical issues.

Artwork

Because we have seen how well students respond to visual stimuli, especially to art, we have included ten reproductions of paintings in *Encounters: Essays for*

Exploration and Inquiry. These works are not merely decorative. Nor are they included simply as stimuli for writing exercises and assignments. Rather, each painting is closely linked with one or more professional or student essays. Although the table of contents identifies each of these links, it does not indicate how the essayists associate the art with their ideas.

In her essay, "Odalisque," Elizabeth MacDonald discusses paintings by de Chirico and Ingres and comments along the way on a photograph of Rita Hayworth (not reprinted). Kristen E. Hughes takes inspiration from Picasso's *Guernica,* in "I Will Be My Own Hero." Felix Trutat's *Reclining Bacchante,* though not specifically mentioned by John Berger in "Ways of Seeing: Men Looking at Women," is powerfully exemplified by his argument and by the student essay that cites Berger—Maile Meloy's "The Voice of the Looking-Glass." Joan Didion refers to Georgia O'Keeffe's paintings, and Mary Gordon refers equally favorably to the work of Mary Cassatt. China Forbes alludes to Matisses's *Odalisque in Red Trousers* in her essay "Naked," while art critic John Canaday analyzes family portraits by Charles Wilson Peale and Edgar Degas.

Finally, Lisa Fifield's *Running Elk* can be linked with issues of gender and culture in the essays by Leslie Marmon Silko, Loren Eiseley, and Barry Lopez—among others—but these links must be made in the reader's imagination; they are not suggested or worked out in the essays. Image and imagination working together create the links.

The fact that visual images stimulate students' imaginations is apparent not only in the student essays reprinted in *Encounters: Essays for Exploration and Inquiry* but also in the many ways other visual texts, especially personal and family photographs, stimulate thought and evoke feeling—in the reader and in the classroom. Two other outstanding examples of what happens when students confront these images and begin to make use of them in their writing can be found in Maile Meloy's "The Voice of the Looking-Glass" and Han N. Pham's "Down the Unwritten Path."

To help students learn to make better use of visual imagery in their own essays, we have included a detailed introduction to the artwork section that discusses how to interpret and make use of paintings and photographs.

Instructor's Manual

Additional advice about using *Encounters* in your writing classes appears in the *Instructor's Manual* that accompanies *Encounters.* The first portion of the manual includes advice about teaching writing, relates reading and writing, works with visual texts, and develops course syllabi in conjunction with a college handbook. The second part deals solely with the essays from the anthology and includes for each essay a summary, a section on style, ideas for in-class activities, ideas for essays, and Internet links pertaining to the essay.

Acknowledgments

We would like to thank the following reviewers of both the first and second editions of *Encounters* for their helpful comments and suggestions: Victoria Boynton, *SUNY College at Cortland*; Jonathon Barron, *University of Southern Mississippi*;

David Breeden, *Schreiner College*; Hilda Carey, *Boston College*; Dan Cross, *Belleville Area College*; Ruth Davidson, *Penn State University*; Mary Ruth Donnelly, *Belleville Area College*; Patrice Fleck, *University of Kentucky*; Eric Gardner, *Saginaw Valley State University*; Donald Hammar, *Ricks College*; Anita Plath Helle, *Oregon State University*; Elizabeth Hodges, *Virginia Commonwealth University*; Robert Lorenzi, *Camden County College*; Kathy McClelland, *Auburn University*; Rochelle Nameroff, *California State University, Hayward*; Robert Noreen, *California State University, Northridge*; Scott Orme, *Spokane Community College*; Donnalee Rubin, *Salem State University*; Nancy Schneider, *University of Maine*; Jody Swilky, *Drake University*; Peter Valenti, *Fayetteville State University*; Anne Zanzucci,*University of Rochester*.

We are especially indebted to Dan Cross and Kathy McClelland for their collaborative work on the Instructor's Manual and for their enthusiastic support of our revisions.

We also want to offer our heartfelt thanks to our out-of-town production/ publishing team—Pat Frederickson (project manager), Sharon Miller, (photos), Sue Brekka (permissions), Mary Christianson (designer), Marc Mattson (supplements)— for their splendid work and good cheer while working against the most demanding constraints. In New York, their fine work was buttressed, from the outset, by the encouragement, conceptual guidance, and meticulous management provided by Lisa Moore (Sponsoring Editor) and Laura Barthule (Development Editor, English/Composition). We could not have created this book without them.

As always, we thank our wives—Ann Hoy and Mary DiYanni— for the kind of loving support that only steadfast partners can provide. It is a mystery beyond understanding.

Final Note

We believe that the student and professional essays in *Encounters: Essays for Exploration and Inquiry* will give you and your students a basis for exciting writing courses. We have suggested some ways for using these essays, but we are less concerned with proposing a particular methodology than with emphasizing the richness of the essays in this collection. The essays can tell you much that you need to know about developing classes suited to your own visions and to your students' needs. Implicit in this collection, of course, is our own sense of what we think of as good writing.

We welcome your questions and comments about our selections and about our suggestions for teaching. We can be reached through McGraw-Hill or through our respective institutions. Please call or e-mail us.

Pat C. Hoy II   ph3@is2.nyu.edu
Robert DiYanni   rdiyanni@pace.edu

INTRODUCTION FOR THE STUDENT

Indeed much of the attraction of writing is that it opens life.

SAM PICKERING

The book cover for this collection of essays invites you to begin thinking about yourself and your writing in new, reflective ways. Sitting wherever you are, looking out onto a part of the world—your room, the scene outside your window, the open space around the park bench—sitting there in that very space, you can also look into your self. Within such a convoluted context, looking out and looking in, writers write; they begin the intriguing, and sometimes frustrating, process of rubbing themselves up against the world, trying to make sense simultaneously of their lives (or themselves) and the world around them. From that vantage point, where you can look out and look within, you can find the beginnings for your writing.

But, of course, there is more; you are not alone. Besides yourself and the scene outside your window, besides your experience and whatever else you eventually come to learn about that world outside, there is also the work of other writers, other thinkers—others who have come before you and have begun to make sense of experience. Those others have left for you the work they have already done.

Once upon a time, those other writers were starting just where you are—at the beginning, at that place where you look within and look without, learning to make sense of what you see. A critical part of that process of turning experience and insight into words involves looking and then looking again, and then thinking about what you have seen.

Read an essay once, look at a painting once, and it may not seem to say much to you; it may not stir your imagination. But take the time to look again, and you may very well find something that did not seem to be there at first glance. We come to know whatever we know piecemeal, by accumulation, by reflection. Rarely does clarity come to us all at once. Looking, relooking, noting the differences and reflecting about them—that is what it takes. Inevitably, if you include *writing* in that process—looking, jotting down notes and impressions, waiting a day if you can, looking again, noting differences, writing out your thoughts—you will almost certainly discover that your writing enabled you to see better, yielded something you could not have predicted. Writing has discovery in it.

The essays in this collection, written both by students and by professional writers, invite you to make discoveries as you read them, write about them, and reflect upon them. At the beginning of the book, we give you examples of student writing that is grounded in some of the essays, photographs, and paintings in this

1

collection. These student essays are there so that you can see how others have responded to the essays and paintings from this collection. The student essays are there, too, to give you insight into how essays actually evolve. In some cases, you will observe the entire process followed by the student writers as they respond to assignments, develop draft essays, collaborate with other writers (classmates and teachers), and revise their work. Looking at the ways these other student writers work, you can begin to discover ways of working that are suited to your individual needs as a reader and as a writer. There is not one right way; there are many ways. This book should help you discover your own ways of reading and writing.

Let us imagine that you are picking up this book for the first time, that you have not been introduced to it by your teacher or by others who have looked into it. No one else has given you a map for your reading. If you look at the first table of contents, you will note that the book has four parts: (1) A Spectrum of Student Writing, (2) A Spectrum of Professional Writing, (3) Students Respond to Three Professional Writers in Depth, and (4) Paintings and Photographs for Thinking and Writing. Although this table of contents may seem forbidding to you because, for the most part, you see nothing but a long list of authors, titles, paintings, and photographs, it permits you to see at a glance how the book is organized and what is in it. The other tables of contents will help you see the collection in other ways.

The second table, an annotated table of contents, offers teasing invitations into the essays themselves—brief quotations, hints about what awaits you. The third table, a thematic table of contents, does some *connecting* work for you, highlighting and configuring a number of topics: family and community; gender, and sexuality; writing and language; race; courage; the mysteries; science and the natural world; and aspects of popular culture. Although there are, of course, many other ways for you to group the essays in the collection, these initial configurations give you a sense of how various essays might be related to one another. The fourth table, a rhetorical table of contents, highlights writing techniques. Instead of suggesting *what* the essays mean, it suggests *how* the essays mean. This table groups essays according to some of the ways writers create meaning.

Mark your place in this introduction, and turn to the annotated table of contents (p. xiii), the one with the inviting quotations. Begin to read, skipping around as you see fit, until you land on an idea or an essay that grabs your attention. Turn to that essay, start reading, and stay with the essay until the writer causes you to lose interest. Then turn back again to the annotated table of contents and repeat the process two or three times, sampling other essays in the collection. During that recursive process, take the time, at least once, to look at the reproductions of art. When you have finished your sampling, prepare for reflection.

Open your reading journal (any notebook that you will be able to use again and again to record your thoughts), and list the essays that you sampled. Write down the authors' names and the titles. Ask yourself these questions, and jot down notes about each of them: What do the essays I sampled have in common? Why did I choose those essays so readily? What do my selections say about my personal interests? What ideas interested me in those essays? What caused me to stop reading and turn back to the table of contents? What, if anything, did the art reproductions have to do with the essays I sampled?

As you sampled the essays, questioned them, wrote about them, and reflected upon what you had done, you were, at the same time, inadvertently configuring a group of essays; you were grouping them according to something that interested you, something that may have been hidden from you at the outset. Now, try that process one more time as you look back at the essays you sampled before. Repeat the reading and reflecting, but slow down a bit. Then reflect, in writing, about what happened during your reexamination: What did you learn? Did your own writing reveal anything to you?

The reading, writing, and reflecting that you have just completed previews and encapsulates a process that you will repeat over and over during your college years. What may seem strange and unfamiliar about it now will more than likely become second nature. This process is fundamental to learning, and it resembles a more formal research process. You begin with an inclination or a hunch and set out to investigate it by reading, questioning what you read, taking notes, reflecting, doing more reading and more reflecting until you have an idea worth writing about. Getting the idea occupies you at first, and then you turn to evaluating the idea and building up, through reading and writing, your confidence in that idea. That investigative and evaluative process leads finally to your research essay, in which you present and justify your findings. But without the initial curiosity, without the preliminary reading and questioning, without the reflecting, there will more than likely be no idea, nothing to write about. Reading, writing, and reflecting carry you along.

STUDENT WRITERS AT WORK:
Drafting and Revising Essays

Let us look now at the work of two students as they move through the reading, writing, and reflecting process in writing essays. We'll catch glimpses of them doing a lot of preliminary work on the way to completing their essays, work that involves reading, questioning, writing, and reflecting. In the beginning, these students are set in motion by writing exercises given them by their instructors, but there comes a point in the process where they are on their own to make sense of what they're learning. We cannot show you what it looked like inside their heads as they sorted things out, but we can help you see how these students got to a place where they began to have something to say and were learning how to say it effectively.

What these students are doing, you can do as well. Observing how they did much of their preliminary work should help you do yours. But, remember, these examples are not prescriptive. No two students will ever work in exactly the same way. You will have to figure out what works best for you. These examples simply suggest possibilities and allow you to look in on other students doing their work.

Let us look first at the work of Maile Meloy, who was learning to make use of her own experience. In her freshman writing course, she and the other students had already learned to tell stories about their experiences and to make use of the stories in *exploratory* essays, such as those written by Michael Cohen, China Forbes, and Gian Neffinger (pp. 39–48). These informal essays explore ideas; they are written so that you as a reader actually have the pleasure of observing the writers as they think about their ideas, developing them as they go along in their essays. Writers of exploratory essays are always looking for elusive answers to nagging questions. Exploratory essays are grounded in the familiar, everyday world in which we all live. These essays depend on stories of experience, but they need not confine themselves exclusively to such stories. On many occasions, exploratory essayists make use of paintings, other essays, movies—anything that helps the writers develop their ideas.

Maile Meloy's instructor wanted students to start thinking about art as well as about their own experiences. To help students get started, the instructor asked them to respond to two different writing exercises. For the first, they were asked to describe a picture or photograph that meant something to them. They were asked both to describe the picture and to explain its importance, all in about 200 to 400 words. Students in the class chose many different kinds of pictures. Some selected masterpieces hanging in prominent museums. Others chose posters from their bedrooms at home or from their college dorm rooms. Still others selected pictures from newspaper and magazine advertisements. Maile, along with several other classmates, chose to write about a photograph.

> I have a photograph of myself at graduation, with my hair down and fuchsia and plumeria leis piled around my neck. I am laughing, with my mouth open, head tilted, and eyes cast to the side, at something the photographer has said. It is not posed; I am caught in a spontaneous, joyful moment by the gaze of the camera. I have looked at that picture a lot. It is the way I want to be seen in everyday, spontaneous moments, when soft studio lights are not at my rescue and I am vulnerable. I am pleased with the image.
>
> When asked for the photograph, my instinctive response was, "But it's the only copy I have," which I blurted out before I realized how narcissistic I sounded. We are not to let on that we monitor ourselves so closely. We are to be head-tossing and laughing-eyed without being conscious of our beauty. Loveliness is to ooze naively from our pores. Why would I need pictures of myself? Because I like them. They are interesting to me. I like to see myself in relation to other people, see myself how other people see me. I study photographs of myself intently, critically--always appraising, always analyzing, carefully recording the information I see there.
>
> I take other opportunities to survey and record—most women do. I have mastered a swift glance over my right shoulder at mirrors and windows as I walk by, careful not to linger and let voyeurs hidden behind reflective glass see my interest in my own image. The left profile is less reassuring, and with scarcely a conscious thought I place people to my right, when it can be subtly maneuvered, so that their view is optimal. This self-observation is not vanity. It is a play for approval, and a request to be treated well, with respect and admiration.

For the second exercise, students were asked to tell a story or to present a situation that had some *connection* with what they had written about in the first exercise—their picture and its importance. Maile chose to write about her mother and her thoughts about appearance, particularly the appearance of women. Notice how Maile's thoughts about appearance conflict to some extent with her mother's. Notice, too, how Maile linked her second exercise with her first.

My mother despises our appearance-oriented environment and lives in fear that I have bought into it. She has sometimes lamented that I was not born unattractive; she is afraid I will have everything given to me, that I'll never know what it is to really earn rewards. She too has bought into the system, however, and perhaps it is that which she laments. Five foot two, beautiful and blonde, a southern-Californian ex-Homecoming Queen, she has been handed a lot on that tarnished silver platter of prettiness. And while carefully maintaining that prettiness, she has despised it. My petite mother always wanted to be tall, dark-haired and magnificent so that people would take her seriously. Unable to transform her appearance, she instead majored in microbiology, which she hated, in an attempt to earn the respect that she craved.

She has since abandoned microbiology and her model-loveliness is beginning to abandon her. It makes me nervous. Old slides of her from college and early marriage are stunning but disconcerting, serving as my own personal *memento mori*. They are my reminder of the death and disappearance of youth and of what is culturally defined as desirable. I wish I could look forward to such changes, to rejoice in the richness that replaces outward worth. But I shudder with the vanity of youth and dread the wrinkles and sagging flesh of age.

Because of my dread of becoming what she is, and what other older women are, I expect intimidation and jealousy. And because I watch other women to compare them to myself and judge myself accordingly, I experience intimidation and jealousy.

Maile's two exercises were read in class by members of her work group. They were also read and commented on by the instructor. Her readers asked Maile questions about her experience and her thinking. Her instructor encouraged her to think about something she had read that had some bearing on the stories she was telling; her instructor also encouraged other students to tell Maile about what they knew or had read that might shed some light on the complicated questions raised by her stories, questions about appearance and image.

They wanted to know, for example, what her central idea might be. They asked Maile whether she was interested primarily in the ways an attractive personal appearance had detrimental as well as beneficial consequences for a woman. They also wondered whether Maile, in her exercises, seemed overly concerned about her own looks, and suggested that she might think about how women in general respond to the perceived need to be attractive, especially to men.

Maile's draft follows, along with annotations and interlinear comments by her instructor. Notice how Maile used a pair of epigraphs (brief quotations at the beginning of her draft) that she gleaned from her reading. (You can read the Berger piece on pp. 114–115.) Notice, too, how Maile introduced brief quotations from other writers into the text of her essay, without letting the voices of those other writers take over her draft. She maintained control, using their words and thoughts to stimulate and clarify her own thinking. Maile used those quotations to clarify her ideas for her readers as well.

Maile Meloy
Paper #3
Expos 17, DiYanni
4/11/99

The girl was ugly. I was bored during the
whole journey.

Casanova
History of My Life

A woman must continually watch herself.
She is almost continually accompanied
by her own image of herself. Men look
at women. Women watch themselves
being looked at.

John Berger
Ways of Seeing

Reverse the order of your epigraphs?

From the moment I became conscious of cause and
effect I have been conscious of the importance of
my own appearance. Little girls (and little boys)
learn quickly that the way women are treated

quickly? early? both?

This second sentence is not quite right. Try alternatives?

depends on?

is relative to the way they appear. [Because, as John Berger says in his book, *Ways of Seeing*, "how she appears to others, and ultimately how she appears to men, is of crucial importance for what is normally thought of as the success of her life," *It* is a woman's ever-present task to monitor her image, not to survey a situation to determine the appropriate action a man does, but to survey herself and define the way she wishes others to act toward her.]

Move this Berger "Because..." part to the end of the paragraph?

Consider making this bracketed part a sentence in itself.

I have a photograph of myself at graduation, with my hair down and fuchsia and plumeria leis piled around my neck. I am laughing, with my mouth open, head tilted, and eyes cast to the side, at something the photographer has said. It is not posed; I am caught in a spontaneous, joyful moment by the gaze of the camera. ¶ I have looked at that picture a lot. It is the way I want to be seen in everyday, spontaneous moments, when soft studio lights are not at my rescue and I am vulnerable. I am pleased with the image.

New paragraph needed here?

No new paragraph here.

And/ I am

When asked for the photograph, my instinctive response *is,* was, "But it's the only copy I have," which I blurted out before I realized how narcissistic I sounded. We are not to let on that we monitor ourselves so closely. We are to be head-tossing and laughing-eyed without being conscious of our beauty. ~~Loveliness is to ooze naively from our pores.~~ ¶ Why *do* I would I need pictures of myself? Because I like them. They are interesting to me. I like to see myself in relation to other people *to* see myself as other people see me. I study photographs of myself intently, critically---always appraising, always analyzing, carefully recording *what* ~~the information~~ I see there.

regarding? evaluating? assessing?

I take other opportunities to survey and
record. Most women do. I have mastered a swift
glance over my right shoulder at mirrors and windows as I walk by, careful not to linger and let
voyeurs [hidden behind reflective glass] see my
interest in my own image. The left profile is
less reassuring, and with scarcely a conscious
thought I place people to my right. ~~when it can be
subtly maneuvered, so that their view is optimal.~~
¶ This self-regard ~~It~~ is not vanity. ~~this self-observation.~~ It is a
play for approval, and a request to be treated
well, with respect and admiration. It says, "I
don't want to bore you during the entire
journey."

Do you need this bracketed material?

Clarify

My mother despises the appearance-oriented
environment in which women live, and she fears that I
have bought into it. She has sometimes lamented
that I was not born unattractive; she is afraid I
will have everything given to me, that I'll never
know what it is to really earn rewards. She too has
bought into the system, however, and perhaps it is
that which she laments. Five foot two, beautiful
and blonde, a southern-Californian ex-Homecoming
Queen, she has been handed a lot on the tarnished
silver platter of prettiness. And while carefully
maintaining that prettiness, she has despised it.
She has always wanted to be tall, dark-haired and
magnificent so that people would take her
seriously. [(It is interesting to note that her
friend Diane, who is tall, dark-haired, and
magnificent, has wanted since her first bas mitzvah
to be short, cute, and blonde.)] My mother, trapped ~~trapped~~
in her surfer-girl image and unable to transform
her appearance, instead majored in microbiology,
which she hated, in an attempt to earn the respect
~~that~~ she craved.

Delete sentence in bracket?

She has since abandoned microbiology and her
model-loveliness is beginning to abandon her. It
makes me nervous. Old slides of her from college
and early marriage ~~are~~ gorgeous ~~but~~ disconcerting, *[show how she was. But these images are]*
serving as a reminder of the death and *[to remind us? one? me?]*
disappearance of youth and of what is culturally
defined as desirable. I wish I could look forward
to such changes, to rejoice in the inner richness
that replaces outward worth, but I shudder with the
vanity of youth and dread the wrinkles and sagging
flesh of age.

Because of my dread of becoming what she is,
and what other older women are, I expect intimidation and jealousy. And because I watch other women,
~~to~~ compare*ing* myself to them and judge*ing* myself accord- *[measuring myself against?]*
ingly, I experience intimidation and jealousy.
The dynamics of this watching myself/watching you
watching me phenomenon create what Margaret Atwood
has dubbed "that pale-mauve hostility that you so
often find between women." It is a shared secret,
that we watch ourselves so carefully while
feigning nonchalance. We appraise other women as a
man would, appraise ourselves as a man would, and
weigh the results. It is strangely comforting to
find the other wanting. I think most women hate
this trap, and hate the pale-mauve hostility. But
we learn it as we learn to walk and to wear our
hair in pigtails the way daddy likes it. It is our
way of surviv*ing* in the world we are born into: one
in which, like it or not, we must continually
impress men. As Berger says, a woman's "own sense
of being in herself is supplanted by a sense of
being appreciated as herself by another." *[This is a richly suggestive notion. It could be elaborated a bit more.]*

We are taught this meticulous self-
observation. At the onset of puberty, among the
other ridiculously sexist boy-catching hints we
receive, girls are often instructed to "learn how

to take a compliment." In other words, we are
expected to accept another person's sense of us as
they have expressed it, and to consider it a
reward. By accepting it we add it to our expectations of ~~ourself~~ *ourselves*--our checklist as we glance into
the mirrors of shop windows, listen to ourselves
speak, or choose our clothes, opinions, and other
accessories.

Nice. I like this shift and mix of "things" and "more-than-things."

When a girl "takes a compliment," she accepts
the reward and accepts, as well, the requirement
~~which~~ *that* earned her the compliment. ~~They both~~ *Both* become
internalized. She now needs to be able to earn
that other person's sense of her from herself. She
practices her "disarming smile" in mirrors,
concentrates on "poise," and makes sure she's
being "a good listener." Not all compliments are
"taken," of course, although they may be
acknowledged with a polite "thank you." Some are
discarded because they do not fit her image as the
watcher in her sees it, and these rejects can be
disconcerting as they suggest a discrepancy between
the internal surveyor and the external one. ~~but~~ *But*
true compliments, the ones that congratulate a
girl's or woman's mutable, monitored perception of
herself, are internalized and added to the
checklist.

Begin a new sentence?

I do not want to be John Berger's pathetically
trapped woman, to merely "appear," and to be a composite of other people's perceptions of me. I do
not want to value appearance over action. ~~but~~ *But* I
cannot escape the habit of constantly having one
eye on my own image. In windows, mirrors, *and in*
photographs, *in* other people's glances, and *in* my own
mind I am haunted, *by images of myself. I am* continually critiquing my
appearance, my reactions, my gestures, ~~and~~ my
speech. ~~Sondheim observes of~~ *Of* one of ~~his~~ *the* women
characters *a Steven Sondheim song sings:* "Look at her looking, forever in that

mirror. What does she see?" ¶She sees the self she
must continually present: the self the world
perceives.

Maile—You've done it again: you've
written what will soon become a
truly wonderful essay. The insights
here are sharp, rich, complex. The
language is often brilliant and
beautiful. But the paper needs one
more draft—for stylistic scrutiny, ref
ining, tightening, fine-tuning. Consider
the various editing suggestions I've indicated within your paper.

Then let's talk——

Two of Maile's classmates read her draft in a class workshop. They expressed
interest in her idea that women see themselves at the mercy of the male gaze, and
they feel obliged to look good for men. One thought that Maile was overstating
the case for this notion, but the other student agreed with Maile and asked if she
could find other evidence to illustrate and support her idea.

Maile also talked with her instructor in a private conference following his
reading of the full essay draft. They discussed many positive features of Maile's
essay, and they considered ways it could be strengthened both in terms of stylistic
refinement and further elaboration of its idea about the relationship of women's
thinking and behavior to their physical appearance.

After receiving responses from both her classmates and her instructor, Maile
prepared another draft of her essay. In this next draft, she introduced an experience she had while walking on a city street—an encounter with a homeless
person. When Maile saw the woman, it seemed like nothing more than an unexpected encounter, and she quickly put the experience aside. But later, as she read
her draft, the experience came back to her; it clarified what she was thinking
about. Maile decided, finally, to use that experience to begin her essay, placing it
directly before her previous draft's introduction. You will notice other changes
Maile made in her essay: changes in phrasing; the addition of details to heighten
our awareness; ideas and quotations from a book of feminist literary criticism that
she linked up with her experience and the story about her mother. (Notice, too,
that Maile reversed the order of her epigraphs.)

What follows represents approximately half of Maile's second full draft of her
essay. The portions described above are included, along with a few additional
paragraphs. This draft is presented without marginal or interlinear comments.

A woman must continually watch herself. She is almost
continually accompanied by her own image of herself. Men look
at women. Women watch themselves being looked at.

John Berger
Ways of Seeing

The girl was ugly. I was bored during the whole journey.

Casanova
History of My Life

   I have been haunted for several days by the image of one of
the homeless people in the city. She sits huddled in a
doorstep in a beige coat with a scarf tied around her head, and
she clutches a large white plastic bag. The first time I saw
her I found myself staring, wondering at her face, which was
colored a deep pink. As I neared her, I could make out the
cakey texture of makeup and I caught the sickeningly sweet
chemical smell of the pink powder that covered her entire face:
forehead, wrinkled cheeks, lips, eyes, eyebrows, and ears, and
that was smeared across the lapels of her coat and mixed with
the pattern of her headwrap. I fixed my eyes back on the
sidewalk, which was covered with white face powder, and braced
for the inevitable request for money. It didn't come. She
didn't even notice me; her eyes were riveted to a spot in the
corner of the the doorstep. I glanced back at that spot as I
passed, expecting to see a mirror into which she was staring so
intently. There was nothing there. Only the concrete wall
stared back at her.

   Later in the day she was gone, and only a white outline of
her seated form remained in the scattered face powder on the
sidewalk, along with a sandwich in a baggie that someone must
have given her, abandoned there with one bite taken.
Disconcerted, I sought my own reflection in a shop window, to
replace that of the trembling, staring, caricature of misplaced
female vanity I had seen that morning. Even as I caught my own

eye, I saw the irony in my means of escape. This poor, ill
woman, to whom her own presented, made-up self is more important
than food, has been in my thoughts as a final stage in the obsession with our appearance that women learn from early childhood.
There but for the grace of something—-perhaps our own awareness
of our appearances trap—-go all women.

Why do I need pictures of myself? Because I like them. They
are interesting to me. I like to see myself in relation to other
people, to see myself how other people see me. I study
photographs of myself intently, critically—-always appraising,
always analyzing, carefully assessing what I see there.

I take other opportunities to survey and assess. Most women
do. I have mastered a swift glance over my right shoulder at
mirrors and windows as I walk by, careful not to linger and let
voyeurs behind the glass see my interest in my own image. The
left profile is less reassuring, and with scarcely a conscious
thought I place people to my right. This self-observation is not
vanity. It is a play for approval, and a request to be treated
well, with respect and admiration. It says, "I don't want to
bore you during the entire journey."

Sandra M. Gilbert and Susan Gubar quote Laura Riding as an
epigraph to the first chapter of *The Madwoman in the Attic:*

And the lady of the house was seen only as she appeared
in each room, according to the nature of the lord of the
room. None saw the whole of her, none but herself. For
the light which she was was both her mirror and her body.
None could tell the whole of her, none but herself.

The chapter, entitled "The Queen's Looking Glass," makes some
important observations about "images of women," especially as
portrayed in the Grimm brothers' fairy tale, "Little Snow
White." They note that "female bonding is extraordinarily
difficult in patriarchy: women almost inevitably turn against
women because the voice of the looking-glass sets them against
each other" (38). Thus we are set up as rivals for each other by
the male voice of the looking glass, and Gilbert and Gubar see
little hope for female solidarity. They share Anne Sexton's view
that Snow White must inevitably become the wicked Queen. Having

escaped from one display case (the glass coffin), she has traded it for another, the mirror in the Prince's home (41-42). To escape her new prison she must become the witch. She must become assertive and therefore monstrous and misogynistic to destroy the "angel woman" Galatea in herself (42).

That the perfect Snow White should become the evil Queen is horrifying to me, although Gilbert and Gubar endorse the witch's actions and sympathize with her. It rings true, however, and it turns me to look at my relationship with my own mother. She despises the appearance-oriented environment in which women live, and she fears that I have bought into it. She has sometimes lamented that I was not born unattractive; she is afraid I will have everything given to me, that I'll never know what it is to really earn rewards. She too has bought into the system, however, and perhaps it is that which she laments. Five feet two, beautiful and blonde, a southern-Californian ex-Homecoming Queen, she has been handed a lot on the tarnished silver platter of prettiness. And while carefully maintaining that prettiness, she has despised it. She has always wanted to be tall, dark-haired and magnificent so that people would take her seriously. My mother, trapped in her surfer-girl image and unable to transform her appearance, instead majored in microbiology, which she hated, in an attempt to earn the respect she craved.

She has since abandoned microbiology and her model-loveliness is beginning to abandon her. It makes me nervous. Old pictures of her from college and early marriage are breathtaking, with her tousled hair, her smooth tan skin, her perfect cheekbones, and her brilliant Homecoming Queen smile. (Holly Near, singing of her own Queen experience, has observed, "That's what Homecoming Queens do, is smile.") These images, however, are disconcerting. They are reminders for me of the death and disappearance of youth and of what is culturally defined as desirable. I wish I could look forward to such changes, to rejoice in the inner richness that replaces outward worth, but I shudder with the vanity of youth and dread the wrinkles and sagging flesh of age. I delight with Snow White that I am still "the fairest of them all."

As good as that second draft is, it benefited from further reflection and revision. Maile decided, for example, that she preferred her original introduction to the one based on the old woman in the street. So she moved the paragraphs about the woman back to a later section of her essay. Maile also elaborated on a reference to a Stephen Sondheim song, which she used to conclude her essay. And she made other adjustments of word choice and sentence style.

Here is the final version of Maile's essay, one that she built up over a period of about four weeks. Remember that this fine essay did not emerge full-blown from Maile's mind all at once. She thought about it repeatedly over an extended period of time. She relied on her experiences, she read, she wrote, collaborated with other classmates, worked with her instructor, revised, and continued to refine and develop her idea until she had an essay that pleased her. Her idea about appearance, her sense of the way women monitor themselves, her conviction that both men and women have something to do with this monitoring—all these notions grew out of Maile's experiences, her living and her reading. She cared about these experiences, cared about making sense of them, and her concern shows in her essay. That concern carried her through the writing and motivated her; it carries the reader along as well in Maile's final essay.

The Voice of the Looking-Glass

Maile Meloy

A woman must continually watch herself. She is almost continually accompanied by her own image of herself. Men look at women. Women watch themselves being looked at.

JOHN BERGER
WAYS OF SEEING

The girl was ugly. I was bored during the whole journey.

CASANOVA
HISTORY OF MY LIFE

From the moment I became conscious of cause and effect I have been conscious of the importance of my own appearance. Little girls (and little boys) learn early that the way women are treated is determined by the way they appear. John Berger, in *Ways of Seeing,* has gotten it right. It is a woman's ever-present task to monitor her image, not to survey a situation to determine the appropriate action, as a man does, but to survey herself and define by her presentation the way she wishes others to act toward her.

I have a photograph of myself at graduation, with my hair down and fuschia and plumeria leis piled around my neck. I am laughing, with my mouth open, head tilted, and eyes cast to the side, at something the photographer has said. The picture is not posed; I am caught in a spontaneous, joyful moment by the gaze of the camera.

I have looked at that picture a lot. It is the way I want to be seen in everyday, spontaneous moments, when soft studio lights are not at my rescue and I am vulnerable: I am pleased with the image. When I am asked for the photograph, my instinctive response is, "But it's the only copy I have," which I blurt out before I realize how narcissistic I sound. We are not to let on that we monitor ourselves so closely. We are to be head-tossing and laughing-eyed without being conscious of our beauty.

Why do I need pictures of myself? Because I like them. They are interesting to me. I like to see myself in relation to other people, to see myself the way other people see me. I study photographs of myself intently, critically—always appraising, always analyzing, carefully assessing what I see there.

I take other opportunities to survey and assess. Most women do. I have mastered a swift glance over my right shoulder at mirrors and windows as I walk by, careful not to linger and let voyeurs behind the glass see my interest in my own image. The left profile is less reassuring, and with scarcely a conscious thought I place people to my right. This self-observation is not vanity. It is a play for approval, and a request to be treated well, with respect and admiration. It says, "I don't want to bore you during the entire journey."

The result of the demand for women to be beautiful, combined with a woman's need for approval, according to Berger, is that a woman's "own sense of being in herself is supplanted by a sense of being appreciated by another." Laura Riding's epigraph to the first chapter of Sandra M. Gilbert and Susan Gubar's *The Madwoman in the Attic* addresses this replacement of a woman's self-image with a male's-eye view:

> And the lady of the house was seen only as she appeared in each room, according to the nature of the lord of the room. None saw the whole of her, none but herself. For the light which she was was both her mirror and her body. None could tell the whole of her.

The chapter, entitled "The Queen's Looking Glass," makes some important observations about "images of women," especially as portrayed in the Grimm brothers' fairy tale "Little Snow White." They note that "female bonding is extraordinarily difficult in patriarchy: women almost inevitably turn against women because the voice of the looking glass sets them against each other" (38). Thus we are set up as rivals for each other by the male voice of the looking glass, and Gilbert and Gubar see little hope for female solidarity. They share Anne Sexton's view that Snow White must inevitably become the wicked Queen. Having escaped from one display case (the glass coffin), she has traded it for another, the mirror (41–42). The Prince's home itself is a prison, the same one her mother encountered, where she appears "according to the nature of the lord of the room." To escape her new prison she must become the witch. She must become assertive and therefore monstrous and misogynistic to destroy the "angel woman" Galatea in herself (42).

That the perfect Snow White should become the evil Queen is horrifying to me, although Gilbert and Gubar endorse the witch's actions and sympathize with her. It rings true, however, and it turns me to look at my relationship with my own mother. She despises the appearance-oriented environment in which women live, and she fears that I have bought into it. She has sometimes lamented that I was not born unattractive; she is afraid I will have everything given to me, that I'll never know what it is to really earn rewards. She too has bought into the system, however, and perhaps it is that which she laments. Five feet two, beautiful and blonde, a southern-Californian ex-Homecoming Queen, she has been handed a lot on the tarnished silver platter of prettiness. And while carefully maintaining that prettiness, she has despised it. She has always wanted to be tall, dark-haired and magnificent so that people would take her seriously. My mother, trapped in her surfer-girl image and unable to transform her appearance, instead majored in microbiology, which she hated, in an attempt to earn the respect she craved.

She has since abandoned microbiology, and her model-loveliness is beginning to abandon her. It makes me nervous. Old pictures of her from college and early marriage are breathtaking, with her tousled hair, her smooth tan skin, her perfect cheekbones, and her brilliant Homecoming Queen smile. (Holly Near, singing of her own Queen experience, has observed, "That's what Homecoming Queens do, is smile.") These images, however, are disconcerting. They are reminders for me of the death and disappearance of youth and of what is culturally defined as desirable. I wish I could look forward to such changes, to rejoice in the inner richness that replaces outward worth, but I shudder with the vanity of youth and dread the wrinkles and sagging flesh of age. I delight with Snow White that I am still "the fairest of them all."

Because of my dread of becoming what my mother is, and what other older women are, I expect intimidation and jealousy. And because I watch other women, measuring myself against them and judging myself accordingly, I experience intimidation and jealousy. The dynamics of this watching myself/watching you watching me phenomenon create what Margaret Atwood has dubbed "that pale-mauve hostility that you often find among women." It is a shared secret, that we watch ourselves so carefully while feigning nonchalance. We appraise other women as a man would, appraise ourselves as a man would, and weigh the results. It is strangely comforting to find the other wanting. I think most women hate this trap, and hate the pale-mauve hostility. But we learn it as we learn to walk and to wear our hair in pigtails the way daddy likes it. It is our way of surviving in the world we are born into: one in which, like it or not, we must continually impress men.

We are taught our meticulous self-observation; it is a learned activity. At the onset of puberty, among the other ridiculously sexist boy-catching hints we receive, girls are often instructed to "learn how to take a compliment." We are expected to accept another person's sense of us as they have expressed it, and to consider it a reward. By accepting it we add it to our expectations of ourself—our checklist as we glance into the mirrors of shop windows, listen to ourselves speak, or choose our clothes, opinions, and other accessories.

When a girl "takes a compliment," she accepts the reward and accepts, as well, the requirement that earned her the compliment. Both become internalized. She now needs to be able to earn that other person's sense of her from herself. She practices her "disarming smile" in mirrors, concentrates on "poise," and makes sure she's being "a good listener." Not all compliments are "taken," of course, although they may be acknowledged with a polite "thank you." Some are discarded because they do not fit her image as the watcher in her sees it, and these rejects can be disconcerting as they suggest discrepancy between the internal surveyor and the external one, but true compliments, the ones that congratulate a girl's or woman's mutable, monitored perception of herself, are internalized and added to the checklist.

Sometimes the internal surveyor goes out of control. I have been haunted for several days by the image of one of the homeless people in the city. She sits huddled in a doorstep in a beige coat with a scarf tied around her head, and she clutches a large white plastic bag. The first time I saw her I found myself staring, wondering at her face, which was colored a deep pink. As I neared her, I could make out the cakey texture of makeup and I caught the sweet chemical smell of the pink powder that covered her entire face: forehead, wrinkled cheeks, lips, eyes, eyebrows, and ears, and that was smeared across the lapels of her coat and mixed with the pattern of her headwrap. I fixed my eyes back on the sidewalk, which was covered with white face powder, and braced for the inevitable request for money. It didn't come. She didn't even notice me; her eyes were riveted to a spot in the corner of the doorstep. I glanced back at that spot as I passed, expecting to see a mirror into which she was staring so intently. There was nothing there. Only the concrete wall stared back at her.

Later in the day she was gone, and only a white outline of her seated form remained in the scattered face powder on the sidewalk, along with a sandwich in a baggie that someone must have given her, abandoned there with one bite taken. Disconcerted, I sought my own reflection in a shop window, to replace that of the trembling, staring caricature of female vanity I had seen that morning. Even as I caught my own eye, I saw the irony in my means of escape. This poor, ill woman, to whom her own made-up self is more important than food, exists at the outer edge of the obsession with appearance that women learn from childhood.

I do not want to be John Berger's pathetically trapped woman, to merely "appear," and to be a composite of other people's perceptions of me. I do not want to value appearance over action, but I cannot escape the habit of constantly having one eye on my own image. In mirrors and windows, in photographs, in other people's glances, and in my own mind I am haunted by images of myself. I am continually critiquing my appearance, my reactions, my gestures, and my speech. I am already caught in the queen's looking glass, already in conspiracy with the made-up old woman in the street.

A Stephen Sondheim character sings of his mistress, "Look at her looking, forever in that mirror. What does she see?" He need not ask, for she sees through his eyes. She sees herself as lover, as desirable object, and as rival before she sees herself as a woman. She sees herself in relation to him and in light of his expectations, and she sees her imperfections in that light. She sees Snow White fading and growing old and yet she clings to the façade. It is what she knows.

*   *   *

Let's look now at a different kind of essay, an *analytical/argumentative* one written by Robynn Stacy Maines, who became excited about Gretel Ehrlich's essay "Looking for a Lost Dog" (pp. 240–242). Once Robynn discovered that the essay was not really about the lost dog, she was able to pay attention to the way Ehrlich developed her ideas about thinking. What she found in that essay interested her so much that she wanted to write about it. She wanted to analyze Ehrlich's essay, break it down into its many parts, look at it, see how it worked, and then write an essay about her discoveries. But we're getting ahead of ourselves. Let's go back to the beginning—to the process of discovery.

Students were asked to respond to the following writing exercise:

Exercise 1

Select an essay by one of the contemporary essayists in this collection and write a 500-word analysis focusing on the essay's images or metaphors, or both.

Here is Robynn's response to the exercise, along with marginal and interlinear annotations that show the comments of one of her student readers and her instructor.

In Gretel Ehrlich's "Looking for a Lost Dog," the first significant metaphor or image is the dog. The essay begins by representing it simply as itself: a lost dog. But as the essay's theme begins to emerge, the dog takes on a metaphorical essence: of things lost. Ehrlich's first straight forward approach to the idea at play is in her sentence in paragraph eleven: "To find what's lost; to lose what's found." It is at this point that the dog becomes symbolic. He represents the concept that the things we go looking for are not necessarily the things we will find. The dog is not, at least in this episode, found, but though many other and perhaps more significant things are.

The underlying idea of the essay emerges clearly in paragraph eleven, but it is in paragraph nine that we get our first real taste of what that idea may resemble. Ehrlich uses the image of the trees with lost blossoms and her feeling of having "caught strangers undressed" to jolt us into feeling, if not fully comprehending yet, the sensation of her unfolding idea. We experience the reaction of surprise that catching strangers undressed

Marginal annotations:

This implies a paradoxical dimension, doesn't it?

Well put.

Do you need this last sentence?

Why skip ahead? Talk about 9 first and then develop into 11.

Could you try to combine these sentences into one?

would generate.] [And so we are effectively prepared to understand the idea that the essay begins to bring out.]

What idea? Be more specific in your reference to the idea of Erlich's essay.

   Ehrlich next introduces the greater significance of losing and finding. Here is where the waterfall image comes into play in order to help illustrate how even the most obvious and pre-sent things—-truths perhaps, about ourselves, about what we truly need from life—-can be concealed, just as the falls are hidden behind rose thickets. In fact, these things appear "lost"—-for we can't see them—-precisely because we are too close to them. And Ehrlich then takes the metaphor further to include the mind, and how it can feel at times that we are "losing our minds" when in fact, we are merely too close to them to see them, under-stand them, clearly. And so we feel overwhelmed, the way one might feel about an impressionist painting up close: it seems to have no meaning until you distance yourself and take in the congru-ent whole.

Lovely.

Good metaphor.

   [This being too close to what is lost to know how to find it, how to recognize it, is like one end of a cord which ties up a bundle.] The other end is in the form of the symbolism of walking, meandering and as in the Thoreau quote in paragraph twelve, water. Through these images Ehrlich demonstrates the other notion that completes the idea: that to find something, or to soothe loss or to calm maddening desire, one must set out "with a purpose but no destination" (paragraph 17). Water seems random, and it is as a substance. But it has a nature, a method, as Thoreau said, always "seeking the shortest course to the sea" (paragraph 12).

Awkward sentence.

You must read Annie Dillard. (Let's talk about her work in conference.)

Isn't this really three ideas?

   And so Ehrlich's walk itself, which had a pur-pose: to find the dog, also was without a destination. The discoveries, however, were enormous, gentle and

a walk   a

both

Erlich

unexpected. Before her walk ~~she~~ was feeling
discontented, longing for things either lost or
not yet found: love, more from life. Her distress
had created so much "noise" that it had become
depressing. By taking a <u>meandering</u>, purposeful
yet destinationless walk, she came to discover
things that were different from what she thought
she needed, but which removed the longing
nonetheless.

> Good use of "meandering".
>
> Good analysis.

   The cottonwood "lunatic with birdsong" is perhaps the most compelling image, appropriately,
because the picture and sound of it pulls together
those two cord ends, drawing up the whole bundle
that is the theme. The tree is full of birds, but ← *Good metaphor.*
to see only the birds is to miss the grandeur of
the "symphony" of the whole tree. And the use of
lunacy is potent because it recalls her earlier
mention of losing one's mind. The fullness of
Ehrlich's idea culminates with the image of this
tree which is so much more, heaving upward, like
her own raucous mind, full of noise yet astonishing
in its *quiet* presence.

> Good analysis in this paragraph.

   And so, by the end "it is enough to make a
shadow" because living itself is enough, and <u>full</u>
<u>of discovery</u> enough, to outweigh whatever is lost.

> I don't understand this phrase. Can you elaborate just a bit?

   The second writing exercise called for a second look, a reconsideration of the
selected essay.

Exercise 2

   Return to the essay you analyzed in Exercise 1 and provide an overview of it
by discussing its structure and organization. You can do this overview in different
ways, the simplest perhaps being to describe what the writer does in each para-

graph or group of paragraphs, taken in order. Or you can decide for yourself what features of the essay's organization or structure to comment on.

Robynn wrote the following response:

The first major structural component of "Looking For a Lost Dog" may be the title itself, for it embodies ~~at first glance,~~ a simple introduction to the situation around which the essay's theme will be woven. It tells us that we are going to hear about the process of looking for a dog, yet its simplicity, its overly direct, almost obvious nature, implies that the dog and the process of looking will ~~come to~~ take on greater meaning. Otherwise, how much depth could simply trying to find a dog possess? The first two paragraphs hold more or less to the first sense of the title: "I started off this morning looking for my lost dog." This first line is blunt, to the point. Ehrlich gets the obvious aspect of the story out of the way immediately in paragraphs one and two with snappy descriptions of the dog and how he's been lost before. We're almost compelled to skim right through this part, for even within their quickness, there is the faintest impression that more is coming which we become anxious to discover: ". . . his right leg is crooked where it froze to the ground," and "When we put our ears to the ground, we could hear the hole that had swallowed him." What oddities, what different angles to take ~~in~~ regarding otherwise normal things. We don't know it yet, but Ehrlich has planted the ~~subconscious~~ seed of her theme.

   Paragraphs three and four then, are the tender sprout. Ehrlich's humorous description of herself "cupping my hands behind my ears—-mule-like—-and pricking them all the way forward or back to hear what's happened or what's ahead," (paragraph 3)

Tighten a little.

and the quote from her friend about life being
polyphonic and hearing having "to do with the great
suspiration of life everywhere," (paragraph 4)
bring the concept of seeing—or hearing—life in
unexpected ways into sharp focus. In fact, she
plays some~~what~~ thing of a trick on us here, allowing us
to believe we've got her figured out. We can gloat
a little, thinking how cleverly we've uncovered
her idea. But read on we must, for the
satisfaction of having our cleverness confirmed.

"But back to the dog." (paragraph 5) What?
There's more? Of course, we think, she must try
to find the dog by looking and listening
differently than she normally would. We still
feel ourselves right along with her, ahead a
little even, as she begins to meander into
descriptions of the countryside. Lovely, we may
think, but isn't it getting a bit off the point?
And then, there's the bit on Navajo "hand
tremblers." The quotation at the end: "Lots of
noise, but noise that's hard to hear" is at first
glance baffling. It has the very effect of what it
says. We find ourselves suddenly confused by the
"noise" of this and the last paragraph's
illustrative qualities, and begin to wonder if in
fact they did have a place. Perhaps we weren't so
clever. Better read on.

Paragraph 7 and the image of the falls leads us
into more description and more uncertainty, until
the end of the paragraph: "The falls roar, but
they're overgrown . . . and the closer I get, the
harder it is to see the water. Perhaps that is how
it will be in my search for the dog." Aha! There
is more here. Not only must we look at things in
different ways, but there is a reason why we don't
see things clearly. Sometimes they are hidden! We
are almost too excited at seeing this idea sprout a

new stem to stop and wonder what it may be that keeps the things we look for hidden.

Ehrlich gives us a reprieve for a moment with paragraph eight, where she launches into a story about how the dog was bitten by rattlesnakes and nearly died. But she inserts a quiet reminder here that the dog is a metaphor. We should be on the lookout for more of what he represents.

Paragraph nine carries us visually on Ehrlich's walk with vibrant pictures of the landscape and the sensations it brings her. The images of glaring mountains, "the black sky (hanging) over like a frown," and the sensation of being pulled downstream by the "string of cottonwoods whose tender leaves are the color of limes," are so beautiful, they transfix us and make us nearly forget that there is a theme to discover fully here. And so in this dazed state, Ehrlich pounces with the image of the blossomless trees making her feel as if she "has caught strangers undressed." Drawn into her description as we are, we can't help but feel the astonishment that such a sight would provoke. We are effectively snapped into the mindset of witnessing the unexpected. And so we are sensationally prepared for the first congruent taste of the essay's theme which is carried to us much like the birds in paragraph 10 on fierce spring winds. It drops neatly and concisely into place with the first sentence of paragraph 11: "To find what's lost; to lose what's found." It's so simple, like the title, but by this point, we have enough information to know that "to find what's lost" takes a new kind of vision and an eye toward the unexpected. But the second half of that sentence: "to lose what's found" is what really compels us. Ehrlich loses no time in drawing on our curiosity by giving us an example of something that can seem lost at times: the mind. And immediately, she rebukes the concept that the mind can be lost by comparing it to the falls: "We can lose sight of what is too close." She is off and running now with the theme at work. She keeps on a steady course, ironically, by bringing in a Thoreau quote about a saunterer having the nature of water: it appears random, yet "is all the while sedulously seeking the shortest course to the sea."

Paragraph 13 and its meanderings into Ehrlich's "longings—for what I'm not, for what is impossible, for people I love who can't be in my life . . ." seem at first undirected, misplaced, as do the descriptions in paragraphs 14 and 15 about Ehrlich's seeming irrational expectations of herself. But then, if we allow ourselves a reminder, we are struck by the earlier Thoreau quote: "The saunterer, in the good sense, is no more vagrant than the meandering river . . ." Paragraph 16 is a sort of preparation for the unity to come in that it plays the organized image of a Japanese garden against the tumultuous one of the "tortured junipers and tumbled boulders." She nearly stumbles, yet catches the perfect sight of an unexpected locust in a bird's nest. Everything is out of place, but strangely perfected and wonderful to behold.

"Some days I think this one place isn't enough," (paragraph 17) tells us what she believes she has lost, that she wants to find more from life perhaps. But then she comes across the "towering cottonwood . . . lunatic with birdsong" and the completion of the essay's idea is before us. "Today it is enough to make a shadow" (paragraph 18) because by allowing herself to meander, with

vision for the unexpected, she has learned to let
go of what she thought she needed and instead   *Lovely.*
discover what she'd really lost: those elements of
discovery in life itself that sustain us beyond any
loss lesser than that of life itself.

**A fine analysis of the essay's idea—
and a good overview of it. When you
write your essay draft, however, do
not structure it according to a linear
march through Erlich's paragraphs.
Very nice insights throughout. Great
work throughout this analysis,
Robynn.**

Notice how in this second exercise Robynn continued to analyze the images of Ehrlich's essay. This time, however, she was able to comment more extensively on how the images affect the reader—both herself as an individual reader and other readers as well.

Notice, too, how she found new ways to frame her understanding of Ehrlich's achievement in "Looking for a Lost Dog." And notice how often Robynn quoted specific phrases and passages from Ehrlich's writing to illustrate the observations she made about the essay.

Robynn looked very closely at individual paragraphs, paying attention to the language and images in those paragraphs. In the process of analyzing, she saw more in Ehrlich's essay than she did when she wrote her first exercise. Looking again paid off. She, like Ehrlich in her search, found more than she bargained for.

Once the exercises had been completed and Robynn had a chance to think about them and about Ehrlich's essay, she was ready to begin work on the first draft of her essay. She was ready to find a way to tell readers what she had discovered.

Robynn's first draft contained many excellent features. It was based on a clear idea about Ehrlich's essay; that idea was Robynn's thesis. Look back to the last half of her first paragraph. The draft presented aptly chosen passages from Ehrlich's essay to illustrate that thesis. And in the draft, Robynn made important connections between Ehrlich's images, quoting Ehrlich's language to illustrate and demonstrate the idea and movement of mind so central to "Looking for a Lost Dog."

In her second draft, Robynn worked hard to improve many of her sentences and to retain her emphasis on Ehrlich's imagery. Her analysis of imagery was the key to her own thesis. Writing this second draft, Robynn wanted to eliminate the sense that she was plodding through Ehrlich's essay paragraph by paragraph, listing in order the things she noticed. She focused primarily on Ehrlich's images rather than on where they appeared in the essay.

Here are a few paragraphs from Robynn's second draft:

This meandering of thought continues into Ehrlich's friend's observation that life is polyphonic and that hearing "has to do with the great suspiration of life everywhere." The concept of seeing—or hearing—life in unexpected ways, all at once comes into sharp focus. ~~like turning a random corner during a walk through a city and coming suddenly upon a cathedral.~~ In fact, Ehrlich plays something of a trick on us here, allowing us to believe we've got her figured out. The use of this rather grand concept and especially the ominous sounding "suspiration" just feels like revelation. ~~We can gloat a little, thinking how cleverly we've uncovered her idea.~~ We're drawn forward ~~though~~ by our desire to have that ~~cleverness~~ revelation affirmed.

Prepared as we are for ~~a philosophical~~ verification of our conclusion, we are jolted by the next sentence: "But back to the dog." This ~~sharp~~ unexpected return to the ordinary, to the bluntness of the beginning is surprising. ~~Ehrlich has returned us to a simple story about a lost dog and we are thrown off balance with this unexpected turn. But then we think, of course, she must try to find the dog by looking and listening differently than she normally would. We still feel ourselves right along with her, ahead a little even~~ As she begins to meander once again, lovely into descriptions of the countryside, we begin to feel lost. ~~lovely, we may think, but isn't she getting a bit off the point?~~ By the time she brings us to the description of Navajo "hand tremblers" and the quotation at the end, "Lots of noise, but noise that's hard to hear," we may feel thoroughly baffled. But all of this has the very effect of what ~~it~~ Erlich is communicating: we ~~find ourselves suddenly~~ are confused

by the "noise" of this and the last paragraph's
illustrative qualities, ~~and begin to wonder if in~~
~~fact they do have a place.~~

The image of the falls with its own noise leads
us into more description and more uncertainty,
until the end of the paragraph: "The falls roar,
but they're overgrown . . . and the closer I get,
the harder it is to see the water. *Perhaps that is*
how it will be in my search for the dog." (my italics) In one sentence,
confusion culminates in meaning. ~~Aha! we~~
~~think, there is more here.~~ Not only must we look
at things in different ways, but there is a reason
why we don't see things clearly: sometimes they are
ready to explore this new idea with Erlich,
hidden. We are ~~almost too excited at seeing this~~
ready for its pertinence to finding the dog.
~~idea sprout a new stem to stop and wonder what it~~
~~may be that keeps the things we look for hidden.~~   Is this the
                                                              best verb?
     But
     ~~And~~ then again, with our curiosity peaked,   ↗ Instead of taking us on the expected route of
Ehrlich (diverges) ~~back to the dog, this time into a~~   the search, she wanders into an ordinary story about how
applying philosophy to the ~~story about how~~ he was bitten by rattlesnakes and
nearly died. ~~and how they've been worried about him~~
~~(about losing him?)~~ By continuing to return us to
prosaic images of the
the dog just when we feel ready to explore her
underlying ideas, Ehrlich inserts a quiet reminder
                           He represents the things we look for consciously, which
that the dog is a metaphor. He also ~~plays the role~~   lead us to other,
acts as a pivot point
~~of fulcrum~~ for the twists and turns of the essay,   less obvious
                                                            discoveries.
so that within the mirroring effect, the dog is the
anchor for the wandering from confusion to   twists and
understanding which takes place throughout.   turns don't have
                                                            a fulcrum.

The crossouts and the interlinear rewriting, as well as the marginal revisions,
are exclusively Robynn's. In looking carefully at her revisions, you will notice how
much clearer they make her essay. Even so, Robynn continued to work on revising
her essay, partly because she saw how far it had already come from those early
exercises. But the more she worked, the more she looked back into Ehrlich's essay
and into her own, the more she kept seeing, and she wanted to comment on those
observations and improve her analysis.

Here, then, is the final version of Robynn's analytical essay on Gretel Ehrlich's
"Looking for a Lost Dog."

Finding a Dog Not Lost in "Looking for a Lost Dog"

Robynn Stacy Maines

In "Looking for a Lost Dog" Gretel Ehrlich employs an effective strategy in making the essay itself, its structure and the actual experience of reading it, an intricate reflection of its theme. Wherever Ehrlich delivers elements of her idea through metaphor, imagery or anecdote, she simultaneously adds a physical dimension to the essay itself, like raising a mirror against another, creating mutual reflections of the central idea both in the essay and in the experience of reading it.

The essay begins with a sort of drifting into reverie, the prose itself resembling the wanderings of the mind. Physical descriptions of the dog lead to a story of how he fell into a hole once, and how they could hear him whining. This image spills over into musings about the positioning of our ears making us narcissistic, so that "we can only hear what's right next to us or else the internal monologue inside." It has such a rambling effect that we almost miss the significance of "the internal monologue inside." In fact, Ehrlich carries us right by it on the meandering stream of her own "internal monologue" into a humorous description of herself "cupping my hands behind my ears—mule-like—and pricking them all the way forward or back to hear what's happened or what's ahead." It's as if she herself, in her own inner conversation, doesn't notice that she's foreshadowed her own thoughts.

Her approach almost compels us to skim right through this part, so that we come close to overlooking a few of the other gems throughout this opening segment. Without being obvious though, they radiate the faintest impression that more is coming, and despite the lightheartedness, we become eager to discover the meaning behind these things: "his right leg is crooked where it froze to the ground," and "when we put our ears to the ground, we could hear the hole that had swallowed him." What oddities, what different angles to take in regard to otherwise normal things. We are not aware of it at this point in reading the essay, but Ehrlich has introduced us to a portion of her idea, that things are not always as they appear. She has also employed the subtle mirroring, for the very rambling nature of her prose introduces us to another key component of her theme: the importance of meandering as a means of discovery.

This meandering of thought continues into Ehrlich's friend's observation that life is polyphonic and that hearing "has to do with the great suspiration of life everywhere." The concept of seeing—or hearing—life in unexpected ways, all at once comes into sharp focus. The use of this rather grand concept and especially the ominous-sounding "suspiration" just feels like revelation, and we are drawn forward by a desire to have that revelation affirmed.

Prepared as we are for verification of our conclusion, we are jolted by the next sentence: "But back to the dog." This unexpected turn into the ordinary throws us off balance, the more so because she doesn't return to the dog at all, but instead begins to meander once again, this time into lovely descriptions of the countryside. We begin to feel lost. By the time she brings us to the description of Navajo "hand tremblers" and the quotation at the end, "Lots of noise, but noise that's hard to hear," we may feel thoroughly baffled. But all of this embodies the very effect of what Ehrlich is communicating: we are confused by the "noise" of this and the last paragraph's illustrative qualities, and begin to wonder if they signify something not yet discovered.

The image of the falls with its own noise leads us into more description and more uncertainty, until the end of the paragraph: "The falls roar, but they're overgrown . . . and the closer I get, the harder it is to see the water. *Perhaps that is how it will be in my search for the dog"* (my italics). In one sentence, confusion culminates in meaning. Not only must we look at things in different ways, but there is a reason why we don't see things clearly: sometimes they are hidden. We are ready to explore this new idea, ready for its pertinence to finding the dog when, again with our curiosity piqued, Ehrlich diverges once more.

Instead of taking us on the expected route of applying philosophy to the search, Ehrlich wanders into an ordinary story about how the dog was bitten by rattlesnakes and nearly died. By continuing to return us to prosaic images of the dog just when we feel ready to explore her underlying ideas, Ehrlich inserts a quiet reminder that the dog is a metaphor. He represents the things we look for consciously, but which lead us instead to other, less obvious discoveries. He also acts as a pivot point for the twists and turns of the essay, so that within the mirroring effect, the dog is the anchor for the wandering from confusion to understanding which takes place throughout our reading.

Ehrlich moves us forward with this sense of random thinking and into random walking with vibrant pictures of the landscape and the sensations it brings her. The images of glaring mountains, "the black sky (hanging) over like a frown," and the sensation of being pulled downstream by the "string of cottonwoods whose tender leaves are the color of limes," are so beautiful that they transfix us and make us nearly forget that there is a theme to discover. And so having effectively lulled us into something of a mesmerized state, Ehrlich surprises us with the image of the blossomless trees making her feel as if she "has caught strangers undressed." Drawn into her description as we are, we can't help but feel the astonishment that such a sight would provoke. We are effectively snapped into the mind-set of witnessing the unexpected and sensationally prepared for the first congruent taste of the essay's theme, which is carried to us much like the birds flying north on fierce spring winds.

It drops neatly and concisely into place with the first sentence of paragraph 11: "To find what's lost; to lose what's found." It's so simple, like the title. By this point, however, we have enough information to know that "to find what's lost" takes a new kind of vision and an eye toward the unexpected.

Ehrlich's straightforward placement of a major thematic concept here has a satiating quality, for it rewards our sense of comprehension. But the second half of that sentence—"to lose what's found"—compels us to venture beyond this initial understanding. This is a perfect example of the mirroring quality present through-out the essay. The words themselves "to lose what's found" mirror the preceding words "to find what's lost." But that is only one dimension of the strategy. The other and even more profound effect is that the concept itself is a reflection of the message we've already come to understand up to this point in the essay. What's more, the introduction of it is so confusing, yet obviously pertinent, that we fall prey to our own rambling curiosity.

Ehrlich loses no time in drawing on our curiosity by giving us an example of something that can seem lost at times: the mind. She then immediately rebukes the concept that the mind can be lost by comparing it to the falls: "We can lose sight of what is too close." We can feel overwhelmed, the way one might feel about an impressionist painting up close: it seems to have no meaning until you distance yourself and take in the congruent whole. Ehrlich is off and running now with the theme at work. She keeps on a steady course, ironically, by bringing in a Thoreau quotation about a saunterer having the nature of water: it appears random, yet "is all the while sedulously seeking the shortest course to the sea."

Being so close to what is lost that you can't find or recognize it, is like one end of a cord which ties up a bundle. The other end is in the symbolism of walking, meandering, and the nature of water. Through these images Ehrlich demonstrates the other notion that completes the idea: that to find something, or to soothe loss or calm maddening desire, one must set out "with a purpose but no destination." Water appears random, yet it has a nature, a method, as Thoreau said, always "seeking the shortest course to the sea."

The meandering of the essay into Ehrlich's "longings—for what I'm not, for what is impossible, for people I love who can't be in my life" seems at first undi-rected, misplaced, as do the descriptions of Ehrlich's seemingly irrational expecta-tions of herself. But then, if we allow ourselves a reminder, we are struck by the Thoreau quotations: "The saunterer, in the good sense, is no more vagrant than the meandering river" and "if I can only walk with sufficient carelessness I am sure to be filled." Ehrlich's walk, as well as her "internal monologue," has carried her to this place of inner speculation. Her "hybrid anguish spends itself as recklessly and purposefully as water" so that whatever it is that is empty, or lost, inside her can be filled, or found. This intrusion of emotion is no intrusion at all, but the destination of her meandering. Its misplaced, sudden sensation is appropriate, for its effect on the reader mirrors the idea that the most obvious and present things are often those which are most difficult to recognize.

The momentum of the essay toward the end reflects that of Ehrlich's thoughts as one begins to play rapidly into the next. Ehrlich's strange notion that she could "sniff out a scent" causes her to question herself and then to relate this to a similar situation in Japan when she thought she would "break into fluent Japanese." It is as if we are witnessing her mind's connections, for the image of the Japanese garden seems to grow out her thoughts of Japan. This apparently discursive run of images recalls the beginning of the essay and its similar ramblings. The difference is that now nothing is ignored or breezed by. The organized image of a Japanese garden plays directly against the tumultuous one of the "tortured junipers and tumbled boulders." She nearly stumbles, yet catches the perfect sight of an unexpected locust in a bird's nest. Everything is out of place, but strangely perfect.

This perfect sensation allows us to not worry about the dog, even if we do wonder about him. We've come to understand that his purpose was not to provide a destination, but to create impetus for the meandering. And so Erlich's walk itself, which started out with the purpose of finding the dog, also is without destination. The discoveries, however, are enormous, gentle and unexpected. Before her walk she was discontented and longing for things either lost or not yet found: love, more from life. Her distress had created so much "noise" that it had become depressing. By taking a meandering, purposeful yet destinationless walk, she came to discover things that were different than what she thought she needed, but which removed the longing nonetheless.

The cottonwood "lunatic with birdsong" is perhaps the most compelling image, appropriately, because the picture and sound of it pull together those two cord ends, drawing up the whole bundle that is the theme. The tree is full of birds, but to see only the birds is to miss the grandeur of the "symphony" of the whole tree. And the use of lunacy is potent because it recalls her earlier mention of losing one's mind. The fullness of Erlich's idea culminates with the image of this tree which is so much more, heaving upward, like her own raucous mind, full of noise yet astonishing in its presence.

And so, by the end "it is enough to make a shadow," because living itself is enough, and full of discovery enough, to outweigh whatever is lost.

*   *   *

Watching these two student writers at work, you can see how their interests developed, how they began by reading, writing, and reflecting. Again and again, they revised their work. Often after initial drafting, they did more reading, listened to their classmates and their instructors, and then wrote again, all in an effort to say what they had discovered and to say it clearly and effectively. Maile wrote an essay that depended very much on stories about her own experiences, but she enriched those stories and her essay with ideas and quotations from other written sources. Robynn focused on a close, analytical reading of Gretel Ehrlich's essay; her evidence came from that essay. She created an essay out of a close reading of another essay. In each case, these students' excitement and enthusiasm came from their discoveries and their desire to tell others what they were learning. Remember, they started with nothing more than an inclination and a little reading. Everything else followed.

The essays and the accompanying reproductions in this book call you, each of you, into reflection—asking you to think about that world outside your window, the fascinating world within, and the many representations of those worlds that appear in the essays and paintings. Therein you find your sources, the beginnings for your writing.

A SPECTRUM OF STUDENT WRITING

The nine essays in this section of the anthology were all written by students for their first-year college writing courses. The final version of each essay (the version printed here) was preceded by a series of exercises and drafts and by comments from classmates and from the writing teacher.

Pedagogical notes are provided for each of the subsections that follow, notes that will help you identify the kind of essay you are reading.

EXPLORATORY ESSAYS:
Conducting an Inquiry through the Analysis of Experience

In this group of essays, students tell stories about their own experiences, and they use these stories to develop and illustrate ideas. These essays, grounded in the familiar and commonplace, explore as they go along; the writers are looking for the elusive answers to nagging questions. You get to see them thinking, working out their ideas. Michael Cohen wonders about the burden of living in New York City; China Forbes, about being naked; Gian Neffinger, about the fragility of beauty. Their conclusions are tentative; their ideas are fluid, capable of further analysis. The exploration of a good idea can go on and on; as experience and evidence change, so do the ideas, over time, ever so slightly.

You Can Shave the Beast, but Will the Fur Grow Back?

Michael Cohen

I live in Brooklyn, New York City. I was born and bred there. I am one of eight million New Yorkers. New York City is sometimes described as a "melting pot," meaning we are like different Kool-Aid powders that dissolve into a uniform color and flavor. My view differs, though. I think we are eight million different insoluble liquids layered one on top of the other, appearing like oil floating on water. When stirred, these liquids are rustled from their respective positions, almost coming together, only to revert to their original separated composition a second later. I'm sorry, Dr. King, we haven't all "sat at the same table" yet. This polarization and social indifference, I believe, stems from the ruthless, heart-hardening, cutthroat environment of our city. But underneath this coarseness, I wonder if there isn't a sliver of pillow-soft care and empathy for those wishing to escape the city's coldness?

New Yorkers are stereotypically known as a crass and rude group, devoid of compassion. Having visited other places in the world, I can frankly attest that I have never experienced apathy so widely spread throughout a populace as I have felt living in New York. The "New York attitude" isn't unique to lower-class individuals who are down on their luck; it transcends class, wealth, stature, and race. It's evident in the Wall Street white collar, the ghetto rogue, the chubby mother of three—and me. It's a compelling force. I've been trained, conditioned like one of Dr. Pavlov's dogs, to behave this way; to bark on demand, to push as I'm being shoved, to hate when hated.

I was sucked into the vacuum of hate at an early age. When I was twelve years old, I got a taste of the caustic malice that would grow, like a cancer, steady and imperceptible, eventually decomposing my soul as I got older. I was riding my bicycle in my relatively safe neighborhood (keep in mind, safe, compared to places like Harlem and Bed-Stuy, might not be considered so safe in terms of average America; you still had to be smart and keep your head up on the street), minding my own business, and rode by two kids who were walking. As I passed them, one of them spat at me and said, "fuckin' Jew." I continued riding, my ear drenched in this person's gooey, bacteria-laden saliva, and my innocence told me this was normal because when I reached the next intersection a man making a left turn drove by me and yelled out a similar epithet from his car. The exact words don't matter. It's the faces, the sneers of hatred, the furrowed brows of enmity that have caused me to become another jaded member of this regressing social zoo. The very hate I was taught to loathe, for my race has been scapegoated and hated since the dawn of mankind, was now slowly becoming part of me. Being swept away by the malevolent New York attitude caused me to ignore this paradox that was taken captive by my anger, shackled to the back wall of my conscience, pleading me to listen, to stop hating. This overpowering ethic was bestial, fit for animals, not humans. I'm not talking about any lovable bunny rabbits or timid deer, mind you. I'm talking about vicious animals, like New York, cat-sized, hairy, filthy, germ-carrying rats that don't scurry when something bigger comes their way, that line their holes with a dead one's crumbs, that gnaw their way into basements so they can pillage someone's food supply.

I was surrounded by these animals; therefore, I could only expect to become a fuming, smileless, growling animal—like them.

I got older and learned to drive. Now I was the one yelling "you fuckin' guido!" or "muthafuckin' nigga'!" or "bastard spic!" It was natural animal instinct. Anyway, who'd you expect me to love!? The nightly eleven o'clock newscasts I saw on my TV weren't filled with ivory-clean, safe, suburban "nothing doing" stories. I saw murdered priests, burnt synagogues, shootings, arsons, gang rapes, babies disposed of in trash dumpsters, death, and more death. I saw Rashid Baz and Lemrick Nelson. Baz, an Arab livery driver, sprayed bullets with reckless abandon into a van transporting a group of Hasidic young men on the Brooklyn Bridge. He killed one. Why'd he do it? No excuse could explain it, not the Koran, not the Muslim fundamentalist doctrine, not anything. Nelson, today a free man, was found with a bloody knife on his person the night Yankel Rosenbaum was murdered in Crown Heights, Brooklyn. The blood was positively identified as Rosenbaum's. Nelson was part of the angry mob that surrounded Rosenbaum and chanted, like something out of *Lord of the Flies,* "Kill the Jew! Kill the Jew!" But this hunt wasn't fictional; it happened on an everyday Brooklyn street. For such atrocities I can only accept one reason: we are New Yorkers; we are animals, predators; we grew up angry and wanted to see the bloodshed of others we didn't like. A consistent diet of spoon-fed images of hate-drenched violence penetrated our consciences. Now, we are immune, desensitized. It's okay to hate, for there's no one to love. Having pondered this, I've told myself that this attitude can't possibly evolve into a formula for happiness, but being too busy clawing and biting my way around in the real world, I was not keen enough to contemplate change yet.

I wonder if I acquired an education, would I become human or merely a smarter, craftier animal? Every morning I take the subway to Manhattan so I can acquire this education. On an elevated platform I wait for the F-train. Off in the distance, to my left, I see the old parachute ride apparatus in Coney Island that looks like the Space Needle in Seattle. It serves no function nowadays, except to remind us how we've degenerated. When that apparatus was working, Coney

Island was in its heyday. On hot days, hundreds of thousands would flock there to enjoy the beach, the rides, the carnival-like atmosphere, and Nathan's franks. It was a happy New York. Today, Coney Island is dilapidated and scary. High crime, drug traffic, and poverty have ravaged the area, not unlike dozens of other neighborhoods throughout the city. To my right, I see the Twin Towers, formally known as the World Trade Center, standing tall, very tall. I take for granted, sometimes, that it is one of the tallest skyscrapers in the world. To me, it's just another big building. But now, from so far away, it shines like a polished jewel, surveying the mind-blowing industrious pace of its city below. Looking up close from the plaza between One and Two World Trade Center, one can understand and can't deny that these structures probably can withstand the impact of a 747 jumbo jet, as its structural engineers proudly contend. It thrives nonstop, lit throughout the night. When six Muslims bombed it two years ago it merely coughed black smoke for a couple of days and resumed its frantic pace soon afterwards. It is an icon of the unrelenting, dog-eat-dog capitalism and greed that embodies New York and has driven many to ledge-jumping. I stand between these two polar edifices, wondering if I am another gear in this machine of a city, if I will ever escape New York's contagious, mass-produced animal destiny.

Travis Bickle, the title character in the Martin Scorsese film *Taxi Driver*, drove and saw "filth and scum" daily. Disgusted, he felt they should be "washed away, just the way rain washes away the dirt on the street." Bickle built up an arsenal of guns and hate. He consummated his frustration by killing a pimp and a gangster and was lauded as a New York hero because he helped return a twelve-year-old prostitute to her white American family. Through violence, he transformed his discontent. My ideology differs from Bickle's, but I wonder if it's possible for me to affect my environment, to enact a change from its current bleak decline. Can I be like Bickle and separate myself from the vacuum suck of this powerful city?

Or can I be like the Flatiron Building on the lower Fifth Avenue corner, where a fork splits Broadway and Fifth from their brief intersection? The Flatiron has a unique teardrop shape. From the long sides of the building it appears as any other normal building. The way the windows are situated on its face gives the illusion that the Flatiron has the equivalent sides and depth of a normal square or rectangular building, like the Empire State Building, would have. But as you walk around its base and turn the corner, the building curves smoothly, appearing thin and sleek, defying the expectation of another square side. It was built early in this century. It is a timeless, classic work of architectural art. It bucks the trend of New York buildings that appear gaudy and modern to grab attention, only to fall out of vogue when their trendy quality is dated. I wish to elude my carnivorous counterparts' bloodthirsty jaws in this pan-competitive city, but will I stand modest and proud in the end, like the Flatiron, having survived my inner battle for compassion in a soul-less environment?

The F-train takes me home at the end of my day. It is packed as I get on. I'm one amongst Black, Hindu, Asian, White, Jewish, Hispanic, and so on. With each stop, weary bodies depart and file themselves away in their respective neighborhoods. After forty minutes I grab my backpack and prepare to get off, too. Through the window I see a majestic sun setting in pretty tones of orange and red.

As I get off the train I see the Coney Island parachute apparatus straight ahead. Its days in the sun are long gone. It looks at me, its construct antiquated, as if it's weeping, warning me, "You're next. Your fate . . . like mine." I turn around, shunning its somber expression, trying to find a glimmer of hope in something, only to face the daunting World Trade Center. Straight-faced, like a banker letting you know your loan request has been denied, it tells me, with a confident clean-shaven-and-starched-collar-executive coolness, "Don't even think about it. You can't change a thing. Not a chance." I want to defy this unfair proclamation. I want to break out and become human, with my own mind, my own will to care. I want to rise above and break the mold of the carbon copy, mean beast this city wants me to become. I refuse to regress.

As I descend the stairs, from the platform to the street below, I accidentally bump hard into somebody. I offer an apology to this fellow and stick my hand out in goodwill. He responds with a vile grunt and an ice-cold stare and mumbles, "Fuck off," before hurriedly scurrying away. Predictable, like a hackneyed cliché from the tobacco-chewing mouth of a vociferous Texas football coach in a half-time motivational talk with his players, is the behavior of this rough-hewn New Yorker.

I tried leading this horse to water. He refused to drink. This new-found compassion to lead, to rectify, has lifted my soul halfway out of the hostile, rancorous dark New York mire. The remaining half of my soul is being held back by the stubborn horses whose reins I'm holding onto. They refuse to join me, to whinny and trot along the green meadows of tolerance. They keep bucking. But letting go will only pull me back in.

Naked

China Forbes

In the spring I was born naked. I was stuffed into a chamois cloth and presented to my mother.

In the summer I was naked, stumbling over cold flat stones and cool, dew-laced grass until I tumbled giggling into my mother's arms. On the patio she sat with a book, sheltered by the weave of wisteria that perfumed the air. Leaving the book open, face down on the white table that wobbled with the burden of lemonades, my mother looked down to me with violet eyes and smiled. We would chat while I stood on my favorite rock that came right up out of the patio floor. I held the iron pole beside it with one outstretched arm, and my other hand on my waist so with hip cocked to the side, I became Marilyn Monroe until I tired of it. Usually when I played Monroe I was in my suit, but not always. For in the summer I was mostly, freely, happily, obliviously naked.

Our house was long and flat-roofed. It meandered down a sloping hill that was our front lawn. The lawn stretched on in every direction until it met with several different barriers: a wall of trees, a gravel drive, an apple orchard. My parents, sister, and I were entirely secluded, and I thought, self-sufficient. We rarely met with the outside world—save trips to the dump via Dairy Queen with Dad. I was, therefore, immodest, and associated summer, early fall, and spring with nudity.

In the fall, my older sister would go to school. She should wear her hair in two braids, put on dresses, and carry a lunch box. In the afternoons she came home with bright paintings under her arm, and stories about apple seeds. I would play in my toy box while she'd sit in the rocker and read.

I was fascinated by the idea of school, of a place where my sister would go and always return with new things. When she left in the morning, she would walk importantly down the drive to Plympton Rd. where the school bus would pick her up. And on this particular morning, I was outside when she marched off to school. As she disappeared between the leaves, I started to follow, slowly keeping my distance. My bare, soft feet pressed into the gravel, and I was slightly chilled with goose bumps. It was a long drive, and I walked it without the air of determination my sister always had. I was curious. With my stomach poking out, I reached the mouth of the drive where the bus was just stopping. My sister turned and saw me standing there, mute and bashful, and cackled. I looked into the bus, through the windows that reflected the turning leaves, and saw the huge, open mouths of the students, climbing over each other to get to the window, their bodies shaking, their faces pressed to the glass. As the door folded open, there was a burst of sound escaping suddenly like the whistle of steam from a kettle. Once my sister had stepped up into the bus, and the door had closed off the noise, it pulled away. I hurried back up the drive, just until I was between the trees, just so long as I was inside the barrier.

That was fourteen years ago. But last summer, I was naked. At eighteen I stepped out of hiding, on purpose.

I had a boyfriend. As far as boyfriends go he was all right. He said a lot of nice things, made a lot of stupid mistakes, and was usually there when I wanted him to be. I suppose I loved him, though that's hard to say now. I used to say it all the time. It was an easy thing for me to yell after him as he left my doorstep. I never understood why my friends couldn't tell it to their boyfriends when they wanted to. It was a "stupid mistake" to speak the truth at the wrong time. I always stripped down as soon as I could. I just said it one day, he said it too, and we were happy.

Then summer came. We were separated by vacation plans. He was a counselor at a tennis camp, and I was living with my sister. For weeks we accepted our parting with optimism, like two children before Christmas, knowing it wouldn't be too long. I tried to hurry it along by taking a bus up to Vermont to see my Grandparents, who live near the camp. I told him I was coming, to take two days off. But when I got there, he couldn't get away. He had no transportation. He had no time off. We spoke on the phone from a distance of thirty miles.

"I think we should break up," he said.

"What?"

"It's ridiculous to keep this up. I never see you."

"That's your fault."

"Maybe."

"I can't believe you're saying this. Over the phone."

"How else could I? I never see you . . . I can't love someone I never see."

"Right."

"I'm going to be in California for four years, we'll never be together for more than three or four days again. Do you want that?"

I was crying.

"Look, I've gotta go, it's 6:30. Dinner."

"Uh huh."

"I'm gonna go."

After two days I wrote a letter. I mailed it the day I left for Europe. It was eight pages of words I had never been able to say to him; more than "I love you." They explained things, told him exactly how I felt. They were soft words, and so honest that I surprised myself. They remembered times we spent in high school, waiting to graduate together. They were sad words, admitting the loss I felt. They told him he was right. And they told him I still loved him.

In three weeks I got back from Europe. There was no letter.

This fall, sitting between the pillows on the futon, my roommates discussed art. We were hanging posters and I tacked up Matisse postcards on my bulletin board: a woman reclines on a chaise lounge in red harem pants, naked from the waist up. The walls of the room are orange and yellow flowers, and a blue and white patterned screen surrounds her. Her hands are behind her head and she is resting, calm. One roommate caught sight of a bared breast, and stopped.

"What is that?"

"What?"

"That's naked!"

"I know it's naked. Haven't you seen a nude before?"

"Not in a painting. I've seen myself."

"You've never seen nude painting? Aren't there museums in Newfoundland?"

"Yes, but they don't exhibit that."

"But it's important, it's beautiful."

"That's not beautiful, it's disgusting."

"It's art."

"It's disgusting."

I wondered if I had unconsciously taped the centerfold on my wall.

I see others carefully covering up their tracks like criminals, spreading the dust thin over the unique grooves they refuse to leave behind. They twist words into measured speeches, keeping silent the taboo feelings. They do it out of fear. They do it out of habit. They learn it young on school buses. They create barriers and never cross them. Because when we see nudity, when we hear nudity, we turn away, close the door to the dressing room in awkward haste or simple ridicule. So I keep reminding myself: I was born naked. I was born naked.

House of Cards

Gian Neffinger

My uncle is an artist, a master craftsman. He does not paint or sculpt or write or draw, at least not particularly well; these things are not his specialty. My Uncle Pete is a master builder of the House of Cards. He says he built his first such house when he was four, and although grandmother tends to doubt this claim, it is certain that he has worked at his skill for some time.

At family gatherings he would build the most magnificent structures imaginable, anything from a cottage complete with windows to a modern skyscraper eight stories tall. No high-rise was ever more of a feat to construct than one of Uncle Pete's masterpieces. At the crucial moment, when all of the family cringed and looked away, his hand was steady, his movements effortlessly precise. And when the occasional indoor breeze did drift through and fell his fragile giant, he simply sighed and sipped his coffee.

When at last he had finished, resisting the inexorable temptation to add just one more wing, he stood back to witness the sum of all the whims that went into its creation. Having duly admired it, he then turned his attention to another matter, that of choosing The Card. After careful analysis he rendered his decision: "That's the one." At this cue my cousin Andy and I began to salivate with anticipation. Who would get to pull out *the* card?

The Pulling of the Card was always saved as an after-dinner treat, but well before the appointed hour, Andy and I would examine the card in question and envision the fateful event like a child adoring a package under the tree on Christmas Eve. Surely it was great fun, watching Uncle Pete enlist each card into his conspiracy to defy the universal law of gravitation, but what made all of his efforts worthwhile to us was not the spectacle of completion but the spectacle of destruction. For upon the pulling of that one card, all of the delicate relationships that held the structure aloft dissolved, and that brilliant conspiracy was reduced to a scattered pile of playing cards, each as ordinary as the next. It was amazing how little disturbance it took; just to bump it would suffice. The only good way to get a sense of the delicate precision involved in creating it was to touch it gently, to try to alter it ever so slightly, and have it crumple to nothing. Andy and I used to promise each other the most outrageous things we could think of in exchange for the other's turn to tinker with The Card.

It was a unique phenomenon, the fall of a house of cards. Having not actually witnessed it, you might guess it would be fun to watch, but for all the wrong reasons. Mother never understood at all; she thought we were just being beastly, destroying the card house just as we destroyed our Lego airplanes and our matchbox cars and our new Sunday slacks. It was not anything malicious at all. "Malicious" is laughing at the blood dribbling from Tyler Evans' nose after my friend Pete clocked him. But Andy and I never had anything against Uncle Pete's houses; in fact we liked them. Malice had nothing to do with it.

Part of the appeal of getting to pull The Card was the sense of power—that's the part Andy and I fought over. Of course, we fought over everything that even vaguely resembled a privilege. But I remember, when no one was around, I used to go into the china cabinet, carefully bring out the beautiful, rose-colored heirloom teapot and hold it out at arm's length over the hard wood floor. The first time I tried this I was nervous—after all, what if I slipped? that would require some wild explaining—even if I did tell the truth, no one would believe me, and they would suspect something far more treacherous instead. That first time I got scared; I clutched the teapot against me and proceeded to carefully return it to its proper place. But something drew me back, until, after several visits, I would grandly swing my arm out to its full extension, as if presenting a trophy of war, and I would admire the finely crafted treasure, pausing only to glance at the unforgiving oak surface below. And I would think to myself, "I could, of course. I could just drop it, and no amount of surgery and no amount of prayer could ever bring it back." And oh, how I smiled!

When the house fell, when the invisible hand of physics let go and the cards fell in chaos, something powerful happened. Having that power between thumb and forefinger was a grand feeling. After all of the care that had gone into its assembly, it seemed ironic that it must all end with the tiniest of movements. Perhaps it was irony that made the moment magic. It would certainly seem equal to the task; it was irony that made the *Titanic* legend great. Had it not been billed as the Unsinkable Ship, its sinking would not have been so remarkable, and the world would never have had cause to learn that eight-ninths of an iceberg's mass lie concealed below the water's surface.

Whatever the meaning hidden in that final moment of splendor, one thing is sure: a sudden demise grants a certain timelessness. A. E. Housman, in his poem "To an Athlete Dying Young," tells of a champion who died in his prime, before his renown faded. He took his championship crown to his grave, where he could never be dethroned. Thus went the *Titanic*. It met its end as the pinnacle of naval technology, and now, whenever anyone thinks of the mightiest ship ever to cruise the open sea, none think of Old Ironsides, bobbing in its secure harbor with its heavy cargo of tourists; none think of the newest, most massive cruise liners or battleships, for the *Titanic* owns the title of mightiest—has owned it since that fateful night, and will own it forever.

So goes the house of cards—quickly, gloriously. No such house ever lasted long enough to suffer the indignities of time and fortune. Most great monuments are not nearly as lucky. Their features are worn away by time, or tourists; their renown is drowned in the wake of Progress. Their beauty is never apprehended; it just slowly fades away.

When I first came across the tragic hero in literature, I felt as if I had met him somewhere before. Here was a man, arguably a great man, who reached the pinnacle of his greatness in his own destruction. In his ruin, he proves himself, revealing, to the swift, the moral: "What a piece of work is a man!" and leaving even the stupid with a sense of wonder at the spectacle they have witnessed. The exceptional character placed in an unnatural circumstance makes for an extraordinary event, stretching the boundaries of our comprehension.

My Uncle Pete builds tragic heroes as a hobby; my cousin and I stage the plays: we circle, examine, touch gently, then grasp The Card, pause for a moment, and pull.

To this day I've never met anyone who could build a house of cards as well as Uncle Pete. To this day Andy and I take turns performing the after-dinner ritual; we have long since retired our Legos and our matchbox cars, but I don't know if we'll ever surrender our childhood rights to The Card. After all, better us than the breeze. What does a breeze know about beauty?

MID-SPECTRUM ESSAYS:
Veering toward Argument by Combining Analysis of Texts and Experience

These essays manage to combine exploration and analysis, bringing together stories of experience as well as textual evidence from essays, novels, and paintings. We are able to see the writers exploring their ideas while also being rigorously analytical and persuasive. Kristen E. Hughes, contemplating Picasso's *Guernica*, hits upon an idea about masculinity and then tells us what it means to be a female hero. Elizabeth MacDonald, working under the influence of the images of Ingres, de Chirico, and Hayworth, gives us a sense of what it means to suffer in the service of beauty. And Han N. Pham takes us "Down the Unwritten Path," leading us into cultural continuities and discontinuities as she draws on the experience of her Vietnam-born parents and grandparents and the evidence gleaned from Frances Fitzgerald's *Fire in the Lake.*

I Will Be My Own Hero

Kristen E. Hughes

I'll walk, but not in old heroic traces,
And not in paths of high morality,
And not among the half-distinguished faces,
The clouded forms of long-past history.

— CHARLOTTE BRONTË

In Picasso's *Guernica,* a bull stands implacably over a screaming woman with a dead child in her arms. Above and aloof from her and the other broken humans below, the bull may represent the German Luftwaffe, which bombed the small town of Guernica in 1937, or the ruthless *caudillo* Franco, or even the masculine pursuit of war itself. The bull's eyes remain expressionless despite the chaos and destruction around him, his ears and horns are simple and sharp. As I looked up at the bull a few years ago in Madrid, I found I hated and feared his strength, his virile indifference to the pain in the faces of the other figures in *Guernica;* yet I also felt awe and admiration. In a perverse way I love his pride and his independence. Sometimes I wonder if there is any of him in me. I wonder too if I want him there.

I used to have a secret hope that inside me there was a Hero who would take over my life and who only suffered from a lack of confidence. I always hoped that my Hero would take charge and make the decision to go adventuring, like Ulysses, across the world. I wanted to be able to say what Tennyson's Ulysses said: "I am become a name;/ For always roaming with a hungry heart/ Much have I seen and known." I yearned also to have "drunk delight of battle with my peers,/Far on the ringing plains of windy Troy" (10-12). What I lacked, I told myself, was opportunity. If the place and time were right, I could be brave and adventuresome, I imagined. I consoled myself for a long time, believing that somewhere within me was a "hungry heart" that would earn me power and glory: I would be Ulysses or Elizabeth the First, a monarch like the best of them. But only a few years ago I began to question what it was exactly that I was worshiping and what it was that I wanted to be.

I always wanted to be a boy when I was younger because I thought that only men (or very unusual women) could become heroic adventurers, and become "honour'd" in the world: they were the ones the inspirational poems were written about. Once on a Saturday morning when my father was home from work, the desire nagged bitterly. We sat in the kitchen, and it was dark enough that the lights were still on, yet the rays of the morning sun were slanting into my eyes through the trees and the French windows, and they glinted on Craig's curly blond hair. My mother and my father sat debating my brother's prospects around the breakfast dishes and the strewn remains of the morning paper. As Daddy planned his boy's future, his voice swelled with male pride I wanted so much to ridicule. Eventually I scooted my chair back from the table and walked away. When I was only halfway up the stairs my eyes were full of tears. Reaching my room I lay on my bed and sobbed and sobbed, pressing my pillow into my face, wishing that my father would show the personal interest in me Craig never seemed to appreciate.

I waited a long time for that recognition, and the waiting tempered my needs. As I gained my own footing, paying attention to what was going on around me, I began to question much of what I considered masculine. One day at school there was the usual argument in the common room during lunch hour. That day Tammy took on the five of us, and eventually, exasperated or defeated, she stormed off pouting. Later, after I had forgotten the whole scene, she walked back into the room after our group had broken up—Tammy tells me now that it was after classes. Her face was damp, and her hair a tangled mess. She begged me to come into the hall with her, and because she looked so worried, so pale, I followed her and listened.

"Kristen, there's something I need to tell you, if you'll listen. And you have to promise never to tell anyone else, not ever; it's been worrying me all day. Will you promise me?" She was pleading with an unusual intensity, and I couldn't imagine what she wanted to say.

"I'm not sure," I stammered, "that's a very difficult promise to . . ."

"Please, will you promise me?" she repeated. I swore I would never tell. She went on: "I need someone to understand, I can't go on like this. My mother has two broken ribs—Dad did it a couple of nights ago. He came home very late, after eating dinner with friends from work, and found an empty wine bottle on the living room floor. He accused Mummy of being an alcoholic. I was upstairs but came down when I heard the noise. But it was only after I left that he hit her. I don't know what to do, and this isn't the first time."

I don't remember the rest of what Tammy said; it has blended in my memory with other stories she has told me since. Shocked and confused, I tried to find out what she wanted to do. Nothing, was the answer. I remember the blinking T.V. screen behind her head announcing the week's events in school, the black wires dangling from the ceiling to the box on the wall.

Tammy says now that her father has the mental age of a five-year-old and that he doesn't know what he is doing, and that is why he breaks her mother's ribs. The violence in men, she would say, is the violence of the boy who rips the wings off flies, and burns ants by concentrating sunlight through a magnifying glass, just as my golden-haired brother used to do not so long ago. On lazy summer afternoons, as if practicing an obscure sacrificial rite, my brother would construct a pyre of grass and dry leaves on our stone patio and lure insects to them with crumbs of food; then, as he angled his glass just so, the pyre and the bodies would go up in flames. The composed and aloof expression on his face suggested that the whole experience was nothing but an experiment for him. He went on calmly to teach the art to our younger brother. Like Tammy's father, he seemed unaware of the pain he might be causing, or the memories he was leaving behind.

These days I no longer adore Ulysses. Though I occasionally desire his "hungry heart," when I think that he had to drink "delight in battle" to satisfy his hunger, I feel betrayed. I am horrified by the thought of my hero fighting, killing, standing proud on the "ringing plains of Troy" bloody sword in hand. Tammy's father and my brother played havoc with that illusion of mine, and I have found too that my own hungry heart can lead me astray.

I too have destroyed life. The six little bodies were those of baby gerbils. All together they had fit snugly into the palm of my hand and wriggled under the water less and less until their movements had stopped, and they were dead. My gerbils had been reproducing every month—every month there was a new litter of ugly, blind, pink babies—and eventually I decided that I could stand the mess and the visitors' oohs and aahs no longer. So I came up with a master plan: I sentenced the babies to a watery death. My father offered to help, but I refused to allow him the honor. It was my operation, and I was going to carry it out with the skill, nerve, and command of a general under fire. But I found that I didn't have the heart for it. I have no respect for what I did.

I wanted, and still want, the admiration of my father. I want the attention of independent boys. I want to be a hero myself. But I no longer stand in awe of the male hero's virile power. I have resented my own father's indifference and have seen the aftermath of violence, and have had boyfriends leave me without a trace of regret. Their tough indifference has wounded me. Alice Walker says, "I saw in [Martin Luther King, Jr.] . . . the hero for whom I had waited so long." She saw in him a model of nonviolence. I am sure, though, that it was not just her adoration for Dr. King that made Walker what she is now; it was her own determination, her own inner resolve. It is not by aspiring to be a great man, or even by following one that I can find my answers. So now I am involved in a new search for a hero within me, but this time the hero will not be a bull, or a Ulysses, or even a Tudor queen.

There is a man, a solitary, adventurous, and heroic man, in Gabriel García Márquez's *One Hundred Years of Solitude,* whose grand illusion of war is shattered, and he can no longer act the soldier. Colonel Aureliano Buendía lives out the remainder of his life in the solitude of his workshop, making, melting, and remaking little gold fishes. "He had had to start thirty-two wars and had had to violate all of his pacts with death and wallow like a hog in the dungheap of glory in order to discover the privileges of simplicity almost forty years later" (163). But Buendía's are not the privileges of old age that I want for myself. He never makes anything that lasts. He melts down the fishes he crafts. He only makes to destroy and to remake. Soldiering was all that he knew. Years after Buendía's death his great-great-nephew—his namesake—looks for the history of his parentage. All the local priest remembers of the old colonel is that a street in town had once borne his name.

After Aureliano Buendía gave up his warring, he could never find the man within himself who could live a quiet life well; he did not have the inner resources he needed to turn his energies to life and the community where he lived. He left nothing of lasting value.

Perhaps it was Nathan, more than any of those other men, who opened my eyes. With Nathan I tried to claim something I had no right to. I didn't know it at the time. Nathan was proud, and inevitably I loved him. I saw in him the boy I wanted to be. He was a dark knight with a beautiful cold smile, a would-be rower, and a chain-smoker at the age of sixteen. I never knew exactly who he was. He was a stranger to me as Colonel Aureliano Buendía had been a stranger to his own mother. Nathan had a faraway look in his eyes, as if he was always dreaming of some other place. I longed to tame him, make him interested in me. But he never even asked me how I felt, and he never praised me. I would dress up for him and suffer for days waiting for him to call.

When Nathan finally got around to coming, he would say, "Kris, I'm going out to a film with the guys tonight and then we're going to get trashed at Kim's house since his parents are in Majorca."

"What about tomorrow?" I would ask.

"Sorry, out rowing tomorrow. Do you want to hear a great song we invented yesterday? It goes like this.

"I woke up this morning, tanananana,

"And wha'du you know, tanananana, . . ."

And I would listen just to hear him talk.

One night he left me for another girl, no explanations, nothing. I hated him and his righteous arrogance, but I think I still love the wild spirit in him. I still yearn to live a life that seems an answer to my own desires. But I can't be indifferent to those around me, can't quite see how my heart can close itself to all the others.

The soldier, the bull, the boy have reasons for killing and inflicting pain, I think, and I cannot understand them. On the one hand they want to gain glory and exalt themselves. A natural part of the glory-making is defeating others, triumphing in battle, controlling other lives. On the other hand, the childish delight in torture, in violence, only exists in some of them. I have seen it in Tammy's father, in my brother, in Pinkie, and in me. Pinkie, the seventeen-year-old gangster and Catholic boy in Graham Greene's *Brighton Rock*, believed the only life after death was in Hell:

> Pinkie stood looking down on the greying hair; he felt no pity at all; he wasn't old enough for pity. . . . A leather-jacket buzzed up the pane and the Boy caught it in his hand. It vibrated like a tiny watch spring in his palm. He began to pull off the legs and wings one by one. "She loves me," he said, "she loves me not. I've been out with my girl, Spicer." (134)

The girl, Rose, he threatened with vitriol, and subsequently married so that she wouldn't implicate him in a murder. She was willing; she idolized him and thought she shared something with him, that they were the same: Catholic and quiet. Violent, Pinkie was frigid and a virgin. He derived his pleasure not from sex, not from Rose, but from cutting people up with his razor blade, from torture. I see some of the dispassionate glee that Pinkie feels when he is thinking about vitriol, or a razor, in the eyes of the toro as he stands over Guernica's destruction. I also see that delight in the eyes of some men, and I turn away. I want to follow a new hero who will also turn away.

Tammy's revelation to me about her father changed the way I thought about heroism and the seductive power of virility. I recognize that the fear I felt looking up at the bull on the huge canvas of *Guernica* two years ago in Spain came from my knowledge of the pain and terror Tammy's father inflicts on her and her mother. What I learned from Nathan was more important than he was to me: what I had been seeking was not to be found where I had been looking. I realized that Nathan worked very hard for his "hard" cool image; and though he never told me what joy it brought him, I know now that it would never satisfy me.

I am finding a new Hero in myself to follow. She can be violent at times, because she can be everything, but she will always be sorry. No matter how hungry her heart, indifference will not suit her. She has an indomitable will but is never proud for long.

WORKS CITED

Brontë, Charlotte. "Stanzas." In *The New Oxford Book of Victorian Verse*. Ed. Christopher Ricks. New York: Oxford University Press, 1990.

Greene, Graham. *Brighton Rock.* New York: Viking, 1953.

Márquez, Gabriel García. *One Hundred Years of Solitude.* Trans. Gregory Rabassa. New York: Avon, 1971.

Tennyson, Lord Alfred. "Ulysses." In *The New Oxford Book of Victorian Verse.* Ed. Christopher Ricks. New York: Oxford University Press, 1990.

Walker, Alice. "The Civil Rights Movement: What Good Was It?" *In Search of Our Mothers' Gardens.* New York: Harcourt Brace, 1984. 119–29.

Odalisque

Elizabeth MacDonald

I am in eighth grade—perhaps two weeks, or even a week before all the trouble started—and walking one evening with a friend on the east side of Manhattan. I catch sight of my reflection in a plateglass window and, in these formative years, observe what I am becoming. My hair is short and less feminine at this time, my face rounder, my body plumper. I was happy with what I saw.

I am in ninth grade and my waist is the thickness of a bottleneck. Lying on my bed I hear my parents talking about me as they walk along the hall.

"This diet has gone on too long," my mother is saying, "she's gotten very weak."

"She is very thin," says my father.

I am in tenth grade and fatter than I have ever been. In a book written during the Twiggy-influenced sixties I read that every day that you fast you lose two pounds of fat. This seems easier than recovering the discipline that I had once in such abundance and have now lost. I begin a regimen in which I eat enormous amounts for a few days and fast on the others. I want very much to regain the beauty that was once mine, to rediscover the indestructible, perfect creature of angles and spare planes that lies hidden under this amorphous mass of lumps. I want more than anything to be thin again. This seems to be a way. For a desperate girl who has no assurance that she will ever be desirable almost no price is too high.

I do not remember the first time that I made myself throw up. It may have been in eleventh grade, but the circumstances have faded under the shame and horror. As I understand it, many people try self-induced vomiting. Few are successful on the first attempt and most give up. Some of us persist: some of us even become quite talented.

In that talent I originally found salvation. Self-indulgence and beauty seemed, for the first time, compatible. I could give myself everything I wanted and retain the figure of the ascetic. I could have my cake, and I could eat it too. Nothing, however, is that easy. Maintaining the façade becomes indispensable. Every compliment is a knife in the gut and an impulse to retain what I have, though I pay, and pay dearly. There is a line in Yeats' "Adam's Curse" that cries bitterness—

> To be born woman is to know—
> Although they do not talk of it at school—
> That we must labor to be beautiful

I have only just discovered that I have been misquoting these lines for years. In my mind the last line, though essentially the same, has always had a slightly different nuance.

> . . . We must suffer to be beautiful.

The most famous photograph of Rita Hayworth, as Gilda, immortalizes her as an extraordinary beauty. In black satin she stands, mysterious and gorgeous—a stunning beauty, with allure and come-hither confidence. Her skin glows alabaster against a black background and on her beautiful face, slightly turned to the side, is a look of encouragement and, conversely, knowing distance. She tilts her chin up in the arrogance of her beauty: she knows very well that she stops traffic and hearts. Her hair is long, her waist is small, and her strapless dress clings to her perfect figure. Her self-presentation is more than feminine; it is the essence of female. Rita Hayworth played a woman all men wanted and all women wanted to be. She sets the standard of what it is to be an ideal woman—a flesh Goddess.

I have heard that she could not reconcile her beauty and herself, that she felt herself to be an illusion created by lights and other people's vision of what she should be. You could never tell that from this photograph. This woman revels in nothing more than her sexuality and beauty. And for all that, all the power and joy in her physical presence that she presents to the world in this still, Rita Hayworth never believed in the image she presented. She felt that the façade was fraudulent and that she was two people inhabiting a beautiful shell whose two sides were irreconcilable. Her most famous quotation is a cry of pain. "Every man I ever knew went to bed with Gilda and woke up with me." They saw in her the realization of all their dreams and found that she was just a woman. Men looked in her for Gilda and a goddess. Inside she knew that she was as mortal as Mary Sixpack and she could not bear the split between her image and what she felt to be her real self. She suffered in her beauty.

In the margins of most of my notebooks is the sketch of a woman's head in a three-quarter view. Her hair is long and her cheekbones are far more pronounced than mine will ever be, no matter how thin I get. Her jaw is very defined. I gave her a name once, a name that has much to do with ethereality and fragility and a name as imaginary as is Gilda. I only christen the sketches that turn out well with that name. I only want to draw a Gilda, and I only want to be a Gilda, even knowing what Gilda did to Rita Hayworth.

I would never presume to compare my looks with those of Rita Hayworth, but I am a woman, and I know about laboring. I too have learned that there is a price to be paid for beauty. I live the same deception as she did. I am not what I seem, and the deception battles my soul.

"Yes, I am attracted," I overheard him say once, "but I don't think she's my type." He did not know me at that point. I was a shell and a body, long hair and green eyes and long legs and a small waist, nice curves for one so thin. I know that he wants the flesh envelope that I walk in. I and others have seen him looking at me, my hair, my face, my legs. He has twisted around in chairs to watch me as I go by, and I know that he is aware of me whenever I am around him. My physicality is a magnet. He wants and he wants, but he just wants a body. He does not want me. He himself is easy in his corporeality: he has the athlete's presence and the athlete's ability to live within his skin and take pleasure in the way his body works. I think I felt that if he—so easy in his skin—believed in my entirety then I too would believe. Only my body sold. Uninterested in the interior, he cannot divorce himself of his attraction for the façade, and I am caught. The façade always sells first, and therefore the façade must always be maintained, no matter what.

I met him for breakfast one morning this winter when the snow was falling softly. I walked alone in the quiet of early morning. I could feel the snow collecting on the gauze of my hair. Alone with him in a near-empty dining hall, I felt cold, and my food had no taste. I ate very little. After breakfast I disappeared.

Sometimes, when I have disappeared and I am unrecognizable, invisible, I run my hands over the planes of my face, telling myself that I am, I am, I am. I exist, I am alive, I tell myself, running my fingertips over the sockets of bone in which those green eyes lie, and I discover the line of my jaw beneath my skin. My eyelashes tickle my hands, and my hands worship my flesh and my bones. I am reassuring myself that somewhere under my rib cage my heart beats, that though invisible I am not gone.

I remember the first time I threw up blood.

The modern artist Giorgio de Chirico painted in a classical manner. His subjects seem to be informed by Italian Renaissance models but the classical vision has been tortured and twisted and made strange. His paintings recede into depth in skewed perspective, and nature has been warped into something that is both recognizable and alien. In his lonely, dark settings the shadows are like none ever seen in reality but are still frighteningly real. "There are more enigmas in the shadow of a man who walks in the sun," he said, "than in all the religions of past, present and future." In the medium he devoted his life to he could find no answers: mysteries were easier than a simple darkness, the shadow of a man in the sun. The lines of his paintings are invariably ruler straight, but there is no peace or ease to be found in his art. His paintings are disorienting: they are the representation of a human imbalance and uncertainty in the world.

I am uneasy in my shell.

The neoclassical artist Ingres painted figures of dubious anatomical construction but used the questions to glorify the beauty of the human shape rather than to disorient the viewer. It is the male body that is said to represent best the human form for its shape follows the lines of the core and is undisguised by curves and softness. Ingres painted women. In "The Turkish Bath" many women lie in splendor, impossibly twisted into sensuous shapes. He celebrates the disguising curves and softness, emphasizing them, asserting roundness as beautiful. In another celebration of Woman, "La Grande Odalisque," a beautiful woman reclines alone [see color insert]. I first saw this painting in grisaille, a technique that simulates statuary, molding the human shape in shades of gray.

The body of this Turkish harem slave is everything that I wish I could permit mine to be. It is voluptuous and smooth; it is classically feminine. In the line of breast and hip, of round arm and thigh, globes and arcs connect and flow, defining grace and beauty. Hers is a celebration of existence, of the flesh and the senses. Nude she reclines, luxuriating in herself as a living being and a body. Her setting reflects and enhances the luxury of her being: royal blue, oriental cushions, self-indulgence and self-love. She cares for her own pleasure. Her skin is pale, and the feminine aspects of her figure have been emphasized to the point of distortion. Her shoulders are narrow; her waist is small, and her lower back is far too long. The elongation highlights the flesh at the hip and leads into her legs. They appear shorter than they would were she thin. Her feet and hands are fragile, her visible eye luminous, and the bones of her face have a delicate beauty. She is direct and beautiful. She is sensuous and sensual. She is enigmatic and she is feminine. Her glance over her round shoulder beckons and arrogantly asserts her power. Nude, she revels in herself as a sexual being. She does not hide.

In my dreams, though, I take on the attributes not of the Odalisque, but of my impossibly idealized sketch. The world celebrates my fragility and stunning physical presence. I define gorgeous. The earth congratulates itself that I pass time on its surface. I am delicate and so breathtakingly beautiful that I put Gilda to shame.

Ingres chose not to make his Odalisque's body anatomically correct. By the standards of reality it is warped and strangely twisted, wrong like de Chirico's perspective. Her arm and her lower back are far too long, her leg twists around her other leg. Her body is more than imperfect, it is impossible, but in its impossibility the necessities of bone and blood have been sacrificed to the beauty of line and form. Where de Chirico skews perspective to disorient, Ingres twists a body and liberates it. Without the bones that constrain the normal human figure, she is freer in her flesh. She is more conscious of her own power and presence. She inhabits her body in joy, accepting it, loving her curves and sensuality, hedonism inherent in the hookah and crumpled sheets. She flows feminine.

In Ingres' world—though not in mine—she need not suffer to be easy in her skin.

Down the Unwritten Path

Han N. Pham

> To the Traditional Vietnamese, the nation consisted of a landscape and the past of the family. . . . the family was the essence, the cell as it were, that contained the design for the whole society.
>
> FRANCES FITZGERALD
FIRE IN THE LAKE

My family has never posed for a family portrait, as most families do. Perhaps this is because we've never had the time or the patience to drag ourselves down to the local photographer and smile with clenched sincerity, eyes checking watch, fingernails tapping impatiently on the corner table. Or perhaps it is because we've never placed much value in "normal" family traditions: the family vacations untaken, the sweet babybooks never bought, the dinner table never used except for the solitary click clicking of a pair of chopsticks. Sometimes. And always alone. In any case, our family history is inscribed in each of us; its struggles mark us, but most notably it marks the women in my family—my grandmother, my mother, me. We, the life-givers and unspoken historians of our family legacy, carry with us, in our faces, in our actions, the unwritten history of our family—past, present, and perhaps, future.

I

Imagine now, just a picture of a woman laughing. That's all. A woman so small in her stature that she could fade into the gray carpet, the gray wall. Only she doesn't. Somehow her vitality has leaked out into her clothing, from the magenta pumps with elfin toes, to the white blouse peeking out from under the

suit so blue it seems the tailor took a portion of the deep blue sky stretched somewhere between dawn and twilight, added a dash of the Caribbean Sea, and filled
the entire length with white sunlight until it was bursting, bursting with blue.
This suit, left alone, could have danced waltzes with more passion than most
people. Yet it was the woman within who brought the final touch.

My mother is the woman laughing in the picture.

She is the kind of mother that carries with her a sweet scent of motherhood
wherever she goes: her arms are soft, her eyes kind, her full pink lips are always
trembling to kiss you. Lips that never thought that they would have to utter to her
children, "Your father is leaving me." Not us. Not my brother and me. Just her
alone. She never expected it to happen to her, this fragmentation of the family, this
abrupt dismissal by her husband. But she accepted it with the quiet obedience so
characteristic of any woman raised in Old Vietnam. Looking at her, within her, listening to the words that fall from lips that might have well been my grandmother's, or her mother's before her, I hear the essence of all the Vietnamese
cultural values that her mother instilled in her and she sought to instill in me:
Obey your parents. Obey your husband. Be ladylike. You are a girl; not a boy.
Then I realize that she is, for me, for my children, the last rickety bridge that
sways somewhere between Old Vietnam and my new America.

II

I am sitting cross-legged on the floor, the soles of my pink feet staring at me
with a chubby softness. I watch my grandmother, who is leaning heavily against
the back of the broken recliner, her rough-skinned hands lying awkwardly in her
lap, palms upward, slightly tilted toward one another as if one hand is asking the
other, "What are we to do now?"

I am interviewing her for a required English project, a report entitled "Words
of the Wise and Experienced." I am asking her about her childhood, the way she
was raised. She tells me, in a throaty voice that dips now and then into bitterness,
that she was raised to work every day, in the fields, in the kitchen, at home, at
school. She was not spoiled like *American* children, her small black eyes focusing
quickly on me before they slip back out of focus. She could cook, clean, sew, raise
chickens, a garden, children—every accomplishment needed of a wife ticked off
on wrinkled fingers swollen with arthritis.

Looking at her weary face, I try to ask a simpler question, a happier one. "And
your husband?" I ask.

She mouths a few sentences in trailing Vietnamese whispers. "He was chosen
for me. He not pretty-boy. But my parents chose him, and you must always listen
to your parents. So we married, and he was my husband." She stops, as if that was

all there was to her marriage. He was her husband. Perhaps she believed her parents when they told her that if she listened to them, then she would always have happiness.

My grandfather stayed behind with his mistress, their former chambermaid, when my grandmother left Vietnam with her daughter and son-in-law and their children, all staking their futures on a leaking boat, filled with peasants and squawking poultry that rained colored feathers, which rocked out onto the black, rolling sea under the cover of night. She would not see my grandfather again for ten years, when she was reunited with him in America. With him came my half-uncle, child of the other woman. To save face, she allows him to call her "Mother."

III

In Vietnam, perhaps in any Asian culture, a woman's life is taking care of her family, in pleasing her husband. A woman without a family is poor, and pitied. A woman whose husband speaks poorly of her, who abuses and mocks her, is a shame to the community. A woman who speaks up against this is an embarrassment. But, perhaps the worst, is a woman whose husband has left her. She then becomes the forgotten spirit of the community, someone to look down upon, to sidle by with a snicker and whispered remarks, a woman to be shunned.

Two generations of my family's women have experienced unhappiness in their married life. Two women wove small deceptions to hide their shame. My grandmother accepted into her life, without a murmur, a strange fifteen-year-old boy who called her "Mother." My mother, when my father moved into his own house many miles away, taught me to say that my father was at work and would return home late every time someone called him. She begged me to learn to tell happy family stories when I visited my other grandmother, my father's mother, in Los Angeles. Through her, I learned how to smile in the face of misery at home, at school, anywhere.

IV

It has been about two years since my father left.

It may be a little shorter, or a little longer; I have accepted it so well I have forgotten. There was never an event that caused my father to storm out of the house, no outburst, no slamming of the door. Sometimes, in my sleep, with eyes shut tight, I can hear past echoes of my father yelling at my mother, of my brother yelling at my father, of my mother crying and yelling at the world for an outlet from the pain. I know now that my father did not leave because of a mistress, as so many are quick to ask me when they find out. It is as FitzGerald related in one section of her book, *"a [Vietnamese] man is not an independent character . . . but a social role—he must always act in the correct manner, no matter what it costs him."* My father left because he could no longer play the role of the strong Vietnamese husband, who had complete control of his household, whose wife was always pretty and delicate, whose children were quiet and obedient. He could not play his Vietnamese role to perfection in America.

He, too, had his secret shame.

V

So many generations have flowed between the rice paddy fields and the hedges of cane, so that "the sense of limitation and enclosure was as much a part of traditional life as of the life of the nation." In the end, the lives of the Vietnamese people concentrated solely on the land and the family. The land was the constant element that sheltered the family from outside influences and helped the family to perpetuate its sacred values and traditional roles of the family: husband and wife, father and son, mother and daughter. However, every tradition, every value, stemmed from the land and was tied intricately to it—"as long as Vietnamese Society remained a closed system, intellectual foundations remained flawless and immobile . . . without their land, they were without a social identity"—*Fire in the Lake*.

So, by passing from Vietnam into America, my family forsook its identity, and began anew.

VI

The arguments have faded long ago. My father no longer tries to run away; he comes every Friday to pick up my mother so they can pass the weekend together. He always smiles quietly at me, and laughs, eyes glistening with a suspicious moistness every time I hug him and pat his balding head, forgiving him. My mother still does everything to please him. Even when he left, she helped him buy furniture and decorations for his home. She proudly proclaims that his garden is the prettiest on the block; she spent many hours crouched on the soft, green grass, happily weeding and making a nest for the seeds she had bought, carefully pouring her love into the earthen beds so that on the day the flowers peeked above their rims of soil to surround that lonely house far away, my father, too, would drink the love that fell from their perfumed petals, poured from the hands of my mother, given freely from the hearts of his family.

The shame has passed.

VII

The suffocating Vietnamese culture that taught my mother, and her mother, and many mothers before to always obey, and tread softly, and speak quietly, is giving way to mine: an American culture where the women stand tall beside the men, where one opinion is weighed against the other on the basis of intelligence, not sex. The women need never flinch, or bow their heads. I can stamp my feet, yell as loud as I want, and never hide here. No one will ever be able to tell me that I must obey my husband, and bear the burdens of the struggles of my family alone, as if I am afraid to be shunned by the community when I let on that I am not perfect, that my family is not the perfect Vietnamese family.

VIII

On the face of my grandmother is the story of Old Vietnam, complete with cultural, social, and family values, etched in the lines of her cheeks, her mouth, her eyes. Then, encountering the picture of my mother, described in the beginning of her laughing at work, taken during our own family crises, you would never realize that the woman so vibrant with laughter had not laughed for many months. But, if you look carefully, you might be able to see the threads of my family's future in the picture, in my mother's stance, and the way her head falls back as she laughs.

Imagine now, only a woman, young or old, in a picture laughing. Laughing with her feet planted firmly on the ground, toes spread out wide to claim her space. Laughing with her body tall and straight, shoulders thrown back with confidence. Laughing with a bob of black hair bouncing back from a head bent backwards, as if leaning back from the weight of the huge smile, open to show two rows of glistening white teeth and a curled pink tongue, that tickles the face open with happiness. Laughing, with twinkling black Asian eyes squeezed tight above a snub nose that rises above the round cheeks like a little hill about to topple over.

This image of the woman, my mother, is the final piece to the fragmented picture described in the beginning, where initially you could only see a woman, in vibrant clothes, laughing. Here you see the entire being: my mother, whole, happy, and strong. And, just as easily, perhaps you can picture me, in the same stance, with the same confidence, laughing, or my daughter after me, or the daughter after that. For the picture could be any of us, now, in the future, laughing with the strength that generations of women before us have passed on to us.

Together, we are the women of our family, holding in our actions, our tears, and our laughter the living etches of our family history—from the Old Vietnam that is my grandmother sitting wearily against the back of the broken recliner, across the rickety bridge that is my mother struggling to find laughter, continuing on to me—the daughter who carries our family's fresh, unwritten pages on into America.

*   *   *

Han N. Pham's essay—one version of it at least—ends here, with the beautiful images of her mother as a rickety bridge uniting her mother's and her old world of Vietnam with her and her daughter's new world of America, the pages of their lives here remaining to be written.

As readers and writers ourselves, we love the essay as it stands. As teachers, however, we wondered whether there wasn't something more that Han could include, something more about her mother and her father. So we asked her the following questions:

- What is there from your grandmother's tradition that has been transported to America and that allows your mother to laugh in the picture of her you describe?
- Can you explain a bit further the connection between what remains from your grandmother's tradition in making your mother the woman she became and you the woman you are becoming?
- How does your father figure into the equation with you and your mother? Can you tell us more about the image of your father living by himself and yet your mother feeling a need to help him?

After thinking about these questions, Han wrote an additional section, which follows. She prefaced her new concluding extension with a note to us that reads in part: "The clue—the image of my father living by himself and my mother giving in to him . . . In the investment of herself for his benefit there is love . . . He is forgiven no matter what he has done . . . You were right in assuming that the clue lay with my father. Read on."

IX

Reflections on "Down the Unwritten Path"

I remember the period of time surrounding my father's leaving and the careful shattering of our family structure so well, as if it was an old movie reel creaking slow images past the eyes of my mind. I remember yelling at my mother, my voice catching as it reeled toward the heights of our vaulted ceiling in desperate, demanding tones: Why don't you stand up to him? Why do you let him treat you that way? Why are you so obedient? I remember her staring at me in a strange way as I screamed out that last word, "obedient."

She knew that I didn't understand. But now I do.

"Down the Unwritten Path" forced me to give voice to the feelings that had struggled unheard; the same concepts that had caused me to emblazon an angry "weak" against my family have now led to the word that is the foundation for these pages—"strong": the sacred concepts of family, its roles, and its honor. It is no exaggeration to say that these concepts were as essential to my family as they were to Vietnam, one viewing itself as a miniature model of the larger, who, in turn, viewed herself as a nation merely perpetuating an enlarged role of the family—an endless cycle of complete roundness, a healthy circle pouring joy and prosperity from past generations into the new.

When my grandmother traveled to America, leaving behind her a nation still smoking in the ruins of the Vietnam War, she brought with her a strange commodity that she had already instilled in her daughter, who had just begun her married life in America—stability. I remember scoffing at the thought of the typical Asian man-and-woman relationship, so barbaric in its command that husband speak, wife obey. When my grandmother accepted my half-uncle into her life, when my mother never yelled back when she should have, could have, when she helped nurture my father's garden and pick out his furniture, I called it "obedience."

I was wrong.

Although this essay is clearly a tribute to the women in my family, the key truly does lie in their relationship with their men: their husbands, fathers, and sons. It is not obedience that keeps harsh words from spilling out in reply to the same, nor is it obedience that causes a woman to "give" so unselfishly to her husband. It is, rather, a deep, ancient understanding that the family is total—that determination, perseverance, and a strong love are needed to do these little tasks that the "civilized" world, with former citizens like me, scoff at. They are not taught to remain silent in the time of crises; their actions alone state that they understand the situation, and are willing to wait silently as they "ride out the storm" very much like the mother who learns to purse her lips while waiting for her obstinate child to learn by doing what she has told him he should not do. These actions do not depict a weak flower, swayed by the winds of struggle; they depict, instead, the silent dignity and honor that surround women who stand, face into the wind, weathering it by planting seeds to await the spring rains and whispering strength into the ears of "Americanized" children asking questions for a school report.

Love, honor, roles, relationships, strength, determination, family—these are the words that form an endless chain into the past, connecting my grandmother, my mother, and me with the other side of the sacred circle—our brothers, husbands, and fathers. They are all boats that help us weather the storm as they carry us to the New World and toward other lands.

ARGUMENTATIVE ESSAYS:
Making a Case through the Analysis of Texts

These essays focus on the close analysis of texts—photographs, an essay, and a painting. These three writers did a great deal of exploring before they began writing their essays; as they wrote their preliminary drafts, they were not only trying to figure out what the photographs, essay, or painting meant to them but also looking into just how that meaning was conveyed. Analyzing, they were taking the texts apart and putting them back together in their minds, all as a way of understanding what they were reading.

In their essays, they tell us the results: what the texts mean to them and how they convey their meaning. These essays are more direct, more certain about their conclusions than the exploratory essays in the first group. But you still get to see these writers thinking as they make their claims about the texts and use the evidence they select from those texts (photographs, essay, painting) to help us understand their interpretive claims. Anna Norris argues that because photographs are as complex as written texts, they must be *read* carefully, considering their context, their genre, and the photographer's aesthetic choices. David Reich adds a new twist to the meaning of standard English, taking a stand against one of Amy Tan's claims in her essay "Mother Tongue." Jessica Underwood interprets George de la Tour's seventeenth-century painting *The Penitent Magdalen,* looking into mythical, cultural, biographical, and religious aspects of the painting.

How to Read Photographs

Anna Norris

A photograph is not an objective window onto reality; therefore, it is always being manipulated in some way, to some specific end.

In 1936 Laszlo Moholy-Nagy, photographer and Bauhaus professor, wrote: "The illiterate of the future will be ignorant of the use of camera and pen alike." Photographs are as complex as text is, and a viewer's reaction to them can be controlled, or guided, through the manipulation of several fundamental elements. They consist, roughly, of the photographer's aesthetic and formal choices, the preexisting social context or genre in which the photograph appears, and its immediate surroundings (for example the editorial choices in a publication), all of which provide layers of information that create the desired effect.

The first thing to understand is that a photograph is never simply the trace of an event. The visual world is abstracted through the photographer's choices. There is no objectivity; the photographer always chooses how to respond to a situation. It is important to bear this in mind because the myth of objectivity is supported by the equally prevalent myth of photographic veracity. However, we will see that even though the photographer's personal vision creates the original picture, the photograph can be used to support an idea that the photographer disagrees with or at least never intended to address. Public belief in the absolute truth of photographic imagery makes this practice possible. It is important to be aware of the way photographs function to read the individual photograph and realize its possibilities.

Maybe the most immediate element that influences how a photograph is read is its visual effect—the thing that creates a response in a viewer. Everyone makes an aesthetic judgment: is the picture good, bad, mediocre? It is important for a viewer to realize what aesthetic traditions are informing the reaction to an individual image. Often when a viewer thinks a photograph is "good," it simply means that the image is similar to one that the person has seen before in some professional context. That is why the "best" travel photographs look like postcards, and the "best" portraits look like something out of a magazine. This aspect of reading photographs is the most startling to analyze because it exposes just how prevalent visual formulas are—the same basic picture appears over and over. These formulas have evolved over the course of visual history and reappear in new forms against the currents of culture. It is unlikely, in fact, that one can make an entirely new image. Thus photographs' power comes in how they are used.

Portraits, for example, are well-loved because we recognize parts of our own humanity in each other's faces. With portraits we write our personal history as it happens, but they also serve specific cultural functions, as they have throughout the history of art. Today's traditions in formal portraiture follow a pre-existing formula that has a message built in. Take the high school senior portrait as an example. The pictures all look the same; the student is smiling and the lighting is soft, the background is controlled. The pictures have meaning to a friend through the visual reference to an individual, but that personal recognition is not the only information in the picture. It uses a formula which is a standardized visual code (the smile, the lighting, the framing) that establishes a visual common ground with other pictures of that kind, and within each describes a cultural norm that, through its proliferation, reflects what is respectable and therefore acceptable. I remember my high school senior class as having been made up of almost every subculture thinkable: punks, goths, skaters, cowboys, preps, everyone. But in the yearbook the class looks like a homogenous group of middle-class American teenagers. This is not representative, but we appear that way because it was necessary to make a nice portrait, and a nice portrait meant we all had to look acceptable. Although a few of the students appeared to be representative of cultures other than the white middle class, most of the students went to the photographer's studio with the knowledge of the sort of formula that was necessary to uphold to have a nice portrait for the relatives and the yearbook. It is the cultural idea that creates the pictures.

One way to substantiate this idea is to look at traditions of photographic portraiture in other cultures. There have been mainstream traditions of portrait-making that, for example, don't even necessitate the presence of the subject. In some African societies, if twins were born and sometime during childhood one of them died, the family might have a portrait made in which the surviving girl twin was photographed, and then photographed again wearing boy's clothing to represent her deceased male sibling. The two pictures would be displayed in the same frame and seen as a perfectly acceptable remembrance of both twins. In the early days of photography in the U.S., it was common to have pictures made of an infant that had just died, as a way to remember the child. However, no one wanted to remember the child dead, so often in the final print the child's eyes were painted open such that he or she appeared alive. These practices are not purely representational, but the pictures are no less representational than those from our own traditions. The idea is not just to remember a person, but to use culturally recognized symbols in order both to remember the person in a particular way and to perpetuate those cultural traditions to which the picture refers. The senior portrait shows not just our faces, but also our performance for the camera. If the purpose were to represent the class as a group of independently thinking people with their own values and goals, we would have each been encouraged to design a portrait that showed the things about ourselves we considered important. However, that is not the way a yearbook functions, and therefore that is not the kind of photograph it seeks or includes.

This basic idea—that pictures are fashioned to serve a specific purpose—is crucial to understand, because once the viewer has the tools to bypass the construct that gives meaning to the picture, it becomes possible to understand both how and why the construct functions and what the picture has the potential to convey.

As we have seen, visual imagery is sometimes used to reinforce social/political standpoints. We have already looked at how a seemingly innocuous pre-existing context creates seemingly new photographs that perpetuate a social attitude, and now we move to a wider area in order to explore some of the many elements that influence the ways individual photographs are read. The following is a simple example to show how a photograph interacts with the photographs around it and how even without lengthy textual explanation, it is designed to influence the viewer's opinion about a situation. The two photographs "Financial District, 1998" and "Spectators at the African-American Day Parade, Harlem, 1998" could be seen simply as examples of public murals in different neighborhoods within a city. A surface reading of the photographs would tell you that they are of murals painted in different styles to fit the neighborhood. In the Financial District of New York we see a scene of nineteenth-century luxury, a lakeside park filled with fashionably dressed ladies out to enjoy the day and watch the sailing. In Harlem, however, the murals do not glorify the satisfied lifestyle of the upper class in some romantic age, designed to be pleasing to the eye and remind us of the pleasures of money, but instead depict present-day working people of different races dedicated to fighting against the discrimination and limited opportunities that the monied class imposes on their entire community. The photographer has paired these photographs on purpose and is drawing on the traditions of photojournalism with its implied objectivity to give credence to her stance. Although the device may be a little heavy-handed, the Financial District mural is shown with the American flag in the side of the frame, to perhaps hint at the hypocrisy of that symbol, as there is a woman with a small child begging for coins on the sidewalk below the mural. The picture in Harlem does not show the people walking placidly down the street with their minds on their own business, but with the help of the caption ("Spectators at the African-American Day Parade, Harlem, 1998") shows the people filling the streets in celebration of their own culture. The example shows one way visual imagery is commonly used to influence public opinion. Imagine the murals' locations reversed. Would residents of Harlem glorify a society that was intent on exploiting the African continent, and would business people in the Financial District incite the population to fight against those in power? The effect a picture has on a viewer depends not only on where the picture is seen, but also on how it is contextualized. Here, placing the two pictures together reveals that the photographer has an opinion about the use of public art and about social class in New York City. Individually, each of these photographs is a representation of a place or an event, but each also suggests the photographer's opinion of the event. Yet viewed separately, out of context with one another, that opinion would not be nearly so

clear. The context that these photographs provide for one another clarifies the photographer's ideas about the events.

When reading photographs, the intent is not to detract from their beauty and the power they have to create strong emotional responses; it is because of these sensual aspects of photographs that their outer world functions at all. But because these responses are so culturally based, it is important to consider how they come about. Remember that the picture is not an objective record of an event, place, person, etc., but that it is created through the photographer's choices. But the photographer usually relinquishes power over the contextualization of the pictures in order to put them before the public eye, and thus has little influence in how a viewer reads them. The photographs are subject to existing cultural traditions, which sometimes take the form of the precise visual formulas that perpetuate themselves in the service of some political function. Once the viewer understands that individual pictures interact with each other, it becomes clear that their meaning is not static, but that how they are read depends on the other pictures and text around them. What this means is that although anything could happen to a picture, it is as possible for it to remain true to the situation it was meant to portray as to create a wild distortion. How should a viewer approach photographs? Viewers should simply remember that photographs require thoughtful reading. Their truth is complicated by the reality that produces them.

"Mother Tongue" and Standard English: Amy Tan's Literary Fusion and Ours

David Reich

In her essay "Mother Tongue," Amy Tan writes about the language she grew up with, the "broken English" that her immigrant Chinese mother spoke at home (198). This language shaped the way she "saw things, expressed things, made sense of the world" (198), but it also caused her a great deal of suffering. For one thing, it actually made her feel ashamed of her mother; though her mother was a mature woman, many Americans treated her as if she were a child because of her poor English (198). In addition, Ms. Tan herself was discouraged from becoming a writer because of a general perception that Asians have difficulty with language (201).

At first, Ms. Tan's way of dealing with language discrimination was to prove that she could speak standard English as well as anyone; she always took pains to use perfect grammar and complex structure in order to impress people with her "mastery over the language" (201). Thus, for Ms. Tan, standard English represented an escape from the stigma of home's "broken" English—in other words, an escape from home. Because it represented an escape from home, her standard English also represented an escape from all she associated with home—all of her early childhood memories, all of her relationships with people, and all of the important things in her life—so that in the end her standard English was a language that was in many ways "bland" (200), in many ways barren of the thought and emotion that was inside her since it focused on rejecting one part of her life instead of affirming another part. When Ms. Tan realized that in writing standard English she was escaping the world that mattered to her and was deliberately writing to nobody at all, she resolved to switch instead to a language she knew much better—her "mother tongue." Once she switched, she made sure to write with a reader in mind—her mother—so that the things she wrote were always personal efforts at communication and sense, and the language she used was always loaded with the imagery of very real human interactions (201–202).

When Ms. Tan began to write using her mother tongue—the language of her soul—the things she wrote became expressions of her soul. Surprisingly, though, Ms. Tan's switch to a more authentic language did not involve a rejection of standard English in the same way that her earlier switch from one language to another had involved a rejection of her mother tongue. In fact, her writing is rendered in grammatical English, which Ms. Tan had initially perceived as "standard"—that is, as foreign and sterile. The important part of Ms. Tan's mother tongue is its imagery and the way in which it is true to life, not its brokenness, so that the reader (and the writer, too) loses little and gains much when she translates her mother's many "Englishes" into comprehensible and "perfect" form (201–202).

There is something very unusual and exciting about standard English that allows Ms. Tan to incorporate her mother tongue into it. Standard English, after all, can be as much a mother tongue as any other subspecies of the language. It is in fact my own mother tongue, the language of my upbringing, and is for me as "vivid, direct," and "full of observation and imagery" (198) as Ms. Tan's mother tongue. But standard English is also different from other mother tongues, and in some sense isn't a mother tongue at all, because it is larger than any particular ethnicity; it's not even "white" English. Because it is spoken in several countries and by people of many different backgrounds, it cannot be associated with a particular world view in the way that Ms. Tan's mother tongue can be associated with the world view of Chinese immigrants or the relationship between a particular mother and daughter. Standard English is larger than other "Englishes" (196)—it is a framework for living rather than a program for living—so that a person like me, who is in quest of his mother tongue, must realize that he cannot so simply say that "my mother tongue is standard English." Instead, he must look more deeply into the English he speaks in order to identify the essential part of his internal language, and only then can he try to understand its relationship to the standard English with which he publicly expresses himself in speech and writing.

I learned my real mother tongue at home, as did Ms. Tan. Through it I learned to value and articulate certain ideas and to think in particular ways, so that ever since, those issues and ways of thinking and forms of articulation have been among the most important influences in my life. In her essay "And We Walk Through," Christella Wong provides a clear way of thinking about the functions of standard English and mother tongue. Language, she writes, is a "door between worlds," serving both as "entrance and barrier" (1). Ms. Tan's mother tongue was initially a barrier or a "closed door" because the difference between her mother's broken English and society's standard English caused her to abandon, for a time, that deeply understood mother tongue in favor of a more sterile language. On the other hand, standard English was for me an "open door," a powerful link between my private world and the public world around me, because the shared vocabulary of the two worlds allowed me to move between them with ease. Moreover, as a writer, I feel comfortable living in the world of standard English—it is not a means to an end but rather an end in itself—so that when I write about something, I am often interested and even struck by what I write. At this point, the language of my writing becomes more than an external thing, more than an assay into the outside world—it becomes the language of my soul. It is also at this point—when living in a world of language becomes an end in itself rather than a means to an end—that Ms. Tan's writing becomes the language of her soul. Once she begins to live in the world of her writing, it does not matter whether she is writing in broken English or English that is grammatically correct; all that matters is that she is writing and that she understands what she writes. Thus, when Ms. Tan chooses to incorporate her mother tongue into standard English, to fuse her two worlds, standard English becomes her open door.

Language, after all, is transcendent, allowing individuals to communicate and take communion with the world around them. The fusion of standard English and mother tongue, of the outer voice with the inner, is the point of transcendence for all writers, their transition from struggling with language to living it. For Amy Tan, justification as a writer lies in the process of living her text, not in the process of changing it. As long as she lives her text, and integrates her mother tongue with standard English so that language is a medium and not an impediment, and so that the world around her is exciting and can be understood in an intimate but also slightly distanced way, she is being honest and true to herself. And if honest and true, she will then be interested in what she herself has to say, and in some sense, though she speaks a mother tongue with a particular reader in mind, she is really speaking to herself, to her own excitement, and she herself—not her mother—has become the primary reader for her own work.

Once Ms. Tan becomes her own reader, she transcends the limitations of both mother tongue and standard English, and everything she writes becomes both absolutely public and intensely personal. In this sense, as a writer who has achieved a measure of transcendence, Amy Tan inhabits that rare space where a writer's private domain becomes the domain of all her readers, so that what she creates in some sense concerns everybody as well as nobody, and is, in another sense, the estate of each individual reader. Ms. Tan's readers therefore sympathize with her story even if it isn't written in their own mother tongue. They are responding to what is distilled from that mother tongue, which is less a particular ethnicity than a literary province where the speakers of a language may use its familiar textures to communicate thoughts and emotions that are universal and real. Even more, they sympathize with her because of her lucid writing, her undogmatic conviction, and her ability to draw her readers into her text—into her life. She makes them feel at home there, in the mesh of her life and text, so that they are forced to concede, even before they are intellectually convinced, and whether or not her words make any sense in a large way, that what she says has validity, and that the language she speaks is not only her "mother tongue," but all of ours.

WORKS CITED

Tan, Amy. "Mother Tongue." In *The Best American Essays 1991*. Ed. Joyce Carol Oates and Robert Atwan. New York: Ticknor, 1991. 196–202.

Wong, Christella. "And We Walk Through." In Pat C. Hoy II, *Expository Writing 16, Fall Term 1992–1993*. Harvard University, 1992. 1.

Georges de la Tour's
The Penitent Magdalen

Jessica Underwood

Carl Jung, pioneer in the exploration of the human psyche, postulated that an individual's unconscious contains "not only personal, but also impersonal, collective components in the form of inherited categories or archetypes" (333). A rather dry and academic way to describe a concept which has captured the imagination of so many, but this is Jung's first elaboration of the "collective unconscious." It is from this deep source that artists, usually unknowingly and unintentionally, gather much of their subject matter. From a Jungian point of view, this is why certain art has the ability to "speak" to its viewer, because it reflects thematic content common to every person's being. Noel Cobb, in *Archetypal Imagination,* says that "the work of artists . . . contributes to the self-discovery and individuation of archetypal psychology itself" (53). In other words, the two fields, psychology and art, one the attempt to understand the human mind, its emotion and expression, the other the physical product of that need to express, feed into each other. Here we are not looking at "mind" as the conscious realm of the intellectual, but as that part of the self that is largely uncontrolled, which is the wellspring of creativity. Freud called it the "id." In religious schools of thought, it has been looked upon as "soul."

The archetypes ubiquitous in art are seen by the Jungian school to be especially prevalent in religious rendering, to the extent that there is a "shifting, indefinable borderline between religion and art. Sometimes one cannot be separated from the other" (Jaffe 260). Religious art then, always concerned with answering the basic questions of human existence, also contains the archetypes that rule the unconscious, the threads that connect humanity and reach across the centuries. Perhaps this is why I, a largely agnostic female Jewish teenager, was able to find solace in the painting of a long dead Catholic Frenchman. The communication of the soul transcends the boundaries imposed by culture and the conscious, temporally bound, world.

A short time ago, feeling mired down and oppressed, I walked up to the Metropolitan Museum of Art. I wandered aimlessly through those great halls, breathing in the smells of ancient stone and oils. Art has the virtue of not intruding upon your thoughts unless you allow it in. Either you force it upon yourself intellectually, or by a strange combination of the eye's simple affinity for color, light, and composition, jumbled with your myriad of personal associations and your emotional state, the work of art seemingly draws you in. In other words, Jung's "collective unconscious" activates itself. I stumbled upon a special exhibition: Georges de la Tour's four representations of Mary Magdalen, all, for a short period, brought together in a single room. Each depicts a contemplative and quietly emotional woman, sitting in a chair, bathed by candlelight and holding a skull. The paintings, however, are quite different in subtler ways: the age of the woman, the addition and subtraction of symbolic objects, the woman's clothing, and the specificity and intensity of her emotional state. One of the Magdalens grabbed my attention as soon as I entered the room, and drew me forward as if inviting me to unlock its secrets. Painted in oils sometime between 1638 and 1643, quite large at 52 x 40 inches, and thought to be the third in the series, it stunningly represents Magdalen, according to Maureen Howard, at the "dramatic moment of her conversion" (199). At the time that I first saw *The Penitent Magdalen,* however, she was simply a young woman whose expression, of strong yet contained emotion, spoke to me through my fog of preoccupation as if to remind me that I was not alone in my quest for solace.

Although there is an emotional intensity to the painting, it also conveys a sense of peace and stillness; Magdalen herself seems almost to be carved of alabaster. The only movement is the implicit flicker of the candle on the table. Magdalen's body dominates the picture, but the eye is first drawn to the light source, and to the gilded mirror that reflects it. Both stand on a table, perhaps her dressing table, as it also holds jewelry and a basket. The frame of the mirror is elaborately decorated, suggesting wealth, as do the pearl necklace and the rich red of Magdalen's skirt. Magdalen herself sits with her head turned nearly away from us, but her pain, yearning, and inner movement of spirit are clearly conveyed on her face, in her slightly open mouth and the heightened emotion of her eyes, visible even in one-quarter profile. It is the face, and the clean lines of her neck and bosom, that are bathed most brightly by the candlelight. Her hair is long and smooth, sweeping cleanly across the side of her face and down her back. She looks to be about twenty-five.

She wears a low cut white blouse and a long red skirt: both are simple, but there is an affluence to the cloth. The skirt covers her feet, but you can see her hands, clasped as they are over the skull in profile. The hands are still, but they express the same intensity of emotion as her face. The play of light brings drama to the work and serves to lock the spectators' attention on a trinity of images: Magdalen's repentant face, her prayerful hands resting on the smooth skull, and the candle, flickering in the richly embossed mirror.

The questions raised here take us into the symbolic. What is meant by the candle, mirror, and the skull in the painting? They are certainly not accidental——they are strategically placed, and moreover, they are different in each of the other three paintings. And what of Mary Magdalen herself? A recurrent figure in Christian art, she seems to hold great significance, not only in Western civilization, but to Georges de la Tour himself. (He did, after all, paint her four times.) Even if one is not fully aware of Magdalen's role in Christianity, as I was not, it is still somehow quite obvious that the woman is in the throes of some kind of spiritual or emotional crisis and awakening. Magdalen has reached a crossroads in her life. This I identify as the painting's central theme: this moment of significant change, of catharsis, that represents a new beginning, is imbued with a peaceful sense of mortality (the skull, the self-consuming candle). In one still moment, La Tour has represented the many stages of life, its cycles of death and rebirth.

The details of La Tour's own life are, unfortunately, sketchy. "It is known that he was born in Vic-sur-Seille in 1593, and that in 1620 . . . he settled in Luneville, where he spent his mature career" (Spear 37), but there is little consensus about where he studied or traveled. La Tour is thought to have been dramatically influenced by the 17th-century Italian painter Caravaggio, due to similarities in subject matter, and especially in his dramatic use of candlelight for illumination. And as ambiguous as the biographical details of his life are, "equally problematic are the questions of chronology—La Tour dated only two known pictures" (Spear 37). None of the Magdalen paintings are definitively dated. Tempting as it is to make the correlation, any claim that La Tour's inspiration in depicting Magdalen's spiritual awakening was correlated to some personal or spiritual renaissance of his own is pure speculation. However, because the subject matter is rendered so passionately, and because of Magdalen's archetypal importance in addition to her spiritual stature, I would like to consider the possibility.

Magdalen herself is ubiquitous in religious art. Her biography, like La Tour's, is somewhat muddled. According to art historian Anne Plogsterth, she is the major woman of the *New Testament,* outweighing even the Virgin Mary, as Magdalen was Jesus' principle female disciple. The *Gnostic Gospels,* a collection of writing by early followers of Christ, claim that "Jesus loved Mary Magdalen more than all other apostles, called her Apostle of the Apostles and 'the Woman Who Knew the All,' and often kissed her. He said she would excel every other disciple in the coming Kingdom of Light, where she would rule" (Walker 613). La Tour, who was not privy to the *Gnostic Gospels* (which were not rediscovered until the 20th century), would have known of Magdalen only through accounts of her in the *New Testament,* combined with vague and mythic notions stemming from the considerable mystique that surrounded her cult, especially in France, where she was popularly supposed to have died. The grotto where she was said to have lived as a mystic, where bones were unearthed that were believed to be hers and worshipped as relics, was in Vezelay, a town near Marseilles. Mary Magdalen, in the *New Testament,* is also the woman out of whom Jesus cast seven devils, and the woman who begged Jesus to raise Lazarus from the dead. Magdalen started her career as a sacred prostitute, a vocation that she supposedly renounced upon her conversion to the teachings of Christ. She was present at the crucifixion, and in Mark 16:9, it is said that Jesus appeared to her first after the resurrection. With so many different accounts of her actions, it is probable that Mary is a combination of several historical women, but the mythical significance that she acquired became much more important than historical fact. Her many different aspects make her all the more compelling as a symbol of femininity, as a woman who embodies contradiction.

In early Christianity, Mary Magdalen was very much a dominant figure, surrounded by mystique, and, just as Jesus was often associated with deities like Dionysus, she was affiliated with very powerful goddesses. She was also often confused and incorporated with Mary, mother of Jesus, in an overt combination of the virgin and the whore, the one a pure matriarch, the other a sensuous lover. Maria Warner, in her study of the Virgin Mary, states: "Together, the Virgin and the Magdalene form a diptych of Christian patriarchy's idea of women. There is no place in the conceptual architecture of early Christian society for a single woman who is neither a virgin nor a whore" (Qualls-Corbett 146). Although these aspects of womanhood were sometimes conflated in popular belief, during the early development of official Church doctrine, in an odd twist that has stymied women for centuries, motherhood, the female's "highest duty," became separated from eroticism, and her social acceptability became contingent upon the disavowal of her sexuality. Mary Magdalen became a revered saint ostensibly because she renounced her wanton nature: "She offered hope to mortals who could not attain the perfect state of the Virgin and who sought to be forgiven for their sins" (146). It is interesting to note that Peter, to whom so much of the misogyny of the New Testament has been attributed, was said to have been openly resentful of Mary's power as Jesus' favorite disciple.

However, her sexual side was too compelling to be forgotten. Like Ishtar and Astarte in ancient times, the Christian age made her the protectress of prostitutes; indeed medieval whores were known as magdalens. In art, Magdalen became the Biblical sex symbol of religious representation, exciting in that she was a "fallen woman," holy in that she redeemed herself. In Plogsterth's words, "she conveyed the lurid past idea—she was a nice little excuse to paint a real tart—kinky pictures that were Biblical." Many of her conversion pictures depict her with one or both breasts bared, like Francisco Goya's *Mary Magdalene*. Furthermore, as Nancy Qualls- Corbett argues:

> Mary Magdalen remained a prominent figure in Christian tradition also for a
> psychological reason. The archetypal dimension of the erotic feminine nature
> elects a figure to carry its projection; Mary Magdalen carried this projection. The
> salient point is that human beings, in their spiritual search, must find an image
> of the feminine which relates to the erotic aspects of the goddess. (146)

On an unconscious, deeply psychological level, at least, Mary Magdalen's supposed repudiation of eroticism, and of her role as sacred prostitute, might as well never have taken place.

Plogsterth claims that La Tour "was remarkably restrained, different than the rest of his period," in painting her in a nonsexual fashion. There were earlier paintings that began to mute her sexual aspect. El Greco's *Magdalen* shows her at the moment of conversion, with the omnipresent skull, a look of yearning or religious ecstasy upon her face, bathed in a holy light. A painting by La Tour's main influence, Caravaggio, *La Maddalena,* depicts a young woman, a single tear running down her face, slumped in a chair. On the floor are scattered jewels and an oil lamp. But *The Penitent Magdalen* is strikingly different in her absolute dignity, her intense reserve of quiet emotion.

La Tour's restraint can be seen as a product of the artistic climate in France at the time. Although contingent upon the Baroque, French Classicists resisted the gilded excesses of the Italians, although Italy's return to emotional religious faith after the cool secular humanism of the Renaissance was echoed in France (Huyghe 268). La Tour saw a powerful reassertion of royal power, after decades of religious war and weak monarchy, with the ascension of Louis XIV, the Sun King. Louis claimed the privileges of "divine right" of kings, and Catholic France experienced a surge in faith that had been shaken in the bloody Huguenot wars that followed the Protestant Reformation. *The Penitent Magdalen* combines this luminous religiosity with the simplicity of Classicism and the focus on individuality that was championed in the Renaissance and carried through into the Baroque period.

La Tour died in 1652, at the age of sixty-one. *The Penitent Magdalen* then, dated sometime between 1638 and 1643, was painted in his late forties or middle fifties, the time of "mid-life crisis" for many men. This is the time when, according to Carl Jung, it is essential to develop the feminine side of consciousness, the anima. The anima is man's eternal image of woman, not the image of this or that particular woman, but a definite feminine image. This image is fundamentally unconscious, a hereditary factor of primordial origin engraved in the living organic system of the man, an imprint or "archetype" of all the ancestral experiences of the female (qtd. in Qualls-Corbett 89). According to Jung:

> after the middle of life, . . . loss of the anima means a diminution of vitality, of flexibility and of human kindness. The result, as a rule, is premature rigidity, crustiness, stereotypes, fanatical one-sidedness, obstinacy, pedantry, or else resignation, weariness, sloppiness, [and] irresponsibility. (qtd. in Qualls-Corbett 108)

As the anima is also responsible for artistic expression, it is therefore essential that the middle-aged painter explore it, as his continued vitality as an artist is at stake. The anima is also intimately connected with any inner spiritual journey that a man must undertake: "the feminine in man not only excites him but acts as [his] soul guide" (Qualls-Corbett 90). Much as Beatrice is seen to have acted as Dante's anima in his allegorical masterwork the [*Inferno*], so can it be surmised that Mary Magdalen, on an unconscious level, represented Georges de la Tour's anima.

As an adult, a sense of completeness is achieved through a union of the conscious and unconscious contents of the mind. Out of this union arises what the Jungians call "the transcendent function of the psyche" (Henderson 146), by which a man can achieve his highest goal: the full realization of the potential of his individual Self, the Self being, of course, a universal archetype. As a middle-aged painter, La Tour's choice to paint Mary Magdalen at the very moment of her own spiritual transcendence may very well symbolize his own inner journey.

The objects in the painting, like Magdalen herself, can be seen to hold meaning beyond their surface associations. Psychologically, mirrors are very significant in human development. They symbolize vanity on one level (and this may be all that La Tour consciously intended), but they also signify self-awareness, the ability to see one's reflection and connect to it as an outer representation of the Self. There-fore I do not think it coincidental that the penitent Mary Magdalen, upon her con-version to Christianity, is in the presence of a mirror, or that—in this painting—the flickering candle is reflected in the mirror. In the related paintings of Magdalen by other artists, the placement of the symbolic objects is different; in one, she is study-ing her reflection, in another, the skull is reflected, and in the earliest, there is no mirror at all. If Magdalen's mirror is the ultimate symbol for both her burgeoning self-awareness and her rebirth into the light of Christianity, then already reflected in that rebirth is her certain mortality, the candle on the wane that will eventually extinguish itself. Death and rebirth are central facets to Christianity; Jesus is reborn and ascends every Spring. This is, of course, an ancient idea, intimately connected to the growth, harvest, and replanting of food staples; the Great Goddesses of old, all of whom were fertility goddesses, often had son-lovers who died and were reborn every Spring.

The goddess herself is eternal, yet the son-lover is slain or sacrificed to be res-urrected again. Inanna's young love was the shepherd Dummuzi, who was sacri-ficed to the nether world six months every year, as was Ishtar's son-lover, Tammuz. In Egypt, there were Isis and Osiris, in Libya, Cybele and Attis. The theme is repeated as each young man meets an untimely cruel death, and is even-tually brought to earth or life once again. It continues through the eras to the more familiar Greek mythology (Qualls-Corbett 59). The Harlot Mary Magdalen, so often confused with both Jesus' mother and with ancient Great Goddesses, is inti-mately connected with Jesus' death and rebirth every Spring: it was she who saw and first reported his Ascension. Just as Jesus dies and is reborn in Heaven, so will be Mary Magdalen, now holy. The flame, reflected in the mirror signifying rebirth, is rising: ascending. This same idea of rebirth and death and rebirth again is por-trayed in Mary's hands, clasped, as if in prayer, over the skull.

In *The Penitent Magdalen,* a voyage of self-discovery takes place in three layers: first there is the experience of the subject herself, Mary Magdalen. Mag-dalen can be seen here as two separate archetypes: as the sacred prostitute, she is the erotic aspect of the Female, and as an individual on a journey of the soul; she is symbolic of the Self. These two archetypes both feed into the second layer of self-discovery, that of the artist himself; as the Female, Magdalen may be seen as the artist's anima, guiding him on his discovery and unification of the Self. In depicting his anima as an individual, a Self on a lonely pilgrimage, La Tour creates a Magdalen who is able to transcend the boundaries of time, religion, and culture and to complete the third layer of self discovery: his own. As Cobb says in *Arche-typal Imagination,* "The concerns of the soul are not bound by time, nor should they be allowed the exclusive domain of psychologists. Even the subjects of his-tory become subjects of the soul—when they have been touched by imagination" (53). In art, the physical embodiment of the "collective unconscious," transcen-dent communication—the verbiage of the soul—is always possible.

I walked out of the Met that day, pensive but infinitely calmer. Just as *The Penitent Magdalen* had seen her own mortality and rebirth in the mirror, I had seen my inner quest reflected in her expression. Art, breaker of the barriers of nationality, sex, religion, and culture, had touched me, through its ability to endlessly echo the Self, down through the centuries. Although La Tour's act of creation was an individual one, and Mary Magdalen's spiritual journey was one that she underwent alone, their quests had together formed an intricate web, a web exposed in a few, masterly daubs of oil paint on canvas. Their acts of creation (and recreation) had become a part of me, and my own inner movement of spirit.

WORKS CITED

Cobb, Noel. *Archetypal Imagination: Glimpses of the Gods in Life and Art.* Hudson, NY: Lindisfarne, 1992.

Henderson, Joseph L. "Ancient Myths and Modern Man." *Man and His Symbols.* Ed. Carl G. Jung. New York: Dell, 1968. 115–186.

Howard, Maureen, ed. *The Metropolitan Museum of Art Guide.* New York: The Metropolitan Museum of Art, 1983.

Huyghe, Rene, ed. *Larousse Encyclopedia of Renaissance and Baroque Art.* Paris: Librairie Larousse, 1961.

Jaffe, Aniela. "Symbolism in the Visual Arts." *Man and His Symbols.* Ed. Carl G. Jung. New York: Dell, 1968. 255–322.

Jung, Carl G., "The Personal and Collective Unconscious." *A World of Ideas.* 5th ed. Lee A. Jacobus. Boston: Bedford, 1998. 321–333.

———, ed. *Man and His Symbols.* New York: Dell, 1968.

Plogsterth, Anne. Personal Interview. 17 Apr. 1998. 321–333.

Qualls-Corbett, Nancy. *The Sacred Prostitute: Eternal Aspect of the Feminine.* Toronto: Inner City, 1988.

Spear, Richard E. *Caravaggio and his Followers.* New York: Harper, 1975.

Walker, Barbara. *The Women's Encyclopedia of Myths and Secrets.* San Francisco: Harper, 1983.

A SPECTRUM OF PROFESSIONAL WRITING

Lee K. Abbott
(b. 1947)

Lee K. Abbott was raised in southern New Mexico in the small town of Las Cruces. He received a B.A. (1970), an M.A. (1973) from New Mexico State University, and an M.F.A. from the University of Arkansas in 1977. In 1989 he became a professor of English at Ohio State University. His stories, collected in five volumes, have appeared in a variety of magazines and literary journals, including *Harper's* and *The Kenyon Review*. Abbott has been awarded numerous prizes, and his stories have been included in *Best American Short Stories* (1985 and 1987), *The Pushcart Prize* volumes (1987 and 1989), and the *O. Henry Prize Stories* (1984). His work has also been twice nominated for a Pulitzer Prize.

In "The True Story of Why I Do What I Do," Abbott explains not only his reasons for writing but also his sense of "truth." The essay is interesting for the questions it raises about how writers reveal their various truths and why some of them rely on fiction to convey those truths. It is also noteworthy for its highly individual and engaging voice.

The True Story of Why I Do What I Do

All stories are true stories, especially the artful lies we invent to satisfy the wishful thinker in us, for they present to us, in disguise often and at great distance, the way we are or would want to be. Told to us in a lingo as unique as a fingerprint, they address our up-and-down, our here-and-now. They come, I think, from a desire, as irresistible as love itself, to fix on the page a moment, suffered or made up, when something—one puny thing or idea or person—revealed itself and so turned off the Boom-Boom-Boom which usually deafens us to ourselves. Happily-ended or not, stories are the truth we leave behind, like crumbs, to say how we've come and what was there to see.

To be inspirational, as high-minded and upward-looking as the foolish half of me mostly aims to be, I have to tell you about my father—as crazed, driven and cross-hearted a hero as I have ever known. His analogues have appeared in dozens of my stories: he's the gentleman, in golf togs or business suit, throwing the epic tantrum, careening hither and thither in a men's locker or banker's office; he's the one, in the fiction I invent, with the outraged moral intelligence, the one who hectors and harangues, the one telling another (usually me, you can guess) how to behave and when to beware and what is likely to be the dry end of things we love.

In fiction, he is imperious, forbidding as a Puritan God, sharp-minded as an out-of-town lawyer, stiff as pig bristle, wiry and unforgiving; in fiction, the made-up landscape I am a sometime citizen in, he suffers and is redeemed (or he is not), does the wrong thing and is shamed (or is not), comes to insight and is crushed (or is not). In fiction, given its unities and shape and its epiphanies, I comprehend my father. I know exactly what he meant when he told me that you could tell a gentleman by his hand shake and his shoe shine. I know, and can articulate, what significance there is in the properly mowed lawn, what wisdom there is in the order of dried dishes. In fiction, I know—maybe as Flannery O'Connor did—why the heathen rage.

In life, however—which, messy and improbable and ephemeral, is not good fiction—I had no idea what made his world spin round and round. The facts were clear to me, not the flesh. He went to Dartmouth, I knew. He pole-vaulted cross-handed. One brother died on the Bataan Death March; his sister in a boating accident on Lake Sasebo in Maine. His father went blind in the last years of his life; his mother squandered an inheritance of at least one million dollars. He was a roué, I heard, a slick-haired rake who hung out on the pier at Old Orchard Beach and went down to Miami in the winter. He married my mother, the over-pampered daughter of a Canadian insurance executive, in Harligen, Texas, while he was at gunnery school in WWII. They lived in Panama, where I was born. He ran the National Guard in Illinois, where my brother was born. He played one year of professional golf. He became a career military man, went to England, Korea, Germany, resigned his commission twice because somebody, or something, infuriated him.

If it is true, as Willa Cather says, that the "basic material a writer works with is acquired before the age of fifteen," then by the time I was a sophomore in high school in Las Cruces, New Mexico, already telling my teachers and myself that I was going to be a writer, the material I had acquired I'd got from him: a duke's mixture of soirées, of country clubs and officers' clubs, of colorful compadres named Red and Goonch and Uncle Inches—the whole of it tragic and tearful to the aggressively poetic kid I was then. My mother was a drunk, institutionalized when I was twelve; my father was a drinker. He had psoriasis on his knobby knees and knobby elbows, he smoked like the dickens, he threw a wedge at the TV, he dressed in pink polkadots for the Club Championship, he banished me to my room forever, he expected my brother and me to know the truth and speak it invariably—this was my material, a hodge-podge of goo and muck and human blah-blah-blah the responsibility for which I was absolutely unaware of until the inspirational summer afternoon I am partly here to yap about.

Once upon a time (Isn't this the rhetoric, in truth, that opens every fairytale we survive and want to write about?), my father and I found ourselves alone at home. I want to say it was a Sunday, for in my memory the day, if not the events themselves, have a liturgical, quasi-holy "feel." In my memory, that attic atop the shoulders where everything truly felt is found, there is that Sunday light, crooked and mote-filled and lazy, and that Sunday time, heavy and ever in danger of wobbling to a halt. My father, in his bermuda shorts and golf shirt, is in the TV room, drinking the rum thing he preferred; he had the habit, annoying I think now, of dumping his half-used ice cubes back in the freezer, a habit the girl who became my wife told me was disgusting every time I made her a Coke and it tasted like hooch. I am in the living room, I think, listening to records; more likely, I am reading—*Sports Illustrated,* the *National Geographic, Life* magazine.

My taste in those days ran to the quick, the immediate—prose of the slash-and-burn kind. *Mila 18* by Leon Uris, *The Naked and the Dead* (still an excellent book, by the way), Alistair MacClean's high seas adventures. I saw myself writing a book like those one day—a book, conceived out of testosterone and *Nugget*-style macho, a book as pithy and direct as a dust jacket blurb: "Mr. Abbott," the endorsement would run, "writes like an assassin. He's the 'Aaarrgghh' the yellow yammer when they spy the vast What-Not opening to greet them." I had, I thought then, no experience (this was long before I realized that Henry James was correct when he said that "experience was an atmosphere of the mind"). I was just a kid, after all. Skinny, with a flat-top and fifteen pimples, half my mind tilted toward girls, the other half tilted toward glory (which would, in the reasoning I was the victim of, get me girls).

The hours passed that Sunday afternoon as they always do when I cast myself back into the dangerous tides that are my past: the clock above the antique writing desk chiming on the quarter-hour, the father wandering between the refrigerator and liquor cabinet, Pee Wee Reese or Dizzy Dean saying in the TV room what the Dodgers were doing; the son in another room cobbling together in his fertile but screwy imagination a tale of swashbuckling and hair-raising, a narrative of guns and grateful bimbos and nick-of-time derring-do. We were in our elements, him and me: one, the older, tuned to the stupid clatter of the exterior world; the other, the younger flesh of him, tuned to the twilight interior world of fetch-and-keep, of fantasy. Then he burst into the living room, eyed me as if wondering for the last time whether I was up to the burden he was about to pitch my way, and said, a little drunkenly, "Come with me."

He had been thinking about himself, it is clear now. An inventory, check mark after check mark after check mark, had been taken: three heart attacks, a fist-sized hunk of his lung removed at William Beaumont General Hospital in Ft. Bliss, the yips on the putting green, Homeric-like anger, frustration at a life twisted which-away, hopes high as heaven he believed in, bitterness at being less than the hero he'd promised himself he'd be. I didn't know this at the time I followed him outdoors and into the utility rooms at the end of the car port. I knew only that he was semi-sloshed. I knew only that he was fifty-six years old, gray-headed and tough. I knew he hated going to work at the post office, his job in those days, where he supervised and inspected and, unhappiest of all for him, had to tattle on those who stole money or stamps or swiped somebody's *Playboy* magazine.

"See this, Kit?" he said. He was standing in the center of the utility room, lawn mower here, gas can there, the walls hung with tools I never got the sense of. Golf clubs were in there, a bucket of practice balls, cans of oil, greasy rags, a hoe, a rake, a cheap hardware store of goodies that smelled old and used and too sweet. "You want to be a writer, huh?" he said, sweeping his arms, then pulling me after him. He snarled the word; it was sound which scorned ignorance and innocence. Against the wall, high as the ceiling, were stacked his footlockers and steamer trunks, from the Army of the United States and from the regiments that were the families of his own father, innkeeper Lyman Kittredge Abbott of Portland, Maine. I like to think now that I knew we were coming to something, my father and I, that he was going to say words to me and I, perhaps for the first time, was going to understand him precisely. I like to think now that I was smart enough to know that I was in the presence of a truth grander than the two of us, a truth the price of which we go paying forever, a truth more dire than the knowing that we die and do not rise. This is the moment, I like to think of myself thinking then, when you discover how hard the world is, when what you've cleaved to is cleaved from you with a broadaxe.

Then he assaulted those lockers and trunks. In a fury, huffing and puffing, he snatched them down, one by one, hollering "Timber!" when the uppermost went tumbling. They crashed and banged, and I tried backing up a little, as he flung one behind him and scrambled over another to reach a third. He was hollering, you have to know, all the New England notes of his voice echoing in that now cramped room, and maybe I was some scared. This was the temper I'd witnessed elsewhere—on the golf course, behind the wheel of his Ford, in the living room when someone in the big world made a ding-a-ling out of himself. But there was more than anger here: there was pain, the particular kind of which was personal and buried deep in his bones, pain for which there is no Latin name or medicine or machine, other than fiction, to account for.

"Write it all down!" he was shouting. "Write it all goddam down!"

And it was here, from a certain X-spot in the world, 1855 Cruse, that my father, teetering from booze and the awful weight of his own life, was taking seriously, in a manner I couldn't yet, what purpose writing ought to have. Here it is, he was in effect saying. Crated and stored, catalogued and preserved, year by used-up year, place by rotten place. Here it is: the come and go of it, the building and collapse of it, the joy and weep of it. Here it is, he was saying. All the tissues and nerves and human jingle-jangle, that want and excess of it, the rigamarole and whirling, damaged creatures we are. And all you have to do, son and boy, is write it down. Write it all goddam down.

This, I submit, is the inspirational part. If we write for any larger purpose than a simple good time—and, believe me, there is nothing at all wrong with a good time—it is, I think, because we all feel, less and more, the obligation we have to our fathers, to our mothers, to all the folks, linked by biology or not, who have raised us; an obligation, as essential to our moral natures as our hearts are to long life, to the places we were raised in and in the knowledge we learned there. We want, I hope, because there is no other way to do it, to write it down, to transform it, to set it straight. At our best, we do not write for the money alone, though money is nice; nor do we write for fame, though fame is likewise nice. We write, beginner and professional alike, because, though half-frightened, we want to know what is in the trunks and lockers we lug forward through time, what vital secrets they can be sprung to reveal.

Considerations

Thinking

Explain the paradox at the beginning of Abbott's opening sentence: "All stories are true stories, especially the artful lies we invent to satisfy the wishful thinker in us."

What, according to Abbott, is the primary function of stories? What do stories enable writers to do?

Is this essay about Abbott's father? About the writer's relationship with his father? About the father's response to the son's ambition? Explain.

Connecting

To what extent can you relate to Abbott's comment that he "had no idea what made his [father's] world spin round and round"? To what extent do you understand your parents' goals and dreams, their hopes and fears and feelings?

Lee K. Abbott was a young man, still in school, during the scene he describes with his father telling him to "Write it all down! Write it all goddam down!" What is the relationship between Abbott's writerly vocation and his father's demand?

Compare Abbott's assessment of the value of stories with Tim O'Brien's in "How to Tell a True War Story."

Writing

Write a piece explaining why you do what you do or why you want to do whatever it is that you envision yourself doing with your life. Try to account for what has motivated you, what may have pushed, prodded, propelled you in the direction you are heading.

Compare Abbott's notions about the truths of fiction with Scott Russell Sanders's notion of the falseness of fact in "Wayland."

Gloria Anzaldúa
(b. 1942)

Gloria Anzaldúa was raised in southwest Texas. She describes herself as "a border woman," living between the Mexican and Anglo cultures. Her books include two edited volumes: *This Bridge Called My Back: Writing by Radical Women of Color* (1983) and *Haciendo Caras: Making Face/Making Soul* (1990). The following selection, from *Borderlands/La Frontera* (1987), crosses language borders by mixing Spanish and English while combining various essay genres, such as autobiography, critical theory, and argument.

How to Tame a Wild Tongue

"We're going to have to control your tongue," the dentist says, pulling out all the metal from my mouth. Silver bits plop and tinkle into the basin. My mouth is a motherlode.

The dentist is cleaning out my roots. I get a whiff of the stench when I gasp. "I can't cap that tooth yet, you're still draining," he says.

"We're going to have to do something about your tongue," I hear the anger rising in his voice. My tongue keeps pushing out the wads of cotton, pushing back the drills, the long thin needles. "I've never seen anything as strong or as stubborn," he says. And I think, how do you tame a wild tongue, train it to be quiet, how do you bridle and saddle it? How do you make it lie down?

Who is to say that robbing a people of its language is less violent than war?

RAY GWYN SMITH

I remember being caught speaking Spanish at recess—that was good for three licks on the knuckles with a sharp ruler. I remember being sent to the corner of the classroom for "talking back" to the Anglo teacher when all I was trying to do was tell her how to pronounce my name. "If you want to be American, speak 'American.' If you don't like it, go back to Mexico where you belong."

"I want you to speak English. Pa' hallar buen trabajo tienes que saber hablar el inglés bien. Qué vale toda tu educación si todavía hablas inglés con un 'accent'," my mother would say, mortified that I spoke English like a Mexican. At Pan American University, I and all Chicano students were required to take two speech classes. Their purpose: to get rid of our accents.

Attacks on one's form of expression with the intent to censor are a violation of the First Amendment. El Anglo con cara de inocente nos arrancó la lengua. Wild tongues can't be tamed, they can only be cut out.

Overcoming the Tradition of Silence

Ahogadas, escupimos el oscuro.
Peleando con nuestra propia sombra
el silencio nos sepulta.

En boca cerrada no entran moscas. "Flies don't enter a closed mouth" is a saying I kept hearing when I was a child. *Ser habladora* was to be a gossip and a liar, to talk too much. *Muchachitas bien criadas,* well-bred girls don't answer back. *Es una falta de respeto* to talk back to one's mother or father. I remember one of the sins I'd recite to the priest in the confession box the few times I went to confession: talking back to my mother, *hablar pa' 'tras, repelar. Hocicona, repelona, chismosa,* having a big mouth, questioning, carrying tales are all signs of being *mal criada.* In my culture they are all words that are derogatory if applied to women—I've never heard them applied to men.

The first time I heard two women, a Puerto Rican and a Cuban, say the word "*nosotras,*" I was shocked. I had not known the word existed. Chicanas use *nosotros* whether we're male or female. We are robbed of our female being by the masculine plural. Language is a male discourse.

> And our tongues have become
> dry   the wilderness has
> dried out our tongues   and
> we have forgotten speech.
>
> IRENA KLEPFISZ

Even our own people, other Spanish speakers *nos quieren poner candados en la boca.* They would hold us back with their bag of *reglas de academia.*

> *Oyé como ladra:*
> *el lenguaje de la frontera*
>
> *Quien tiene boca se equivoca.*
>
> MEXICAN SAYING

"*Pocho,* cultural traitor, you're speaking the oppressor's language by speaking English, you're ruining the Spanish language," I have been accused by various Latinos and Latinas. Chicano Spanish is considered by the purist and by most Latinos deficient, a mutilation of Spanish.

But Chicano Spanish is a border tongue which developed naturally. Change, *evolución, enriquecimiento de palabras nuevas por invención o adopción* have created variants of Chicano Spanish, *un nuevo lenguaje. Un lenguaje que corresponde a un modo de vivir.* Chicano Spanish is not incorrect, it is a living language.

For a people who are neither Spanish nor live in a country in which Spanish is the first language; for a people who live in a country in which English is the reigning tongue but who are not Anglo; for a people who cannot entirely identify with either standard (formal, Castilian) Spanish nor standard English, what recourse is left to them but to create their own language? A language which they can connect their identity to, one capable of communicating the realities and values true to themselves—a language with terms that are neither *español ni inglés,* but both. We speak a patois, a forked tongue, a variation of two languages.

Chicano Spanish sprang out of the Chicanos' need to identify ourselves as a distinct people. We needed a language with which we could communicate with ourselves, a secret language. For some of us, language is a homeland closer than the Southwest—for many Chicanos today live in the Midwest and the East. And because we are a complex, heterogeneous people, we speak many languages. Some of the languages we speak are

1. Standard English
2. Working class and slang English
3. Standard Spanish
4. Standard Mexican Spanish
5. North Mexican Spanish dialect
6. Chicano Spanish (Texas, New Mexico, Arizona, and California have regional variations)
7. Tex-Mex
8. *Pachuco* (called *caló*)

My "home" tongues are the languages I speak with my sister and brothers, with my friends. They are the last five listed, with 6 and 7 being closest to my heart. From school, the media, and job situations, I've picked up standard and working class English. From Mamagrande Locha and from reading Spanish and Mexican literature, I've picked up Standard Spanish and Standard Mexican Spanish. From *los recién llegados,* Mexican immigrants, and *braceros,* I learned the North Mexican dialect. With Mexicans I'll try to speak either Standard Mexican Spanish or the North Mexican dialect. From my parents and Chicanos living in the Valley, I picked up Chicano Texas Spanish, and I speak it with my mom, younger brother (who married a Mexican and who rarely mixes Spanish with English), aunts, and older relatives.

With Chicanas from *Nuevo México* or *Arizona* I will speak Chicano Spanish a little, but often they don't understand what I'm saying. With most California Chicanas I speak entirely in English (unless I forget). When I first moved to San Francisco, I'd rattle off something in Spanish, unintentionally embarrassing them. Often it is only with another Chicana *tejano* that I can talk freely.

Words distorted by English are known as anglicisms or *pochismos.* The *pocho* is an anglicized Mexican or American of Mexican origin who speaks Spanish with an accent characteristic of North Americans and who distorts and reconstructs the language according to the influence of English. Tex-Mex, or Spanglish, comes most naturally to me. I may switch back and forth from English to Spanish in the same sentence or in the same word. With my sister and my brother Nune and with Chicano *tejano* contemporaries I speak in Tex-Mex.

From kids and people my own age I picked up *Pachuco*. *Pachuco* (the language of the zoot suiters) is a language of rebellion, both against Standard Spanish and Standard English. It is a secret language. Adults of the culture and outsiders cannot understand it. It is made up of slang words from both English and Spanish. *Ruca* means girl or woman, *vato* means guy or dude, *chale* means no, *simón* means yes, *churro* is sure, talk is *periquiar*, *pigionear* means petting, *que gacho* means how nerdy, *ponte águila* means watch out, death is called *la pelona*. Through lack of practice and not having others who can speak it, I've lost most of the *Pachuco* tongue.

Chicano Spanish

Chicanos, after 250 years of Spanish/Anglo colonization, have developed significant differences in the Spanish we speak. We collapse two adjacent vowels into a single syllable and sometimes shift the stress in certain words such as *maíz/maiz*, *cohete/cuete*. We leave out certain consonants when they appear between vowels: *lado/lao, mojado/mojao*. Chicanos from South Texas pronounce *f* as *j* as in *jue* (*fue*). Chicanos use "archaisms," words that are no longer in the Spanish language, words that have been evolved out. We say *semos, truje, haiga, ansina*, and *naiden*. We retain the "archaic" *j*, as in *jalar*, that derives from an earlier *h* (the French *halar* or the Germanic *halon* which was lost to standard Spanish in the sixteenth century), but which is still found in several regional dialects such as the one spoken in South Texas. (Due to geography, Chicanos from the Valley of South Texas were cut off linguistically from other Spanish speakers. We tend to use words that the Spaniards brought over from Medieval Spain. The majority of the Spanish colonizers in Mexico and the Southwest came from Extremadura—Hernán Cortés was one of them—and Andalucía. Andalucians pronounce *ll* like a *y*, and their *d*'s tend to be absorbed by adjacent vowels: *tirado* becomes *tirao*. They brought *el lenguaje popular, dialectos y regionalismos*.)

Chicanos and other Spanish speakers also shift *ll* to *y* and *z* to *s*. We leave out initial syllables, saying *tar* for *estar*, *toy* for *estoy*, *hora* for *ahora* (*cubanos* and *puertorriqueños* also leave out initial letters of some words). We also leave out the final syllable such as *pa* for *para*. The intervocalic *y*, the *ll* as in *tortilla, ella, botella*, gets replaced by *tortia* or *tortiya, ea, botea*. We add an additional syllable at the beginning of certain words: *atocar* for *tocar*, *agastar* for *gastar*. Sometimes we'll say *lavaste las vacijas*, other times *lavates* (substituting the *ates* verb endings for the *aste*).

We used anglicisms, words borrowed from English: *bola* from ball, *carpeta* from carpet, *máchina de lavar* (instead of *lavadora*) from washing machine. Tex-Mex argot, created by adding a Spanish sound at the beginning or end of an

English word such as *cookiar* for cook, *watchar* for watch, *parkiar* for park, and *rapiar* for rape, is the result of the pressures on Spanish speakers to adapt to English.

We don't use the word *vosotros/as* or its accompanying verb form. We don't say *claro* (to mean yes), *imagínate,* or *me emociona,* unless we picked up Spanish from Latinas, out of a book, or in a classroom. Other Spanish-speaking groups are going through the same, or similar, development in their Spanish.

Linguistic Terrorism

Deslenguadas. Somos los del español deficiente. We are your linguistic nightmare, your linguistic aberration, your linguistic *mestisaje,* the subject of your *burla.* Because we speak with tongues of fire we are culturally crucified. Racially, culturally, and linguistically *somos huérfanos*—we speak an orphan tongue.

Chicanas who grew up speaking Chicano Spanish have internalized the belief that we speak poor Spanish. It is illegitimate, a bastard language. And because we internalize how our language has been used against us by the dominant culture, we use our language differences against each other.

Chicana feminists often skirt around each other with suspicion and hesitation. For the longest time I couldn't figure it out. Then it dawned on me. To be close to another Chicana is like looking into the mirror. We are afraid of what we'll see there. *Pena.* Shame. Low estimation of self. In childhood we are told that our language is wrong. Repeated attacks on our native tongue diminish our sense of self. The attacks continue throughout our lives.

Chicanas feel uncomfortable talking in Spanish to Latinas, afraid of their censure. Their language was not outlawed in their countries. They had a whole lifetime of being immersed in their native tongue; generations, centuries in which Spanish was a first language, taught in school, heard on radio and TV, and read in the newspaper.

If a person, Chicana or Latina, has a low estimation of my native tongue, she also has a low estimation of me. Often with *mexicanas y latinas* we'll speak English as a neutral language. Even among Chicanas we tend to speak English at parties or conferences. Yet, at the same time, we're afraid the other will think we're *agringadas* because we don't speak Chicano Spanish. We oppress each other trying to out-Chicano each other, vying to be the "real" Chicanas, to speak like Chicanos. There is no one Chicano language just as there is no one Chicano experience. A monolingual Chicana whose first language is English or Spanish is just as much a Chicana as one who speaks several variants of Spanish. A Chicana from Michigan or Chicago or Detroit is just as much a Chicana as one from the Southwest. Chicano Spanish is as diverse linguistically as it is regionally.

By the end of this century, Spanish speakers will comprise the biggest minority group in the United States, a country where students in high schools and colleges are encouraged to take French classes because French is considered more "cultured." But for a language to remain alive it must be used. By the end of this century English, and not Spanish, will be the mother tongue of most Chicanos and Latinos.

So, if you want to really hurt me, talk badly about my language. Ethnic identity is twin skin to linguistic identity—I am my language. Until I can take pride in my language, I cannot take pride in myself. Until I can accept as legitimate Chicano Texas Spanish, Tex-Mex, and all the other languages I speak, I cannot accept the legitimacy of myself. Until I am free to write bilingually and to switch codes without having always to translate, while I still have to speak English or Spanish when I would rather speak Spanglish, and as long as I have to accommodate the English speakers rather than having them accommodate me, my tongue will be illegitimate.

I will no longer be made to feel ashamed of existing. I will have my voice: Indian, Spanish, white. I will have my serpent's tongue—my woman's voice, my sexual voice, my poet's voice. I will overcome the tradition of silence.

> My fingers
> move sly against your palm
> Like women everywhere, we speak in code.
>
> MELANIE KAYE/KANTROWITZ

"Vistas," corridos, y comida:

My Native Tongue

In the 1960s, I read my first Chicano novel. It was *City of Night* by John Rechy, a gay Texan, son of a Scottish father and a Mexican mother. For days I walked around in stunned amazement that a Chicano could write and could get published. When I read *I Am Joaquín* I was surprised to see a bilingual book by a Chicano in print. When I saw poetry written in Tex-Mex for the first time, a feeling of pure joy flashed through me. I felt like we really existed as a people. In 1971, when I started teaching High School English to Chicano students, I tried to supplement the required texts with works by Chicanos, only to be reprimanded and forbidden to do so by the principal. He claimed that I was supposed to teach "American" and English literature. At the risk of being fired, I swore my students to secrecy and slipped in Chicano short stories, poems, a play. In graduate school, while working toward a Ph.D., I had to "argue" with one adviser after the other, semester after semester, before I was allowed to make Chicano literature an area of focus.

Even before I read books by Chicanos or Mexicans, it was the Mexican movies I saw at the drive-in—the Thursday night special of $1.00 a carload—that gave me a sense of belonging. *"Vámonos a las vistas,"* my mother would call out and we'd all—grandmother, brothers, sister, and cousins—squeeze into the car. We'd wolf down cheese and bologna white bread sandwiches while watching Pedro Infante in melodramatic tearjerkers like *Nosotros los pobres,* the first "real" Mexican movie (that was not an imitation of European movies). I remember seeing *Cuando los hijos se van* and surmising that all Mexican movies played up the love a mother has for her children and what ungrateful sons and daughters suffer when they are not devoted to their mothers. I remember the singing-type "westerns" of Jorge Negrete and Miquel Aceves Mejía. When watching Mexican movies, I felt a sense of homecoming as well as alienation. People who were to amount to something didn't go to Mexican movies, or *bailes,* or tune their radios to *bolero, rancherita,* and *corrido* music.

The whole time I was growing up, there was *norteño* music sometimes called North Mexican border music, or Tex-Mex music, or Chicano music, or *cantina* (bar) music. I grew up listening to *conjuntos,* three- or four-piece bands made up of folk musicians playing guitar, *bajo sexto,* drums, and button accordion, which Chicanos had borrowed from the German immigrants who had come to Central Texas and Mexico to farm and build breweries. In the Rio Grande Valley, Steve Jordan and Little Joe Hernández were popular, and Flaco Jiménez was the accordion king. The rhythms of Tex-Mex music are those of the polka, also adapted from the Germans, who in turn had borrowed the polka from the Czechs and Bohemians.

I remember the hot, sultry evenings when *corridos*—songs of love and death on the Texas-Mexican borderlands—reverberated out of cheap amplifiers from the local *cantinas* and wafted in through my bedroom window.

Corridos first became widely used along the South Texas/Mexican border during the early conflict between Chicanos and Anglos. The *corridos* are usually about Mexican heroes who do valiant deeds against the Anglo oppressors. Pancho Villa's song, *"La cucaracha,"* is the most famous one. *Corridos* of John F. Kennedy and his death are still very popular in the Valley. Older Chicanos remember Lydia Mendoza, one of the great border *corrido* singers who was called *la Gloria de Tejas.* Her *"El tango negro,"* sung during the Great Depression, made her a singer of the people. The ever-present *corridos* narrated one hundred years of border history, bringing news of events as well as entertaining. These folk musicians and folk songs are our chief cultural mythmakers, and they made our hard lives seem bearable.

I grew up feeling ambivalent about our music. Country-western and rock-and-roll had more status. In the fifties and sixties, for the slightly educated and *agringado* Chicanos, there existed a sense of shame at being caught listening to our music. Yet I couldn't stop my feet from thumping to the music, could not stop humming the words, nor hide from myself the exhilaration I felt when I heard it.

There are more subtle ways that we internalize identification, especially in the forms of images and emotions. For me food and certain smells are tied to my identity, to my homeland. Woodsmoke curling up to an immense blue sky; woodsmoke perfuming my grandmother's clothes, her skin. The stench of cow manure and the yellow patches on the ground; the crack of a .22 rifle and the reek of cordite. Homemade white cheese sizzling in a pan, melting inside a folded *tortilla*. My sister Hilda's hot, spicy *menudo, chile colorado* making it deep red, pieces of *panza* and hominy floating on top. My brother Carito barbequing *fajitas* in the backyard. Even now and 3,000 miles away, I can see my mother spicing the ground beef, pork, and venison with *chile*. My mouth salivates at the thought of the hot steaming *tamales* I would be eating if I were home.

Si le preguntas a mi mamá, "¿Qué eres?"

> Identity is the essential core of who
> we are as individuals, the conscious
> experience of the self inside.
>
> GERSHEN KAUFMAN

Nosotros los Chicanos straddle the borderlands. On one side of us, we are constantly exposed to the Spanish of the Mexicans, on the other side we hear the Anglos' incessant clamoring so that we forget our language. Among ourselves we don't say *nosotros los americanos, o nosotros los españoles, o nosotros los hispanos*. We say *nosotros los mexicanos* (by *mexicanos* we do not mean citizens of Mexico; we do not mean a national identity, but a racial one). We distinguish between *mexicanos del otro lado* and *mexicanos de este lado*. Deep in our hearts we believe that being Mexican has nothing to do with which country one lives in. Being Mexican is a state of soul—not one of mind, not one of citizenship. Neither eagle nor serpent, but both. And like the ocean, neither animal respects borders.

> *Dime con quien and as y te diré quien eres.*
> (Tell me who your friends are and I'll tell you who you are.)
>
> MEXICAN SAYING

Si le preguntas a mi mamá, "¿Qué eres?" te dirá, "Soy mexicana." My brothers and sister say the same. I sometimes will answer *"soy mexicana"* and at others will say *"soy Chicana" o "soy tejana." But I identified as "Raza"* before I ever identified as *"mexicana"* or "Chicana."

As a culture, we call ourselves Spanish when referring to ourselves as a linguistic group and when copping out. It is then that we forget our predominant Indian genes. We are 70–80 percent Indian. We call ourselves Hispanic or Spanish-American or Latin American or Latin when linking ourselves to other Spanish-speaking peoples of the Western hemisphere and when copping out. We call ourselves Mexican-American to signify we are neither Mexican nor American, but more the noun "American" than the adjective "Mexican" (and when copping out).

Chicanos and other people of color suffer economically for not acculturating. This voluntary (yet forced) alienation makes for psychological conflict, a kind of dual identity—we don't identify with the Anglo-American cultural values and we don't totally identify with the Mexican cultural values. We are a synergy of two cultures with various degrees of Mexicanness or Angloness. I have so internalized the borderland conflict that sometimes I feel like one cancels out the other and we are zero, nothing, no one. *A veces no soy nada ni nadie. Pero hasta cuando no lo soy, lo soy.*

When not copping out, when we know we are more than nothing, we call ourselves Mexican, referring to race and ancestry; *mestizo* when affirming both our Indian and Spanish (but we hardly ever own our Black) ancestry; Chicano when referring to a politically aware people born and/or raised in the United States; *Raza* when referring to Chicanos; *tejanos* when we are Chicanos from Texas.

Chicanos did not know we were a people until 1965 when Cesar Chavez and the farmworkers united and *I Am Joaquín* was published and *la Raza Unida* party was formed in Texas. With that recognition, we became a distinct people. Something momentous happened to the Chicano soul—we became aware of our reality and acquired a name and a language (Chicano Spanish) that reflected that reality. Now that we had a name, some of the fragmented pieces began to fall together— who we were, what we were, how we had evolved. We began to get glimpses of what we might eventually become.

Yet the struggle of identities continues, the struggle of borders is our reality still. One day the inner struggle will cease and a true integration take place. In the meantime, *tenémos que hacer la lucha. ¿Quién está protegiendo los ranchos de mi gente? ¿Quién está tratando de cerrar la fisura entre la india y el blanco en nuestra sangre? El Chicano, si, el Chicano que anda como un ladrón en su propia casa.*

Los Chicanos, how patient we seem, how very patient. There is the quiet of the Indian about us. We know how to survive. When other races have given up their tongue we've kept ours. We know what it is to live under the hammer blow of the dominant *norteamericano* culture. But more than we count the blows, we count the days the weeks the years the centuries the aeons until the white laws and commerce and customs will rot in the deserts they've created, lie bleached. *Humildes* yet proud, *quietos* yet wild, *nosotros los mexicanos-Chicanos* will walk by the crumbling ashes as we go about our business. Stubborn, persevering, impenetrable as stone, yet possessing a malleability that renders us unbreakable, we, the *mestizas* and *mestizos,* will remain.

Considerations

Thinking

What argument does Anzaldúa make for the need for a Chicano Spanish? Why does she characterize it as "a forked tongue"? And why does she say that "often it is only with another Chicana *tejano* that [she] can talk freely"?

What cultural values are associated with the different languages and dialects Anzaldúa describes? Which are most important to her and why?

Connecting

To what extent does Anzaldúa's discussion of her languages reflect your own linguistic experience? Did you find yourself connected to or disconnected from her discourse? Where, especially, and why?

Relate what Anzaldúa says about language to what Amy Tan says about her "Englishes" in "Mother Tongue."

Writing

Write an essay describing, illustrating, and exploring the different languages or dialects you use. Explain where and when you use them, with whom you use them, and why.

James Baldwin
(1924–1987)

James Baldwin was born in Harlem and became, at fourteen, a preacher. At seventeen, he abandoned the ministry and devoted himself to the craft of writing. Baldwin received institutional support in the form of fellowships to help sustain him while he wrote his first two novels: *Go Tell It on the Mountain* (1953) and *Giovanni's Room* (1956). Sandwiched between these two works was a collection of essays, *Notes of a Native Son* (1955), which many readers consider his finest work.

In his essays, Baldwin struggled to define himself as an American, as a writer, and as a black man, all of which, for Baldwin, were inextricably intertwined. In coming to terms with what was the most difficult thing in his life (his blackness), Baldwin revealed himself to be a passionate and eloquent writer, whose most frequent subject has been the relations between the races.

The Discovery of What It Means
to Be an American

"It is a complex fate to be an American," Henry James observed, and the principal discovery an American writer makes in Europe is just how complex this fate is. America's history, her aspirations, her peculiar triumphs, her even more peculiar defeats, and her position in the world—yesterday and today—are all so profoundly and stubbornly unique that the very word "America" remains a new almost completely undefined and extremely controversial proper noun. No one in the world seems to know exactly what it describes, not even we motley millions who call ourselves Americans.

I left America because I doubted my ability to survive the fury of the color problem here. (Sometimes I still do.) I wanted to prevent myself from becoming *merely* a Negro; or, even, merely a Negro writer. I wanted to find out in what way the *specialness* of my experience could be made to connect me with other people instead of dividing me from them. (I was as isolated from Negroes as I was from whites, which is what happens when a Negro begins, at bottom, to believe what white people say about him.)

In my necessity to find the terms on which my experience could be related to that of others, Negroes and whites, writers and non-writers, I proved, to my astonishment, to be as American as any Texas G.I. And I found my experience was shared by every American writer I knew in Paris. Like me, they had been divorced from their origins, and it turned out to make very little difference that the origins of white Americans were European and mine were African—they were no more at home in Europe than I was.

The fact that I was the son of a slave and they were the sons of free men meant less, by the time we confronted each other on European soil, than the fact that we were both searching for our separate identities. When we had found these, we seemed to be saying, why, then, we would no longer need to cling to the shame and bitterness which had divided us so long.

It became terribly clear in Europe, as it never had been here, that we knew more about each other than any European ever could. And it also became clear that, no matter where our fathers had been born, or what they had endured, the fact of Europe had formed us both was part of our identity and part of our inheritance.

I had been in Paris a couple of years before any of this became clear to me. When it did, I, like many a writer before me upon the discovery that his props have all been knocked out from under him, suffered a species of breakdown and was carried off to the mountains of Switzerland. There, in that absolutely alabaster landscape, armed with two Bessie Smith records and a typewriter, I began to try to recreate the life that I had first known as a child and from which I had spent so many years in flight.

It was Bessie Smith, through her tone and her cadence, who helped me to dig back to the way I myself must have spoken when I was a pickaninny, and to remember the things I had heard and seen and felt. I had buried them very deep. I had never listened to Bessie Smith in America (in the same way that, for years, I would not touch watermelon), but in Europe she helped to reconcile me to being a "nigger."

I do not think that I could have made this reconciliation here. Once I was able to accept my role—as distinguished, I must say, from my "place"—in the extraordinary drama which is America, I was released from the illusion that I hated America.

The story of what can happen to an American Negro writer in Europe simply illustrates, in some relief, what can happen to any American writer there. It is not meant, of course, to imply that it happens to them all, for Europe can be very crippling, too; and, anyway, a writer, when he has made his first breakthrough, has simply won a crucial skirmish in a dangerous, unending and unpredictable battle. Still, the breakthrough is important, and the point is that an American writer, in order to achieve it, very often has to leave this country.

The American writer, in Europe, is released, first of all, from the necessity of apologizing for himself. It is not until he is released from the habit of flexing his muscles and proving that he is just a "regular guy" that he realizes how crippling this habit has been. It is not necessary for him, there, to pretend to be something he is not, for the artist does not encounter in Europe the same suspicion he encounters here. Whatever the Europeans may actually think of artists, they have killed enough of them off by now to know that they are as real—and as persistent—as rain, snow, taxes or businessmen.

Of course, the reason for Europe's comparative clarity concerning the different functions of men in society is that European society has always been divided into classes in a way that American society never has been. A European writer considers himself to be part of an old and honorable tradition—of intellectual activity, of letters—and his choice of a vocation does not cause him any uneasy wonder as to whether or not it will cost him all his friends. But this tradition does not exist in America.

On the contrary, we have a very deep-seated distrust of real intellectual effort (probably because we suspect that it will destroy, as I hope it does, that myth of America to which we cling so desperately). An American writer fights his way to one of the lowest rungs on the American social ladder by means of pure bullheadedness and an indescribable series of odd jobs. He probably *has* been a "regular fellow" for much of his adult life, and it is not easy for him to step out of that lukewarm bath.

We must, however, consider a rather serious paradox: though American society is more mobile than Europe's, it is easier to cut across social and occupational lines there than it is here. This has something to do, I think, with the problem of status in American life. Where everyone has status, it is also perfectly possible, after all, that no one has. It seems inevitable, in any case, that a man may become uneasy as to just what his status is.

But Europeans have lived with the idea of status for a long time. A man can be as proud of being a good waiter as of being a good actor, and, in neither case, feel threatened. And this means that the actor and the waiter can have a freer and more genuinely friendly relationship in Europe than they are likely to have here. The waiter does not feel, with obscure resentment, that the actor has "made it," and the actor is not tormented by the fear that he may find himself, tomorrow, once again a waiter.

This lack of what may roughly be called social paranoia causes the American writer in Europe to feel—almost certainly for the first time in his life—that he can reach out to everyone, that he is accessible to everyone and open to everything. This is an extraordinary feeling. He feels, so to speak, his own weight, his own value.

It is as though he suddenly came out of a dark tunnel and found himself beneath the open sky. And, in fact, in Paris, I began to see the sky for what seemed to be the first time. It was borne in on me—and it did not make me feel melancholy—that this sky had been there before I was born and would be there when I was dead. And it was up to me, therefore, to make of my brief opportunity the most that could be made.

I was born in New York, but have lived only in pockets of it. In Paris, I lived in all parts of the city—on the Right Bank and the Left, among the bourgeoisie and among *les misérables,* and knew all kinds of people, from pimps and prostitutes in Pigalle to Egyptian bankers in Neuilly. This may sound extremely unprincipled or even obscurely immoral: I found it healthy. I love to talk to people, all kinds of people, and almost everyone, as I hope we still know, loves a man who loves to listen.

This perceptual dealing with people very different from myself caused a shattering in me of preconceptions I scarcely knew I held. The writer is meeting in Europe people who are not American, whose sense of reality is entirely different from his own. They may love or hate or admire or fear or envy this country—they see it, in any case, from another point of view, and this forces the writer to reconsider many things he had always taken for granted. This reassessment, which can be very painful, is also very valuable.

This freedom, like all freedom, has its dangers and its responsibilities. One day it begins to be borne in on the writer, and with great force, that he is living in Europe as an American. If he were living there as a European, he would be living on a different and far less attractive continent.

This crucial day may be the day on which an Algerian taxi-driver tells him how it feels to be an Algerian in Paris. It may be the day on which he passes a café terrace and catches a glimpse of the tense, intelligent and troubled face of Albert Camus. Or it may be the day on which someone asks him to explain Little Rock and he begins to feel that it would be simpler—and, corny as the words may sound, more honorable—to *go* to Little Rock than sit in Europe, on an American passport, trying to explain it.

This is a personal day, a terrible day, the day to which his entire sojourn has been tending. It is the day he realizes that there are no untroubled countries in this fearfully troubled world; that if he has been preparing himself for anything in Europe, he has been preparing himself—for America. In short, the freedom that the American writer finds in Europe brings him, full circle, back to himself, with the responsibility for his development where it always was: in his own hands.

Even the most incorrigible maverick has to be born somewhere. He may leave the group that produced him—he may be forced to—but nothing will efface his origins, the marks of which he carries with him everywhere. I think it is important to know this and even find it a matter for rejoicing, as the strongest people do, regardless of their station. On this acceptance, literally, the life of a writer depends.

The charge has often been made against American writers that they do not describe society, and have no interest in it. They only describe individuals in opposition to it, or isolated from it. Of course, what the American writer is describing is his own situation. But what is *Anna Karenina* describing if not the tragic fate of the isolated individual, at odds with her time and place?

The real difference is that Tolstoy was describing an old and dense society in which everything seemed—to the people in it, though not to Tolstoy—to be fixed forever. And the book is a masterpiece because Tolstoy was able to fathom, and make us see, the hidden laws which really governed this society and made Anna's doom inevitable.

American writers do not have a fixed society to describe. The only society they know is one in which nothing is fixed and in which the individual must fight for his identity. This is a rich confusion, indeed, and it creates for the American writer unprecedented opportunities.

That the tensions of American life, as well as the possibilities, are tremendous is certainly not even a question. But these are dealt with in contemporary literature mainly compulsively; that is, the book is more likely to be a symptom of our tension than an examination of it. The time has come, God knows, for us to examine ourselves, but we can only do this if we are willing to free ourselves of the myth of America and try to find out what is really happening here.

Every society is really governed by hidden laws, by unspoken but profound assumptions on the part of the people, and ours is no exception. It is up to the American writer to find out what these laws and assumptions are. In a society much given to smashing taboos without thereby managing to be liberated from them, it will be no easy matter.

It is no wonder, in the meantime, that the American writer keeps running off to Europe. He needs sustenance for his journey and the best models he can find. Europe has what we do not have yet, a sense of the mysterious and inexorable limits of life, a sense, in a word, of tragedy. And we have what they sorely need: a new sense of life's possibilities.

In this endeavor to wed the vision of the Old World with that of the New, it is the writer, not the statesman, who is our strongest arm. Though we do not wholly believe it yet, the interior life is a real life, and the intangible dreams of people have a tangible effect on the world.

Considerations

Thinking

Why does Baldwin say that it is "a complex fate" to be an American? Why was it a particularly complex fate for him? To what extent do you share Baldwin's experience? To what extent are you persuaded by his claims about his own experience?

What does Baldwin suggest about origins—about what and where a person is born and how he or she is raised? What does a person's origins—race, ethnicity, cultural background, language—reveal about him or her?

Connecting

Throughout the second and third sections of this essay, Baldwin contrasts Europe with America. What differences does he emphasize? And what are his reasons for establishing contrasts?

How can living in another country help a writer or other artist—or indeed anyone? To what extent can living in a different state or section of the country help you better understand your origins, cultural perspective, and values?

Writing

Write an essay in which you explore what it means for you to be an American. Consider some of the following: your race, ethnic background, sex, cultural, religious, and social values.

Write an essay in which you explore the following comment from paragraph 27: "Every society is really governed by hidden laws, by unspoken but profound assumptions on the part of the people, and ours is no exception."

Roland Barthes
(1915–1980)

Roland Barthes was born in France and studied French literature and classics at the University of Paris. After teaching in universities in Bucharest and Alexandria, he joined the National Center for Scientific Research, where he pursued research studies in sociology and language. As a leader of France's new critics, Barthes drew on the insights of Karl Marx and Sigmund Freud as well as on the work of the influential linguist Ferdinand de Saussure to expand the science of semiology, the study of signs and symbols underlying all aspects of human culture. The following essay on toys is taken from his book *Mythologies*.

Toys

French toys: one could not find a better illustration of the fact that the adult Frenchman sees the child as another self. All the toys one commonly sees are essentially a microcosm of the adult world; they are all reduced copies of human objects, as if in the eyes of the public the child was, all told, nothing but a smaller man, a homunculus to whom must be supplied objects of his own size.

Invented forms are very rare: a few sets of blocks, which appeal to the spirit of do-it-yourself, are the only ones which offer dynamic forms. As for the others, French toys *always mean something,* and this something is always entirely socialized, constituted by the myths or the techniques of modern adult life: the Army, Broadcasting, the Post Office, Medicine (miniature instrument-cases, operating theatres for dolls), School, Hair-Styling (driers for permanent-waving), the Air Force (Parachutists), Transport (trains, Citroens, Vedettes, Vespas, petrol-stations), Science (Martian toys).

The fact that French toys *literally* prefigure the world of adult functions obviously cannot but prepare the child to accept them all, by constituting for him, even before he can think about it, the alibi of a Nature which has at all times created soldiers, postmen and Vespas. Toys here reveal the list of all the things the adult does not find unusual: war, bureaucracy, ugliness, Martians, etc. It is not so much, in fact, the imitation which is the sign of an abdication, as its literalness: French toys are like a Jivaro head, in which one recognizes, shrunken to the size of an apple, the wrinkles and hair of an adult. There exist, for instance, dolls which urinate; they have an oesophagus, one gives them a bottle, they wet their nappies; soon, no doubt, milk will turn to water in their stomachs. This is meant to prepare the little girl for the causality of house-keeping, to condition her to her future role as mother. However, faced with this world of faithful and complicated objects, the child can only identify himself as owner, as user, never as creator; he does not invent the world, he uses it: there are, prepared for him, actions without adventure, without wonder, without joy. He is turned into a little stay-at-home householder who does not even have to invent the mainsprings of adult causality; they are supplied to him ready-made: he has only to help himself, he is never allowed to discover anything from start to finish. The merest set of blocks, provided it is not too refined, implies a very different learning of the world: then,

[handwritten note top-left: "Bart is a marxist"]

the child does not in any way create meaningful objects, it matters little to him whether they have an adult name; the actions he performs are not those of a user but those of a demiurge. He creates forms which walk, which roll, he creates life, not property: objects now act by themselves, they are no longer an inert and complicated material in the palm of his hand. But such toys are rather rare: French toys are usually based on imitation, they are meant to produce children who are users, not creators.

[handwritten margin note: "Playing then depicted as totally dull and passive"]

The bourgeois status of toys can be recognized not only in their forms, which are all functional, but also in their substances. Current toys are made of a graceless material, the product of chemistry, not of nature. Many are now moulded from complicated mixtures; the plastic material of which they are made has an appearance at once gross and hygienic, it destroys all the pleasure, the sweetness, the humanity of touch. A sign which fills one with consternation is the gradual disappearance of wood, in spite of its being an ideal material because of its firmness and its softness, and the natural warmth of its touch. Wood removes, from all the forms which it supports, the wounding quality of angles which are too sharp, the chemical coldness of metal. When the child handles it and knocks it, it neither vibrates nor grates, it has a sound at once muffled and sharp. It is a familiar and poetic substance, which does not sever the child from close contact with the tree, the table, the floor. Wood does not wound or break down; it does not shatter, it wears out, it can last a long time, live with the child, alter little by little the relations between the object and the hand. If it dies, it is in dwindling, not in swelling out like those mechanical toys which disappear behind the hernia of a broken spring. Wood makes essential objects, objects for all time. Yet there hardly remain any of these wooden toys from the Vosges, these fretwork farms with their animals, which were only possible, it is true, in the days of the craftsman. Henceforth, toys are chemical in substance and colour; their very material introduces one to a coenaesthesis of use, not pleasure. These toys die in fact very quickly, and once dead, they have no posthumous life for the child.

[handwritten margin note: "aren't they only dead when the child declares it dead & yet dead only in use / their memory will live on"]

Considerations

Thinking

Barthes suggests that French toys "mean something," that they are not mere objects of play. What is his point about the kinds of things the toys signify?

Do you agree with Barthes' critique of French toys as stifling creativity? What sorts of toys stifle the creative imagination of children and what sorts perhaps stimulate and develop that imaginative capacity?

Connecting

To what extent does Barthes' idea about the significance of French toys apply to American toys? According to Barthes, what functions do French (and analogously American) toys serve? That is, what do the toys do for children besides simply amuse them? Might Barthes' critique of toys be extended to other forms of entertainment, such as movies or video games? Why or why not?

Writing

In the manner of Barthes' discussion of toys, write an essay in which you explore the significance of some aspect of popular culture. Your goal is to examine the significance, the forms of meaning of one aspect of popular culture. Some possibilities: fast food, television sit-coms, wrestling, boxing, hockey (or another team sport), beer (or wine), casino gambling, and so on.

John Berger
(b. 1926)

John Berger is a writer and a critic of international repute. His books include the novels *G* and *A Fortunate Man,* and the critical works *About Looking* and *Ways of Seeing*—among a number of others. His art criticism is animated by a social and cultural critical impulse. He aims to see works of art in context, considering the societal values they embody, and encouraging his readers to see such works in relation to other images from contemporary life, especially those in film, advertising, and photography.

The following selection, "Ways of Seeing: Men Looking at Women," is excerpted from Berger's brief but important book about the cultural values revealed and concealed in Western art. Berger focuses here on ways women see themselves in the regard of men, and how men's looking at women influences the ways they look at themselves.

Ways of Seeing:
Men Looking at Women

According to usage and conventions which are at last being questioned but have by no means been overcome, the social presence of a woman is different in kind from that of a man. A man's presence is dependent upon the promise of power which he embodies. If the promise is large and credible his presence is striking. If it is small or incredible, he is found to have little presence. The promised power may be moral, physical, temperamental, economic, social, sexual—but its object is always exterior to the man. A man's presence suggests what he is capable of doing to you or for you. His presence may be fabricated, in the sense that he pretends to be capable of what he is not. But the pretense is always towards a power which he exercises on others.

By contrast, a woman's presence expresses her own attitude to herself, and defines what can and cannot be done to her. Her presence is manifest in her gestures, voice, opinions, expressions, clothes, chosen surroundings, taste—indeed there is nothing she can do which does not contribute to her presence. Presence for a woman is so intrinsic to her person that men tend to think of it as an almost physical emanation, a kind of heat or smell or aura.

To be born a woman has been to be born, within an allotted and confined space, into the keeping of men. The social presence of women has developed as a result of their ingenuity in living under such tutelage within such a limited space. But this has been at the cost of a woman's self being split into two. A woman must continually watch herself. She is almost continually accompanied by her own image of herself. Whilst she is walking across a room or whilst she is weeping at the death of her father, she can scarcely avoid envisaging herself walking or weeping. From earliest childhood she has been taught and persuaded to survey herself continually.

And so she comes to consider the surveyor and the surveyed within her as the two constituent yet always distinct elements of her identity as a woman.

She has to survey everything she is and everything she does because how she appears to others, and ultimately how she appears to men, is of crucial importance for what is normally thought of as the success of her life. Her own sense of

114

being in herself is supplanted by a sense of being appreciated as herself by another.

Men survey women before treating them. Consequently how a woman appears to a man can determine how she will be treated. To acquire some control over this process, women must contain it and interiorize it. That part of a woman's self which is the surveyor treats the part which is the surveyed so as to demonstrate to others how her whole self would like to be treated. And this exemplary treatment of herself by herself constitutes her presence. Every woman's presence regulates what is and is not "permissible" within her presence. Every one of her actions—whatever its direct purpose or motivation—is also read as an indication of how she would like to be treated. If a woman throws a glass on the floor, this is an example of how she treats her own emotion of anger and so of how she would wish it to be treated by others. If a man does the same, his action is only read as an expression of his anger. If a woman makes a good joke this is an example of how she treats the joker in herself and accordingly of how she as a joker-woman would like to be treated by others. Only a man can make a good joke for its own sake.

One might simplify this by saying: *men act and women appear.* Men look at women. Women watch themselves being looked at. This determines not only most relations between men and women but also the relation of women to themselves. The surveyor of woman in herself is male: the surveyed female. Thus she turns herself into an object—and most particularly an object of vision: a sight.

Considerations

Thinking

What distinction does Berger make with regard to a man's and a woman's "presence"? With regard to a man's and a woman's power? With regard to the relationship between power and presence for men and women?

How important, according to Berger, is a woman's image of herself? To what extent is her self-image influenced by the male gaze?

To what extent do you share Berger's belief that "*men act* and *women appear*"? Why?

Do women, as Berger suggests, turn themselves into objects? If so, to what extent are men complicit in that transformation? Why?

Connecting

To what extent can you, as a man or a woman, relate to what Berger says about men and women in this piece? Why?

After reading Maile Meloy's "The Voice of the Looking-Glass," account for the ways in which Meloy uses Berger. Consider how you might use Meloy's techniques in your own writing.

Examine various images of women in the media, in public life, in business, and at home. To what extent do the images of women found in one or more of those places support, illustrate, or qualify Berger's ideas about women?

After reading Elizabeth MacDonald's "Odalisque" and Berger's ideas about women, what do you think Berger would have to say about "Odalisque"? Why?

Writing

Write an essay in which you examine images of women in advertising or in Western painting in light of Berger's claims. You can begin with Trutat's *Reclining Bacchante* and Ingres's *La Grande Odalisque* (see the essay by Elizabeth MacDonald). You may wish to include consideration of Cassatt's *The Family* (color insert).

Write an essay in which you examine the depiction of women by one or more writers in this book, again, in light of Berger's argument. You may wish to read one essay or more than one. You may also wish to go beyond those included in the book. But for a start, look at these: Joan Didion's "Georgia O'Keeffe," Nancy Mairs's "On Being a Cripple," Alice Walker's "Beauty: When the Other Dancer Is the Self."

Sven Birkerts
(b. 1951)

Sven Birkerts is the author of five collections of essays, most recently *Readings*. His other works include *The Gutenberg Elegies: The Fate of Reading in an Electronic Age, An Artificial Wilderness: Essays on Twentieth-Century Literature, The Electric Life: Essays on Modern Poetry,* and *Tolstoy's Dictaphone: Technology and the Muse.* His essays and reviews appear regularly in the *Atlantic, Harper's,* the *New York Times Book Review,* and the *New Republic.* He has received Guggenheim and Lila-Wallace awards and teaches at Mount Holyoke College. He is also a member of the Core Faculty of the Bennington Writing Seminars.

"The Idea of the Internet" raises interesting questions about the loss of individuality, the morphing of the self, and what Birkerts sees as our "large-scale refusal to contemplate the systemic influence" of the "microchip and the electronic media."

The Idea of the Internet

Thinking about the Internet these days, I find myself less preoccupied with the system itself—how it all works, what it can and cannot do—and much more with the importance of the *idea* of the Internet, and in what ways, frontal or oblique, that idea impinges on our cultural life.

The Internet is a phenomenon that in certain ways demands to be treated more as idea than thing. Although for any one user it is always some particular process of sending or receiving information, no transaction happens apart from the core potentiality—the instant linkages possible—of the system.

The pressure, the impact, the implications of this potentiality are what interest me. How has it affected our thinking across a spectrum?

We can take air travel as a partial analogy. Here is a technological innovation that has concrete, practical effects: It gets me from here to there rapidly and allows me a certain range of activity otherwise not available. I can fly to another city, give a lecture, and return without having to cancel a class. But what is, in my view, far more consequential is that the idea of air travel has entirely infiltrated my experience of living in the world, and would have done so even if I never had recourse to flight; has done so because I live in a social world conditioned by an understanding of time and space different from that of generations of forebears. Los Angeles has become a locale that is, in part, a function of access, of the hours it would take to get there (rather than the days, as formerly), even if I never go there. And therefore Los Angeles—the idea of Los Angeles, the idea that cannot be separated entirely from the geographical entity—is different.

This is fairly obvious, but I cannot ignore its bearing on the idea of the Internet.

Before I question in what ways the idea of the Internet changes the contours of our experience, I need to make certain observations about the arrival of the technology into our collective midst.

Primarily, although the concept itself is somewhat revolutionary, and is for this reason the subject of a good deal of public attention and debate, the actual implementation by individuals does not manifest a revolutionary—or all-transforming—character. By and large, its functions—like air travel, say—as an augmentation. The Internet is a new thing, a new process, but one brings it into the fold of habit, makes a place for it, and although life does change, it does not change utterly. For this reason, we often see the individual response to the media excitement taking the form of a bemused shrug. Air travel, too, may be a monumental transformation of the existing, but if we fly twice a year to another city, we will likely not regard its effect on our lives as being monumental.

Think of it another way, as analogous to global warming. The scientists who study climate are right to be alarmed about the possibility of a temperature increase of two or three degrees over a period of several decades, even if our local—that is, experiential—response is a shrug. Climate scientists project the increase systematically and register a vast array of intertwined consequences, which in their sum may in significant ways change life as we know it. The individual, blind to the possibility of systematic consequence, ponders a warmer spring, a hotter summer, perhaps even savors the thought of less snow on the ground come winter. Two degrees can be accommodated easily enough.

I have these thoughts when people accuse me of making far too much of the microchip and the electronic network. But if I sometimes profess a certain alarm, it is at least in part alarm about the large-scale refusal to contemplate the systemic influence of these innovations, the fact that our picture of the world is being subtly but significantly altered.

In what sense do I mean this?

I mean, I suppose, that when a massive electronic nervous system rapidly establishes itself inside the geographical corpus, allowing, as the sketchy preliminary systems like telegraph and telephone never did, rapid transfer of large quantities of information, complex interactivity, and so on, then the idea of connectivity truly becomes part of our sense of things. What high-speed air travel has done to the idea of place, the Internet is, in its way, doing to the idea of individuality and isolated selfhood. It is injecting a new range of possibility into our conception of relation—among other things.

This is not necessarily bad, but it is a significant change and needs to be contemplated as such. There are those like psychologist-technotheorist Sherry Turkle who prognosticate diverse scenarios of liberation. Mediated communication, Turkle believes—and this is the thrust of her recent book, *Life on the Screen: Identity in the Age of the Internet*—will render human boundaries at once more permeable and more provisional; it will encourage the self to morph in diverse ways, slipping in and out of roles in ways that reflect its essential instability. Out of the chaos will arise new systems of relation; we will stand free of the powerful constraints imposed by face-to-face situations.

Thinking in these terms, we begin to consider that the isolated self, the subjective individual, may be less a natural given than a phase in a larger evolutionary process. Is bounded autonomy a desirable characteristic in an age dominated by network communications and mediated (and increasingly virtual) experience?

But we cannot regard such transformation blithely—it is something more than a *Time* or *Newsweek* feature story. For upon our long-standing notions of self (public and private) are predicated our laws, our social customs, our civic institutions, our conceptions of community, of art—of *everything*. It matters greatly how we come to understand the norms and possibilities of interaction. Communication, as the theorist Mikhail Bakhtin understood, is *dialogic*: It always happens between a specific sender and a specific receiver. When the process is transformed, by immediacy over distance, by the possibilities of anonymity and invisibility, and by the sense of endless potential networks running in every direction, we cannot expect anything to remain the same. This, the dissolving of what George W. S. Trow called the "grid of two hundred million" into the subjective space of the self, is the idea of the Internet, and it is an idea now in our midst. The temperature rises by a few degrees and everything changes—ocean levels, currents, vegetation belts. Bring a system of total connectivity—the idea of such a system—forward, and you will feel how a sense of unreality begins to shadow our perceptions. We will no longer stand on the same ground; the atmospheres of relation will have changed. Pundits everywhere will ascribe the new strangeness to the coming of the millennium.

Considerations

Thinking

Birkerts introduces two analogies in his essay: the one about air travel is fairly innocuous, neutral; the one about global warming tends toward warning. What do you make of that warning?

Birkerts makes use of three other thinkers in his essay: Sherry Turkle, Mikhail Bakhtin, and George W. S. Trow. How does he use each to advance his own idea about the Internet? Does he strengthen or weaken his case by incorporating the thoughts of these writers? Explain.

Connecting

Consider how Birkerts and Berndt Heinrich use analogies to advance ideas in their respective essays in this anthology. Note the similarities and differences in their use of these analogies. Select the two most effective uses and explain your choices in terms of the analogies' rhetorical value.

Explain the relationship between Birkerts' initial use of the global warming analogy early in his essay and his extension of that analogy in the essay's ending. How does that extension of the analogy reinforce Birkerts' idea about Internet?

Writing

In a short written presentation for your class, explain the difference between Birkerts' own judgment about the Internet (as you see it expressed in this essay) and what he calls "the Idea of the Internet."

Go to the library and do a little more reading from two of Birkerts' collections of essays: *The Gutenberg Elegies* and *Readings* (from which "Idea" was taken). Your aim is to try to find out more about what Birkerts means in "Idea" when he makes this claim: "Thinking in these terms, we begin to consider that the isolated self, the subject individual, may be less a natural given than a phase in a larger evolutionary process." Write a short essay revealing your interpretation of that claim in terms of this essay and others that you read.

Or after doing your reading, consider this response on the Internet to Birkerts' collection, *The Gutenberg Elegies:* http://www2.theatlantic.com/atlantic/atlweb/aandc/gutenbrg/ wschirev.htm. Does this review of Birkerts' book strike you as a fair assessment? Explain in a short e-mail response to the reviewer.

Rosellen Brown
(b. 1939)

Rosellen Brown has published four novels: *Before and After* (1992), *Civil Wars* (1984), *Tender Mercies* (1978), and *The Autobiography of My Mother* (1976). She has also published three collections of poetry, a collection of stories, and *The Rosellen Brown Reader* (1992), which contains essays, stories, and poetry. Her work has been selected for *O. Henry Prize Stories, Best American Short Stories,* and *Pushcart Prizes.*

Brown has received an award in literature from the American Academy of Arts and Letters, and fellowships from the Guggenheim Foundation, the Ingram Merrill Foundation, the Bunting Institute, the Howard Foundation, and twice from the National Endowment for the Arts. She was a *Ms.* magazine "Woman of the Year" in 1984, the same year *Civil Wars* won the Janet Kafka Prize for the best novel by an American woman.

Her piece in this anthology was the introductory essay for *Mojo,* a collection of Keith Carter's photographs—three of which are reprinted in this book (cover and following page 760).

Mojo

A pagan spirituality roams loose in these pages. It's a notoriously complicated and even personal force, this *mojo*. In fact it seems to me as I search Keith Carter's photographs and let them move in on my spirit, that the meaning of this strange word, so playful and mysterious on the tongue, must gather gradually out of the images themselves.

What shows itself on these pages and what commonality binds them? Do they constitute a world of individuals and their unique experiences, a universe of separate selves, or is there a shared landscape and a set of lived assumptions here? Carter's *Blue Man* series was so profoundly of and about East Texas that he claimed the place better than anyone before him; you could feel the pull of the very soil on the shoes of its inhabitants, and you believed you could hear the famous panther cry in those tangled, vinyl woods. Is there in *mojo* another kind of surface tension, some subtle kinship, that holds these scenes and portraits together, keeps them from flying off into the discrete existences of the merely anthologized?

There is, to begin with, a profound stillness in many of these photographs. Look, for example, at the serene stop-time moment in which a slender African-American acolyte stands ready at a baptism, with a look of sufficiency and assurance on him, as if he knows something we can't see. His large hands hang empty by the sides of his robe, grasping for nothing. They are not needy hands; they seem wholly resolved. We know this is only an instant's satisfaction in the midst of a life of movement, an instant in which even the horizon is so flat and uninflected that it seems bewitched. Still his portrait represents a moment this boy will never be able to deny: how he stood, once, in a long becalmed space, steeped in an inner peace with something just slightly less public than a smile on his lips.

Then there are the many pictures of death, a more extreme stasis: the alligator hung from a tree, so ancient, so wildly commanding, with its armored back dense as a tree itself. Yet, mastered, vanquished, it seems to have grown out of life into another form nearly as vigorous. And later we have a vision of its underside, this creature's own or a relative's, held up by an unsmiling girl with a stunning neutrality, as if it were—had always been—a thoroughly inanimate object.

And we are given the butchered cow, hoisted up (which only reminds us of the fate that awaits a few live barnyard pigs jauntily trotting in a file behind a couple of dogs); the beetles and insects, some neatly arranged for study, some loosely scattered, husks of the cast-off bodies of mysterious silent creatures—and the butterfly, weird and harshly beautiful, who seems to seal (or is it emerging from?) the mouth of a man with unsurprised eyes. Here, it seems to me, is where Keith Carter asks a kind of question—or if he doesn't ask it exactly, it gathers force from his images and asks itself: Does something continue to shimmer, to vibrate, in or around those empty shells? Is there some kind of imminence, or at least the resonance of loss?

Consider the dog who at first seems to be sleeping, casually, in an easy posture, on a picnic bench. On closer look, she turns out to be garlanded with wild flowers, turns out to have gone strange around the eyes. The eyes, in fact, are empty, veiled over. The dog is newly dead. This was someone's beloved dog then, that's becoming clear, and the subsiding energy of the live animal and someone's love and care haven't quite been quenched yet, even by grief. It's impossible, suddenly, not to remember the other pictures of dogs in the series, how alive and acute they seem; all of them appear to be listening to something with their finely attuned concentration. It has always been the hallmark of Carter's vision that he accords animals no less attention and respect than he does humans. Whatever hierarchy contains us all is not so absolute that we are seen to be more interesting, more innately powerful, or more feeling. So there is a palpable connection between the lovingly bedecked dog, so freshly dead, and the hand hovering over a very old man's head ("Wedding Ring") that seems to be smoothing it gently toward its final sleep.

Oddly related, there is the striking view of a young boy sitting, perhaps in a school or museum hallway, holding a giant model of an insect, a massive segmented pseudo-specimen with bulky wings, utterly and permanently unanimated. The boy gives no clue to what he is thinking—perhaps he's going to study the model, name its parts, learn some statistics. Where the model fits on the continuum between the live animals and the dead isn't quite clear; no border has been crossed here between the quick and the dead. Instead, playing at the edge between live and not-live, the mock-up in the boy's real, vital hands is faintly amusing, faintly disquieting. If photographs are positives, the presence of the negative lies behind them always. As in a good poem, each embodies its antithesis—movement behind stillness, chaos behind clarity, and, inevitably, death behind life.

It isn't surprising that Keith Carter pursues this edgy fascination into a series of photographs in which our memories seem to be filled with things we've never seen, mysteriously abandoned tableaux where only the vivid spoors of the living remain: a wallful of handprints, the smudge-handed child or children who made them long gone. A mirror with the bull's-eye of a bullet hole through it, silent questions, dangerous ones, penetrating the glass, radiating into an impressionistic landscape. The shaky line of dominoes from an abandoned game, a kind of architecture both disciplined and spontaneous. The empty nest of a bird larger than any one I ever hope to encounter up close, but—always there's an implied question in these photographs, a small mystification, a provocative detail, a contrast or contradiction—the frail and scruffy tree looks too delicate to support its guest.

Apparently it does serve, though: the gigantic nest fits in the bare branches as comfortably as a cup in the hand. A little procession of children through the woods is caught, ghostly, in their movement, and right in the middle a set of twins—doubles rendered a little bit strange in this context, as if one represented the solid side of existence and the other, perhaps, the visible white smoke of quick movement just captured. There in the center, the twins are the little "pique" of interest Roland Barthes wrote about, that unexpected snag for our attention that we pass right by if we're not looking as hard as we can.

Some of Carter's photographs are serious games played with scale, which inevitably emphasizes the characteristics of large and small, weak and strong. A lumberingly heavy man offers his chest to a litter of infinitely vulnerable kittens, who climb it as if it's the world. A woman stands over a barrel, smoke or steam rising from its surface, cradling what looks like a very small puppy. It contrasts the helplessness of the animal with the massiveness and danger of the material world. And, in "Swimmers," two pubescent boys in bathing suits, their half-fledged bodies open to our sight, face us in attitudes that look both prayerful and terrified. They are neither, of course, but the coincidence of this split-second of vision freezes them, in a convivial crowd of young men and noise and motion, just at the point where their unprotected fragility still shows, on the brink of their disappearance into manhood.

If Keith Carter's landscape is in some sense bounded by the invisible line between movement/stasis, and strength/weakness, it is also vivified, uncynically, with a religious presence. A lady in her white uniform sits, Bible in lap, her hands as relaxed as those of the boy acolyte, but her posture that of a resolved, habituated congregant. Where he looks purely expectant, she seems almost complacent: no surprises are going to unseat her from her divinely inspired posture of assurance. In "Oak Tree," in a dark tree as secure as a great body with numerous arms, like Shiva, sits a tiny birdhouse in the shape of a church. A wonderful emblem out of a whole lived life is Willie's Bible, lying well used and solid, fingered and worn, against the most pristine, almost idealized, white lace. The book is such a piece of a life, or a succession of lives, that it is a simple statement, brimming with real, not institutionalized, religious feeling. As for the chairs waiting in church with their fans propped up, Carter has captured what seems almost a visible image, a sort of Shroud of Turin, on the homely curtains lit from behind. These are the places where his vision of ordinary life inbued with spirit comes close to folk art: This is a daily, modest reverence caught and heightened by the camera's curious eye.

And finally, we come upon that pagan spirit that would never speak in the pages of anyone's Bible, the counterpoint to "ordinary" religion that brings us closest to the *mojo* of curses and spells, to the "mojo hand" of hexes, and from there into darker, hidden energies. The mud man, for example, stands in a scrubby brush like some natural excrescence of the earth, or one of those not-quite-Christian putti who pee unapologetically in Italian gardens. In a related image, a young woman clings to her lover amidst shimmering water and the bizarre eruptions of cypress knees, the two of them joyous earth sprites, natural forces—anima—sprung straight from the forest.

Carter obviously shares Walker Evans's belief that people's houses describe their inhabitants. A lucky horseshoe hangs benignly above photographs and ads for kielbasa—who says everything should be explicable and everyone's ideas of beauty interchangeable? A crystal ball swirls in smoke without apparent explanation. A row of candles sits ambiguously on a mantel or altar, above which an enigmatic image appears—Christlike or saintlike, painting or mirror?—full of disembodied relics. The lighting is pure Catavaggio, but the obeisance feels secretive, personal, darkly idiosyncratic.

No book of Southern photographs is complete without its bottle tree, but Carter's is much more homely than most. For one thing this is a close-up, and the bottles are so new that their easily deciphered, familiar labels—Slice, a 7-Up can—don't inspire much mystery. Nor is the tree even a tree: it's a post, and at its base lies a rubble of battles fallen off their nails. There is an element of sadness, though it's not unmixed with humor, in the seedy demystification of this old African tradition, as if duty, not conviction, hung the whole business for some reason barely remembered. But then, some might say, what is any conventional religion but barely remembered passion?

Conversely, the woman in the striped dress and head-rag who is flailing the air with her gone-to-seed garlic, roots and all, whatever she may really be doing seems to be invoking some profound vegetative force. Carter catches a gloriously vital instant, a joyous spark of connection between this woman in a field, whose face we don't see, and some spirit abroad in the wide-open air.

Carter makes no comment on these backyard phenomena, the pathetic bottle tree or the garlic whipping through space (though, taken from below, the picture of the woman enlarges her stature and gives us a vast blank sky against which she seems to be making magic). There is one delightful portrait of a young black girl so serene, so youthful and intelligent, that the glowing light bulb beside her seems almost a fanciful embodiment of her liveliness, pure spirit made material. But in general, Carter rarely engages his subjects eye-to-eye. The photographs find their point of entry into these lives by quietly observing, by catching a telling or typical moment, a gesture. Everything they record has the feel of *habit* to it, not a one-time chance or freak occurrence but the expression of a way of being. Real life.

Since Keith Carter is a notably modest man, it seems very much in keeping with his personality that he does not force into his photographs much acknowledgment of his presence. He doesn't stalk his subjects, nor does he ask them to represent themselves as they'd like to be seen. These are not "objective" documentations like August Sander's, or defenses against judgment like Diane Arbus's. Nor are they political, unless a little black child holding the famous portrait of George Washington can be called political because its ironies are so painful, or the collection of black "role model" dolls ranged beneath the remnant of a bulletin board that cheerfully promises "YES" above their raised and empty hands. His photographs give us the sense that he has either stumbled upon a peculiar moment accidentally—a smiling dog!—or has waited patiently for a defining image to emerge out of a life almost the way the photographic image clarifies under the surface of the developing solution, deepening as we watch for it.

In the end, Keith Carter's *mojo* is just that kind of feeling, the culmination of many moments of being in a representative instant, but an instant charged with the inexplicable animating energy of the particular. The poet Lorca tried to define his concept of *duende*—the feeling that for him separated ordinary speech or stolid verse from serious poetry—by quoting Goethe. *"A mysterious power,"* he called it, *"that all may feel and no philosophy can explain."* To be more precise than that would be to circumscribe the limitless invitations Keith Carter holds out to us to enter these worlds through the narrow opening of his aperture.

Lorca ends one of his odes with a plea to the contradictory forces out of which his *duende* and, I think, Keith Carter's *mojo* are so sweetly and perilously made:

> *Give us that daily bread, for we wish it,*
> *flower with alder, threshed tenderness, world without end;*
> *earth's will be done, for we wish it,*
> *who offers her harvest to all.*

Considerations

Thinking

At the beginning of her essay on Keith Carter's photographs, Rosellen Brown suggests that "a pagan spirituality roams loose in these pages." She is referring to the pages of Carter's book *Mojo*. In *Encounters*, we have included two of Carter's photographs from that book—Garlic and Starball (following page 760)—that should give you a sense of what Brown means by a "pagan spirituality." Consult those photographs and your college dictionary, and see if you can figure out what Brown means by that important phrase. Check your sense of the phrase against what Brown tells you later in her essay.

Connecting

Brown creates word pictures of many of Carter's photographs from *Mojo*. Compare her word pictures with the actual photographs that we have reprinted in this anthology. How do the word images stand up to the photographs themselves? What are the distinguishing qualities of each form of representation?

Writing

What do you make of Brown's claim, "If photographs are positives, the presence of the negative lies behind them always. As in a good poem, each embodies its antithesis—movement behind stillness, chaos behind clarity, and, inevitably, death behind life"? Write an essay that considers this claim in light of two or three photographs that are reprinted in this anthology.

On several occasions in Brown's essay, she suggests that Carter's photographs raise questions for our consideration. Identify two of those instances of questioning in Brown's essay and explain how the questions themselves help Brown develop her ideas and her essay.

Assemble a collection of photographs of your family. Write an introductory essay for this collection accounting for the nature of your family as it is represented within the context of the photographs. Consult Anna Norris's essay "How to Read Photographs" (pp. 69–73) to help you think about the way context affects meaning.

Jane Brox
(b. 1956)

Jane Brox is the author of *Here and Nowhere Else: Late Seasons of a Farm and Its Family,* which received the 1996 New England PEN award. Her essays have appeared in *The Georgia Review, The Gettysburg Review, Salamander,* and other journals. "Influenza 1918" is from *Five Thousand Days Like This One,* a collection of essays on the interweaving of industrial and agricultural life in the lower Merrimack River valley at the turn of the century. Her essay is striking for the precision of its language and the specificity of its detail.

Influenza 1918

In ordinary times, the bankers, lawyers, and mill owners who lived on Tower Hill opened their doors to a quiet broken only by the jostle of a laden milk wagon, the first stirrings of a wind in the elms, or the quavering notes of a sparrow. It was the height of country; the air, sweet and clear. Looking east from their porches they could survey miles of red-brick textile mills that banked the canals and the sluggish Merrimack, as well as the broad central plain mazed with tenements. To their west was a patchwork of small dairy holdings giving over to the blue distance. But for the thirty-one mornings of October 1918 those men adjusted gauze masks over their mouths and noses as they set out for work in the cold-tinged dawn, and they kept their eyes to the ground so as not to see what they couldn't help but hear: the clatter of motorcars and horse-drawn wagons over the paving stones, as day and night without ceasing the ambulances ran up the hill bringing sufferers from the heart of the city and the hearses carried them away.

It had started as a seemingly common thing—what the line-storm season always brings, born on its wind and on our breath, something that would run its course in the comfort of camphor and bed rest. At first there had been no more than six or eight or ten cases a day reported in the city, and such news hardly took up a side column in the papers, which were full of soldiers' obituaries and reports of a weakening Germany. As September wore on, however, the death notices of victims of the flu began to outnumber the casualties of war. Finally it laid low so many the Lawrence Board of Health set aside its usual work of granting permits to keep roosters, charting the milk supply, and inspecting tenements. The flu took up all its talk—how it was to be treated, how contained, how to stay ahead of the dead. The sufferers needed fresh air and isolation, and their care had to be consolidated to make the most of the scarce nurses and orderlies. So the board took a page from other stricken cities and voted to construct a makeshift tent hospital on their highest, most open land that offered the best air, which was the leeward side of Tower Hill where a farm still spread across the slope.

At home the mill workers breathed in the smells of rubbish and night soil that drifted up from the alleyways. Where they lived was low-lying, so much smells, together with smoke and ash, hung in the air. Their heat was sparse. They were crowded into their rooms. The flu cut right through, spreading ahead of its own rumors, passing on a handshake and on the wind and with the lightest kiss. No spitting. No sharing food. Keep your hands clean. Avoid crowds. Walk everywhere. Sleep with your windows open.

They slept to the sound of rain—rain pouring from their gutterless roofs turning the alleyways into thick mud, rain on the wandering hens pecking at stones in the streets, rain on the silenced pigeons puffed and caged in their coops. At times the rain was hard, driven from the north like mare's hooves on their roofs, drowning the parsley and oregano set in enamel basins on the window ledges. Other times it fell soft and fine out of a pale gray sky, making circles fragile as wrists on the surfaces of the canals before being lost to the brown, frothy water there. And sometimes it was no more than a mist that settled in the low places, obscuring the bottoms of the stairwells and the barrels and the piles of sawdust, only to shift and reveal the same world as always. Then the rain would gather its strength again, seeming to rake their lives all that much harder. Scrap coal couldn't keep away its chill.

A doctor may as well have gone house to house down Common, Haverhill, and Jackson streets, so numerous were the cases. Often his knock would go unanswered, since it wasn't the family who had sought him out. More likely the sickness had been reported by their landlord or neighbor—afraid that the influenza would spread—so the doctor heard a sudden silence within and a face at the window disappearing into shadow. What kept the families from responding wasn't a lack of a common language so much as the fear that the doctor would tack a card to the door warning of the infection within, and the greater fear that their sick children would be ordered to the tent hospital. Once there, they wouldn't be seen again until they were dead or cured.

When the doctor finally gained entrance—at times with the help of the police—he could find whole families had been laid low, with the sick tending those who were sicker. They had sacks of camphor around their necks, or mustard spread on their chests, a cup of chamomile by the cot. Whiskey. Garlic and onions weighed in the air. Some sufferers lay in windowless rooms where the damp had kept in the smoke from a low coal fire, and what light there was wavered from a kerosene lamp. Almost always the disease had gone beyond a cough and aches and a runny nose. There was blood mixed in with their phlegm, and they couldn't move from their beds. In the worst cases their skin was tinted blue.

One doctor could see hundreds of cases a day, and in his haste to complete his records, he sometimes left out the ages of the victims and often the names. They come down now in the *Influenza Journal* distinguished only by their address or their nationality: *four Cases, 384 Common Street (downstairs).* Or: *Mother and Child. Baby Rossano. Father and Son. A Syrian fellow. Polish man.* When the rain finally let up and days of mist lifted to bring on clear dry air, the number of influenza cases still didn't slow. Every woman who gave birth, it seems, died. The elderly, schoolchildren, and infants, yes—but strangest of all was how it took the young and healthy who had never been sick in their lives. Just yesterday they had worked a full day.

The entrance to the tent hospital on Tower Hill was clotted with ambulances arriving with patients and standing ambulances awaiting their dispatch orders. Many were still horse drawn, and the mares stood uneasy in the confusion. The motorized cars idled and choked the air with gasoline, the tang of which overlay the warm, familiar smells of hay and animal sweat. Everyone wore gauze masks, and there was no talk but orders. *Don't back up. Bring that one over here.* Nurses checked the pulse and color of patients and listened to their lungs. *We need more masks. Find me a doctor. Help me with this one.* The gate was patrolled by a military guard to assure that only the sufferers and those who tended them went beyond. Waiting black hacks stood three deep.

Every day at 5 A.M. a soldier blew reveille. The quick, bright notes parted the confusion at the entrance and gleamed above the hospital grounds—a far call from a country those patients no longer came from. The general din at the gate may as well have been the sound of a market day in a port city, and they, drowsing on a ship that had pulled away. They didn't stir. It was no concern of theirs, each in his or her own tent, the tent flap open to the back of a neighboring tent. Tents were arranged in rows, in wards, and in precincts, making a grid of the old hay-field. Its crickets were silent. Its summer birds had flown. Electrical wires hung on makeshift poles, and you could hear them swaying in the storms. The soaked canvas flanks of the tents ballooned in a wind and settled back on their frames. Boardwalks had been laid down between the tents, and footfalls, softened by the drenched wood, came near and receded. The nuns' habits swished. What country was this? A cough. A groan. The stricken tossed in their fevers. Their muscles ached. One moment they had the sweats; the next, chills. In forty-five different languages and dialects they called for water and warmth.

Many were cared for in words they couldn't understand. The student nurses and the Good Shepherd Sisters spoke English and French, but to the Germans and Italians and Syrians their voices may just as well have been more soft rain. A face half covered with gauze leaned near their own. They were given water to drink. Cool cloths were placed on their brows. They were wrapped in blankets and wheeled outside for more air. Someone listened to their hearts and then to their bogged-down lungs. A spoonful of thick serum was lifted to their lips. Their toes and fingertips turned blue from a lack of oxygen. In many pneumonia set in.

It was the same suffering in each tent, in each ward, in each precinct of the hospital. And the same in the surrounding country, in all cities, in all the known nations of the world. It struck those already stricken with war in the military camps, the troop ships, the trenches, in the besieged villages along the Meuse, in the devastated plain called the Somme, in the Argonne woods. It struck those who knew nothing of the war—all the Eskimos in a remote outpost, villagers in China. Some died without having given it a name. Others called it "the grippe," the glue—influenza—meaning "under the influence of the stars," under Orion and the Southern Cross, under the Bear, the Pole Star, and the Pleiades.

When care failed in the Tower Hill hospital, the Good Shepherd Sisters closed the eyes of the dead, blessed the body in the language that they knew, blessed themselves, and closed the tent flap. The sisters on the next shift said a last prayer in front of each closed tent and turned to the living.

In the central city those who were spared became captive to a strange, altered music. All the sounds of their streets—voices and songs, teams hauling loads over paving stones, elm whips cracking the air and animals, bottles nudging one another in the back of a truck, the deliberate tread of the iceman on their stairs— all these were no longer heard. Or weren't heard as usual. Survivors strained at the absence, as if they were listening for flowing water after a cold snap, water now trapped and nearly silenced by clear ice. Schools and movie houses had been ordered closed and bolted shut; public gatherings were curtailed. Workers, their numbers halved, walked down Essex Street to the mills in a slackened ribbon. Their tamped-down gossip touched only on who had been stricken, who had died in the night. They traded preventions and cures, some wearing masks, others with garlic hung around their necks. More pronounced than the usual smells of the fouled canals or lanolin or grease were the head-clearing scents of camphor and carbolic soap.

The flow of supply wagons slowed as well. There was no commerce in bolts of velvet, silk puffs, worsted suits, or pianos. Bakers who used to shape one hundred granary loaves a day—split and seeded and washed with a glaze of milk— took to preparing fifty or sixty unadorned loaves. In the corner groceries, scab spread on the early apple crop, grapes softened then soured, and pears turned overripe in their crates.

The absence filled with uncommon sounds. Children with nowhere to go played in the streets and in the parks as if it were another kind of summer. They sang their jump-rope songs and called out sides in the letups between rains. The pharmacies swarmed with customers looking for Vaporub, germicide, and ice. And all the carpenters—whether they had formerly spent their days roughing out tenements or carving details into table legs—had turned to making pine boxes. Their sawing and the sound of bright nails driving into soft wood could be heard long into the night. Even so, coffins remained scarce and expensive.

The streets running up to Tower Hill rushed with ambulances, police cars, and fire engines. The alleyways and side streets were clogged with passing funerals. Meager corteges where everywhere—there, out of the corner of an eye, or coming straight on. In hopes of slowing the spread of the epidemic, the board of health had limited the size of the funerals to one carriage. They prohibited church services for the dead, and forbade anyone other than the immediate family to accompany the coffin. So, a black hack or a utility wagon with a loose knot of mourners following on foot behind was all. Some of the grieving were sick themselves, some barely recovered, and they had trouble keeping up if the hack driver was proceeding faster than he should—there were so many, had been so many, and someone else was waiting for his services. The processions appeared to be blown by a directionless wind down home streets past the millworks and across the bridge to the burial grounds on the outskirts of the city.

The mourners entered a place started with freshly closed graves and open graves with piles of earth next to them—clay, sea-worn gravel, sodden sandy loam. The gravediggers kept on shoveling—they had long stopped looking up from their work. Even so, they couldn't stay ahead, and most of the coffins had to be escorted to the yard and left near the entrance along with others to await a later burial. Few of the processions were accompanied by ministers or priests. The parents or children or sisters of the deceased bowed their heads and said their own prayers. Perhaps they threw a handful of earth on the set-aside box. Maybe they lay a clutch of asters on the top. So plain and unsacred, it may just as well have been a death in the wilderness. Small. A winter spider crawling across an old white wall.

"We knew it was serious, but we didn't know how serious," my father says. The farm is less than five miles to the west of Lawrence, but by the time news reached here, it was muted and slowed—no more than a rumor on the sea winds biting in from Cape Ann. Their eastward view was open then, and they could see the leeward slope of Tower Hill, though it was far enough away to appear plainly blue. On the first of October 1918 they woke to see the flanks of those white canvas tents set in columns and rows across the hill. And that night the horizon was so crowded with lights that it must have seemed as if the heart of the city had grown closer.

As in the city, whole families on some farms were stricken, others spared. His family was spared—all he knew of the flu then was white chips of camphor in an old sock around his neck, and his mother whispering to his father in the evenings: "You'll bring it here" His aunt and uncle, who had a nearby farm, and his cousins all came down with it in turn, until the whole household was confined to their beds. No doctor came. My grandfather, after he had tended his own herd, saw to theirs—to their water and feed, and to their milking. He drew water for the house and brought them bread. He'd light the fires and bring in a day's supply of wood. Even so, with the windows open the rooms felt as cold as quarried granite.

The youngest boy died. The parents, still weak, were slow to perform the offices of the strong. They washed the body and had to rest. It seemed to take most of a day to make a respectable, small pine coffin. They cleaned the front room, set the coffin in the bay window, and took their turns sitting beside it. Not even small things were the same. Not the rust-colored chrysanthemums blooming against the kitchen door. Not the lingering fragrance of thyme and mint in the yard.

And the large things to be done—the work that had waited all through their sickness—waited still and weighed heavier. It was late enough in the year so that the weeding didn't matter anymore. But carrots, potatoes, and cabbages had to be harvested and stored. Wood to be gotten in. The late apple tree was laden with fruit—Ben Davis apples would cling to the branches all winter if you let them. Enough work to fill their days for as long as they could foresee.

There are two small, walled-in graveyards in the middle of our farm. They seem odd and adrift now among our fields and woods, though in the early part of this century there had been a Methodist church adjoining them. It was pulled down for salvage sometime in the forties, and its granite steps are now my parents' doorstone. My father would sit on one of the pews when he pulled off his work boots. Now he's buried among those graves, just up the hill, behind a white birch. But in those years only the names of the settlers—Richardson, Coburn, Clough—had been chiseled into the stones. It wasn't a place for recent immigrants to be buried, so his uncle's family walked behind the coffin to Lawrence and set their child beside all the recent victims in the city. The mounds of earth beside the open graves were composed of heavier and stonier soils than any they had cultivated in the arid land they had been born to. Impossible to return to that country now, though they said their words in Arabic before turning west out of the gate.

For another week after the funeral they could still see the tents, white in the new days, just like yesterday. Then at the end of October the epidemic broke, the fires were banked. The tent hospital was taken down in a driving rain, and the stricken were moved to winter quarters at the General Hospital. At night Tower Hill once again appeared darker than the night sky. Predictable quiet returned to the neighborhood of mill owners, bankers, lawyers. The schools opened again, then the theaters. The policemen and firemen took off their gauze masks. On the twelfth of November, even the Red Cross workers marched in the Victory Day parade. When the city looked up, they counted more dead of the flu than of the war.

The winter of 1918 was so cold that the water over the Lawrence dam froze and had to be dynamited. The following spring, the field where the tent hospital had stood was seeded in hay. It was mown three times that summer and winds swept the timothy and redtop. Here, after the child had become bone, a liturgy was said for him. A child whose life is no longer given a name or a length, so short it is remembered by the one fact of his death.

On summer evenings, my father would sit on his porch, looking into our own horizon. The long simple line of the hill was gone. Pine and maple had grown up and buildings squared off against the sky. Once in a while out of nowhere he'd mention the lights of the tent hospital, as if he could still see them, strange and clear.

Author's Note

I am indebted to the Immigrant City Archives Historical Society of Lawrence, Massachusetts, where I was able to consult the *Records of the Board of Health, January 1918–April 1931,* and the *Board of Health Influenza Journal, 1918–1920.* In addition, the Archives house recordings of oral histories. Listening to these voices was invaluable to my understanding of the atmosphere of the time. The recordings made of the recollections of Daniel Murphy and Sister Jeanne d'Arc were particularly helpful. I am also indebted to Alfred Crosby's *America's Forgotten Pandemic: The Influenza of 1918* (Cambridge: Cambridge University Press, 1989) and to two local newspapers, the *Lawrence Telegram* and the *Lawrence Sun American* (September–November 1918).

Considerations

Thinking

Brox's essay is historical, in that it describes a historical event—the great influenza outbreak of 1918. Why do you think she chose to focus on a small town in Massachusetts rather than reporting on what was actually a worldwide epidemic?

What are some of the implications that emerge from Brox's essay? That is, what is implied there about disease, about human life and death? Could such an epidemic occur today?

Connecting

To what extent can the influenza epidemic of 1918 be compared with the spread of AIDS in the 1990s?

Compare Brox's description of the spread of influenza in Lawrence, Massachusetts, with Richard Selzer's description of AIDS in Haiti in his essay "A Mask on the Face of Death."

Writing

Write an essay in which you describe a historical event by focusing in closely on a local scene. You can choose to do some historical research, as Brox has done, or you might decide to write your essay based on your field research, as Richard Selzer does.

Write a paragraph analyzing the structure or organization of Brox's essay. Divide her essay into parts and explain what she presents in each, and with what effects.

John Canaday
(1907–1985)

John Canaday was born in Fort Scott, Kansas, and educated at the University of Texas and Yale University. He has taught art history at various universities. He has also served as administrator and lecturer at the Philadelphia Museum of Art, and as art critic for the *New York Times*. Canaday has written numerous books on art, including *Mainstreams of Modern Art* and *What Is Art?* from which "The Peale and Bellelli Families" has been excerpted. Through his use of comparison and contrast, Canaday illuminates both paintings with greater clarity than he might have explained either painting in isolation.

The Peale and Bellelli Families

Peale began work on the group portrait of his family [see the inserts] about 1773. Nine of the people in the picture are family members by birth or by marriage. The tenth is a matriarchal family nurse who stands in the background, hands folded, with all the dignity of a great natural monument. For good measure Peale includes three familial portrait busts on the shelf to the right and as an afterthought adds the portrait head of a member who joined the family after the picture was half-finished, the dog Argus.

Argus, as a pup, was left to the Peales by a grateful old Revolutionary soldier who pulled him out from under his blouse in return for a free meal. The Revolution had come and gone since Peale began the picture. For many years he kept it unfinished in his studio as a kind of demonstration piece. In finishing it, he added the portrait of Argus, by then venerable, and the following inscription at center right: "C. W. Peale painted these Portraits *of his family* in 1773. wishing to finish every work he had undertaken—compleated this picture in 1809!"

A little arithmetic shows that the picture was completed thirty-six years after it was begun. This explains why Peale, who was sixty-eight years old at the time, appears in it as a young man of thirty-two. He stands to the left side, holding a palette and bending over to inspect a drawing on which his brother, St. George Peale, is at work.

The Peale Family is a delightful painting. John Adams, who saw it in 1776 in the painter's Philadelphia studio, wrote in a letter: "There was a pleasant, a happy cheerfulness in their countenances, and a familiarity in their air towards each other." And the intention of the picture is no more complicated than that. It presents an ideal façade of family life, informal, affectionate, harmonious, and secure. The canvas on the easel in the background, the picture-within-a-picture upon which Charles Willson Peale has been at work, originally bore the phrase *Concordia Animae* as a clue to the meaning of the whole painting. But Peale later eliminated these words, "the design being," he wrote to his son, "sufficient to tell the subject," as indeed it is. A glance at *The Peale Family* is enough to show that the ten people in it are happily united as a group. They are pleasantly disposed and share the limelight without competing for it (although Argus, it must be confessed, remains what he was when he was introduced into the composition, a postscript).

Compositionally, the subjects are divided into two groups, six figures clustered at the left and three at the right side, or, if you include the nurse, four. She stands in a nicely selected relationship to the family proper, expressive of her position in the household, closely allied with the other figures yet slightly removed, painted as she is in more subdued tones and standing as she does in the only attitude not physically bound to the rest by contact of a hand or a shoulder.

If all the figures had been massed together, they would have looked crowded and monotonous. Hence the division into two groups. But this is a family, a harmoniously united family, so it is necessary that we also be conscious of the two groups as a unit. And we are: the two halves are united by a slight overlapping and by a scattering of fruit across the table, a trivial detail, yet an important one in binding the two halves together—as well as a pretty bit of still life gratuitously offered. The halves are even more strongly held together by the fact that St. George (extreme left), sketching his mother as she holds a grandchild (extreme right), glances toward her as he draws. This play of interest across the breadth of the picture is a psychologically effective tie, nullifying any feeling of disunity that might have been produced by the physical division into two groups.

Within this firmly knit composition each figure is pleasantly varied. We are conscious of each one as an individual, but we cannot look long at one without being led to another. The composition is not brilliant or complicated; it need be neither to fulfill the painter's conception, which is direct and simple.

Peale's style has a suggestion of dryness in it, like a pinch of salt in a dish that might otherwise have been too bland. There are occasional awkwardnesses in drawing—the hands of the sister standing at the left, one resting on the shoulder of Charles Willson Peale, the other on the shoulder of his wife, are a touch oversize. These hands are not quite as fortunately incorporated as the rest. They remind us that the picture is a group of separate studies synthesized into a whole. Also, the arm of the grandmother cannot bear close examination. Instead of terminating as it should, it continues as a tubelike form and disappears into the shadows a moment too late to conceal from us that it is overlong, and handless. But these imperfections have their own appeal; they account for the suggestion of engaging provincialism that distinguishes the work of this early American painter from that of the facile English portrait painters he would have liked to emulate.

Pictures of this general type, which go by the name of "conversation pieces," are frequent in eighteenth-century and early nineteenth-century painting. Based on the assumption that life is a matter of agreeable surfaces, they are usually built around a theme with incidental reference to some pleasurable activity associated with the subjects, like the exercise in drawing that occupies St. George and Charles Willson here.

The picture is a happy interpretation of family life but not a very searching one, even for a pre-Freudian age. Families are more complicated than this. Family relationships produce frictions and irritations as minor evils, agonizing psychological conflicts as major ones. The brothers, sisters, and in-laws gathered around the Peale table were human beings, and certainly not immune to these difficulties. Just as certainly, in other aspects of their family life they rose to joys more intense than the casual affections so uniformly expressed in the group. Peale does not hint that these human beings have more than an agreeably tepid experience of life, nor does he make much effort, if any, to differentiate one from another psychologically. He was certainly aware of the psychological individuality of his sitters and of the crosscurrents of emotional relationships, but if it even occurred to him that it would be interesting to explore these in a painting, he rejected the idea as inappropriate in a family portrait.

The particular circumstances of individual relationships in all their psychological subtleties fascinated another artist, a young Frenchman who painted a family group in 1859 when he was less than thirty years old. This, you may remember, is younger than Peale was when he began his family portrait. But at that age this Frenchman, Edgar Degas, was already an urbane cosmopolite. He was a doubter, a speculator upon human nature, and basically a pessimist. He spent the better part of a year in Italy in spite of his father's repeated insistence that he return to Paris, for Degas had begun work on a large painting of his aunt, Baroness Bellelli, his two young cousins, and the Baron. In this family there was a less happy state of affairs than the one Peale would have us believe existed in his. Degas reveals it through a composition as original as any in the history of painting, and, as Peale said of his own, "sufficient to tell the subject." "Sufficient" is an understatement. Superlatives are dangerous, but there is less danger than usual in describing *The Bellelli Family* [see the inserts] as the finest psychological group portrait ever painted. The temperament of each of the four members is individualized for us, and, beyond that, their interrelationship is analyzed. Before you read the following paragraphs, you may want to ask yourself on the evidence of the picture what these people were like. In that case try to decide what the relationship of the father to the rest of the family might be, what the emotional tie of each of the little girls is to each of the parents, and what the difference is, temperamentally, between these two children. The chances are that you will learn as much from the picture itself as you will know when you have read the following summary, with the exception of specific historical facts.

From references in family letters we gather that the Baron was a man of uneven temperament, given to moods and, at least during the time Degas visited the family, conscious of frustrations and discouragements both in his personal life and in his career. His only son had died (the family is still in mourning in the portrait) and the Baron was marking time as a political exile from his native Naples. His disturbed life made him half a stranger in his own household, a condition aggravated by an increasing rift with his wife. Social conventions of respectability in the mid-nineteenth century placed limitations on a woman in the Baroness's situation. A reserved, intelligent, and patient woman—if we can accept the judgment of her young nephew—she seems to have shouldered even more of the responsibility for the home and the children than did the average wife of her time. Of the two little girls, the elder, Giovanna, was placid and closely attached to her mother, whereas the younger, Giuliana, was more energetic and restless, temperamentally sympathetic to her father but, by force of circumstance, more securely bound within the lives of her mother and sister.

The most casual observer must notice that in Degas's portrait the father is separated from the rest of the family by a series of vertical lines, which, violating normal compositional rules, separate a generous third of the picture from the rest. In addition, he sits unconventionally, with his back toward us and his profile in shadow. His features are painted less decisively than those of the other figures. He is the only one of the family who is not completely revealed to us as a person; we are left with the feeling that we do not know him as we know the mother and daughters. He has a life beyond this room; perhaps he leads a life more important to him than the life we are seeing here; he is an outsider.

But this vagueness, incompleteness, and isolation are reversed in the figure of the wife. She stands with decision, dignity, and forbearance, dominating the room by her quietness. Of all the figures, hers is the simplest and strongest in silhouette; that is why we return to her always, no matter how interesting the rest of the picture may be in its greater detail and variety.

Her right hand rests on the shoulder of Giovanna, the more placid daughter, who was like her and closest to her. This little girl is held within the larger silhouette of the mother's figure; her way of standing echoes her mother's, as does her general silhouette—and she stands quietly. She is the only one of the family who looks at us, although the others are aware of our presence. She looks at us unquestioningly, content to stay within her mother's support and protection.

But the other child, Giuliana, partially breaks away from the pair. She occupies the side of the picture separated from the father, yet we feel strongly her connection with him. She is the only one whose glance could, and in a moment might, meet her father's. She sits restlessly, one leg tucked up under her, as if impatient with sitting for her artist-cousin, unable to remain still, the volatile member of the group. Just as she is divided in her loyalty to her mother and her father, so she does not belong wholly to either in the composition of the painting.

It is apparent, then, that Degas set about expressing a specific set of circumstances with the help of appropriate compositional means. When we know the circumstances, the picture takes on some peripheral interest; but it is a great picture because it is expressive of the interrelationships of four people, whether or not we know the specific circumstances. The picture has a life of its own beyond the immediate reasons for its creation. If the identity of the painter and the family were unknown to us, any meaning *The Bellelli Family* might lose would be of little consequence.

The Bellellis are not important to us as individuals. It makes no difference how they looked. Their troubles were never of any significance except to themselves. The relationships so brilliantly revealed were neither unique nor on the grand scale. The picture's greatness lies in its ability to stir us to thought beyond the limited considerations of a single family's not unusual circumstances. And it does so because Degas has crystallized his material into forms of perfect order, rid of all confusions, incidentals, vagaries, and distractions. In the resultant clarity our sensibilities and understanding may expand.

Degas was one of the greatest of all pictorial composers, and *The Bellelli Family,* an early painting, is only one (though one of the best) of a succession of startlingly original compositions. Degas is preeminent in this unconventionality without freakishness. Other great masters of pictorial composition time and again demonstrate their ability to use conventional devices more skillfully than their contemporaries. But Degas invents compositions without direct precedent, and each of these compositions is so special to its subject that none is directly useful to followers hunting a formula. The composition of *The Peale Family* might be adapted to any number of group portraits, but that of *The Bellelli Family* could not.

Considerations

Thinking

What is the main point Canaday makes in his comparison and contrast of the Degas and Peale paintings? What points of comparison does Canaday survey? What differences does he identify? And what does he conclude from his observations?

As a strategy of explanation, how useful is Canaday's example of comparison and contrast? Why? What would be gained and/or lost if his discussion were to be reorganized so as to bounce back and forth more often between details of each picture rather than analyzing the paintings one at a time?

Connecting

Use what you have learned from analyzing the composition of figures in a painting to interpret two of the other paintings in the inserts in *Encounters.*

Compare Canaday's approach to discussing paintings with the approach of either John Berger in "Ways of Seeing," or Rosellen Brown (discussing photographs) in "Mojo."

Writing

Choose any two paintings in *Encounters* (or outside the book) and write your own comparative analysis, utilizing what you have learned from reading Canaday's or other writers' essays on art.

Write an essay about families (perhaps your own family) in which you include descriptions of at least two photographs and/or paintings.

Judith Ortiz Cofer
(b. 1952)

Judith Ortiz Cofer is a novelist, poet, and essayist whose work has appeared in magazines and literary reviews such as *Glamour, The Georgia Review,* and *The Kenyon Review.* Her work includes *The Line of the Sun,* a novel; *Terms of Survival* and *Reaching for the Mainland,* poetry collections; *Peregrina,* a chapbook; and *Silent Dancing,* essays and poems. She has won fellowships from the National Endowment for the Arts, the Florida and Georgia Councils for the Arts, and the Bread Loaf Writers' Conference.

"Silent Dancing" focuses on the way imported cultural values affected the lives of Puerto Ricans who moved in the 1950s into a newly formed ethnic enclave in Paterson, New Jersey, just across the Hudson River from New York City. Cofer is especially interested in the way the new culture affects those who move into it. In "Silent Dancing" she gives us glimpses of that turmoil through a retrospective look at a home movie filmed during her childhood in her new home.

Silent Dancing

We have a home movie of this party. Several times my mother and I have watched it together, and I have asked questions about the silent revelers coming in and out of focus. It is grainy and of short duration, but it's a great visual aid to my memory of life at that time. And it is in color—the only complete scene in color I can recall from those years.

We lived in Puerto Rico until my brother was born in 1954. Soon after, because of economic pressures on our growing family, my father joined the United States Navy. He was assigned to duty on a ship in Brooklyn Yard—a place of cement and steel that was to be his home base in the States until his retirement more than twenty years later. He left the Island first, alone, going to New York City and tracking down his uncle who lived with his family across the Hudson River in Paterson, New Jersey. There my father found a tiny apartment in a huge tenement that had once housed Jewish families but was just being taken over and transformed by Puerto Ricans, overflowing from New York City. In 1955 he sent for us. My mother was only twenty years old, I was not quite three, and my brother was a toddler when we arrived at *El Building,* as the place had been christened by its newest residents.

My memories of life in Paterson during those first few years are all in shades of gray. Maybe I was too young to absorb vivid colors and details, or to discriminate between the slate blue of the winter sky and the darker hues of the snow-bearing clouds, but that single color washes over the whole period. The building we lived in was gray, as were the streets, filled with slush the first few months of my life there. The coat my father had bought for me was similar in color and too big; it sat heavily on my thin frame.

I do remember the way the heater pipes banged and rattled, startling all of us out of sleep until we got so used to the sound that we automatically shut it out or raised our voices above the racket. The hiss from the valve punctuated my sleep (which has always been fitful) like a nonhuman presence in the room—a dragon sleeping at the entrance of my childhood. But the pipes were also a connection to all the other lives being lived around us. Having come from a house designed for a single family back in Puerto Rico—my mother's extended-family home—it was curious to know that strangers lived under our floor and above our heads, and that the heater pipe went through everyone's apartments. (My first spanking in Paterson came as a result of playing tunes on the pipes in my room to see if there

145

would be an answer.) My mother was as new to this concept of beehive life as I was, but she had been given strict orders by my father to keep the doors locked, the noise down, ourselves to ourselves.

It seems that Father had learned some painful lessons about prejudice while searching for an apartment in Paterson. Not until years later did I hear how much resistance he had encountered with landlords who were panicking at the influx of Latinos into a neighborhood that had been Jewish for a couple of generations. It made no difference that it was the American phenomenon of ethnic turnover which was changing the urban core of Paterson, and that the human flood could not be held back with an accusing finger.

"You Cuban?" one man had asked my father, pointing at his name tag on the Navy uniform—even though my father had the fair skin and light-brown hair of his northern Spanish background, and the name Ortiz is as common in Puerto Rico as Johnson is in the United States.

"No," my father had answered, looking past the finger into his adversary's angry eyes. "I'm Puerto Rican."

"Same shit." And the door closed.

My father could have passed as European, but we couldn't. My brother and I both have our mother's black hair and olive skin, and so we lived in El Building and visited our great-uncle and his fair children on the next block. It was their private joke that they were the German branch of the family. Not many years later that area too would be mainly Puerto Rican. It was as if the heart of the city map were being gradually colored brown—*café con leche*[1] brown. Our color.

The movie opens with a sweep of the living room. It is "typical" immigrant Puerto Rican decor for the time: The sofa and chairs are square and hard-looking, upholstered in bright colors (blue and yellow in this instance), and covered with the transparent plastic that furniture salesmen then were so adept at convincing women to buy. The linoleum on the floor is light blue; if it had been subjected to spike heels (as it was in most places), there were dime-sized indentations all over it that cannot be seen in this movie. The room is full of people dressed up: dark suits for the men, red dresses for the women. When I have asked my mother why most of the women are in red that night, she has shrugged, "I don't remember. Just a coincidence." She doesn't have my obsession for assigning symbolism to everything.

The three women in red sitting on the couch are my mother, my eighteen-year-old cousin, and her brother's girlfriend. The novia *is just up from the Island, which is apparent in her body language. She sits up formally, her dress pulled over her knees. She is a pretty girl, but her posture makes her look insecure, lost in her full-skirted dress, which she has carefully tucked around her to make room for my gorgeous cousin, her future sister-in-law. My cousin has grown up in Paterson and is in her last year of high school. She doesn't have a trace of what Puerto Ricans call* la mancha *(literally, the stain: the mark of the new immigrant—something about the posture, the voice, or the humble demeanor that makes it obvious to everyone the person has just arrived on the main-*

---

[1]*café con leche:* Coffee with cream. In Puerto Rico it is sometimes prepared with boiled milk. [All footnotes in this essay are author notes—EDS.]

land). *My cousin is wearing a tight, sequined, cocktail dress. Her brown hair has been lightened with peroxide around the bangs, and she is holding a cigarette expertly between her fingers, bringing it up to her mouth in a sensuous arc of her arm as she talks animatedly. My mother, who has come up to sit between the two women, both only a few years younger than herself, is somewhere between the poles they represent in our culture.*

It became my father's obsession to get out of the barrio, and thus we were never permitted to form bonds with the place or with the people who lived there. Yet El Building was a comfort to my mother, who never got over yearning for *la isla*. She felt surrounded by her language: The walls were thin, and voices speaking and arguing in Spanish could be heard all day. *Salsas* blasted out of radios, turned on early in the morning and left on for company. Women seemed to cook rice and beans perpetuallythe strong aroma of boiling red kidney beans permeated the hallways.

Though Father preferred that we do our grocery shopping at the supermarket when he came home on weekend leaves, my mother insisted that she could cook only with products whose labels she could read. Consequently, during the week I accompanied her and my little brother to *La Bodega*—a hole-in-the-wall grocery store across the street from El Building. There we squeezed down three narrow aisles jammed with various products. Goya's and Libby's—those were the trademarks that were trusted by *her mamá,* so my mother bought many cans of Goya beans, soups, and condiments, as well as little cans of Libby's fruit juices for us. And she also bought Colgate toothpaste and Palmolive soap. (The final *e* is pronounced in both these products in Spanish, so for many years I believed that they were manufactured on the Island. I remember my surprise at first hearing a commercial on television in which Colgate rhymed with "ate.") We always lingered at La Bodega, for it was there that Mother breathed best, taking in the familiar aromas of the foods she knew from Mamá's kitchen. It was also there that she got to speak to the other women of El Building without violating outright Father's dictates against fraternizing with our neighbors.

Yet Father did his best to make our "assimilation" painless. I can still see him carrying a real Christmas tree up several flights of stairs to our apartment, leaving a trail of aromatic pine. He carried it formally, as if it were a flag in a parade. We were the only ones in El Building that I knew of who got presents on both Christmas day AND *dia de Reyes*, the day when the Three Kings brought gifts to Christ and to Hispanic children.

Our supreme luxury in El Building was having our own television set. It must have been a result of Father's guilt feelings over the isolation he had imposed on us, but we were among the first in the barrio to have one. My brother quickly became an avid watcher of Captain Kangaroo and Jungle Jim, while I loved all the series showing families. By the time I started first grade, I could have drawn a map of Middle America as exemplified by the lives of characters in "Father Knows Best," "The Donna Reed Show," "Leave It to Beaver," "My Three Sons," and (my favorite) "Bachelor Father," where John Forsythe treated his adopted teenage daughter like a princess because he was rich and had a Chinese houseboy to do everything for him. In truth, compared to our neighbors in El Building, *we* were rich. My father's Navy check provided us with financial security and a standard of life that the factory workers envied. The only thing his money could not buy us was a place to live away from the barrio—his greatest wish, Mother's greatest fear.

In the home movie the men are shown next, sitting around a card table set up in one corner of the living room, playing dominoes. The clack of the ivory pieces was a familiar sound. I heard it in many houses on the Island and in many apartments in Paterson. In "Leave It to Beaver," the Cleavers played bridge in every other episode; in my childhood, the men started every social occasion with a hotly debated round of dominoes. The women would sit around and watch, but they never participated in the games.

Here and there you can see a small child. Children were always brought to parties and, whenever they got sleepy, were put to bed in the host's bedroom. Babysitting was a concept unrecognized by the Puerto Rican women I knew: A responsible mother did not leave her children with any stranger. And in a culture where children are not considered intrusive, there was no need to leave the children at home. We went where our mother went.

Of my preschool years I have only impressions: the sharp bite of the wind in December as we walked with our parents toward the brightly lit stores downtown; how I felt like a stuffed doll in my heavy coat, boots, and mittens; how good it was to walk into the five-and-dime and sit at the counter drinking hot chocolate. On Saturdays our whole family would walk downtown to shop at the big department stores on Broadway. Mother bought all our clothes at Penney's and Sears, and she liked to buy her dresses at the women's specialty shops like Lerner's and Diana's. At some point we'd go into Woolworth's and sit at the soda fountain to eat.

We never ran into other Latinos at these stores or when eating out, and it became clear to me only years later that the women from El Building shopped mainly in other places—stores owned by other Puerto Ricans or by Jewish merchants who had philosophically accepted our presence in the city and decided to make us their good customers, if not real neighbors and friends. These establishments were located not downtown but in the blocks around our street, and they were referred to generically as *La Tienda, El Bazar, La Bodega, La Botánica.* Everyone knew what was meant. These were the stores where your face did not turn a clerk to stone, where your money was as green as anyone else's.

One New Year's Eve we were dressed up like child models in the Sears catalogue: my brother in a miniature man's suit and bow tie, and I in black patent-leather shoes and a frilly dress with several layers of crinoline underneath. My mother wore a bright red dress that night, I remember, and spike heels; her long black hair hung to her waist. Father, who usually wore his Navy uniform during his short visits home, had put on a dark civilian suit for the occasion: We had been invited to his uncle's house for a big celebration. Everyone was excited because my mother's brother Hernan—a bachelor who could indulge himself with luxuries—had bought a home movie camera, which he would be trying out that night.

Even the home movie cannot fill in the sensory details such a gathering left imprinted in a child's brain. The thick sweetness of women's perfumes mixing with the ever-present smells of food cooking in the kitchen: meat and plantain *pasteles,* as well as the ubiquitous rice dish made special with pigeon peas—*gandules*—and seasoned with precious *sofrito*[2] sent up from the Island by somebody's mother or smuggled in by a recent traveler. *Sofrito* was one of the items that women hoarded, since it was hardly ever in stock at La Bodega. It was the flavor of Puerto Rico.

The men drank Palo Viejo rum, and some of the younger ones got weepy. The first time I saw a grown man cry was at a New Year's Eve party: He had been reminded of his mother by the smells in the kitchen. But what I remember most were the boiled *pasteles*—plantain or yucca rectangles stuffed with corned beef or other meats, olives, and many other savory ingredients, all wrapped in banana leaves. Everybody had to fish one out with a fork. There was always a "trick" pastel—one without stuffing—and whoever got that one was the "New Year's Fool."

There was also the music. Long-playing albums were treated like precious china in these homes. Mexican recordings were popular, but the songs that brought tears to my mother's eyes were sung by the melancholy Daniel Santos, whose life as a drug addict was the stuff of legend. Felipe Rodríguez was a particular favorite of couples, since he sang about faithless women and brokenhearted men. There is a snatch of one lyric that has stuck in my mind like a needle on a worn groove: *De piedra ha de ser mi cama, de piedra la cabezera . . . la mujer que a mi me quiera . . . ha de quererme de veras. Ay, Ay, Ay, corazón, porque no amas.*[3] . . . I must have heard it a thousand times since the idea of a bed made of stone, and its connection to love, first troubled me with its disturbing images.

The five-minute home movie ends with people dancing in a circle—the creative filmmaker must have set it up, so that all of them could file past him. It is both comical and sad to watch silent dancing. Since there is no justification for the absurd movements that music provides for some of us, people appear frantic, their faces embarrassingly intense. It's as if you were watching sex. Yet for years I've had dreams in the form of this home movie. In a recurring scene, familiar faces push themselves forward into my mind's eyes, plastering their features into distorted close-ups. And I'm asking them: "Who is *she*? Who is the old woman I don't recognize? Is she an aunt? Somebody's wife? Tell me who she is."

"See the beauty mark on her cheek as big as a hill on the lunar landscape of her face—well, that runs in the family. The women on your father's side of the family wrinkle early; it's the price they pay for that fair skin. The young girl with the

[2]*sofrito:* A cooked condiment. A sauce composed of a mixture of fatback, ham, tomatoes, and many island spices and herbs. It is added to many typical Puerto Rican dishes for a distinctive flavor.
[3]*De piedra ha de ser . . . amas:* Lyrics from a popular romantic ballad (called a *bolero* in Puerto Rico). Freely translated: "My bed will be made of stone, of stone also my headrest (or pillow), the woman who (dares to) loves me, will have to love me for real. Ay, Ay, Ay, my heart, why can't you (let me) love. . . . "

green stain on her wedding dress is *La Novia*—just up from the Island. See, she lowers her eyes when she approaches the camera, as she's supposed to. Decent girls never look at you directly in the face. *Humilde,* humble, a girl should express humility in all her actions. She will make a good wife for your cousin. He should consider himself lucky to have met her only weeks after she arrived here. If he marries her quickly, she will make him a good Puerto Rican-style wife; but if he waits too long, she will be corrupted by the city—just like your cousin there."

"She means me. I do what I want. This is not some primitive island I live on. Do they expect me to wear a black mantilla on my head and go to mass every day? Not me. I'm an American woman, and I will do as I please. I can type faster than anyone in my senior class at Central High, and I'm going to be a secretary to a lawyer when I graduate. I can pass for an American girl anywhere—I've tried it. At least for Italian, anyway—I never speak Spanish in public. I hate these parties, but I wanted the dress. I look better than any of these *humildes* here. *My* life is going to be different. I have an American boyfriend. He is older and has a car. My parents don't know it, but I sneak out of the house late at night sometimes to be with him. If I marry him, even my name will be American. I hate rice and beans—that's what makes these women fat."

Your *prima*[4] is pregnant by that man she's been sneaking around with. Would I lie to you? I'm your *Tía Política,*[5] your great-uncle's common-law wife—the one he abandoned on the Island to go marry your cousin's mother. *I* was not invited to this party, of course, but I came anyway. I came to tell you that story about your cousin that you've always wanted to hear. Do you remember the comment your mother made to a neighbor that has always haunted you? The only thing you heard was your cousin's name, and then you saw your mother pick up your doll from the couch and say: 'It was as big as this doll when they flushed it down the toilet.' This image has bothered you for years, hasn't it? You had nightmares about babies being flushed down the toilet, and you wondered why anyone would do such a horrible thing. You didn't dare ask your mother about it. She would only tell you that you had not heard her right, and yell at you for listening to adult conversations. But later, when you were old enough to know about abortions, you suspected.

"I am here to tell you that you were right. Your cousin was growing an *Americanito* in her belly when this movie was made. Soon after she put something long and pointy into her pretty self, thinking maybe she could get rid of the problem before breakfast and still make it to her first class at the high school. Well, *Niña,*[6] her screams could be heard downtown. Your aunt, her mamá, who had been a midwife on the Island, managed to pull the little thing out. Yes, they probably flushed it down the toilet. What else could they do with it—give it a Christian burial in a little white casket with blue bows and ribbons? Nobody wanted that baby—least of all the father, a teacher at her school with a house in West Paterson that he was filling with real children, and a wife who was a natural blonde.

[4]*prima:* Female cousin.
[5]*Tía Política:* Aunt by marriage.
[6]*Niña:* Girl.

"Girl, the scandal sent your uncle back to the bottle. And guess where your cousin ended up? Irony of ironies. She was sent to a village in Puerto Rico to live with a relative on her mother's side: a place so far away from civilization that you have to ride a mule to reach it. A real change in scenery. She found a man there—women like that cannot live without male company—but believe me, the men in Puerto Rico know how to put a saddle on a woman like her. *La Gringa,*[7] they call her. Ha, ha, ha. *La Gringa* is what she always wanted to be. . . . "

The old woman's mouth becomes a cavernous black hole I fall into. And as I fall, I can feel the reverberations of her laughter. I hear the echoes of her last mocking words: *La Gringa, La Gringa!* And the conga line keeps moving silently past me. There is no music in my dream for the dancers.

When Odysseus visits Hades to see the spirit of his mother, he makes an offering of sacrificial blood, but since all the souls crave an audience with the living, he has to listen to many of them before he can ask questions. I, too, have to hear the dead and the forgotten speak in my dream. Those who are still part of my life remain silent, going around and around in their dance. The others keep pressing their faces forward to say things about the past.

My father's uncle is last in line. He is dying of alcoholism, shrunken and shriveled like a monkey, his face a mass of wrinkles and broken arteries. As he comes closer I realize that in his features I can see my whole family. If you were to stretch that rubbery flesh, you could find my father's face, and deep within *that* face—my own. I don't want to look into those eyes ringed in purple. In a few years he will retreat into silence, and take a long, long time to die. *Move back, Tio,* I tell him. *I don't want to hear what you have to say. Give the dancers room to move. Soon it will be midnight. Who is the New Year's Fool this time?*

Considerations

Thinking

How does Cofer use color to underscore her ideas in the first third of her essay?

How do you account for the different attitudes that Cofer's mother and father had about isolating the family within El Building? Can you detect Cofer's attitude about those differences? How does that family conflict over values manifest itself in other ways throughout the essay?

How would you characterize the differences in values within Cofer's extended family—expecially those between the men and the women and those between the newly arrived Puerto Ricans and those who have begun to adapt to the new culture?

---

[7]*La Gringa:* Derogatory epithet used here to ridicule a Puerto Rican girl who wants to look like a blonde North American.

Connecting

Cofer uses both television and the home movie to develop her ideas. Is one of these forms of visual evidence more effective than the other, or do the two kinds of evidence simply allow her to reveal different things? Explain.

Make a list of the various times when silence comes into play in the essay. What is the overall effect of silence on the final impression that Cofer creates? Do you want to remain silent in face of what you learn, or do you want to speak out? What might your decision have to do with your own ethnicity?

Read Sharman Apt Russell's "Homebirth." What connections can you make between the women in that essay and the women in "Silent Dancing"—and between the men in the two essays?

Writing

Select a moment from your own life when you chose to remain silent and you now realize you should have spoken up. Write an essay that gives readers a clear perspective on how you feel about that decision now.

Choose a family photograph or a home video that you were a part of. Write about your choice, telling us about what was going on outside the frame of the photograph or the video, what observers now cannot see or know about without your help. In light of what the photograph or video represents to you now, try to account for the significance of what remains unseen or unexamined.

Bernard Cooper
(b. 1951)

Bernard Cooper is the author of *Maps to Anywhere, A Year of Rhymes,* and *Truth Serum,* from which his essay "Burl's" is taken. Cooper's essays have appeared in *Harper's Magazine, The Los Angeles Times Magazine,* and *The Paris Review,* among other periodicals. Among his literary awards are an O. Henry prize and a PEN/USA Ernest Hemingway Award. In "Burl's," Cooper explores the subject of sexual identity through narrating a series of intertwined personal experiences.

Burl's

I

I loved the restaurant's name, a compact curve of a word. Its sign, five big letters rimmed in neon, hovered above the roof. I almost never saw the sign with its neon lit; my parents took me there for early summer dinners, and even by the time we left—father cleaning his teeth with a toothpick, mother carrying steak bones in a doggie bag—the sky was still bright. Heat rippled off the cars parked along Hollywood Boulevard, the asphalt gummy from hours of sun.

With its sleek architecture, chrome appliances, and arctic temperature, Burl's offered a refuge from the street. We usually sat at one of the booths in front of the plate-glass windows. During our dinner, people came to a halt before the news-vending machine on the corner and burrowed in their pockets and purses for change.

The waitresses at Burl's wore brown uniforms edged in checked gingham. From their breast pockets frothed white lace handkerchiefs. In between reconnaissance missions to the table, they busied themselves behind the counter and shouted "Tuna to travel" or "Scorch that patty" to a harried short-order cook who manned the grill. Miniature pitchers of cream and individual pats of butter were extracted from an industrial refrigerator. Coca-Cola shot from a glinting spigot. Waitresses dodged and bumped one another, frantic as atoms.

My parents usually lingered after the meal, nursing cups of coffee while I played with the beads of condensation on my glass of ice water, tasted Tabasco sauce, or twisted pieces of my paper napkin into mangled animals. One evening, annoyed with my restlessness, my father gave me a dime and asked me to buy him a *Herald Examiner* from the vending machine in front of the restaurant.

Shouldering open the heavy glass door, I was seared by a sudden gust of heat. Traffic roared past me and stirred the air. Walking toward the newspaper machine, I held the dime so tightly it seemed to melt in my palm. Duty made me feel large and important. I inserted the dime and opened the box, yanking a *Herald* from the spring contraption that held it as tight as a mousetrap. When I turned around, paper in hand, I saw two women walking toward me.

Their high heels clicked on the sun-baked pavement. They were tall, broad-shouldered women who moved with a mixture of haste and defiance. They'd teased their hair into nearly identical black beehives. Dangling earrings flashed in the sun, brilliant as prisms. Each of them wore the kind of clinging, strapless outfit my mother referred to as a cocktail dress. The silky fabric—one dress was purple, the other pink—accentuated their breasts and hips and rippled with insolent highlights. The dresses exposed their bare arms, the slope of their shoulders, and the smooth, powdered plane of flesh where their cleavage began.

I owned at the time a book called *Things for Boys and Girls to Do.* There were pages to color, intricate mazes, and connect-the-dots. But another type of puzzle came to mind as I watched those women walking toward me: What's Wrong With This Picture? Say the drawing of a dining room looked normal at first glance; on closer inspection, a chair was missing its leg and the man who sat atop it wore half a pair of glasses.

The women had Adam's apples.

The closer they came, the shallower my breathing was. I blocked the sidewalk, an incredulous child stalled in their path. When they saw me staring, they shifted their purses and linked their arms. There was something sisterly and conspiratorial about their sudden closeness. Though their mouths didn't move, I thought they might have been communicating without moving their lips, so telepathic did they seem as they joined arms and pressed together, synchronizing their heavy steps. The pages of the *Herald* fluttered in the wind. I felt them against my arm, light as batted lashes.

The woman in pink shot me a haughty glance and yet she seemed pleased that I'd taken notice, hungry to be admired by a man, or even an awestruck eight-year-old boy. She tried to stifle a grin, her red lipstick more voluptuous than the lips it painted. Rouge deepened her cheekbones. Eye shadow dusted her lids, a clumsy abundance of blue. Her face was like a page in *Things for Boys and Girls to Do,* colored by a kid who went outside the lines.

At close range, I saw that her wig was slightly askew. I was certain it was a wig because my mother owned several; three Styrofoam heads lined a shelf in my mother's closet; upon them were perched a Page-Boy, an Empress, and a Baby-Doll, all in shades of auburn. The woman in the pink dress wore her wig like a crown of glory.

But it was the woman in the purple dress who passed nearest me, and I saw that her jaw was heavily powdered, a half-successful attempt to disguise the telltale shadow of a beard. Just as I noticed this, her heel caught on a crack in the pavement and she reeled on her stilettos. It was then that I witnessed a rift in her composure, a window through which I could glimpse the shades of maleness that her dress and wig and makeup obscured. She shifted her shoulders and threw out her hands like a surfer riding a curl. The instant she regained her balance, she smoothed her dress, patted her hair, and sauntered onward.

Any woman might be a man. The fact of it clanged through the chambers of my brain. In broad day, in the midst of traffic, with my parents drinking coffee a few feet away, I felt as if everything I understood, everything I had taken for granted up to that moment—the curve of the earth, the heat of the sun, the reliability of my own eyes—had been squeezed out of me. Who were those men? Did they help each other get inside those dresses? How many other people and things were not what they seemed? From the back, the impostors looked like women once again, slinky and curvaceous, purple and pink. I watched them disappear into the distance, their disguises so convincing that other people on the street seemed to take no notice, and for a moment I wondered if I had imagined the whole encounter, a visitation by two unlikely muses.

Frozen in the middle of the sidewalk, I caught my reflection in the window of Burl's, a silhouette floating between his parents. They faced one another across a table. Once the solid embodiments of woman and man, pedestrians and traffic appeared to pass through them.

II

There were some mornings, seconds before my eyes opened and my senses gathered into consciousness, that the child I was seemed to hover above the bed, and I couldn't tell what form my waking would take—the body of a boy or the body of a girl. Finally stirring, I'd blink against the early light and greet each incarnation as a male with mild surprise. My sex, in other words, didn't seem to be an absolute fact so much as a pleasant, recurring accident.

By the age of eight, I'd experienced this groggy phenomenon several times. Those ethereal moments above my bed made waking up in the tangled blankets, a boy steeped in body heat, all the more astonishing. That this might be an unusual experience never occurred to me; it was one among a flood of sensations I could neither name nor ignore.

And so, shocked as I was when those transvestites passed me in front of Burl's, they confirmed something about which I already had an inkling: the hazy border between the sexes. My father, after all, raised his pinky when he drank from a teacup, and my mother looked as faded and plain as my father until she fixed her hair and painted her face.

Like most children, I once thought it possible to divide the world into male and female columns. Blue/Pink. Rooster/Hens. Trousers/Skirts. Such division were easy, not to mention comforting, for they simplified matter into compatible pairs. But there also existed a vast range of things that didn't fit neatly into either camp: clocks, milk, telephones, grass. There were nights I fell into a fitful sleep while trying to sex the world correctly.

Nothing typified the realms of male and female as clearly as my parents' walk-in closets. Home alone for any length of time, I always found my way inside them.

I could stare at my parents' clothes for hours, grateful for the stillness and silence, haunting the very heart of their privacy.

The overhead light in my father's closet was a bare bulb. Whenever I groped for the chain in the dark, it wagged back and forth and resisted my grasp. Once the light clicked on, I saw dozens of ties hanging like stalactites. A monogrammed silk bathrobe sagged from a hook, a gift my father had received on a long-ago birthday and, thinking it fussy, rarely wore. Shirts were cramped together along the length of an aluminum pole, their starched sleeves sticking out as if in a half-hearted gesture of greeting. The medicinal odor of mothballs permeated the boxer shorts that were folded and stacked in a built-in drawer. Immaculate underwear was proof of a tenderness my mother couldn't otherwise express; she may not have touched my father often, but she laundered his boxers with infinite care. Even back then, I suspected that a sense of duty was the final erotic link between them.

Sitting in a neat row on the closet floor were my father's boots and slippers and dress shoes. I'd try on his wingtips and clomp around, slipping out of them with every step. My wary, unnatural stride made me all the more desperate to effect some authority. I'd whisper orders to imagined lackeys and take my invisible wife in my arms. But no matter how much I wanted them to fit, those shoes were as cold and hard as marble.

My mother's shoes were just as uncomfortable, but a lot more fun. From a brightly colored array of pumps and slingbacks, I'd pick a pair with the glee and deliberation of someone choosing a chocolate. Whatever embarrassment I felt was overwhelmed by the exhilaration of being taller in a pair of high heels. Things will look like this someday, I said to myself, gazing out from my new and improved vantage point as if from a crow's nest. Calves elongated, arms akimbo, I gauged each step so that I didn't fall over and moved with what might have passed for grace had someone seen me, a possibility I scrupulously avoided by locking the door.

Back and forth I went. The longer I wore a pair of heels, the better my balance. In the periphery of my vision, the shelf of wigs looked like a throng of kindly bystanders. Light streamed down from a high window, causing crystal bottles to glitter, the air ripe with perfume. A makeup mirror above the dressing table invited my self-absorption. Sound was muffled. Time slowed. It seemed as if nothing bad could happen as long as I stayed within those walls.

Though I'd never been discovered in my mother's closet, my parents knew that I was drawn toward girlish things—dolls and jump rope and jewelry—as well as to the games and preoccupations that were expected of a boy. I'm not sure now if it was my effeminacy itself that bothered them as much as my ability to slide back and forth, without the slightest warning, between male and female mannerisms. After I'd finished building the model of an F-17 bomber, say, I'd sit back to examine my handiwork, pursing my lips in concentration and crossing my legs at the knee.

III

One day my mother caught me standing in the middle of my bedroom doing an imitation of Mary Injijikian, a dark, overeager Armenian girl with whom I believed myself to be in love, not only because she was pretty but because I wanted to be like her. Collector of effortless A's, Mary seemed to know all the answers in class. Before the teacher had even finished asking a question, Mary would let out a little grunt and practically levitate out of her seat, as if her hand were filled with helium. "Could we please hear from someone else today besides Miss Injijikian," the teacher would say. *Miss Injijikian.* Those were the words I was repeating over and over to myself when my mother caught me. To utter them was rhythmic, delicious, and under their spell I raised my hand and wiggled like Mary. I heard a cough and spun around. My mother froze in the doorway. She clutched the folded sheets to her stomach and turned without saying a word. My sudden flush of shame confused me. Weren't boys supposed to swoon over girls? Hadn't I seen babbling, heartsick men in a dozen movies?

Shortly after the Injijikian incident, my parents decided to send me to gymnastics class at the Los Angeles Athletic Club, a brick relic of a building on Olive Street. One of the oldest establishments of its kind in Los Angeles, the club prohibited women from the premises. My parents didn't have to say it aloud: they hoped a fraternal atmosphere would toughen me up and tilt me toward the male side of my nature.

My father drove me downtown so I could sign up for the class, meet the instructor, and get a tour of the place. On the way there, he reminisced about sports. Since he'd grown up in a rough Philadelphia neighborhood, sports consisted of kick-the-can or rolling a hoop down the street with a stick. The more he talked about his physical prowess, the more convinced I became that my daydreams and shyness were a disappointment to him.

The hushed lobby of the athletic club was paneled in dark wood. A few solitary figures were hidden in wing chairs. My father and I introduced ourselves to a man at the front desk who seemed unimpressed by our presence. His aloofness unnerved me, which wasn't hard considering that no matter how my parents put it, I knew their sending me here was a form of disapproval, a way of banishing the part of me they didn't care to know.

A call went out over the intercom for someone to show us around. While we waited, I noticed that the sand in the standing ashtrays had been raked into perfect furrows. The glossy leaves of the potted plants looked as if they'd been polished by hand. The place seemed more like a well-tended hotel than an athletic club. Finally, a stoop-shouldered old man hobbled toward us, his head shrouded in a cloud of white hair. He wore a T-shirt that said "Instructor"; his arms were so wrinkled and anemic, I thought I might have misread it. While we followed him to the elevator, I readjusted my expectations, which had involved fantasies of a hulking drill sergeant barking orders at a flock of scrawny boys.

The instructor, mumbling to himself and never turning around to see if we were behind him, showed us where the gymnastics class took place. I'm certain the building was big, but the size of the room must be exaggerated by a trick of memory, because when I envision it, I picture a vast and windowless warehouse. Mats covered the wooden floor. Here and there, in remote and lonely pools of light, stood a pommel horse, a balance beam, and parallel bars. Tiers of bleachers rose into darkness. Unlike the cloistered air of a closet, the room seemed incomplete without a crowd.

Next we visited the dressing room, empty except for a naked middle-aged man. He sat on a narrow bench and clipped his formidable toenails. Moles dotted his back. He glistened like a fish.

We continued to follow the instructor down an aisle lined with numbered lockers. At the far end, steam billowed from the doorway that led to the showers. Fresh towels stacked on a nearby table made me think of my mother; I knew she liked to have me at home with her—I was often her only companion—and I resented her complicity in the plan to send me here.

The tour ended when the instructor gave me a sign-up sheet. Only a few names preceded mine. They were signatures, or so I imagined, of other soft and wayward sons.

IV

When the day of the first gymnastics class arrived, my mother gave me money and a gym bag and sent me to the corner of Hollywood and Western to wait for a bus. The sun was bright, the traffic heavy. While I sat there, an argument raged inside my head, the familiar, battering debate between the wish to be like other boys and the wish to be like myself. Why shouldn't I simply get up and go back home, where I'd be left alone to read and think? On the other hand, wouldn't life be easier if I liked athletics, or learned to like them?

No sooner did I steel my resolve to get on the bus than I thought of something better: I could spend the morning wandering through Woolworth's, then tell my parents I'd gone to the class. But would my lie stand up to scrutiny? As I practiced describing phantom gymnastics, I became aware of a car circling the block. It was a large car in whose shaded interior I could barely make out the driver, but I thought it might be the man who owned the local pet store. I'd often gone there on the pretext of looking at the cocker spaniel puppies huddled together in their pen, but I really went to gawk at the owner, whose tan chest, in the V of his shirt, was the place I most wanted to rest my head. Every time the man moved, counting stock or writing a receipt, his shirt parted, my mouth went dry, and I smelled the musk of sawdust and dogs.

I found myself hoping that the driver was the man who ran the pet store. I was thrilled by the unlikely possibility that the sight of me, slumped on a bus bench in my T-shirt and shorts, had caused such a man to circle the block. Up to that point in my life, lovemaking hovered somewhere in the future, an impulse a boy might aspire to but didn't indulge. And there I was, sitting on a bus bench in the middle of the city, dreaming I could seduce an adult. I showered the owner of the pet store with kisses and, as aquariums bubbled, birds sang, and mice raced in a wire wheel, slipped my hand beneath his shirt. The roar of traffic brought me to my senses. I breathed deeply and blinked against the sun. I crossed my legs at the knee in order to hide an erection. My fantasy left me both drained and changed. The continent of sex had drifted closer.

The car made another round. This time the driver leaned across the passenger seat and peered at me through the window. He was a complete stranger, whose gaze filled me with fear. It wasn't the surprise of not recognizing him that frightened me, it was what I did recognize—the unmistakable shame in his expression, and the weary temptation that drove him in circles. Before the car behind him honked, he mouthed "hello" and cocked his head. What now, he seemed to be asking. A bold, unbearable question.

I bolted to my feet, slung the gym bag over my shoulder, and hurried toward home. Now and then I turned around to make sure he wasn't trailing me, both relieved and disappointed when I didn't see his car. Even after I became convinced that he wasn't at my back—my sudden flight had scared him off—I kept turning around to see what was making me so nervous, as if I might spot the source of my discomfort somewhere on the street. I walked faster and faster, trying to outrace myself. Eventually, the bus I was supposed to have taken roared past. Turning the corner, I watched it bob eastward.

Closing the kitchen door behind me, I vowed never to leave home again. I was resolute in this decision without fully understanding why, or what it was I hoped to avoid; I was only aware of the need to hide and a vague notion, fading fast, that my trouble had something to do with sex. Already the mechanism of self-deception was at work. By the time my mother rushed into the kitchen to see why I'd returned so early, the thrill I'd felt while waiting for the bus had given way to indignation.

I poured out the story of the man circling the block and protested, with perhaps too great a passion, my own innocence. "I was just sitting there," I said again and again. I was so determined to deflect suspicion away from myself, and to justify my missing the class, that I portrayed the man as a grizzled pervert who drunkenly veered from lane to lane as he followed me halfway home.

My mother cinched her housecoat. She seemed moved and shocked by what I told her, if a bit incredulous, which prompted me to be more dramatic. "It wouldn't be safe," I insisted, "for me to wait at the bus stop again."

No matter how overwrought my story, I knew my mother wouldn't question it, wouldn't bring the subject up again; sex of any kind, especially sex between a man and a boy, was simply not discussed in our house. The gymnastics class, my parents agreed, was something I could do another time.

And so I spent the remainder of that summer at home with my mother, stirring cake batter, holding the dustpan, helping her fold the sheets. For a while I was proud of myself for engineering a reprieve from the athletic club. But as the days wore on, I began to see that my mother had wanted me with her all along, and forcing that to happen wasn't such a feat. Soon a sense of compromise set in; by expressing disgust for the man in the car, I'd expressed disgust for an aspect of myself. Now I had all the time in the world to sit around and contemplate my desire for men. The days grew long and stifling and hot, an endless sentence of self-examination.

Only trips to the pet store offered any respite. Every time I went there, I was too electrified with longing to think about longing in the abstract. The bell tinkled above the door, animals stirred within their cages, and the handsome owner glanced up from his work.

V

I handed my father the *Herald*. He opened the paper and disappeared behind it. My mother stirred her coffee and sighed. She gazed at the sweltering passersby and probably thought herself lucky. I slid into the vinyl booth and took my place beside my parents.

For a moment, I considered asking them about what had happened on the street, but they would have reacted with censure and alarm, and I sensed there was more to the story than they'd ever be willing to tell me. Men in dresses were only the tip of the iceberg. Who knew what other wonders existed—a boy, for example, who wanted to kiss a man—exception the world did its best to keep hidden.

It would be years before I heard the word "transvestite," so I struggled to find a word for what I'd seen. "He-she" came to mind, as lilting as "Injijikian." "Burl's" would have been perfect, like "boys" and "girls" spliced together, but I can't claim to have thought of this back then.

I must have looked stricken as I tried to figure it all out, because my mother put down her coffee cup and asked if I was O.K. She stopped just short of feeling my forehead. I assured her I was fine, but something within me had shifted, had given way to a heady doubt. When the waitress came and slapped down our check—"Thank You," it read, "Dine out more often"—I wondered if her lofty hairdo or the breasts on which her nametag quaked were real. Wax carnations bloomed at every table. Phony wood paneled the walls. Plastic food sat in a display case: fried eggs, a hamburger sandwich, a sundae topped with a garish cherry.

Considerations

Thinking

What makes "Burl's" an essay and not just a series of anecdotes? What connections link Cooper's scenes in terms of ideas and values?

What does Cooper convey about his experience in paragraphs 13–16? What perspective on gender does his essay as a whole provide? Where do you find Cooper's perspective most effectively presented?

Connecting

What connections link the following people and incidents in Cooper's essay: Mary Injijikian, the gymnastics class, the driver of the circling car, the owner of the pet store?

Where does Cooper's introduction end and his conclusion begin? How would you divide the middle or body of Cooper's essay?

How do the details in the paragraphs about Cooper's parents connect with the details about the transvestites?

Writing

Write an essay in which you explore an idea about gender. You can use Cooper as a starting point, or you can use an incident from your own experience.

Write an essay in which you compare Cooper's essay about gender identity with one of the following about another aspect of identity: "Silent Dancing," "The Discovery of What it Means to Be an American," "On Being a Cripple," or "Mother Tongue."

William Cronon
(b. 1954)

William Cronon is Professor of History, Geography, and Environmental Studies at the University of Wisconsin, Madison. He is an American historian specializing in environmental history, frontier history, and the history of the American West. His books include *Changes in the Land: Indians, Colonists, and the Ecology of New England; Nature's Metropolis: Chicago and the Great West;* and *Uncommon Ground: Toward Reinventing Nature,* in which a version of his essay "The Trouble with Wilderness" appears. In this essay Cronon complicates conventional ideas about the meaning of wilderness.

The Trouble with Wilderness

The time has come to rethink wilderness.

This will seem a heretical claim to many environmentalists, since the idea of wilderness has for decades been a fundamental tenet—indeed, a passion—of the environmental movement, especially in the United States. For many Americans wilderness stands as the last remaining place where civilization, that all too human disease, has not fully infected the earth. It is an island in the polluted sea of urban-industrial modernity, the one place we can turn for escape from our own too-muchness. Seen in this way, wilderness presents itself as the best antidote to our human selves, a refuge we must somehow recover if we hope to save the planet. As Henry David Thoreau once famously declared, "In Wildness is the preservation of the World."

But is it? The more one knows of its peculiar history, the more one realizes that wilderness is not quite what it seems. Far from being the one place on earth that stands apart from humanity, it is quite profoundly a human creation—indeed, the creation of very particular human cultures at very particular moments in human history. It is not a pristine sanctuary where the last remnant of an untouched, endangered, but still transcendent nature can for at least a little while longer be encountered without the contaminating taint of civilization. Instead, it is a product of that civilization, and could hardly be contaminated by the very stuff of which it is made. Wilderness hides its unnaturalness behind a mask that is all the more beguiling because it seems so natural. As we gaze into the mirror it holds up for us, we too easily imagine that what we behold is Nature when in fact we see the reflection of our own unexamined longings and desires. For this reason, we mistake life that wilderness can be the solution to our culture's problematic relationships with the nonhuman world, for wilderness is itself no small part of the problem.

To assert the unnaturalness of so natural a place will no doubt seem absurd or even perverse to many readers, so let me hasten to add that the nonhuman world we encounter in wilderness is far from being merely our own invention. I celebrate with others who love wilderness the beauty and power it contains. Each of us who has spent time there can conjure images and sensations that seem all the more hauntingly real for having engraved themselves so indelibly on our memories. Such memories may be uniquely our own, but they are also familiar enough to be instantly recognizable to others. Remember this? The torrents of mist shooting out from the base of a great waterfall in the depths of a Sierra canyon, the tiny droplets cooling your face as you listen to the roar of the water and gaze up toward the sky through a rainbow that hovers just out of reach. Remember this too: looking out across a desert canyon in the evening air, the only sound a lone raven calling in the distance, the rock walls dropping away into a chasm so deep that its bottom all but vanishes as you squint into the amber light of the setting sun. And this: the moment beside the trail as you sit on a sandstone ledge, your boots damp with the morning dew while you take in the rich smell of the pines, and the small red fox—or maybe for you it was a raccoon or a coyote or a deer— that suddenly ambles across your path, stopping for a long moment to gaze in your direction with cautious indifference before continuing on its way. Remember the feelings of such moments, and you will know as well as I do that you were in the presence of something irreducibly nonhuman, something profoundly Other than yourself. Wilderness is made of that, too.

And yet: what brought each of us to the places where such memories became possible is entirely a cultural invention. Go back 250 years in American and European history, and you do not find nearly so many people wandering around remote corners of the planet looking for what today we would call "the wilderness experience." As late as the eighteenth century, the most common usage of the word "wilderness" in the English language referred to landscapes that generally carried adjectives far different from the ones they attract today. To be a wilderness then was to be "deserted," "savage," "desolate," "barren"—in short, a "waste," the word's nearest synonym. Its connotations were anything but positive, and the emotion one was most likely to feel in its presence was "bewilderment"—or terror.

Many of the word's strongest associations then were biblical, for it is used over and over again in the King James Version to refer to places on the margins of civilization where it is all too easy to lose oneself in moral confusion and despair. The wilderness was where Moses had wandered with his people for forty years, and where they had nearly abandoned their God to worship a golden idol. "For Pharaoh will say of the Children of Israel," we read in Exodus, "They are entangled in the land, the wilderness hath shut them in." The wilderness was where Christ had struggled with the Devil and endured his temptations: "And immediately the Spirit driveth him into the wilderness. And he was there in the wilderness for forty days tempted of Satan; and was with the wild beasts; and the angels ministered unto him." The "delicious Paradise" of John Milton's Eden was surrounded by "a steep wilderness, whose hairy sides / Access denied" to all who sought entry. When Adam and Eve were driven from that garden, the world they entered was a wilderness that only their labor could redeem. Wilderness, in short, was a place to which one came against one's will, and always in fear and trembling. Whatever value it might have arose solely from the possibility that it might be "reclaimed" and turned toward human ends—plants, say, or a city upon a hill. In its raw state, it had little or nothing to offer civilized men and women.

But by the end of the nineteenth century all this had changed. The wastelands that had once seemed worthless had for some people come to seem almost beyond price. That Thoreau in 1862 could declare wildness to be the preservation of the world suggests the sea change that was going on. Wilderness had once been the antithesis of all that was orderly and good—it had been the darkness, one might say, on the far side of the garden wall—and yet now it was frequently likened to Eden itself. When John Muir arrived in the Sierra Nevada in 1869, he would declare, "No description of Heaven that I have ever heard or read of seems half so fine." He was hardly alone in expressing such emotions. One by one, various corners of the American map came to be designated as sites whose wild beauty was so spectacular that a growing number of citizens had to visit and see them for themselves. Niagara Falls was the first to undergo this transformation, but it was soon followed by the Catskills, the Adirondacks, Yosemite, Yellowstone, and others. Yosemite was deeded by the U.S. government to the State of California in 1864 as the nation's first wildland park, and Yellowstone became the first true national park in 1872.

By the first decade of the twentieth century, in the single most famous episode in American conservation history, a national debate had exploded over whether the city of San Francisco should be permitted to augment its water supply by damming the Tuolumne River in Hetch Hetchy valley, well within the boundaries of Yosemite National Park. The dam was eventually built, but what today seems no less significant is that so many people fought to prevent its completion. Even as the fight was being lost, Hetch Hetchy became the battle cry of an emerging movement to preserve wilderness. Fifty years earlier, such opposition would have been unthinkable. Few would have questioned the merits of "reclaiming" a wasteland like this in order to put it to human use. Now the defenders of Hetch Hetchy attracted widespread national attention by portraying such an act not as improvement or progress but as desecration and vandalism. Lest one doubt that the old biblical metaphors had been turned completely on their heads, listen to John Muir attack the dam's defenders. "Their arguments," he wrote, "are curiously like those of the devil, devised for the destruction of the first garden so much of the very best Eden fruit going to waste; so much of the best Tuolumne water and Tuolumne scenery going to waste." For Muir and the growing number of Americans who shared his views, Satan's home had become God's own temple.

The sources of this rather astonishing transformation were many, but for the purposes of this essay they can be gathered under two broad headings: the sublime and the frontier. Of the two, sublime is the older and more pervasive cultural construct being one of the most important expressions of that broad transatlantic movement we today label at romanticism; the frontier is more peculiarly American, though it too had its European antecedents and parallels. The two converged to remake wilderness in their own image, freighting it with moral values and cultural symbols that it carries to this day. Indeed, it is not too much to say that the modern environmental movement is itself a grandchild of romanticism and post-frontier ideology, which is why it is no accident that so much environmentalist discourse takes its bearings from the wilderness these intellectual movements helped create. Although wilderness may today seem to be just one environmental concern among many, it in fact serves as the foundation for a long list of other such concerns that on their face seem quite remote from it. That is why its influence is so pervasive and, potentially, so insidious.

To gain such remarkable influence, the concept of wilderness had to become loaded with some of the deepest core values of the culture that created and idealized it: it had to become sacred. This possibility had been present in wilderness even in the days when it had been a place of spiritual danger and moral temptation. If Satan was there, then so was Christ, who had found angels as well as wild beasts during his sojourn in the desert. In the wilderness the boundaries between human and nonhuman, between natural and supernatural, had always seemed less certain than elsewhere. This was why the early Christian saints and mystics had often emulated Christ's desert retreat as they sought to experience for themselves the visions and spiritual testing he had endured. One might meet devils and run the risk of losing one's soul in such a place, but one might also meet God. For some that possibility was worth almost any price.

By the eighteenth century this sense of the wilderness as a landscape where the supernatural lay just beneath the surface was expressed in the doctrine of the *sublime,* a word whose modern usage has been so watered down by commercial hype and tourist advertising that it retains only a dim echo of its former power. In the theories of Edmund Burke, Immanuel Kant, William Gilpin, and others, sublime landscapes were those rare places on earth where one had more chance than elsewhere to glimpse the face of God. Romantics had a clear notion of where one could be most sure of having this experience. Although God might, of course, choose to show himself anywhere, he would most often be found in those vast, powerful landscapes where one could not help feeling insignificant and being reminded of one's own mortality. Where were these sublime places? The eighteenth-century catalogue of their locations feels very familiar, for we still see and value landscapes as it taught us to do. God was on the mountaintop, in the chasm, in the waterfall, in the thundercloud, in the rainbow, in the sunset. One has only to think of the sites that Americans chose for their first national parks—Yellowstone, Yosemite, Grand Canyon, Rainier, Zion—to realize that virtually all of them fit one or more of these categories. Less sublime landscapes simply did not appear worthy of such protection; not until the 1940s, for instance, would the first swamp be honored, in Everglades National Park, and to this day there is no national park in the grasslands.

Among the best proofs that one had entered a sublime landscape was the emotion it evoked. For the early romantic writers and artists who first began to celebrate it, the sublime was far from being a pleasurable experience. The classic description is that of William Wordsworth as he recounted climbing the Alps and crossing the Simplon Pass in his autobiographical poem *The Prelude.* There, surrounded by crags and waterfalls, the poet felt himself literally to be in the presence of the divine—and experienced an emotion remarkably close to terror:

> The immeasurable height
> Of woods decaying, never to be decayed,
> The stationary blasts of waterfalls,
> And in the narrow rent at every turn
> Winds thwarting winds, bewildered and forlorn,

> The torrents shooting from the clear blue sky,
> The rocks that muttered close upon our ears,
> Black drizzling crags that spake by the way-side
> As if a voice were in them, the sick sight
> And giddy prospect of the raving stream,
> The unfettered clouds and region of the
> Heavens,
> Tumult and peace, the darkness and the light—
> Were all like workings of one mind, the features
> Of the same face, blossoms upon one tree;
> Characters of the great Apocalypse,
> The types and symbols of Eternity,
> Of first, and last, and midst, and without end.

This was no casual stroll in the mountains, no simple sojourn in the gentle lap of nonhuman nature. What Wordsworth described was nothing less than a religious experience, akin to that of the Old Testament prophets as they conversed with their wrathful God. The symbols he detected in this wilderness landscape were more supernatural than natural, and they inspired more awe and dismay than joy or pleasure. No mere mortal was meant to linger long in such a place, so it was with considerable relief that Wordsworth and his companion made their way back down from the peaks to the sheltering valleys.

Lest you suspect that this view of the sublime was limited to timid Europeans who lacked the American know-how for feeling at home in the wilderness, remember Henry David Thoreau's 1846 climb of Mount Katahdin, in Maine. Although Thoreau is regarded by many today as one of the great American celebrators of wilderness, his emotions about Katahdin were no less ambivalent than Wordsworth's about the Alps.

> It was vast, Titanic, and such as man never inhabits. Some part of the beholder, even some vital part, seems to escape through the loose grating of his ribs as he ascends. He is more lone than you can imagine. . . . Vast, Titanic, inhuman Nature has got him at disadvantage, caught him alone, and pilfers him of some of his divine faculty. She does not smile on him as in the plains. She seems to say sternly, why came ye h3ere before your time? This ground is not prepared for you. Is it not enough that I smile in the valleys? I have never made this soil for thy feet, this air for thy breathing, these rocks for thy neighbors. I cannot pity nor fondle thee here, but forever relentlessly cave thee hence to where I *am* kind. Why seek me where I have not called thee, and then complain because you find me but a stepmother?

This is surely not the way a modern backpacker or nature lover would describe Maine's most famous mountain, but that is because Thoreau's description owes as much to Wordsworth and other romantic contemporaries as to the rocks and clouds of Katahdin itself. His words took the physical mountain on which he stood and transmuted it into an icon of the sublime: a symbol of God's presence on earth. The power and the glory of that icon were such that only a prophet might gaze on it for long. In effect, romantics like Thoreau joined Moses and the children of Israel in Exodus when "they looked toward the wilderness, and behold, the glory of the Lord appeared in the cloud."

But even as it came to embody the awesome power of the sublime, wilderness was also being tamed—not just by those who were building settlements in its midst but also by those who most celebrated its inhuman beauty. By the second half of the nineteenth century, the terrible awe that Wordsworth and Thoreau regarded as the appropriately pious stance to adopt in the presence of their mountaintop God was giving way to a much more comfortable, almost sentimental demeanor. As more and more Tourists sought out the wilderness as a spectacle to be looked at and enjoyed for its great beauty, the sublime in effect became domesticated. The wilderness was still sacred, but the religious sentiments it evoked were more those of a pleasant parish church than those of a grand cathedral or a harsh desert retreat. The writer who best captures this late romantic sense of a domesticated Sublime is undoubtedly John Muir whose descriptions of Yosemite and the Sierra Nevada reflect none of the anxiety or terror one finds in earlier writers. Here he is, for instance, sketching on North Dome in Yosemite Valley:

> No pain here, no dull empty hours, no fear of the past, no fear of the future. These blessed mountains are so compactly filled with God's beauty, no petty personal hope or experience has room to be. Drinking this champagne water is pure pleasure, so is breathing the living air, and every movement of limbs is pleasure, while the body seems to feel beauty when exposed to it as it feels the campfire or sunshine, entering not by the eyes alone, but equally through all one's flesh like radiant heat, making a passionate ecstatic pleasure glow not explainable.

The emotions Muir describes in Yosemite could hardly be more different from Thoreau's on Katahdin or Wordsworth's on the Simplon Pass. Yet all three men are participating in the same cultural tradition and contributing to the same myth: the mountain as cathedral. The three may differ in the way they choose to express their piety—Wordsworth favoring an awe-filled bewilderment, Thoreau a stern loneliness, Muir a welcome ecstasy—but they agree completely about the church in which they prefer to worship. Muir's closing words on North Dome diverge from his older contemporaries only in mood, not in their ultimate content:

> Perched like a fly on this Yosemite dome, I gaze and sketch and bask, oftentimes settling down into dumb admiration without definite hope of ever learning much, yet with the longing, unresting effort that lies at the door of hope, humbly prostrate before the vast display of God's power, and eager to offer self-denial and renunciation with eternal toil to learn any lesson in the divine manuscript.

Muir's "divine manuscript" and Wordsworth's "Characters of the great Apocalypse" were in fact pages from the same holy book. The sublime wilderness had ceased to be a place of satanic temptation and become instead a sacred temple, much as it continues to be for those who love it today.

But the Romantic sublime was not the only cultural movement that helped transform wilderness into a sacred American icon during the nineteenth century. No less important was the powerful romantic attraction of primitivism, dating back at least to Rousseau—the belief that the best antidote to the ills of an overly refined and civilized modern world was a return to simpler, more primitive living. In the United States, this was embodied most strikingly in the national myth of the frontier. The historian Frederick Jackson Turner wrote in 1893 the classic academic statement of this myth, but it had been part of American cultural traditions for well over a century. As Turner described the process, easterners and European immigrants, in moving to the wild unsettled lands of the frontier, shed the trappings of civilization, rediscovered their primitive racial energies, reinvented direct democratic institutions, and thereby reinfused themselves with a vigor, an independence, and a creativity that were the source of American democracy and national character. Seen in this way, wild country became a place not just of religious redemption but of national renewal, the quintessential location for experiencing what it meant to be an American.

One of Turner's most provocative claims was that by the 1890s the frontier was passing away. Never again would "such gifts of free land offer themselves" to the American people. "The frontier has gone," he declared, "and with its going has closed the first period of American history." Built into the frontier myth from its very beginning was the notion that this crucible of American identity was temporary and would pass away. Those who have celebrated the frontier have almost always looked backward as they did so, mourning an older, simpler, truer world that is about to disappear forever. That world and all of its attractions, Turner said, depended on free land—on wilderness. Thus, in the myth of the vanishing frontier lay the seeds of wilderness preservation in the United States, for if wild land had been so crucial in the making of the nation, then surely one must save its last remnants as monuments to the American past—and as an insurance policy to protect its future. It is no accident that the movement to set aside national parks and wilderness areas began to gain real momentum at precisely the time that laments about the passing frontier reached their peak. To protect wilderness was in a very real sense to protect the nation's most sacred myth of origin.

Among the core elements of the frontier myth was the powerful sense among certain groups of Americans that wilderness was the last bastion of rugged individualism. Turner tended to stress communitarian themes when writing frontier history, asserting that Americans in primitive conditions had been forced to band together with their neighbors to form communities and democratic institutions. For other writers, however, frontier democracy for communities was less compelling than frontier freedom for individuals. By fleeing to the outer margins of settled land and society—so the story ran—an individual could escape the confining strictures of civilized life. The mood among writers who celebrated frontier individualism was almost always nostalgic; they lamented not just a lost way of life but the passing of the heroic men who had embodied that life. Thus Owen Wister in the introduction to his classic 1902 novel *The Virginian* could write of "a vanished world" in which "the horseman, the cow-puncher, the last romantic figure upon our soil" rode only "in his historic yesterday" and would "never come again." For Wister, the cowboy was a man who gave his word and kept it ("Wall Street would have found him behind the times"), who did not talk lewdly to women ("Newport would have thought him old-fashioned"), who worked and played hard, and whose "ungoverned hours did not unman him." Theodore Roosevelt wrote with much the same nostalgic fervor about the "fine, manly qualities" of the "wild rough-rider of the plains." No one could be more heroically masculine, thought Roosevelt, or more at home in the western wilderness:

> There he passes his days, there he does his life-work, there, when he meets death, he faces it as he has faced many other evils, with quiet, uncomplaining fortitude. Brave, hospitable, hardy, and adventurous, he is the grim pioneer of our race; he prepares the way for the civilization from before whose face he must himself disappear. Hard and dangerous though his existence is, it has yet a wild attraction that strongly draws to it his bold, free spirit.

This nostalgia for a passing frontier way of life inevitably implied ambivalence, if not downright hostility, toward modernity and all that it represented. If one saw the wild lands of the frontier as freer, truer, and more natural than other, more modern places, then one was also inclined to see the cities and factories of urban-industrial civilization as confining, false, and artificial. Owen Wister looked at transition" that had followed "the horseman of the plains," and did not like what he saw: "a shapeless state, a condition of men and manners as unlovely as is that moment in the year when winter is gone and spring not come, and the face of Nature is ugly." In the eyes of writers who shared Wister's distaste for modernity, civilization contaminated its inhabitants and absorbed them into the faceless, collective, contemptible life of the crowd. For all of its troubles and dangers, and despite the fact that it must pass away, the frontier had been a better place. If civilization was to be redeemed, it would be by men like the Virginian who could retain their frontier virtues even as they made the transition to post-frontier life.

The mythic frontier individualist was almost always masculine in gender: here, in the wilderness, a man could be a real man, the rugged individual he was meant to be before civilization sapped his energy and threatened his masculinity. Wister's contemptuous remarks about Wall Street and Newport suggest what he and many others of his generation believed—that the comforts and seductions of civilized life were especially insidious for men, who all too easily became emasculated by the feminizing tendencies of civilization. More often than not, men who felt this way came, like Wister and Roosevelt, from elite class backgrounds. The curious result was that frontier nostalgia became an important vehicle for expressing a peculiarly bourgeois form of anti-modernism. The very men who most benefited from urban-industrial capitalism were among those who believed they must escape its debilitating effects. If the frontier was passing, then men who had the means to do so should preserve for themselves some remnant of its wild landscape so that they might enjoy the regeneration and renewal that came from sleeping under the stars, participating in blood sports, and living off the land. The frontier might be gone, but the frontier experience could still be had if only wilderness were preserved.

Thus the decades following the Civil War saw more and more of the nation's wealthiest citizens seeking out wilderness for themselves. The elite passion for wild land took many forms: enormous estates in the Adirondacks and elsewhere (disingenuously called "camps" despite their many servants and amenities), cattle ranches for would-be roughriders on the Great Plains, guided big-game hunting trips in the Rockies, and luxurious resort hotels whereby railroads pushed their way into sublime landscapes. Wilderness suddenly emerged as the landscape of choice for elite tourists, who brought with them strikingly urban ideas of the countryside through which they traveled. For them, wild land was not a site for productive labor and not a permanent home; rather, it was a place of recreation. One went to the wilderness not as a producer but as a consumer, hiring guides and other backcountry residents who could serve as romantic surrogates for the rough riders and hunters of the frontier, if one was willing to overlook their new status as employees and servants of the rich.

In just this way, wilderness came to embody the national frontier myth, standing for the wild freedom of America's past and seeming to represent a highly attractive natural alternative to the ugly artificiality of modern civilization. The irony, of course, was that in the process wilderness came to reflect the very civilization its devotees sought to escape! Ever since the nineteenth century, celebrating wilderness has been an activity mainly for well-to-do city folks. Country people generally know far too much about working the land to regard unworked land as their ideal. In contrast, elite urban tourists and wealthy sportsmen projected their leisure-time frontier fantasies onto the American landscape and so created wilderness in their own image.

There were other ironies as well. The movement to set aside national parks and wilderness areas followed hard on the heels of the final Indian wars, in which the prior human inhabitants of these areas were rounded up and moved onto reservations. The myth of the wilderness as "virgin," uninhabited land had always been especially cruel when seen from the perspective of the Indians who had once called that land home. Now they were forced to move elsewhere, with the result that tourists could safely enjoy the illusion that they were seeing their nation in its pristine, original state, in the new morning of God's own creation. Among the things that most marked the new national parks as reflecting a post-frontier consciousness was the relative absence of human violence within their boundaries. The actual frontier had often been a place of conflict, in which invaders and invaded fought for control of land and resources. Once set aside within the fixed and carefully policed boundaries of the modern bureaucratic state, the wilderness lost its savage image and became safe: a place more of reverie than of revulsion or fear. Meanwhile, its original inhabitants were kept out by dint of force, their earlier uses of the land redefined as inappropriate or even illegal. To this day, for instance, the Blackfeet continue to be accused of "poaching" on the lands of Glacier National Park that originally belonged to them and that were ceded by treaty only with the proviso that they be permitted to hunt there.

The removal of Indians to create an "uninhabited wilderness"—uninhabited as never before in the human history of the place—reminds us just how invented, just how constructed, the American wilderness really is. To return to my opening argument: there is nothing natural about the concept of wilderness. It is entirely a creation of the culture that holds it dear, a product of the very history it seeks to deny. Indeed, one of the most striking proofs of the cultural invention of wilderness is its thoroughgoing erasure of the history from which it sprang. In virtually all of its manifestations, wilderness represents a flight from history. Seen as the original garden, it is a place outside of time from which human beings had to be ejected before the fallen world of history could properly begin. Seen as the frontier, it is a savage world at the dawn of civilization, whose transformation represents the very beginning of the national historical epic. Seen as the bold landscape of frontier heroism, it is the place of youth and childhood, into which men escape by abandoning their pasts and entering a world of freedom where the constraints of civilization fade into memory. Seen as the sacred sublime, it is the home of a God who transcends history by standing as the One who remains untouched and unchanged by time's arrow. No matter what the angle from which we regard it, wilderness offers us the illusion that we can escape the cares and troubles of the world in which our past has ensnared us.

This escape from history is one reason why the language we use to talk about wilderness is often permeated with spiritual and religious values that reflect human ideals far more than the material world of physical nature. Wilderness fulfills the old romantic project of secularizing Judeo-Christian values so as to make a new cathedral not in some petty human building but in God's own creation, Nature itself. Many environmentalists who reject traditional notions of the godhead and who regard themselves as agnostics or even atheists nonetheless express feelings tantamount to religious awe when in the presence of wilderness—a fact that testifies to the success of the romantic project. Those who have no difficulty seeing God as the expression of our human dreams and desires nonetheless have trouble recognizing that in a secular age Nature can offer precisely the same sort of mirror.

Thus it is that wilderness serves as the unexamined foundation on which so many of the quasi-religious values of modern environmentalism rest. The critique of modernity that is one of environmentalism's most important contributions to the moral and political discourse of our time more often than not appeals, explicitly or implicitly, to wilderness as the standard against which to measure the failings of our human world. Wilderness is the natural unfallen antithesis of an unnatural civilization that has lost its soul. It is a place of freedom in which we can recover the true selves we have lost to the corrupting influences of our artificial lives. Most of all, it is the ultimate landscape of authenticity. Combining the sacred grandeur of the sublime with the primitive simplicity of the frontier, it is the place where we can see the world as it really is, and so know ourselves as we really are— or ought to be.

But the trouble with wilderness is that it quietly expresses and reproduces the very values its devotees seek to reject. The flight from history that is very nearly the core of wilderness represents the false hope of an escape from responsibility, the illusion that we can somehow wipe clean the slate of our past and return to the tabula rasa that supposedly existed before we began to leave our marks on the world. The dream of an unworked natural landscape is very much the fantasy of people who have never themselves had to work the land to make a living—urban folk for whom food comes from a supermarkets or a restaurant instead of a field, and for whom the wooden houses in which they live and work apparently have no meaningful connection to the forests in which trees grow and die. Only people whose relation to the land was already alienated could hold up wilderness as a model for human life in nature, for the romantic ideology of wilderness leaves precisely nowhere for human beings actually to make their living from the land.

This, then, is the central paradox: wilderness embodies a dualistic vision in which the human is entirely outside the natural. If we allow ourselves to believe that nature, to be true, must also be wild, then our very presence in nature represents its fall. The place where we are is the place where nature is not. If this is so— if by definition wilderness leaves no place for human beings, save perhaps as contemplative sojourners enjoying their leisurely reverie in God's natural cathedral—then also by definition it can offer no solution to the environmental and other problems that confront us. To the extent that we celebrate wilderness as the measure with which we judge civilization, we reproduce the dualism that sets humanity and nature at opposite poles. We thereby leave ourselves little hope of discovering what an ethical, sustainable, *honorable* human place in nature might actually look like.

Worse: to the extent that we live in an urban-industrial civilization but at the same time pretend to ourselves that our *real* home is in the wilderness, to just that extent we give ourselves permission to evade responsibility for the lives we actually lead. We inhabit civilization while holding some part of ourselves—what we imagine to be the most precious part—aloof from its entanglements. We work our nine-to-five jobs in its institutions, we eat its food, we drive its cars (not least to reach the wilderness), we benefit from the intricate and all too invisible networks with which it shelters us, all the while pretending that these things are not an essential part of who we are. By imagining that our true home is in the wilderness, we forgive ourselves the homes we actually inhabit. In its flight from history, in its siren song of escape, in its reproduction of the dangerous dualism that sets human beings outside of nature—in all of these ways, wilderness poses a serious threat to responsible environmentalism at the end of the twentieth century.

By now I hope it is clear that my criticism in this essay is not directed at wild nature per se, or even at efforts to set aside large tracts of wild land, but rather at the specific habits of thinking that flow from this complex cultural construction called wilderness. It is not the things we label as wilderness that are the problem—for nonhuman nature and large tracts of the natural world *do* deserve protection—but rather what we ourselves mean when we use that label. Lest one doubt how pervasive these habits of thought really are in contemporary environmentalism, let me list some of the places where wilderness serves as the ideological underpinning for environmental concerns that might otherwise seem quite remote from it. Defenders of biological diversity, for instance, although sometimes appealing to more utilitarian concerns, often point to "untouched" ecosystems as the best and richest repositories of the undiscovered species we must certainly try to protect. Although at first blush an apparently more "scientific" concept than wilderness, biological diversity in fact invokes many of the same sacred values, which is why organizations like the Nature Conservancy have been so quick to employ it as an alternative to the seemingly fuzzier and more problematic concept of wilderness. There is a paradox here, of course. To the extent that biological diversity (indeed, even wilderness itself) is likely to survive in the future only by the most vigilant and self-conscious management of the ecosystems that sustain it, the ideology of wilderness is potentially in direct conflict with the very thing it encourages us to protect.

The most striking instances of this have revolved around "endangered species," which serve as vulnerable symbols of biological diversity while at the same time standing as surrogates for wilderness itself. The terms of the Endangered Species Act in the United States have often meant that those hoping to defend pristine wilderness have had to rely on a single endangered species like the spotted owl to gain legal standing for their case—thereby making the full power of sacred land inhere in a single numinous organism whose habitat then becomes the object of intense debate about appropriate management and use. The ease with which antienvironmental forces like the wise-use movement have attacked such single-species preservation efforts suggests the vulnerability of strategies like these.

Perhaps partly because our own conflicts over such places and organisms have become so messy, the convergence of wilderness values with concerns about biological diversity and endangered species has helped produce a deep fascination for remote ecosystems, where it is easier to imagine that nature might somehow be "left alone" to flourish by its own pristine devices. The classic example is the tropical rain forest, which since the Ages has become the most powerful modern icon of unfallen, sacred land—a veritable Garden of Eden—for many Americans and Europeans. And yet protecting the rain forest in the eyes of First World environmentalists all too often means protecting it from the people who live there. Those who seek to preserve such "wilderness" from the activities of native peoples run the risk of reproducing the same tragedy—being forcibly removed from an ancient home—that befell American Indians. Third World countries face massive environmental problems and deep social conflicts, but these are not likely to be solved by a cultural myth that encourages us to "preserve" peopleless landscapes that have not existed in such places for millennia. At its worst, as environmentalists are beginning to realize, exporting American notions of wilderness in this way can become an unthinking and self-defeating form of cultural imperialism.

Perhaps the most suggestive example of the way that wilderness thinking can underpin other environmental concerns has emerged in the recent debate about "global change." In 1989 the journalist Bill McKibben published a book entitled *The End of Nature,* in which he argued that the prospect of global climate change as a result of unintentional human manipulation of the atmosphere means that nature as we once knew it no longer exists. Whereas earlier generations inhabited a natural world that remained more or less unaffected by their actions, our own generation is uniquely different. We and our children will henceforth live in a biosphere completely altered by our own activity, a planet in which the human and the natural can no longer be distinguished because the one has overwhelmed the other. In McKibben's view, nature has died, and we are responsible for killing it. "The planet," he declares, "is utterly different now."

But such a perspective is possible only if we accept the wilderness premise that nature, to be natural, must also be pristine—remote from humanity and untouched by our common past. In fact, everything we know about environmental history suggests that people have been manipulating the natural world on various scales for as long as we have a record of their passing. Moreover, we have unassailable evidence that many of the environmental changes we now face also occurred quite apart from human intervention at one time or another in the earth's past. The point is not that our current problems are trivial, or that our devastating effects on the earth's ecosystems should be accepted as inevitable or "natural." It is rather that we seem unlikely to make much progress in solving these problems if we hold up to ourselves as the mirror of nature a wilderness we ourselves cannot inhabit.

To do so is merely to take to a logical extreme the paradox that was built into wilderness from the beginning: if nature dies because we enter it, then the only way to save nature is to kill ourselves. The absurdity of this proposition flows from the underlying dualism it expresses. Not only does it ascribe greater power to humanity than we in fact possess—physical and biological nature will surely survive in some form or another long after we ourselves have gone the way of all flesh—but in the end it offers us little more than a self-defeating counsel of despair. The tautology gives us no way out: if wild nature is the only thing worth saving, and if our mere presence destroys it, then the sole solution to our own unnaturalness, the only way to protect sacred wilderness from profane humanity, would seem to be suicide. It is not a proposition that seems likely to produce very positive or practical results.

And yet radical environmentalists and deep ecologists all too frequently come close to accepting this premise as a first principle. When they express, for instance, the popular notion that our environmental problems began with the invention of agriculture, they push the human fall from natural grace so far back into the past that all of civilized history becomes a tale of ecological declension. Earth First! founder Dave Foreman captures the familiar parable succinctly when he writes:

> Before agriculture was midwifed in the Middle East, humans were in the wilderness. We had no concept of "wilderness" because everything was wilderness and *we were a part of it*. But with irrigation ditches, crop surpluses, and permanent villages, we became *apart from* the natural world. . . . Between the wilderness that created us and the civilization created by us grew an ever-widening rift.

In this view, the farm becomes the first and most important battlefield in the long war against wild nature, and all else follows in its wake. From such a starting place, it is hard not to reach the conclusion that the only way human beings can hope to live naturally on earth is to follow the hunter-gatherers back into a wilderness Eden and abandon virtually everything that civilization has given us. It may indeed turn out that civilization will end in ecological collapse or nuclear disaster, whereupon one might expect to find any human survivors returning to a way of life closer to that celebrated by Foreman and his followers. For most of us, though, such a debacle would be cause for regret, a sign that humanity had failed to fulfill its own promise and failed to honor its own highest values—including those of the deep ecologists.

In offering wilderness as the ultimate hunter-gatherer alternative to civilization, Foreman reproduces an extreme but still easily recognizable version of the myth of frontier primitivism. When he writes of his fellow Earth Firsters that "we believe we must return to being animal, to glorying in our sweat, hormones, tears, and blood" and that "we struggle against the modern compulsion to become dull, passionless androids," he is following in the footsteps of Owen Wister. Although his arguments give primacy to defending biodiversity and the autonomy of wild nature, his prose becomes most passionate when he speaks of preserving "the wilderness experience." His own ideal "Big Outside" bears an uncanny resemblance to that of the frontier myth: wide open spaces and virgin land with no trails, no signs, no facilities, no maps, no guides, no rescues, no modern equipment. Tellingly, it is a land where hardy travelers can support themselves by hunting with "primitive weapons (bow and arrow, atlatl, knife, sharp rock)." Foreman claims that "the primary value of wilderness is not as a proving ground for young Huck Finns and Annie Oakleys," but his heart is with Huck and Annie all the same. He admits that "preserving a quality wilderness experience for the human visitor, letting her or him flex Paleolithic muscles or seek visions, remains a tremendously important secondary purpose." Just so does Teddy Roosevelt's Rough Rider live on in the greener garb of a new age.

However much one may be attracted to such a vision, it entails problematic consequences. For one, it makes wilderness the locus for an epic struggle between malign civilization and benign nature, compared with which all other social, political, and moral concerns seem trivial. Foreman writes, "The preservation of wildness and native diversity is *the* most important issue. Issues directly affecting only humans pale in comparison." Presumably so do any environmental problems whose victims are mainly people, for such problems usually surface in landscapes that have already "fallen" and are no longer wild. This would seem to exclude from the radical environmentalist agenda problems of occupational health and safety in industrial settings, problems of toxic waste exposure on "unnatural" urban and agricultural sites, problems of poor children poisoned by lead exposure in the inner city, problems of famine and poverty and human suffering in the "overpopulated" places of the earth—problems, in short, of environmental justice. If we set too high a stock on wilderness, too many other corners of the earth become less than natural and too many other people become less than human, thereby giving us permission not to care much about their suffering or their fate.

It is no accident that these supposedly inconsequential environmental problems affect mainly poor people, for the long affiliation between wilderness and wealth means that the only poor people who count when wilderness is *the* issue are hunter-gatherers, who presumably do not consider themselves to be poor in the first place. The dualism at the heart of wilderness encourages its advocates to conceive of its protection as a crude conflict between the "human" and the "nonhuman"—or, more often, between those who value the nonhuman and those who do not. This in turn tempts one to ignore crucial differences *among* humans and the complex cultural and historical reasons why different peoples may feel very differently about the meaning of wilderness.

Why, for instance, is the "wilderness experience" so often conceived as a form of recreation best enjoyed by those whose class privileges give them the time and resources to leave their jobs behind and "get away from it all"? Why does the protection of wilderness so often seem to pit urban recreationists against rural people who actually earn their living from the land (excepting those who sell goods and services to the tourists themselves)? Why in the debates about pristine natural areas are "primitive" peoples idealized, even sentimentalized, until the moment they do something unprimitive, modern, and unnatural, and thereby fall from environmental grace? What are the consequences of a wilderness ideology that devalues productive labor and the very concrete knowledge that comes from working the land with one's own hands? All of these questions imply conflicts among different groups of people, conflicts that are obscured behind the deceptive clarity of "human" versus "nonhuman." If in answering these knotty questions we resort to so simplistic an opposition, we are almost certain to ignore the very subtleties and complexities we need to understand.

But the most troubling cultural baggage that accompanies the celebration of wilderness has less to do with remote rain forests and peoples than with the ways we think about ourselves—we American environmentalists who quite rightly worry about the future of the earth and the threats we pose to the natural world. Idealizing a distant wilderness too often means not idealizing the environment in which we live, the landscape that for better or worse we call home. Most of our most serious environmental problems start right here, at home, and if we are to solve those problems, we need an environmental ethic that will tell us as much about using nature as about not using it. The wilderness dualism tends to cast any use as *ab*use, and thereby denies us a middle ground in which responsible use and non-use might attain some kinship. My own belief is that only by exploring this middle ground will we learn ways of imagining a better world for all of us: humans and nonhumans, rich people and poor, women and men, First Worlders and Third Worlders, white folks and people of color, consumers and producers— a world better for humanity in all of its diversity and for all the rest of nature too. The middle ground is where we actually live. It is where we—all of us, in our different places and ways—make our homes.

That is why, when I think of the times I myself have come closest to experiencing what I might call the sacred in nature, I often find myself remembering wild places much closer to home. I think, for instance, of a small pond near my house where water bubbles up from limestone springs to feed a series of pools that rarely freeze in winter and so play home to waterfowl that stay here for the protective warmth even on the coldest of winter days, gliding silently through steaming mists as the snow falls from gray February skies. I think of a November evening long ago when I found myself on a Wisconsin hilltop in rain and dense fog, only to have the setting sun break through the clouds to cast an otherworldly golden light on the misty farms and woodlands below, a scene so unexpected and joyous that I lingered past dusk so as not to miss any part of the gift that had come my way. And I think perhaps most especially of the blown-out, bankrupt farm in the sand country of central Wisconsin where Aldo Leopold and his family tried one of the first American experiments in ecological restoration, turning ravaged and infertile soil into carefully tended ground where the human and the nonhuman could exist side by side in relative harmony. What I celebrate about such places is not *just* their wildness, though that certainly is among their most important qualities; what I celebrate even more is that they remind us of the wildness in our own back yards, of the nature that is all around us if only we have eyes to see it.

Indeed, my principal objection to wilderness is that it may teach us to be submissive or even contemptuous of such humble places and experiences. Without our quite realizing it, wilderness tends to privilege some parts of nature at the expense of others. Most of us, I suspect, still follow the conventions of the romantic sublime in finding the mountaintop more glorious than the plains, the ancient forest nobler than the grasslands, the mighty canyon more inspiring than the humble marsh. Even John Muir, in arguing against those who sought to dam his beloved Hetch Hetchy valley in the Sierra Nevada, argued for alternative dam sites in the gentler valleys of the foothills—a preference that had nothing to do with nature and everything with the cultural traditions of the sublime. Just as problematically, our frontier traditions have encouraged Americans to define "true" wilderness as requiring very large tracts of roadless land—what Dave Foreman calls the Big Outside. Leaving aside the legitimate empirical question in conservation biology of how large a tract of land must be before a given species can reproduce on it, the emphasis on big wilderness reflects a romantic frontier belief that one hasn't really gotten away from civilization unless one can go for days at a time without encountering another human being. By teaching us to fetishize sublime places and wide open country, these peculiarly American ways of thinking about wilderness encourage us to adopt too high a standard for what counts as "natural." If it isn't hundreds of square miles big, if it doesn't give us God's-eye views or grand vistas, if it doesn't permit us the illusion that we are alone on the planet, then it really isn't natural. It's too small, too plain, or too crowded to be *authentically* wild.

In critiquing wilderness as I have done in this essay, I'm forced to confront my own deep ambivalence about its meaning for modern environmentalism. On the one hand, one of my own most important environmental ethics is that people should always be conscious that they are part of the nature world, inextricably tied to the ecological systems that sustain their lives. Any way of looking at nature that encourages us to believe we re separate from nature—as wilderness tends to do—is likely to reinforce environmentally irresponsible behavior. On the other hand, I also think it no less crucial for us to recognize and honor nonhuman nature as a world we did not create, a world with its own independent, nonhuman reasons for being as it is. The autonomy of nonhuman nature seems to me an indispensable corrective to human arrogance. Any way of looking at nature that helps us remember—as wilderness also tends to doxj that the interests of people are not necessarily identical to those of every other creature or of the earth itself is likely to foster responsible behavior. To the extent that wilderness has served as an important vehicle for articulating deep moral values regarding our obligations and responsibilities to the nonhuman world, I would not want to jettison the contributions it has made to our culture's ways of thinking about nature.

If the core problem of wilderness is that it distances us too much from the very things it teaches us to value, then the question we must ask is what it can tell us about home, the place where we live. How can we take the positive values we associate with wilderness and bring them closer to home? I think the answer to this question will come by broadening our sense of the otherness that wilderness seeks to define and protect. In reminding us of the world we did not make, wilderness can teach profound feelings of humility and respect as we confront our fellow beings and the earth itself. Feelings like these argue for the importance of self-awareness and self-criticism as we exercise our own ability to transform the world around us, helping us set responsible limits to human mastery—which without such limits too easily becomes human hubris. Wilderness is the place where, symbolically at least, we try to withhold, our power to dominate.

Wallace Stegner once wrote of

> the special human mark, the special record of human passage, that distinguishes man from all other species. It is rare enough among men, impossible to any other form of life. *It is simply the deliberate and chosen refusal to make any marks at all*. . . . We are the most dangerous species of life on the planet, and every other species, even the earth itself, has cause to fear our power to exterminate. But we are also the only species which, when it chooses to do so, will go to great effort to save what it might destroy.

The myth of wilderness, which Stegner knowingly reproduces in these remarks, is that we can somehow leave nature untouched by our passage. By now it should be clear that this for the most part is an illusion. But Stegner's deeper message then becomes all the more compelling. If living in history means that we cannot help leaving marks on a fallen world, then the dilemma we face is to decide what kinds of marks we wish to leave. It is just here that our cultural traditions of wilderness remain so important. In the broadest sense, wilderness teaches us to ask whether the Other must always bend to our will, and, if not, under what circumstances it should be allowed to flourish without our intervention. This is surely a question worth asking about everything we do, and not just about the natural world.

When we visit a wilderness area, we find ourselves surrounded by plants and animals and physical landscapes whose otherness compels our attention. In forcing us to acknowledge that they are not of our making, that they have little or no need of our continued existence, they recall for us a creation far greater than our own. In the wilderness, we need no reminder that a tree has its own reasons for being, quite apart from us. The same is less true in the gardens we plant and tend ourselves: there it is far easier to forget the otherness of the tree. Indeed, one could almost measure wilderness by the extent to which our recognition of its otherness requires a conscious, willed act on our part. The romantic legacy means that wilderness is more a state of mind than a fact of nature, and the state of mind that today most defines wilderness is *wonder*. The striking power of the wild is that wonder in the face of it requires no act of will, but forces itself upon us—as an expression of the nonhuman world experienced through the lens of our cultural history—as proof that ours is not the only presence in the universe.

Wilderness gets us into trouble only if we imagine that this experience of wonder and otherness is limited to the remote corners of the planet, or that it somehow depends on pristine landscapes we ourselves do not inhabit. Nothing could be more misleading. The tree in the garden is in reality no less other, no less worthy of our wonder and respect, than the tree in an ancient forest that has never known an ax or a saw—even though the tree in the forest reflects a more intricate web of ecological relationships. The tree in the garden could easily have sprung from the same seed as the tree in the forest, and we can claim only its location and perhaps its form as our own. Both trees stand apart from us; both share our common world. The special power of the tree in the wilderness is to remind us of this fact. It can teach us to recognize the wildness we did not see in the tree we planted in our own back yard. By seeing the otherness in that which is most unfamiliar, we can learn to see it too in that which at first seemed merely ordinary. If wilderness can do this—if it can help us perceive and respect a nature we had forgotten to recognize as natural—then it will become part of the solution to our environ mental dilemmas rather than part of the problem.

This will happen, however, only if we abandon the dualism that sees the tree in the Eden as artificial—completely fallen and unnatural—and the tree in the wilderness as natural—completely pristine and wild. Both trees in some ultimate sense are wild; both in a practical sense now depend on our management and care. We are responsible for both, even though we can claim credit for neither. Our challenge is to stop thinking of such things according to a set of bipolar moral scales in which the human and the nonhuman, the unnatural and the natural, the fallen and the unfallen, serve as our conceptual map for understanding and valuing the world. Instead, we need to embrace the full continuum of a natural landscape that is also cultural, in which the city, the suburb, the pastoral, and the wild each has its proper place, which we permit ourselves to celebrate without needlessly denigrating the others. We need to honor the Other within and the Other next door as much as we do the exotic Other that lives far away—a lesson that applies as much to people as it does to (other) natural things. In particular, we need to discover a common middle ground in which all of these things, from the city to the wilderness, can somehow be encompassed in the word "home." Home, after all, is the place where finally we make our living. It is the place for which we take responsibility, the place we try to sustain so we can pass on what is best in it (and in ourselves) to our children.

The task making a home in nature is what Wendell Berry has called "the forever unfinished lifework of our species." "The only thing we have to preserve nature with," he writes, "is culture; the only thing we have to preserve wildness with is domesticity." Calling a place home inevitably means that we will *use* the nature we find in it, for there can be no escape from manipulating and working and even killing some parts of nature to make our home. But if we acknowledge the autonomy and otherness of the things and creatures around us—an autonomy our culture has taught us to label with the word "wild"—then we will at least think carefully about the uses to which we put them, and even ask if we should use them at all. Just so can we still join Thoreau in declaring that "in Wildness is the preservation of the World," for *wildness* (as opposed to wilderness) can be found anywhere: in the seemingly tame fields and woodlots of Massachusetts, in the cracks of a Manhattan sidewalk, even in the cells of our own bodies. As Gary Snyder has wisely said, "A person with a clear heart and open mind can experience the wilderness anywhere on earth. It is a quality of one's own consciousness. The planet is a wild place and always will be." To think ourselves capable of causing "the end of nature" is an act of great hubris, for it means forgetting the wildness that dwells everywhere within and around us.

Learning to honor the wild—learning to remember and acknowledge the autonomy of the Other—means striving for critical self-consciousness in all of our actions. It means that deep reflection act of use, and means too that we must always consider the possibility of non-use. It means looking at the part of nature we intend to turn toward our own ends and asking whether we can use it again and again and again—sustainably—without its being diminished in the process. It means never imagining that we can flee into a mythical wilderness to escape history and the obligation to take responsibility for our own actions that history inescapably entails. Most of all, it means practicing remembrance and gratitude, for thanksgiving is the simplest and most basic of ways for us to recollect the nature the culture, and the history that have come together to make the world as we know it. If wildness can stop being (just) out there and start being (also) in here, if it can start being as humane as it is natural, then perhaps we can get on with the unending task of struggling to live rightly in the world—not just in the garden, not just in the wilderness, but in the home that encompasses them both.

Considerations

Thinking

Why does Cronon want people to rethink the concept of wilderness? What, for Cronon, is the trouble with how many people currently and conventionally think of "wilderness"?

How does Cronon define "wilderness," and how does he distinguish it from "wildness"? Is this a valid and useful distinction? Why or why not?

What does Cronon suggest about the relationship between nature and culture?

Connecting

Cronon relates contemporary ideas about wilderness to ideas about the wild from the past. To that end he quotes a number of writers, including Wordsworth and Thoreau. What is his purpose in doing so?

Use Cronon's ideas about wilderness and the wild in connection with your reading of either Dillard's "Living like Weasels" or Grice's "The Black Widow." What relationship do you see between Cronon's ideas and Dillard's or Grice's essay?

Writing

Write an essay in which you explore the meaning(s) and significance of a term important in contemporary environmentalism. Some possibilities: *environment* or *environmental, ecology* or *ecological, nature* or *natural.*

Visit the Nature Company and then write an essay that explains and explores the idea of nature purveyed there.

Arthur C. Danto
(b. 1924)

Arthur C. Danto is the Johnsonian Professor of Philosophy at Columbia University. His work is distinguished by the ease and elegance that accompany his moves across academic disciplines. He is the art critic for *The Nation* and the author of several books of philosophy, including *The Philosophical Disenfranchisement of Art, Narration and Knowledge,* and *Connection to the World.* He is the recipient of the Lionel Trilling Award and the George S. Polk Award for criticism, Guggenheim Fellowships, and two appointments as a Fulbright scholar.

In "Gettysburg," Danto examines Civil War memorial art in general and the Gettysburg battlefield in particular as a way of exploring the moral boundaries of war.

Gettysburg

Then the whole of things might be different
From what it was thought to be in the beginning,
before an angel bandaged the field glasses.

JOHN ASHBERY

Pity-and-terror, the classically prescribed emotional response to tragic representation, was narrowly restricted to drama by the ancient authorities. In my view, tragedy has a wider reference by far, and pity-and-terror is aroused in me by works of art immeasurably less grand than those which unfold the cosmic undoings of Oedipus and Agamemnon, Antigone, Medea, and the women of Troy. The standard Civil War memorial, for example, is artistically banal by almost any criterion, and yet I am subject to pity-and-terror whenever I reflect upon the dense ironies it embodies. I am touched that the same figures appear and reappear in much the same monument from village to village, from commons to green to public square, across the American landscape. The sameness only deepens the conveyed tragedy, for it is evidence that those who subscribed funds for memorials, who ordered their bronze or cast-iron cement effigies from catalogues or from traveling sales representatives, so that the same soldier, carrying the same musket, flanked by the same cannons and set off by the same floral or patriotic decorations, were blind to the tragedy that is, for me, the most palpable quality of these cenotaphs. That blindness is a component of the tragedy inherent in the terrible juxtaposition of the most deadly armaments and ordnance known up to that time, with what, under those conditions, was the most vulnerably clad soldiery in history.

The Civil War infantryman is portrayed in his smart tunic and foraging cap. Take away the musket, the bayonet and the cartridge case, and he would be some uniformed functionary—messenger, conductor, bellhop, doorman. This was the uniform he fought in, as we know from countless drawings and photographs that have come down to us from the Civil War. Armed, carrying a knapsack, he moved across the battlefield as though on dress parade. But the weapons he faced were closer in design and cold effectiveness to those standard in the First World War, fifty years in his future, than to those confronted by Napoleon's troops at the Battle of Waterloo, fifty years in his past. What moves me is the contradiction between the code of military conduct, symbolically present in his garments but absent from his gun. We see, instead of the chivalry and romanticism of war as a form of art, the chill implacable indifference to any consideration other than maiming and death, typical of the kind of total combat the Civil War became. That contradiction was invisible when the memorials were raised, and it is its invisibility today that moves me to pity-and-terror.

The rifled musket—one with a helically grooved bore giving a stabilizing spin to the bullet and making possible a flat trajectory—was known in the eighteenth century, but it was used then primarily for hunting. The smooth-bore musket was military issue. There is an affecting Yankee pragmatism in the fact that the citizen-soldiers of the American Revolution should have used their hunting weapons to such effect against the celebrated "Brown Bess"—a smooth-bore musket with its barrel shortened and browned—that the rifled musket had to be adopted by British and European armies. But the Brown Bess had been Wellington's weapon in Belgium, in the style of warfare conducted on the classical battlefield, with disciplined infantry firing in ranks at short distance: a row of blasts from these muskets, as from deadly popguns, could be pretty effective in stopping or driving back an opposed line. Even the rifled musket, at that time, used the round ball. The elongated, cylindroconoidal bullet was invented only afterward, by Captain John Norton, in 1823, and though it has been acclaimed as the greatest military invention since the flintlock, Wellington could not see how it improved on the Brown Bess, as indeed it did not if battle were conducted as Wellington understood it. The elongated bullet, with its lowered wind resistance making its charge much more powerful, was understood by Sir William Napier as profoundly altering the nature of infantry, turning the infantry soldier into a "long-range assassin." Napier intuited that a change in the conduct of battle at any point would entail a change at every point—like what Heidegger calls a *Zeugganzes*—a complex of instruments, men and arms forming a total system which functions *as* a totality. Napier's objection implies the very code that the Civil War uniform embodies, and defines a certain moral boundary, the other side of which is not war so much as slaughter. Rifling, the Norton bullet and the percussion cap, established as superior to the flintlock by 1839, certainly changed the face of warfare. There was no room in the new complex for the cavalry charge, as had to be learned in the Charge of the Light Brigade in 1854, and relearned in the Civil War. In any case, the standard Civil War issue was the 1861-model Springfield rifle: percussion lock, muzzle-loading, .58 caliber, shooting a 480-grain conical Minié bullet. It was effective at a thousand yards, deadly accurate at three hundred. The smooth-bore was of limited effectiveness at one hundred to one hundred twenty yards. Civil War soldiers faced the kind of fire that made obsolete the way they were used by generals who learned about battle at West Point and had studied the Napoleonic paradigms. The guns faithfully depicted in the Civil War memorial statue made the style and gallantry of the men who carried them obsolete. Even the brass button would be a point of vulnerability in battles to come.

The 1903 and 1917 Springfield models were used by American infantry in the First World War. Increased muzzle velocity flattened trajectory; the ammunition clip, easy to change, speeded charging the magazine. But those rifles were fired over the cusp of trenches and the steel helmets protected the riflemen's heads. Of course, helmets have existed since ancient times and, in fact, were worn by Prussian and Austrian observers at Gettysburg, though more for ostentation than protection. They were brightly polished. "The sword carries greater honor than the shield" could be repeated by a military historian in very recent years, giving a reason why Robert E. Lee should have achieved greater honor through losing glamorously than his opponent, George Meade, earned through winning stolidly, by fighting a defensive battle. Lee had been mocked as "The King of Spades" when he used entrenchments at Chancellorsville. The steel helmet reduced injuries in the First World War by about seventy-five percent. The casualties at Gettysburg, for the three days of the battle, totaled about 51,000, of which 7,058 were outright deaths. The Roman legions were better protected, and their sanitary conditions were better than those prevailing in the 1860s. A wound in the July heat festered and went gangrenous quickly. There were 33,264 wounded. The wagon train that carried the Confederate wounded away under driving rains on July 5 was seventeen miles long. Over 10,000 were unaccounted for, and I suppose their bones would still be turned up at Gettysburg had the battlefield not become a military park. In any case I am uncertain they would have worn helmets if they had had them, for they were men who lived and died by an exalted concept of honor. You went to your death like a soldier, head held high under your jaunty cap. "As he passed me he rode gracefully," Longstreet wrote, years after, of Pickett leading his stupendous charge, "with his jaunty cap raked well over on his right ear and his long auburn locks, nicely dressed, hanging almost to his shoulders. He seemed rather a holiday soldier than the general at the head of a column which was about to make one of the grandest, most desperate assaults recorded in the annals of war." Longstreet thought the great charge a terrible mistake. He thought Lee wrong from the start at Gettysburg. Lee was deaf to Longstreet for the same reason that mourners and patriots across America were blind to the message of their memorials. Longstreet is my hero.

I recently trudged the battle lines at Gettysburg. The scene of that great collision had, according to the architectural historian Vincent Scully, been transformed by the National Park Service into a work of art, and I was curious to see, in the first instance, how the locus of agony and glory should have been preserved and transfigured under the glass bell of aesthetic distance into a memorial object. An interest in memorial art and in the moral boundaries of war would have sufficed to move me as a pilgrim to what, since the Gettysburg Address, we have thought of as consecrated ground. But I had also been enough unsettled by a recent remark of Gore Vidal's that had come up in the civil strife between *Commentary* and *The Nation,* in regard to Norman Podhoretz's patriotism, to want to think out for myself whether, as Vidal claimed, the American Civil War is our Trojan War. Podhoretz had pretended to a greater interest in the Wars of the Roses than in the Civil War, and this had greatly exercised Vidal, whose family had participated on both sides and thus had internalized the antagonisms that divided the nation. The Trojan War was not of course a civil conflict. A better paradigm might have been the epic wars between the Pandavas and Kauravas, as recounted in the *Mahabharata* and given moral urgency in the *Bhagavad Gita,* where the fact that it is a *civil* war was deemed by the great warrior Arjuna—until he was persuaded otherwise by the god Krishna—a compelling reason not to fight. No one's remembered ancestors participated in the Trojan War when it in fact was their Trojan War in the sense Vidal must have intended, when the Homeric poems had emerged out of the mists to define the meaning of life, strife, love and honor for a whole civilization. The Civil War, if it were to be our Trojan War in that sense, would have to be so even for those whose families were elsewhere and indifferent when it took place. It has not received literary embodiment of the right sort to affect American consciousness as the *Iliad* affected Greek consciousness (Troy affected Roman consciousness through the *Aeneid*). And so a further question that directed me was whether the artistic embodiment of a battlefield into a military park might serve to make it our Trojan War in the required way, where one could not pretend an indifference to it because it was now the matrix of our minds and our beings.

Like Tewkesbury, where the climactic battle of the Wars of the Roses took place in 1471, the name Gettysburg has an irresistibly comic sound, good for a giggle in music hall or vaudeville. It could, like Podunk, serve as everyone's name for Nowheresville, the boondocks, the sticks. It was one of hundreds of "-burgs" and "-villes" named after forgotten worthies (James Gettys had been given the site by William Penn), indicating, before the place "became terrible"—Bruce Catton's phrase—simply where life went on. Gettysburg in 1863 was the seat of Adams County and a poky grove of Academe, with a college and a seminary. But Gettysburg was no Troy: the battle was *at* but not *for* Gettysburg. When Lee withdrew on July 5, its 2,400 inhabitants had ten times that number of dead and wounded to deal with, not to mention mounds of shattered horses: the miasma of putrefaction hung over the town until winter. Gettysburg became host to a cemetery large in proportion to its size, though there is a strikingly prophetic Romanesque gatehouse at Evergreen Cemetery, which gave its name to Cemetery Hill and Cemetery Ridge, and which seemed waiting to welcome the alien dead: you can see artillery emplacements in front of it in a surviving photograph. You can count the houses in Gettysburg in another photograph of the time, looking east from Seminary Ridge. That the battle was there, between Cemetery Ridge and Seminary Ridge, was an artifact of the war. Gettysburg was not somebody's prize. Longstreet called it "ground of no value." It was a good place for a battle, but though it is clear that there had to be a battle someplace soon, it could have happened in any number of other burgs or villes. Meade, knowing there was to be a battle, would have preferred Pipes Creek as its site. Lee was heading for Harrisburg, a serious city and the capital of the state, and decided to *accept* battle instead, knowing he would have to do so somewhere, and Gettysburg, by geological accident, was as good a place as any to fight.

In his novel *Lincoln,* Gore Vidal puts Mary Lincoln in the War Room with her husband. She is supposed to have had, according to the novel, a certain military intuition, and Vidal describes her looking at a map, pointing to the many roads leading in and out of Gettysburg, and saying, in effect, My goodness—whoever controls Gettysburg controls everything. Perhaps this in fact is intended to underscore Mary Lincoln's acute frivolity: if it meant, really, to show how the mind of a general got lodged in the pretty head of the President's wife, it simply shows the limits of Vidal's own military intuition. Gettysburg was not that kind of place. It was not, for example, like Monte Cassino, anchoring a line because it controlled roads up the Italian peninsula, so that when it fell, its defenders were obliged to fall back to the next line of defense. Gettysburg really *was* nowhere, of no importance and no consequence: like Waterloo it was illuminated by the sheer *Geworfenheit* of war. The essence of war is accident.

This is how it happened to happen there. It was known in Washington in late June that Lee was somewhere in Pennsylvania, but not known where he was exactly. Despite the telegraph and the *New York Times,* there is a sense in which men were as much in the dark in regard to one another's whereabouts as they might have been in England in the fifteenth century, fighting the Wars of the Roses. Lee had heard rumors that the Army of the Potomac was somewhere east of him, but he had no clear idea of where. This, too, was a matter of accident. In classical warfare, the cavalry served as the eyes of the army. But Lee's glamorous and vain cavalry leader, Jeb Stuart, was off on a toot of his own, seeking personal glory. He turned up only on the last day of the battle of Gettysburg, trailing some useless trophies. Buford, a Union cavalry general, sent out to look for the suspected Confederate troops, more or less bumped into General Pettigrew's brigade marching along the Chambersburg Pike into Gettysburg to requisition shoes. They collided, as it were, in the fog, and each sent word that the enemy was near. Buford perceived that it was good ground for a battle and sent for reinforcements. Lee perceived that it was a good *moment* for battle and began to concentrate his forces. It happened very fast: the next day was the first day of the engagement, July 1.

Here is Longstreet's description of the site:

> Gettysburg lies partly between Seminary Ridge on the West and Cemetery Ridge on the South-east, a distance of about fourteen hundred yards dividing the crests of the two ridges.

This is a soldier's description, not the imagined description of a novelist's personage: you can deduce the necessary orders to infantry and artillery from Longstreet's single sentence. The battle seethed and boiled between the two ridges, as if they were its containing walls. Gettysburg had the bad luck to lie partly between the ridges. It had the good luck to lie between them *partly*. There was only one accidental, civilian death: the battle took place, mainly, to the south of the village. The ridges formed two facing natural ramparts, as though two feudal lords had built their walls within catapult distance of each other.

GETTYSBURG • JULY 3, 1863 • 2:30 P.M.

To visualize the terrain, draw a vertical line and label it Seminary Ridge. This is where the Confederate Army formed its line, along the crest. They seized it after a heated battle with Buford's forces, which, despite reinforcements, were driven fourteen hundred yards east to Cemetery Ridge. Now draw a line parallel and to the right of Seminary Ridge, only curve it to the right at the top, to form a sort of fishhook. This was the shape of the Union line, indeed called "The Fish-hook," on July 2 and 3. (Gettysburg is a dot between the lines, just about where the hook begins its curve.) Where the barb would be is Culp's Hill. Farther back along the shaft is Cemetery Hill. At the eye of the hook is Big Round Top, at a distance of about four miles from Cemetery Hill. About half its height, and upshaft, is Little Round Top. The four hills served as battle towers. The rampart itself slopes to the west to form what is designated a *glacis* in the vocabulary of fortification. It was a formidable defensive position, but Seminary Ridge too would have been a formidable defensive position. "If we could only take position here and have them attack us through this open ground!" Lee's chief of artillery, Porter Alexander, recalled having thought. "We were in no such luck—the boot, in fact, being upon the other foot." A defensive war was not what had brought Lee north and onto enemy territory. He had to attack if there was to be battle.

Longstreet did not think there needed to be battle. Standing beside Lee, he surveyed the Union position with his field glasses for a very long time, turned to Lee and said,

> If we could have chosen a point to meet our plans of operation, I do not think we could have found a better one than that upon which they are now concentrating. All we have to do is throw our army around by their left, and we shall interpose between the Federal Army and Washington. We can get a strong position and wait, and if they fail to attack us we shall have everything in condition to move back tomorrow night in the direction of Washington.

"No," said General Lee—the words are famous and fateful—"the enemy is there and I am going to attack him there."

Perhaps Longstreet was wrong: Meade was as cautious a man as he. Why need Meade have attacked them, even though between Washington and its army? Lee's supply line was long and vulnerable, and Meade might have ringed any position he would take and wait out a siege. Still, wars are fought not so much by generals as by governments, and Longstreet knew that Washington would pressure Meade to attack, needing a victory and in fear for Washington itself. And Lee was probably right: if he could crush Meade's army here, where it was, he would have free access to Washington or Baltimore or Philadelphia. He needed or thought he needed a *brilliant* victory. He had invaded the North not for conquest but to astonish. And he could sustain a defeat as Meade could not. If Meade were defeated, pressure to negotiate would be exerted on Lincoln by the Peace Party in the Union. There might be foreign recognition. And morale would have been disastrously lowered since the Union had just undergone a series of brutal defeats. He might, on the symbolic date of July Fourth, achieve independence for the South.

Whereas if he lost at Gettysburg, well, he could have swaggered back to his own territory, as after a dashing raid, trailing glory. Besides, rounding the Federal left would have baffled his troops, who had driven the enemy back to that position. Morale is a precious factor, a form of power. Lee would have to *smash* the Union left. He would have to take Little Round Top, as he nearly succeeded in doing on the second day of battle.

A battlefield has something of the metaphysical complexity of a work of art: it stands to the terrain on which it is spread as a work of art stands to the physical object to which it belongs. Not every part of the physical object is really a part of the work of art—we do not take the weave of canvas into consideration in identifying the meaning of a picture, for example, since there is no coherent way in which we can read the roughness of his surfaces into, say, the iconographic program of Tintoretto's Scuola di San Rocco. We rarely consider the fact that a surface is dry when interpreting a painting. Richard Wollheim, in his recent Mellon Lectures, borrowed from phenomenology the useful term "thematization," and would use it to say that not every part or property of the physical object is "thematized" by the work. Doubtless the concept can be taken further—I am seeking to thematize the contradiction, which most would not even see as there, in Civil War memorial statuary. But what I want to say here is that battle thematizes certain features of the terrain, transforming them into what soldiers call "ground." At Gettysburg, the flanking hills of the Federal line were thematized in this sense on the second day of battle; Cemetery Hill and the sweep of field and meadow between the ridges were thematized on the third and last day. It is doubtful the two ridges would have been so thematized in an imagined encounter between Napoleon and Wellington: their artillery would not have reached far enough, and besides, the explosive shell had not been invented in 1815. (Its invention meant the end of the wooden battleship.) What would be the point of lobbing cannon balls across the fields? One follows the structure of battle by grasping successive thematizations. War is a deadly artist. A battlefield is already more than halfway to a work of art.

On July 2, Lee strove to take either or both Culp's Hill and Little Round Top. Meade's defensive line along Cemetery Ridge would have been untenable had Lee succeeded: he would have had to draw back to Pipes Creek, and it would have been a defeat. The fighting that afternoon was fierce but uncoordinated—each commander had difficulties with his generals—and the outcome of the engagement was sufficiently ambiguous that Lee could interpret it as a victory. Still, no thanks to General Daniel Sickles, the tempestuous Federal general who had left Little Round Top undefended, both the contested hills remained, it may have seemed precariously, in Union hands. Had Meade's engineering chief, Gouverneur Warren, not happened to see that no one was holding the crest at Little Round Top and on his own authority diverted troops to its defense in the very nick of time, the outcome of that day's fighting would have been different.

It is worth contemplating Little Round Top from the perspective of weaponry. Little Round Top was called "the Rocky Hill" by the Confederates—armies improvise a nomenclature with their thematizations. Its slopes are strewn with heavy boulders of the kind that, piled up, gave the name "Devil's Den" to an adjacent site. It is full of ad hoc shelters and one-man fortresses, and offers an object lesson in the military imagination. It cried out for a kind of weapon—the grenade—which was to be indispensable to infantry in the World Wars but which was considered extinct at the time of the Civil War because of the increase in range and accuracy of muzzled arms. Grenades had been intensely employed in seventeenth-century tactics (when a grenadier was a special physical type, like a shot-putter). It came into its own again in the Russo-Japanese war. The field mortar, with its high trajectory, would also have done wonders at Devil's Den, with its freestone breastworks and God-given sniper nests. Civil War battle seems to have been imagined as something that takes place on a field, between massed armies. The grenade and mortar, conceived of as suited to storming fortresses, were inscrutable in 1863, even though all the technology was in place for the manufacture of the lightweight grenades that re-entered the armory half a century later. The weaponry determined the order of thematization, and particularly the field between the ridges on which Pickett's charge was to take place on July 3 was something generals understood or thought they understood. Longstreet knew they did not.

On July 3, Lee had determined to attack Meade's center. This was his reasoning: Meade, he believed, would infer that Lee was seeking to turn his flanks and would renew the attack on the anchoring hills. So Meade would move reinforcements to right and left, leaving the center weak. Meade's reasoning was this: Lee would reason as he in fact reasoned, so the right thing was to reinforce the center. In classical warfare there is a kind of language—armies communicate through guns (as the United States and the Soviet Union today communicate through nuclear testing): a cannonade announces a charge. All that morning the Federal officers and men watched the enemy concentrate its artillery—150 guns focused on the Union center. "A magnificent sight," according to Henry Hunt, chief of artillery on the Union side: "Never before had such a sight been witnessed on this continent, and rarely, if ever, abroad." The Union employed about 200 pieces in that battle, and a duel opened up at about 1 P.M. that lasted nearly two hours: nothing on that scale had ever taken place before. But the state of explosive chemistry in the mid-nineteenth century raised severe cognitive problems for the Confederate force. What was used then was black gunpowder, which created dense smoke. The exploding shells cast a smoke screen over Cemetery Ridge, concealing from Confederate artillery chief Porter Alexander that he was shooting too high, and that his shells were falling behind the Union line. By accident, he hit a dozen caissons of ammunition to Meade's rear. Union Major General Hunt decided to conserve ammunition for the attack to come, and ordered fire to cease. Alexander took this as a sign that he had silenced the Federal guns, and signaled Pickett to move forward. Smoke still hung blackly over Cemetery Ridge, but at a certain moment of no return a breeze lifted it and Pickett's men saw, in Allan Nevins's words, "the full panoply of Union strength in its terrifying grandeur, a double line of infantry in front, guns frowning beside them, and reserves in thick platoons further back." Until that moment, none of Lee's officers had any real idea of what power had been building up behind the sullen ridge. Had his cavalry been operative, Lee would not have charged. He fought blind.

It was in Pickett's grand charge up the slopes of Cemetery Ridge that the tragic contradiction between arms and uniform became palpable. Pickett's superb veterans, fresh in this battle, marched according to a magnificent code into a wall of fire. It was the brutal end to an era of warfare, the last massed charge. The triumph of slaughter over chivalry gave rise to Sherman's horrifying march through Georgia and South Carolina, to total war, to the firebombing of Dresden, to Hiroshima and Nagasaki, to the rolled grenade in the full jetliner. "It was the most beautiful thing I ever saw," exclaimed Colonel Fremantle, a British observer at Longstreet's side. The sentiment was widely shared. Pickett's charge was what war was all about in that era; it had the kind of beauty that made Lee remark, at the Battle of Fredericksburg, "It is well that war is so terrible—we should grow too fond of it." Longstreet wrote: "That day at Gettysburg was one of the saddest in my life." I think he was more or less alone in this feeling. I do not think Gettysburg was perceived as the awful defeat it was by the South, at least not then, since news of Grant's victory at Vicksburg had not yet come, nor do I think it was received as a great victory, least of all in Washington, or by Lincoln, who cared only that Meade should press his advantage. What no one could see, just because the doors of the future always are closed, was that beauty on that occasion was only the beginning of terror.

The bodies were rolled into shallow trenches, and the armies moved off to other encounters. Some 3,500 Union dead are today neatly buried in concentric arcs alongside Evergreen Cemetery. Seventeen acres were set aside for this, weeks after the battle, and it was here, before the landscaping was altogether completed, that Lincoln delivered the address which is so enshrined in the national consciousness today that it requires an effort of severe deconstruction to perceive it as a cry of victory as gloating as anything that issued from the coarse throat of Ajax. The Gettysburg Battlefield Memorial Association was chartered in 1864 and began acquiring land which was absorbed into the National Military Park established, without debate so far as I can discover, by an act of Congress in 1895. In 1933 it came under the jurisdiction of the National Park Service, which transformed it in an unforgiving way. There is an historical preservation I applaud but a political overlay that distresses me.

It is always moving to visit a battlefield when the traces of war itself have been erased by nature or transfigured by art, and to stand amid memorial weapons, which grow inevitably quaint and ornamental with the evolution of armamentary technology, mellowing under patinas and used, now, to punctuate the fading thematizations of strife. The first cannon to be fired at the Battle of Gettysburg stands by the memorial to Buford near MacPherson's Farm, like a capital letter to mark the beginning of a ferocious sentence. Four cannons form Cushing's battery stand, like four exclamation points, to mark its end at the point where Pickett's men penetrated the Union line only to be surrounded. General Francis Walker uses a Homeric metaphor to describe Pickett's charge:

> As the spear of Menelaus pierced the shield of his antagonist, cut through the shining breastplate, but spared the life, so the division of Pickett, launched from Seminary Ridge, broke through the Union defense, and for the moment thrust its head of column within our lines, threatening destruction to the Army of the Potomac.

When I was a soldier, I was often struck, as by a paradox, that at the very moment that artillery was pounding somewhere, somewhere else men and women in soft clothing were touching glasses and carrying on flirtations; and that before and after this moment, but in this place, the peaceful pursuit of human purposes would go innocently forward, that families would picnic where men were being killed. And I was overwhelmed after the war by the thick peace that had settled back over places I had seen sharded: Salerno, Velletri, Cassino, Anzio. There is that sense today at Gettysburg, as tourists consult their maps and point across to not very distant hills and ridges, or listen to patient guides rehearse the drama of those three days in July 1863. The statue of General Lee, on his elegant horse, Traveller, stands just where Lee himself stood, and faces, across the open field traversed by Pickett's division, to where an appropriately less flamboyant effigy of Meade looks west from Cemetery Ridge. The copse of trees that Lee had singled out as the point to head for still stands not far from Meade's statue, segregated by an iron fence, as if a sacred grove. Ranks of cannons point across, from ridge to ridge, and the sites are strewn with touching, simple monuments, placed by the units that were there so that it would always be remembered that they were there. The most florid monument celebrates the Pennsylvania presence (there are 537 Pennsylvanians buried in the National Cemetery, and 867 New Yorkers—the largest representation by state there). There is an art history of Gettysburg to be written, but the meaning that comes through, even without it, is that a momentous collision occurred here, and that it was connected with the high and generous feelings that are appropriate, after a battle, between those who fought it.

The Park Service's pamphlet of 1950 recommends an itinerary with fourteen stops—it maps onto the Stations of the Cross if you have an appetite for numerical correspondences. It is chronological. You begin where the battle began, at MacPherson's Ridge at 8 A.M. on July 1. You now follow a trail south along Seminary Ridge, and you may pause in front of Lee's statue and recite the thought Faulkner insisted was in the breast of every Southern boy: it is, there, eternally "still not yet two o'clock on that July afternoon in 1863." Edging the Peach Orchard, where Sickles formed a reckless salient and lost a leg, you mount Round Top and head north to The Copse of Trees and Meade's headquarters. You pause at the cemetery and end, not quite appropriately, at Culp's Hill. In 1950, as today, you would leave 1863 from time to time and enter the present, for the acreage of the Battle Park is intersected, here and there, with fragments of mere unthematized Pennsylvania, along whose roads tractors and trucks drive past restaurants and service stations on one or another civilian errand. The almost cubist interpenetration of past and present, war and peace, is semiotically moving in its own right.

The itinerary of 1950 was dropped from revised editions of the pamphlet, in 1954 and 1962, and today the visit has a different structure. Today you enter the park, amidst many monuments, along "High-Water Mark Trail." There are no Confederate markers among the celebratory monuments: instead, there is "High-Water Mark Monument," erected by "us" to show how far "they" reached. It was not really a high-water mark. There was no flood: this was not Genghis Khan, but one of the gentlest occupations the world has ever seen. It was, exactly as General Walker put it, a spear point which penetrated but did not slay—a Homeric poet would have supposed a god or goddess deflected the weapon. Lee was the spearman—Menelaus, if the analogy appeals (except Menelaus triumphed). If we construe the Military Park as a monumentary text, it now reads *not* as the history of a great battle between heroic adversaries, but as the victory of the Union. The text begins where the victory was won. As a text, the park is now a translation into historical landscape of the Gettysburg Address. Small wonder it "fell like a wet blanket," as Lincoln afterward said. Small wonder the *Harrisburg Patriot* editorialized the "silly remarks" this way: "For the credit of the Nation we are willing that the veil of oblivion shall be dropped and that they shall be no more repeated or thought of." Half the men who fell there did not fight for what Lincoln said was achieved there, and of those who might have, Lincoln's were not in every case the reasons they were there. It was an inappropriate political speech on an occasion that called for generosity, vaunting and confessional. The language is concealingly beautiful, evidence that Auden is after all right that time worships language "and forgives / Everyone by whom it lives."

I can understand, or might be able to understand, how a literary scholar, though patriotic, might find the Wars of the Roses of greater interest than the American Civil War, even if he should have no special concern with the ambitions of Lancaster and York. Henry VI, the subject of an early tragedy of Shakespeare, founded Kings College, Cambridge. But the main reason, I should think, for being interested in the civil wars of the fifteenth century in England is connected with one main reason for being interested in our Civil War. The Wars of the Roses were of an unparalleled brutality and were fought by mercenaries. It was total warfare, and the sickening experience of having one's land run over by one's countrymen but acting like brigands and in the royal pay lingered for centuries in British consciousness. Henry VI also founded Eton, on whose playing fields the British Empire is said to have been won by practices governed by the rules of fair combat and respect for the opponent. The unspeakable conduct of battle on the Continent—think of the Thirty Years War—until the eighteenth century, when Anglicization began to define the moral outlines of military conduct, must have confirmed the legacy of the Wars of the Roses in the English mind.

My sense is that the high-minded perception of the soldierly vocation is embodied in the uniform, the insignia, the flags and the vulnerability of the militia depicted in sculpture of the Civil War. The other form of war is embodied in the weapons. If there is a high-water mark in the history of modern war, it was in Pickett's gallant and foregone assault. It has been growing darker and darker ever since. I am not certain this is a basis for seeing the Civil War as "our" Trojan War. In a sense, something is not a Trojan War if it is *ours*: the Trojan War speaks to what is universal and human, regardless of political division and national culture. I am not certain that the idea of Union has any more meaning than or as much meaning as Helen of Troy, as justification for pitched combat. If the Civil War is to address humanity as the Trojan War does, it must itself be addressed at a different level than any that has so far been reached. Gettysburg is a good place to begin.

Considerations

Thinking

What do you think Danto means by "the triumph of slaughter over chivalry" in this sentence about Pickett's charge at Cemetery Ridge: "The triumph of slaughter over chivalry gave rise to Sherman's horrifying march through Georgia and South Carolina, to total war, to the firebombing of Dresden, to Hiroshima and Nagasaki, to the rolled grenade in the full jetliner"? What does that phrase about slaughter and chivalry have to do with those Civil War memorials that interest Danto so profoundly?

What is Danto's complaint about the "concealingly beautiful" language of Lincoln's Gettysburg Address, and what does that complaint have to do with what Danto calls (borrowing Richard Wollheim's language from phenomenology) "thematization"?

Connecting

Throughout this essay, Danto refers to other wars, especially the Trojan War. How does he make use of those other wars, and why does he object so much to Gore Vidal's notion that Gettysburg was "our" Trojan War?

Consider these stanzas from Robert Lowell's poem "For the Union Dead":

> On a thousand small town New England greens,
> the old white church holds their air
> of sparse, sincere rebellion; frayed flags
> quilt the graveyards of the Grand Army of the Republic.

> The stone statues of the abstract Union Soldier
> grow slimmer and younger each year—
> wasp-waisted, they doze over muskets
> and muse through their sideburns . . .

What do you think Danto would say to Lowell about this image of the soldiers? What do you think Lowell would say to Danto about his essay?

Writing

After reading Lincoln's Gettysburg Address, write a letter to Danto about his assessment of the address, explaining why you agree or disagree with that assessment.

Go to a military battlefield or to a museum that contains the artifacts of war. Select one artifact, research it, and write an essay about an idea of yours that arises from your research and reflection.

Joan Didion
(b. 1934)

Joan Didion is a writer of great diversity. She has published five nonfiction works: *Slouching Toward Bethlehem, The White Album, Salvador, Miami,* and *After Henry;* four novels: *Run River, Play It As It Lays, The Book of Common Prayer,* and *Democracy;* and sketches, reviews, and screenplays. In all of Didion's work, there is a subtle, understated longing for a less complex, more stable world than the one we live in, but there is no whining, no refusal to go forward. Neither is hers a solipsistic vision. Facing the personal, facing the self, is to face the world on the barest of terms: alone.

We catch glimpses of Didion's toughness by the way she writes about and admires Georgia O'Keeffe's "hardness." She turns that hardness into something far more intriguing than fluttering eyelashes and submissiveness. And in "On Self-Respect" Didion confronts the difficulty and necessity of living according to one's convictions.

Georgia O'Keeffe

"Where I was born and where and how I have lived is unimportant," Georgia O'Keeffe told us in the book of paintings and words published in her ninetieth year on earth. She seemed to be advising us to forget the beautiful face in the Stieglitz photographs. She appeared to be dismissing the rather condescending romance that had attached to her by then, the romance of extreme good looks and advanced age and deliberate isolation. "It is what I have done with where I have been that should be of interest." I recall an August afternoon in Chicago in 1973 when I took my daughter, then seven, to see what Georgia O'Keeffe had done with where she had been. One of the vast O'Keeffe "Sky Above Clouds" [see inserts] canvases floated over the back stairs in the Chicago Art Institute that day, dominating what seemed to be several stories of empty light, and my daughter looked at it once, ran to the landing, and kept on looking. "Who drew it," she whispered after a while. I told her. "I need to talk to her," she said finally.

My daughter was making, that day in Chicago, an entirely unconscious but quite basic assumption about people and the work they do. She was assuming that the glory she saw in the work reflected a glory in its maker, that the painting was the painter as the poem is the poet, that every choice one made alone—every word chosen or rejected, every brush stroke laid or not laid down—betrayed one's character. *Style is character.* It seemed to me that afternoon that I had rarely seen so instinctive an application of this familiar principle, and I recall being pleased not only that my daughter responded to style as character but that it was Georgia O'Keeffe's particular style to which she responded: this was a hard woman who had imposed her 192 square feet of clouds on Chicago.

"Hardness" has not been in our century a quality much admired in women, nor in the past twenty years has it even been in official favor for men. When hardness surfaces in the very old we tend to transform it into "crustiness" or eccentricity, some tonic pepperiness to be indulged at a distance. On the evidence of her work and what she has said about it, Georgia O'Keeffe is neither "crusty" nor eccentric. She is simply hard, a straight shooter, a woman clean of received wisdom and open to what she sees. This is a woman who could early on dismiss most of her contemporaries as "dreamy," and would later single out one she liked as "a very poor painter." (And then add, apparently by way of softening the judg-

200

ment: "I guess he wasn't a painter at all. He had no courage and I believe that to create one's own world in any of the arts takes courage.") This is a woman who in 1939 could advise her admirers that they were missing her point, that their appreciation of her famous flowers was merely sentimental. "When I paint a red hill," she observed coolly in the catalogue for an exhibition that year, "you say it is too bad that I don't always paint flowers. A flower touches almost everyone's heart. A red hill doesn't touch everyone's heart." This is a woman who could describe the genesis of one of her most well-known paintings—the "Cow's Skull: Red, White and Blue" owned by the Metropolitan—as an act of quite deliberate and derisive orneriness. "I thought of the city men I had been seeing in the East," she wrote. "They talked so often of writing the Great American Novel—the Great American Play—the Great American Poetry. . . . So as I was painting my cow's head on blue I thought to myself, 'I'll make it an American painting. They will not think it great with the red stripes down the sides—Red, White and Blue—but they will notice it.'"

The city men. The men. They. The words crop up again and again as this astonishingly aggressive woman tells us what was on her mind when she was making her astonishingly aggressive paintings. It was those city men who stood accused of sentimentalizing her flowers: "I made you take time to look at what I saw and when you took time to really notice my flower you hung all your associations with flowers on my flower and you write about my flower as if I think and see what you think and see—and I don't." *And I don't.* Imagine those words spoken, and the sound you hear is *don't tread on me.* "The men" believed it impossible to paint New York, so Georgia O'Keeffe painted New York. "The men" didn't think much of her bright color, so she made it brighter. The men yearned toward Europe so she went to Texas, and then New Mexico. The men talked about Cézanne, "long involved remarks about the 'plastic quality' of his form and color," and took one another's long involved remarks, in the view of this angelic rattlesnake in their midst, altogether too seriously. "I can paint one of those dismal-colored paintings like the men," the woman who regarded herself always as an outsider remembers thinking one day in 1922, and she did: a painting of a shed "all low-toned and dreary with the tree beside the door." She called this act of rancor "The Shanty" and hung it in her next show. "The men seemed to approve of it," she reported fifty-four years later, her contempt undimmed. "They seemed to think that maybe I was beginning to paint. That was my only low-toned dismal-colored painting."

Some women fight and others do not. Like so many successful guerrillas in the war between the sexes, Georgia O'Keeffe seems to have been equipped early with an immutable sense of who she was and a fairly clear understanding that she would be required to prove it. On the surface her upbringing was conventional. She was a child on the Wisconsin prairie who played with china dolls and painted watercolors with cloudy skies because sunlight was too hard to paint and, with her brother and sisters, listened every night to her mother read stories of the Wild West, of Texas, of Kit Carson and Billy the Kid. She told adults that she wanted to be an artist and was embarrassed when they asked what kind of artist she wanted to be: she had no idea "what kind." She had no idea what artists did. She had never seen a picture that interested her, other than a pen-and-ink Maid of Athens in one of her mother's books, some Mother Goose illustrations printed on cloth, a tablet cover that showed a little girl with pink roses, and the painting of Arabs on horseback that hung in her grandmother's parlor. At thirteen, in a Dominican convent, she was mortified when the sister corrected her drawing. At Chatham Episcopal Institute in Virginia she painted lilacs and sneaked time alone to walk out to where she could see the line of the Blue Ridge Mountains on the horizon. At the Art Institute in Chicago she was shocked by the presence of live models and wanted to abandon anatomy lessons. At the Art Students League in New York one of her fellow students advised her that, since he would be a great painter and she would end up teaching painting in a girls' school, any work of hers was less important than modeling for him. Another painted over her work to show her how the Impressionists did trees. She had not before heard how the Impressionists did trees and she did not much care.

At twenty-four she left all those opinions behind and went for the first time to live in Texas, where there were no trees to paint and no one to tell her how not to paint them. In Texas there was only the horizon she craved. In Texas she had her sister Claudia with her for a while, and in the late afternoons they would walk away from town and toward the horizon and watch the evening star come out. "That evening star fascinated me," she wrote. "It was in some way very exciting to me. My sister had a gun, and as we walked she would throw bottles into the air and shoot as many as she could before they hit the ground. I had nothing but to walk into nowhere and the wide sunset space with the star. Ten watercolors were made from that star." In a way one's interest is compelled as much by the sister Claudia with the gun as by the painter Georgia with the star, but only the painter left us this shining record. Ten watercolors were made from that star.

Considerations

Thinking

What do you think about hardness—"a straight shooter, a woman clean of received wisdom and open to what she sees"—in a woman? In a man?

To what extent does Didion's celebration of O'Keeffe's aggressiveness turn on itself, raising the possibility that O'Keeffe may have needed the men to set her work in motion?

Referring to the men, O'Keeffe makes this judgment: "I made you take time to look at what I saw and when you took time to really notice my flower you hung all your associations with flowers on my flower and you write about my flower as if I think and see what you think and see—and I don't." Aren't we bound inevitably to hang all our associations on whatever we are looking at? To what extent can we ever see what is there before us—seeing the object as it really is?

Connecting

In his famous preface to *The Renaissance,* a collection of essays about painters, Walter Pater says that the critic's primary aim is not—as Matthew Arnold had claimed—to see the object (whether painting, book, poem, personality) as it really is, but to "know one's impression of the object as it really is." Which of these men seems closer to describing the way Didion gives us O'Keeffe's work?

What is the connection between Texas and New Mexico and what *you* see in O'Keeffe's paintings? Do those flowers actually have anything to do with the American southwest? Speculate.

Just how much of Didion do you find in her analysis of O'Keeffe?

Writing

Look at O'Keeffe's "Sky Above Clouds" in the inserts in this book. Go to your college library and look at a collection of O'Keeffe's paintings. Imagine why Didion's seven-year-old daughter, after looking at "Sky Above Clouds," exclaimed to her mother about O'Keeffe, "I need to talk to her." Didion offers an explanation of why she thinks her daughter wanted to see O'Keeffe. Assume that you are Didion's daughter; consider your mother's conjecture, and write your own reasons for wanting to talk to O'Keeffe.

In his essay "Not Looking at Pictures," E. M. Forster says that paintings send him off on "alien visions." He has a hard time holding his imagination to the painting. Select one of O'Keeffe's paintings, focus on just what you can see there in the painting, and write about it. Then set your mind free and write about your associations. Which reaction do you prefer? Explain.

On Self-Respect

Joan Didion

Once, in a dry season, I wrote in large letters across two pages of a notebook that innocence ends when one is stripped of the delusion that one likes oneself. Although now, some years later, I marvel that a mind on the outs with itself should have nonetheless made painstaking record of its every tremor, I recall with embarrassing clarity the flavor of those particular ashes. It was a matter of misplaced self-respect.

I had not been elected to Phi Beta Kappa. This failure could scarcely have been more predictable or less ambiguous (I simply did not have the grades), but I was unnerved by it; I had somehow thought myself a kind of academic Raskolnikov, curiously exempt from the cause-effect relationships which hampered others. Although even the humorless nineteen-year-old that I was must have recognized that the situation lacked real tragic stature, the day that I did not make Phi Beta Kappa nonetheless marked the end of something, and innocence may well be the word for it. I lost the conviction that lights would always turn green for me, the pleasant certainty that those rather passive virtues which had won me approval as a child automatically guaranteed me not only Phi Beta Kappa keys but happiness, honor, and the love of a good man; lost a certain touching faith in the totem power of good manners, clean hair, and proven competence on the Stanford-Binet scale. To such doubtful amulets had my self-respect been pinned, and I faced myself that day with the nonplused apprehension of someone who has come across a vampire and has no crucifix at hand.

Although to be driven back upon oneself is an uneasy affair at best, rather like trying to cross a border with borrowed credentials, it seems to me now the one condition necessary to the beginnings of real self-respect. Most of our platitudes notwithstanding, self-deception remains the most difficult deception. The tricks that work on others count for nothing in that very well-lit back alley where one keeps assignations with oneself: no winning smiles will do here, no prettily drawn lists of good intentions. One shuffles flashily but in vain through one's marked cards—the kindness done for the wrong reason, the apparent triumph which involved no real effort, the seemingly heroic act into which one had been shamed. The dismal fact is that self-respect has nothing to do with the approval of others

—who are, after all, deceived easily enough; has nothing to do with reputation, which, as Rhett Butler told Scarlett O'Hara, is something people with courage can do without.

To do without self-respect, on the other hand, is to be an unwilling audience of one to an interminable documentary that details one's failings, both real and imagined, with fresh footage spliced in for every screening. *There's the glass you broke in anger, there's the hurt on X's face; watch now, this next scene, the night Y came back from Houston, see how you muff this one.* To live without self-respect is to lie awake some night, beyond the reach of warm milk, phenobarbital, and the sleeping hand on the coverlet, counting up the sins of commission and omission, the trusts betrayed, the promises subtly broken, the gifts irrevocably wasted through sloth or cowardice or carelessness. However long we postpone it, we eventually lie down alone in that notoriously uncomfortable bed, the one we make ourselves. Whether or not we sleep in it depends, of course, on whether or not we respect ourselves.

To protest that some fairly improbable people, some people who *could not possibly respect themselves,* seem to sleep easily enough is to miss the point entirely, as surely as those people miss it who think that self-respect has necessarily to do with not having safety pins in one's underwear. There is a common superstition that "self-respect" is a kind of charm against snakes, something that keeps those who have it locked in some unblighted Eden, out of strange beds, ambivalent conversations, and trouble in general. It does not at all. It has nothing to do with the face of things, but concerns instead a separate peace, a private reconciliation. Although the careless, suicidal Julian English in *Appointment in Samarra* and the careless, incurably dishonest Jordan Baker in *The Great Gatsby* seem equally improbable candidates for self-respect, Jordan Baker had it, Julian English did not. With that genius for accommodation more often seen in women than in men, Jordan took her own measure, made her own peace, avoided threats to that peace: "I hate careless people," she told Nick Carraway. "It takes two to make an accident."

Like Jordan Baker, people with self-respect have the courage of their mistakes. They know the price of things. If they choose to commit adultery, they do not then go running, in an access of bad conscience, to receive absolution from the wronged parties; nor do they complain unduly of the unfairness, the undeserved embarrassment, of being named co-respondent. In brief, people with self-respect exhibit a certain toughness, a kind of moral nerve; they display what was once called *character,* a quality which, although approved in the abstract, sometimes loses ground to other, more instantly negotiable virtues. The measure of its slipping prestige is that one tends to think of it only in connection with homely children and United States senators who have been defeated, preferably in the primary, for reelection. Nonetheless, character—the willingness to accept responsibility for one's own life—is the source from which self-respect springs.

Self-respect is something that our grandparents, whether or not they had it, knew all about. They had instilled in them, young, a certain discipline, the sense that one lives by doing things one does not particularly want to do, by putting fears and doubts to one side, by weighing immediate comforts against the possibility of larger, even intangible, comforts. It seemed to the nineteenth century admirable, but not remarkable, that Chinese Gordon put on a clean white suit and held Khartoum against the Mahdi; it did not seem unjust that the way to free land in California involved death and difficulty and dirt. In a diary kept during the winter of 1846, an emigrating twelve-year-old named Narcissa Cornwall noted coolly: "Father was busy reading and did not notice that the house was being filled with strange Indians until Mother spoke about it." Even lacking any clue as to what Mother said, one can scarcely fail to be impressed by the entire incident: the father reading, the Indians filing in, the mother choosing the words that would not alarm, the child duly recording the event and noting further that those particular Indians were not, "fortunately for us," hostile. Indians were simply part of the *donnée*.

In one guise or another, Indians always are. Again, it is a question of recognizing that anything worth having has its price. People who respect themselves are willing to accept the risk that the Indians will be hostile, that the venture will go bankrupt, that the liaison may not turn out to be one in which *every day is a holiday because you're married to me.* They are willing to invest something of themselves; they may not play at all, but when they do play, they know the odds.

That kind of self-respect is a discipline, a habit of mind that can never be faked but can be developed, trained, coaxed forth. It was once suggested to me that, as an antidote to crying, I put my head in a paper bag. As it happens, there is a sound physiological reason, something to do with oxygen, for doing exactly that, but the psychological effect alone is incalculable: it is difficult in the extreme to continue fancying oneself Cathy in *Wuthering Heights* with one's head in a Food Fair bag. There is a similar case for all the small disciplines, unimportant in themselves; imagine maintaining any kind of swoon, commiserative or carnal, in a cold shower.

But those small disciplines are valuable only insofar as they represent larger ones. To say that Waterloo was won on the playing fields of Eton is not to say that Napoleon might have been saved by a crash program in cricket; to give formal dinners in the rain forest would be pointless did not the candlelight flickering on the liana call forth deeper, stronger disciplines, values instilled long before. It is a kind of ritual, helping us to remember who and what we are. In order to remember it, one must have known it.

To have that sense of one's intrinsic worth which constitutes self-respect is potentially to have everything: the ability to discriminate, to love and to remain indifferent. To lack it is to be locked within oneself, paradoxically incapable of either love or indifference. If we do not respect ourselves, we are on the one hand forced to despise those who have so few resources as to consort with us, so little perception as to remain blind to our fatal weaknesses. On the other, we are peculiarly in thrall to everyone we see, curiously determined to live out—since our self-image is untenable—their false notions of us. We flatter ourselves by thinking this compulsion to please others an attractive trait: a gist for imaginative empathy, evidence of our willingness to give. *Of course* I will play Francesca to your Paolo, Helen Keller to anyone's Annie Sullivan: no expectation is too misplaced, no role too ludicrous. At the mercy of those we cannot but hold in contempt, we play roles doomed to failure before they are begun, each defeat generating fresh despair at the urgency of divining and meeting the next demand made upon us.

It is the phenomenon sometimes called "alienation from self." In its advanced stages, we no longer answer the telephone, because someone might want something; that we could say *no* without drowning in self-reproach is an idea alien to this game. Every encounter demands too much, tears the nerves, drains the will, and the specter of something as small as an unanswered letter arouses such disproportionate guilt that answering it becomes out of the question. To assign unanswered letters their proper weight, to free us from the expectations of others, to give us back to ourselves—there lies the great, the singular power of self-respect. Without it, one eventually discovers the final turn of the screw: one runs away to find oneself, and finds no one at home.

Considerations

Thinking

Does Didion actually define the term "self-respect"? What are the characteristic qualities or features that Didion includes in her discussion of self-respect? Can you add any others? To what extent is self-respect "a kind of ritual"? Why do you think Didion begins by discussing what she calls "misplaced self-respect"?

Connecting

What is the relationship between what Didion identifies as "small disciplines" and "larger ones"?

Use "On Self-Respect" to analyze the character of Georgia O'Keeffe in Didion's essay about this modern American painter. To what extent does O'Keeffe embody the qualities Didion identifies as characterizing self-respect?

Writing

Write a letter to Didion responding to her discussion of self-respect. You can explain why you agree with certain things she says in the essay. You may wish to question or challenge some of Didion's ideas and assumptions. You might also identify other qualities you think are essential for self-respect, or you might provide additional examples. Select another abstract term, such as "integrity" or "courage," and write an essay exploring what the term means in practice. Choose your examples from your experience, observation, and reading.

Annie Dillard
(b. 1945)

Annie Dillard has taught creative writing at Wesleyan University in Connecticut. She lived for a time in Roanoke, Virginia, a setting she used to wonderful effect in her first book, *Pilgrim at Tinker Creek,* which won a Pulitzer Prize. Since then, Dillard has spent quite a lot of time living on Puget Sound, as well as writing a number of books, including *Living by Fiction,* a critical study; *Teaching a Stone to Talk,* a collection of essays; and *An American Childhood,* a portion of her autobiography. Dillard's essays can be demanding both intellectually and emotionally.

Her essay "Living Like Weasels" is both surprising and intellectually provocative. One of its most notable features is its images suggesting the weasel's tenacity—images that Dillard introduces in the opening paragraphs of her essay.

Living Like Weasels

A weasel is wild. Who knows what he thinks? He sleeps in his underground den, his tail draped over his nose. Sometimes he lives in his den for two days without leaving. Outside, he stalks rabbits, mice, muskrats, and birds, killing more bodies than he can eat warm, and often dragging the carcasses home. Obedient to instinct, he bites his prey at the neck, either splitting the jugular vein at the throat or crunching the brain at the base of the skull, and he does not let go. One naturalist refused to kill a weasel who was socketed into his hand deeply as a rattlesnake. The man could in no way pry the tiny weasel off, and he had to walk half a mile to water, the weasel dangling from his palm, and soak him off like a stubborn label.

And once, says Ernest Thompson Seton—once, a man shot an eagle out of the sky. He examined the eagle and found the dry skull of a weasel fixed by the jaws to his throat. The supposition is that the eagle had pounced on the weasel and the weasel swiveled and bit as instinct taught him, tooth to neck, and nearly won. I would like to have seen that eagle from the air a few weeks or months before he was shot: was the whole weasel still attached to his feathered throat, a fur pendant? Or did the eagle eat what he could reach, gutting the living weasel with his talons before his breast, bending his beak, cleaning the beautiful airborne bones?

I have been reading about weasels because I saw one last week. I startled a weasel who startled me, and we exchanged a long glance.

Twenty minutes from my house, through the woods by the quarry and across the highway, is Hollins Pond, a remarkable piece of shallowness, where I like to go at sunset and sit on a tree trunk. Hollins Pond is also called Murray's Pond; it covers two acres of bottomland near Tinker Creek with six inches of water and six thousand lily pads. In winter, brown-and-white steers stand in the middle of it, merely dampening their hooves; from the distant shore they look like miracle itself, complete with miracle's nonchalance. Now, in summer, the steers are gone. The water lilies have blossomed and spread to a green horizontal plane that is terra firma to plodding blackbirds, and tremulous ceiling to black leeches, crayfish, and carp.

This is, mind you, suburbia. It is a five-minute walk in three directions to rows of houses, though none is visible here. There's a 55 mph highway at one end of the pond, and a nesting pair of wood ducks at the other. Under every bush is a muskrat hole or a beer can. The far end is an alternating series of fields and woods, fields and woods, threaded everywhere with motorcycle tracks—in whose bare clay wild turtles lay eggs.

So. I had crossed the highway, stepped over two low barbed-wire fences, and traced the motorcycle path in all gratitude through the wild rose and poison ivy of the pond's shoreline up into high grassy fields. Then I cut down through the woods to the mossy fallen tree where I sit. This tree is excellent. It makes a dry, upholstered bench at the upper, marshy end of the pond, a plush jetty raised from the thorny shore between a shallow blue body of water and a deep blue body of sky.

The sun had just set. I was relaxed on the tree trunk, ensconced in the lap of lichen, watching the lily pads at my feet tremble and part dreamily over the thrusting path of a carp. A yellow bird appeared to my right and flew behind me. It caught my eye; I swiveled around—and the next instant, inexplicably, I was looking down at a weasel, who was looking up at me.

Weasel! I'd never seen one wild before. He was ten inches long, thin as a curve, a muscled ribbon, brown as fruitwood, soft-furred, alert. His face was fierce, small and pointed as a lizard's; he would have made a good arrowhead. There was just a dot of chin, maybe two brown hairs' worth, and then the pure white fur began that spread down his underside. He had two black eyes I didn't see, any more than you see a window.

The weasel was stunned into stillness as he was emerging from beneath an enormous shaggy wild rose bush four feet away. I was stunned into stillness twisted backward on the tree trunk. Our eyes locked, and someone threw away the key.

Our look was as if two lovers, or deadly enemies, met unexpectedly on an overgrown path when each had been thinking of something else: a clearing blow to the gut. It was also a bright blow to the brain, or a sudden beating of brains, with all the charge and intimate grate of rubbed balloons. It emptied our lungs. It felled the forest, moved the fields, and drained the pond; the world dismantled and tumbled into that black hole of eyes. If you and I looked at each other that way, our skulls would split and drop to our shoulders. But we don't. We keep our skulls. So.

He disappeared. This was only last week, and already I don't remember what shattered the enchantment. I think I blinked, I think I retrieved my brain from the weasel's brain, and tried to memorize what I was seeing, and the weasel felt the yank of separation, the careening splashdown into real life and the urgent current of instinct. He vanished under the wild rose. I waited motionless, my mind suddenly full of data and my spirit with pleadings, but he didn't return.

Please do not tell me about "approach-avoidance conflicts." I tell you I've been in that weasel's brain for sixty seconds, and he was in mine. Brains are private places, muttering through unique and secret tapes—but the weasel and I both plugged into another tape simultaneously, for a sweet and shocking time. Can I help it if it was a blank?

What goes on in his brain the rest of the time? What does a weasel think about? He won't say. His journal is tracks in clay, a spray of feathers, mouse blood and bone: uncollected, unconnected, loose-leaf, and blown.

I would like to learn, or remember, how to live. I come to Hollins Pond not so much to learn how to live as, frankly, to forget about it. That is, I don't think I can learn from a wild animal how to live in particular—shall I suck warm blood, hold my tail high, walk with my footprints precisely over the prints of my hands?—but I might learn something of mindlessness, something of the purity of living in the physical senses and the dignity of living without bias or motive. The weasel lives in necessity and we live in choice, hating necessity and dying at the last ignobly in its talons. I would like to live as I should, as the weasel lives as he should. And I suspect that for me the way is like the weasel's: open to time and death painlessly, noticing everything, remembering nothing, choosing the given with a fierce and pointed will.

I missed my chance. I should have gone for the throat. I should have lunged for that streak of white under the weasel's chin and held on, held on through mud and into the wild rose, held on for a dearer life. We could live under the wild rose wild as weasels, mute and uncomprehending. I could very calmly go wild. I could live two days in the den, curled, leaning on mouse fur, sniffing bird bones, blinking, licking, breathing musk, my hair tangled in the roots of grasses. Down is a good place to go, where the mind is single. Down is out, out of your ever-loving mind and back to your careless senses. I remember muteness as a prolonged and giddy fast, where every moment is a feast of utterance received. Time and events are merely poured, unremarked, and ingested directly, like blood pulsed into my gut through a jugular vein. Could two live that way? Could two live under the wild rose, and explore by the pond, so that the smooth mind of each is as everywhere present to the other, and as received and as unchallenged, as falling snow?

We could, you know. We can live any way we want. People take vows of poverty, chastity, and obedience—even of silence—by choice. The thing is to stalk your calling in a certain skilled and supple way, to locate the most tender and live spot and plug into that pulse. This is yielding, not fighting. A weasel doesn't "attack" anything; a weasel lives as he's meant to, yielding at every moment to the perfect freedom of single necessity.

I think it would be well, and proper, and obedient, and pure, to grasp your one necessity and not let it go, to dangle from it limp wherever it takes you. Then even death, where you're going no matter how you live, cannot you part. Seize it and let it seize you up aloft even, till your eyes burn out and drop; let your musky flesh fall off in shreds, and let your very bones unhinge and scatter, loosened over fields, over fields and woods, lightly, thoughtless, from any height at all, from as high as eagles.

Considerations

Thinking

What does Dillard mean by suggesting that we can live like the weasel? To what extent are weasel life and human life analogous? In what ways do they differ, and how are those differences suggested in Dillard's essay?

What do you think is Dillard's purpose in "Living Like Weasels"? Where do you find her argument most clearly articulated?

Connecting

What is the relationship between the story Dillard tells in the first paragraph and the story she recounts in the second paragraph?

Explain how Dillard connects her experience with weasels with her reading about them.

Compare Dillard's presentation of her experience with the weasel with Gordon Grice's description of his experiences with a black widow spider in "The Black Widow" (pp. 314–317).

Writing

Write an essay in which you explore your relationship to the natural world. You may wish to base your essay on one or more experiences you have had in nature. Or you may wish to center your essay on a literary work that reflects a concern with nature.

Write an essay describing some of your own encounters with animals and what you have learned from those experiences.

Andre Dubus
(1936–1999)

Andre Dubus was born in Lake Charles, Louisiana, later served in the Marine Corps, and then attended the University of Iowa. He is the author of nine works of fiction and two of nonfiction; they include *Separate Flights, Adultery & Other Choices, Dancing After Hours, Broken Vessels* (nonfiction), and *Meditations from a Movable Chair* (nonfiction). He lost the use of both legs in 1986 when he stopped on I-93 outside Boston to assist accident victims and was struck by an on-coming car.

Dubus received the PEN/Malamud Award, the Rea Award for excellence in short fiction, the Jean Stein Award from the American Academy of Arts and Letters, and fellowships from both the Guggenheim and MacArthur Foundations. Until his death in 1999, he lived in Haverhill, Massachusetts.

"Giving Up the Gun" explores issues associated with owning guns and suggests why, eventually, he chose to give them up.

Giving Up the Gun

In the winter of 1990, sitting in my wheelchair in a sleeping compartment on a train from Portland, Oregon, to Chicago, I gave up my guns and the protection I believed they gave people I loved, and strangers whose peril I might witness, and me. At home in Massachusetts, I had a metal gun box with two locks, and in it were eight handguns, one a small twenty-two-caliber revolver that is four and a half inches long. In my wallet on the train, I had a Massachusetts license to carry firearms. In the space on the card for occupation, a police officer had typed *Author;* in the space under *Reason for Issuing License,* he had typed *Protection.*

For thirteen years, I had a license, renewing it every five years. I still have the one that was with me on the train, but it expired four years ago, in 1991, and the guns have been locked in their box since I returned from Oregon. Thirteen years before I rode that train, someone I love was raped in Boston by a man who held a knife at her throat. I went to my local police chief and told him I wanted a license, and that my father had taught me to shoot, and the Marine Corps had, and I would safely own a gun, and no woman would ever be raped if I were with her. I cursed and wept and he was sympathetic and said he would immediately start the background investigation by the state. A detective made a rolled impression of my right index finger, and I went to a photographer for a picture.

In about three weeks, I had my license and I went to a sporting-goods store to choose and buy a gun: a Charter Arms thirty-eight-caliber snubnosed revolver, because it cost less than a Smith & Wesson or a Colt. I did not own a suit and rarely wore a sport coat, so a shoulder holster would not do. The store owner made me a shadow holster: a leather one whose belt slot was low, so that most of the holster and the gun were above my waist. I could wear a pullover shirt, or sweater, or even a loose-fitting T-shirt, and you could not see the gun. So my thirteen years as an armed man began.

For a long time, I put the gun on my belt only when I went to Boston with a woman. Then I was certain that she was safe, and I was also certain that I would never have to use the gun; that simply being prepared for rapists or other violent men would keep them from my path. And if that failed, I was certain that I would not have to shoot anyone; I would only have to hold the gun in my hand and point it at a man while the woman with me called the police. Maybe I would have to fire a shot straight up in the air, if this man I did not believe would be part of

214

my life appeared anyway, intent on removing me with his fists or a weapon, and taking the woman. If a shot in the air did not change his dark direction and send him running, if instead he attacked, I would shoot his leg or shoulder. This was all very tidy, and I believed it.

After a few years, and a lot of newspaper stories, I began asking myself questions whose answers were not in my brain, my body, my gun, but in my soul, though I did not know that. What if I went with a man to watch the Red Sox or a movie, and we saw several men or one big one attacking a woman or a man, not to steal, but to harm or rape or kill? I was no hand-to-hand fighter, and did not intend to be. I also did not intend to watch a crucifixion in any form. I started bringing a gun every time I went to Boston: to Fenway Park, to jazz clubs, to dinner in restaurants, to movies.

When I fired the Charter Arms thirty-eight at a target, it often spit tiny fragments of lead toward my face. I sold it at a gun store and bought a used three-eighty semiautomatic, which looks like a very small forty-five, and I put it in the pocket of my jeans, with my keys and coins, and it was flat enough to be concealed. Through the years, when I had the money, I bought other guns. One was a Smith & Wesson snub-nosed thirty-eight that fit in the shadow holster. By now, I had begun loading guns with hollow-point bullets, so if I had to shoot a human being in the shoulder or leg, the bullet would not go through him and hit someone else; it would shatter into pieces inside his body. The guns were to protect other people. No one would rape me. If someone wanted my money, he could have it. If someone felt like beating me, I could run. But I had the gun, and I believed that nothing would happen, simply because I was prepared for it; and that if something did happen, it would be as I had imagined it. My confidence in this was foolish, and the foolishness was as concealed from my soul as the gun in my pocket or holster was concealed from the eyes of other people.

Alabama has stricter handgun laws than Massachusetts, or it did in 1985, when I went by train with my wife and our three-year-old daughter, and brought guns for hunting, target shooting, and to put in my pocket or in a holster under my coat, if I felt I needed it in Tuscaloosa. I went there to earn money, to hold the writing chair for a semester at the University of Alabama. Because I grew up in Louisiana, where guns in homes were ordinary, where an adult could carry a gun if it was not concealed, and men who worked in woods or swamps often wore holstered handguns so they could shoot snakes, I assumed that Alabama in 1985 would be like Louisiana in the forties and fifties. A few days after we moved into the large and free house that came with the job in Tuscaloosa, I went to the sheriff's office and showed a deputy my Massachusetts permit, and asked him if I could carry a handgun. He said that no one could carry a handgun in Alabama; that a resident, after a background investigation, could buy one and take it home but could not take it out of the home. The deputy was a friendly man, and after we talked for a while, he told me to get a letter from the English department, showing that I was employed in Alabama. He said the letter and my Massachusetts license would make everything all right.

"If it went to court," he said, "the judge would throw it out."

"What if there's trouble, and I have to use it?"

"Then it's never a problem."

Tuscaloosa did not feel like a place where I needed a gun. Of course if you feel the need to carry a gun, you need one everywhere. But the territory of violence was in my imagination: cities were places where predators lived; towns and small cities were not. Unarmed, I drove and walked in Tuscaloosa, until I bought the four-and-a-half-inch-long twenty-two revolver, stainless steel, with brown plastic handgrips. It holds five rounds, and you load and unload it by removing the cylinder, which means the gun is as safe as a handgun can be: the cylinder is either in place or it is not; and if it is, you handle the gun as though it is loaded, even when you know it is not. Because of the training given me by my father and the Marine Corps, I always assume a gun is loaded. I also attribute to a gun the ability to load itself, even fire itself, without being touched by a human hand.

I love guns, especially well-made pistols and revolvers. Many of them are beautiful, and their shape and balanced weight are pleasing to hold. I love the relaxed concentration of aiming a gun and squeezing its trigger, the thrill of hitting a bull's-eye or a can. When I hold a gun, I do not imagine the death of a human being, which is the purpose of most handguns. I know people who are frightened or appalled by guns and do not want to hold one, spin its cylinder or pull its slide to the rear and watch and hear it move forward, hear that perfect and final click as the slide pushes a bullet into the chamber. These people are right: they see a bullet entering a human body. In the gun store in Alabama, I held the tiny twenty-two as another person might hold a pocket watch or a ring, a hammer or a golf club. To me, that gun, like all my guns, was somehow alive, with a history and a future; with a soul. I loved it, and bought it.

Before I could take it home, I had to wait about a week for permission from the state of Alabama. At home, I took out the cylinder, loaded it with four rounds of hollow-points, leaving an empty chamber under the hammer, and put the gun in the right pocket of my jeans, with my coins, keys, and lighter, and it was always there, when I left the house for Mass or work, errands or shopping, or pleasure. I had not fired it, and did not expect to until I went home to Massachusetts, where in my basement I had a target for twenty-two-caliber weapons. The little gun in my pocket amused me. It was, I said, for gentle places, where there would be no trouble. I called it "Misty."

If it had not been in my pocket the night I aimed it at a man's stomach, I do not know what would have happened on that crowded sidewalk across the street from the university. The night was a Friday, my wife and daughter were out of town, visiting relatives in the North, the evening was warm, and I began it with happy hour on the patio of a restaurant we writers liked. Most of the writers I knew were graduate students, and we liked this place because we could drink cheaply and afford Mexican appetizers until six o'clock. One of the women that evening on the patio was a graduate student who was separated from her husband, and had a young daughter she was afraid would live with the father. Later, she and her husband lived together and remained married, but that night it did not seem possible, and she was in pain.

She had driven me to the bar, and at six o'clock, when the prices of drinks changed and the writers dispersed and went to other cheap bars or home for dinner, the woman and I drove to a video store. We had decided while drinking that we wanted to watch *Rebel Without a Cause*. We rented it to watch at my house, but we wanted first to sit in a quiet air-conditioned bar and drink club sodas and talk about divorce, and she drove there; it was twilight now and the streetlamps were on. She parked around the corner from a block of bars and restaurants facing the campus. We walked to the corner. Then a man with no hands came around it and stopped in front of me. He was stocky and short, and I looked down at his face. I was taking a cigarette from a pack when he asked me for money. I offered him a cigarette; I did not know how he would smoke it, but I felt that he did not want my help. Somehow, with his stumps or an elbow, he got it to his lips. I was not watching; I was taking money from my wallet and slipping it into the left pocket of his pants. Then I gave him a light. He said: "I saw that."

I do not remember what he did with the cigarette. I said: "You can buy me a drink."

"Where?"

I nodded at the bar beside us. He said: "I can't go in there."

"Why?"

"I'm eighty-sixed."

"Let's go anyway."

The three of us went inside; it was crowded with students, and dark, with loud talk and laughter and music from the jukebox, and I went to the bar. The bartender was a young man. He said: "Sir, that man can't come in here."

"Why?"

"He makes trouble."

I wondered what kind of trouble a man with no hands could make. We went outside. The man without hands said: "Let's go to my place."

"No thanks; we're going down the street."

He crossed the street to a liquor store on the opposite corner, and the woman and I watched. He came out with a case of beer on his right shoulder, his stump holding it in place. He lifted the other to wave, and we waved at him. Then a young blond man was standing with us; he had come out of the bar. He looked like an undergraduate. He said: "Mister, that man is trouble."

"What can he do, without hands?"

"Believe me, he's trouble."

He was an affable young man, and the three of us chatted for a while. He invited us to have a drink, but we thanked him and walked down the block to a well-lighted bar where you could nearly always sit among quiet strangers. We did that, and drank club sodas with wedges of lime and dashes of bitters, and talked about divorce. We assumed her daughter would not live with her. I had never known a woman who had lost custody of her child, but I knew her pain. We talked about it and drank club sodas for two hours or more, and I no longer felt the happy-hour margaritas. While we were becoming sober, the young blond man, in the bar at the corner, was probably drinking too much. It is easy to conclude that someone dangerous at night, outside of a bar, is drunk; but I shall never know whether that man was drunk and was doing something he would not want to do in his normal state, or was a violent man whose trajectory met mine on a sidewalk in Alabama.

When the woman and I left our seats at the bar, I was tired because of what we had talked about, and neither of us was certain we still wanted to watch the movie. Deciding to see it had been delightful when the sun was shining and we were drinking in its light on the patio. Now it was nearly ten o'clock. We stepped out of the air-conditioned bar, into the warm air and streetlights, and I held her elbow, guiding her through a group of large black men who had come down a stairway from an upstairs bar. I felt her body tense, and I looked at her face. She looked afraid. I do not know why. In Alabama, except for that Friday night, I saw no trouble between white and black people, and I did not hear any bigotry. This was one of many reasons I loved my time there.

When I left Louisiana in the spring of 1958, integration was inchoate. In my sophomore year of college, black students had enrolled. In the student union, they sat with one another; I do not remember any black men playing on a varsity team. I grew up feeling compassion for black people; you could not live in a segregated town, even as a young boy, and not see injustice. I also felt involved in this injustice, and stained by it; I still do. I did not want black people to drink at different public water fountains, go into different public bathrooms, sit in the balcony of one movie theater (they could not go into our other two theaters); I did not want them to ride on the back of the bus, but they did, and there I was at the front of the bus, even if black people had to stand in its crowded rear. And my parents had taught me, their only son, always to offer my seat to a woman. I did not want black people to live in their part of town, with its dirt roads and hovels. I did not want them to be subservient, and their work to be menial, but they were and it was; and I grew and learned and played in the sun.

This was in Lafayette, Louisiana, a small city then, and I do not remember any violence engendered by black boys or men. Nor do I remember white boys or men assaulting black people. As I write this in 1995, black people in America are still beyond the pale; white people have created and maintained ghettos where understandable hopelessness and rage keep true freedom of the body and spirit at bay. It is a world I was born to skirt, for I am white, and it is a world I can avoid by simply having enough money to buy a house on an acre and a quarter of land in Massachusetts. I would not wheel about in my chair in a ghetto, because I am afraid; and I am afraid because I believe that only God's grace can keep many black people from feeling anger about anyone who is white; and we often turn away from God's grace; or His voice is lost in the clamor of simply being alive.

In Lafayette in the forties and fifties, we were not afraid of black people. Some of us—I think most of us—were respectful, some were scornful, some were hateful. I doubt that any of us, boys and girls, men and women, felt that we and black people were equal, despite what our priests told us. How can you feel equal, save in the heart of God, with someone who is always excluded? I believe I saw no violence between white and black boys because we were never with one another in schools, or on playgrounds, or in swimming pools, or even in groups on the street or, as we grew older, in bars and nightclubs; and I believe also that black people were afraid of us. Many of them moved among us with the caution of wild birds. In my boyhood, there were no lynchings in Louisiana; or I do not remember any. But how could any black person in the segregated South not be aware of this horror?

In Tuscaloosa in 1985, black people were everywhere, in the stores, on the sidewalks, on the campus and in classrooms, in bars and theaters and churches. I do not know why the woman seemed afraid as we strolled through the group of black men, standing happily at ease on a hot night. She and I walked nearly the length of the block, were at the corner where we had talked with the man without hands and the young blond man, when I heard a man's voice say: "Nigger."

I stopped and turned. The young blond man stood about twenty-five feet from me, in front of the plate-glass window of a restaurant; in his right hand was an open pocketknife with a long and wide blade, and he was looking at a small black man. Behind the black man was a wall, and his back touched it. The blond man slowly moved toward him. I put my right hand in the pocket of my jeans, gripped the revolver and pulled it out and cocked it and aimed it at the blond man's stomach. I knew nothing about the accuracy of this little gun; if I fired at his shoulder or leg, I might not hit him at all. I saw the gun sight at the front of the barrel, his stomach, the silver blade of his knife, and his face. To his right, some young white men were telling him not to do this; but to me, they were as distant as campus buildings hundreds of yards away. I still do not know how many of them stood there. My hand aiming the gun was steady and I said loudly: "Put away the knife."

He looked at me, recognized me, and said: "Fuck you."

I had no images of my history or my future, not even of pulling the trigger or not pulling the trigger. The voices of his friends, indeed all sounds on the sidewalk and street and coming from the bar on the corner, only a few feet to my right, were like wind you have been hearing for hours. All of me focused on the knife; it had to disappear; and I was mysteriously calm. I said: "Put it back in your pocket, or I'll shoot."

"Fuck you." He was not moving. I glanced at the black man, standing against the wall. The woman stood to my left; either she was silent or I did not hear her; she too was as distant from me as everyone else on the sidewalk, save the blond man and the black man at the wall. I remember only one instant of one wish: that the black man would run away. I said: "I mean it."

He spread his arms from his body, and said: "Fuck you. Shoot. Go ahead. Shoot."

The voices of his friends rose, I could see their hands and faces to his right, and they were pleading with him; but they did not touch him. By now, probably the group of black men the woman and I had walked through had gathered, watching us; I did not see them; but when it ended, they were standing near us. The young man's arms were still spread, and he said: "Shoot me. Go ahead. Shoot me."

Over the barrel of the gun, I looked at his stomach; my arm was extended; the gun was steady. I said: "It's a twenty-two hollow-point, son. It'll spread your guts all over that window."

"All right." He started walking toward me, his friends on his right moving with him, talking to him. Then he was close to me, and everything had changed. I pointed the gun in the air, held its hammer with my thumb, gently squeezed the trigger, and lowered the hammer into place. Then I held the gun at my side. He still held the knife; when he was two feet from me, he stopped and said: "Tell you what. I'll give my buddy the knife, and you give her the gun, and you and me'll fight it out."

I imagined the back of my head hitting the sidewalk. He was young and he looked strong and he would knock me down and the concrete would fracture my skull and I would die here. I said: "I don't want to fight."

I do not remember the sentence he spoke then, only the word *nigger;* then all I felt was resignation. I would have to fight him, receive whatever pain and injury he dealt, until someone stopped him, or he was done with me. I was not angry; I felt nothing about him.

"That's it," I said, and I dropped the revolver into the woman's large purse. Then one of his friends stood between us, his face close to mine, and said: "Mister, I know you can whip his ass. But please leave. I've got to get him out of here before the cops come."

"Okay," I said, and held the woman's elbow and walked away, around the corner. We stopped, and I took the gun from her purse. Then a cruiser came onto the street of bars, quietly, but with flashing lights, and I looked around the corner and watched it stop; two police officers got out and walked to the young blond man. The woman and I went to her car and, as she started it, I said: "Men are funny. If that guy had said: 'I know he can whip *your* ass,' I would have had to fight him. But he said: 'You can whip his ass.' So he let me off the hook."

Then she was trembling.

"Violence scares me," she said. "I have to go home."

"Me too."

She drove me there, and I took the video, to return it to the store, and went inside and filled a glass with ice and took it and a Coke to the front porch. I sat on the steps in the warm night and looked at trees and the sky. I needed the company of women and children; I wanted my wife and daughter to be upstairs, sleeping. I sat for a long time. Saturday morning, I phoned my wife, then a man who was a poet, a hunter, a fisherman, and who lived in the country near Tuscaloosa, and I told him about Friday night, and said I wanted to go out and hunt squirrels with him, to be in the beautiful woods and use a gun the way it ought to be used.

Monday, my wife and daughter were home, and I went to Mass at noon. After Mass, I talked to the young chaplain and a young nun. We stood in front of the chapel, in warm sunlight. The nun was pretty and wore jeans; I always liked seeing her and talking to her; being attracted to a woman and knowing that what we shared was God and my attraction could not become carnal was lovely. I told them about the man and the knife and my gun. I said: "I understand turning the other cheek. But what about turning somebody else's cheek? Christ doesn't say anything about that. What about the woman they were going to stone for adultery? What would He have done if they had picked up rocks and started throwing them at her? It wasn't His time yet. He couldn't stand in front of her and get killed. He had to wait to be crucified. Would He throw rocks at them?" I looked at the priest's eyes, and nodded toward the nun. "What would you do if some guys tried to rape her?"

"I'd fight them."

Still I had no peace. A young man could be dead because of one moment on a Friday night. I did not know what else I could have done but aim my gun at him until either the knife or the black man was gone. I still do not know. I could have kept the gun in my pocket and tried to disarm him. When I was a Marine officer candidate, the sergeant who taught hand-to-hand fighting said: "If someone pulls a knife on you in a bar, run; if you can't run, throw an ashtray or bottle at his face and charge him." Then the sergeant showed us one way to grab the man's wrist, move behind him, and push his arm into a hammerlock. It was a move you would have to practice. I thought about this, during those days and nights in Tuscaloosa, while I kept hoping to know what I should have done. Sometimes, seeing the young man's face, I saw myself trying to grab his wrist, saw his knife piercing my flesh, my aorta. But none of this applied: that night on the sidewalk, my only instinct had been to aim a gun. I had no conflict, because I had only one choice. Now I wanted more choices, and I wanted to know what they were.

At Thanksgiving, my wife and daughter and I rode on the train to Baton Rouge to visit my oldest sister, Kathryn. In the evening, after dinner, people came to Kathryn's house. One was a priest, and one was a nun in her fifties. I imagined the eyes of Christ were like her eyes: in them were strength and depth, and she was cheerful and wise. The priest was in his thirties, short and graceful and athletically built. He lifted weights and had a black belt in karate, and he engaged in contact karate matches. His eyes were like John the Baptist's, or the way I imagined his to be: they were dark and bright with embers that could become rage. He and the nun and I stood with drinks; I felt he would have an answer for me, and I told him my story. He said: "Within the realm of human possibility, you did what you could. You wanted no one to be harmed. And no one was. I beat up a man on Christmas Eve, then said the midnight Mass."

"You did?"

"I was delivering food to the poor. When I got to his house, he was beating his wife. I took her and the children to another house, then went back to talk to him. Then he tried to beat me."

So I had my answer, and the comfort of it. Within the realm of human possibility, I had done what I could.

I have written all of this to try to discover why, sitting in my wheelchair on a train, I gave up my guns. But I do not know. Eight months after that Thanksgiving in Baton Rouge, I was driving home from Boston, armed with a pistol, and I stopped on the highway and got out of my car to help two people who had driven over an abandoned motorcycle. Then a car hit me, and I have been in a wheelchair for over nine years. My body can no longer do what I want to do, and it cannot protect my two young daughters, and my grandchildren, from perils I used to believe I could save people from. I have not learned the virtue of surrender—which I want—but I have learned the impossibility of avoiding surrender. I am also more afraid now. For the first three years and eight months after my injury, until those moments on the train, I believed I needed a gun more than I ever had. Alone in my house, I kept a small twenty-two Beretta semiautomatic in my shoulder bag, its loaded magazine in one of the bag's pockets, and for the first time in my life, the gun was to protect myself.

I only know this: on the train, images came to me: I was alone in my house, on the couch, watching a movie on video, and a man kicked my door open and came in, to steal, beat, kill; and I shoved the magazine into the pistol and worked its slide and aimed the gun, but he kept coming at me, and I shot his leg, but he kept coming, and I shot his chest, again and again, till he stopped coming. Then, as I looked out the train window at snow on the ground, one sentence came to me: With my luck, I'll kill someone.

That was all. *Luck* was not the accurate word, and I do not know what the accurate word is. But with that sentence, I felt the fence and gate, not even the lawn and porch and door to the house of sorrow I would live in if I killed someone. Then I felt something detach itself from my soul, departing, rising, vanishing; and I said to God: *It's up to You now.* This is not the humble and pure and absolutely spiritual love of turning the other cheek. It is not an answer to turn someone else's cheek. On the train, I gave up answers that are made of steel that fire lead, and I decided to sit in a wheelchair on the frighteningly invisible palm of God.

Considerations

Thinking

What do you make of Dubus's resolution to give up his gun and place himself in the "frighteningly invisible palm of God"—having only a few years earlier lost the use of his legs to a highway act of mercy? Is there a contradiction at work here or not? Explain.

Why do you think Dubus interrupts his story about the confrontation between himself and the blond man to tell the story about racism in Lafayette, Louisiana?

Connecting

What connections can you make between Dubus's attitude at the end of this essay and Leonard Kriegel's attitude at the end of "Falling into Life"? Are their resolutions about life akin or vastly different? Explain.

Consider the same question about resolution with respect to Dubus and Nancy Mairs in "On Being a Cripple."

Read Tim O'Brien's "How to Tell a True War Story" and then assess whether you think Dubus has told the truth in his story. Explain.

Writing

Consider the difference between Dubus's opening narrative and the story he tells about the encounter with the blond man. Figure out what he is telling us in that long opening narrative and why. What is the relationship between that narrative and the story of the encounter? Write an account of your findings for the class.

Select a moment from your own life that involved giving up something that you loved or depended on very much. Write an essay that makes use of that moment to help you develop a related idea.

Figure out why you think Dubus actually decided to give up his guns. Write a short essay that substantiates your conclusion. Cite evidence from the text, along with your reflections and explanation about the meaning of that evidence, as you understand it.

Gerald Early
(b. 1952)

Gerald Early is the Merle S. Kling Professor of Modern Letters and director of Afro-American Studies at Washington University in St. Louis. He is the author of *Tuxedo Junction: Essays on American Culture* and the editor of numerous books, including *Lure and Loathing: Essays on Race, Identity, and the Ambivalence of Assimilation.* He won the 1994 National Book Critics Circle Award in Criticism for *The Culture of Bruising Essays on Prizefighting, Literature, and Modern American Culture,* from which "Life With Daughters: Watching the Miss America Pageant" has been taken. In this essay Early interrogates the culture of the beauty pageant as he raises questions about gender and race.

Life With Daughters:
Watching the Miss America Pageant

The theater is an expression of our dream life—of our unconscious aspirations.

> – DAVID MAMET, "A TRADITION OF THE THEATER AS ART,"
> *WRITING IN RESTAURANTS*

Aunt Hester went out one night,—where or for what l do not know,—and happened to be absent when my master desired her presence.

> – FREDERICK DOUGLASS,
> *NARRATIVE OF THE LIFE OF FREDERICK DOUGLASS*

Adults, older girls, shops, magazines, newspapers, window signs—all the world had agreed that a blue-eyed, yellow-haired, pink-skinned doll was what every girl child treasured.

> – TONI MORRISON, *THE BLUEST EYE*

It is now fast become a tradition—if one can use that word to describe a habit about which I still feel a certain amount of shamefacedness—for our household to watch the Miss America contest on television every year. The source of my embarrassment is that this program remains, despite its attempts in recent years to modernize its frightfully antique quality of "women on parade," a kind of maddeningly barbarous example of the persistent, hard, crass urge to sell: from the plugs for the sponsor that are made a part of the script (that being an antique of fifties and sixties television; the show does not remember its history so much as it seems bent on repeating it) to the constant references to the success of some of the previous contestants and the reminders that this is some sort of scholarship competition, the program has all the cheap earnestness of a social uplift project being played as a musical revue in Las Vegas. Paradoxically, it wishes to convince the public that it is a common entertainment while simultaneously wishing to convey that it is more than mere entertainment. The Miss America pageant is the worst sort of "Americanism," the soft smile of sex and the hard sell of toothpaste and hair dye ads wrapped in the dreamy ideological gauze of "making it through one's own effort." In a perverse way, I like the show; it is the only live television left other than sports, news broadcasts, performing arts award programs, and speeches by the president. I miss live TV. It was the closest thing to theater for the masses. And the Miss America contest is as it has been for some time, the most perfectly rendered theater in our culture, for it so perfectly captures what we yearn for: a low-class ritual, a polished restatement of vulgarity, that wants to open the door to high-class respectability by way of plain middle-class anxiety and ambition. Am I doing all right? the contestants seem to ask in a kind of reassuring, if numbed, way. The contest brings together all the American classes in a show-biz spectacle of classlessness and tastelessness.

My wife has been interested in the Miss America contest since childhood, and so I ascribe her uninterrupted engagement with America's cultural passage into fall (Miss America, like college and pro football, signifies for us as a nation the end of summer; the contest was invented, back in 1921, by Atlantic City merchants to prolong the summer season past Labor Day) as something mystically and uniquely female. She, as a black woman, had a long-standing quarrel with the contest until Vanessa Williams was chosen the first black Miss America in September 1983. Somehow she felt vindicated by Williams for all those years as a black girl in Dallas, watching white women win the crown and thumb their noses at her, at her blackness, at her straightened hair, her thick lips, her wide nose. She played with white Barbie dolls as a little girl and had, I suppose, a "natural," or at least an understandable and predictable, interest in seeing the National White Barbie Doll chosen every year because for such a long time, of course, the Miss America contest, with few exceptions, was a totemic preoccupation with and representation of a particularly stilted form of patriarchal white supremacy. In short, it was a national white doll contest. And well we know that every black girl growing up in the fifties and early sixties had her peculiar love-hate affair with white dolls, with mythicized white femininity. I am reminded of this historical instance: everyone knows that in the *Brown versus Topeka Board of Education* case (the case that resulted in the Supreme Court decision to integrate public schools) part of the sociological evidence used by the plaintiffs to show the psychological damage suffered by blacks because of Jim Crow was an account by Kenneth Clarke of how, when offered a choice between a black doll and a white doll, little black girls invariably chose the white doll because they thought it "prettier."

On the front page of the January 6, 1962, *Pittsburgh Courier,* a black weekly, is a picture of a hospitalized black girl named Connie Smith holding a white doll sent to her by Attorney General Robert Kennedy. Something had occurred between 1954, when the Supreme Court made its decision, and 1962 that made it impossible for Kennedy to send the girl a black doll, and this impossibility was to signal, ironically, that the terms of segregation and the terms of racial integration, the very icon of them, were to be exactly the same. Kennedy could not send the girl a black doll, as it would have implied, in the age of integration, that he was, in effect, sending her a Jim Crow toy, a toy that would emphasize the girl's race. In the early sixties such a gesture would have been considered condescending. To give the black girl a white doll in the early sixties was to mainstream the black girl into the culture, to say that she was worthy of the same kind of doll that a white girl would have. But how can it be that conservatism and liberalism, segregation and integration, could produce, fantastically, the same results, the identical iconography: a black girl hugging a white doll because everyone thinks it is best for her to have it? How can it be that at one time the white doll is the sign of the black girl's rejection and inferiority and fewer than ten years later it is the sign of her acceptance and redemption? Those who are knowledgeable about certain aspects of the black mind or the collective black consciousness realize, of course, that the issues of segregation and integration, of conservatism and liberalism, of acceptance and rejection, of redemption and inferiority, are all restatements of the same immovable and relentless reality of the meaning of American blackness; that this is all a matter of the harrowing and compelling intensity that is called, quaintly, race pride. And in this context, the issue of white dolls, this fetishization of young white feminine beauty, and the complexity of black girlhood becomes an unresolved theme stated in a strident key. Blacks have preached for a long time about how to heal their daughters of whiteness: in the November 1908 issue of *The Colored American Magazine,* E. A. Johnson wrote an article entitled "Negro Dolls for Negro Babies," in which he said, "I am convinced that one of the best ways to teach Negro children to respect their own color would be to see to it that the children be given colored dolls to play with. . . . To give a Negro child a white doll means to create in it a prejudice against its own color, which will cling to it through life." Lots of black people believed this and, for all I know, probably still do, as race pride, or the lack thereof, burns and crackles like a current through most African-American public and private discourse. Besides, it is no easy matter to wish white dolls away.

A few years ago I was thumbing through an album of old family photographs and saw one of me and my oldest sister taken when I was four and she was nine. It struck me, transfixed me really, as it was a color photo and most of the old family pictures taken when I was a boy were black-and-white because my mother could not afford to have color pictures developed. We, my sister and I, are sitting on an old stuffed blue chair and she is holding a white doll in her hand, displaying it for the picture. I remember the occasion very well, as my sister was to be confirmed in our small, all-black Episcopal church that day, and she was, naturally, proud of the moment and wanted to share it with her favorite toy. That, I remembered, was why these were color pictures. It was a special day for the family, a day my mother wanted to celebrate by taking special pictures. My mother is a very dark woman who has a great deal of race pride and often speaks about my sisters' having black dolls. I was surprised, in looking at the picture recently, that they ever owned a white one, that indeed a white one had been a favorite.

My wife grew up—enjoyed the primary years of black girlhood, so to speak—during the years 1954 through 1962; she was about five or six years younger than my oldest sister. She lived in a southern state, or a state that was a reasonable facsimile of a southern state. She remembers that signs for colored and white bathrooms and water fountains persisted well into the mid-sixties in Texas. She remembers also Phyllis George, the Miss America from Denton, Texas, who went on to become a television personality for several years. She has always been very interested in George's career, and she has always disliked her. "She sounds just like a white girl from Texas," my wife likes to say, always reminding me that while both blacks and whites in Texas have accents, they do not sound alike. George won the contest in 1971, my wife's freshman year at the University of Pennsylvania and around the time she began to wear an Afro, a popular hairstyle for young black women in the days of "our terrible blackness" or "our black terribleness." It was a year fraught with complex passages into black womanhood for her. To think that a white woman from Texas should win the Miss America title that year! For my wife, the years of watching the Miss America contest were nothing more, in some sense continue to be nothing more, than an expression of anger made all the worse by the very unconscious or semiconscious nature of it. But if the anger has been persistent, so has her enormous capacity to "take it"; for in all these years it has never occurred to her to refuse to watch because, like the black girl being offered the white doll, like all black folk being offered white gifts, she has absolutely no idea how that is done, and she is not naïve enough to think that a simple refusal would be an act of empowerment. Empowerment comes only through making demands of our bogeymen, not by trying to convince ourselves we are not tormented. Yet, paradoxically, among blacks there is the bitter hope that a simplistic race pride will save us, a creed that masks its complex contradictions beneath lapping waves of bourgeois optimism and bourgeois anguish; for race pride clings to the opposing notions that the great hope (but secret fear) of an African-American future is, first, that blacks will always remain black and, second, that the great fear (but secret hope) of an African-American future is that blacks will not always remain black but evolve into something else. Race pride, which at its most insistent argues that blackness is everything, becomes, in its attempt to be the psychological quest for sanity, a form of dementia that exists as a response to that form of white dementia that says blackness is nothing. Existing as it does as a reactive force battling against a white preemptive presumption, race pride begins to take on the vices of an unthinking dogma and the virtues of a disciplined religious faith, all in the same instance. With so much at stake, race pride become both the act of making a virtue of a necessity and making a necessity of a virtue and, finally, making a profound and touching absurdity of both virtue and necessity. In some ways my wife learned her lessons well in her youth: she never buys our daughters white dolls.

My daughters, Linnet, age ten, and Rosalind, age seven, have become staunch fans of beauty contests in the last three years. In that time they have watched, in their entirety, several Miss America pageants, one Miss Black America contest, and one Miss USA. At first, I ascribed this to the same impulse that made my wife interested in such events when she was little: something secretly female, just as an interest in professional sports might be ascribed to something peculiarly male. Probably it is a sort of resentment that black girls harbor toward these contests. But that could not really be the case with my daughters. After all, they have seen several black entrants in these contests and have even seen black winners. They also have black dolls.

Back in the fall of 1983 when Vanessa Williams became Miss America, we, as a family, had our picture taken with her when she visited St. Louis. We went, my wife and I, to celebrate the grand moment when white American popular culture decided to embrace black women as something other than sexual subversives or fat, kindly maids cleaning up and caring for white families. We had our own, well, royalty, and royal origins means a great deal to people who have been denied their myths and their right to human blood. White women reformers may be ready to scrap the Miss America contest. (And the contest has certainly responded to the criticism it has been subjected to in recent years by muting some of the fleshier aspects of the program while, in its attempts to be even more the anxiety-ridden middle-class dream-wish, emphasizing more and more the magic of education and scholarly attainments.) It is now the contest that signifies the quest for professionalism among bourgeois women, and the first achievement of the professional career is to win something in a competition. But if there is a movement afoot to bring down the curtain finally on Miss America, my wife wants no part of it: "Whites always want to reform and end things when black people start getting on the gravy train they've been enjoying for years. What harm does the Miss America contest do?" None, I suppose, especially since black women have been winning lately.

Linnet and Rosalind were too young when we met Vanessa Williams to recall anything about the pictures, but they are amazed to see themselves in a bright, color Polaroid picture with a famous person, being part of an event that does not strike a chord in their consciousness because they cannot remember being alive when it happened. I often wonder if they attach any significance to the pictures at all. They think Vanessa is very pretty, prettier than their mother, but they attach no significance to being pretty—that is to say, no real value; they would not admire someone simply because he or she was good-looking. They think Williams is beautiful, but they do not wish that she were their mother. And this issue of being beautiful is not to be taken lightly in the life of a black girl. About two years ago Linnet started coming home from school wishing aloud that her hair was long and blond so that she could fling it about, the way she saw many of her white classmates doing. As she attends a school that is more than 90 percent white, it seemed inevitable to my wife that one of our daughters would become sensitive about her appearance. At this time Linnet's hair was not straightened and she wore it in braids. Oddly, despite the fact that she wanted a different hairstyle that would permit her hair to "blow in the wind," so to speak, she vehemently opposed having it straightened, although my wife has straightened hair, after having worn an Afro for several years. I am not sure why Linnet did not want her hair straightened; perhaps, after seeing her teenaged cousin have her hair straightened on several occasions, the process of hair straightening seemed distasteful or disheartening or frightening. Actually, I do not think Linnet wanted to change her hair to be beautiful; she wanted to be like everyone else.[1] But perhaps this is simply wishful thinking here or playing with words because Linnet must have felt her difference as being a kind of ugliness. Yet she is not a girl who is subject to illusion. Once, about a year earlier, when she had had a particularly rough day in school, I told her, in a father's patronizing way with a daughter, that I thought she was the most beautiful girl in the world. She looked at me strangely when I said that and then replied matter-of-factly: "I don't think I'm beautiful at all. I think I'm just ordinary. There is nothing wrong with that, is there, Daddy?

Just to be ordinary?" "Are you unhappy to be ordinary?" I asked. She thought for a moment, then said quietly and finally, "No. Are you?"

Hair straightening, therefore, was not an option and would not have been even if Linnet had wanted it, because my wife was opposed to having Linnet's hair straightened at her age. At first, Linnet began going to school with her hair unbraided. Unfortunately, this turned out to be a disastrous hairdo, as her hair shrank during the course of a day to a tangled mess. Finally, my wife decided to have both Linnet and Rosalind get short Afro haircuts. Ostensibly, this was to ease the problem of taking swim lessons during the summer. In reality, it was to end Linnet's wishes for a white hairstyle by, in effect, foreclosing any possibility that she could remotely capture such a look. Rosalind's hair was cut so that Linnet would not feel that she was being singled out. (Alas, the trials of being both the second and the younger child!) At first, the haircuts caused many problems in school. Some of the children—both black and white—made fun of them. Brillo heads, they were called, and fungus and Afro heads. One group of black girls at school refused to play with Linnet. "You look so ugly with that short hair," they would say. "Why don't you wear your hair straight like your mom. Your mom's hair is so pretty." Then, for the first time, the girls were called niggers by a white child on their school bus, although I think neither the child nor my daughters completely understood the gravity of that obscenity. People in supermarkets would refer to them as boys unless they were wearing dresses. Both girls went through a period when they suffered most acutely from that particularly American disease, that particularly African-American disease, the conjunction of oppression and exhibitionistic desire: self-consciousness. They thought about their hair all the time. My wife called the parents of the children who teased them. The teasing stopped for the most part, although a few of the black girls remained so persistent that the white school counselor suggested that Linnet's and Rosalind's hair be straightened. "I'm white," he said, "and maybe I shouldn't get into this, but they might feel more comfortable if they wore a different hairstyle." My wife angrily rejected that bit of advice. She had them wear dresses more often to make them look unmistakably like girls, although she refused out of hand my suggestion of having their ears pierced. She is convinced that pierced ears are just a form of mutilation, primitive tattooing, or scarring passing itself off as something fashionable. Eventually, the girls became used to their hair. Now, after more than a year, they hardly think about it, and even if Linnet wears a sweat suit or jeans, no one thinks she is a boy because she is budding breasts. Poor Rosalind still suffers on occasion in supermarkets because she shows no outward signs of sexual maturity. Once, while watching Linnet look at her mother's very long and silken straight hair, the hair that the other black girls at school admire, always calling it pretty, I asked her if she would like to have hers straightened.

"Not now," she said. "Maybe when I'm older. It'll be something different."

"Do you think you will like it?" I asked.

"Maybe," she said.

And in that "maybe," so calmly and evenly uttered, rests the complex contradictions, the uneasy tentative negotiations of that which cannot be compromised yet can never be realized in this flawed world as an ideal; there is, in that "maybe,"

the epistemology of race pride for black American women so paradoxically symbolized by their straightened hair. In the February 1939 issue of *The Atlantic
Monthly,* a black woman named Kimbal Goffman (possibly a pseudonym) wrote
an essay entitled "Black Pride" in which she accused blacks of being ashamed of
their heritage and, even more damningly in some of her barbs obviously aimed at
black women, of their looks:

> Why are so many manufacturers becoming rich through the manufacture of bleach-
> ing preparations? Why are hair-straightening combs found in nearly every Negro
> home? Why is the following remark made so often to a newborn baby, when
> grandma or auntie visits it for the first time? "Tell Mother she must pinch your nose
> every morning. If she doesn't, you're gonna have a sure 'nough darky nose."

According to Goffman, blacks do not exploit what society has given them;
they are simply ashamed to have what they have, tainted as it is with being associated with a degraded people, and long to be white or to have possessions that
would accrue a kind of white status. In the essay, blacks in general receive their
share of criticism but only black women are criticized in a gender-specific way
that their neurotic sense of inferiority concerning physical appearance is a particularly dangerous form of reactionism as it stigmatizes each new generation.
According to Goffman, it is black women, because they are mothers, who perpetuate their sense of inferiority by passing it on to their children. In this largely Du
Boisian argument, Goffman advises, "Originality is the backbone of all progress."
And, in this sense, originality means understanding blackness as something
uncontrolled or uninfluenced by what whites say it is. This is the idealism of race
pride that demands both purity and parity. Exactly one year later, in the February
1940 issue of *The Brown American,* a black magazine published in Philadelphia,
Lillian Franklin McCall wrote an article about the history of black women beauty
shop owners and entrepreneurs entitled "Appointment at Seven." The opening
paragraph is filled with dollar signs:

> The business of straightening milady's insistent curls tinkles cash registers in the
> country to the tune of two million and a half dollars a year. And that covers
> merely the semi-monthly session with the hairdresser for the estimated four mil-
> lion of Eve's sepia adult daughters by national census. Today there is a growing
> trend to top off the regular, "Shampoo and wave," with a facial; and, perhaps, a
> manicure. New oil treatments and rinses prove a lure, too, so milady finds her
> beauty budget stepped up from approximately $39 yearly for an average $1.25
> or $1.50 "hair-do," to $52.00 per year if she adds a facial to the beauty rite, and
> $10 more, for the manicure.

In a Booker T. Washington tone, McCall goes on to describe how the establish-
ment of a black beauty culture serves as a source of empowerment for black women:

> Brown business it is, in all its magnitude for Miss Brown America receives her
> treatments from the hands of Negro beauticians and her hair preparations and
> skin dreams come, usually from Negro laboratories.

She then tells the reader that leading companies in this field were founded by black women: Madam C. J. Walker, Mrs. Annie Turbo Malone, Madame Sara Spencer Washington. And one is struck by the absences that this essay evokes, not only in comparison to Goffman's piece but also to Elsie Johnson McDougald's major manifesto on black women, "The Task of Negro Womanhood" that appeared in Alain Locke's seminal 1925 anthology of African-American thought, *The New Negro*. In McDougald's piece, which outlines all the economic status and achievements of black women at the time, there is absolutely no mention of black beauty culture, no mention of Madame C. J. Walker, although her newspaper ads were among the biggest in black newspapers nationwide during the twenties. (And why did McDougald not mention black women's beauty workers and businesspeople along with the nurses, domestics, clerks, and teachers she discusses at length? It can scarcely be because she, as a trained and experienced writer on black sociological matters, did not think of it.) It is not simply money or black woman's industry or endeavor that makes the black woman present or a presence; it is beauty culture generally that finally brings her into being, and specifically, her presence is generated by her hair. What for one black woman writer, Goffman, is an absence and thus a sign of degradation, is for another a presence and a sign of economic possibilities inherent in feminine aesthetics.

What did I see as a boy when I passed the large black beauty shop on Broad and South streets in Philadelphia where the name of its owner, Adele Reese, commanded such respect or provoked such jealousy? What did I see there but a long row of black women dressed immaculately in white tunics, washing and styling the hair of other black women? That was a sign of what culture, of what set of politics? The sheen of those straightened heads, the entire enterprise of the making of black feminine beauty: Was it an enactment of a degradation inspirited by a bitter inferiority or was it a womanly laying on of hands where black women were, in their way, helping themselves to live through and transcend their degradation? As a boy, I used to watch and wonder as my mother straightened my sisters' hair every Saturday night for church on Sunday morning. Under a low flame on the stove, the hot comb would glow dully; from an open jar of Apex bergamot hair oil or Dixie Peach, my mother would extract blobs and place them on the back of one hand, deftly applying the oil to strands of my sisters' hair with the other. And the strange talk about a "light press" or a "heavy press" or a "close press" to get the edges and the ends; the concern about the hair "going back" if caught in the rain. Going back where, I wondered. To Africa? To the bush? And the constant worry and vigil about burning, getting too close to the scalp. I can remember hearing my sisters' hair sizzle and crackle as the comb passed through with a kind of pungent smell of actually burning hair. And I, like an intentional moth, with lonely narrow arcs, hovered near this flame of femininity with a fascinated impertinence. Had I witnessed the debilitating nullity of absence or was it the affirmation of an inescapable presence? Had I witnessed a mutilation or a rite of devotion? Black women's hair is, I decided even as a boy, unintelligible. And now I wonder, is the acceptance of the reigns of black women

as Miss America a sign that black beauty has become part of the mainstream culture? Is the black woman now truly a presence?

We, I and my wife and our daughters, sat together and watched the latest
Miss America contest. We did what we usually do. We ate popcorn. We laughed at
all the talent numbers, particularly the ones when the contestants were opera
singers or dancers. We laughed when the girls tried to answer grand social questions—such as "How can we inspire children to achieve and stay in school?" or
"How can we address the problem of mainstreaming physically disadvantaged
people?"—in thirty seconds. In fact, as Rosalind told me after the show, the main
reason my daughters watch the Miss America pageant is that "it's funny." My
daughters laugh because they cannot understand why the women are doing what
they are doing, why they are trying so hard to please, to be pleasing. This must
certainly be a refreshing bit of sanity, as the only proper response for such a contest is simply to dismiss it as hilarious; this grandiose version of an elocution,
charm school, dance and music recital, which is not a revelation of talent but a
reaffirmation of bourgeois cultural conditioning. And this bit of sanity on my
daughters' part may prove hopeful for our future, for our American future, for our
African-American future, if black girls are, unlike my wife when she was young,
no longer angry. When it was announced that Miss Missouri, Debbye Turner, the
third black to be Miss America, was the winner, my children were indifferent. It
hardly mattered to them who won, and a black woman's victory meant no more
than if any other contestant had prevailed. "She's pretty," Linnet said. She won two
dollars in a bet with my wife, who did not think it possible that another black
Miss America would be chosen. "Vanessa screwed up for the whole race," she told
me once. "It's the race burden, the sins of the one become the original sins of us
all." Linnet said simply, "She'll win because she is the best." Meritocracy is still a
valid concept with the young.

For me, it was almost to be expected that Miss Turner would win. First, she
received more precontest publicity than any other contestant in recent years,
with the possible exception of the black woman who was chosen Miss Mississippi a few years ago. Second, after the reign of Vanessa Williams, one would
think that the Miss America powers that be very much wanted to have another
black win and have a successful reign so that the contest itself could both prove
its good faith (to blacks) and forestall criticism from white feminists and liberals
(who are always put in a difficult position when the object of their disapproval is
a black woman). As with the selection of Williams, the contest gained a veneer of
postmodernist social and political relevance not only by selecting a black again
but by having an Asian, a kidney donor, and a hearing-impaired woman among
the top ten finalists. This all smacks of Affirmative Action or the let's-play-fair-
with-the-underrepresented doctrine, which, as Miss Virginia pointed out after
the contest, smacks of politics. But the point she missed, of course, is the point
that all people who oppose Affirmative Action miss. The selection process for the
Miss America contest has always been political. Back in the days when only white
college women, whose main interest in most instances was a degree in MRS,
could win, the contest was indeed just as political as it is now, a clear ideological

bow to both patriarchal ideals and racism. It is simply a matter of which politics you prefer, and while no politics are perfect, some are clearly better than others. But in America, it must be added, the doctrine of fair play shouldn't even be graced with such a sophisticated term as "political." It is more our small-town, bourgeois Christian, muscular myth of ethical rectitude, the tremendous need Americans feel to be decent. So Miss Turner is intended to be both the supercession of Vanessa Williams—a religious vet student whose ambitions are properly, well, postmodernist Victorianism, preach do-goodism, evoke the name of God whenever you speak of your ambitions, and live with smug humility—and the redemption of the image of black women in American popular culture, since the Miss America contest is one of the few vehicles of display and competition for women in popular culture.

And if my daughters have come to one profound penetration of this cultural rite, it is that the contest ought to be laughed at in some ways, as most of the manifestations of popular culture ought to be for being the shoddy illusions that they are. For one always ought to laugh at someone or a group of someones who are trying to convince you that nothing is something—and that is not really the same as someone trying to convince you that you can have something for nothing, because in the popular culture business, the price for nothing is the same as the price for something; this "nothing is something" is, in fact, in most cases what the merchandising of popular culture is all about. (But as my mother reminded me as a boy: Nothing is nothing and something is something. Accept no substitutes!) For my children, the contest can be laughed at because it is so completely meaningless to them; they know it is an illusion despite its veneer as a competition. And it is that magical word "competition," which is used over and over again all night long by the hosts and hostesses of the Miss America show (a contest, like most others these days, from the SATs to professional sports, that is made up of a series of competitions within the framework of larger competitions in such a pyramid that the entire structure of the outside world, for the bourgeois mind, is a frightful maze, a strangulating skein of competitions), that is the touchstone of reality, the momentous signifier that the sponsors of the pageant hope will give this extravaganza new significance and new life. For everything that we feel is important now is a matter of competition, beating out someone else for a prize, for some cheap prestige, a moment of notice before descending to cipherhood again; competition ranging from high culture (literary prizes, which seem to be awarded every day in the week, and classical music competitions for every instrument in a symphony orchestra, because of course for high culture one can never have enough art) to mid-culture (the entire phenomenon of American education, from academic honors to entrance requirements for prestigious schools, because of course for the middle class one can never have enough education or enough professionalism) to low culture (playing the lottery and various forms of gambling, because of course for the lower class one can never hope enough for money). And the most stringent and compulsively expressed the competition is (and the Miss America contest has reached a new height of hysteria in both the stridency and compulsion of the competition), the more legitimate and noteworthy it is.

Everyone in our culture wants to win a prize. Perhaps that is the grand lesson we have taken with us from kindergarten in the age of the perversions of Dewey-style education: Everyone gets a ribbon, and praise becomes a meaningless narcotic to soothe egoistic distemper. And in our bourgeois coming-of-age, we simply crave more and more ribbons and praise, the attainment of which becomes all the more delightful and satisfying if they are gotten at someone else's expense. Competition, therefore, becomes in the end a kind of laissez-faire psychotherapy that structures and orders our impossible rages of ambition, our rages to be noticed. But competition does not produce better people (a myth we have swallowed whole); it does not even produce better candidates; it simply produces more desperately grasping competitors. The "quality" of the average Miss America contestant is not significantly better now than it was twenty-five years ago, although the desires of today's contestants may meet with our approval (who could possibly disapprove of a black woman who wishes to be a vet in this day of careerism as the expression of independence and political empowerment), but then the women of twenty-five years ago wanted what their audiences approved of as well. That is not necessarily an advance or progress; that is simply a recognition that we are all bound by the mood and temper of our time. So, in this vast competition, this fierce theatrical warfare where all the women are supposed to love their neighbor while they wish to beat her brains out, this warfare so pointedly exposed before the nation, what we have chosen is not the Royal American Daughter (although the contest's preoccupation with the terminology of aristocracy mirrors the public's need for such a person as the American princess) but rather the Cosmopolitan Girl. As the magazine ad states:

> Can a girl be too busy? I'm taking seventeen units at Princeton, pushing on with my career during vacations and school breaks, study singing and dancing when I can, try never to lose track of my five closest chums, steal the time for Michael Jackson and Thomas Hardy, work for an anti-drug program for kids and, oh yes, I hang out with three horses, three cats, two birds and my dog Jack. My favorite magazine says "too busy" just means you don't want to miss anything. . . . I love that magazine. I guess you can say I'm That Cosmopolitan Girl.

When one reads about these women in the Miss America contest, that is precisely what they sound like: the Cosmopolitan Girl who knows how to have serious fun, and she has virtually nothing with which to claim our attention except a moralistic bourgeois diligence. To use a twenties term: she sounds "swell." She is an amalgam of both lead characters portrayed by Patty Duke on her old TV show: the studious, serious kid and the "typical" wacky but good-hearted suburban teenager, or, to borrow Ann Douglas's concept, she is the Teen Angel: the bourgeois girl who can do everything, is completely self-absorbed with her leisure, and has a heart of gold. Once again, with the Miss America contest we have America's vehement preoccupation with innocence, with its inability to deal with the darkness of youth, the darkness of its own uselessly expressed ambition, the dark complexity of its own simplistic morality of sunshine and success, the darkness, righteous rage, and bitter depth of its own daughters. Once again, when the new

Miss America, victorious and smiling, walks down the runway, we know that runway, that victory march, to be the American catwalk of supreme bourgeois self-consciousness and supreme illusion. We are still being told that nothing is something.

Nonetheless, the fact that Miss Turner won struck both my wife and me as important, as something important for the race. We laughed during the contest, but we did not laugh when she was chosen. We wanted her to win very much; it is impossible to escape that need to see the race uplifted, to thumb your nose at whites in a competition. It is impossible for blacks not to want to see their black daughters elevated to the platforms where white women are. Perhaps this tainted desire, an echoing "Ballad of the Brown Girl" that resounds in the unconscious psyche of all black people, is the unity of feeling that is the only race pride blacks have ever had since they became Americans; for race pride for the African American, finally, is something that can only be understood as existing on the edge of tragedy and history and is, finally, that which binds both together to make the African American the darkly and richly complicated person he or she is. In the end, both black women magazine writers quoted earlier were right: race pride is transcending your degradation while learning to live in it and with it. To paraphrase an idea of Dorothy Sayers, race pride must teach blacks that they are not to be saved *from* degradation but saved *in* it.

A few days after the contests I watched both my daughters playing Barbies, as they call it. They squat on the floor on their knees, moving their dolls around through an imaginary town and in imaginary houses. I decided to join them and squatted down too, asking them the rules of their game, which they patiently explained as though they did not mind having me, the strange adult, invade their children's world. I told them it was hard for me to squat and asked if I could simply sit down, but they said that one always plays Barbies while squatting. It was a rule that had to be obeyed. As they went along, explaining relationships among their myriad dolls and the several landscapes, as complicated a genealogy as anything Faulkner ever dreamed up, a theater as vast as the entire girlhood of the world, they told me that one particular black Ken doll and one particular black Barbie doll were married and that the dolls had a child. Then Rosalind held up a white doll that someone, probably a grandparent, had given them (my wife is fairly strict on the point of our daughters' not having white dolls, but I guess a few have slipped through), explaining that this doll was the daughter of the black Ken and Barbie.

"But," I said, "how could two black dolls have a white daughter?"

"Oh," said Rosalind, looking at me as if I were an object deserving of only her indulgent pity, "we're not racial. That's old-fashioned. Don't you think so, Daddy? Aren't you tired of all that racial stuff?"

Bowing to that wisdom which, it is said, is the only kind that will lead us to Christ and to ourselves, I decided to get up and leave them to their play. My knees had begun to hurt and I realized, painfully, that I was much too old, much too at peace with stiffness and inflexibility, for children's games.

NOTES

1. Richard Wright tells a story in his 1956 account of the Bandung conference, entitled *The Color Curtain,* that emphasizes the absence of the black woman. He relates how a white woman journalist knocks on his hotel room door during the course of the conference and confides the strange behavior of her roommate—a black woman journalist from Boston. Her roommate walks around in the middle of the night and the white woman often covertly spies her in "a dark corner of the room . . . bent over a tiny blue light, a very low and a very blue flame. . . . It seemed like she was combing her hair, but I wasn't sure. Her right arm was moving and now and then she would look over her shoulder toward my bed." The white woman thinks that the black woman is practicing voodoo. But Wright soon explains that the black woman is simply straightening her hair.

> "But why would she straighten her hair? Her hair seems all right" [the white woman journalist asks].
> "Her hair is all right. But it's not straight. It's kinky. But she does not want you, a white woman, to see her when she straightens her hair. She would feel embarrassed "
> "Why?"
> "Because you were born with straight hair, and she wants to look as much like you as possible. . . . "
> The woman stared at me, then clapped her hands to her eyes and exclaimed:
> "Oh!"
> I leaned back and thought: here in Asia, where everybody was dark, the poor American Negro woman was worried about the hair she was born with. Here, where practically nobody was white, her hair would have been acceptable; no one would have found her "inferior" because her hair was kinky; on the contrary, the Indonesians would perhaps have found her different and charming.

The conversation continues with an account of the black woman's secretive skin-lightening treatments. What is revealing in this dialogue, which takes on both political and psychoanalytic proportions, is the utter absence of the black woman's voice, her presence. She is simply the dark, neurotic ghost that flits in the other room while the black male and the white female, both in the same room, one with dispassionate curtness and the other with sentimentalized guilt, consider the illness that is enacted before them as a kind of bad theater. Once again, the psychopathology of the black American is symbolized by the black woman's straightened hair, by her beauty culture.

Considerations

Thinking

What is Early's view of the Miss America pageant? What does he dislike about it? What does he like? Why? How do the views of his wife and daughters compare with his view of the pageant? How do you understand Early's paradoxical statement "race pride becomes both the act of making a virtue of necessity and making a necessity of a virtue"?

Connecting

What connections does Early make between the Miss America pageant and barbie dolls?

What connection does Early make between racial pride and hair styles?

Why does Early include quotations from Lillian Franklin McCall's 1940 magazine article on the history of women beauty shop owners and entrepreneurs?

How does the connection Early makes between *Cosmopolitan* magazine and the Miss America pageant relate to his overall idea in the essay?

Writing

Write an essay in which you inquire into the values of a popular cultural competition, such as sports car racing, body-building contests, ice-skating competitions, the NCAA basketball tournament, the Super Bowl, or the like. Explain what is at stake in the competition. Identify and analyze the social and cultural values it reflects.

Gretel Ehrlich
(b. 1946)

Educated at Bennington, the UCLA Film School, and the New School for Social Research, Gretel Ehrlich now lives in California, where she grew up. *The Solace of Open Spaces,* her first book of essays about her life in Wyoming, won the Harold B. Vurcell Memorial Award. She has also written a novel *(Heart Mountain)* about Japanese internment during World War II, a second collection of essays *(Islands, Universe, and Home),* and, most recently, a long narrative *(A Match to the Heart)* detailing her physical and spiritual recovery after being struck by lightning. Her other awards include a Whiting Foundation grant for "Spring," and a Guggenheim Fellowship.

"Looking for a Lost Dog" turns from the dog to a pursuit of the "peregrine saunterings of the mind." As Ehrlich follows her own deep longings, her interest shifts to the struggle that takes place in our lives between "impulse and reason, logic and passion." "Spring" takes up the question of indeterminacy, focusing on the undercurrents that inform illusions of permanence, stillness, and the linear nature of time.

Looking for a Lost Dog

The most valuable thoughts which I entertain are anything but what *I* thought. Nature abhors a vacuum, and if I can only walk with sufficient carelessness I am sure to be filled.

— HENRY DAVID THOREAU

I started off this morning looking for my lost dog. He's a red heeler, blotched brown and white, and I tell people he looks like a big saddle shoe. Born at Christmas on a thirty-below-zero night, he's tough, though his right front leg is crooked where it froze to the ground.

It's the old needle-in-the-haystack routine: small dog, huge landscape, and rugged terrain. While moving cows once, he fell in a hole and disappeared. We heard him whining but couldn't see him. When we put our ears to the ground, we could hear the hole that had swallowed him.

It's no wonder human beings are so narcissistic. The way our ears are constructed, we can only hear what's right next to us or else the internal monologue inside. I've taken to cupping my hands behind my ears—mule-like—and pricking them all the way forward or back to hear what's happened or what's ahead.

"Life is polyphonic," a Hungarian friend in her eighties said. She was a child prodigy from Budapest who had soloed on the violin in Paris and Berlin by the time she was twelve. "Childishly, I once thought hearing had mostly to do with music," she said. "Now that I'm too old to play the fiddle, I know it has to do with the great suspiration of life everywhere."

But back to the dog. I'm walking and looking and listening for him, though there is no trail, no clue, no direction to the search. Whimsically, I head north toward the falls. They're set in a deep gorge where Precambrian rock piles up to ten thousand feet on either side. A raven creaks overhead, flies into the cleft, glides toward a panel of white water splashing over a ledge, and comes out cawing.

To find what is lost is an art in some cultures. The Navajos employ "hand tremblers," usually women, who go into a trance and "see" where the lost article or person is located. When I asked one such diviner what it was like when she was in trance, she said, "Lots of noise, but noise that's hard to hear."

Near the falls the ground flattens into a high-altitude valley before the mountains rise vertically. The falls roar, but they're overgrown with spruce, pine, willow, and wild rose, and the closer I get, the harder it is to see the water. Perhaps that is how it will be in my search for the dog.

We're worried about Frenchy because last summer he was bitten three times by rattlesnakes. After the first bite he walked toward me, reeled dramatically, and collapsed. I could see the two holes in his nose where the fangs went in, and I felt sure he was dying. I drove him twenty miles to the vet; by the time we arrived, Frenchy resembled a monster. His nose and neck had swollen as though a football had been sewn under the skin.

I walk and walk. Past the falls, through a pass, toward a larger, rowdier creek. The sky goes black. In the distance snow on the Owl Creek Mountains glares. A blue ocean seems to stretch between, and the black sky hangs over like a frown. A string of cottonwoods whose new, tender leaves are the color of limes pulls me downstream. I come into the meadow with the abandoned apple orchard. The trees have leaves but have lost most of their blossoms. I feel as if I had caught strangers undressed.

The sun comes back, and the wind. It brings no dog, but ducks slide overhead. An Eskimo from Barrow, Alaska, told me the reason spring has such fierce winds is so birds coming north will have something to fly on.

To find what's lost; to lose what's found. Several times I've thought I might be "losing my mind." Of course, minds aren't literally misplaced—on the contrary, we live too much under them. As with viewing the falls, we can lose sight of what is too close. It is between the distant and close-up views that the struggle between impulse and reason, logic and passion takes place.

The feet move; the mind wanders. In his journals Thoreau wrote: "The saunterer, in the good sense, is no more vagrant than the meandering river, which is all the while sedulously seeking the shortest course to the sea."

Today I'm filled with longings—for what I'm not, for what is impossible, for people I love who can't be in my life. Passions of all sorts struggle soundlessly, or else, like the falls, they are all noise but can't be seen. My hybrid anguish spends itself as recklessly and purposefully as water.

Now I'm following a game trail up a sidehill. It's a mosaic of tracks—elk, deer, rabbit, and bird. If city dwellers could leave imprints in cement, it would look this way: tracks would overlap, go backward and forward like the peregrine saunterings of the mind.

I see a dog's track, or is it a coyote's? I get down on my hands and knees to sniff out a scent. What am I doing? I entertain expectations of myself as preposterous as when I landed in Tokyo—I felt so at home there that I thought I would break into fluent Japanese. Now I sniff the ground and smell only dirt. If I spent ten years sniffing, would I learn scents?

The tracks veer off the trail and disappear. Descending into a dry wash whose elegant, tortured junipers and tumbled boulders resemble a Japanese garden, I trip on a sagebrush root. I look. Deep in the center of the plant there is a bird's nest, but instead of eggs, a locust stares up at me.

Some days I think this one place isn't enough. That's when nothing is enough, when I want to live multiple lives and be allowed to love without limits. Those days, like today, I walk with a purpose but no destination. Only then do I see, at least momentarily, that everything is here. To my left a towering cottonwood is lunatic with birdsong. Under it I'm a listening post while its great gray trunk—like a baton or the source of something—heaves its green symphony into the air.

I walk and walk: from the falls, over Grouse Hill, to the dry wash. Today it is enough to make a shadow.

Considerations

Thinking

About halfway through this essay, references to the dog get more and more scarce. Where do you last sense the dog's presence? What do you think his disappearance suggests about the essay's meaning?

What do you suppose Ehrlich means by this revelation: "My hybrid anguish spends itself as recklessly and purposefully as water"? Cite evidence from the essay to back up your interpretation.

Look carefully at the last two paragraphs. What signs do you find of solace? Of compromise?

Connecting

How does Ehrlich help you understand Thoreau's idea that "the most valuable thoughts which I entertain are anything but what *I* thought"?

What do you suppose Ehrlich's Hungarian friend meant about hearing "the great suspiration of life everywhere"? Why do you think Ehrlich quotes her?

Make five columns on a blank sheet of paper and list one of the senses at the top of each. Read through the essay again and keep track of the references to each of the five senses. How does that exercise alter your sense of the essay's meaning? Now read Robynn Stacy Maines's essay "Finding a Dog Not Lost in 'Looking for a Lost Dog.'" How does Maines's essay help you understand Ehrlich's? Explain.

Writing

Select a sentence from Ehrlich's essay—as she did from Thoreau's—to use as the epigraph for your own essay. Develop that essay to deepen the understanding of the sentence you chose.

Jot down a list of the people and the quotations Ehrlich introduces in her essay. Then make a list of her most compelling images. Write a paragraph about each list, explaining how the list helps you understand the essay.

Spring

Gretel Ehrlich

We have a nine-acre lake on our ranch and a warm spring that feeds it all winter. By mid-March the lake ice begins to melt where the spring feeds in, and every year the same pair of mallards come ahead of the others and wait. Though there is very little open water, they seem content. They glide back and forth through a thin estuary, brushing watercress with their elegant, folded wings, then tip end-up to eat and, after, clamber onto the lip of ice that retreats, hardens forward, and retreats again.

Mornings, a transparent pane of ice lies over the melt-water. I peer through and see some kind of waterbug—perhaps a leech—paddling like a sea turtle between green ladders of lakeweed. Cattails and sweet grass from the previous summer are bone dry, marked with black mold spots, and bend like elbows into the ice. They are swords that cut away the hard tenancy of winter. At the wide end, a mat of dead water plants has rolled back into a thick, impregnable breakwater. Near it, bubbles trapped under the ice are lenses focused straight up to catch the coming season.

It's spring again, and I wasn't finished with winter. That's what I said at the end of summer too. I stood on the ten-foot-high haystack and yelled, "No!" as the first snow fell. We had been up since four in the morning, picking the last bales of hay from the oat field by hand, slipping under the weight of them in the mud, and by the time we finished the stack, six inches of snow had fallen.

It's spring, but I was still cataloguing the different kinds of snow: snow that falls dry but is rained on; snow that melts down into hard crusts; wind-driven snow that looks blue; powder snow on hard pack on powder—a Linzer torte of snow. I look up. The troposphere is the five-mile-wide sleeve of air out of which all our weather shakes. A bank of clouds drives in from the south. Where in it, I wonder, does a snowflake take on its thumbprint uniqueness? Inside the cloud, where schools of flakes like schools of fish are flung this way and that? What gives the snowflake its needle, plate, column, branching shapes—the battering wind or the dust particles around which water vapor clings?

Near town the river ice breaks up and lies stacked in industrial-sized hunks on the banks—big as railway cars—and is flecked black by wheeling hurricanes of plowed topsoil. That's how I feel when winter breaks up inside me: heavy, upended, inert against the flow of a new season. I had thought about ice during the cold months too. How it is movement betrayed, water seized in the moment of falling. In November, ice thickened over the lake like a cataract and from the air looked like a Cyclops: one bad eye. Under its milky spans over irrigation ditches, the sound of water running south was muffled. One solitary spire of ice hung noiselessly against dark rock at the falls, as if mocking or mirroring the broomtail comet on the horizon. Then, in February, I tried for words not about ice but words hacked from it—the ice at the end of the mind, so to speak—and failed.

Those were winter things, and now it is spring, though one name can't describe what, in Wyoming, is a three-part affair: false spring, the vernal equinox, and the spring in June, when flowers come and the grass grows.

Spring means restlessness. The physicist I've been talking to all winter says if I look more widely, deeply, and microscopically all at once, I might see how springlike the whole cosmos is. What I see as order and stillness, the robust, time-bound determinacy of my life, is really a mirage suspended above chaos. "There's a lot of random jiggling going on everywhere," he tells me. Winter's tight sky hovers. Under it, hayfields are green, then white, then green growing under white. The confinement I've felt since November resembles the confinement of sub-atomic particles, I'm told. A natural velocity finally shows itself. Particles move and become waves.

Sap rises in trees and in me, and the hard knot of perseverance I cultivated to meet winter dissipates; I walk away from the obsidian of bitter nights. Now snow comes wet and heavy, but the air it traverses feels light. I sleep less and dream not of human entanglements but of animals I've never seen: a caterpillar fat as a man's thumb, made of linked silver tubes, has two heads—one human, one a butterfly's.

Last spring at this time I was coming out of a bout with pneumonia. I went to bed on January 1 and didn't get up until the end of February. Winter was a cocoon in which my gagging, basso cough shook the dark figures at the end of my bed. Had I read too much Hemingway? Or was I dying? I'd lie on my stomach and look out. Nothing close-up interested me. All engagements of mind—the circumlocutions of love interests and internal gossip—appeared false. Only my body was true. And my body was trying to close down, go out the window without me.

I saw things out there. Our ranch faces south down a long treeless valley whose vanishing point is two gray hills folded one in front of the other like two hands, beyond which is space, cerulean air, pleated clouds, and red mesas standing up like breaching whales in a valley three thousand feet below. Afternoons, our young horses played, rearing up on back legs and pawing oh so carefully at each other, reaching around, ears flat back, nipping manes and withers. One of those times their falsetto squeals looped across the pasture and hung, but when I tried to intone their sounds of delight, I found my lungs had no air.

It was thirty-five below zero that night. Our plumbing froze and because I was very weak my husband had to bundle me up and help me to the outhouse. Nothing close at hand seemed to register with me: neither the cold nor the semi-coziness of an uninsulated house. But the stars were lurid. For a while I thought I saw dead horses, eating one another's manes and tails, spinning above my head in the ice fall.

Scientists talk animatedly about how insignificant we humans are when placed against the time scale of geology and the cosmos. I had heard it a hundred times but never felt it truly. Back in bed, I felt the black room was a screen through which parts of my body traveled, leaving the rest behind. I thought I was a sun flying over a barge whose iron holds soaked me up until I became rust, floating on a bright river. A ferocious loneliness took hold of me. That night a luscious, creamy fog rolled in like a roll of fat hugging me, but it was snow.

Recuperation is like spring: dormancy and vitality collide. In any year I'm like a bear, a partial hibernator. During January thaws I stick my nose out and peruse the frozen desolation as if reading a book whose language I don't know. In March I'm ramshackle, weak in the knees, giddy, dazzled by broken-backed clouds, the passing of Halley's comet, the on-and-off strobe of sun. Like a sheepherder, I x out each calendar day as if time were a forest through which I could clear-cut a way to the future. The physicist straightens me out on this point too. The notion of "time passing," like a train through a landscape, is an illusion, he says. I hold the Big Ben clock taken from a dead sheepherder's wagon. The clock measures intervals of time, not the speed of time, and the calendar is a scaffolding we hang as if time were rushing water we could harness. Time-bound, I hinge myself to a linear bias—cause and effect all laid out in a neat row.

Julius Caesar had a sense of humor about time. The Roman calendar with its kalends, nones, and ides—counting days—changed according to who was in power. Caesar serendipitously added days, changed the names of certain months, and when he was through, the calendar was so skewed, January fell in autumn.

Einsteinian time is too big for even Julius Caesar to have touched. It stretches and shrinks and dilates. Indecipherable from space, time is not one thing but an infinity of space-times, overlapping and interfering. There is no future that is not now, no past that is not now. Time includes every moment.

It's the Ides of March today.

I've walked to a hill a mile from the house. It's not really a hill but a mountain slope that heaves up, turns sideways, and comes straight down to a foot-wide creek. Everything I can see from here used to be a flatland covered with shallow water. "Used to be" means several hundred million years ago, and the land itself was not really "here" at all but part of a continent floating near Bermuda. On top is a fin of rock, a marine deposition from Jurassic times created by small waves moving in and out from the shore.

I've come here for peace and quiet and to see what's going on in this secluded valley away from ranch work and sorting corrals, but what I get is a slap on the ass by a prehistoric wave, gains and losses in altitude and aridity, outcrops of mud composed of rotting volcanic ash which fell continuously for ten thousand years, a hundred million years ago. The soils are a geologic flag—red, white, green, and gray. On one side of the hill, mountain mahogany gives off a scent like orange blossoms; on the other, colonies of sagebrush root wide in ground the color of Spanish roof tiles. And it still looks like the ocean to me. "How much truth can a man stand, sitting by the ocean, all that perpetual motion . . . ," Mose Allison, the jazz singer, sings.

The wind picks up and blusters. Its fat underbelly scrapes uneven ground, twisting toward me like taffy, slips up over the mountain and showers out across the Great Plains. The sea smell it carried all the way from Seattle has long since been absorbed by pink gruss—the rotting granite that spills down the slopes of the Rockies. Somewhere over the Midwest the wind slows, tangling in the hair of hardwood forests, and finally drops into the corridors of cities, past Manhattan's World Trade Center, ripping free again as it skims the Atlantic's green swell.

Spring jitterbugs inside me. Spring is wind, symphonic and billowing. A dark cloud pops like a blood blister, spraying red hail down. The sky widens, breaking itself. Wind concusses. It is a cloth that sails so birds have something to fly on.

A message reports to my brain, but I can't believe my eyes. The sheet of wind had a hole in it: an eagle just fell out of the sky as if down the chute of a troubled airplane. Landed, falling. Is there a leg broken? The sides of this narrow valley, a seashore 170,000 years ago, now lift like a medic's litter to catch up this bird.

Hopping, she flaps seven feet of wing and sways near a dead fawn whose carcass had recently been feasted upon. When I approached, all I could see of the animal was a rib cage rubbed red with fine tissue and the decapitated head lying peacefully against sagebrush, eyes closed.

Friends who have investigated eagles' nests have literally feared for their lives. An eagle's talons are a powerful jaw. Their grip is so strong the talons can slice through flesh to bone in one motion.

I had come close to seeing what was wrong, to seeing what I could do. An eagle with a bum leg will starve to death, but when I approached again she lifted her wings threateningly and, craning her neck, first to one side, then to the other, she stared hard, giving me "the eagle eye." Best to leave her alone. My husband dragged a road-killed deer up the mountain slope so she could eat, and I brought a bucket of water.

A golden eagle is not golden but black with yellow spots on the neck and wings. Looking at her, I had wondered how feathers—the rachis, vane, and quill—came to be.

Birds are glorified flying lizards. Positioned together, feathers are like hundreds of smaller wings, evolved from reptilian scales. Ancestral birds had thirteen pairs of cone-shaped teeth that grew in separate sockets like a snake's, rounded ribs, and bony tails. Archaeopteryx was half bird, half dinosaur, and glided instead of flying; ichthyornis was a fish-bird, a relative of the pelican; diatryma was a seven-foot-tall giant with a huge beak and with wings so absurdly small they must have been useless, though later the wing bone sprouted from them. *Aquila chrysaëtos,* the modern golden eagle, has seven thousand contour feathers, no teeth, and weighs about one pound. I think about the eagle on the hill. How big she was, how each time she spread her wings it was like a thought stretching between two seasons.

Back at the house, I relax with a beer. At 5:03 the vernal equinox occurs. I go outside and stand in the middle of a hayfield with my eyes closed. The universe is restless, but I want to feel celestial equipoise: twelve hours of daylight, twelve of dark, and the earth ramrod straight on its axis. Straightening my posture to resist the magnetic tilt back into dormancy, spiritual and emotional reticence, I imagine the equatorial sash, now nose-to-nose with the sun, sizzling like a piece of bacon, and the earth slowly tilting.

In the morning I walk to the valley. The eagle isn't there. The hindquarters of the road-killed deer have been eaten. Coyote tracks circle the carcass. Did they have eagle for dinner too?

Afternoon. I return. Far up on the opposite hill I see her, flapping and hopping to the top. When I stop, she stops and turns her head. Even at two hundred yards, I can feel the heat of her stare.

Later, looking through my binoculars, I try to see the world with eagle eyes. After glassing the crescent moon, I dream it has grown full and doubled. One moon is pink and spins fast; the other is an eagle's head, turning slowly in the opposite direction. Then both moons descend, and it is day.

At first light I clamber up the hill. Now the dead deer my husband brought is only a hoop of ribs, two forelegs, and hair. The eagle is not here or along the creek or on either hill. I climb the slope and sit. After a long wait she careens out from the narrow slit of the red-walled canyon whose creek drains into this valley. Surely it's the same bird. Flying by, she cocks her head and looks at me. I smile. What is a smile to her? Now she is not flying but lifting above the planet, far from me.

Late March. The emerald of the hayfields brightens. A flock of gray-capped rosy finches who overwintered here swarms a leafless apple tree, then falls from the smooth boughs like cut grass. The tree was planted by the Texan who homesteaded this ranch. As I walk past, one of the boughs, shaped like an undulating dragon, splits off from the trunk and drops.

Space is an arena where the rowdy particles that are the building blocks of life perform their antics. All spring, things fall; the general law of increasing disorder is on the rise. What is it to be a cause without an effect, an effect without a cause, to abandon time-bound thinking, the use of tenses, the temporally related emotions of impatience, expectation, hope, and fear? But I can't. At the edge of the lake I watch ducks. Like them, my thinking rises and falls on the same water.

Another day. Feeling small-minded, I take a plane ride over Wyoming. As we take off, the plane resists accepting air under its wings. Is this how an eagle feels? Ernst Mach's principle tells me that an object's resistance against being accelerated is not the intrinsic property of matter but a measure of its interaction with the universe; that matter has inertia only because it exists in relation to other matter.

Airborne, we fly southeast from Heart Mountain across the Big Horn River, over the long red wall where Butch Cassidy trailed stolen horses, across the high plains to Laramie. Coming home, we hit clouds. Turbulence, like many forms of trouble, cannot always be seen. We bounce so hard my arms sail helplessly above my head. In evolution, wing bones became arms and hands; perhaps I'm de-evolving.

From ten thousand feet I can see that spring is only half here: the southern part of the state, being higher in altitude, is white; the northern half is green. Time is one of spring's greening forms, a clock whose hands are blades of grass moving vertically, up through the fringe of numbers, spreading across the middle of the face, sinking again as the sun moves from one horizon to the other. Time doesn't go anywhere; the shadow of the plane, my shadow, moves across it.

To sit on a plane is to sit on the edge of sleep, where the mind's forge bright-ens into incongruities. Down there I see disparate wholenesses strung together and the string dissolving. Mountains run like rivers; I fly through waves and waves of chiaroscuro light. The land looks bare but is articulate. The body of the plane is my body, pressing into spring, pressing matter into relation with matter. Is it even necessary to say the obvious? That spring brings on surges of desire? From this disinterested height I say out loud what Saint Augustine wrote: "My love is my weight. Because of it I move."

Directly below us now is the fine old Wyoming ranch where Joel, Mart, Dave, Hughy, and I have moved thousands of head of cattle. Joel's father, Smokey, was one of two brothers who put the outfit together. They worked hard, lived frugally, and even after his brother died, Smokey did not marry until his late fifties. As tes-timony to a long bachelorhood, there is no kitchen in the main house. The cook-house stands separate from all the other buildings. In back is a bedroom and bath, which has housed a list of itinerant cooks ten pages long.

Over the years I've helped during roundup and branding. We'd rise at four. Smokey, then in his eighties, cooked flapjacks and boiled coffee on the wood cookstove. There was a long table. Joel and Smokey always sat at one end. They were look-alikes, both skin-and-bones tall, with tipped-up dark eyes set in narrow faces. Stern and vigilant, Smokey once threw a young hired hand out of the cookhouse because he hadn't grained his saddle horse after a long day's ride. "On this outfit we take care of our animals first," he said. "Then, if there's time, we eat."

Even in his early twenties, Joel had his father's dignity and razor-sharp wit. They both wore white Stetsons, identically shaped. Only their hands were differ-ent: Joel had eight fingers and one thumb—the other he lost while roping.

Ten summers ago my parents and I visited their ranch. We drank homemade whiskey left over from Prohibition days, ate steaks cut from an Angus bull, four kinds of vegetables, watermelon, ice cream and pie. Despite a thirteen-year differ-ence in our ages, Smokey wanted Joel to marry me. As we rose from the meal, he shook my father's hand. "I guess you'll be my son's father-in-law," he said. That was news to all of us. Joel's face turned crimson. My father threw me an astonished look, cleared his throat, and thanked his host for the fine meal.

One night Joel *did* come to my house and asked if I would take him into my bed. It was a gentlemanly proposition—doffed hat, moist eyes, a smile grimacing with loneliness.

"You're an older woman. Think of all you could teach me," he said jauntily but with a blush. He stood ramrod straight, waiting for an answer. My silence turned him away like a rolling wave, and he drove to the home ranch, spread out across the Emblem Bench, thirty-five miles away.

The night Joel died, I was staying at a friend's farm in Missouri. I had fallen asleep early, then awakened suddenly, feeling claustrophobic. I jumped out of bed and stood in the dark. I wanted to get out of there, drive home to Wyoming, and I didn't know why. Finally, at seven in the morning, able to sleep, I dreamed about a bird landing on, then lifting out of a tree along a riverbank. That was the night Joel's pickup rolled. He wasn't found until daylight and died on the way to the hospital.

Now I'm sitting on a fin of Gypsum Springs rock, looking west. The sun is setting. What I see are three gray cloud towers letting rain down at the horizon. The sky behind these massifs is gilded gold, and long fingers of land—benches where Charolais cattle graze—are pink. Somewhere over Joel's grave, the sky is bright. The road where he died shines like a dash in a Paul Klee painting. But here it is still winter: snow, dry as Styrofoam when squeezed together, tumbles into my lap. I think about flying and falling. The place in the sky where the eagle fell is dark. Why does a wounded eagle get well and fly away? Why do the head wounds of a young man cut him down? Useless questions.

Sex and death are the riddles thrown into the hopper, thrown down on the planet like red and black hailstones. Where one hits the earth, makes a crater, and melts, perhaps a weed can germinate; perhaps not. If I dice life into atoms, the trajectories I find are so wild, so random, anything could happen: life or nonlife. But once we have a body, who can give it up easily? Our own or others'? We check our clocks and build our beautiful narratives, under which indeterminacy seethes.

Sometimes, lying in bed, I feel like a flounder with its two eyes on one side pointing upward into nothingness. The casings of thought rattle. Then I realize there are no casings at all. Is it possible that the mind, like space, is finite but has no boundaries, no center or edge? I sit cross-legged on old blankets. My bare feet strain against the backs of my knees. Just as morning comes and the indigo lifts, the leaflessness of the old apple tree looks ornate. *Nothing in this world is plain.*

"Every atom in your body was once inside a star," another physicist says, trying to humor me. Not all atoms in all kinds of matter are shared. But who wouldn't find that idea appealing? Outside, shadows trade places with a sliver of sun, which trades places with shadow. A Pacific storm blows in from the south like a jib sail reaching far out, backhanding me with a tropical gust. It snows into my mouth, between my breasts, against my shins. Spring teaches me what space and time teach me: that I am a random multiple; that the many fit together; that my swell is a collision of particles. Spring is music, a seething minor, a twelve-tone scale. Odd harmonies amass and lift up only to dissolve.

Spring presses harder and harder and is feral. The first thunder cracks the sky into a larger domain. Sap rises in obdurateness. For the first time in seven months, rain slants down in a slow pavanne—sharp but soft, like desire. I drive the highway that crosses the wild-horse range. Near Emblem a lone black stud horse trots across the landscape. He travels north, then turns in my direction as if coming to me. Now, when I dream of Joel, he is riding that horse and he knows he is dead. One night he rides to my house, all smiles and shyness, and I let him in.

Considerations

Thinking

Look carefully at the first eight paragraphs of Ehrlich's essay "Spring"—up to the first white-space break in the essay. Consider these paragraphs Ehrlich's beginning. Read this section in isolation. What are the things it tells you? What is Ehrlich suggesting? Identify various kinds of movement in these paragraphs; make a list.

Ehrlich keeps letting the physicist into her essay. Why does she do that? How, exactly, does he help her with her main idea?

That physicist tells Ehrlich that "the notion of 'time passing,' like a train through a landscape, is an illusion." If he is right, what is the consequence of being "time-bound," hinged to a "linear bias"?

Connecting

Ehrlich comments often about her *body* throughout this essay. Make a list of those comments, or highlight them in your text. Think of each as a piece of evidence. Considered together, what do those comments about her body tell you about Ehrlich's main idea concerning spring?

Why are Einstein and Julius Caesar in this essay?

What do Ehrlich's two essays "Spring" and "Looking for a Lost Dog" have in common besides their authorship?

Writing

The novelist and essayist Tom Wolfe has said that "Spring is the season of the rising sap." Assume that you are Gretel Ehrlich and that you know how she thinks and how she writes from reading "Spring" and "Looking for a Lost Dog." In the guise of Ehrlich, write Wolfe a letter telling him what you think about his remark.

After reading Ehrlich's two essays in this anthology, see if you can figure out her central preoccupation—let's call it the central facet of her imagination, something that informs all that she writes about. Go to the library or search the Internet to find one more of her essays, selected randomly. Does that essay change your mind about that central facet? Write a short essay explaining and defending your idea about Ehrlich's central preoccupation.

Loren Eiseley
(1907–1977)

Although Loren Eiseley was an anthropologist by profession—a professor and once the provost of the University of Pennsylvania—he considered himself a writer. Other labels, some self-generated (social philosopher, scientist, naturalist, fugitive, drifter), satisfied him less. What he wrote most and liked best were the pieces he called "concealed" essays, essays in which "personal anecdote [is] allowed gently to bring under observation thoughts of a more purely scientific nature." His works include *The Immense Journey, Darwin's Century, The Firmament of Time, The Unexpected Universe, The Invisible Pyramid, The Night Country, All the Strange Hours, The Star Thrower,* three volumes of poetry, and *The Lost Notebooks of Loren Eiseley.* His many awards include the Joseph Wood Krutch Medal, in 1976, for significant contribution toward the improvement of life and the environment.

"The Dance of the Frogs" takes us into that territory between the scientific world of rationality and the more ineffable world of the spirit.

The Dance of the Frogs

I

He was a member of the Explorers Club, and he had never been outside the state of Pennsylvania. Some of us who were world travelers used to smile a little about that, even though we knew his scientific reputation had been, at one time, great. It is always the way of youth to smile. I used to think of myself as something of an adventurer, but the time came when I realized that old Albert Dreyer, huddling with his drink in the shadows close to the fire, had journeyed farther into the Country of Terror than any of us would ever go, God willing, and emerge alive.

He was a morose and aging man, without family and without intimates. His membership in the club dated back into the decades when he was a zoologist famous for his remarkable experiments upon amphibians—he had recovered and actually produced the adult stage of the Mexican axolotl, as well as achieving remarkable tissue transplants in salamanders. The club had been flattered to have him then, travel or no travel, but the end was not fortunate. The brilliant scientist had become the misanthrope; the achievement lay all in the past, and Albert Dreyer kept to his solitary room, his solitary drink, and his accustomed spot by the fire.

The reason I came to hear his story was an odd one. I had been north that year, and the club had asked me to give a little talk on the religious beliefs of the Indians of the northern forest, the Naskapi of Labrador. I had long been a student of the strange mélange of superstition and woodland wisdom that makes up the religious life of the nature peoples. Moreover, I had come to know something of the strange similarities of the "shaking tent rite" to the phenomena of the modern medium's cabinet.

"The special tent with its entranced occupant is no different from the cabinet," I contended. "The only difference is the type of voices that emerge. Many of the physical phenomena are identical—the movement of powerful forces shaking the conical hut, objects thrown, all this is familiar to Western physical science.

What is different are the voices projected. Here they are the cries of animals, the voices from the swamp and the mountain—the solitary elementals before whom the primitive man stands in awe, and from whom he begs sustenance. Here the game lords reign supreme; man himself is voiceless."

A low, halting query reached me from the back of the room. I was startled, even in the midst of my discussion, to note that it was Dreyer.

"And the game lords, what are they?"

"Each species of animal is supposed to have gigantic leaders of more than normal size," I explained. "These beings are the immaterial controllers of that particular type of animal. Legend about them is confused. Sometimes they partake of human qualities, will and intelligence, but they are of animal shape. They control the movements of game, and thus their favor may mean life or death to man."

"Are they visible?" Again Dreyer's low, troubled voice came from the back of the room.

"Native belief has it that they can be seen on rare occasions," I answered. "In a sense they remind one of the concept of the archetypes, the originals behind the petty show of our small, transitory existence. They are the immortal renewers of substance—the force behind and above animate nature."

"Do they dance?" persisted Dreyer.

At this I grew nettled. Old Dreyer in a heckling mood was something new. "I cannot answer that question," I said acidly. "My informants failed to elaborate upon it. But they believe implicitly in these monstrous beings, talk to and propitiate them. It is their voices that emerge from the shaking tent."

"The Indians believe it," pursued old Dreyer relentlessly, "but do *you* believe it?"

"My dear fellow"—I shrugged and glanced at the smiling audience—"I have seen many strange things, many puzzling things, but I am a scientist." Dreyer made a contemptuous sound in his throat and went back to the shadow out of which he had crept in his interest. The talk was over. I headed for the bar.

II

The evening passed. Men drifted homeward or went to their rooms. I had been a year in the woods and hungered for voices and companionship. Finally, however, I sat alone with my glass, a little mellow, perhaps, enjoying the warmth of the fire and remembering the blue snowfields of the North as they should be remembered—in the comfort of warm rooms.

I think an hour must have passed. The club was silent except for the ticking of an antiquated clock on the mantel and small night noises from the street. I must have drowsed. At all events it was some time before I grew aware that a chair had been drawn up opposite me. I started.

"A damp night," I said.

"Foggy," said the man in the shadow musingly. "But not too foggy. They like it that way."

"Eh?" I said. I knew immediately it was Dreyer speaking. Maybe I had missed something; on second thought, maybe not.

"And spring," he said. "Spring. That's part of it. God knows why, of course, but we feel it, why shouldn't they? And more intensely."

"Look—" I said. "I guess—" The old man was more human than I thought. He reached out and touched my knee with the hand that he always kept a glove over—burn, we used to speculate—and smiled softly.

"You don't know what I'm talking about," he finished for me. "And, besides, I ruffled your feelings earlier in the evening. You must forgive me. You touched on an interest of mine, and I was perhaps overeager. I did not intend to give the appearance of heckling. It was only that . . ."

"Of course," I said. "Of course." Such a confession from Dreyer was astounding. The man might be ill. I rang for a drink and decided to shift the conversation to a safer topic, more appropriate to a scholar.

"Frogs," I said desperately, like any young ass in a china shop. "Always admired your experiments. Frogs. Yes."

I give the old man credit. He took the drink and held it up and looked at me across the rim. There was a faint stir of sardonic humor in his eyes.

"Frogs, no," he said, "or maybe yes. I've never been quite sure. Maybe yes. But there was no time to decide properly." The humor faded out of his eyes. "Maybe I should have let go," he said. "It was what they wanted. There's no doubting that at all, but it came too quick for me. What would you have done?"

"I don't know," I said honestly enough and pinched myself.

"You had better know," said Albert Dreyer severely, "if you're planning to become an investigator of primitive religions. Or even not. I wasn't, you know, and the things came to me just when I least suspected—But I forget, you don't believe in them."

He shrugged and half rose, and for the first time, really, I saw the black-gloved hand and the haunted face of Albert Dreyer and knew in my heart the things he had stood for in science. I got up then, as a young man in the presence of his betters should get up, and I said, and I meant it, every word: "Please, Dr. Dreyer, sit down and tell me. I'm too young to be saying what I believe or don't believe in at all. I'd be obliged if you'd tell me."

Just at that moment a strange, wonderful dignity shone out of the countenance of Albert Dreyer, and I knew the man he was. He bowed and sat down, and there were no longer the barriers of age and youthful ego between us. There were just two men under a lamp, and around them a great waiting silence. Out to the ends of the universe, I thought fleetingly, that's the way with man and his lamps. One has to huddle in, there's so little light and so much space. One—

III

"It could happen to anyone," said Albert Dreyer. "And especially in the spring. Remember that. And all I did was to skip. Just a few feet, mark you, but I skipped. Remember that, too.

"You wouldn't remember the place at all. At least not as it was then." He paused and shook the ice in his glass and spoke more easily.

"It was a road that came out finally in a marsh along the Schuylkill River. Probably all industrial now. But I had a little house out there with a laboratory thrown in. It was convenient to the marsh, and that helped me with my studies of amphibia. Moreover, it was a wild, lonely road, and I wanted solitude. It is always the demand of the naturalist. You understand that?"

"Of course," I said. I knew he had gone there, after the death of his young wife, in grief and loneliness and despair. He was not a man to mention such things. "It is best for the naturalist," I agreed.

"Exactly. My best work was done there." He held up his black-gloved hand and glanced at it meditatively. "The work on the axolotl, newt neoteny. I worked hard. I had—" he hesitated—"things to forget. There were times when I worked all night. Or diverted myself, while waiting the result of an experiment, by midnight walks. It was a strange road. Wild all right, but paved and close enough to the city that there were occasional street lamps. All uphill and downhill, with bits of forest leaning in over it, till you walked in a tunnel of trees. Then suddenly you were in the marsh, and the road ended at an old, unused wharf.

"A place to be alone. A place to walk and think. A place for shadows to stretch ahead of you from one dim lamp to another and spring back as you reached the next. I have seen them get tall, tall, but never like that night. It was like a road into space."

"Cold?" I asked.

"No. I shouldn't have said 'space.' It gives the wrong effect. Not cold. Spring. Frog time. The first warmth, and the leaves coming. A little fog in the hollows. The way they like it then in the wet leaves and bogs. No moon, though; secretive and dark, with just those street lamps wandered out from the town. I often wondered what graft had brought them there. They shone on nothing—except my walks at midnight and the journeys of toads, but still . . ."

"Yes?" I prompted, as he paused.

"I was just thinking. The web of things. A politician in town gets a rake-off for selling useless lights on a useless road. If it hadn't been for that, I might not have seen them. I might not even have skipped. Or, if I had, the effect—How can you tell about such things afterwards? Was the effect heightened? Did it magnify their power? Who is to say?"

"The skip?" I said, trying to keep things casual. "I don't understand. You mean, just skipping? Jumping?"

Something like a twinkle came into his eyes for a moment. "Just that," he said. "No more. You are a young man. Impulsive? You should understand."

"I'm afraid—" I began to counter.

"But of course," he cried pleasantly. "I forget. You were not there. So how could I expect you to feel or know about this skipping. Look, look at me now. A sober man, eh?"

I nodded. "Dignified," I said cautiously.

"Very well. But, young man, there is a time to skip. On country roads in the spring. It is not necessary that there be girls. You will skip without them. You will skip because something within you knows the time—frog time. Then you will skip."

"Then I will skip," I repeated, hypnotized. Mad or not, there was a force in Albert Dreyer. Even there under the club lights, the night damp of an unused road began to gather.

IV

"It was a late spring," he said. "Fog and mist in those hollows in a way I had never seen before. And frogs, of course. Thousands of them, and twenty species, trilling, gurgling, and grunting in as many keys. The beautiful keen silver piping of spring peepers arousing as the last ice leaves the ponds—if you have heard that after a long winter alone, you will never forget it." He paused and leaned forward, listening with such an intent inner ear that one could almost hear that far-off silver piping from the wet meadows of the man's forgotten years.

I rattled my glass uneasily, and his eyes came back to me.

"They come out then," he said more calmly. "All amphibia have to return to the water for mating and egg laying. Even toads will hop miles across country to streams and waterways. You don't see them unless you go out at night in the right places as I did, but that night—

"Well, it was unusual, put it that way, as an understatement. It was late, and the creatures seemed to know it. You could feel the forces of mighty and archaic life welling up from the very ground. The water was pulling them—not water as we know it, but the mother, the ancient life force, the thing that made us in the days of creation, and that lurks around us still, unnoticed in our sterile cities.

"I was no different from any other young fool coming home on a spring night, except that as a student of life, and of amphibia in particular, I was, shall we say, more aware of the creatures. I had performed experiments"—the black glove gestured before my eyes. "I was, as it proved, susceptible.

"It began on that lost stretch of roadway leading to the river, and it began simply enough. All around, under the street lamps, I saw little frogs and big frogs hopping steadily toward the river. They were going in my direction.

"At that time I had my whimsies, and I was spry enough to feel the tug of that great movement. I joined them. There was no mystery about it. I simply began to skip, to skip gaily, and enjoy the great bobbing shadow I created as I passed onward with that leaping host all headed for the river.

"Now skipping along a wet pavement in spring is infectious, particularly going downhill, as we were. The impulse to take mightier leaps, to soar farther, increases progressively. The madness worked into me. I bounded till my lungs labored, and my shadow, at first my own shadow, bounded and labored with me.

"It was only midway in my flight that I began to grow conscious that I was not alone. The feeling was not strong at first. Normally a sober pedestrian, I was ecstatically preoccupied with the discovery of latent stores of energy and agility which I had not suspected in my subdued existence.

"It was only as we passed under a street lamp that I noticed, beside my own bobbing shadow, another great, leaping grotesquerie that had an uncanny suggestion of the frog world about it. The shocking aspect of the thing lay in its size, and the fact that, judging from the shadow, it was soaring higher and more gaily than myself.

"'Very well,' you will say"—and here Dreyer paused and looked at me tolerantly—"'Why didn't you turn around? That would be the scientific thing to do.'

"It would be the scientific thing to do, young man, but let me tell you it is not done—not on an empty road at midnight—not when the shadow is already beside your shadow and is joined by another, and then another.

"No, you do not pause. You look neither to left nor right, for fear of what you might see there. Instead, you dance on madly, hopelessly. Plunging higher, higher, in the hope the shadows will be left behind, or prove to be only leaves dancing, when you reach the next street light. Or that whatever had joined you in this midnight bacchanal will take some other pathway and depart.

"You do not look—you cannot look—because to do so is to destroy the universe in which we move and exist and have our transient being. You dare not look, because, beside the shadows, there now comes to your ears the loose-limbed slap of giant batrachian feet, not loud, not loud at all, but there, definitely there, behind you at your shoulder, plunging with the utter madness of spring, their rhythm entering your bones until you too are hurtling upward in some gigantic ecstasy that it is not given to mere flesh and blood to long endure.

"I was part of it, part of some mad dance of the elementals behind the show of things. Perhaps in that night of archaic and elemental passion, that festival of the wetlands, my careless hopping passage under the street lights had called them, attracted their attention, brought them leaping down some fourth-dimensional roadway into the world of time.

"Do not suppose for a single moment I thought so coherently then. My lungs were bursting, my physical self exhausted, but I sprang, I hurtled, I flung myself onward in a company I could not see, that never outpaced me, but that swept me with the mighty ecstasies of a thousand springs, and that bore me onward exultantly past my own doorstep, toward the river, toward some pathway long forgotten, toward some unforgettable destination in the wetlands and the spring.

"Even as I leaped, I was changing. It was this, I think, that stirred the last remnants of human fear and human caution that I still possessed. My will was in abeyance; I could not stop. Furthermore, certain sensations, hypnotic or otherwise, suggested to me that my own physical shape was modifying, or about to change. I was leaping with a growing ease. I was—

"It was just then that the wharf lights began to show. We were approaching the end of the road, and the road, as I have said, ended in the river. It was this, I suppose, that startled me back into some semblance of human terror. Man is a land animal. He does not willingly plunge off wharfs at midnight in the monstrous company of amphibious shadows.

"Nevertheless their power held me. We pounded madly toward the wharf, and under the light that hung above it, and the beam that made a cross. Part of me struggled to stop, and part of me hurtled on. But in that final frenzy of terror before the water below engulfed me I shrieked, *'Help! In the name of God, help me! In the name of Jesus, stop!'*"

Dreyer paused and drew in his chair a little closer under the light. Then he went on steadily.

"I was not, I suppose, a particularly religious man, and the cries merely revealed the extremity of my terror. Nevertheless this is a strange thing, and whether it involves the crossed beam, or the appeal to a Christian deity, I will not attempt to answer.

"In one electric instant, however, I was free. It was like the release from demoniac possession. One moment I was leaping in an inhuman company of elder things, and the next moment I was a badly shaken human being on a wharf. Strangest of all, perhaps, was the sudden silence of that midnight hour. I looked down in the circle of the arc light, and there by my feet hopped feebly some tiny froglets of the great migration. There was nothing impressive about them, but you will understand that I drew back in revulsion. I have never been able to handle them for research since. My work is in the past."

He paused and drank, and then, seeing perhaps some lingering doubt and confusion in my eyes, held up his black-gloved hand and deliberately pinched off the glove.

A man should not do that to another man without warning, but I suppose he felt I demanded some proof. I turned my eyes away. One does not like a webbed batrachian hand on a human being.

As I rose embarrassedly, his voice came up to me from the depths of the chair.

"It is not the hand," Dreyer said. "It is the question of choice. Perhaps I was a coward, and ill prepared. Perhaps"—his voice searched uneasily among his memories—"perhaps I should have taken them and that springtime without question. Perhaps I should have trusted them and hopped onward. Who knows? They were gay enough, at least."

He sighed and set down his glass and stared so intently into empty space that, seeing I was forgotten, I tiptoed quietly away.

Considerations

Thinking

There seem to be two Eiseleys in this essay—the young scientist and the older man looking back, reflecting. What does this sentence, uttered by the younger man, tell you about their differences: "I have seen many strange things, many puzzling things, but I am a scientist"?

Recounting his dance with the frogs, Dreyer tries to account for the force that moved him so close to the water. How effectively does his language serve him? Explain.

Connecting

Do you believe in the "mad dance of the elementals behind the show of things"?

Was Dreyer, as he claimed, "free," released from "demoniac possession," when he turned away at the wharf, or was he more free when he skipped with the frogs? How do you know?

How does Eiseley actually entice you to believe in the dance? What are his techniques?

Writing

Decide whether you think "The Dance of the Frogs" is a tale or an essay, and make that decision the point of an essay. Support your conclusion by citing evidence from specimen pieces (other tales, other essays) or from any other general sources about those two forms of literature. You might also consider other Eiseley essays.

Write a short essay about how Eiseley uses light and shadow to convey meaning.

E. M. Forster
(1879–1970)

E. M. Forster is known to us primarily through his novels and the movies that have been based on them, especially *A Room with a View* and *Howards End*. Forster was also a fine essayist, deft, with a wry sense of humor and a quiet, understated contempt for pomposity. His two most important collections of essays—*Abinger Harvest* and *Two Cheers for Democracy*—although personal and familiar, offer a far-reaching sense of history.

"Not Looking at Pictures" shows us Forster at his self-depreciating best, using humour to inform us about the importance of art. He claims to be ignorant of art's formal concepts while celebrating its ability to set our minds off on "some alien vision."

Not Looking at Pictures

Pictures are not easy to look at. They generate private fantasies, they furnish material for jokes, they recall scraps of historical knowledge, they show landscapes where one would like to wander and human beings whom one would like to resemble or adore, but looking at them is another matter, yet they must have been painted to be looked at. They were intended to appeal to the eye, but almost as if it were gazing at the sun itself the eye often reacts by closing as soon as it catches sight of them. The mind takes charge instead and goes off on some alien vision. The mind has such a congenial time that it forgets what set it going. Van Gogh and Corot and Michelangelo are three different painters, but if the mind is indisciplined and uncontrolled by the eye, they may all three induce the same mood, we may take just the same course through dreamland or funland from them, each time, and never experience anything new.

I am bad at looking at pictures myself, and the late Roger Fry enjoyed going to a gallery with me now and then, for this very reason. He found it an amusing change to be with someone who scarcely ever saw what the painter had painted. "Tell me, why do you like this, why do you prefer it to that?" he would ask, and listen agape for the ridiculous answer. One day we looked at a fifteenth-century Italian predella, where a St. George was engaged in spearing a dragon of the plesiosaurus type. I laughed. "Now, *what* is there funny in this?" pounced Fry. I readily explained. The fun was to be found in the expression upon the dragon's face. The spear had gone through its hooped-up neck once, and now startled it by arriving at a second thickness. "Oh dear, here it comes again, I hoped that was all" it was thinking. Fry laughed too, but not at the misfortunes of the dragon. He was amazed that anyone could go so completely off the lines. There was no harm in it—but really, really! He was even more amazed when our enthusiasms coincided: "I fancy we are talking about different things," he would say, and we always were; I liked the mountain-back because it reminded me of a peacock, he because it had some structural significance, though not as much as the sack of potatoes in the foreground.

Long years of wandering down miles of galleries have convinced me that there must be something rare in those coloured slabs called "pictures," something which I am incapable of detecting for myself, though glimpses of it are to be had through the eyes of others. How much am I missing? And what? And are other modern sight-seers in the same fix? Ours is an aural rather than a visual age, we do not get so lost in the concert hall, we seem able to hear music for ourselves, and to hear it as music, but in galleries so many of us go off at once into a laugh or a sigh or an amorous day-dream. In vain does the picture recall us. "What have your obsessions got to do with me?" it complains. "I am neither a theatre of varieties nor a spring-mattress, but paint. Look at my paint." Back we go—the picture kindly standing still meanwhile, and being to that extent more obliging than music—and resume the looking-business. But something is sure to intervene—a tress of hair, the half-open door of a summer-house, a Crivelli dessert, a Bosch fish-and-fiend salad—and to draw us away.

One of the things that helps us to keep looking is composition. For many years now I have associated composition with a diagonal line, and when I find such a line I imagine I have gutted the picture's secret. Giorgione's Castelfranco Madonna has such a line in the lance of the warrior-saint, and Titian's Entombment at Venice has a very good one indeed. Five figures contribute to make up the diagonal; beginning high on the left with the statue of Moses, it passes through the heads of the Magdalene, Mary, and the dead Christ, and plunges through the body of Joseph of Arimathea into the ground. Making a right angle to it, flits the winged Genius of Burial. And to the right, apart from it, and perpendicular, balancing the Moses, towers the statue of Faith. Titian's Entombment is one of my easiest pictures. I look at photographs of it intelligently, and encourage the diagonal and the pathos to reinforce one another. I see, with more than usual vividness, the grim alcove at the back and the sinister tusked pedestals upon which the two statues stand. Stone shuts in flesh; the whole picture is a tomb. I hear sounds of lamentation, though not to the extent of shattering the general scheme; that is held together by the emphatic diagonal, which no emotion breaks. Titian was a very old man when he achieved this masterpiece; that too I realise, but not immoderately. Composition here really has been a help, and it is a composition which no one can miss; the diagonal slopes as obviously as the band on a threshing-machine, and vibrates with power.

Unfortunately, having no natural esthetic aptitude, I look for diagonals everywhere, and if I cannot find one think the composition must be at fault. It is a word which I have learnt—a solitary word in a foreign language. For instance, I was completely baffled by Velasquez's Las Meninas. Wherever was the diagonal? Then the friend I was with—Charles Mauron, the friend who, after Roger Fry, has helped me with pictures most—set to work on my behalf, and cautiously underlined the themes. There is a wave. There is a half-wave. The wave starts up on the left, with the head of the painter, and curves down and up through the heads of the three girls. The half-wave starts with the head of Isabel de Velasco, and sinks out of the canvas through the dwarfs. Responding to these great curves, or inverting them, are smaller ones on the women's dresses or elsewhere. All these waves are not merely pattern; they are doing other work too—e.g., helping to bring out the effect of depth in the room, and the effect of air. Important too is the pushing forward of objects in the extreme left and right foregrounds, the easel of the painter in the one case, the paws of a placid dog in the other. From these, the composition curves back to the central figure, the lovely child-princess. I put it more crudely than did Charles Mauron, nor do I suppose that his account would have been Velasquez's, or that Velasquez would have given any account at all. But it is an example of the way in which pictures should be tackled for the benefit of us outsiders: coolly and patiently, as if they were designs, so that we are helped at last to the appreciation of something non-mathematical. Here again, as in the case of the Entombment, the composition and the action reinforced one another. I viewed with increasing joy that adorable party, which had been surprised not only by myself but by the King and Queen of Spain. There they were in the looking-glass! Las Meninas has a snap-shot quality. The party might have been taken by Philip IV, if Philip IV had had a Kodak. It is all so casual—and yet it is all so elaborate and sophisticated, and I suppose those curves and the rest of it help to bring this out, and to evoke a vanished civilisation.

Besides composition there is colour. I look for that, too, but with even less success. Colour is visible when thrown in my face—like the two cherries in the great grey Michael Sweertz group in the National Gallery. But as a rule it is only material for dream.

On the whole, I am improving, and after all these years, I am learning to get myself out of the way a little, and to be more receptive, and my appreciation of pictures does increase. If I can make any progress at all, the average outsider should do better still. A combination of courage and modesty is what he wants. It is so unenterprising to annihilate everything that's made to a green thought, even when the thought is an exquisite one. Not looking at art leads to one goal only. Looking at it leads to so many.

Considerations

Thinking

What do you think of Forster's claim that when confronted with pictures, "the mind takes charge . . . and goes off on some alien vision"? Is that what happens to you when you look at paintings? Or do you see and recognize compositional elements within the paintings?

Roger Fry was a distinguished art critic earlier in this century. Why does Forster bring him into the essay? How does his "presence" contribute to Forster's ideas about looking, or not looking, at art?

Connecting

What does Forster mean by "esthetic aptitude"? Does he seem to have it despite his claims to the contrary? Explain, based on what you find throughout the essay.

Writing

Forster died in 1970 at the age of 91, having lived through the first 70 years of this century. He makes this judgment about the age in which he lived: "Ours is an aural rather than a visual age, we do not get so lost in the concert hall, we seem able to hear music for ourselves, and to hear it as music, but in galleries so many of us go off at once into a laugh or a sigh or an amorous day-dream." What do you suppose Forster would say about the culture of your age or generation? Write a short piece in which you imagine Forster's reaction to the world you now live in only 30 years after his death. Focus on music and art.

Select one of the paintings that Forster writes about in the essay and go to the library or the Internet to find a reproduction. Or better, go to a museum to see the actual painting. Record your reaction to the painting when you first examine it. Where does your mind go as you look at it? Then go back to the painting later and look again, paying attention to its compositional qualities. Record your observations. Compare your observations with Forster's, and write a short appraisal of his judgments.

Paul Fussell
(b. 1924)

Paul Fussell, the Donald T. Regan Professor of English at the University of Pennsylvania, is the author of *The Great War and Modern Memory,* which won the National Book Award in 1976 along with the National Book Critics Circle Award and the Ralph Waldo Emerson Award from Phi Beta Kappa. Fussell's other works include *The Boy Scout Handbook and Other Observations, Thank God for the Atom Bomb,* and *Wartime: Understanding and Behavior in the Second World War.* His essays on war, class, and culture seek to expose our excesses; they reveal as well Fussell's penetrating wit and acerbic sensibility. Occasionally, as in "Indy," they also reveal a touch of sentimentality about American rituals, albeit couched in irony.

"Indy" is Fussell's attempt to put the Indy 500 into national perspective, thereby revealing the ritual that informs the race. In what Fussell sees as a taming of the machine, he sees as well an alternative to war.

Indy

Nineteen eighty-two was a bad year for motor racing. Making a practice run at the Indianapolis Motor Speedway, driver Gordon Smiley was killed, just a week after driver Gilles Villeneuve was killed in Belgium. These two horrors let loose a cascade of objections to motor racing, most of them based on the assumption that human beings are rational creatures, despite the evidence to the contrary that was pouring in from the South Atlantic, where in the Falkland Islands Argentinians and British were shooting and shelling each other to death over matters of national pride and publicity. While that mass murder was in progress, some journalists chose to find auto racing a scandal. In *Time* magazine, Tom Callahan deplored the whole enterprise of the Indianapolis 500: "Some 450,000 people," he wrote, "will perch or picnic at the Speedway on Sunday. Nobody knows how many of them are ghouls spreading their blankets beside a bad intersection." This reprehension of ghoulishness was attended by four gruesome color photographs of Smiley's bloody accident designed to gratify the ghoul in all readers. At the same time, Frank Deford was setting off his anti-Indy blast in *Sports Illustrated,* finding the race not a sport but a mere hustling of automotive products ("The drivers at Indy look much less like athletes than like a lot of congested billboards"). He concluded that among the spectators lurk a significant number of "barbarians." George Vecsey, in the sports pages of *The New York Times,* suggested that the Indy race is becoming too dangerous to be regarded as a sport. "I can see accidents," he said, "on the Long Island Expressway."

Were these people right? Is the Indy 500 a sporting event, or is it something else? And if something else, is it evil or benign? I went there to find out.

Although the automotive industry moved to Detroit early in this century, Indianapolis is still a motor city, swarming with car washes and auto-parts stores, and the sign on the road into town from the airport, WELCOME TO INDIANAPOLIS: CROSSROADS OF AMERICA, seems to imply that you're entering a place best reached by car. Here, nobody walks. One day I walked two and a half miles along Sixteenth Street to the Speedway, and in that one hour found myself literally the only person not in an automobile. Returning a few hours later, I was still the only walker, with the exception of a man who accosted me and tried to borrow sixty-two cents.

To a Northeasterner, Indianapolis seems at first a strangely retrograde repository of piety and patriotism. When I arrived, an editorial in the only paper in town was raising a populist voice in a call for school prayer, and a front-page box offered "Today's Prayer" just above "Today's Chuckle." After a short sojourn in Indianapolis one is no longer surprised at the imperious sign in the store window, GO TO CHURCH SUNDAY. Catholics wishing to arrive at the 500-mile race very early Sunday morning, like everyone else, have their needs cared for by the Archdiocese of Indianapolis, which has ruled that the race-going faithful may fulfill their holy Sunday obligation "by attending Mass the evening before." Indianapolis seems the sort of place where the President expects no one to guffaw or shout, "Oh, come off it!" when he asserts that someone or something is "in my prayers." In fact, the President would love Indianapolis. Driving to the Speedway, the motorist passes a billboard advertising (of course) cars, but bellowing also GOD BLESS AMERICA. At the Speedway, even at qualifying trials weeks before the race, the national anthem is played at every opportunity, and the official program carries odd vainglorious ads like one inserted by the International Association of Machinists and Aerospace Workers: "PRIDE—Pride helped build America into the greatest nation on earth."

"Naptown" is what many locals call Indianapolis, and it does seem a somnolent place. Although it's a city and not a town, it's hard not to think of the Hoosier Booth Tarkington and those long, warm, sleepy afternoons when Penrod and Sam found nothing whatever to do. As I experienced the slowness of the Indianapolis pace— every transaction seems to drag on interminably, every delay is welcomed with friendly patience—I began to wonder whether speed and danger were not celebrated there one day a year just for the sheer relief and novelty of it, life being, on all other days, so safe, slow, and predictable. But friendly as well, it must be said. An elderly man flushing the urinal next to mine at the Speedway Motel, astonished at the noisy vigor of the flush, turned to me and although we'd not been introduced, kindly made me the audience for his observation, "Gawd, the *suction* on that son of a bitch! If you dropped it *in* there, you'd really lose it!" Ron Dorson, an authority on the anthropology of Indy, observes that although "in most public social settings . . . it is considered socially deviant for strangers to approach one another," at the Speedway things are different. There, "it becomes perfectly acceptable to engage total strangers in conversation about lap times, automotive technology, Speedway management, or race-driver intrigue." Something of pioneer individualism seems to linger in this friendliness, and on race Sunday, when you behold the infield crowded with campers, tents, trailers, and R.V.s, their occupants cooking and drawing water and cosseting children and making love in the friendliest fashion, you realize what the Indy setting really is. It's an early-nineteenth-century American pioneer campsite surrounded, as if fortuitously, by an early-twentieth-century two-and-a-half-mile track. And you almost begin to wonder if it's not the camping out, that primeval American ceremony of innocence, rather than the race and its excitements and hazards, that has drawn these multitudes here.

I'd say the people can be divided into three social classes: the middles, who on race day, in homage to the checkered flag, tend to dress all in black and white and who sit in reserved seats; the high proles, who watch standing or lolling in the infield, especially at the turns, "where the action is"; and the uglies, the over-advertised, black-leathered, beer-sodden, pot-headed occupiers of that muddy stretch of ground in the infield at the first turn known as the Snake Pit. These are the ones who, when girls approach, spiritlessly hold up signs reading SHOW US YOUR TITS. These uglies are sometimes taken to be the essence of Indy, and they are those Frank Deford probably has in mind when he speaks of "barbarians." But they are not the significant Indy audience. The middle class is—all those nice unstrenuous types arriving at the Speedway in cars bearing Purdue and Indiana State stickers.

The middles are privileged to participate in an exclusive social event, the classy pit promenade. Beginning three hours before the start, anyone who can wangle a pit pass strolls slowly up and down in the space between the pits and the track proper, all dressed up and watched enviously—that is the hope, at least—by the tens of thousands of social inferiors confined to the stands. On race morning in Indianapolis this is the stylish place to be, a place where one wouldn't dare show oneself unshaven or in dirty clothes. Many spandy-clean black-and-white getups are to be seen there, including trousers with two-inch black-and-white squares. Even though the social tone is compromised a bit by the presence of journalistic onlookers (that's how I got there), the thing struck me as comparable with some of the great snob social operations of the world, like appearing in or near the royal box at Ascot or visibly sipping champagne while watching the cricket at Lord's or even nodding slightly to well-dressed friends while ambling slowly down the Champs Élysées. But this Indy promenade is distinctly for middle-class people. The upper-middle class is not to be found at Indy. If you're the sort of person drawn to the U.S. Open or the America's Cup races at Newport, you're not likely to be seen at the Speedway.

From the outset devotees of motor racing have felt anxieties about its place on the class-status ladder. Is motor racing on a par with cockfighting and female mud wrestling, or is it up there with pro football and even, perhaps, tennis? The surprise registered by an Indianapolis paper after the race in 1912 speaks volumes, socially: "There has been no better-mannered gathering in Indianapolis. . . . There was no pushing, no crowding, no profanity, no discourtesies." When the Chief Steward issues his portentous injunction, "Gentlemen, start your engines," we may feel that the first word insists a bit too much. Presumably, if women drivers were to become a regular feature at Indy, the formula would have to include "Ladies and . . . ," which some might think a further advance toward gentility. Janet Guthrie, who has so far been the only woman to participate (three times), says: "I think that racing's image needs all the help it can get. It has traditionally been a lowbrow image." Before being killed in the Austrian Grand Prix in 1975, Mark Donohue, who had graduated not just from college but from Brown, raced at Indy and sensed what an anomaly he was there. "I was considered different from the other Indy drivers," he said. "I had gone to college, I was articulate, and I didn't swear a lot."

The sense that racing will naturally sink proleward unless rigorously disciplined is what one takes away from a reading of the rule book promulgated by the

United States Auto Club, the official supervisor of Indy racing. Cars are not to bear "undignified names," "improper language or conduct" is forbidden, and everything must be neat and clean at all times, just as a gentleman would wish: "*Appearance:* cars, crews, and all pit personnel whose appearance detracts from the character of the program may be excluded." (What's that aimed at, long hair? Terrible acne? Effeminate gestures?)

A similar aspiration to respectability seems partially responsible for the euphemisms that abound at Indy. Just as the self-conscious middle class may remark that someone has passed away (sometimes *over*), the Indy public-address announcer will inform the spectators that "We have a fatality." Instead of saying that there's been a terrible smash-up on the third turn, he'll say, "We have a yellow light." A car never hits the wall, it "gets into" it, or even "kisses" it. When a hurtling car comes into contact with the concrete wall, the driver may be said to have "visited cement city." Driver Danny Ongais, badly injured in a crash in 1981, spoke of it later not as the crash or even the accident but as "the incident." Everywhere there is the gentleman's feeling that if you pretend something has not happened, it has not. Thus the rule prohibiting cars from adding oil during the race. Adding oil would publicly acknowledge, as racing journalist Terry Reed points out, "that a car is blowing (or leaking) its original supply on the track, making the course even more hazardous." Almost immediately after Gordon Smiley's car and body nauseatingly stained the wall, it was repainted, white and pure. After that his tire marks on the third turn ran oddly into an immaculate expanse of white.

As Danny Ongais's indirection suggests, there are psychological as well as social reasons for all this euphemism. Racing is now deadly dangerous, with speeds over 200 miles an hour the rule. That makes more true than ever Jackie Stewart's point: "Motor racing will always be dangerous because you are always going too fast for things around you." Johnny Rutherford adds: "Very few drivers—maybe only a handful—are capable of running two hundred miles an hour." An example of one guy who wasn't, some say in Indianapolis, was the late Gordon Smiley. At least that's the way they rationalize in order to admit to no defect in the conditions, only in the weaker aspirants, thus making racing seem a wholesome and natural illustration of Darwinian selection. A pervasive atmosphere of risk shrouds a top driver's professional life. In June 1970, Jackie Stewart had occasion to realize that in the past months he'd "seen more of life and death than most people see in two lifetimes. Four weeks after Jimmy died, it was Mike Spence at Indianapolis; four weeks later, another friend, Ludovico Scarfiotti; four weeks more, to the day, it was Jo Schlesser in Rouen; and two weeks ago, Bruce McLaren at Goodwood. Now it's Piers. It just keeps on." The U.S.A.C. rule book says explicitly that "Automobile racing is a hazardous undertaking," and it implies it all the way through as when it notes that all drivers are required to remove dentures before starting or when it lays down precise specifications for easily detached steering wheels, "to aid in removing injured drivers from cars."

I have been really scared quite a bit, most notably in the infantry in the Second World War, when shells whined closer and closer and I waited for the final one to tear me to pieces. But I had another moment of sheer terror on May 22,

1982, at eleven in the morning, on the third day of qualifying at Indy, when I
entered the Speedway through an underpass running beneath the track itself and
for the first time heard those cars screaming by just overhead. They give off not
just an almost unbearable sudden noise, but shocking heat and concussion as
well. In their appalling *whoosh* is the quintessential menace of the Machine. Not
even an observer feels entirely safe at the Speedway, and indeed the spectators are
in actual danger all the time—from hurtling machines, tires, and fragments, and
from the deadly methanol fuel, which burns with a scarcely visible flame, consuming ears and noses and fingers before onlookers are even aware that the victim is on fire. No wonder "13" is, by U.S.A.C. edict, never used in car numbering.

No wonder, either, that the rituals of the Indy world are so strenuously male,
macho as all get-out. Women, even wives and girlfriends, weren't allowed in the
pits until 1970. In 1976 Janet Guthrie, intent on breaking the male barrier for the
first time, couldn't get her car to go fast enough to qualify for a starting position,
but on her way to her car to try, as the journalist Dan Gerber remembers,

> she is stopped by two slightly beer-crazed twenty-year-olds.
> "Hey, Janet," one of them calls, "You gonna qualify?"
> "I hope so," she replies, smiling, perhaps a little nervously.
> "Well, we don't," the other boy calls back to her. "We hope you crash and
> burn where we can see you."

Actually, to understand just how male Indy is, you have only to scrutinize the
famous Borg-Warner trophy, awarded annually to the winner after he has drunk
from the traditional quart bottle of milk—not carton, bottle, for this is Indy
which, except for speed, has made very few concessions to the modern world. On
top of the Borg-Warner trophy is a silver male figure ten inches tall, signaling the
finish of a race by vigorously deploying a checkered flag, despite the curious fact
that he's quite naked and exhibiting a complete set of realistic male genitals,
instead of what we might expect of Indiana, a cache-sexe, consisting maybe of a
windblown bit of fabric. There he stands, quite immodestly undraped—unlike,
say, the modest figure in front of Rockefeller Center—proclaiming for all to see the
ideal maleness toward which Indy aspires.

The ideal whiteness too. Indy, as Ron Dorson says, is "a show staged by white
people for a white audience." Blacks are so rare among the spectators that you
notice them specifically, and of course there are no black drivers, nor threat of any.
(There was once a Jewish driver, Mauri Rose, but that's another story.) At a local
cocktail party I broached the black topic as politely as I could and was told by one
woman that blacks abjured the race because you had to sit for hours in the hot
sun and, as is well known, blacks can't bear to sit in the sun. Phoned for his views,
the local NAACP spokesman fulminated, asserting that the situation is a scandal
but that all black representations had been ineffective. Once Indy is over and the
Speedway emptied for another year, you see a lot of blacks there working for a
week to sweep up the six million pounds of litter the crowd leaves (together with
odd left-behinds like sets of teeth, and each time, two or three quite decent cars
inexplicably abandoned forever in the infield).

The combined weight of the litter suggests the size of the crowd, estimated (the Speedway declines to issue a precise count) at around 400,000. That's half the total population of the state of Montana. And the size of the crowd suggests another thing that's being celebrated besides speed. A name for it would be gigantism. Indy is the biggest of everything, "the largest single-day sporting event in the world," as local publicity says, and as Roger Penske adds, for the drivers it's "the biggest race in the world to win"; both the purse and the publicity are the largest. There is more press coverage—over 4,000 media people are there—than of any similar event. So gigantic is the track that a spectator sees only a tiny segment of it. Thus the public-address announcer is indispensable, performing over (naturally) "the world's largest public-address system" to tell you what you are missing. This means that every event is mediated through language: "We have a yellow light." The Indy public-address and radio announcers have always become public personages, even stars, and young Paul Page, who recently succeeded Sid Collins as the radio "Voice of the Indianapolis Five Hundred," is as famous there as, say, Alistair Cooke is elsewhere.

It's not just the announcing that makes Indy so curiously a language event. It's the advertising, the sight of grown men proud to be walking around in caps that say VALVOLINE or GOODYEAR. The cars themselves, plastered with decals (CHAMPION, DIEHARD, STP), have been called "the world's fastest billboards." So precise are the contracts between advertisers and drivers that drivers are allowed to appear bareheaded only for the brief moment between removing the helmet and clapping on the required prole-cap, reading DOMINO'S PIZZA or QUAKER STATE. Officially, Indy is a celebration of "progress" in the motor-car and rubber-tire industries (the tires are supplied gratis by Goodyear). It's supposed to be a testing ground for improvements destined to make their way into your passenger car. But unofficially, it's a celebration of the charm of brand names, a recognition of their totemic power to confer distinction on those who wear, utter, or display them— and secondary distinction on those in the stands who recognize and respond to them. You achieve vicarious power by wearing the right T-shirt or cap and thus allying yourself with successful enterprises like BUDWEISER or GATORADE. By this display of "legible clothing," as Alison Lurie calls it, you fuse your private identity with external commercial success, redeeming your insignificance and becoming, for the moment, somebody. (A cruel and ironic end for Whitman's highly American awareness of the Self and the Other.) Even the lucky wearers of the coveted pit passes are vouchsafed this feeling of power, for the badges, not content to be merely what they are, are also little ads—for CHEVROLET CAMARO, the year I was there. A person unable to read (a real "barbarian," maybe) would get very little out of Indy.

Obviously there's much more going on here than is commonly imagined by what Naptowners are likely to refer to as "the eastern press," and there's certainly more going on than an overpowering desire to see someone killed. There is a powerful and in my view benign element of ritual purgation about Indy, and the things purged are precisely such impurities as greed, vulgarity, snobbery, and sadism.

The events just before the race, presented always in the same order and with the same deliberate, ample timing, are enough to hint at this ritual element. It is a Sunday morning, a time once appropriate for other rituals of purgation. When I inquired why the race was held on Sunday despite protests from the local Baptists about profaning the Sabbath and the inconvenience of closed liquor stores, I was told that Monday, the holiday, was always available as a rain date. But the race seems to gravitate to a Sunday for deeper reasons.

We've entered the Speedway very early, at 7:00 or 8:00 in the morning, although the crazies will have poured in, already blotto on beer and clad in T-shirts proclaiming the wearer TOO DRUNK TO FUCK, when the gates open at 5:00. We're all anticipating the hour of start, 11:00, the hour when church services traditionally begin. By 9:30 virtually everyone involved in the unvarying pre-start ceremonies is in place. At 9:45, as—I'm quoting the official program—"the Purdue University Band plays 'On the Banks of the Wabash,'" the race cars, still inert, silent, dead things, a threat to no one, are pushed by hand from the pits to their starting positions on the too narrow track, where they are formed up into the eleven rows of a viciously hazardous but thoroughly traditional three-abreast arrangement. At 10:34 the Chief Steward makes a stately ritual circuit in the pace car, officially inspecting the track for impurities one last time. At 10:44, all rise: "The Star-Spangled Banner." At 10:47, heads bowed for the invocation, delivered by a local divine, who prays for a safe race and reminds us of the dead of all our wars—and all past Indys. One minute later, "Taps." It is Memorial Day, you suddenly remember. Two minutes after "Taps," the band plays, very slowly, "Back Home in Indiana." By this time I find that I am crying, for me always an empirical indication, experienced at scores of weddings and commencements, that I am taking part in a ritual. By the time the portentous voice issued its command to the gentlemen, I was ready to be borne out on a litter. And the race hadn't even started yet.

If, while witnessing these things, you come to understand that Indy has something more to do with Memorial Day than coincidence, you also realize that there's some ritual meaning in the event's occurring at the moment recognized as the division between spring and summer. For Dan Gerber, listening as a boy annually to the Voice of the Indianapolis Five Hundred meant release. "It meant school was getting out and I could get sunburned and go fishing and spend three months on Lake Michigan." It has meant something similar to me: the university year has ended, grades have been turned in, no more pressure, no more anxiety, from that quarter at least, until fall. Indy, says the man who for years has commanded the corps of six hundred ushers, "is spring tonic to me." I know what he means.

As with a great many contemporary experiences, the meaning of Indy is elusive because it won't fit familiar schemes of classification. Rationalists, trying to make sense of its competitive dimension, will conclude that news about it belongs on the sports page. But then Warner Wolf, the TV sports commentator, appalled by the destruction of Villeneuve and Smiley, argues that racing is not a sport at all and indignantly defames it as merely a thing about machines. Although there probably is a legitimate sport called "motor sport," indulged in largely by amateurs, Wolf is right in perceiving that what takes place at Indy is not really a sport. The essence of Indy is in its resemblance to other rituals in which wild, menacing, nonhuman things are tamed.

I am thinking of the rodeo and the bullfight. Subduing beasts that, unsubdued, would threaten man—that's the ritual enacted by rodeo, and, with some additional deepening of the irrational element, of the bullfight as well. Just as at Indy, you can get hurt trying to subdue wild horses, killed trying to dominate bulls. Virility, *cojones,* figure in each of these, as the little silver man indicates they do at Indy. Warner Wolf is also right when he notes that Indy is a thing about machines, but it's about machines only the way rodeos would be about broncos if no men were there to break them and bullfights about *toros* if no *toreros* were there to command them. Indy enacts the ritual taming and dominating of machines, emphasizing the crucial distinction between man and machine, the one soft and vulnerable but quick with courage and resource, the other hard and threatening but witless and unimaginative, stupid, indeed. The cars are at Indy so that men can be shown able to dominate them, and the wonder and glory of the dominators is the point. Indy is thus like a great Sunday-morning proclamation of the dignity of man, and no number of discarded chicken bones or trampled beer cans can change that. Like former Sunday morning rituals, Indy insists that people are worth being saved. If the machine should win, onlookers—sadists excepted—do not feel pleasure. The reasons the extinction of the space shuttle *Challenger* was so distressing are many, but one was certainly the spectacle of the machine, in that case, winning. Those aboard lost their lives not to something like a hurricane or an earthquake, but to a machine. The servant had suddenly turned master, and a vicious, violent master at that.

Do some people, regardless, come to see drivers killed? Probably, but as irrelevant a tiny number of the sick as those who enjoy seeing a bullfight ruined by a goring. If you see someone die at Indy, you are seeing that the machine has won, and that's opposed to everything the ritual is saying. No one enjoyed the moment in the 1987 race when a tire flew off one of the cars and killed a spectator. That was a victory for the machine, and like all such victories, it was messy and inartistic. A longtime student of the race, Sam Posey, seems to get the point when he considers the pleasure spectators take in identifying themselves with the driver-tamer of the machine. When things go wrong and the crowd sees a driver killed, he says, "They are terribly shocked and extremely depressed. They wish they had not been there." What the spectator wants to see is the machine crashing, disintegrating, wheels flying off, and in the end the man springing out and waving, "I'm okay." "Because that's the moment of the greatest thrill," says Posey. "That's when man has conquered the machine. The machine has bitten back, but the man jumps out laughing and therefore the spectator's dream of immortality is confirmed." Immortality: hence, value, and value much longer lasting than that conferred on the congeries of steel, aluminum, and rubber by the mere age of the machine.

I was at Indy during a week when every day brought worse news and more terrible images of people's limbs blown off in the South Atlantic, and perhaps the contrast between that spectacle and the Greatest Spectacle in Racing made Indy seem especially therapeutic. No one was hurt all the time I was there, the only injuries being sunburns and hangovers. I went looking for something mean, but what I found was not that at all. If Indy is in one sense about beer, in a deeper sense it's about milk, as the winning driver's victory refreshment suggests. A full-page ad in the official program, inserted by "Your Local Indiana Dairy Farmer," designated milk "the Drink of Champions" and noted that "over the past six years milk has powered the 'Fastest Rookie.'" Indy, the program also said, is "an American Tradition." It would be hard to find one ministering more comprehensively to the national spirit.

[handwritten in margin: it is a way of life]

Considerations

Thinking

Why do you suppose Fussell likens the Indy 500 to "an early-nineteenth-century American pioneer campsite" and calls it a "primeval American ceremony of innocence"? Does he make similar comparisons elsewhere in the essay?

Why do you suppose Fussell includes the information about blacks in his essay? Why not Asians, Chicanos, other nonwhites?

What exactly does Fussell mean by that "powerful" and "benign element of ritual purgation" that takes place at Indy? How does Fussell's crying relate to that purgation? Is his crying consistent with what you can discern about his attitude toward the race and the crowd? Explain.

Connecting

Select a spectator event that you are familiar with and recall the crowds. Can you figure out a class structure in that crowd comparable to the "social classes" Fussell discerned at the racetrack?

Compare the way Fussell peoples his essay with local characters and uses their dialogue with the way Gretel Ehrlich uses her characters in "Looking for a Lost Dog." What does that comparison reveal about writing techniques?

What is the relationship between Fussell and all those sports writers he quotes? How does he use them in his essay?

Writing

Write an essay in which you consider what Fussell calls "the spectator's dream of immortality." Extend your inquiry to another sport or activity that you know a great deal about.

If Fussell went to the Indy 500 "looking for something mean," what do you think he found? Write your response to someone else in your class, exchange responses, and compare them.

Jaclyn Geller
(b. 1963)

Jaclyn Geller is studying for her Ph.D. at New York University where she teaches in the expository writing program. Her work has appeared in *On the Issues* and *Salmagundi,* and she is completing a collection of essays *(Here Comes the Bride)* for Four Walls Eight Windows press.

In "The Celebrity Bride as Cultural Icon" Geller turns to history, popular culture, and *People* magazine as sources for her *reading* of a collection of photographs that capture the essence of celebrity weddings.

The Celebrity Bride as Cultural Icon

In pseudo-aristocratic fashion, John F. Kennedy, Jr., kisses the hand of his new bride as she smiles at him seductively. Grasping a bunch of white roses, supermodel Christie Brinkley flashes a professional smile as she takes yet another trip down the aisle. The shiny-faced television actress Candice Cameron beams from beneath a massive, flower-studded headpiece, leaning down to embrace a red-haired flower girl whose tiny body is sheathed in heavy white satin.

In "Celebrity Weddings '97," *People* magazine's annual February rite of passage in celebration of St. Valentine's Day, the reader is treated to what appears to be spontaneous eruptions of joy. There is a wedding—actually many weddings. The natural course of events has taken place; two fragmentary halves have become a Platonic whole. Loneliness has been alleviated. A reciprocal identity has been forged. The central—the only—source of earthly happiness has been achieved for two individuals.

A trance-like inevitability characterizes these wedding photographs: personal fulfillment, sexual satisfaction and economic solvency have been neatly compressed in a gesture of order and resolution supported by a community. The plethora of brocade and lace, pearls, roses, crystal, china and champagne appear to be physical manifestations of each couple's self-sustaining love. Clad in a "white Pamela Dennis dress," singer Judy Collins poses, arm in arm, with feminist activists Marlo Thomas and Gloria Steinem. The copy reads, "Fittingly, it was songwriter Leonard Cohen who said it best. When singer Judy Collins wed industrial designer Louis Nelson last spring, Cohen's gift to his longtime friends was two dozen roses and a note that read simply, `I love you. It's about time.'"

Reading between the lines—or in this case behind the image—there is something else going on here. Even a cursory knowledge of social history and a general sense of the modern evolution of gender roles clues one into the cultural values being celebrated. *People's* wedding photographs are anything but natural or spontaneous. They contain a series of rigidly stylized poses that idealize marriage, obscuring the institution's inequities, incongruities and contradictions. One sees, in the series of apparently random, haphazard images, the preservation of a code of sexual relations. The model Angie Everhart assumes a softcore porn pose, pouting at the camera and lifting the skirts of her plush satin gown to display her legs. Wrapped around her right thigh is a lace garter. Swathed in virginal white, she displays her perfectly toned body as a bandanna clad makeup artist combs her mane of thick red hair. She is both virgin and coquette, embodying the modern ideology of femininity, described by scholar Joseph Boone as "a paradoxical combination of chaste innocence, sexual overtures and economic opportunism."

Like many of *People's* celebrity brides, Everhart is a pure, visual exemplification of this ethos. Indeed, the popularity of marriage-oriented magazines attests to the continuing dominance of 18th- and 19th-century notions of female domesticity. The historian Lawrence Stone has described how, in the 1700s, the conception of female delicacy emerged in Western Europe in full force: "By a strange twist of cultural fate, the sex which is the toughest and most resilient of the two became identified with both physical and psychological delicacy and ability—defects in fact artificially induced in the interests of conformity to the current ideal of beauty. The cultivation of feminine debility had the same symbolic significance as the crushing of the feet of upper-class Chinese women . . . Loving parents now believed that their daughters' chances on the marriage market would be seriously impaired unless they had the correct, rigidly upright posture, emaciated bodies, palid complexion and languid airs, and were prepared to faint at the slightest provocation." As opposed to the salacious woman of medieval lore, the modern female was delicate, sensitive and sentimental. Granted total immunity from sexual feelings, she was a romance-driven creature, born and bred for marriage and motherhood.

Decarnalized, she was more dependent than ever on a pleasing exterior to lure a husband, for the long-standing tradition of arranged nuptials was eroding and sexual attraction was gaining credibility as a motive for marriage.

Today's celebrity bride is an immensely powerful stereotype of femininity. She wields the kind of cultural influence that popular heroines of 18th- and 19th-century novels did, prior to the invention of the camera. She is glamorous and popular. More often than not, she is young. If older, she is remarrying, often, after years of hardship, to become young again. *People* likens the newly married, middle-aged author Mary Higgins Clark to a teenager in love. If young, she tends to exemplify the ambitious female parvenu. The drama of Carolyn Bessette's "grand entrance into the Kennedy clan" is heightened by the "sleek" Nacisco Rodriguez gown "that has already launched countless imitations."

The celebrity bride is our culture's standard bearer for marriage. Like the romance of the heroine of the previous century's fictions, she enjoys epiphanic happiness based on the belief in her own self-improvement through marriage. "Marriage is a different kind of commitment, very valuable, I think, and very life affirming," proclaims Judy Collins, who is photographed at the altar of St. John the Divine Cathedral in New York, clasping her groom's arm, while looking past him into the crowd of wedding guests.

Victoria Duffy, the 29-year-old bride of 59-year-old actor Dennis Hopper, is captured in two separate images. In the first, she stands with Hopper on the balcony of an apartment overlooking New York's Fifth Avenue. Wearing a white dress, she is the tangible symbol of female decarnalization. While no longer a literal symbol of virginity, the costume denotes female purity—that marked disinterest in the sexual that is essential to our culture's perception of the married woman. Duffy's cumbersome white gown is counter-balanced by Hopper's black suit; their attire demonstrates a total separation between the male and the female, signifying two distinct natures, two discrete social roles. Hopper lunges toward the waif-like Duffy, grasping her waist and kissing her neck passionately, displaying his sexual appetite. She smiles demurely, looking down; her head is turned away from his embrace, and in a gesture of apathy, she views the traffic on the avenue below. She is the picture of modest, female restraint: delicate, poised and appropriately disinterested.

In a complementary image, Duffy stands at Hopper's side. Behind the couple is a row of four bridesmaids dressed in lavender, sleeveless gowns, each looking bored and distracted. In front of the pair is Hopper's 6-year-old son from a previous relationship. Duffy beams down at the boy with maternal benevolence. He stands in rigid defiance, his back turned to her. The message underlying the photograph's composition is clear: friendship has been relegated to the background; all previous relationships are now subordinate to the marriage bond. Standing in the foreground is the married couple, two counterparts of a newly formed unit, which, Joseph Boone points out, reflects a fantasy of social coherence and stability, bolstering "the myth of a tightly knit social order." The female participant assumes and publicly affirms her role as nurturer, imposing her maternal will on a sullen, unwilling recipient.

Images of female delicacy abound in *People*'s view of celebrity weddings. The bride swoons, not from sexual ecstasy but from the thrill of self-completion. Surrounded by beaming friends and family members, immersed in contrived elegance, and outfitted in the only ritual garment that she may ever wear, the contemporary bride revels in the privilege of her own centrality. No other ceremony or rite of passage in her life will compare to this one; there will be no comparable expenditure of money, no similar outpouring of gifts and emotion, no other moment at which she is the focal point of so many people's attention. She has reached the narrative apex of her own existence, and both posed and candid wedding photographs assert this fact. Through her entry into the realm of sanctioned conjugal relations, the woman has, each image asserts, become whole. *People* quotes scandal queen Gennifer Flowers: "I'm ready to shut out the darkness, go for the light, and get on with my life." In her wedding photograph, Flowers kisses the hand of her husband, real estate broker Finis Shelnutt, in a gesture of religious self-abnegation.

The language of religious epiphany is used deliberately in contemporary wedding literature, suggesting the sacrosanct status of an institution that was, at one time, merely an economic arrangement between families in which women were bartered to solidify dynastic alliances. Both the visual and the verbal rhetoric of current presentations of marriage suggest our culture's beatification of the institution. In celebrity wedding photographs, the bride herself is a paragon of worshipful intensity, lulled into a state of dreamy, ecstatic reverie by the gestures of her own performance.

People's equation of weddings with femininity is clearly demonstrated by its section on bridal dresses. That there is no equivalent portion of the wedding issue devoted to grooms' attire suggests that the wedding is a day on which the woman alone casts an image of herself through her fashion choices. Both the composition of the ten bridal photographs and the language used by the magazine's five judges is symbolically charged.

The actress Vivian Wu's sumptuous gown is described as "expensive and upper-class couture-looking," suggesting a classic marriage narrative—the financially advantageous match. Wu's ascent from an anonymous girlhood in Shanghai to material comfort through her marriage to a wealthy producer is celebrated by the judges in their praise of her "great style."

"Va-va-va voom!" exclaim the judges, about model Eva Herzigova's clingy, bias-cut gown, praising the dress as "provocative without being vulgar." Herzigova is extolled as the woman who ensnares a man through sexual wiliness, suggesting, without flaunting, the physical satisfaction that she will provide her mate. The lower portion of her gown covers her feet entirely, presenting an image of discomfort and immobility, but the dress's plunging neckline displays her cleavage. Her attire is that of the contemporary bride envisioned as a dependent, sexual toy.

"A lot of young women want a dress like this," say the judges when they come to Candice Cameron's beaded Pucci gown. The enormous dress, with its cumbersome train, sits on Cameron's petite frame like a jungle gym covered in brocade. The pubescent, 20-year-old actress beams angelically at the camera, incarnating another key marriage plot: the child bride who plays house with her new partner. The contemporary bride's conscious self-heroization is most clearly stated by *People's* judges in their embrace of Mary Higgins Clark's green and gold gown: "This is a mystery writer who chose a romance story."

Yet "Celebrity Weddings '97" seems TO be neither a sweetly innocent album of romance nor an elaborate piece of camp. Rather, it is a conduct book, a genre piece informed by the conventions of a didactic, domestic literature that originated in the 18th century. Blanford Parker's study, "The Triumph of Augustan Poetics," argues that Romanticism arose within the void of early modernity, when, after centuries of post-Reformation violence, religion had been discredited. The 17th century's satirical world view perceived both Catholicism and Protestantism as forms of pathology. The former with its layers of institutional corruption, was a rotting edifice. The latter, with its vehement enthusiasm, rested on the shaky foundations of private vision. Out of the heap of ashes that had been religion, the self, mythologized, ascended like a phoenix. By 1740 or so, there was nothing much left to worship. The subjects of perception, cognition, the natural world, and, especially amorous attachment, assumed mythic importance, not as analogues of a creative deity but as an end in themselves. Viewing a sunset or kissing a woman became acts of secular self-worship. In contemporary, secular culture, the wedding has emerged as our most definitive ritual, a form of institutional heterosexuality that extols a single relationship—the companionate marriage—above all others.

The wedding codifies our notions of sexual identity, enshrining an image of the contemporary woman as domestic, delicate, sexually coy, romance-driven and maternal. To view celebrity marriage photographs knowingly is to understand them as evidence of the modern, sacramental approach to amorous love. It is also to perceive the generative power of such texts. The ultimate celebrity bride captured in *People,* Jacqueline Kennedy, in her off-the-shoulder gown and her pearl necklace, has spawned two generations of imitators—women who naturalize femininity through their performance as brides.

Considerations

Thinking

What is the effect of Geller's re-creation of images in the first paragraph? How do those images forecast the idea she will develop in her essay? Consider both the images she re-creates and the particular language that she uses to recreate them. Are there hints of Geller's attitude in the selected language?

What are the cultural values that Geller finds inscribed in those wedding photos as she reads "between the lines—or in this case behind the image"?

If indeed "Celebrity Wedding '97" is "a conduct book," what are the long-range social implications for those whose lives are governed by the "book"? Whose lives are touched by or influenced by that book?

Connecting

In what ways might this essay serve as evidence for Anna Norris's argument in "How to Read Photographs" (pp. 69–73)? Explain.

Compare the way Geller uses "the language of religious epiphany" with the way Richard Rodriguez uses religious motifs in his essay "Late Victorians"? Both writers deal with popular culture; both discover religious implications in their primary subjects—feminism and homosexuality. What does a comparison of their religious allusion tell us about their sense of our culture? Do you agree with those implicit suggestions? Explain.

Writing

Geller claims that "today's celebrity bride is an immensely powerful stereotype of femininity." What are the characteristics Geller associates with that "powerful stereotype"? Write a short essay in which you assess the reliability of Geller's claim, based on your knowledge of femininity and your own *reading* of popular culture.

Select something *readable* from popular culture—a collection of images, a celebrity, a phenomenon—and write an essay about your discoveries. Cite evidence that you have gathered from your observations and from your reading.

Diana Hume George
(b. 1948)

Diana Hume George, a poet, essayist, and literary critic, is also a professor of English at Pennsylvania State University (Behrend College). *Blake and Freud,* a book of literary criticism, was nominated for a Pulitzer Prize. She is also the author of *Oedipus Anne: The Poetry of Anne Sexton* and a volume of her own poetry, *The Resurrection of the Body.* George's work has appeared in the *Missouri Review,* the *Georgia Review,* the *Ontario Review, Spoon River Quarterly,* and *Best American Essays 1990.*

"Wounded Chevy at Wounded Knee," written on the occasion of a visit to the site of the 1890 massacre at Wounded Knee, South Dakota, gives George an opportunity to write a searching inquiry into the modern plight of Native Americans, while coming to terms with her own long-standing confusion about her relationship to these "indigenous peoples of North America." She is the mother of a "half-Indian son."

Wounded Chevy at Wounded Knee

Pine Ridge Sioux Reservation, July 1989

"If you break down on that reservation, your car belongs to the Indians. They don't like white people out there." This was our amiable motel proprietor in Custer, South Dakota, who asked where we were headed and then propped a conspiratorial white elbow on the counter and said we'd better make sure our vehicle was in good shape. To get to Wounded Knee, site of the last cavalry massacre of the Lakota in 1890 and of more recent confrontations between the FBI and the American Indian Movement, you take a road out of Pine Ridge on the Lakota reservation and go about eight miles. If you weren't watching for it you could miss it, because nothing is there but a hill, a painted board explaining what happened, a tiny church, and a cemetery.

The motel man told us stories about his trucking times, when by day his gas stops were friendly, but by night groups of Indian men who'd been drinking used to circle his truck looking for something to steal—or so he assumed. He began carrying a .357 Magnum with him "just in case." Once he took his wife out to Pine Ridge. "She broke out in hives before we even got there." And when they were stopped on the roadside and a reservation policeman asked if they needed help, she was sure he was going to order her out of the car, steal it, and, I suppose, rape and scalp her while he was at it. As the motel man told us these contradictory stories, he seemed to be unaware of the irony of warning us that the Indians would steal our car if they got a chance and following with a story about an Indian who tried to help them just in case they might be having trouble.

He did make a distinction between the reservation toughs and the police. He wasn't a racist creep, but rather a basically decent fellow whose view of the world was narrowly white. I briefly entertained the notion of staying awhile, pouring another cup of coffee, and asking him a few questions that would make him address the assumptions behind his little sermon, but I really wanted to get on my way, and I knew he wasn't going to change his mind about Indians here in the middle of his life in the middle of the Black Hills.

Mac and I exchanged a few rueful remarks about it while we drove. But we both knew that the real resistance to dealing with Indian culture on these trips that have taken us through both Pueblo and Plains Indian territories hasn't come from outside of our car or our minds, but rather from within them. More specifically, from within me. For years Mac has read about the Plains Indians with real attentiveness and with an openness to learning what he can about the indigenous peoples of North America. He reads histories, biographies, novels, and essays, thinks carefully about the issues involved, remembers what he has read, informs himself with curiosity and respect about tribes that have occupied the areas we visit. For a couple of years he urged me toward these materials, many of which have been visible around our home for years: *Black Elk Speaks, In a Sacred Manner We Live, Bury My Heart at Wounded Knee,* studies of Indian spiritual and cultural life. While we were in Lakota country this time, he was reading Mari Sandoz's biography of Crazy Horse. But he has long since given up on getting me to pay sustained attention to these rich materials, because my resistance has been firm and long-standing. I am probably better informed about Indian life than most Americans ever thought of being, but not informed enough for a thoughtful reader and writer. My resistance has taken the form of a mixture of pride and contempt: pride that I already know more than these books can tell me, and contempt for the white liberal intellectual's romance with all things Indian. But my position has been very strange perhaps, given that I was married to an American Indian for five years, lived on a reservation, and am the mother of a half-Indian son.

I've been mostly wrong in my attitudes, but it's taken me years to understand that. Wounded Knee is where I came to terms with my confusion, rejection, and ambivalence, and it happened in a direct confrontation with past events that are now twenty years old. My resistance broke down because of an encounter with a young Lakota named Mark, who is just about my own son's age.

I grew up in the 1950s and 1960s in a small white community on the edge of the Cattaraugus Seneca Indian Reservation in western New York State. Relations between Indians and whites in my world were bitter, and in many respects replicated the dynamics between whites and blacks in the South, with many exceptions due to the very different functions and circumstances of these two groups of people of color in white America. The school system had recently been integrated after the closing of the Thomas Indian School on the reservation. The middle-class whites wanted nothing to do with the Indians, whom they saw as drunkards and degenerates, in many cases subhuman. When I rebelled against the restraints of my white upbringing, the medium for asserting myself against my parents and my world was ready-made, and I grabbed it.

I began hanging out on the reserve with young Indians and shifted my social and sexual arena entirely to the Indian world. I fell in love with an idea of noble darkness in the form of an Indian carnival worker, got pregnant by him, married him, left the white world completely, and moved into his. Despite the fact that this was the sixties, my actions weren't politically motivated; or, rather, my politics were entirely personal at that point. While my more aware counterparts might have done some of the same things as conscious political and spiritual statements, I was fifteen when I started my romance with Indians, and I only knew that I was in love with life outside the constricting white mainstream, and with all the energy that vibrates on the outer reaches of cultural stability. My heart and what would later become my politics were definitely in the right place, and I have never regretted where I went or what I came to know. But for twenty years that knowledge spoiled me for another kind of knowing.

Whatever my romantic notions were about the ideal forms of American Indian wisdom—closeness to the land, respect for other living creatures, a sense of harmony with natural cycles, a way of walking lightly in the world, a manner of living that could make the ordinary and profane into the sacred—I learned that on the reservation I was inhabiting a world that was contrary to all these values. American Indian culture at the end of the road has virtually none of these qualities. White America has destroyed them. Any culture in its death throes is a grim spectacle, and there can be no grimmer reality than that endured by people on their way to annihilation.

I did not live among the scattered wise people or political activists of the Seneca Nation. I did not marry a nominal American Indian from a middle-class family. I married an illiterate man who dropped out of school in the seventh grade and was in school only intermittently before that. He traveled around the East with carnivals, running a Ferris wheel during the summer months, and logged wood on the reservation during the winter—when he could get work. Home base was an old trailer without plumbing in the woods, where his mother lived. He drank sporadically but heavily, and his weekends, often his weekdays, were full of pool tables, bar brawls, the endlessness of hanging out with little to do. He didn't talk much. How I built this dismal life into a romanticized myth about still waters running deep gives me an enduring respect for the mythopoeic, self-deluding power of desire, wish, will.

When I was married to him my world was a blur of old cars driven by drunk men in the middle of the night, of honky-tonk bars, country music, late night fights with furniture flying, food stamps and welfare lines, stories of injury and death. The smell of beer still sickens me slightly. I was sober as a saint through all of this, so I didn't have the insulation of liquor, only of love. I lived the contrary of every white myth about Indian life, both the myths of the small-town white racists and those of the smitten hippies. When I finally left that life behind, extricating myself and my child in the certain knowledge that to stay would mean something very like death for both of us, I removed myself in every respect. I knew how stupid white prejudice was, understood the real story about why Indians drank and wasted their lives, felt the complexities so keenly that I couldn't even try to explain them to anyone white. But similarly, I knew how birdbrained the lovechild generation's romance with Indian culture was.

My husband went on to a career of raping white women that had begun during—or maybe before—our marriage. When he was finally caught, convicted, and sent to Attica, I was long since done with that part of my life. My son pulled me back toward it with his own love for his father, and I still keep in touch with my husband's mother on the reservation, sometimes helping her to handle white bureaucracy, but that's all. I heard at a remove of miles, of eons, it seemed, about the early deaths of young men I'd known well—deaths due to diabetes, to lost limbs, or to car wrecks at high speed—and I felt something, but I didn't have to deal with it. When I tried to think about that past life in order to put it into some kind of perspective, no whole picture emerged. When I tried to write about it, no words would come. And when I tried to be open to learning something new about Indians in America on my trips, my heart closed up tight, and with it my mind.

When I went to Wounded Knee, the wounds of these other Indians half a continent and half a lifetime away were a part of the landscape.

We pull off to the side of the road to read the billboard that tells what happened here. "Massacre of Wounded Knee" is the header, but upon close inspection you see that "Massacre" is a new addition, painted over something else. "Battle," perhaps? What did it used to say, I wonder, and hope I'll run into a local who can tell me. While I'm puzzling over this, an old Chevy sputters into the pull-off and shakes to a stop. It's loaded with dark faces, a young man and an older woman with many small children. The man gets out and walks slowly to the front of the car, rolling up his T-shirt over his stomach to get air on his skin. As he raises the hood, a Comanche truck pulls in beside him with one woman inside. It's very hot, and I weave a little in the glare of sun. Suddenly I see the past, superimposed on this hot moment. I've seen it before, again and again, cars full of little Indian kids in the heat of summer on the sides of roads. I glance again, see the woman in the front seat, know that she's their mother or their aunt. She looks weary and resigned, not really sad. She expects this.

And then in another blink it's not only that I have seen this woman; I have *been* this woman, my old car or someone else's packed with little kids who are almost preternaturally quiet, wide-eyed and dark-skinned and already knowing that this is a big part of what life is about, sitting in boiling back seats, their arms jammed against the arms of their brother, their sister, their cousin. There is no use asking when they'll get there, wherever "there" is. It will happen when it happens, when the adults as helpless as they are, figure out what to do. In the meantime they sweat and stare. But I am not this woman anymore, not responsible for these children, some of whose intelligent faces will blank into a permanent sheen of resignation before they're five. I am a tourist in a new Plymouth Voyager, my luggage rack packed with fine camping equipment, my Minolta in my hand to snap pictures of the places I can afford to go.

When Mac suggests that we offer to help them, I am not surprised at my flat negative feeling. He doesn't know what that means, I surmise, and I don't have any way to tell him. Help them? Do you want to get anywhere today, do you have the whole afternoon? The young man's shoulders bend over the motor. He is fit and beautiful, his good torso moves knowingly but powerlessly over the heat rising from beneath the hood. I recognize him, as well as the woman. He has no job. He talks about getting off the reservation, finding work, living the dreams he still has. He'll talk this way for a few more years, then give up entirely. He drinks too much. He has nothing to do. Drinking is the only thing that makes him really laugh, and his only way to release rage. I also know that whatever else is wrong with it the car is out of gas, and that these people have no money. Okay, sure, I say to Mac, standing to one side while he asks how we can help. Close to the car now, I see that the woman is the young man's mother. These kids are his brothers and sisters.

The car is out of gas and it needs a jump. The battery is bad. The woman in the other car is the young man's aunt, who can give him a jump but has no money to give him for gas—or so she says. I know her, too. She is more prosperous than her relatives, and has learned the hard way never to give them any money because she needs it herself, and if she gives it to them she'll never see it again. She made her policy years ago, and makes it stick no matter what. She has to.

Well, then, we'll take them to the nearest gas station. Do they have a gas can? No, just a plastic washer-fluid jug with no top. Okay, that will have to do. How far is the nearest gas? Just up the road a couple of miles. But they don't have any money because they were on their way to cash his mother's unemployment check when they ran out of gas, and the town where they can do that is many miles away. So can we loan them some money for gas? We can. He gets in the front seat. I get in the back, and as we pull away from the windy parking area, I look at the woman and the kids who will be sitting in the car waiting until we return. She knows she can't figure out how soon that will be. She stares straight ahead. I don't want to catch her eye, nor will she catch mine.

Right here up this road. Mark is in his early twenties. Mac asks him questions. He is careful and restrained in his answers at first, then begins to open up. No there's no work around here. Sometimes he does a little horse breaking or fence mending for the ranchers. All the ranches here are run by whites who had the money to make the grim land yield a living. They lease it from the Lakota. Mark went away to a Job Corps camp last year, but he had to come back because his twenty-one-year-old brother died last winter, leaving his mother alone with the little ones. He froze to death. He was drinking at a party and went outside to take a leak. Mark said they figured he must have just stopped for a minute to rest, and then he fell asleep. They found him frozen in the morning. Mark had to come back home to bury his brother and help his mother with the kids.

As we bounce over the dirt road, I stare at the back of Mark's head and at his good Indian profile when he turns toward Mac to speak. He is so familiar to me that I could almost reach out to touch his black straight hair, his brown shoulder. He is my husband, he is my son. I want to give him hope. He speaks about getting out of here, going to "Rapid"—Lakota shorthand for Rapid City—and making a life. He is sick of having nothing to do, he wants work, wants an apartment. But he can't leave yet; he has to stay to help his mother. But things are going to be okay, because he has just won a hundred thousand dollars and is waiting for them to send the check.

What?

"You know the Baja Sweepstakes?" He pronounces it "Bay-jah." "Well, I won it, I think I won it, I got a letter. My little brother sent in the entry form we got with my CD club and he put my name on it, and it came back saying that I'm one of a select few chosen people who've won a hundred thousand dollars. That's what it said, it said that, and I had to scratch out the letters and if three of them matched it means I win, and they matched, and so I sent it back in and now I'm just waiting for my money. It should come pretty soon and then everything will be okay." He repeats it over and over again in the next few minutes: he's one of a select few chosen people.

As he speaks of this, his flat voice becomes animated. Slowly I begin to believe that he believes this. Whatever part of him knows better is firmly shelved for now. This hope, this belief that hundreds of thousands of dollars are on the way, is what keeps him going, what keeps him from walking out into the sky—or to the out-house in the winter to take a leak and a nap in the snow. What will you do with the money, I ask. Well, first he is going to buy his mother and the kids a house.

The first gas stop is a little shack that's closed when we finally get there. Sandy wind and no sign of life. Miles on down the road is a small Lakota grocery store with only a few items on the shelves and a sign that reads "Stealing is not the Lakota way." Mac hands Mark a five dollar bill. You can kiss that five bucks good-bye, I say to Mac. I know, he nods. When Mark comes back out he has the gas, and also a big cup of 7-Up and a bag of nachos. You want some, he asks me? He hands Mac a buck fifty in change. On the way back I hold the gas can in the back seat, placing my hand over the opening. Despite the open windows, the van fills with fumes. My head begins to ache. I am riding in a dream of flatness, ranch fences, Mark's dark head in front of me wishing away his life, waiting for the break that takes him to Rapid. Later I learn that we are in Manderson, and this is the road where Black Elk lived.

Mark is talking about white people now. Yes, they get along okay. For "yes" he has an expression of affirmation that sounds sort of like "huh." Mari Sandoz spells it "hou" in her books on the Lakota. The Lakota are infiltrated in every way by whites, according to Mark. Lots of people in charge are white, the ranchers are white. And there's a place in Rapid called Lakota Hills, fancy houses meant for Lakotas, but whites live in them. Later it occurs to us that this is probably a development named Lakota Hills that has nothing at all to do with the Indians, but it has their name and so Mark thinks it belongs to them. I am angry for him that we borrow their name this way and paste it on our air-conditioned prosperity. I don't have anything to say to him. I lean back and close my eyes. It would be easy to be one of them again. I remember now how it's done. You just let everything flatten inside.

And when we return to Wounded Knee, the pull-off is empty. Mother, children, car, aunt, all are gone. There's nothing but wind and dust. This doesn't surprise me. Mark's mother knows better than to wait for her son's return if other help comes along. Mark means well, but maybe she has learned that sometimes it's hours before he gets back with gas—hours and a couple of six-packs if he has the chance. Now we face the prospect of driving Mark around the reservation until we can find them. I have just resigned myself to this when his aunt pulls back in and says they're broken down again a couple of miles up. We can leave now. Mark thanks us, smiles, and shyly allows us the liberty of having his aunt take a picture of all three of us. I am feeling a strange kind of shame, as though I had seen him naked, because he told us his secret and I knew it was a lie.

Unemployment, high rates of suicide and infant mortality, fetal alcohol syndrome, death by accident, and drinking-related diseases such as diabetes: these are now the ways that American Indians are approaching their collective demise. Over a century ago, American whites began this destruction by displacing and killing the *pte,* the Indian name for the buffalo the Plains Indians depended upon. We herded them together in far crueler ways than they had herded the bison, whose sacredness the Indians respected even as they killed them for food and shelter. The history of our genocide is available in many historical and imaginative sources. What is still elusive, still amazingly misunderstood, is how and why the Indians seem to have participated in their own destruction by their failure to adapt to changed circumstances.

Whites can point to the phenomenal adjustments of other non-Caucasian groups in America, most recently the Asians, who were badly mistreated and who have nevertheless not only adapted but excelled. Indians even come off badly in comparison to the group in some respects most parallel to them, American blacks, whose slowness in adapting seems at first glance to have more justification. Blacks were, after all, our slaves, brought here against their will, without close cultural ties to keep them bound together in a tradition of strength; and on the whole blacks are doing better than Indians. However slowly, a black middle class is emerging in America. What's the matter with Indians? Why haven't they adjusted better as a group?

The American Indian Movement is of course strong in some areas, and Indians have articulate, tough leaders and savvy representatives of their cause who are fighting hard against the tide of despair gripping the heart of their race. But they're still losing, and they know it. Estimates of unemployment on the Pine Ridge and Rosebud reservations run as high as 85 percent. Health officials at Pine Ridge estimate that as many as 25 percent of babies born on the reservation now have fetal alcohol syndrome. This culturally lethal condition cannot be overemphasized, since it means that the next generation of Lakota are genetically as well as socioeconomically crippled; one of the consequences of fetal alcohol syndrome is not only physical disability but mental retardation. The prospects are extremely depressing for Lakota leaders whose traditional values are associated with mental acuity and imaginative wisdom. Mark is vastly ignorant and gullible, but he is intelligent enough. Many of his younger brothers and sisters are not only underprivileged and without educational advantages, but also—let the word be spoken—stupid. When the light of inquiry, curiosity, mental energy, dies out in the eyes of young Indians early in their stunted lives because they have nowhere to go and nothing to do, it is one kind of tragedy. When it is never present to die out in the first place, the magnitude of the waste and devastation is exponentially increased. Indian leaders who are now concentrating on anti-alcohol campaigns among their people are doing so for good reasons.

Indian leaders disagree about culpability at this point. Essentially the arguments become theories of genocide or suicide. On one end of the spectrum of blame is the theory that it is all the fault of white America. The evidence that can be marshaled for this point of view is massive: broken treaties, complete destruction of the Indian ways of life, welfare dependency established as the cheapest and easiest form of guilt payment, continued undermining of Indian autonomy and rights. The problem with this perspective, say others, is that it perpetuates Indian desperation and permits the easy way out—spend your life complaining that white America put you here, and drink yourself into the oblivion of martyrdom instead of taking responsibility for your own life. Some Indians say they've heard enough about white America's culpability, and prefer to transfer responsibility—not blame, but responsibility—to the shoulders of their own people. "White people aren't doing this to us—we're doing it to ourselves," said one Pine Ridge health official on National Public Radio's *Morning Edition* recently. She sees the victim stance as the lethal enemy now. The situation is as nearly hopeless as it is possible to be. Assimilation failed the first time and would fail if tried concertedly again, because Indian culture is rural and tribal and tied to open land, not urban airlessness. The Indian model is the encampment or village—the latter more recently and under duress—and not the city. Even the more stationary pueblo model is by definition not urban. The only real hope for Indian prosperity would be connected to vast tracts of land—not wasteland, but rich land. Nor are most Indians farmers in the sense that white America defines the farm. Though they might be, and have been, successful farmers under pressure, this is not their traditional milieu. Supposing that many tribes could adapt to the farming model over hunting and gathering, they would need large tracts of fine land to farm, and there are none left to grant them.

When the American government gave the Lakota 160 acres apiece and said "Farm this," they misunderstood the Indians completely; and even if Indians had been able to adapt readily—a change approximately as difficult as asking a yuppie to become a nomad moving from encampment to encampment—the land they were given was inadequate to the purpose. Grubbing a living out of the land we have given them, in what John Wesley Powell called "the arid region" west of the one hundredth meridian, takes a kind of know-how developed and perfected by white Americans, and it also takes capital. It is no coincidence that the large ranches on Pine Ridge are almost entirely leased by whites who had the initial wherewithal to make the land yield.

The Sioux were a people whose lives were shaped by a sense of seeking and vision that white America could barely understand even if we were to try, and we do not try. The life of a Sioux of a century and a half ago was framed by the Vision Quest, a search for goals, identity, purpose. One primary means of fulfillment was self-sacrifice. Now, as Royal Hassrick has written, "No longer is there anything which they can deny themselves, and so they have sacrificed themselves in pity." Whereas they were once people whose idea of being human was bound to creative self-expression, their faces now reflect what Hassrick calls "apathy and psychic emaciation." Collectively and individually they have become a people without a vision.

Why do they drink themselves into obliteration and erasure? Why not? When white America approaches the problem from within our own ethnocentric biases, we can't see why people would allow themselves to be wasted in this way, why they would not take the initiative to better themselves, to save themselves through the capitalist individuality that says, "*I* will make it out of this." But in fact part of their problem is that they have tried to do this, as have most Indian peoples. They've bought the American dream in part, and become greedy for money and material goods. Life on an Indian reservation—most any reservation—is a despairing imitation of white middle-class values. In this respect Indians are like all other minority groups in ghettos in America, and this explains why Mark has a

CD player instead of the more modest possessions we would not have begrudged him. If he is anything like the Indians I lived with, he also has a color TV, though he may well live in a shack or trailer without plumbing and without siding.

Their own dreams have evaded them, and so have ours. Mark and his brothers and sisters have been nourished on memories of a culture that vanished long before they were born and on the promises of a different one, from whose advantages they are forever excluded. Does Mark really believe he has won the sweepstakes? What he got was obviously one of those computer letters that invite the recipient to believe he has won something. Without the education that could teach him to read its language critically, or to read it adequately at all, he has been deceived into believing that a *deus ex machina* in the form of the Baja Sweepstakes will take him out of his despair.

In 1890, the year of the final defeat of the Sioux at Wounded Knee, the Ghost Dance was sweeping the plains. Begun by a few leaders, especially the Paiute seer Wovoka, the Ghost Dance promised its practitioners among the warriors that the buffalo would return and the white man would be defeated. Ghost Dancers believed that their ceremonial dancing and the shirts they wore would make them proof against the white man's bullets. Among the Sioux warriors at Wounded Knee, the willing suspension of disbelief was complete. It made the warriors reckless and abandoned, throwing normal caution and survival strategy to the wind.

A tragically inverted form of the self-delusion embodied in the Ghost Dance is practiced today on the Pine Ridge and other Sioux reservations. The original Ghost Dance has beauty and vitality, as well as desperation, as its sources. Now many Sioux men who would have been warriors in another time behave as though liquor and passivity will not kill them. Mark chooses to suspend his disbelief in white promises and to wait for a hundred thousand dollars to arrive in the mail.

Hank Doctor was my husband's best friend on the Seneca reservation. He was raunchy, hard drinking, outrageous in behavior and looks. His hair was long and scraggly, his nearly black eyes were genuinely wild, and his blue jeans were always caked with dust and falling down his hips. His wit was wicked, his laugh raucous, dangerous, infectious. Hank was merciless toward me, always making white-girl jokes, telling me maybe I better go home to my mama, where I'd be safe from all these dark men. He wanted me to feel a little afraid of his world, told me horrible stories about ghost-dogs that would get me on the reservation if I ventured out at night—and then he'd laugh in a way that said hey, white girl, just joking, but not entirely. He alternated his affection toward me with edgy threats, made fun of the too-white way I talked or walked, took every opportunity to make me feel foolish and out of place. He was suspicious that I was just slumming it as a temporary rebellion—maybe taking notes in my head—and that I'd probably run for home when the going got too tough. Of course he was right, even though I didn't know it at the time. I liked him a lot.

A few years ago, my son Bernie went through a period when he chose to remove himself from my world and go live in his father's, from which I'd taken him when he was three. I didn't try to stop him, even though I knew he was hanging out with people who lived dangerously. I used to lie in bed unable to go to sleep because I was wondering what tree he'd end up wrapped around with his dad. He was a minor, but I was essentially helpless to prevent this. If I'd forced the issue, it would only have made his desire to know a forbidden world more intense. He lived there for months, and I slowly learned to get to sleep at night. Mothers can't save their children. And he had a right.

The day I knew he'd ultimately be okay was when he came home and told me about Hank. He wondered if I'd known Hank. He'd never met him before because Hank had been out west for years. Now he was back home, living in a shack way out in the country, terribly crippled with diabetes and other ailments from drinking, barely able to walk. Hank would have been in his mid-forties at this time. Bernie and his dad took rabbits to Hank when they went hunting so that Hank would have something to eat. During these visits, Hank talked nonstop about the old days, reminding big Bernard of all their bar brawls, crowing to young Bernie that the two of them could beat anyone when they fought as a team, recounting the times they'd dismantled the insides of buildings at four in the morning. He told his stories in vivid, loving detail. His gift for metaphor was precise and fine, his memory perfect even if hyperbolic. He recalled the conversations leading up to fights, the way a person had leaned over the bar, and who had said what to whom just before the furniture flew.

Bernie was impressed with him, but mostly he thought it was pathetic, this not-yet-old man who looked like he was in his seventies, with nothing to remember but brawls. I told Bernie to value Hank for the way he remembered, the way he could make a night from twenty years ago intensely present again, his gift for swagger and characterization, his poetry, his laughter. In another time Hank would have been a tribal narrator, a story catcher with better exploits to recount. He would have occupied a special place in Seneca life because of his gifts.

My son left the reservation valuing and understanding important things about his father's world, but not interested in living in its grip. He lives in Florida where he's a chef in a resort, and he's going to college. A month ago his daughter, my granddaughter, was born. She is named Sequoia, after the Cherokee chief who gave his people an alphabet and a written language. Bernie took her to the reservation on his recent visit north and introduced the infant Sequoia to her great-grandmother. My husband's mother says that big Bernard is drinking again, using up her money, and she doesn't know how much more she can take. I know she'll take as much as she has to. I hope I'll see Bernard someday soon to say hello, and maybe we can bend together over our granddaughter, for whom I know we both have many hopes.

Just before we leave Wounded Knee, I walk over to Aunt Lena's Comanche and point to the tribal sign that tells the story. "It says 'Massacre' there, but it used to say something else." I ask her if she knows what it said before. She looks over my shoulder and laughs. "That's funny," she says, "I've lived here all my life, but you know, I never did read that sign." We're miles down the road before I realize that I never finished reading it myself.

Considerations

Thinking

What do you think George means by the "energy that vibrates on the outer reaches of cultural stability"—the energy that may have caused her to fall in love "with the idea of noble darkness in the form of an Indian carnival worker"?

What is that other kind of knowledge that George had to wait twenty years to find because it had been "spoiled" all those years by another form of knowledge?

In what ways does George find Native American culture "in its death throes"?

Connecting

Early in the essay, George makes a connection between the plight of blacks and the plight of Native Americans. Later, she says, "I lived the contrary of every white myth about Indian life, both the myths of the small-town white racists and those of the smitten hippies." What are the far-reaching implications of that claim—for George and for the rest of us in America?

When George brings up the Asians (and the blacks again), it is to substantiate her notion that "the Indians seem to have participated in their own destruction by their failure to adapt to changed circumstances." What do you think of that idea, and what do you think the reasons might be for such participation?

Writing

Write an essay about what you think George means by the "mythopoeic, self-deluding power of desire, wish, will." Explore the dark and the light side of such power, calling on experience, George's essay, and your reading.

Write an essay about what George calls the "victim stance," but do not feel compelled to concentrate only on Native Americans. Do not be quick to make up your mind about the nature of "victims"; think about why they might be justified in claiming to be a victim and why using such claims to defer action might be self-defeating.

Nadine Gordimer
(b. 1923)

South Africa's most widely read writer, Nadine Gordimer, was born in Springs, South Africa, and educated at the University of Witwatersrand. Since 1949, the year of publication of *Face to Face,* her first collection of stories, Gordimer has produced a steady stream of books, mostly fiction, much of which takes for its subject racial problems in South Africa.

Her essays and occasional writings have been collected in *The Essential Gesture* (1991). Although the following selection, "Where Do Whites Fit In?" was originally published in 1959, long before the recent political change to black majority rule that has occurred in South Africa, the issues Gordimer raises and the questions she asks are relevant today. Gordimer's essay is especially noteworthy for the way she honestly confronts essential problems and imagines the consequences of not resolving them.

Where Do Whites Fit In?

Where do whites fit in in the New Africa? *Nowhere,* I'm inclined to say, in my gloomier and least courageous moods; and I do believe that it is true that even the gentlest and most westernised Africans would like the emotional idea of the continent entirely without the complication of the presence of the white man for a generation or two. But *nowhere,* as an answer for us whites, is in the same category as remarks like *What's the use of living?* in the face of the threat of atomic radiation. We are living; we are in Africa. *Nowhere* is the desire to avoid painful processes and accept an ultimate and final solution (which doesn't exist in the continuous process that is life itself); the desire to have over and done with; the death wish, if not of the body, at least of the spirit.

For if we're going to fit in at all in the new Africa, it's going to be sideways, where-we-can, wherever-they'll-shift-up-for-us. This will not be comfortable; indeed, it will be hardest of all for those of us (I am one myself) who want to belong in the new Africa as we never could in the old, where our skin-colour labelled us as oppressors to the blacks and our views labelled us as traitors to the whites. We want merely to be ordinary members of a multi-coloured, any-coloured society, freed both of the privileges and the guilt of the white sins of our fathers. This seems to us perfectly reasonable and possible and, in terms of reason, it is. But belonging to a society implies two factors which are outside reason: the desire to belong, on the one part, and acceptance, on the other part. The new Africa may, with luck, grant us our legal rights, full citizenship and the vote, but I don't think it will accept us in the way we're hankering after. If ever, it will take the confidence of several generations of jealous independence before Africa will feel that she can let us belong.

There is nothing so damaging to the ego as an emotional rebuff of this kind. (More bearable by far the hate-engendered hate that the apartheiders must expect.) And you don't have to be particularly thin-skinned in order to feel this rebuff coming in Africa. Africans are prickling with the desire to be off on their own; the very fact that you welcome the new Africa almost as fervently as they do seems an intrusion in itself. They have had so much of us—let's not go through the whole list again, from tear-gas and taxes to brotherly advice—that all they crave is to have no part of us.

You'll understand that I'm not speaking in economic or even political, but purely in human or, if you prefer it, psychological terms. For the purposes of what

I have to say it may be true that in South Africa, for example, foreign capital and skills would have to be retained, in order to keep the mines and industry going, by wide concessions given by any black independent government with its head screwed on the right way. But the fact that we might go on living in our comfortable houses in the suburbs of Johannesburg under a black republic just as we do under a white near-republic, does not mean that we should feel ourselves accepted as part of the homogeneous society of the new Africa. For a long time to come any white South African must expect to find any black man, from any African territory, considered by the black South African as more of a brother than the white South African himself. No personal bonds of loyalty, friendship or even love will change this; it is a nationalism of the heart that has been brought about by suffering. There is no share in it we can hope to have. I for one can read this already in the faces, voices and eloquently regretful but firm handclasps of my own African friends.

Make no mistake, those moderate African political leaders who offer us whites—with sincerity, I believe—full participation in the new life of Africa offer us only the tangibles of existence. The intangibles that make up emotional participation and the sense of belonging cannot be legislated for.

What are we to do? Shall we go? Shall we leave Africa? For those small white communities who are truly foreign to the African territories in which they live, 'sent out' from a homeland in Europe for a spell of duty on administrative jobs or as representatives of commercial firms, there can't be much question of staying on. But in those territories, such as South Africa and the Rhodesias, where there is a sizeable and settled white population whose *home* is Africa, there is no easy answer; sometimes, it seems no answer at all. I do not attempt to speak, of course, for the stubborn mass that will continue, like a Napoleon in a mad house, to see itself as the undisputed master and make no attempt to consider the reality of living another role. I do not even try to guess what will happen to them; what *can* happen to them in a situation that they find unthinkable. I can only fear that events will deal with them grimly, as events usually do with people who refuse to think. I speak for people like myself, who think almost too much about the whole business and hope to arrive at an honest answer, without self-pity for the whites or sentiment about the blacks.

Some of us in South Africa want to leave; a few of us have gone already. And certainly, when one comes to Europe on a visit, one becomes a little uneasy at the number of friends (well-informed friends with a good perspective on the swerves and lurches of the way the world is going) who take one aside and ask whether one isn't planning to leave Africa? Which brings me to the reasons why some people have left and why these friends in Europe think one should pack up, too. A few have left because they cannot bear the guilt and ugliness of the white man's easy lot here; a few have left because they are afraid of the black man; and most, I should say, have left because of a combination of the two. I doubt if any consciously have left for the long-term reason I have elaborated here—the growing unwelcomeness of the white man in Africa. Yet I feel that if the white man's lot were to become no better and no worse than anyone else's tomorrow and the fear of violence at the hands of the black man (which we all have) were to have been brought to the test and disproved, unwelcomeness might still remain as the factor that would, in the end, decide many of us to give up our home and quit Africa.

I myself fluctuate between the desire to be gone—to find a society for myself where my white skin will have no bearing on my place in the community—and a terrible, obstinate and fearful desire to stay. I feel the one desire with my head and the other with my guts. I know that there must be many others who feel as I do, and who realise that generally the head is the more sensible guide of the two. Those of us who stay will need to have the use of our heads in order to sustain the emotional decision that home is not necessarily where you belong ethnogenically, but rather the place you were born to, the faces you first saw around you, and the elements of the situation among your fellow men in which you found yourself and with which you have been struggling, politically, personally or artistically, all your life.

The white man who wants to fit in in the new Africa must learn a number of hard things. He'd do well to regard himself as an immigrant to a new country; somewhere he has never lived before, but to whose life he has committed himself. He'll have to forget the old impulses to leadership, and the temptation to give advice backed by the experience and culture of Western civilisation—Africa is going through a stage when it passionately prefers its own mistakes to successes (or mistakes) that are not its own. This is an absolutely necessary stage in all political, sociological and spiritual growth, but it is an uncomfortable and disillusioning one to live through. And giving up the impulse to advise and interfere and offer to resume responsibility may not be as easy as we whites think. Even those of us who don't want to be boss (or *baas*, rather) have become used to being bossy. We've been used to assuming leadership or at least tutorship, even if it's only been in liberal campaigns to secure the rights of the Africans to vote and speak for themselves. Out of our very concern to see Africans make a go of the new Africa, we may—indeed, I know we shall—be tempted to offer guidance when we haven't been consulted. The facts that we'll be well-meaning and that the advice may be good and badly needed do not count; the sooner we drum that into our egos the better. What counts is the need of Africa to acquire confidence through the experience of picking itself up, dusting itself down, and starting all over again; and the quickening marvel of often getting things right into the bargain.

It's hard to sit quiet when you think you can tell how a problem may be solved or a goal accomplished, but it may be even harder to give help without recriminations or, worse, smugness when it is sought. If we want to fit in anywhere in Africa, that is what we'll have to teach ourselves to do; answer up, cheerfully and willingly, when we're called upon and shut up when we're not. Already I notice that the only really happy whites I know in Africa—the only ones who are at peace with themselves over their place in the community—are some South African friends of mine who have gone to live in Ghana, and who have an educational job to do on contract from the Government. They are living as equals among the Africans, they have no say in the affairs of the country for the Africans to resent and they are contributing something useful and welcome to the development of Africa. In other words, they are in the position of foreign experts, employed at the Government's pleasure. I can positively feel my fellow-whites in

Africa swelling with indignance at this extreme picture of the white man's future life on the continent; and it makes me feel rather indignant myself. But I think we've got to accept the home truth of the picture, whether we like it or not, and whether or not what we see there seems fair. All that the new Africa will really want from us will be what we can give as "foreign experts"—the technical, scientific and cultural knowledge that white civilisation has acquired many hundreds of years before black civilisation, and on which, whether the Africans like it or not, their own aspirations are based.

I suppose we may get over being a minority minority instead of the majority minority we've been used to being all these past years, but I don't know whether that valuable change of attitude will actually bring us much nearer the integration we seek. Will intermarriage help us? It would, of course, on a large scale, but personally I don't believe that it will happen on a large scale in Africa. Intermarriage has always been regarded as a social stigma by whites, even in those territories where, unlike South Africa, it is not actually a crime, but I have never been able to find out whether, among blacks, it is regarded as a stigma or a step up in the world. (Most whites assume it is regarded as a deeply desired privilege, of course.) I know that, for example, in South Africa many Africans who are not Bechuanas, and have nothing whatever to do with the people of Bechuanaland, have on their walls a picture of Ruth and Seretse Khama. It is difficult to say whether this means that they take pride in the fact that a white woman chose to marry an important African, or whether the picture simply gives them a chance to identify themselves with the ex-chief's successful defiance of white taboo and authority.

Once the social stigma is removed—in the new Africa marriage with an African will be marrying into the ruling class, remember, and no one can measure how much of colour-prejudice is purely class-prejudice, in a country where there has been a great gap between the living standards of black and white—and once (in the case of South Africa) there are no legal disabilities in mixed marriages, I think that intermarriage will increase at two extreme levels of the social scale, but scarcely at all in between. Intellectuals will intermarry because they feel closer to intellectuals, whatever their race or colour, than to the mass, and the humbler and poorly adjusted fringes of both the black and white masses, who have not found acceptance in their own societies, will intermarry in order to find a home somewhere—if not within the confines of their own background, then in someone else's. But I don't think we can hope for intermarriage on an effective scale between ordinary people, and I shouldn't be surprised if independent black Africa frowned upon it, in an unofficial but firm way. Especially in a country like South Africa, where there might remain whites in sufficiently large numbers to create an unease at the possibility that they might try to close their hands once again on those possessions of power from which their fingers had been prised back one by one. It is quite likely that there will be a social stigma, among ordinary people whose sense of nationalism is well stoked up, attached to marrying whites; it may be considered un-African. (Nkrumah has set the official precedent already, by choosing not a Ruth Williams, but a girl who "belongs" to the continent—a bride from Nasser's Egypt.) If white numbers do not dwindle in those areas of the continent which are heavily white-populated, and there is integration in schools and universities and no discrimination against white children, the picture will change in a few generations, of course. I do not see those young people as likely to regard parental race prejudice on either side as anything but fuddy-duddy. But will the whites remain, stick it out anywhere in Africa in sufficient numbers for this to come about? Isn't it much more likely that they will dwindle to small, socially isolated communities, whites in the diaspora?

If one will always have to feel white first, and African second, it would be better not to stay on in Africa. It would not be worth it for this. Yet, although I claim no mystique about Africa, I fear that like one of those oxen I sometimes read about in the Sunday papers, I might, dumped somewhere else and kindly treated, continually plod blindly back to where I came from.

Considerations

Thinking

Gordimer wrote this piece in 1959, yet much of what she has to say seems applicable to the South Africa of today (and tomorrow). Do you think she seems overly pessimistic about the place of whites in a South Africa controlled by blacks? Do you think Gordimer would be more optimistic today, given the recent political events in South Africa? Why or why not?

Connecting

Relate what Gordimer says about the place and position of whites in the South Africa of the future with what Cornel West says in "Race Matters" about race relations in the America of the future.

To what extent are Gordimer's observations about interracial marriage in a future South Africa relevant in America today and tomorrow?

Writing

Write an essay concerning your ambivalence about remaining in a place and leaving it. Consider, if you wish, Gordimer's ambivalence and her reasons for it in discussing your own situation.

Compare Gordimer's discussion of place and home with that of Scott Russell Sanders in "Wayland."

Mary Gordon
(b. 1949)

Mary Gordon was born in Far Rockaway, New York. She graduated with a B.A. from Barnard, where she now teaches, and she has also earned an M.A. from Syracuse University. Her books include the fictional works *Final Payments* (1978), *The Company of Women* (1981), *Men and Angels* (1986), *Temporary Shelter* (1988), and *The Other Side* (1990). The following selection, "Mary Cassatt," is taken from her collection of essays, *Good Boys and Dead Girls and Other Essays* (1991).

In "Mary Cassatt," Gordon raises questions about gender, creativity, and power. She also describes a few of Cassatt's paintings, one of which can be found in the color inserts. One of Gordon's achievements in this essay is her ability to direct us to aspects of Cassatt's art that are worth noticing, appreciating, and thinking about.

Mary Cassatt

When Mary Cassatt's father was told of her decision to become a painter, he said: "I would rather see you dead." When Edgar Degas saw a show of Cassatt's etchings, his response was: "I am not willing to admit that a woman can draw that well." When she returned to Philadelphia after twenty-eight years abroad, having achieved renown as an Impressionist painter and the esteem of Degas, Huysmans, Pissarro, and Berthe Morisot, the *Philadelphia Ledger* reported: "Mary Cassatt, sister of Mr. Cassatt, president of the Pennsylvania Railroad, returned from Europe yesterday. She has been studying painting in France and owns the smallest Pekingese dog in the world."

Mary Cassatt exemplified the paradoxes of the woman artist. Cut off from the experiences that are considered the entitlement of her male counterpart, she has access to a private world a man can only guess at. She has, therefore, a kind of information he is necessarily deprived of. If she has almost impossible good fortune—means, self-confidence, heroic energy and dedication, the instinct to avoid the seductions of ordinary domestic life, which so easily become a substitute for creative work—she may pull off a miracle: she will combine the skill and surety that she has stolen from the world of men with the vision she brings from the world of women.

Mary Cassatt pulled off such a miracle. But if her story is particularly female, it is also American. She typifies one kind of independent American spinster who keeps reappearing in our history in forms as various as Margaret Fuller and Katharine Hepburn. There is an astringency in such women, a fierce discipline, a fearlessness, a love of work. But they are not inhuman. At home in the world, they embrace it with a kind of aristocratic greed that knows nothing of excess. Balance, proportion, an instinct for the distant and the formal, an exuberance, a vividness, a clarity of line: the genius of Mary Cassatt includes all these elements. The details of the combination are best put down to grace; the outlines may have been her birthright.

She was one of those wealthy Americans whose parents took the children abroad for their education and medical care. The James family comes to mind and, given her father's attitude toward her career, it is remarkable that Cassatt didn't share the fate of Alice James. But she had a remarkable mother, intelligent, encouraging of her children. When her daughter wanted to study in Paris, and her husband disapproved, Mrs. Cassatt arranged to accompany Mary as her chaperone.

From her beginnings as an art student, Cassatt was determined to follow the highest standards of craftsmanship. She went first to Paris, then to Italy, where she studied in Parma with Raimondi and spent many hours climbing up scaffolding (to the surprise of the natives) to study the work of Correggio and Parmigianino. Next, she was curious to visit Spain to look at the Spanish masters and to make use of the picturesque landscape and models. Finally, she returned to Paris, where she was to make her home, and worked with Degas, her sometime friend and difficult mentor. There has always been speculation as to whether or not they were lovers; her burning their correspondence gave the rumor credence. But I believe that they were not; she was, I think, too protective of her talent to make herself so vulnerable to Degas as a lover would have to be. But I suppose I don't believe it because I cherish, instead, the notion that a man and a woman can be colleagues and friends without causing an excuse for raised eyebrows. Most important, I want to believe they were not lovers because if they were, the trustworthiness of his extreme praise grows dilute.

She lived her life until late middle age among her family. Her beloved sister, Lydia, one of her most cherished models, had always lived as a semi-invalid and died early, in Mary's flat, of Bright's disease. Mary was closely involved with her brothers and their children. Her bond with her mother was profound: when Mrs. Cassatt died, in 1895, Mary's work began to decline. At the severing of her last close familial tie, when her surviving brother died as a result of an illness he contracted when traveling with her to Egypt, she broke down entirely. "How we try for happiness, poor things, and how we don't find it. The best cure is hard work—if only one has the health for it," she said, and lived that way.

Not surprisingly, perhaps, Cassatt's reputation has suffered because of the prejudice against her subject matter. Mothers and children: what could be of lower prestige, more vulnerable to the charge of sentimentality. Yet if one looks at the work of Mary Cassatt, one sees how triumphantly she avoids the pitfalls of sentimentality because of the astringent rigor of her eye and craft. The Cassatt iconography dashes in an instant the notion of the comfortable, easily natural fit of the maternal embrace. Again and again in her work, the child's posture embodies the ambivalence of his or her dependence. In *The Family* [see inserts in this book], the mother and child exist in positions of unease; the strong diagonals created by their postures of opposition give the pictures their tense strength, a strength that renders sentimental sweetness impossible. In *Ellen Mary Cassatt in a White Coat* and *Girl in the Blue Arm Chair,* the children seem imprisoned and dwarfed by the trappings of respectable life. The lines of Ellen's coat, which create such a powerful framing device, entrap the round and living child. The sulky little girl in the armchair seems about to be swallowed up by the massive cylinders of drawing room furniture and the strong curves of emptiness that are the floor. In *The Bath,* the little girl has all the unformed charming awkwardness of a young child: the straight limbs, the loose stomach. But these are not the stuff of Gerber babies—even of the children of Millais. In this picture, the center of interest is not the relationship between the mother and the child but the strong vertical and diagonal stripes of the mother's dress, whose opposition shapes the picture with an insistence that is almost abstract.

Cassatt changed the iconography of the depiction of mothers and children. Hers do not look out into and meet the viewer's eye; neither supplicating nor seductive, they are absorbed in their own inner thoughts. Minds are at work here, a concentration unbroken by an awareness of themselves as objects to be gazed at by the world.

The brilliance of Cassatt's colors, the clarity and solidity of her forms, are the result of her love and knowledge of the masters of European painting. She had a second career as adviser to great collectors: she believed passionately that America must, for the sake of its artists, possess masterpieces, and she paid no attention to the outrage of her European friends, who felt their treasures were being sacked by barbarians. A young man visiting her in her old age noted her closed mind regarding the movement of the moderns. She thought American painters should stay home and not become "café loafers in Paris. Why should they come to Europe?" she demanded. "When I was young it was different. . . . Our Museums had not great paintings for the students to study. Now that has been corrected and something must be done to save our young over here."

One can hear the voice of the old, irascible, still splendid aunt in that comment and see the gesture of her stick toward the Left Bank. Cassatt was blinded by cataracts; the last years of her life were spent in a fog. She became ardent on the subjects of suffragism, socialism, and spiritualism; the horror of the First World War made her passionate in her conviction that mankind itself must change. She died at her country estate near Grasse, honored by the French, recipient of the Légion d'honneur, but unappreciated in America, rescued only recently from misunderstanding, really, by feminist art critics. They allowed us to begin to see her for what she is: a master of line and color whose great achievement was to take the "feminine" themes of mothers, children, women with their thoughts alone, to endow them with grandeur without withholding from them the tenderness that fits so easily alongside the rigor of her art.

Considerations

Thinking

Explain what Gordon means by writing, "Mary Cassatt exemplified the paradoxes of the woman artist." What "miracle," according to Gordon, did Cassatt pull off? Do you agree with Gordon about the miracle and the paradoxes? Why or why not?

Why does Gordon begin her essay with three quotations, two spoken and one written? How effective is this introductory paragraph?

Connecting

To what extent have you found that women artists (and writers) are dismissed as unimportant because of the subjects they choose to depict in their art?

Compare the ways Gordon approaches the life and work of Mary Cassatt with the approach Joan Didion, in her essay, takes to the life and work of Georgia O'Keeffe.

Writing

After looking at reproductions of the Cassatt paintings Gordon describes—*The Family, Ellen Mary Cassatt in a White Coat, Girl in the Blue Arm Chair*—write an essay describing what you see in the paintings.

Write an essay about an artist (any type of artist) you admire. Identify and explain the bases for your admiration of the artist's life and work.

Stephen Jay Gould
(b. 1941)

Stephen Jay Gould is a professor of zoology at Harvard, where he teaches biology, geology, and the history of science. His widely acclaimed works include *Ontogeny and Phylogeny, The Mismeasure of Man, Wonderful Life,* and several collections of essays, including *Ever Since Darwin, The Panda's Thumb, The Flamingo's Smile,* and *Bully for Brontosaurus.* Gould, the recipient of a MacArthur Award, writes scientific essays for *Natural History* magazine.

In "Women's Brains," he sets out to refute Paul Broca's findings that relate brain size and intelligence. In the process of exposing the limitations of Broca's findings, Gould examines a wider range of contemporary social distinctions that result from "biological labeling imposed upon members of disadvantaged groups."

Women's Brains

In the prelude to *Middlemarch,* George Eliot lamented the unfulfilled lives of talented women:

> Some have felt that these blundering lives are due to the inconvenient indefiniteness with which the Supreme Power has fashioned the natures of women: if there were one level of feminine incompetence as strict as the ability to count three and no more, the social lot of women might be treated with scientific certitude.

Eliot goes on to discount the idea of innate limitation, but while she wrote in 1872, the leaders of European anthropometry were trying to measure "with scientific certitude" the inferiority of women. Anthropometry, or measurement of the human body, is not so fashionable a field these days, but it dominated the human sciences for much of the nineteenth century and remained popular until intelligence testing replaced skull measurement as a favored device for making invidious comparisons among races, classes, and sexes. Craniometry, or measurement of the skull, commanded the most attention and respect. Its unquestioned leader, Paul Broca (1824–80), professor of clinical surgery at the Faculty of Medicine in Paris, gathered a school of disciples and imitators around himself. Their work, so meticulous and apparently irrefutable, exerted great influence and won high esteem as a jewel of nineteenth-century science.

Broca's work seemed particularly invulnerable to refutation. Had he not measured with the most scrupulous care and accuracy? (Indeed, he had. I have the greatest respect for Broca's meticulous procedure. His numbers are sound. But science is an inferential exercise, not a catalog of facts. Numbers, by themselves, specify nothing. All depends upon what you do with them.) Broca depicted himself as an apostle of objectivity, a man who bowed before facts and cast aside superstition and sentimentality. He declared that "there is no faith, however respectable, no interest, however legitimate, which must not accommodate itself to the progress of human knowledge and bend before truth." Women, like it or not, had smaller brains than men and, therefore, could not equal them in intelligence. This fact, Broca argued, may reinforce a common prejudice in male society, but it is also a scientific truth. L. Manouvrier, a black sheep in Broca's fold, rejected the inferiority of women and wrote with feeling about the burden imposed upon them by Broca's numbers:

> Women displayed their talents and their diplomas. They also invoked philosophical authorities. But they were opposed by *numbers* unknown to Condorcet or to John Stuart Mill. These numbers fell upon poor women like a sledge hammer, and they were accompanied by commentaries and sarcasms more ferocious than the most misogynist imprecations of certain church fathers. The theologians had asked if women had a soul. Several centuries later, some scientists were ready to refuse them a human intelligence.

Broca's argument rested upon two sets of data: the larger brains of men in modern societies, and a supposed increase in male superiority through time. His most extensive data came from autopsies performed personally in four Parisian hospitals. For 292 male brains, he calculated an average weight of 1,325 grams; 140 female brains averaged 1,144 grams for a difference of 181 grams, or 14 percent of the male weight. Broca understood, of course, that part of this difference could be attributed to the greater height of males. Yet he made no attempt to measure the effect of size alone and actually stated that it cannot account for the entire difference because we know, a priori, that women are not as intelligent as men (a premise that the data were supposed to test, not rest upon):

> We might ask if the small size of the female brain depends exclusively upon the small size of her body. Tiedemann has proposed this explanation. But we must not forget that women are, on the average, a little less intelligent than men, a difference which we should not exaggerate but which is, nonetheless, real. We are therefore permitted to suppose that the relatively small size of the female brain depends in part upon her physical inferiority and in part upon her intellectual inferiority.

In 1873, the year after Eliot published *Middlemarch,* Broca measured the cranial capacities of prehistoric skulls from L'Homme Mort cave. Here he found a difference of only 99.5 cubic centimeters between males and females, while modern populations range from 129.5 to 220.7. Topinard, Broca's chief disciple, explained the increasing discrepancy through time as a result of differing evolutionary pressures upon dominant men and passive women:

> The man who fights for two or more in the struggle for existence, who has all the responsibility and the cares of tomorrow, who is constantly active in combating the environment and human rivals, needs more brain than the woman whom he must protect and nourish, the sedentary woman, lacking any interior occupations, whose role is to raise children, love, and be passive.

In 1879, Gustave Le Bon, chief misogynist of Broca's school, used these data to publish what must be the most vicious attack upon women in modern scientific literature (no one can top Aristotle). I do not claim his views were representative of

Broca's school, but they were published in France's most respected anthropological journal. Le Bon concluded:

> In the most intelligent races, as among the Parisians, there are a large number of women whose brains are closer in size to those of gorillas than to the most developed male brains. This inferiority is so obvious that no one can contest it for a moment; only its degree is worth discussion. All psychologists who have studied the intelligence of women, as well as poets and novelists, recognize today that they represent the most inferior forms of human evolution and that they are closer to children and savages than to an adult, civilized man. They excel in fickleness, inconstancy, absence of thought and logic, and incapacity to reason. Without doubt there exist some distinguished women, very superior to the average man, but they are as exceptional as the birth of any monstrosity, as, for example, of a gorilla with two heads; consequently, we may neglect them entirely.

Nor did Le Bon shrink from the social implications of his views. He was horrified by the proposal of some American reformers to grant women higher education on the same basis as men:

> A desire to give them the same education, and, as a consequence, to propose the same goals for them, is a dangerous chimera. . . . The day when, misunderstanding the inferior occupations which nature has given her, women leave the home and take part in our battles; on this day a social revolution will begin, and everything that maintains the sacred ties of the family will disappear.

Sound familiar?

I have reexamined Broca's data, the basis for all this derivative pronouncement, and I find his numbers sound but his interpretation ill-founded, to say the least. The data supporting his claim for increased difference through time can be easily dismissed. Broca based his contention on the samples from L'Homme Mort alone—only seven male and six female skulls in all. Never have so little data yielded such far-ranging conclusions.

In 1888, Topinard published Broca's more extensive data on the Parisian hospitals. Since Broca recorded height and age as well as brain size, we may use modern statistics to remove their effect. Brain weight decreases with age, and Broca's women were, on average, considerably older than his men. Brain weight increases with height, and his average man was almost half a foot taller than his average woman. I used multiple regression, a technique that allowed me to assess simultaneously the influence of height and age upon brain size. In an analysis of the data for women, I found that, at average male height and age, a woman's brain would weigh 1,212 grams. Correction for height and age reduces Broca's measured difference of 181 grams by more than a third, to 113 grams.

I don't know what to make of this remaining difference because I cannot assess other factors known to influence brain size in a major way. Cause of death has an important effect: degenerative disease often entails a substantial diminution of brain size. (This effect is separate from the decrease attributed to age alone.) Eugene Schreider, also working with Broca's data, found that men killed in accidents had brains weighing, on average, 60 grams more than men dying of infectious diseases. The best modern data I can find (from American hospitals) records a full 100-gram difference between death by degenerative arteriosclerosis and by violence or accident. Since so many of Broca's subjects were very elderly women, we may assume that lengthy degenerative disease was more common among them than among the men.

More importantly, modern students of brain size still have not agreed on a proper measure for eliminating the powerful effect of body size. Height is partly adequate, but men and women of the same height do not share the same body build. Weight is even worse than height, because most of its variation reflects nutrition rather than intrinsic size—fat versus skinny exerts little influence upon the brain. Manouvrier took up this subject in the 1880s and argued that muscular mass and force should be used. He tried to measure this elusive property in various ways and found a marked difference in favor of men, even in men and women of the same height. When he corrected for what he called "sexual mass," women actually came out slightly ahead in brain size.

Thus, the corrected 113-gram difference is surely too large; the true figure is probably close to zero and may as well favor women as men. And 113 grams, by the way, is exactly the average difference between a 5 foot 4 inch and a 6 foot 4 inch male in Broca's data. We would not (especially us short folks) want to ascribe greater intelligence to tall men. In short, who knows what to do with Broca's data? They certainly don't permit any confident claim that men have bigger brains than women.

To appreciate the social role of Broca and his school, we must recognize that his statements about the brains of women do not reflect an isolated prejudice toward a single disadvantaged group. They must be weighed in the context of a general theory that supported contemporary social distinctions as biologically ordained. Women, blacks, and poor people suffered the same disparagement, but women bore the brunt of Broca's argument because he had easier access to data on women's brains. Women were singularly denigrated but they also stood as surrogates for other disenfranchised groups. As one of Broca's disciples wrote in 1881: "Men of the black races have a brain scarcely heavier than that of white women." This juxtaposition extended into many other realms of anthropological argument, particularly to claims that, anatomically and emotionally, both women and blacks were like white children—and that white children, by the theory of recapitulation, represented an ancestral (primitive) adult stage of human evolution. I do not regard as empty rhetoric the claim that women's battles are for all of us.

Maria Montessori did not confine her activities to educational reform for young children. She lectured on anthropology for several years at the University of Rome, and wrote an influential book entitled *Pedagogical Anthropology* (English edition, 1913). Montessori was no egalitarian. She supported most of Broca's work and the theory of innate criminality proposed by her compatriot Cesare Lombroso. She measured the circumference of children's heads in her schools and inferred that the best prospects had bigger brains. But she had no use for Broca's conclusions about women. She discussed Manouvrier's work at length and made much of his tentative claim that women, after proper correction of the data, had slightly larger brains than men. Women, she concluded, were intellectually superior, but men had prevailed heretofore by dint of physical force. Since technology has abolished force as an instrument of power, the era of women may soon be upon us: "In such an epoch there will really be superior human beings, there will really be men strong in morality and in sentiment. Perhaps in this way the reign of women is approaching, when the enigma of her anthropological superiority will be deciphered. Woman was always the custodian of human sentiment, morality and honor."

This represents one possible antidote to "scientific" claims for the constitutional inferiority of certain groups. One may affirm the validity of biological distinctions but argue that the data have been misinterpreted by prejudiced men with a stake in the outcome, and that disadvantaged groups are truly superior. In recent years, Elaine Morgan has followed this strategy in her *Descent of Woman,* a speculative reconstruction of human prehistory from the woman's point of view— and as farcical as more famous tall tales by and for men.

I prefer another strategy. Montessori and Morgan followed Broca's philosophy to reach a more congenial conclusion. I would rather label the whole enterprise of setting a biological value upon groups for what it is: irrelevant and highly injurious. George Eliot well appreciated the special tragedy that biological labeling imposed upon members of disadvantaged groups. She expressed it for people like herself—women of extraordinary talent. I would apply it more widely—not only to those whose dreams are flouted but also to those who never realize that they may dream—but I cannot match her prose. In conclusion, then, the rest of Eliot's prelude to *Middlemarch:*

> The limits of variation are really much wider than anyone would imagine from the sameness of women's coiffure and the favorite love stories in prose and verse. Here and there a cygnet is reared uneasily among the ducklings in the brown pond, and never finds the living stream in fellowship with its own oary-footed kind. Here and there is born a Saint Theresa, foundress of nothing, whose loving heartbeats and sobs after an unattained goodness tremble off and are dispersed among hindrances instead of centering in some long-recognizable deed.

Considerations

Thinking

What do you think of Gould's claim that "science is an inferential exercise, not a catalog of facts"? What exactly do you think he means by "inferential exercise"?

Identify what you think are Gould's primary aims in writing this essay.

See if you can figure out just how Gould develops his argument against Broca's theories. What, in other words, are Gould's rhetorical strategies in this essay? Are those strategies directed solely against Broca, or does Gould have other antagonists in mind?

Connecting

What is the overall effect of Gould's use of George Eliot's *Middlemarch?*

Gould brings two other women, besides Eliot, into his essay. What use does he make of Maria Montessori and Elaine Morgan?

Compare the way Gould uses scientific evidence in this essay with the way Loren Eiseley uses scientific experience in "The Dance of the Frogs." Is one use of science more effective than the other? How do you think the differences are related to the kinds of essays Gould and Eiseley are writing?

Writing

If Gould is right that "science is an inferential exercise, not a catalog of facts," how well would your formal, scientific education measure up against that definition? Write your assessment to a professor of science within your college or university.

Write an essay that examines the effect on our culture of what Gould calls "biological labeling." Consider one problem in depth, rather than making superficial generalizations about a host of problems.

Gordon D. Grice
(b. 1955)

Gordon Grice is a newspaper writer and columnist, whose essays, poems, and short stories have appeared in journals and magazines such as *Harper's Magazine* and the *Chattahoochee Review.* "The Black Widow," originally from *High Plains Literary Review,* now forms part of Grice's book *The Red Hourglass: Lives of the Predators.* The essay is notable for its philosophical perspective.

The Black Widow

I hunt black widow. When I find one, I capture it. I have found them in discarded wheels and tires and under railroad ties. I have found them in house foundations and cellars, in automotive shops and toolsheds, in water meters and rock gardens, against fences and in cinderblock walls. I have found them in a hospital and in the den of a rattlesnake, and once on the bottom of the chair I was sitting in.

Sometimes I raise a generation or two in captivity. The egg sacs produce a hundred or more pinpoint cannibals, each leaving a trail of gleaming light in the air, the group of them eventually producing a glimmering tangle in which most of them die, eaten by stronger sibs. Finally I separate the three or four survivors and feed them bigger game.

Once I let several egg sacs hatch out in a container about eighteen inches on a side, a tight wooden box with a sliding glass top. As I tried to move the box one day, the lid slid off and I fell, hands first, into the mass of young widows. Most were still translucent newborns, their bodies a swirl of brown and cream. A few of the females had eaten enough to molt; they had the beginnings of their blackness. Their tangle of broken web clung to my forearms. They felt like trickling water in my arm hairs.

I walked out into the open air and raised my arms into the stiff wind. The widows answered the wind with new strands of web and drifted away, their bodies gold in the late sun. In about ten minutes my arms carried nothing but old web and the husks of spiderlings eaten by their sibs.

I have never been bitten.

The black widow has the ugliest web of any spider. The orb weavers make those seemingly delicate nets that poets have traditionally used as symbols of imagination, order, and perfection. The sheet-web spiders weave crisp linens on the grass. But the widow makes messy-looking tangles in the corners and bends of things and under logs and debris. Often the web is littered with leaves. Beneath it lie the husks of insect prey, their antennae still as gargoyle horns, cut loose and dropped; on them and the surrounding ground are splashes of the spider's white urine, which looks like bird guano and smells of ammonia even at a distance of several feet. This fetid material draws scavengers—ants, sow bugs, crickets, roaches, and so on—which become tangled in vertical strands of silk reaching from the ground up into the web. The widow comes down and, with a bicycling of the hind pair of legs, throws gummy silk onto this new prey.

When the prey is seriously tangled but still struggling, the widow cautiously descends and bites the creature, usually on a leg joint. This is a killing bite; it pumps neurotoxin into the victim. The widow will deliver a series of bites as the creature dies, injecting substances that liquefy the organs. Finally it will settle down to suck the liquefied innards out of the prey, changing position two or three times to get it all.

Before the eating begins, and sometimes before the victim dies from the slow venom, the widow usually moves it higher into the web. It attaches some line to the prey with a leg-bicycling toss, moves up the vertical web strand that originally snagged the prey, crosses a diagonal strand upward to a higher point on a different vertical strand, and here secures the line. It has thus dragged the prey's body up off the ground. The whole operation is like that of a person moving a load with block and tackle. It occurs in three dimensions—as opposed to the essentially two-dimensional operations of orb weavers and sheet weavers.

You can't watch the widow in this activity very long without realizing that its web is not a mess at all but an efficient machine. It allows complicated uses of leverage and also, because of its complexity of connections, lets the spider feel a disturbance anywhere in the web—usually with enough accuracy to tell the difference at a distance between a raindrop or leaf and viable prey. The web is also constructed in a certain relationship to movements of air so that flying insects are drawn into it. This fact partly explains why widow webs are so often found in the face-down side of discarded car wheels—the wheel is essentially a vault of still air that protects the web, but the central hole at the top allows airborne insects to fall in. An insect that is clumsy and flies in random hops, such as a June beetle, is especially vulnerable to this trap. The widow often seems to choose her building sites according to indigenous smells rather than creating her own stinking waste pile from scratch. The webs turn up, for example, in piles of trash and rotting wood. A few decades ago, the widow was notorious for building its home inside the works of outdoor toilets. Scraping around with a stick before using the toilet was a common practice.

The architectural complexities of the widow web do not particularly impress the widows. They move around in these webs almost blind, yet they never misstep or get lost. In fact, a widow forcibly removed from its web and put back at a different point does not seem confused; it will quickly return to its habitual resting place. Furthermore, widows never snare themselves, even though every strand of the web is a potential trap. A widow will spend a few minutes every day coating the clawed tips of its legs with the oil that lets it walk the sticky strands. It secretes the oil from its mouth, coating its legs like a cat cleaning its paws.

The human mind cannot grasp the complex functions of the web but must infer them. The widow constructs it by instinct. A brain smaller than a pinhead contains the blueprints, precognitive memories the widow unfolds out of itself into actuality. I have never dissected with enough precision or delicacy to get a good specimen of the black widow brain, but I did glimpse one once. A widow was struggling to wrap a praying mantis when the insect's forelegs, like scalpels mounted on lightning, sliced away the spider's carapace and left exposed the clear droplet of bloody brain.

Widows reportedly eat mice, toads, tarantulas—anything that wanders into that remarkable web. I have never witnessed a widow performing a gustatory act of that magnitude, but I have seen them eat scarab beetles heavy as pecans; carabid beetles strong enough to prey on wolf spiders; cockroaches more than an inch long; and hundreds of other arthropods of various sizes. Widows begin life by eating their siblings. An adult female will fight any other female; the winner often eats the loser. A popular game among Mexican children is to stage such fights and bet on the outcome. The children put the widows on a stick and pass it around so that everyone can see. Sometimes one female ties another up and leaves without killing her. I have come across such black pearls wrapped in silk and, upon peeling off the skin, seen the pearls unfold their legs and rush away.

The widow gets her name by eating her lover, though this does not always happen. He distinguishes himself from ordinary prey by playing her web like a lyre. Sometimes she eats him without first copulating; sometimes she snags him as he withdraws his palp from her genital pore. Sometimes he leaves unharmed after mating; in this case, he soon withers and dies on his own. I have witnessed male and female living in platonic relationships in one web. The males' palps, still swollen with sperm, proved that these relationships had not been sexual.

Many widows will eat as much as opportunity gives. One aggressive female had an abdomen a little bigger than an English pea. She snared a huge cockroach and spent several hours subduing it, then three days consuming it. Her abdomen swelled to the size of a largish marble, its glossy black stretching to a tight red-brown. With a different widow, I decided to see whether that appetite was really insatiable. I collected dozens of large crickets and grasshoppers and began to drop them into her web at a rate of one every three or four hours. After catching and consuming her tenth victim, this bloated widow fell from her web, landing on her back. She remained in this position for hours, making only feeble attempts to move. Then she died.

The first thing people ask when they hear about my fascination with the widow is why I am not afraid. The truth is that my fascination is rooted in fear.

I have childhood memories that partly account for my fear. When I was six my mother took my sister and me to the cellar of our farmhouse and told us to watch as she killed a widow. With great ceremony she produced a long stick (I am tempted to say a ten-foot pole) and, narrating her technique in exactly the hushed voice she used for discussing religion or sex, went to work. Her flashlight beam found a point halfway up the cement wall where two marbles hung together—one crisp white, the other a glossy black. My mother ran her stick through the dirty silver web around them, and as it tore it sounded like the crackling of paper in fire. This sound is unique to the widow's powerful web—anybody with a little experience can tell a widow's work from another spider's by ear. The black marble rose on thin legs to fight off the intruder. As the plump abdomen wobbled across the wall, it seemed to be constantly throwing those legs out of its path. The impression it gave was of speed and frantic anger, but actually a widow's movements outside the web are slow and inefficient. My mother smashed the widow onto the stick and carried it up into the light. It was still kicking its remaining legs. Mom scraped it against the sidewalk, grinding it to a paste. Then she returned for the white marble—the widow's egg sac. This, too, came to an abrasive end.

My mother's stated purpose was to teach us how to recognize and deal with a dangerous creature we would probably encounter on the farm. But of course we also took the understanding that widows were actively malevolent, that they waited in dark places to ambush us, that they were worthy of ritual disposition, like an enemy whose death is not sufficient but must be followed with the murder of his children and the salting of his land and whose unclean remains must not touch our hands.

The odd thing is that so many people, some of whom presumably did not first encounter the widow in such an atmosphere of mystic reverence, hold the widow in awe. Various friends have told me that the widow always devours her mate, or that her bite is always fatal to humans—in fact, it almost never is. I have heard told for truth that goods imported from the Orient are likely infested with widows and that women with bouffant hairdos have died of widow infestation. Any contradiction of such tales is received as if it were a proclamation of atheism.

The most startling contribution to the widow's mythical status I have ever encountered was *Black Widow: America's Most Poisonous Spider,* a book that appeared in 1945. Between genuine scientific observations, the authors present the widow as a lurking menace with a taste for human flesh. They describe the experiments of other investigators; one involved inducing a widow to bite a laboratory rat on the penis, after which event the rat "appeared to become dejected and depressed." Perhaps the most psychologically revealing passage is the authors' quotation from another writer, who said the "deadliest Communists are like the black widow spider; they conceal their *red* underneath."

We project our archetypal terrors onto the widow. It is black; it avoids the light; it is a voracious carnivore. Its red markings suggest blood. Its name, its sleek, rounded form invite a strangely sexual discomfort; the widow becomes an emblem for a man's fear of extending himself into the blood and darkness of a woman, something like the legendary Eskimo vampire that takes the form of a fanged vagina.

The widow's venom is, of course, a soundly pragmatic reason for fear. The venom contains a neurotoxin that can produce sweats, vomiting, swelling, convulsions, and dozens of other symptoms. The variation in symptoms from one person to the next is remarkable. The constant is pain. A useful question for a doctor trying to diagnose an uncertain case: "Is this the worst pain you've ever felt?" A "yes" suggests a diagnosis of black widow bite. Occasionally people die from widow bites. The very young and the very old are especially vulnerable. Some people seem to die not from the venom but from the infection that may follow; because of its habitat, the widow carries dangerous microbes.

Some researchers hypothesized that the virulence of the venom was necessary for killing beetles of the scarab family. This family contains thousands of species, including the June beetle and the famous dung beetle the Egyptians thought immortal. All the scarabs have thick, strong bodies and unusually tough exoskeletons, and many of them are common prey for the widow. The tough hide was supposed to require a particularly nasty venom. As it turns out, the venom is thousands of times more virulent than necessary for this purpose. The whole idea is full of the widow's glamour: an emblem of eternal life killed by a creature whose most distinctive blood-colored markings people invariably describe as an hourglass.

No one has ever offered a sufficient explanation for the dangerous venom. It provides no evolutionary advantages: all of the widow's prey items would find lesser toxins fatal, and there is no particular benefit in killing or harming larger animals. A widow that bites a human being or other large animal is likely to be killed. Evolution does sometimes produce such flowers of natural evil—traits that are neither functional nor vestigial but utterly pointless. Natural selection favors the inheritance of useful characteristics that arise from random mutation and tends to extinguish disadvantageous traits. All other characteristics, the ones that neither help nor hinder survival, are preserved or extinguished at random as mutation links them with useful or harmful traits. Many people—even many scientists—assume that every animal is elegantly engineered for its ecological niche, that every bit of an animal's anatomy and behavior has a functional explanation. This assumption is false. Nothing in evolutionary theory sanctions it; fact refutes it.

We want the world to be an ordered room, but in a corner of that room there hangs an untidy web. Here the analytical minds find an irreducible mystery, a motiveless evil in nature, and the scientist's vision of evil comes to match the vision of a God-fearing country woman with a ten-foot pole. No idea of the cosmos as elegant design accounts for the widow. No idea of a benevolent God is comfortable in a world with the widow. She hangs in her web, that marvel of design, and defies teleology.

Considerations

Thinking

What does Grice imply about the black widow spider? What does he suggest more broadly about the natural world? And what does he say about the human mind's attempt to accommodate the black widow? What does Grice mean by saying that the black widow "defies teleology"?

Grice's essay blends personal experience with natural observation and philosophical speculation. What would be gained or lost without one of these components?

Connecting

Compare Grice's essay on the black widow with Annie Dillard's essay "Living Like Weasels." What do their essays have in common? How do they differ?

Compare Grice's essays with Jane Brox's essay "Influenza 1918." How do both writers engage their readers? What does Brox do that Grice does not, and vice versa?

Writing

Write an essay in which you describe your experience with an element of untamed nature. Use your experience—with snakes, spiders, or another animal or insects—as a starting point for reflection about its purpose in nature and its significance in the larger scheme of things.

Write an analysis of Grice's essay, or write a response to the questions he raises and the observations he makes at the end.

Bernd Heinrich
(b. 1940)

Bernd Heinrich is a professor of zoology at the University of Vermont and the winner of a John Burroughs Medal. His passion for the outdoors runs as deep as his desire to understand the complex workings of the natural world. The titles of his books suggest the range of his interests: *A Year in the Maine Woods, Ravens in Winter, One Man's Owl, Bumblebee Economics, The Trees in My Forest,* and most recently, *The Mind of the Raven: Investigations and Adventures with Wolf-Birds.*

Heinrich's books not only reveal fascinating things about the natural world, but also teach us about the art of scientific observation. In his works, we see Heinrich in the natural habitat of his Maine farm; we see him in the outdoor shelters; we see him in the act of observing; we experience his enthusiasms; and we come to understand something of the rigors and limitations of scientific investigation.

"Sex in Trees, " from *The Trees in My Forest,* gives us a peek into the reproductive life of trees and into Heinrich's whimsical imagination.

Sex in Trees

There is more of good nature than of good sense at the bottom of most marriages.

—HENRY DAVID THOREAU

One day in mid April, the alders down by the brook unfurled their hard, tight, purple catkins. Overnight they were transformed into long, loose dangling tassels that trembled in the least bit of a breeze. Wisps of yellow pollen flew off like puffs of smoke. The brook, aptly named Alder Stream, roared full of tannin-stained yellow water collected in rivulets off the hill still under thick banks of snow. Slightly above the alder thickets under the bare poplars, the beaked hazel-nuts were also unfurling their male catkins. As in the alders, the female hazelnut flowers are on the same twigs. But I see these tiny delicate purple wisps only when I look closely. Windblown pollen grains find them.

The alders, hazelnuts, poplars, willows, sugar and red maples, beeches, ashes, and oaks each shed their pollen in a few days. All are done blooming when the first leaf buds open from the beginning of May and on into June. The insect-pollinated trees, the basswoods and chestnuts, wait to flower until summer, weeks after they have leaves. Each species has a schedule, and that schedule is especially strict in matters pertaining to sex.

Flowers are sexual organs, and flowering is not sex but the preliminaries. A great deal of investment goes into sex, and the mechanisms that animals and plants have evolved to achieve sex are a source of wonder and beauty. Without sex there would be no flowers and no bees, nor would there be brightly colored birds and birdsong. There would be no alluring scents that female moths give off at night that attract males from a mile or more downwind. There would be no flash-ing of fireflies through the trees on hot July nights, nor would there be evening serenades of crickets and katydids in August. Scents, sounds, and colors often combined in fantastic forms have the purpose of attracting mates. But trees can't be attracted. They are rooted in place.

In order to achieve sex, each male tree (or the portion of it that is male) sends forth millions of tiny pollen grains. These structures contain sperm, but they are not sperm. Instead, they are analogous to whole male reproductive tracts. When one pollen grain lodges on the stigma of a flower—the receptive part of a compat-

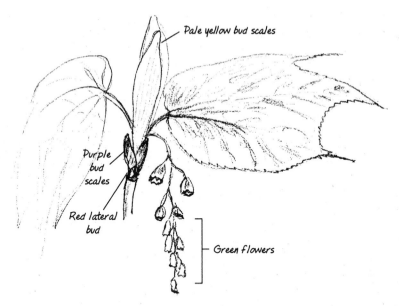

THE TERMINAL BUD OF A STRIPED MAPLE OPENS TO REVEAL BOTH LEAVES AND FLOW-
ERS. THE FLOWERS ARE SMALL AND GREEN, AND THEY ARE BOTH WIND- AND INSECT-
POLLINATED.

ible female reproductive tract of another tree—it sends forth a penislike tube that
grows rapidly, thrusting into the plant's ovary. Only then do the sperm descend
through this self-made tube into the ovary to fertilize the eggs. However, the
female is not passive. She chemically recognizes the proper pollen and permits the
growth of pollen tubes only for mates she chooses. The plant's own pollen is usually rejected or accepted only when none other reaches her.

There are several ways whereby a tree's pollen grains may find appropriate
ovaries. The forte of the angiosperm plants is their ability to harness intermedi-
aries to carry the pollen. Apple trees, for example, have harnessed bees by tailor-
ing the flowers' shapes, colors, scents, and food rewards to suit bees. Apple
flowers are perfumed and colored bright pink. They stand out like billboards to
bees and advertise to them from afar, inviting them to come sip sweet nectar and
take pollen. As bees feed on the flowers' nectar they become dusted with pollen.
They scrape most of this pollen from their bodies and collect it to feed their larvae
back in their hive. However, some of the pollen remains on their body hairs, and
it inadvertently gets deposited on other apple flowers on other trees that the bee
also visits. The bee thus becomes a long-range mating agent for trees rooted in
place. In some other plants, such as saguaro cactus trees, the much larger white
flowers open only at night and provide much more nectar than apple flowers.
They are shaped so that the fur of specific bats that are adapted to eat nectar and

pollen gets dusted with pollen, and this pollen then gets deposited in flowers of the next plant the bat visits. Many other plants are tailored in shape, color, scent, and the food they offer to attract moths, butterflies, flies, beetles, or birds. In turn, the flower bats, hummingbirds, sphinx moths, and bees are highly dependent on the plants for their own livelihood and neither organism can now exist without the other. Through evolution, flowers made these animals what they are, and the animals in turn made flowers.

Almost all of the trees in my forest use wind, rather than bees or other animals, to transfer their pollen. Wind has drawbacks. It is unpredictable. It may be absent when the flowers bloom, or it could blow from the wrong direction. Insects, however, are there to be beckoned at any time, and they can come from any direction. In comparison to a bee flying directly from flower to flower, using the wind to send pollen or to receive it from a neighbor might seem like a big gamble for achieving sex. As in all gambles, however, there are ways of improving the odds. Trees improve their odds of fertilization by dispersing astronomical numbers of pollen grains. More than five million are released from a single birch flower or catkin, and each tree has hundreds of thousands of flowers. Female wind-pollinated flowers have enlarged sticky stigmatic surfaces that aid in catching pollen grains out of the air. In all of the deciduous wind-pollinated trees (ashes, elms, beeches, sugar and red maples, oaks, birches, willows, poplars, and aspens), the narrow window of time when sexual unions occur is very early in the spring before the leaf buds open. If flowers waited until after the leaves unfurled, then they would be partially shielded from the wind and there would be less chance for successful transfer of pollen between flowers.

Animals search ouçflowers even within foliage. After having been rewarded with food from one kind of flower, most animals search persistently for others of the same kind, identifying them by scent, color, and shape. Male and female flowers must be similar in appearance; otherwise the pollinator might fly to flowers of one sex and not the other. Having both sexes on the same flower, such as in the apple, is one common solution that helps solve this problem (so long as the plant also has means to prevent self-pollinating). The sexual system of an apple tree thus differs from that of an animal in that male and female roles are usually not mutually exclusive within one individual. Most plants have little or no sexual identity. An apple blossom is both male and female. It gives and receives pollen. Having both sexes on the same flower, apples have so-called perfect flowers, as opposed to "imperfect" ones (either male or female), as are found on alder, hazelnut, or maple, for example.

Wind-pollinated plants do not have showy flowers. In them the appearance of male and female flowers is irrelevant and the sexes are usually on separate flowers. Sometimes there are even whole trees that have either all male or all female flowers. In willows, for example, some individual trees have only male flowers and others have only female flowers. In American white ash trees and red maples there are (usually) separate male and female trees. Two of the three American chestnuts I have planted have so far produced both male and female flowers on the same tree. However, one produced primarily male flowers. Only the female flowers produce nuts. On hazelnut, alder, beech, and oak, separate male and female flowers are always on the same tree, and to achieve cross-pollination these trees must avoid fertilizing their own ovaries with their own sperm. Trees avoid self-fertilization and achieve cross-pollination in various complex ways. Given all the large investment, and all the complex and wonderful mechanisms that have gone into achieving sexual reproduction, one wonders: What is the point of it?

The point of *reproduction* is to pass on as many of the individual's genes as possible. If a tree's flowers were self-pollinated, then all of its seeds would contain only its own genes. One that must be cross-pollinated automatically halves the number of its genes that it packages into each seed, since the other half comes from an unrelated other parent. Cross-pollination from the perspective of reproduction is thus not a solution. It's an immense problem. What does sex do for the tree? Why bother with it? Why should a tree cross-pollinate when, by so doing, it reduces the number of genes it passes on relative to what could be achieved by self-pollination?

Sex is a mechanism that introduces genetic variety into offspring. Sex dissolves old genetic combinations, scrambles them, and randomly reassembles them into many new mosaics. It's a little bit like having two similar cars (originating from two factories), taking them apart piece by piece, putting all the pieces into one heap, duplicating the pieces many times, and then picking appropriate pieces of each kind randomly to reassemble them again into numerous new cars. Each of these cars will have different percentages of parts in different combinations from the two parent lines.

Every one of these new cars is apt to be slightly different. Some will perform better and some will perform worse in each varied situation. However, genetic variety increases the odds that one or another of these "offspring" will succeed in a changing or variable environment relative to that of the "parents." Of course, the two original cars can't be too different—say a VW "bug" and a Mack truck—else the parts won't mesh and then none survives.

For trees and other plants as well as animals, diseases may be one of the greatest variables of the environment. Right now, for example, blister rust is devastating the white pines and Dutch elm disease the elms. Both of the fungi that cause these diseases are highly effective because they have fine-tuned their biochemistry to that of potential hosts. If they eventually specialize to attack a clone rather than a sexually reproducing tree, then *all* "individuals" of that clone would be equally vulnerable. Since each pine and elm tree is the product of a sexual union, however, there is more chance of individual immunity or resistance, offering them an evolutionary escape mechanism. Given sufficient isolation and time, potentially a whole new population could arise from a new variant. The rewards of sex in trees are not immediate. They are strictly long-term.

In the short term there are often situations when sex is disadvantageous to trees. Perhaps the greatest drawback is when potential mates are not within the trees' sexual reach. Since trees cannot travel, they face a problem. I could see it in my chestnut trees. In the fall of 1996 I examined my American chestnut trees and found that they had both male and female flowers. So far so good. The trees had even produced the typical round, spiny fruit of chestnut trees. However, inside the fruit were only the empty shells of typical-looking brown nuts. I suspect therefore that American chestnut trees don't self-pollinate. The flowers had probably not been cross-pollinated, so no embryos grew although receptacles for them did. Perhaps there were not sufficient numbers of suitable sexual partners nearby, or maybe the critical pollinating insect required by chestnuts was absent. Similarly, I found the ground strewn with sterile nuts under a lone black walnut tree (on a farm in Vermont). I eagerly picked up enough walnuts to fill a grocery bag. Unfortunately, each of thirty-five nuts I cracked was empty. The flowers from which they had grown probably had not been cross-pollinated for lack of a nearby partner.

I have often wondered why most of the trees in my forest use the wind to transfer their pollen and in many cases to disperse their seeds. In tropical forests, the trees hitch both their pollen and seed transfer almost exclusively onto animals, and the animals in turn come to depend on them. Especially in the tropical forests, trees can scarcely be thought of as separate organisms at all. They exist as parts of an unfathomable complex web where each species is linked to others in growth, reproduction, and sex.

Nobody has "the answer" to why northern trees are mostly wind-pollinated rather than animal-pollinated. There are probably many answers. Maybe there is not enough wind in tropical forests, or not enough animals in northern forests. Perhaps there are fewer animals in northern forests simply because the trees don't offer nectar rewards because they use the wind. Cause and effect often become blurred.

Tree distribution is undoubtedly important in determining the kind of pollination system that is needed to accomplish the job. A one-hectare plot (about two and a half acres) of Borneo rain forest selected at random contains about seven hundred species of trees, and the trees of any one species therefore tend to be *isolated* one from another. In contrast, in my forest, a one-hectare area selected at random would likely contain only one-hundredth the variety of trees, and many trees of a single species grow in dense crowds. Different sections of the southern slope down to Alder Stream are dominated respectively by quaking aspen, red maple, and sugar maple. The top of the ridge grows mainly red spruce, while on the western slope of the hill balsam fir and white birch predominate. The alders grow in patches along the side of the brook. In most cases, the individual trees of the same species touch or almost touch each other. I can hardly differentiate individuals. I doubt that pollinators do so. The trees are an *anonymous* crowd; they are not individually labelled by unique sign or location.

Looking at the pollinators' world in human terms, it is as if a street had many unlabelled, identical-looking, and identically scented restaurants all randomly intermingled. Some of them serve ample food of superior quality and some of them serve very poor food or none at all. To enter any one you have to pay at the door, and customers must visit several locales each evening to be satiated. As long as customers feel that on average they get suitable food they'll take chances and keep on coming to that group of anonymous restaurants. The restaurateurs, however, are individuals, and they are in intense competition with one another. In order to stay in business many of the more shrewd or dishonest slyly provide less food. Others must follow suit, with the end result that the customers eventually stop coming to eat on that particular street, because on average they keep paying the same and getting less. Substitute plants with nectar-rewarding flowers for restaurants, and bees for people, and we have the same situation. The plants get a payoff not from having the nectar eaten out of their flowers, but from having the insects enter their flowers, which pollinates them. When the customers no longer enter their flowers, plants need to devise a new mechanism of pollination. Could sex in the wind be the solution?

Considerations

Thinking

Heinrich uses a number of interesting analogies in his essay. Consider two—the one about similar cars and the one at the end of the essay about restaurants. How do these analogies help Heinrich advance his argument? In what ways are these analogies limited?

Consider the last sentence of the essay: "Could sex in the wind be the solution?" How effective is it? In the context of the whole essay and of life as you know and understand it, what are the things that final question makes you think about? Do these questions of your own limit or extend the meaning of the essay as you understand it?

Connecting

Heinrich and Stephen Jay Gould are both science writers. Read their respective essays in this anthology and note the differences in their style—the way they go about developing their arguments. Note similarities and differences. What do they tell you about good science writing?

Repeat the exercise using Heinrich and Lewis Thomas ("The Lives of a Cell," pp. 614–615). What do science writing (the kind you see Heinrich and Thomas practicing) and other writing have in common? Explain.

Writing

Assume that you are Heinrich; you have studied his sentences and his style and his wit. As Heinrich, write Roy Reed a letter about his essay "Spring Comes to Hogeye" (pp. 470–472). Your purpose is to engage him in a bit of friendly banter. In your letter you must also make some use of Gretel Ehrlich's essay "Spring." Have fun.

Write a short explanation of why you think Heinrich chose to head his essay with the epigraph from Thoreau: "There is more of good nature than of good sense at the bottom of most marriages." Explain that epigraph in terms of Heinrich's essay, paying particular attention to the phrases "good nature" and "good sense."

Pat C. Hoy II
(b. 1938)

Pat C. Hoy II has taught English literature and expository writing at the U.S. Military Academy and at Harvard University as well as at Bergen Community College. He is director of the Expository Writing Program at New York University and a professor of English. In another life he was a colonel in the Field Artillery and a Vietnam War veteran. Hoy has published articles, reviews, and familiar essays on a wide range of subjects for periodicals such as the *Sewanee Review,* the *Virginia Quarterly Review, Agni,* and *Twentieth-Century Literature.* His first book of familiar essays, *Instinct for Survival,* was published by the University of Georgia Press in 1992.

In the essay that follows, Hoy reviews a group of books whose subjects are related to war, a topic that haunts his imagination.

War Elegy

As I sit here on this flagless Memorial Day overlooking Washington Square Park from my apartment in the city of New York, my mind turns naturally to war and to E. B. White. This was, after all, his city, and it is impossible, still, to write here apart from him, especially on a national holiday like this one. During the 1930s, and stretching all the way into the late 60s, his *New Yorker* pieces reflect a continuing impatience with national fervor. In 1933 he calls on Einstein, speaking "not about relativity but about nationalism" to warn us of "forces inimical to life," and as late as 1969 White frets about a similar concern during a moment of national celebration. The moon, he grumbled, is "a poor place for flags"—"What a pity that in our moment of triumph we did not forswear the familiar Iwo Jima scene and plant instead a device acceptable to all: a limp white handkerchief, perhaps, symbol of the common cold, which, like the moon, affects us all, unites us all." It was unity that interested White—world unity—and were he with us today, still writing, I suspect that India and Pakistan would replace Leipzig in his mind; and he would try once again to make us see how "a single day's development" could take us back "a thousand years into the dark."

But White would also be concerned, as he was when he buried his pig, about forgetfulness, a failure to mourn those who have suffered and with whom we should be bound. He would not have us cast national unity aside, even though we are inclined to misuse it politically. "The Death of a Pig" remains fresh and provocative because it plays against our deep-seated, but often ignored, need for communal purgation. For White the tragic scene that he and his cast enact over the pig's death is "slapstick—the sort of dramatic treatment that instantly appealed to my old dachshund, Fred, who joined the vigil, held the [enema] bag and, when all was over, presided at the interment."

But there is a serious undercurrent in this ritual. The death is not about the loss of nourishment, White tells us, but about the pig who "had suffered in a suffering world." White brings in a host of characters from the rural community to bear witness to the suffering, and at the end, despite the slapstick and the rhetorical hyperbole, we know that White's "deep hemorrhage intears" express a loss that is bigger than a pig—that this death is a "departure which the community marks solemnly on its calendar, a sorrow in which it feels fully involved." White assures us, finally, that he and Fred will visit the unmarked grave in the woods "singly and together, in seasons of reflection and despair, on flagless memorial days of our own choosing."

Flagless memorial days—suffering and death recounted privately, throughout the year, rather than on specified days of national mourning, that is White's idea about the authenticity of mourning. My concern today, as I look out over Washington Square, is that most of those sauntering happily around the park—pushing as they often do the very limits of free expression—know, as the years pass, less and less about the suffering that others have done on their behalf. As the past recedes from memory, these inheritors of freedom have little basis for remembering, often no basis at all except the stories that others have left, and are leaving behind.

The definitive history of those stories has been written by Samuel Hynes in *The Soldiers' Tale: Bearing Witness to Modern War.* Hynes's elegant book extends the work that Paul Fussell did so well in *The Great War and Modern Memory* and less well in the polemical *Wartime: Understanding and Behavior in the Second World War.* Hynes gains distinction because of the broader scope of his investigation—the two world wars and the war in Vietnam—and the narrower focus on the soldiers' tales within each of the wars. In an earlier book, Hynes, like Russell, investigated the relationship between war and culture. In *The Soldiers' Tale* he distills the essence of the tales themselves, subordinating culture to the experience of war. The larger tale that he eventually constructs emerges from his even-handed analysis of the personal stories—memoirs, letters, journals—of men who actually fought. Beginning with the particulars of their experiences, he reaches for "the recoverable past of war" rather than making a higher claim on "historical truth." What he grasps is a heightened sense of how war feels, what it is like for the soldier.

The power of Hynes's accomplishment derives in large part from the way he uses his own war experiences and from the attitude he brings to the task of recovery; the two go hand in hand. To illustrate just what I mean by these strengths, I want to juxtapose Hynes and Fussell a moment longer. Their own memoirs of war provide the clues we need to understand just how Hynes elicits the reader's trust as he constructs the larger tale.

In *Doing Battle: The Making of a Skeptic* Fussell recovers a persona he had cast aside in 1987 as he began to collect and republish many of his earlier pieces on war, just as he also began to conceptualize *Wartime*. He identified that persona as "the pissed-off infantryman, disguised as a literary and cultural commentator." When Fussell deliberately removed that infantryman from the collected essays, affecting a more appealing form of reasonableness, the writing ironically became polemical, less persuasive. He lost touch with his own teasing ambiguities.

In his memoir Fussell restores that same infantryman but strips him of his military title, leaving us with what seems to be the real McCoy—the veteran "skeptic" who seems still to be riding high on the crest of a wave of unspent anger. Fussell takes us from his privileged early life in Pasadena (1924–43) all the way to the publication of *Wartime* (1990) and his final years of teaching at the University of Pennsylvania, but the central story of the memoir is the "extirpation of Boy Fussell" at the hands of the U.S. Army. From that story we see how war can strip away entitlement and turn innocent fascination into rage. In this most lonely of the soldier's tales, we see too how war continues to fuel Fussell's anger, feed his contempt, set him apart from others, and undercut his ironic stance. He can't get war out of his system.

Fussell is at his best as a writer when he pushes the anger below the surface and dispassionately rubs our noses in the grimy reality of war, asking only that we sit up and take notice. To those inclined to forget the horrors of war, Fussell seems to say, *I will not permit it.* For those without experience, he provides it, delighting as he does in how "wonderfully absurd, bizarre and unforgettable" the sights of war can be:

> The spectacle that caused my mouth to open in wonder, and almost in admira-tion, consisted of five German soldiers spread out prone in a semicircular skirmish line. They were still staring forward, alert for signs of the maquis. Behind them, in the center of the semicircle, was an equally rigid German medic with his Red Cross armband who had been crawling forward to do his work. In his left hand, a roll of two-inch bandage; in his right, a pair of surgical scissors. I could infer a plausible narrative. One or more men in the group had been wounded, and as the medic crawled forward to do his duty, his intention was rudely frustrated by an unspeakable loud sharp crack [of artillery] overhead, and instantly the lights went out for all of them. . . . The little waxwork squad, its soldiers unbloody and unmarked, had all left life at the same instant.

We are left with an eerie image, one of a kind that Hynes will call Battlefield Gothic. Fussell, left with a "sight that somehow brought art and life into strange relation," intensifies the image for us: "It was so cold that the bodies didn't smell, and they'd not begun visibly to decompose, but their open eyes were clouded, and snow had lodged in their ears and the openings in their clothes and the slits in their caps. Their flesh was whitish green. Although they were prone, their knees were bent, as if they were athletes terribly surprised while sprinting. They looked like plaster simulacra excavated from some chill white Herculaneum. No one but me, apparently, saw this sight."

Now, owing to Fussell, we have all seen it, and because of the transfiguration we wonder with him whether to interpret it "as an image of the whole war and its meaning, less a struggle between good and evil than a worldwide disaster impli-cating everyone alike, scarcely distinguishing its victims in the general shambles and ruin." For him the image and the experience linger in his mind "as a prime illustration of modernism, not that it occurred but that it seemed so normal, and that no one seemed to care."

There in that last bit of imagining, we see Fussell taint the image with his own personal suffering—so normal; no one seemed to care—as he points to the emblematic source of the unbalancing anger that causes him during the war to grow "increasingly snotty and sarcastic" and years later to see his less gifted, less experienced academic colleagues as "dolts." Out of Harvard and on the way to his first academic job, he "insisted on playing [his] transfigured self, that is, impu-dent, insolent, sarcastic, and ostentatiously clever and supercilious." Even though that transfigured self is tempered often by a yen for irony and occasionally by a deep, contradictory strain of sentimentality, the angry critic prevails, dominating and wearying us as he goes about his work.

Hynes's memoir, *Flights of Passage: Reflections of a World War II Aviator* (1988), reveals a very different kind of man, one who took with him from the war a more settled and settling resolution. His war in the Pacific, while no less isolating than Fussell's in Europe, took place in the sky and that, coupled with an inherited emotional restraint, seems to have made all the difference. From the outset Hynes is a "true believer in the religion of flight," and his lyrical descriptions retain a romantic flavor whether he is training stateside or flying combat missions in the Pacific:

Over Memphis

Below me light began to come on in houses and farms, and everything that was not a light became dark and indistinct, so that the ground was almost like a night sky. But still I flew on in sunlight. The surface of the plane seemed to absorb and hold the light and color of the sunset; brightness surrounded me. It was as though the earth had died, and I alone was left alive. A sense of my own aliveness filled me. I would never die. I would go on flying forever.

Over the Pacific

And then the island appears ahead, the planes slide into attack formation, the high-speed descent begins, the first plane peels off, and you really see the island for the first time, in your bombsight—a grove of trees on the right, an airstrip, a few buildings—and tracers begin to rise lazily toward you, and little clouds of AA bursts hang in the air as you dive past, and you have dropped and are pulling away, over the trees toward the beach and safety.

They were classic, beautiful strikes, the feeling of planes and men relating in the intricate choreography of a strike-formation, the gut-knotting climax, and the long, calm return. What memory returns to me is images.

How different these images are from Fussell's. And yet Hynes is no giddy flyboy. He suffered the loss of friends, "felt the rage that other pilots felt," and, in the memoir, he exposes the U.S. Navy's complicity in these losses. But from the outset, there is something besides the lilt of flying that holds Hynes steady. "After preflight," he tells us, "we would never quite join the Navy; we had joined instead a smaller, more independent and anarchic group, the community of fliers. The Navy was our antagonist, muscle-bound and dumb like those football-coach officers; but because it was dumb we could beat it. With a little imagination we could circumvent, muddle, and exploit the regulations, and we could fly."

Home from the war, Hynes chose to be discharged in Pensacola because he "wanted to return just once, just for a few days, to that place where I had learned the only skill I had, and where I had been happy in that timeless world of young men, before the dying began." "Perhaps," he goes on, "the impulse to return is a sign that one has grown up, an acknowledgment of the way the good times pass us. We go back in space because we can't go back in time." Some forty years after the war, summing up the experience of his last four-hour flight there in Pensacola, Hynes recalls the end of that wartime adventure: "We had become men with families and responsibilities and futures. The end of flying had made us mortal." And yet the war has not ended for Hynes either. Like Fussell he can't seem to be done with it, but the distance he has acquired from it allows him to elicit trust when he writes about it.

Hynes's discerning judgment, tempered by the claims of war, informs all that he says in *The Soldiers' Tale*. The book's supreme accomplishment lies in the multiplicity of voices—each of the individual soldier's voices that Hynes permits us to hear, accompanied always by the deft analytical voice of the soldier-scholar, making of the many tales the one definitive story about modern war. It is a delicate act of witnessing and reconstruction, complicated by the fragility and whimsicality of memory and language; but, by the end of this book, I have already begun to know what I could never have known through my own soldierly experiences. I know where I fit into the larger narrative of war, where my brothers who fought in Hynes's war fit into that same long, continuing tale. I know how the tale varies from war to war and from theater to theater; and because of Hynes's own discerning presence in this scholarly reconstruction of war, I also know something about the worth of the soldiers' collective investment in the nation's life. I know better what to mourn and what to revile in that common experience that binds us all together as a nation.

Hynes's own witnessing takes two different but related forms. The first consists of the subtle discerning commentary that permits us to understand each witness's contribution to the larger tale. In that commentary Hynes must weigh the value of those other tales, necessarily different from his own. As he creates the collective tale, a tale never heard until now, he must do justice to the others if his own is to be believed.

Here, then, is just a glimpse of how Hynes does that essential work of weighing and valuing. The war, in this example, is my war, Vietnam; the soldier's tale under examination is Philip Caputo's. The particular detail under scrutiny is Caputo's account of the death of Captain Frank Reasoner, a man I knew almost forty years ago when we were both cadets at West Point.

Before turning to the death itself, or even to Caputo, Hynes establishes the context for viewing the death, reminding us that Vietnam narratives, unlike the narratives from other wars, were written after various myths about the war had already been established within our culture. "The soldiers' tale of the war, when it took shape in the postwar years, would draw on [an] . . . existing myth, affirming or denying it, but acknowledging that it existed, that before the war ended it had been judged." Hynes has two myths in mind: "the Myth of the Bad War, which said it was an immoral adventure that should never have begun, in which American boys were killed and a nation was devastated; and the Myth of the War That Was Lost, which said the army could and would have won, if it had been allowed to fight as it wished." Hynes sees in the two myths a common thread: "bitterness and a sense of national shame."

One of the many things about these myths that interests Hynes is the "way the narratives use the traditional language of military values, the Big Words like 'courage' and 'duty' and 'heroism.' Those words survive, but without a clear moral base; they are simply words for extraordinary kinds of behavior." To demonstrate his point he turns, finally, to Caputo's description of "'the hero's' death of Captain Reasoner": "We split a beer and talked about the patrol he was taking out in the afternoon. His company was going into the paddy lands below Charlie ridge, flat, dangerous country with a lot of tree lines and hedgerows. Reasoner finished his beer and left. A few hours later, a helicopter brought him back in; a machine gun had stitched him across the belly, and the young corporal who had pulled Reasoner's body out of the line of fire said, 'He should be covered up. Will someone get a blanket? My skipper's dead.'"

Hynes then goes to work, analyzing this description, emphasizing what it reveals to us about the revised language of war: "How flat and workmanlike that sounds, just a story of a Marine going out to do his job and coming back dead. But then there is the touch of tenderness for the dead captain: "'He should be covered up. . . . My skipper's dead.' The emotional links between soldiers, and between officers and their men, are difficult to render, because though attachments between men in war can be strong—stronger than peacetime friendships—they are mostly inarticulate. Caputo does it delicately here."

Hynes has more to show us about what happened to Reasoner, about his Medal of Honor and the official citation; but he is most concerned about the absence in Caputo's language of the "brave adjectives." Nevertheless this glimpse is enough to reveal the acute witnessing that Hynes does, the way he insinuates himself into the larger account of war, as he explains the narratives that others have written. And there is yet another dimension to his witnessing.

In "Agents and Sufferers," the last chapter of his book, Hynes turns his attention to the victims of the Holocaust and the bombing of Hiroshima and to the prisoners whose long confinements deprived them of their status as active soldiers, made them helpless like the others. Asking whether these victims' stories should be included in the soldiers' tale that he is constructing, Hynes focuses our attention on the brutality surrounding what he considers the ultimate "war against humanity." We see the corpses, experience the torture inflicted on the prisoners in the Japanese camps, and look straight at the disfiguring damage of the Bomb. It is Hynes's way of intensifying questions about the moral complexity of war that have been largely implicit throughout the rest of the book, muted by his own dispassionate and workmanlike analysis of the hundreds of individual tales. But here Hynes points to our darkest side, reminding us that the "elements of our nature as human beings that we thought were immutable can be diminished or destroyed, and that the human heart may be colder and crueler than experience has shown us." He wants us to see clearly that "the process of disillusionment within progress and civilization reached its lowest depth there, in those camps designed by reason and by science for the efficient destruction of human lives."

At the end, as he brings together the experiences of the Holocaust victims, the denuded soldiers in the prison camps, and the innocent civilians at Hiroshima, Hynes also calls our attention to a variation on witnessing that makes us see in a different light what he had been doing throughout the book. He reminds us that "remembering is an action: to witness is to oppose. If you make the truth survive, however terrible it is, you are retaliating against inhumanity, in the only way the powerless have." These stories of suffering, Hynes tells us, "close the soldiers' tale of our century: not because they stand at the chronological end of modern war narratives (wars and their stories go on, as I write, as you read) but because they mark the extreme edge of military destructiveness in our time—as far as humankind has been able to extend the idea of war toward pure victimhood, beyond imaginable conflicts of armies to mass annihilation of the helpless and the innocent, and the end of war stories."

Focused as Hynes is at this moment on a particular aspect of the tale, we cannot help looking back on the inhumanity and the suffering that is always and everywhere an integral part of the soldiers' tale. There, in that final chapter, we come to see how subtly he has woven his own opposition into the fabric of the book—as if by giving us that felt sense of war, he can somehow help us learn to stop the killing and the destruction, to bring an end to the long tale.

Whether we have it in us to be that wise remains to be seen. The legacy of war is compelling, and the evidence of these memoirs suggests that something deeper than politics and nationalism draws us inexorably into the fray. In acknowledging war's power to call us out of our ordinary selves, I want to touch briefly on James Salter's *Burning the Days,* the most beautifully written memoir I've ever read—dangerous in its seduction, compelling in its presentation of the allure of war, and unsettling in its implications.

Salter knows only too well how the deep allure of war is like an obsessive love affair, and in the first half of this haunting book he sweeps us through the seductive phase of his life when love and war tempt him and pull at his spirit. The second half takes us into the aftermath of youthful romance where the spell of writing competes with the afterglow of the war, and loses. Nothing, not even a woman, can quite measure up to the feeling of grandeur that the war, at certain moments, can deliver. Salter calls it "the single daring act" that transforms a man, makes him godly, gives him satisfaction, gives him, as Hynes demonstrates again and again, the sense that he is a part of history. Listen as Salter pinpoints the ecstasy and then draws out the loss:

Over Korea

The flight has split up, we're in two's. By this time MIGs are being called out everywhere. The radio is brimming with voices, among them someone calling out MIGs south of the river at twenty-four thousand feet. How many, someone asks?

"Many, many!"

We head that way and see two, far out, sail past us on the left. We turn to follow, and they climb and begin to turn also. The sky is a burning blue, a sky things seem black in. I am on my back, Immelmanning up to get between them and the river, rolling out slightly beneath the leader, who is turning hard to the right and cannot see me. I duck my head and try to find the gunsight, which is an image projected onto a thick, slanted piece of glass that serves as the windshield. There's nothing there—turning has pulled it all the way off the glass. The MIG begins to level out and the sight drifts into view. About a thousand feet back I press the trigger. The tracers fall behind him. He begins to climb again and I am cutting him off, closing, glancing quickly back to see if my wingman is still there, firing again. A few hits in the right wing, then tremendous joy, at closer range a solid burst in the fuselage. The flashes are intense, brilliant, as of something vital shattering. He abruptly rolls over and I follow, as if we are leaping from a wall. He begins to pull it through. I am still shooting and something flies off the plane—the canopy. A moment later a kind of bundle, the pilot, comes out.

Loss

In the end there is a kind of illness. A feeling of inconsequence, even lightness, takes hold. It is, in a way, like the earliest days, the sense of being an outsider. Others are taking one's place, nameless others who can never know how it was. It is being given to them, the war with all its fading, romantic detail, its disasters and lucky chances. They will be coming home through the intense skies of autumn, settling gracefully in over the boundary of the field. The smooth black runway floats up to meet them. The ships are empty, feather-light, the fuel tanks almost drained, the belts of ammunition vanished; they are bringing back nothing except that thing we prized above all.

How, Salter asks us to consider, can anything ever match it? How can a young man turn away from it? War, Salter implies, is the only experience that is sure to rescue him from "obscurity."

As I turn from these memoirs and Hynes's magisterial tale back into my ordinary life, I feel the snap. It is better, I think, that the people outside the window sauntering in the park do not know what I know, what other soldiers know, else they too might ease their resistance and be drawn to it. On the other hand I have feelings akin to those of Hynes and Fussell. I do not want them to forget.

This past summer, at my sister's house I chanced to find a box of my older brother's belongings, all that's left of a tail gunner's physical life: a handful of letters, a scrapbook, trinkets from Paris, a boy's paraphernalia. I have not yet had the courage to read these letters, written some fifty-odd years ago before his life ended, in the skies over Germany, on a New Year's day. I do not know what the contents of that box will tell me, but I do know that those scant remains will bind the two of us even closer, and that once more I will suffer his loss. I know too that I will mourn again and again at a time of my own choosing. And I will never forget.

Considerations

Thinking

What is the effect on your own imagination of the beginning of "War Elegy"—the part dealing with E. B. White and the people strolling around Washington Square Park in New York City on Memorial Day? What are the implications of that beginning?

Why does Hoy interrupt his review of Hynes's book, *The Soldiers' Tale,* to spend a great deal of time and space comparing Hynes and Fussell? How does that comparison contribute to your understanding of Hynes's accomplishment in *Tale?*

Connecting

Consider what Hoy tells you about that long narrative of war that Hynes constructs and calls "the soldiers' tale." How can Arthur Danto's *Gettysburg* (pp. 185–197) help you put that tale in perspective? Explain.

Hoy tells us that "witnessing" is an important concept in Hynes's book. What are the two kinds of witnessing that Hoy identifies?

What do you think Hoy learns about war from the witnessing done by those three writers—Hynes, Fussell, and Salter—whose books he reviews? Identify specific places in the review essay where Hoy reveals implicitly or explicitly what he learns.

Writing

Write a brief account of how Hoy makes use of his own experience in his review. Explain whether this inclusion of experience strengthens or weakens Hoy's analysis of the other writers' books. Does it diminish his objectivity? Explain.

Write a brief account of what you think Hoy's overarching idea is in this review. In short, what does he have to tell us besides what he has to say about the books he reviews?

Sue Hubbell
(b. 1935)

Sue Hubbell is a self-taught naturalist who has written six books, including *A Country Year: Living the Questions, Far Flung Hubbell: Essays from the American Road,* and most recently, *Waiting for Aphrodite: Journeys into the Times before Bones.* She is a journalist as well as a naturalist whose essays and articles have appeared in the *New Yorker,* the *New York Times Magazine,* and *Smithsonian.*

Before Hubbell became a passionate observer of the little creatures of the earth, she was a librarian at Brown University. Seeking escape from a cloistered life, she and her first husband settled in the Ozarks, where she became a beekeeper, a serious writer, and an explorer. She now divides her time between Maine and Washington, D.C.

"Passionate Science," the first chapter of *Waiting for Aphrodite,* gives us a sense of Hubbell's motivation for observing and writing, and reveals as well her fascination with the limitations of scientific classification schemes, her distrust of taxonomies.

Passionate Science

I went to three different colleges before I managed to snag an undergraduate degree, and considering how callow I was in those days, it is a wonder I learned anything at all. But looking back, I believe I learned three things. Two are irrelevant to our purposes here, but one has some bearing. A professor at the first of those colleges penetrated my attention sufficiently to impress upon me that there was no such thing as objective writing, that every inscription, every traveler's tale, every news account, every piece of technical writing, tells more about the author and his times than it does about the ostensible subject. The best that can be hoped is that the writer will lay out his bias up front.

I'm nearly half a century away from my college days, but everything I've ever read, including the scientific papers on biological subjects that I mine for my own writing, has convinced me that the professor was right. The writers of those papers, men and women I have interviewed and have come to know and admire, have selected their subjects because they have a passion for them. They have observed phenomena with an eye shaped by their experiences in particular places and times and have found interest and significance according to their own gifts, limitations, sadnesses, and sociabilities; their understandings have been shaped by their own peculiar and quirky worlds.

One of the better achievements of Western thought is the scientific method, which, when it works well, makes allowances for all those passions, limitations, and quirks. A good field biologist goes out and looks at the real world, sees something no one else has noticed, writes it down as accurately as he can, and reports it to others through publication. On the basis of his observation, he or someone else may spin a theory that explains it. Other observers with other passions, later observers with other biases, check it out, supplement, amplify, disagree, revise. Science is a process, not a body of received wisdom.

My own interests run to small animals that creep and jump and slither and flutter, the invertebrates—"the little things that run the world," as E. O. Wilson has said. What I hope to do when I write, keeping my old professor in mind, is to tell about the world of invertebrates, which appears to me an interesting and engaging one. I try to lay out my biases up front. I am grateful but astonished that over my writing life—one of the several lives I've had—sober, serious, responsible grownup editors have let me loose in that particular world to satisfy my own curiosity and amuse myself, in return for bringing back reports of what I see. There is a lot of news.

Because we have backbones—vertebrae—we think they are important, so in one of those smug Aristotelian bifurcations, we have divided up the animals into vertebrates and invertebrates. Actually, it was Lamarck, the eighteenth-century French naturalist, inventor of the notion that acquired characteristics could be inherited, who dreamed up the word "invertebrates." But the idea goes back to Aristotle, the original digital thinker, a man who always divided things into two categories. His basic division of animals was into those that had blood and those that lacked it. By blood he meant good, rich, red blood, not the pale ichor that oozes from a bug when you squash it, and in the blooded category he included mammals, birds, reptiles, and fishes—in short, vertebrates, animals with backbones. The bloodless were crustaceans, cephalopods, insects, and snails—in short, invertebrates, or at least the ones he knew about. His scheme made further divisions of the Twenty Questions sort. Does the blooded animal have hair or is it hairless? Legged or legless? If it has legs, are there four or two? This digital, yes or no, approach is familiar to anyone who has used a botanical key. Leaves alternate or opposite? Stems fuzzy or smooth?

Today, however, the basic principle of taxonomy is that living things should be defined by what they have, not what they lack, so taxonomic divisions come in varying numbers, not just in twos. The biological reference text I use divides all animals into thirty-two phylum units, of which animals with backbones are only one. But the Aristotelian way of thinking is powerful and still dominates our view of the world. College courses are taught and textbooks written on "Invertebrate Zoology." The premier zoological research institutions of the world, such as the Smithsonian, have departments of vertebrate and of invertebrate zoology.

Thoughtful taxonomists and zoologists grumble about this backbone fixation. One of them, Robert O'Hara, part philosopher, part zoologist, wondered how humans might be classified if an arthropod were making up the scheme. Arthropoda, meaning "joint-footed," is the biggest phylum of animals, those that by numerical rights, at least, should do the classifying if they were so inclined. The phylum includes spiders, insects, crabs, and lobsters. An arthropod might, according to O'Hara, describe us and our near relatives this way: "The anarthropods are a primitive group with few species and a limited diversity of form. Their reproductive rates prevent them from adapting to their environments closely, and the giantism exhibited by many anarthropods has kept their numbers very low and is no doubt the cause of their general sluggishness."

The invertebrates could get along without us quite nicely, and did for hundreds of millions of years, but we could not get along without them, so dependent are we on the life processes they have initiated and keep going. We humans are a minority of giants stumbling around in the world of little things, often not noticing our neighbors, not even being able to see many of them because they are *very* small. Yet each and every species, constituted from the same basic handful of chemicals as we are, has a complicated and special way of getting on in the world, different from ours and different one from another.

When we learn something about the way invertebrates live, they become familiar to us and we develop some charity and friendliness toward them. I am pleased to know that the woman who lives next door to Arne and me in Washington, D.C., has a home business that is thriving and that her children are doing well in school. I am pleased, also, to know that the bumblebee I see in early springtime, working the azaleas in our front yard, is a solitary mother queen hustling up enough provisions to raise daughters who will help her work during the months ahead. I find it satisfying and enjoyable to watch a periwinkle snuffling through the algae on a seaside rock near our new home in Maine and know that it is having a good feed.

Although we don't know everything about vertebrates, we know quite a lot: occasionally a new bird or fish or mammal or reptile is discovered, but those discoveries are rare, so we know pretty well how many tens of thousands of vertebrate species there are, and we know a good deal about their biology and behavior. But more than 95 percent of the animal species are invertebrates, and we have discovered only a fraction of the suspected tens of millions of them. We know next to nothing about how they get on in their lives or what happens when we lurch through their communities. We don't even have a fix on the number of invertebrate species already known and described, which is surprising in these days of computer technology and catalogs. Nowhere in the world is there any tidy master list of all discovered species with their names neatly registered and affixed. Specialists in a particular group—the fireflies, for instance—usually have a fair notion of how many species there are in that group, but even those are educated estimates, and the numbers within bigger groupings, such as insects or sponges, are guesses. So we don't even know what we know. Anyone venturing among invertebrates is sure to have the pleasure of discovery. And nearly every observation becomes a piece of news from an uncharted world.

That sort of pleasure is certainly one of the reasons zoologists go out into the field . . . and why I follow them there. In working with them I have been struck, as a writer, with the similarity of our occupations. Both journalism and field biology require standing aside a little, playing observer, not participant, taking a look at the real world, interviewing its inhabitants one way or another, watching the manner in which they get along, and reporting what we have seen or heard. But more than that, both writers and biologists share a compulsion to describe to others how we see that world. We keep at it, publishing this bit now, another later, piling up reports of our own realities.

A couple of books ago, I learned just how heady the pleasure of discovery could be and what a compulsion its pursuit becomes. In that book, *Broadsides from the Other Orders,* I was writing on several themes and using the biology and behavior of a particular bug to explore each one. I selected my bug examples in direct proportion to my own curiosity, which is to say ignorance, about them: silverfish, katydids, water striders, daddy longlegs, and so on. For twenty years I had been living, on my farm in Missouri, in close company with camel crickets— pale, silent, humpbacked crickets with stripy brown jumping legs. When I looked them up in guidebooks I found the same three or four tired facts about them, but nothing that satisfied, so I put camel crickets on my list for the book. My procedure, as chapter added to chapter, was to head down to the Library of Congress and spend several weeks reading everything I could find on the new chapter's bug. Usually, by the end of that time I had found the one person who was doing interesting work on it. I would telephone him or her and ask if I could come talk. Entomologists are generous people, and they invariably said yes. But with camel crickets the situation was different. Very little was known about them, and nearly all of it had been discovered by one man who had died by the time I started my reading. A student of his, on the verge of retirement himself, had continued some of the taxonomic work, and he kindly identified the species I had on my farm. He also informed me that my species was a special kind that had piqued his mentor's interest. In fact, he gave me a paper written by that man near the end of his life, in which he described the species as a piece of "unfinished business and a beckoning problem."

Briefly, the paper explained that my camel crickets existed in a small area in and around my farm as an isolated group within a larger population that were thought to be the same species. When the males of this group matured sexually, they became puzzlingly different from the males outside, whom they otherwise resembled. They grew a bright orange bump on the back of what we would like to call their necks but mustn't, because bugs don't have necks. And, the taxonomist told me, no one knew anything about how camel crickets mated, for that act had never been seen: perhaps the orange bump contained a food gift that males allowed the females to bite into during courtship. The contribution of a body part is a part of some insect wooings. Camel crickets of other species are common across the United States. They are nocturnal and live in basements, under piles of stacked lumber, in corners of garages, in country well houses, but none besides mine flaunted an orange bump.

I learned to sex even immatures, captured a few males and females, and began keeping them in a terrarium. I figured out what they liked to eat, gave them water in bottle caps, learned that they were virtually blind and deaf but received a startling array of information through their more-than-body-length antennae. I watched them molt and grow, and took notes on all this as much for myself as for the chapter I was to write for the book. And, yes, I became the first person to see

A MATURE MALE CAMEL CRICKET (3/4 LIFESIZE). NOTE THE BUMP ON HIS PRONOTUM, JUST BEHIND THE HEAD.

them mate and lay eggs. They mated in a contorted position, but the female never nibbled at the male's orange bump.

For comparison, I began raising, in separate terraria, populations of camel crickets from twenty miles south of my farm, outside the range of my group. I discovered, to my surprise, that those males and females matured more slowly than did the ones from my farm and therefore mated much later in the season. This meant that in the wild the two populations would never interbreed. Could they? I isolated immature males and females from both populations and kept them cloistered in single-gender terraria until the ones lacking the orange bump were ready to breed and then mixed them, pair by pair, in still other terraria.

By this time my chapter on camel crickets had long since been written and the book published, but I was still fired with the delight of investigation. In those days I was regularly commuting the 1,010 miles between my Missouri farm and the house in Washington in a van loaded with manuscripts, source books, two dogs, a cat, the unabridged dictionary, and the eleventh edition of the *Encyclopaedia Britannica*. To that pile I added a good many terraria of camel crickets.

In the end I found that the two populations could be induced, in this artificial way, to interbreed and that their offspring were fertile, so that by the common definition they did indeed belong to the same species. That definition holds that a species is made up of individuals that interbreed and produce fertile offspring. But the offspring of these forced matches were frequently deformed; some could not molt successfully and often died before their time. Does the orange bump of the speedily maturing group contain a hormone that hastens development? Are the two groups genetically distinct? Is the orange-bump group a species in formation or, alternatively, a primitive group? My farm bordered a geologically unusual area that contains plants relict from the Ice Age. Might my camel crickets be relict, too, from a time when the season was shorter?

I haven't the equipment, skills, or training to answer those questions, but they spurred me, when I finally admitted that I had to give up the farm, to place it with an organization that will keep it and the camel crickets forever wild and safe. There were, to be sure, additional reasons for that decision, but the presence of the unusual camel crickets contributed to it. It is my hope that someday a young entomologist will stumble across something I've written and go looking for camel crickets with bright orange bumps one springtime. He may answer those questions, but he will ask others. That's the way the process goes.

There will always be people who believe that watching camel crickets is an unsuitable way for a grownup to spend her time and energies. One reason for the lack of information about camel crickets was that although they are an extremely common insect, big and easy to observe, they have little relevance to humans; they neither help nor harm us. Most research is driven by the availability of funding, and funding agencies need to see a payback. Will research on this particular oddly named animal we have never heard of improve human life in some demonstrable way? If we fund the research, will we find a better way to kill the animal if we believe it to be harmful or to encourage it if we find it beneficial? Camel crickets, in that sense, are neither "good" nor "bad" bugs. In this they resemble most of the life on the planet. In the very short run, the one in which research funding takes place, it is hard to show that much of what lives and grows in the world relates to us. We eat salmon but not sea mice, the elusive *Aphrodite,* a genus of worms that live in the ocean deeps, where, some scientists say, there may be as many as ten million other species as unconcerned with our existence as we are ignorant of theirs. Certain black flies cause a terrible tropical disease in humans, river blindness, but camel crickets do not make us sick, nor do most of the more than one million other species of insects. Sensible, practical concerns should and do make salmon and black flies of more importance and interest in the funding of research and the formation of public environmental policy than camel crickets or *Aphrodite* or those other nameless millions. That is the way of the world, or at least of our time in the world.

I must confess, however, that I've never been convinced that to be interesting and important an animal needs to have a relationship to, or use for, human beings. As a matter of fact, otherness, remoteness, and independence engage my curiosity and intellect more than do similarity and utility. And I think there are a number of good long-term reasons why we should persist in our interest in camel crickets and sea mice and all those millions of invertebrates awaiting discovery. Some of those reasons will turn up in the pages that follow. But here, initially, I want to return to this compulsion that we have, writers and naturalists, to become tellers of tales about the world we have traveled in.

My brother, Bil Gilbert, a writer whose preoccupations run to animals with backbones, most especially crows, has often written of our "fascination with other bloods" as the basis of our yearning to understand the ways of others, as an escape from mere human perspective. But it is my son, Brian Hubbell, also a writer, a poet, who has said it best of all. Poets often do. He wrote, in a 1996 issue of the *Beloit Poetry Journal:*

> The Message
>
> Dry September weekday morning,
> time indolence equates to sin,
> I was outside, eyes closed over coffee
> thinking some things I think when
> a grasshopper flew in a certain fury
> arcing off the desiccating asters
> and affixed itself sharply to my upper lip,
> returning startle with a compound stare
> a ceaseless green on green.
>
> Buttoned in its urgent grip
> words came as plain as under
> a falconed pigeon's ring
> or in a half-corked bottle;
> surely the heart of sadness is this knowing:
> each embarks a gulf alone, each with
> his fractured bit of seeing and a need
> but not the tools to tell.

READINGS

Barnes, R. S. K., et al. *The Invertebrates.* Oxford: Blackwell Scientific Publications, 1993.

Brusca, Richard C., and Gary J. Brusca. *Invertebrates.* Sunderland, Mass.: Sinauer Associates, 1990.

Buchsbaum, Ralph, et al. *Animals Without Backbones.* Chicago: University of Chicago Press, 1987.

Clarkson, E. N. K. *Invertebrate Paleontology and Evolution.* London: Chapman & Hall, 1993.

O'Hara, Robert. "Telling the Tree: Narrative Representation and the Study of Evolutionary History." *Biology and Philosophy* 7, no. 2 (1992).

Ruppert, Edward E., and Robert D. Barnes. *Invertebrate Zoology.* New York: Harcourt Brace, 1994.

Considerations

Thinking

The editors of *Encounters* gave this first chapter of Sue Hubbell's most recent book, *Waiting for Aphrodite,* its title "Passionate Science." Did they do a good job, or could there be a better title for this piece? Explain.

How is it, according to Hubbell, that we can have good science if scientists follow their passions and particular interests, "piling up reports of [their] own realities"?

If the chief reason for focusing on the little creatures is not utilitarian, what are the reasons, according to Hubbell?

Connecting

Why do you suppose Hubbell tells the story of the camel crickets? What does it have to do with the rest of the essay? Is it a piece of evidence? Explain.

Look carefully at the way Hubbell makes her case about pursuing her scientific passions. Compare her rhetorical moves with those of Stephen Jay Gould in "Women's Brains." What can you learn about science writing from that comparison?

Writing

What might Hubbell and Bernd Heinrich have to say to one another in a conversation about camel crickets and trees? Construct a snippet of that conversation as you imagine it.

Select some very small thing from the world around you that you suspect others pass by on a daily basis without noticing. Write an essay about that thing, revealing to us the significance of what we are missing. Be sure to think long and hard about the thing itself, but think as well about what *lies behind it,* what it suggests besides itself.

Langston Hughes
(1902–1967)

Langston Hughes was born in Joplin, Missouri. As a young man, he worked as a merchant seaman and traveled widely, living for a time in Paris and Rome. He published his first volume of poems, *The Weary Blues* (1926), three years before he graduated from Lincoln University, where he had won a scholarship. A major figure of the Harlem Renaissance, Hughes wrote prolifically, producing fiction and folklore, drama, song lyrics, essays, memoirs, and children's books as well as many poems.

His nonfiction prose is best represented by his autobiographical writing, from which the following essay, "Salvation," is drawn. In it, Hughes displays a talent for re-creating and dramatizing experience, giving it a quality of life, as if encountered directly and lived intensely.

Salvation

I was saved from sin when I was going on thirteen. But not really saved. It happened like this. There was a big revival at my Auntie Reed's church. Every night for weeks there had been much preaching, singing, praying, and shouting, and some very hardened sinners had been brought to Christ, and the membership of the church had grown by leaps and bounds. Then just before the revival ended, they held a special meeting for children, "to bring the young lambs to the fold." My aunt spoke of it for days ahead. That night I was escorted to the front row and placed on the mourners' bench with all the other young sinners, who had not yet been brought to Jesus.

My aunt told me that when you were saved you saw a light, and something happened to you inside! And Jesus came into your life! And God was with you from then on! She said you could see and hear and feel Jesus in your soul. I believed her. I had heard a great many old people say the same thing and it seemed to me they ought to know. So I sat there calmly in the hot, crowded church, waiting for Jesus to come to me.

The preacher preached a wonderful rhythmical sermon, all moans and shouts and lonely cries and dire pictures of hell, and then he sang a song about the ninety and nine safe in the fold, but one little lamb was left out in the cold. Then he said: "Won't you come? Won't you come to Jesus? Young lambs, won't you come?" And he held out his arms to all us young sinners there on the mourners' bench. And the little girls cried. And some of them jumped up and went to Jesus right away. But most of us just sat there.

A great many old people came and knelt around us and prayed, old women with jet-black faces and braided hair, old men with work-gnarled hands. And the church sang a song about the lower lights are burning, some poor sinners to be saved. And the whole building rocked with prayer and song.

Still I kept waiting to *see* Jesus.

Finally all the young people had gone to the altar and were saved, but one boy and me. He was a rounder's son named Westley. Westley and I were surrounded by sisters and deacons praying. It was very hot in the church, and getting late now. Finally Westley said to me in a whisper: "God damn! I'm tired o' sitting here. Let's get up and be saved." So he got up and was saved.

Then I was left all alone on the mourners' bench. My aunt came and knelt at my knees and cried, while prayers and song swirled all around me in the little

346

church. The whole congregation prayed for me alone, in a mighty wail of moans and voices. And I kept waiting serenely for Jesus, waiting, waiting—but he didn't come. I wanted to see him, but nothing happened to me. Nothing! I wanted something to happen to me, but nothing happened.

I heard the songs and the minister saying: "Why don't you come? My dear child, why don't you come to Jesus? Jesus is waiting for you. He wants you. Why don't you come? Sister Reed, what is this child's name?"

"Langston," my aunt sobbed.

"Langston, why don't you come? Why don't you come and be saved? Oh, Lamb of God! Why don't you come?"

Now it was really getting late. I began to be ashamed of myself, holding everything up so long. I began to wonder what God thought about Westley, who certainly hadn't seen Jesus either, but who was now sitting proudly on the platform, swinging his knickerbockered legs and grinning down at me, surrounded by deacons and old women on their knees praying. God had not struck Westley dead for taking his name in vain or for lying in the temple. So I decided that maybe to save further trouble, I'd better lie, too, and say that Jesus had come, and get up and be saved.

So I got up.

Suddenly the whole room broke into a sea of shouting, as they saw me rise. Waves of rejoicing swept the place. Women leaped in the air. My aunt threw her arms around me. The minister took me by the hand and led me to the platform.

When things quieted down, in a hushed silence, punctuated by a few ecstatic "Amens," all the new young lambs were blessed in the name of God. Then joyous singing filled the room.

That night, for the first time in my life but one—for I was a big boy twelve years old—I cried. I cried, in bed alone, and couldn't stop. I buried my head under the quilts, but my aunt heard me. She woke up and told my uncle I was crying because the Holy Ghost had come into my life, and because I had seen Jesus. But I was really crying because I couldn't bear to tell her that I had lied, that I had deceived everybody in the church, that I hadn't seen Jesus, and that now I didn't believe there was a Jesus anymore, since he didn't come to help me.

Considerations

Thinking

To what extent is Hughes's essay about faith? About the loss of belief? About communal pressure to conform—to see and think as others do?

Why does Hughes begin with what seems like a contradiction: "I was saved from sin when I was going on thirteen. But not really saved"? Why do you think he uses two sentences instead of one for these words?

Connecting

Compare the way Hughes brings his scenes to life with the way Alice Walker does in "Beauty: When the Other Dancer Is the Self."

Consider your own experience in connection with Hughes's. To what extent have you accepted, rejected, or qualified the religious faith(s) you have been exposed to?

Writing

Write an essay in which you explore a turning point in your attitude toward religion and faith.

Compare the pressures toward conforming described in "Salvation" with those Didion describes in "Georgia O'Keeffe."

Zora Neale Hurston
(1902–1960)

Zora Neale Hurston was born in Eatonville, Florida, where she spent her early years. She attended Howard University and in 1925, went to New York City, becoming involved in cultural activities in Harlem. There she met Langston Hughes, who, like Hurston, was interested in the folk elements of African American culture, particularly as reflected in southern life.

Hurston wrote books based on her study of folkways, including *Mules and Men* (1935). She also wrote novels, the best known of which is *Their Eyes Were Watching God* (1937). These and other works, including her essays, were rediscovered and reappreciated as a result of the women's movement and in conjunction with an upsurge in the study of African American literature.

In "How It Feels to Be Colored Me," Hurston discusses her blackness as an aspect of race and of her cultural, social, and personal identity. The essay's tone is confident and upbeat as Hurston celebrates herself as a modern African American woman who knows her worth even when others do not.

How It Feels to Be Colored Me

I am colored but I offer nothing in the way of extenuating circumstances except the fact that I am the only Negro in the United States whose grandfather on the mother's side was *not* an Indian chief.

I remember the very day that I became colored. Up to my thirteenth year I lived in the little Negro town of Eatonville, Florida. It is exclusively a colored town. The only white people I knew passed through the town going to or coming from Orlando. The native whites rode dusty horses, the Northern tourists chugged down the sandy village road in automobiles. The town knew the Southerners and never stopped cane chewing when they passed. But the Northerners were something else again. They were peered at cautiously from behind curtains by the timid. The more venturesome would come out on the porch to watch them go past and got just as much pleasure out of the tourists as the tourists got out of the village.

The front porch might seem a daring place for the rest of the town, but it was a gallery seat for me. My favorite place was atop the gate-post. Proscenium box for a born first-nighter. Not only did I enjoy the show, but I didn't mind the actors knowing that I liked it. I usually spoke to them in passing. I'd wave at them and when they returned my salute, I would say something like this: "Howdy-do-well-I-thank-you-where-you-goin'?" Usually automobile or the horse paused at this, and after a queer exchange of compliments, I would probably "go a piece of the way" with them, as we say in farthest Florida. If one of my family happened to come to the front in time to see me, of course negotiations would be rudely broken off. But even so, it is clear that I was the first "welcome-to-our-state" Floridian, and I hope the Miami Chamber of Commerce will please take notice.

During this period, white people differed from colored to me only in that they rode through town and never lived there. They liked to hear me "speak pieces" and sing and wanted to see me dance the parse-me-la, and gave me generously of their small silver for doing these things, which seemed strange to me for I wanted to do them so much that I needed bribing to stop. Only they didn't know it. The colored people gave no dimes. They deplored any joyful tendencies in me, but I was their Zora nevertheless. I belonged to them, to the nearby hotels, to the county—everybody's Zora.

But changes came in the family when I was thirteen, and I was sent to school in Jacksonville. I left Eatonville, the town of the oleanders, as Zora. When I disembarked from the river-boat at Jacksonville, she was no more. It seemed that I had suffered a sea change. I was not Zora of Orange County any more, I was now a little colored girl. I found it out in certain ways. In my heart as well as in the mirror, I became a fast brown—warranted not to rub nor run.

But I am not tragically colored. There is no great sorrow dammed up in my soul, nor lurking behind my eyes. I do not mind at all. I do not belong to the sobbing school of Negrohood who hold that nature somehow has given them a low-down dirty deal and whose feelings are all hurt about it. Even in the helter-skelter skirmish that is my life, I have seen that the world is to the strong regardless of a little pigmentation more or less. No, I do not weep at the world—I am too busy sharpening my oyster knife.

Someone is always at my elbow reminding me that I am the granddaughter of slaves. It fails to register depression with me. Slavery is sixty years in the past. The operation was successful and the patient is doing well, thank you. The terrible struggle that made me an American out of a potential slave said "On the line!" The Reconstruction said "Get set!"; and the generation before said "Go!" I am off to a flying start and I must not halt in the stretch to look behind and weep. Slavery is the price I paid for civilization, and the choice was not with me. It is a bully adventure and worth all that I have paid through my ancestors for it. No one on earth ever had a greater chance for glory. The world to be won and nothing to be lost. It is thrilling to think—to know that for any act of mine, I shall get twice as much praise or twice as much blame. It is quite exciting to hold the center of the national stage, with the spectators not knowing whether to laugh or to weep.

The position of my white neighbor is much more difficult. No brown specter pulls up a chair beside me when I sit down to eat. No dark ghost thrusts its leg against mine in bed. The game of keeping what one has is never so exciting as the game of getting.

I do not always feel colored. Even now I often achieve the unconscious Zora of Eatonville before the Hegira. I feel most colored when I am thrown against a sharp white background.

For instance at Barnard. "Beside the waters of the Hudson" I feel my race. Among the thousand white persons, I am a dark rock surged upon, and over-swept, but through it all, I remain myself. When covered by the waters, I am; and the ebb but reveals me again.

Sometimes it is the other way around. A white person is set down in our midst, but the contrast is just as sharp for me. For instance, when I sit in the drafty basement that is The New World Cabaret with a white person, my color comes. We enter chatting about any little nothing that we have in common and are seated by the jazz waiters. In the abrupt way that jazz orchestras have, this one plunges into a number. It loses no time in circumlocutions, but gets right down to business. It constricts the thorax and splits the heart with its tempo and narcotic harmonies. This orchestra grows rambunctious, rears on its hind legs and attacks the tonal veil with primitive fury, rending it, clawing it until it breaks through to the jungle beyond. I follow those heathen—follow them exultingly. I dance wildly inside myself; I yell within, I whoop; I shake my assegai above my head, I hurl it true to the mark *yeeeeooww!* I am in the jungle and living in the jungle way. My face is painted red and yellow and my body is painted blue. My pulse is throbbing like a war drum. I want to slaughter something—give pain, give death to what, I do not know. But the piece ends. The men of the orchestra wipe their lips and rest their fingers. I creep back slowly to the veneer we call civilization with the last tone and find the white friend sitting motionless in his seat, smoking calmly.

"Good music they have here," he remarks, drumming the table with his fingertips.

Music. The great blobs of purple and red emotion have not touched him. He has only heard what I felt. He is far away and I see him but dimly across the ocean and the continent that have fallen between us. He is so pale with his whiteness then and I am *so* colored.

At certain times I have no race, I am *me*. When I set my hat at a certain angle and saunter down Seventh Avenue, Harlem City, feeling as snooty as the lions in front of the Forty-Second Street Library, for instance. So far as my feelings are concerned, Peggy Hopkins Joyce on the Boule Mich with her gorgeous raiment, stately carriage, knees knocking together in a most aristocratic manner, has nothing on me. The cosmic Zora emerges. I belong to no race nor time. I am the eternal feminine with its string of beads.

I have no separate feeling about being an American citizen and colored. I am merely a fragment of the Great Soul that surges within the boundaries. My country, right or wrong.

Sometimes, I feel discriminated against, but it does not make me angry. It merely astonishes me. How *can* any deny themselves the pleasure of my company? It's beyond me.

But in the main, I feel like a brown bag of miscellany propped against a wall. Against a wall in company with other bags, white, red and yellow. Pour out the contents, and there is discovered a jumble of small things priceless and worthless. A first-water diamond, an empty spool, bits of broken glass, lengths of string, a key to a door long since crumbled away, a rusty knife-blade, old shoes saved for a road that never was and never will be, a nail bent under the weight of things too heavy for any nail, a dried flower or two still a little fragrant. In your hand is the brown bag. On the ground before you is the jumble it held—so much like the jumble in the bags, could they be emptied, that all might be dumped in a single heap and the bags refilled without altering the content of any greatly. A bit of colored glass more or less would not matter. Perhaps that is how the Great Stuffer of Bags filled them in the first place—who knows?

Considerations

Thinking

Hurston presents herself as happy with who she is, especially with her race. Do you think her experience and attitude are characteristic of most people? Why or why not?

What does Hurston see as the advantages for her of being "colored"?

Connecting

To what extent can Hurston's celebration of herself as a black woman be applied by any reader regardless of race, ethnicity, or gender? Why?

Consider Hurston's discussion of racial difference in connection with that of James Baldwin in "The Discovery of What It Means to Be an American."

Writing

Write an essay in which you explore your identity in terms of gender, race, class, or ethnicity. Try to account for times when you feel this aspect of your identity most acutely and times when it seems invisible or unimportant.

Discuss Hurston's presentation of herself as a black woman in conjunction with June Jordan's images of black women in "Many Rivers to Cross" (the next essay in our collection).

June Jordan
(b. 1936)

June Jordan was born in Harlem and raised in the Bedford-Stuyvesant section of Brooklyn. She has taught at City College of the City University of New York, Sarah Lawrence College, and Yale University, and she has held professorships at the State University of New York, Stony Brook, and at the University of California, Berkeley. In addition to three volumes of essays, she has published fourteen volumes of poetry, drama, and biography. Her work has appeared in such publications as the *New York Times,* the *Village Voice,* and the *New Republic.* Her awards include a Rockefeller Grant in creative writing, the American Library Association's award for the best book of the year, the *New York Times* award for outstanding book of the year, and the Prix de Rome in environmental design. She has also been a National Book Award finalist and a fellow of the National Education Association.

In many of her essays, Jordan worries about the struggle for self-respect and self-love, seeing it as a struggle against despair. In "Many Rivers to Cross," she gives us a sense of how difficult it may have been for her and for other women to gain that self-respect.

Many Rivers to Cross

When my mother killed herself I was looking for a job. That was fifteen years ago. I had no money and no food. On the pleasure side I was down to my last pack of Pall Malls plus half a bottle of J & B. I needed to find work because I needed to be able fully to support myself and my eight-year-old son, very fast. My plan was to raise enough big bucks so that I could take an okay apartment inside an acceptable public school district, by September. That deadline left me less than three months to turn my fortunes right side up.

It seemed that I had everything to do at once. Somehow, I must move all of our things, mostly books and toys, out of the housing project before the rent fell due, again. I must do this without letting my neighbors know because destitution and divorce added up to personal shame, and failure. Those same neighbors had looked upon my husband and me as an ideal young couple, in many ways: inseparable, doting, ambitious. They had kept me busy and laughing in the hard weeks following my husband's departure for graduate school in Chicago; they had been the ones to remember him warmly through teasing remarks and questions all that long year that I remained alone, waiting for his return while I became the "temporary," sole breadwinner of our peculiar long-distance family by telephone. They had been the ones who kindly stopped the teasing and the queries when the year ended and my husband, the father of my child, did not come back. They never asked me and I never told them what that meant, altogether. I don't think I really knew.

I could see how my husband would proceed more or less naturally from graduate school to a professional occupation of his choice, just as he had shifted rather easily from me, his wife, to another man's wife—another woman. What I could not see was how I should go forward, now, in any natural, coherent way. As a mother without a husband, as a poet without a publisher, a freelance journalist without assignment, a city planner without a contract, it seemed to me that several incontestable and conflicting necessities had suddenly eliminated the whole realm of choice from my life.

My husband and I agreed that he would have the divorce that he wanted, and I would have the child. This ordinary settlement is, as millions of women will testify, as absurd as saying, "I'll give you a call, you handle everything else." At any rate, as my lawyer explained, the law then was the same as the law today; the courts would surely award me a reasonable amount of the father's income as child support, but the courts would also insist that they could not enforce their own

355

decree. In other words, according to the law, what a father owes to his child is not serious compared to what a man owes to the bank for a car, or a vacation. Hence, as they say, it is extremely regrettable but nonetheless true that the courts cannot garnish a father's salary, nor freeze his account, nor seize his property on behalf of his children, in our society. Apparently this is because a child is not a car or a couch or a boat. (I would suppose this is the very best available definition of the difference between an American child and a car.)

Anyway, I wanted to get out of the projects as quickly as possible. But I was going to need help because I couldn't bend down and I couldn't carry anything heavy and I couldn't let my parents know about these problems because I didn't want to fight with them about the reasons behind the problems—which was the same reason I couldn't walk around or sit up straight to read or write without vomiting and acute abdominal pain. My parents would have evaluated that reason as a terrible secret compounded by a terrible crime; once again an unmarried woman, I had, nevertheless, become pregnant. What's more I had tried to interrupt this pregnancy even though this particular effort required not only one but a total of three abortions—each of them illegal and amazingly expensive, as well as, evidently, somewhat poorly executed.

My mother, against my father's furious rejections of me and what he viewed as my failure, offered what she could; she had no money herself but there was space in the old brownstone of my childhood. I would live with them during the summer while I pursued my crash schedule for cash, and she would spend as much time with Christopher, her only and beloved grandchild, as her worsening but partially undiagnosed illness allowed.

After she suffered a stroke, her serenely imposing figure had shrunk into an unevenly balanced, starved shell of chronic disorder. In the last two years, her physical condition had forced her retirement from nursing, and she spent most of her days on a makeshift cot pushed against the wall of the dining room next to the kitchen. She could do very few things for herself, besides snack on crackers, or pour ready-made juice into a cup and then drink it.

In June, 1966, I moved from the projects into my parents' house with the help of a woman named Mrs. Hazel Griffin. Since my teens, she had been my hairdresser. Every day, all day, she stood on her feet, washing and straightening hair in her crowded shop, the Arch of Beauty. Mrs. Griffin had never been married, had never finished high school, and she ran the Arch of Beauty with an imperturbable and contagious sense of success. She had a daughter as old as I who worked alongside her mother, coddling customer fantasy into confidence. Gradually, Mrs. Griffin and I became close; as my own mother became more and more bedridden and demoralized, Mrs. Griffin extended herself—dropping by my parents' house to make dinner for them, or calling me to wish me good luck on a special freelance venture, and so forth. It was Mrs. Griffin who closed her shop for a whole day and drove all the way from Brooklyn to my housing project apartment in Queens. It was Mrs. Griffin who packed me up, so to speak, and carried me and the boxes back to Brooklyn, back to the house of my parents. It was Mrs. Griffin who ignored my father standing hateful at the top of the stone steps of the house and not saying a word of thanks and not once relieving her of a single load she wrestled up the stairs and past him. My father hated Mrs. Griffin because he was proud and because she was a stranger of mercy. My father hated Mrs. Griffin because he was like that sometimes: hateful and crazy.

My father alternated between weeping bouts of self-pity and storm explosions of wrath against the gods apparently determined to ruin him. These were his alternating reactions to my mother's increasing enfeeblement, her stoic depression. I think he was scared; who would take care of him? Would she get well again and make everything all right again?

This is how we organized the brownstone: I fixed a room for my son on the top floor of the house. I slept on the parlor floor in the front room. My father slept on the same floor, in the back. My mother stayed downstairs.

About a week after moving in, my mother asked me about the progress of my plans. I told her things were not terrific but that there were two different planning jobs I hoped to secure within a few days. One of them involved a study of new towns in Sweden and the other one involved an analysis of the social consequences of a huge hydro-electric dam under construction in Ghana. My mother stared at me uncomprehendingly and then urged me to look for work in the local post office. We bitterly argued about what she dismissed as my "high-falutin" ideas and, I believe, that was the last substantial conversation between us.

From my first memory of him, my father had always worked at the post office. His favorite was the night shift, which brought him home usually between three and four o'clock in the morning.

It was hot. I finally fell asleep that night, a few nights after the argument between my mother and myself. She seemed to be rallying; that afternoon, she and my son had spent a long time in the backyard, oblivious to the heat and the mosquitoes. They were both tired but peaceful when they noisily re-entered the house, holding hands awkwardly.

But someone was knocking at the door to my room. Why should I wake up? It would be impossible to fall asleep again. It was so hot. The knocking continued. I switched on the light by the bed: 3:30 A.M. It must be my father. Furious, I pulled on a pair of shorts and a t-shirt. "What do you want? What's the matter?" I asked him, through the door. Had he gone berserk? What could he have to talk about at that ridiculous hour?

"OK, all right," I said, rubbing my eyes awake as I stepped to the door and opened it. "What?"

To my surprise, my father stood there looking very uncertain.

"It's your mother," he told me, in a burly, formal voice. "I think she's dead, but I'm not sure." He was avoiding my eyes.

"What do you mean," I answered.

"I want you to go downstairs and figure it out."

I could not believe what he was saying to me. "You want me to figure out if my mother is dead or alive?"

"I can't tell! I don't know!!" he shouted angrily.

"Jesus Christ," I muttered, angry and beside myself.

I turned and glanced about my room, wondering if I could find anything to carry with me on this mission; what do you use to determine a life or a death? I couldn't see anything obvious that might be useful.

"I'll wait up here," my father said. "You call up and let me know."

I could not believe it; a man married to a woman more than forty years and he can't tell if she's alive or dead and he wakes up his kid and tells her, "You figure it out."

I was at the bottom of the stairs. I halted just outside the dining room where my mother slept. Suppose she really was dead? Suppose my father was not just being crazy and hateful? "Naw." I shook my head and confidently entered the room.

"Momma?!" I called, aloud. At the edge of the cot, my mother was leaning forward, one arm braced to hoist her body up. She was trying to stand up! I rushed over. "Wait. Here, I'll help you!" I said.

And I reached out my hands to give her a lift. The body of my mother was stiff. She was not yet cold, but she was stiff. Maybe I had come downstairs just in time! I tried to loosen her arms, to change her position, to ease her into lying down.

"Momma!" I kept saying. "Momma, listen to me! It's OK! I'm here and everything. Just relax. Relax! Give me a hand, now. I'm trying to help you lie down!"

Her body did not relax. She did not answer me. But she was not cold. Her eyes were not shut.

From upstairs my father was yelling, "Is she dead? Is she dead?"

"No!" I screamed at him. "No! She's not dead!"

At this, my father tore down the stairs and into the room. Then he braked.

"Milly?" he called out, tentative. Then he shouted at me and banged around the walls. "You damn fool. Don't you see now she's gone. Now she's gone!" We began to argue.

"She's alive! Call the doctor!"

"No!"

"Yes!"

At last my father left the room to call the doctor.

I straightened up. I felt completely exhausted from trying to gain a response from my mother. There she was, stiff on the edge of her bed, just about to stand up. Her lips were set, determined. She would manage it, but by herself. I could not help. Her eyes fixed on some point below the floor.

"Momma!" I shook her hard as I could to rouse her into focus. Now she fell back on the cot, but frozen and in the wrong position. It hit me that she might be dead. She might be dead.

My father reappeared at the door. He would not come any closer. "Dr. Davis says he will come. And he call the police."

The police? Would they know if my mother was dead or alive? Who would know?

I went to the phone and called my aunt. "Come quick," I said. "My father thinks Momma has died but she's here but she's stiff."

Soon the house was weird and ugly and crowded and I thought I was losing my mind.

Three white policemen stood around telling me my mother was dead. "How do you know?" I asked, and they shrugged and then they repeated themselves. And the doctor never came. But my aunt came and my uncle and they said she was dead.

After a conference with the cops, my aunt disappeared and when she came back she held a bottle in one of her hands. She and the police whispered together some more. Then one of the cops said, "Don't worry about it. We won't say anything." My aunt signalled me to follow her into the hallway where she let me understand that, in fact, my mother had committed suicide.

I could not assimilate this information: suicide.

I broke away from my aunt and ran to the telephone. I called a friend of mine, a woman who talked back loud to me so that I could realize my growing hysteria, and check it. Then I called my cousin Valerie who lived in Harlem; she woke up instantly and urged me to come right away.

I hurried to the top floor and stood my sleeping son on his feet. I wanted to get him out of this house of death more than I ever wanted anything. He could not stand by himself so I carried him down the two flights to the street and laid him on the backseat and then took off.

At Valerie's, my son continued to sleep, so we put him to bed, closed the door, and talked. My cousin made me eat eggs, drink whiskey, and shower. She would take care of Christopher, she said. I should go back and deal with the situation in Brooklyn.

When I arrived, the house was absolutely full of women from the church dressed as though they were going to Sunday communion. It seemed to me they were, every one of them, wearing hats and gloves and drinking coffee and solemnly addressing invitations to a funeral and I could not find my mother anywhere and I could not find an empty spot in the house where I could sit down and smoke a cigarette.

My mother was dead.

Feeling completely out of place, I headed for the front door, ready to leave. My father grabbed my shoulder from behind and forcibly spun me around.

"You see this?" He smiled, waving a large document in the air. "This am insurance paper for you!" He waved it into my face. "Your mother, she left you insurance, see?"

I watched him.

"But I gwine burn it in the furnace before I give it you to t'row away on trash!"

"Is that money?" I demanded. "Did my mother leave me money?"

"Eh-heh!" he laughed. "And you don't get it from me. Not today, not tomorrow. Not until I dead and buried!"

My father grabbed for my arm and I swung away from him. He hit me on my head and I hit back. We were fighting.

Suddenly, the ladies from the church bustled about and pushed, horrified, between us. This was a sin, they said, for a father and a child to fight in the house of the dead and the mother not yet in the ground! Such a good woman she was, they said. She was a good woman, a good woman, they all agreed. Out of respect for the memory of this good woman, in deference to my mother who had committed suicide, the ladies shook their hats and insisted we should not fight; I should not fight with my father.

Utterly disgusted and disoriented, I went back to Harlem. By the time I reached my cousin's place I had begun to bleed, heavily. Valerie said I was hemorrhaging so she called up her boyfriend and the two of them hobbled me into Harlem Hospital.

I don't know how long I remained unconscious, but when I opened my eyes I found myself on the women's ward, with an intravenous setup feeding into my arm. After a while, Valerie showed up. Christopher was fine, she told me; my friends were taking turns with him. Whatever I did, I should not admit I'd had an abortion or I'd get her into trouble, and myself in trouble. Just play dumb and rest. I'd have to stay on the ward for several days. My mother's funeral was tomorrow afternoon. What did I want her to tell people to explain why I wouldn't be there? She meant, what lie?

I thought about it and I decided I had nothing to say; if I couldn't tell the truth then the hell with it.

I lay in that bed at Harlem Hospital, thinking and sleeping. I wanted to get well.

I wanted to be strong. I never wanted to be weak again as long as I lived. I thought about my mother and her suicide and I thought about how my father could not tell whether she was dead or alive.

I wanted to get well and what I wanted to do as soon as I was strong again, actually, what I wanted to do was I wanted to live my life so that people would know unmistakably that I am alive, so that when I finally die people will know the difference for sure between my living and my death.

And I thought about the idea of my mother as a good woman and I rejected that, because I don't see why it's a good thing when you give up, or when you cooperate with those who hate you or when you polish and iron and mend and endlessly mollify for the sake of the people who love the way that you kill yourself day by day silently.

And I think all of this is really about women and work. Certainly this is all about me as a woman and my life work. I mean I am not sure my mother's suicide was something extraordinary. Perhaps most women must deal with a similar inheritance, the legacy of a woman whose death you cannot possibly pinpoint because she died so many, many times and because, even before she became your mother, the life of that woman was taken; I say it was taken away.

And really it was to honor my mother that I did fight with my father, that man who could not tell the living from the dead.

And really it is to honor Mrs. Hazel Griffin and my cousin Valerie and all the women I love, including myself, that I am working for the courage to admit the truth that Bertolt Brecht has written; he says, "It takes courage to say that the good were defeated not because they were good, but because they were weak."

I cherish the mercy and the grace of women's work. But I know there is new work that we must undertake as well: that new work will make defeat detestable to us. That new women's work will mean we will not die trying to stand up: we will live that way: standing up.

I came too late to help my mother to her feet.

By way of everlasting thanks to all of the women who have helped me to stay alive I am working never to be late again.

Considerations

Thinking

In what ways might "Many Rivers to Cross" be considered an essay about betrayal?

Why does Jordan want to honor her cousin Valerie and Mrs. Hazel Griffin?

What are the implications of that one-sentence paragraph near the end of the essay, "I came too late to help my mother to her feet"?

Connecting

After reading this essay, what would you guess is Jordan's attitude about men? As a writer, how does she use the two men in her essay?

How does Jordan use the image of her mother trying to get up from her cot? What does that image have to do with Jordan's central idea?

Writing

Write a short essay about the importance of feminism at your college or in your local community.

Select a powerful image from your own experience and reconstruct it. Set it aside for a few days; then go back to see what you find there in the recorded image. When you go back to the image, write a few paragraphs about what the image means to you.

Jamaica Kincaid
(b. 1949)

Jamaica Kincaid was born in Antigua and immigrated to the United States, where she has been a contributor and staff writer for the *New Yorker*, served on the Harvard faculty, and won distinction for her three books: *Annie John*, *A Small Place*, and *Lucy*. Her collection of stories *At the Bottom of the River* won the Morton Dauwen Zabel Award from the American Academy and Institute of Arts and Letters. Her work has appeared in the *New Yorker*, *Rolling Stone*, and *Paris Review*.

In "On Seeing England for the First Time," Kincaid reveals the difference between the England she inherited and the England she found in reality, as she invites us to think about the "space between the idea of something and its reality"—that space that is always "wide and deep and dark."

On Seeing England for the First Time

When I saw England for the first time, I was a child in school sitting at a desk. The England I was looking at was laid out on a map gently, beautifully, delicately, a very special jewel; it lay on a bed of sky blue—the background of the map—its yellow form mysterious, because though it looked like a leg of mutton, it could not really look like anything so familiar as a leg of mutton because it was England—with shadings of pink and green, unlike any shadings of pink and green I had seen before, squiggly veins of red running in every direction. England was a special jewel all right, and only special people got to wear it. The people who got to wear England were English people. They wore it well and they wore it everywhere: in jungles, in deserts, on plains, on top of the highest mountains, on all the oceans, on all the seas, in places where they were not welcome, in places they should not have been. When my teacher had pinned this map up on the blackboard, she said, "This is England"—and she said it with authority, seriousness, and adoration, and we all sat up. It was as if she had said, "This is Jerusalem, the place you will go to when you die but only if you have been good." We understood then—we were meant to understand then—that England was to be our source of myth and the source from which we got our sense of reality, our sense of what was meaningful, our sense of what was meaningless—and much about our own lives and much about the very idea of us headed that last list.

At the time I was a child sitting at my desk seeing England for the first time, I was already very familiar with the greatness of it. Each morning before I left for school, I ate a breakfast of half a grapefruit, an egg, bread and butter and a slice of cheese, and a cup of cocoa; or half a grapefruit, a bowl of oat porridge, bread and butter and a slice of cheese, and a cup of cocoa. The can of cocoa was often left on the table in front of me. It had written on it the name of the company, the year the company was established, and the words "Made in England." Those words, "Made in England," were written on the box the oats came in too. They would also have been written on the box the shoes I was wearing came in; a bolt of gray linen cloth lying on the shelf of a store from which my mother had bought three yards to make the uniform that I was wearing had written along its edge those three words. The shoes I wore were made in England; so were my socks and cotton undergarments and the satin ribbons I wore tied at the end of two plaits of my hair. My father, who might have sat next to me at breakfast, was a carpenter and cabinet maker. The shoes he wore to work would have been made in England, as were his

363

khaki shirt and trousers, his underpants and undershirt, his socks and brown felt hat. Felt was not the proper material from which a hat that was expected to provide shade from the hot sun should be made, but my father must have seen and admired a picture of an Englishman wearing such a hat in England, and this picture that he saw must have been so compelling that it caused him to wear the wrong hat for a hot climate most of his long life. And this hat—a brown felt hat—became so central to his character that it was the first thing he put on in the morning as he stepped out of bed and the last thing he took off before he stepped back into bed at night. As we sat at breakfast a car might go by. The car, a Hillman or a Zephyr, was made in England. The very idea of the meal itself, breakfast, and its substantial quality and quantity was an idea from England; we somehow knew that in England they began the day with this meal called breakfast and a proper breakfast was a big breakfast. No one I knew liked eating so much food so early in the day; it made us feel sleepy, tired. But this breakfast business was Made in England like almost everything else that surrounded us, the exceptions being the sea, the sky, and the air we breathed.

At the time I saw this map—seeing England for the first time—I did not say to myself, "Ah, so that's what it looks like," because there was no longing in me to put a shape to those three words that ran through every part of my life, no matter how small; for me to have had such a longing would have meant that I lived in a certain atmosphere, an atmosphere in which those three words were felt as a burden. But I did not live in such an atmosphere. My father's brown felt hat would develop a hole in its crown, the lining would separate from the hat itself, and six weeks before he thought that he could not be seen wearing it—he was a very vain man—he would order another hat from England. And my mother taught me to eat my food in the English way: the knife in the right hand, the fork in the left, my elbows held still close to my side, the food carefully balanced on my fork and then brought up to my mouth. When I had finally mastered it, I overheard her saying to a friend, "Did you see how nicely she can eat?" But I knew then that I enjoyed my food more when I ate it with my bare hands, and I continued to do so when she wasn't looking. And when my teacher showed us the map, she asked us to study it carefully, because no test we would ever take would be complete without this statement: "Draw a map of England."

I did not know then that the statement "Draw a map of England" was something far worse than a declaration of war, for in fact a flat-out declaration of war would have put me on alert, and again in fact, there was no need for war—I had long ago been conquered. I did not know then that this statement was part of a process that would result in my erasure, not my physical erasure, but my erasure all the same. I did not know then that this statement was meant to make me feel in awe and small whenever I heard the word "England": awe at its existence, small because I was not from it. I did not know very much of anything then—certainly not what a blessing it was that I was unable to draw a map of England correctly.

After that there were many times of seeing England for the first time. I saw England in history. I knew the names of all the kings of England. I knew the names of their children, their wives, their disappointments, their triumphs, the names of people who betrayed them; I knew the dates on which they were born and the dates they died. I knew their conquests and was made to feel glad if I figured in them; I knew their defeats. I knew the details of the year 1066 (the Battle of Hastings, the end of the reign of the Anglo-Saxon kings) before I knew the details of the year 1832 (the year slavery was abolished). It wasn't as bad as I make it sound now; it was worse. I did like so much hearing again and again how Alfred the Great, traveling in disguise, had been left to watch cakes, and because he wasn't used to this the cakes got burned, and Alfred burned his hands pulling them out of the fire, and the woman who had left him to watch the cakes screamed at him. I loved King Alfred. My grandfather was named after him; his son, my uncle, was named after King Alfred; my brother is named after King Alfred. And so there are three people in my family named after a man they have never met, a man who died over ten centuries ago. The first view I got of England then was not unlike the first view received by the person who named my grandfather.

This view, though—the naming of the kings, their deeds, their disappointments—was the vivid view, the forceful view. There were other views, subtler ones, softer, almost not there—but these were the ones that made the most lasting impression on me, these were the ones that made me really feel like nothing. "When morning touched the sky" was one phrase, for no morning touched the sky where I lived. The mornings where I lived came on abruptly, with a shock of heat and loud noises. "Evening approaches" was another, but the evenings where I lived did not approach; in fact, I had no evening—I had night and I had day and they came and went in a mechanical way: on, off; on, off. And then there were gentle mountains and low blue skies and moors over which people took walks for nothing but pleasure, when where I lived a walk was an act of labor, a burden, something only death or the automobile could relieve. And there were things that a small turn of a head could convey—entire worlds, whole lives would depend on this thing, a certain turn of a head. Everyday life could be quite tiring, more tiring than anything I was told not to do. I was told not to gossip, but they did that all the time. And they ate so much food, violating another of those rules they taught me: do not indulge in gluttony. And the foods they ate actually: if only sometime I could eat cold cuts after theater, cold cuts of lamb and mint sauce, and Yorkshire pudding and scones, and clotted cream, and sausages that came from up-country (imagine, "up-country"). And having troubling thoughts at twilight, a good time to have troubling thoughts, apparently; and servants who stole and left in the middle of a crisis, who were born with a limp or some other kind of deformity, not nourished properly in their mother's womb (that last part I figured out for myself; the point was, oh to have an untrustworthy servant); and wonderful cobbled streets onto which solid front doors opened; and people whose eyes were blue and who had fair skins and who smelled only of lavender, or sometimes sweet pea or primrose. And those flowers with those names: delphiniums, foxgloves, tulips, daffodils, floribunda, peonies; in bloom, a striking display, being cut and placed in large glass bowls, crystal, decorating rooms so large twenty families the size of mine could fit in comfortably but used only for passing through. And the weather was so remarkable because the rain fell gently always, only occasionally in deep gusts, and it colored the air various shades of gray, each an appealing shade for a

[handwritten margin note:] this is all too good to be true— they were taught, essentially, that England was perfect and everything English followed similar logic

dress to be worn when a portrait was being painted; and when it rained at twilight, wonderful things happened: people bumped into each other unexpectedly and that would lead to all sorts of turns of events—a plot, the mere weather caused plots. I saw that people rushed: they rushed to catch trains, they rushed toward each other and away from each other; they rushed and rushed and rushed. That word: rushed! I did not know what it was to do that. It was too hot to do that, and so I came to envy people who would rush, even though it had no meaning to me to do such a thing. But there they are again. They loved their children; their children were sent to their own rooms as a punishment, rooms larger than my entire house. They were special, everything about them said so, even their clothes; their clothes rustled, swished, soothed. The world was theirs, not mine; everything told me so.

If now as I speak of all this I give the impression of someone on the outside looking in, nose pressed up against a glass window, that is wrong. My nose was pressed up against a glass window all right, but there was an iron vise at the back of my neck forcing my head to stay in place. To avert my gaze was to fall back into something from which I had been rescued, a hole filled with nothing, and that was the word for everything about me, nothing. The reality of my life was conquests, subjugation, humiliation, enforced amnesia. I was forced to forget. Just for instance, this: I lived in a part of St. John's, Antigua, called Ovals. Ovals was made up of five streets, each of them named after a famous English seaman—to be quite frank, an officially sanctioned criminal: Rodney Street (after George Rodney), Nelson Street (after Horatio Nelson), Drake Street (after Francis Drake), Hood Street, and Hawkins Street (after John Hawkins). But John Hawkins was knighted after a trip he made to Africa, opening up a new trade, the slave trade. He was then entitled to wear as his crest a Negro bound with a cord. Every single person living on Hawkins Street was descended from a slave. John Hawkins's ship, the one in which he transported the people he had bought and kidnapped, was called *The Jesus*. He later became the treasurer of the Royal Navy and rear admiral.

Again, the reality of my life, the life I led at the time I was being shown these views of England for the first time, for the second time, for the one-hundred-millionth time, was this: the sun shone with what sometimes seemed to be a deliberate cruelty; we must have done something to deserve that. My dresses did not rustle in the evening air as I strolled to the theater (I had no evening, I had no theater; my dresses were made of a cheap cotton, the weave of which would give way after not too many washings). I got up in the morning, I did my chores (fetched water from the public pipe for my mother, swept the yard), I washed myself, I went to a woman to have my hair combed freshly every day (because before we were allowed into our classroom our teachers would inspect us, and children who had not bathed that day, or had dirt under their fingernails, or whose hair had not been combed anew that day, might not be allowed to attend class). I ate that breakfast. I walked to school. At school we gathered in an auditorium and sang a hymn, "All Things Bright and Beautiful," and looking down on us as we sang were portraits of the Queen of England and her husband; they wore jewels and medals and they smiled. I was a Brownie. At each meeting we would form a little group around a flagpole, and after raising the Union Jack, we would say, "I promise to do my best, to do my duty to God and the Queen, to help other people every day and obey the scouts' law."

Who were these people and why had I never seen them, I mean really seen them, in the place where they lived? I had never been to England. No one I knew had ever been to England, or I should say, no one I knew had ever been and returned to tell me about it. All the people I knew who had gone to England had stayed there. Sometimes they left behind them their small children, never to see them again. England! I had seen England's representatives. I had seen the governor general at the public grounds at a ceremony celebrating the Queen's birthday. I had seen an old princess and I had seen a young princess. They had both been extremely not beautiful, but who of us would have told them that? I had never seen England, really seen it, I had only met a representative, seen a picture, read books, memorized its history. I had <u>never set foot, my own foot, in it.</u> *and sunk her presence into its soil*

The space between the idea of something and its reality is always wide and deep and dark. The longer they are kept apart—idea of thing, reality of thing— the wider the width, the deeper the depth, the thicker and darker the darkness. This space starts out empty, there is nothing in it, but it rapidly becomes filled up with obsession or desire or hatred or love—sometimes all of these things, sometimes some of these things, sometimes only one of these things. The existence of the world as I came to know it was a result of this: idea of thing over here, reality of thing way, way over there. There was Christopher Columbus, an unlikable man, an unpleasant man, a liar (and so, of course, a thief) surrounded by maps and schemes and plans, and there was the reality on the other side of that width, that depth, that darkness. He became obsessed, he became filled with desire, the hatred came later, <u>love was never a part of it.</u> Eventually, his idea met the longed-for reality. That the idea of something and its reality are often two completely different things is something no one ever remembers; and so when they meet and find that they are not compatible, the weaker of the two, idea or reality, dies. That idea Christopher Columbus had was more powerful than the reality he met, and so the reality he met died.

And so finally, when I was a grown-up woman, the mother of two children, the wife of someone, a person who resides in a powerful country that takes up more than its fair share of a continent, the owner of a house with many rooms in it and of two automobiles, with the desire and will (which I very much act upon) to take from the world more than I give back to it, more than I deserve, more than I need, finally then, I saw England, the real England, not a picture, not a painting, not through a story in a book, but England, for the first time. In me, the space between the idea of it and its reality had become filled with(hatred), and so when at last I saw it I wanted to take it into my hands and tear it into little pieces and then crumble it up as if it were clay, child's clay. That was impossible, and so I could only indulge in not-favorable opinions.

There were monuments everywhere; they commemorated victories, battles fought between them and the people who lived across the sea from them, all vile people, fought over which of them would have dominion over the people who looked like me. The monuments were useless to them now, people sat on them and ate their lunch. They were like markers on an old useless trail, like a piece of old string tied to a finger to jog the memory, like old decoration in an old house, dirty, useless, in the way. Their skins were so pale, it made them look so fragile, so weak, so ugly. What if I had the power to simply banish them from their land, send boat after boatload of them on a voyage that in fact had no destination, force them to live in a place where the sun's presence was a constant? This would rid them of their pale complexion and make them look more like me, make them look more like the people I love and treasure and hold dear, and more like the people who occupy the near and far reaches of my imagination, my history, my geography, and reduce them and everything they have ever known to figurines as evidence that I was in divine favor, what if all this was in my power? Could I resist it? No one ever has.

And they were rude, they were rude to each other. They didn't like each other very much. They didn't like each other in the way they didn't like me, and it occurred to me that their dislike for me was one of the few things they agreed on.

I was on a train in England with a friend, an English woman. Before we were in England she liked me very much. In England she didn't like me at all. She didn't like the claim I said I had on England, she didn't like the views I had of England. I didn't like England, she didn't like England, but she didn't like me not liking it too. She said, "I want to show you my England, I want to show you the England that I know and love." I had told her many times before that I knew England and I didn't want to love it anyway. She no longer lived in England; it was her own country, but it had not been kind to her, so she left. On the train, the conductor was rude to her; she asked something, and he responded in a rude way. She became ashamed. She was ashamed at the way he treated her; she was ashamed at the way he behaved. "This is the new England," she said. But I liked the conductor being rude; his behavior seemed quite appropriate. Earlier this had happened: we had gone to a store to buy a shirt for my husband; it was meant to be a special present, a special shirt to wear on special occasions. This was a store where the Prince of Wales has his shirts made, but the shirts sold in this store are beautiful all the same. I found a shirt I thought my husband would like and I wanted to buy him a tie to go with it. When I couldn't decide which one to choose, the salesman showed me a new set. He was very pleased with these, he said, because they bore the crest of the Prince of Wales, and the Prince of Wales had never allowed his crest to decorate an article of clothing before. There was something in the way he said it; his tone was slavish, reverential, awed. It made me feel angry; I wanted to hit him. I didn't do that. I said, my husband and I hate princes, my husband would never wear anything that had a prince's anything on it. My friend stiffened. The salesman stiffened. They both drew themselves in, away from me. My friend told me that the prince was a symbol of her Englishness, and I could see that I had caused offense. I looked at her. She was an English person, the sort of English person I used to know at home, the sort who was nobody in England but somebody when they came to live among the people like me. There were many people I could have seen England with; that I was seeing it with this particular person, a person who reminded me of the people who showed me England long ago as I sat

[margin annotations, handwritten:]

things change when the norm and perception of race relations change from country to country

trying to justify to shabby state of affairs and defend her afore mentioned pride in church or at my desk, made me feel silent and afraid, for I wondered if, all these years of our friendship, I had had a friend or had been in the thrall of a racial memory.

I went to Bath—we, my friend and I, did this, but though we were together, I was no longer with her. The landscape was almost as familiar as my own hand, but I had never been in this place before, so how could that be again? And the streets of Bath were familiar, too, but I had never walked on them before. It was all those years of reading, starting with Roman Britain. Why did I have to know about Roman Britain? It was of no real use to me, a person living on a hot, drought-ridden island, and it is of no use to me now, and yet my head is filled with this nonsense, Roman Britain. In Bath, I drank tea in a room I had read about in a novel written in the eighteenth century. In this very same room, young women wearing those dresses that rustled and so on danced and flirted and some-times disgraced themselves with young men, soldiers, sailors, who were on their way to Bristol or someplace like that, so many places like that where so many adventures, the outcome of which was not good for me, began. Bristol, England. A sentence that began "That night the ship sailed from Bristol, England" would end not so good for me. And then I was driving through the countryside in an English motorcar, on narrow winding roads, and they were so familiar, though I had never been on them before; and through little villages the names of which I somehow knew so well though I had never been there before. And the country-side did have all those hedges and hedges, fields hedged in. I was marveling at all the toil of it, the planting of the hedges to begin with and then the care of it, all that clipping, year after year of clipping, and I wondered at the lives of the people who would have to do this, because wherever I see and feel the hands that hold up the world, I see and feel myself and all the people who look like me. And I said, "Those hedges" and my friend said that someone, a woman named Mrs. Rothchild, worried that the hedges weren't being taken care of properly; the farm-ers couldn't afford or find the help to keep up the hedges, and often they replaced them with wire fencing. I might have said to that, well if Mrs. Rothchild doesn't like the wire fencing, why doesn't she take care of the hedges herself, but I didn't. And then in those fields that were now hemmed in by wire fencing that a privi-leged woman didn't like was planted a vile yellow flowering bush that produced an oil, and my friend said that Mrs. Rothchild didn't like this either; it ruined the English countryside, it ruined the traditional look of the English countryside.

It was not at that moment that I wished every sentence, everything I knew, that began with England would end with "and then it all died; we don't know how, it just all died." At that moment, I was thinking, who are these people who forced me to think of them all the time, who forced me to think that the world I knew was incomplete, or without substance, or did not measure up because it was not England; that I was incomplete, or without substance, and did not mea-sure up because I was not English. Who were these people? The person sitting next to me couldn't give me a clue; no one person could. In any case, if I had said to her, I find England ugly, I hate England; the weather is like a jail sentence, the English are a very ugly people, the food in England is like a jail sentence, the hair *a loaded term*

of English people is so straight, so dead looking, the English have an unbearable smell so different from the smell of people I know, real people of course, she would have said that I was a person full of prejudice. Apart from the fact that it is I—that is, the people who look like me—who made her aware of the unpleasantness of such a thing, the idea of such a thing, prejudice, she would have been only partly right, sort of right: I may be capable of prejudice, but my prejudices have no weight to them, my prejudices have no force behind them, my prejudices remain opinions, my prejudices remain my personal opinion. And a great feeling of rage and disappointment came over me as I looked at England, my head full of personal opinions that could not have public, my public, approval. The people I come from are powerless to do evil on grand scale.

The moment I wished every sentence, everything I knew, that began with England would end with "and then it all died, we don't know how, it just all died" was when I saw the white cliffs of Dover. I had sung hymns and recited poems that were about a longing to see the white cliffs of Dover again. At the time I sang the hymns and recited the poems, I could really long to see them again because I had never seen them at all, nor had anyone around me at the time. But there we were, groups of people longing for something we had never seen. And so there they were, the white cliffs, but they were not that pearly majestic thing I used to sing about, that thing that created such a feeling in these people that when they died in the place where I lived they had themselves buried facing a direction that would allow them to see the white cliffs of Dover when they were resurrected, as surely they would be. The white cliffs of Dover, when finally I saw them, were cliffs, but they were not white; you would only call them that if the word "white" meant something special to you; they were dirty and they were steep; they were so steep, the correct height from which all my views of England, starting with the map before me in my classroom and ending with the trip I had just taken, should jump and die and disappear forever.

the height of the Dover mountain a metaphor for her capacity of knowledge on England; yet false knowledge, as false as the "white cliffs" the plunge = reality

Considerations

Thinking

What does England mean for Kincaid? To what extent is her view of England a product of her early education? To what extent is it affected by the world of cultural difference she inhabits?

ominous term

What does the phrase "made in England" come to mean in the essay? With what does Kincaid contrast things "made in England"? Toward what point and with what effect? Why does the command "Draw a map of England" resonate so powerfully in Kincaid's memory and imagination?

Connecting

Kincaid sets up a number of contrasts between England and her Caribbean island home. Identify two different types of these, and explain what Kincaid conveys by emphasizing such differences.

What ironies does Kincaid point up in her discussion of street names in St. John's, Antigua? How does her discussion of Christopher Columbus tie in with her discussion of England?

Writing

Write an essay in which you explore what Kincaid calls "the space between the idea of something and its reality." It may be a place, a situation, an anticipated experience, a person. Whatever you write about, consider the extent to which the weaker of the two, the idea or the reality of the thing, diminishes when the two conflict.

Write an essay exploring the various views of England Kincaid presents. Consider what she says about the white cliffs of Dover in her final paragraph.

Martin Luther King, Jr.
(1929–1968)

Martin Luther King, Jr., won the Nobel Peace Prize in 1964 for his indefatigable effort to secure the blessings of liberty for his people—especially black Americans living in the South. He challenged unfair laws, stood up against demagogues, led peaceful demonstrations through the South, and argued persuasively for change all across America. His successful efforts cost him his life. He was assassinated in Memphis, Tennessee, on April 4, 1968.

"Letter from Birmingham Jail" was written to a group of Christian ministers who had criticized King's effort to integrate restaurants by staging sit-ins at luncheon counters in Birmingham, Alabama. It is an argument against injustice and delay—an urgent appeal to grant African Americans their freedom and independence.

Letter from Birmingham Jail

April 16, 1963

My Dear Fellow Clergymen:

While confined here in the Birmingham city jail, I came across your recent statement calling my present activities "unwise and untimely." Seldom do I pause to answer criticism of my work and ideas. If I sought to answer all the criticisms that cross my desk, my secretaries would have little time for anything other than such correspondence in the course of the day, and I would have no time for constructive work. But since I feel that you are men of genuine good will and that your criticisms are sincerely set forth, I want to try to answer your statement in what I hope will be patient and reasonable terms.

I think I should indicate why I am here in Birmingham, since you have been influenced by the view which argues against "outsiders coming in." I have the honor of serving as president of the Southern Christian Leadership Conference, an organization operating in every southern state, with headquarters in Atlanta, Georgia. We have some eighty-five affiliated organizations across the South, and one of them is the Alabama Christian Movement for Human Rights. Frequently we share staff, educational and financial resources with our affiliates. Several months ago the affiliate here in Birmingham asked us to be on call to engage in a nonviolent direct-action program if such were deemed necessary. We readily consented, and when the hour came we lived up to our promise. So I, along with several members of my staff, am here because I was invited here. I am here because I have organizational ties here.

But more basically, I am in Birmingham because injustice is here. Just as the prophets of the eighth century B.C. left their villages and carried their "thus saith the Lord" far beyond the boundaries of their home towns, and just as the Apostle Paul left his village of Tarsus and carried the gospel of Jesus Christ to the far corners of the Greco-Roman world, so am I compelled to carry the gospel of freedom beyond my own home town. Like Paul, I must constantly respond to the Macedonian call for aid.

Moreover, I am cognizant of the interrelatedness of all communities and states. I cannot sit idly by in Atlanta and not be concerned about what happens in Birmingham. Injustice anywhere is a threat to justice everywhere. We are caught in an inescapable network of mutuality, tied in a single garment of destiny. Whatever affects one directly, affects all indirectly. Never again can we afford to live with the narrow, provincial "outside agitator" idea. Anyone who lives inside the United States can never be considered an outsider anywhere within its bounds.

You deplore the demonstrations taking place in Birmingham. But your statement, I am sorry to say, fails to express a similar concern for the conditions that brought about the demonstrations. I am sure that none of you would want to rest content with the superficial kind of social analysis that deals merely with effects and does not grapple with underlying causes. It is unfortunate that demonstrations are taking place in Birmingham, but it is even more unfortunate that the city's white power structure left the Negro community with no alternative.

In any nonviolent campaign there are four basic steps: collection of the facts to determine whether injustices exist; negotiation; self-purification; and direct action. We have gone through all these steps in Birmingham. There can be no gainsaying the fact that racial injustice engulfs this community. Birmingham is probably the most thoroughly segregated city in the United States. Its ugly record of brutality is widely known. Negroes have experienced grossly unjust treatment in the courts. There have been more unsolved bombings of Negro homes and churches in Birmingham than in any other city in the nation. These are the hard brutal facts of the case. On the basis of these conditions, Negro leaders sought to negotiate with the city fathers. But the latter consistently refused to engage in good-faith negotiation.

Then, last September, came the opportunity to talk with leaders of Birmingham's economic community. In the course of the negotiations, certain promises were made by the merchants—for example, to remove the stores' humiliating racial signs. On the basis of these promises, the Reverend Fred Shuttlesworth and the leaders of the Alabama Christian Movement for Human Rights agreed to a moratorium on all demonstrations. As the weeks and months went by, we realized that we were the victims of a broken promise. A few signs, briefly removed, returned; the others remained.

As in so many past experiences, our hopes had been blasted, and the shadow of deep disappointment settled upon us. We had no alternative except to prepare for direct action, whereby we would present our very bodies as a means of laying our case before the conscience of the local and the national community. Mindful of the difficulties involved, we decided to undertake a process of self-purification. We began a series of workshops on nonviolence, and we repeatedly asked ourselves: "Are you able to accept blows without retaliating?" "Are you able to endure the ordeal of jail?" We decided to schedule our direct-action program for the Easter season, realizing that except for Christmas, this is the main shopping period of the year. Knowing that a strong economic-withdrawal program would be the by-product of direct action, we felt that this would be the best time to bring pressure to bear on the merchants for the needed change.

Then it occurred to us that Birmingham's mayoralty election was coming up in March, and we speedily decided to postpone action until after election day. When we discovered that the Commissioner of Public Safety, Eugene "Bull" Connor, had piled up enough votes to be in the run-off, we decided again to postpone action until the day after the run-off so that the demonstrations could not be used to cloud the issues. Like many others, we waited to see Mr. Connor defeated, and to this end we endured postponement after postponement. Having aided in this community need, we felt that our direct-action program could be delayed no longer.

You may well ask: "Why direct action? Why sit-ins, marches and so forth? Isn't negotiation a better path?" You are quite right in calling for negotiation. Indeed, this is the very purpose of direct action. Nonviolent direct action seeks to create such a crisis and foster such a tension that a community which has constantly refused to negotiate is forced to confront the issue. It seeks so to dramatize the issue that it can no longer be ignored. My citing the creation of tension as part of the work of the nonviolent-resister may sound rather shocking. But I must confess that I am not afraid of the word "tension." I have earnestly opposed violent tension, but there is a type of constructive nonviolent tension which is necessary for growth. Just as Socrates felt that it was necessary to create a tension in the mind so that individuals could rise from the bondage of myths and half-truths to the unfettered realm of creative analysis and objective appraisal, so must we see the need for nonviolent gadflies to create the kind of tension in society that will help men rise from the dark depths of prejudice and racism to the majestic heights of understanding and brotherhood.

The purpose of our direct-action program is to create a situation so crisis-packed that it will inevitably open the door to negotiation. I therefore concur with you in your call for negotiation. Too long has our beloved Southland been bogged down in a tragic effort to live in monologue rather than dialogue.

One of the basic points in your statement is that the action that I and my associates have taken in Birmingham is untimely. Some have asked: "Why didn't you give the new city administration time to act?" The only answer that I can give to this query is that the new Birmingham administration must be prodded about as much as the outgoing one, before it will act. We are sadly mistaken if we feel that the election of Albert Boutwell as mayor will bring the millennium to Birmingham. While Mr. Boutwell is a much more gentle person than Mr. Connor, they are both segregationists, dedicated to maintenance of the status quo. I have hope that Mr. Boutwell will be reasonable enough to see the futility of massive resistance to desegregation. But he will not see this without pressure from devotees of civil rights. My friends, I must say to you that we have not made a single gain in civil rights without determined legal and nonviolent pressure. Lamentably, it is an historical fact that privileged groups seldom give up their privileges voluntarily. Individuals may see the moral light and voluntarily give up their unjust posture; but, as Reinhold Niebuhr has reminded us, groups tend to be more immoral than individuals.

We know through painful experience that freedom is never voluntarily given by the oppressor; it must be demanded by the oppressed. Frankly, I have yet to engage in a direct-action campaign that was "well timed" in the view of those who have not suffered unduly from the disease of segregation. For years now I have heard the word "Wait!" It rings in the ear of every Negro with piercing familiarity. This "Wait" has almost always meant "Never." We must come to see, with one of our distinguished jurists, that "justice too long delayed is justice denied."

We have waited for more than 340 years for our constitutional and God-given rights. The nations of Asia and Africa are moving with jet-like speed toward gaining political independence, but we still creep at horse-and-buggy pace toward gaining a cup of coffee at a lunch counter. Perhaps it is easy for those who have never felt the stinging darts of segregation to say, "Wait." But when you have seen vicious mobs lynch your mothers and fathers at will and drown your sisters and brothers at whim; when you have seen hate-filled policemen curse, kick and even kill your black brothers and sisters; when you see the vast majority of your twenty million Negro brothers smothering in an airtight cage of poverty in the midst of an affluent society; when you suddenly find your tongue twisted and your speech stammering as you seek to explain to your six-year-old daughter why she can't go to the public amusement park that has just been advertised on television, and see tears welling up in her eyes when she is told that Funtown is closed to colored children, and see ominous clouds of inferiority beginning to form in her little mental sky, and see her beginning to distort her personality by developing an unconscious bitterness toward white people; when you have to concoct an answer for a five-year-old son who is asking: "Daddy, why do white people treat colored people so mean?"; when you take a cross-country drive and find it necessary to sleep night after night in the uncomfortable corners of your automobile because no motel will accept you; when you are humiliated day in and day out by nagging signs reading "white" and "colored"; when your first name becomes "nigger," your middle name becomes "boy" (however old you are) and your last name becomes "John," and your wife and mother are never given the respected title "Mrs."; when you are harried by day and haunted by night by the fact that you are a Negro, living constantly at tiptoe stance, never quite knowing what to expect next, and are plagued with inner fears and outer resentments; when you are forever fighting a degenerating sense of "nobodiness"—then you will understand why we find it difficult to wait. There comes a time when the cup of endurance runs over, and men are no longer willing to be plunged into the abyss of despair. I hope, sirs, you can understand our legitimate and unavoidable impatience.

You express a great deal of anxiety over our willingness to break laws. This is certainly a legitimate concern. Since we so diligently urge people to obey the Supreme Court's decision of 1954 outlawing segregation in the public schools, at first glance it may seem rather paradoxical for us consciously to break laws. One may well ask: "How can you advocate breaking some laws and obeying others?" The answer lies in the fact that there are two types of laws: just and unjust. I would be the first to advocate obeying just laws. One has not only a legal but a moral responsibility to obey just laws. Conversely, one has a moral responsibility to disobey unjust laws. I would agree with St. Augustine that "an unjust law is no law at all."

Now, what is the difference between the two? How does one determine whether a law is just or unjust? A just law is a man-made code that squares with the moral law or the law of God. An unjust law is a code that is out of harmony with the moral law. To put it in the terms of St. Thomas Aquinas: An unjust law is a human law that is not rooted in eternal law and natural law. Any law that uplifts human personality is just. Any law that degrades human personality is unjust. All segregation statutes are unjust because segregation distorts the soul and damages the personality. It gives the segregator a false sense of superiority and the segregated a false sense of inferiority. Segregation, to use the terminology of the Jewish philosopher Martin Buber, substitutes an "I-it" relationship for an "I-thou" relationship and ends up relegating persons to the status of things. Hence segregation is not only politically, economically and sociologically unsound, it is morally wrong and sinful. Paul Tillich has said that sin is separation. Is not segregation an existential expression of man's tragic separation, his awful estrangement, his terrible sinfulness? Thus it is that I can urge men to obey the 1954 decision of the Supreme Court, for it is morally right; and I can urge them to disobey segregation ordinances, for they are morally wrong.

Let us consider a more concrete example of just and unjust laws. An unjust law is a code that a numerical or power majority group compels a minority group to obey but does not make binding on itself. This is *difference* made legal. By the same token, a just law is a code that a majority compels a minority to follow and that it is willing to follow itself. This is *sameness* made legal.

Let me give another explanation. A law is unjust if it is inflicted on a minority that, as a result of being denied the right to vote, had no part in enacting or devising the law. Who can say that the legislature of Alabama which set up that state's segregation laws was democratically elected? Throughout Alabama all sorts of devious methods are used to prevent Negroes from becoming registered voters, and there are some counties in which even though Negroes constitute a majority of the population, not a single Negro is registered. Can any law enacted under such circumstances be considered democratically structured?

Sometimes a law is just on its face and unjust in its application. For instance, I have been arrested on a charge of parading without a permit. Now, there is nothing wrong in having an ordinance which requires a permit for a parade. But such an ordinance becomes unjust when it is used to maintain segregation and to deny citizens the First-Amendment privilege of peaceful assembly and protest.

I hope you are able to see the distinction I am trying to point out. In no sense do I advocate evading or defying the law, as would the rabid segregationist. That would lead to anarchy. One who breaks an unjust law must do so openly, lovingly, and with a willingness to accept the penalty. I submit that an individual who breaks a law that conscience tells him is unjust, and who willingly accepts the penalty of imprisonment in order to arouse the conscience of the community over its injustice, is in reality expressing the highest respect for law.

Of course, there is nothing new about this kind of civil disobedience. It was evidenced sublimely in the refusal of Shadrach, Meshach and Abednego to obey the laws of Nebuchadnezzar, on the ground that a higher moral law was at stake. It was practiced superbly by the early Christians, who were willing to face hungry lions and the excruciating pain of chopping blocks rather than submit to certain unjust laws of the Roman Empire. To a degree, academic freedom is a reality today because Socrates practiced civil disobedience. In our own nation, the Boston Tea Party represented a massive act of civil disobedience.

We should never forget that everything Adolf Hitler did in Germany was "legal" and everything the Hungarian freedom fighters did in Hungary was "illegal." It was "illegal" to aid and comfort a Jew in Hitler's Germany. Even so, I am sure that, had I lived in Germany at the time, I would have aided and comforted my Jewish brothers. If today I lived in a Communist country where certain principles dear to the Christian faith are suppressed, I would openly advocate disobeying that country's anti-religious laws.

I must make two honest confessions to you, my Christian and Jewish brothers. First, I must confess that over the past few years I have been gravely disappointed with the white moderate. I have almost reached the regrettable conclusion that the Negro's great stumbling block in his stride toward freedom is not the White Citizen's Counciler or the Ku Klux Klanner, but the white moderate, who is more devoted to "order" than to justice; who prefers a negative peace which is the absence of tension to a positive peace which is the presence of justice; who constantly says: "I agree with you in the goal you seek, but I cannot agree with your methods of direct action"; who paternalistically believes he can set the timetable for another man's freedom; who lives by a mythical concept of time and who constantly advises the Negro to wait for a "more convenient season." Shallow understanding from people of good will is more frustrating than absolute misunderstanding from people of ill will. Lukewarm acceptance is much more bewildering than outright rejection.

I had hoped that the white moderate would understand that law and order exist for the purpose of establishing justice and that when they fail in this purpose they become the dangerously structured dams that block the flow of social progress. I had hoped that the white moderate would understand that the present tension in the South is a necessary phase of the transition from an obnoxious negative peace, in which the Negro passively accepted his unjust plight, to a substantive and positive peace, in which all men will respect the dignity and worth of human personality. Actually, we who engage in nonviolent direct action are not the creators of tension. We merely bring to the surface the hidden tension that is already alive. We bring it out in the open, where it can be seen and dealt with. Like a boil that can never be cured so long as it is covered up but must be opened with all its ugliness to the natural medicines of air and light, injustice must be exposed, with all the tension its exposure creates, to the light of human conscience and the air of national opinion before it can be cured.

In your statement you assert that our actions, even though peaceful, must be condemned because they precipitate violence. But is this a logical assertion? Isn't this like condemning a robbed man because his possession of money precipitated the evil act of robbery? Isn't this like condemning Socrates because his unswerving commitment to truth and his philosophical inquires precipitated the act by the misguided populace in which they made him drink hemlock? Isn't this like condemning Jesus because his unique God-consciousness and never-ceasing devotion to God's will precipitated the evil act of crucifixion? We must come to see that, as the federal courts have consistently affirmed, it is wrong to urge an individual to cease his efforts to gain his basic constitutional rights because the quest may precipitate violence. Society must protect the robbed and punish the robber.

I had also hoped that the white moderate would reject the myth concerning time in relation to the struggle for freedom. I have just received a letter from a white brother in Texas. He writes: "All Christians know that the colored people will receive equal rights eventually, but it is possible that you are in too great a religious hurry. It has taken Christianity almost two thousand years to accomplish what it has. The teachings of Christ take time to come to earth." Such an attitude stems from a tragic misconception of time, from the strangely irrational notion that there is something in the very flow of time that will inevitably cure all ills. Actually, time itself is neutral; it can be used either destructively or constructively. More and more I feel that the people of ill will have used time much more effectively than have the people of good will. We will have to repent in this generation not merely for the hateful words and actions of the bad people but for the appalling silence of the good people. Human progress never rolls in on wheels of inevitability; it comes through the tireless efforts of men willing to be co-workers with God, and without this hard work, time itself becomes an ally of the forces of social stagnation. We must use time creatively, in the knowledge that the time is always ripe to do right. Now is the time to make real the promise of democracy and transform our pending national elegy into a creative psalm of brotherhood. Now is the time to lift our national policy from the quicksand of racial injustice to the solid rock of human dignity.

You speak of our activity in Birmingham as extreme. At first I was rather disappointed that fellow clergymen would see my nonviolent efforts as those of an extremist. I began thinking about the fact that I stand in the middle of two opposing forces in the Negro community. One is a force of complacency, made up in part of Negroes who, as a result of long years of oppression, are so drained of self-respect and a sense of "somebodiness" that they have adjusted to segregation; and in part of a few middle-class Negroes who, because of a degree of academic and economic security and because in some ways they profit by segregation, have become insensitive to the problems of the masses. The other force is one of bitterness and hatred, and it comes perilously close to advocating violence. It is expressed in the various black nationalist groups that are springing up across the nation, the largest and best-known being Elijah Muhammad's Muslim movement. Nourished by the Negro's frustration over the continued existence of racial discrimination, this movement is made up of people who have lost faith in America, who have absolutely repudiated Christianity, and who have concluded that the white man is an incorrigible "devil."

I have tried to stand between these two forces, saying that we need emulate neither the "do-nothingism" of the complacent nor the hatred and despair of the black nationalist. For there is the more excellent way of love and nonviolent protest. I am grateful to God that, through the influence of the Negro church, the way of nonviolence became an integral part of our struggle.

If this philosophy had not emerged, by now many streets of the South would, I am convinced, be flowing with blood. And I am further convinced that if our white brothers dismiss as "rabble-rousers" and "outside agitators" those of us who employ nonviolent direct action, and if they refuse to support our nonviolent efforts, millions of Negroes will, out of frustration and despair, seek solace and security in black-nationalist ideologies—a development that would inevitably lead to a frightening racial nightmare.

Oppressed people cannot remain oppressed forever. The yearning for freedom eventually manifests itself, and that is what has happened to the American Negro. Something within has reminded him of his birthright of freedom, and something without has reminded him that it can be gained. Consciously or unconsciously, he has been caught up by the *Zeitgeist,* and with his black brothers of Africa and his brown and yellow brothers of Asia, South America and the Caribbean, the United States Negro is moving with a sense of great urgency toward the promised land of racial justice. If one recognizes this vital urge that has engulfed the Negro community, one should readily understand why public demonstrations are taking place. The Negro has many pent-up resentments and latent frustrations, and he must release them. So let him march; let him make prayer pilgrimages to the city hall; let him go on freedom rides—and try to understand why he must do so. If his repressed emotions are not released in nonviolent ways, they will seek expression through violence; this is not a threat but a fact of history. So I have not said to my people: "Get rid of your discontent." Rather, I have tried to say that this normal and healthy discontent can be channeled into the creative outlet of nonviolent direct action. And now this approach is being termed extremist.

But though I was initially disappointed at being categorized as an extremist, as I continued to think about the matter I gradually gained a measure of satisfaction from the label. Was not Jesus an extremist for love: "Love your enemies, bless them that curse you, do good to them that hate you, and pray for them which despitefully use you, and persecute you." Was not Amos an extremist for justice: "Let justice roll down like waters and righteousness like an ever-flowing stream." Was not Paul an extremist for the Christian gospel: "I bear in my body the marks of the Lord Jesus." Was not Martin Luther an extremist: "Here I stand; I cannot do otherwise, so help me God." And John Bunyan: "I will stay in jail to the end of my days before I make a butchery of my conscience." And Abraham Lincoln: "This nation cannot survive half slave and half free." And Thomas Jefferson: "We hold these truths to be self-evident, that all men are created equal. . . ." So the question is not whether we will be extremists, but what kind of extremists we will be. Will we be extremists for hate or for love? Will we be extremists for the preservation of injustice or for the extension of justice? In that dramatic scene on Calvary's hill three men were crucified. We must never forget that all three were crucified for the same crime—the crime of extremism. Two were extremists for immorality, and thus fell below their environment. The other, Jesus Christ, was an extremist for love, truth and goodness, and thereby rose above his environment. Perhaps the South, the nation and the world are in dire need of creative extremists.

I had hoped that the white moderate would see this need. Perhaps I was too optimistic; perhaps I expected too much. I suppose I should have realized that few members of the oppressor race can understand the deep groans and passionate yearnings of the oppressed race, and still fewer have the vision to see that injustice must be rooted out by strong, persistent and determined action. I am thankful, however, that some of our white brothers in the South have grasped the meaning of this social revolution and committed themselves to it. They are still all too few in quantity, but they are big in quality. Some—such as Ralph McGill,

Lillian Smith, Harry Golden, James McBride Dabbs, Ann Braden and Sarah Patton Boyle—have written about our struggle in eloquent and prophetic terms. Others have marched with us down nameless streets of the South. They have languished in filthy, roach-infested jails, suffering the abuse and brutality of policemen who view them as "dirty nigger-lovers." Unlike so many of their moderate brothers and sisters, they have recognized the urgency of the moment and sensed the need for powerful "action" antidotes to combat the disease of segregation.

Let me take note of my other major disappointment. I have been so greatly disappointed with the white church and its leadership. Of course, there are some notable exceptions. I am not unmindful of the fact that each of you has taken some significant stands on this issue. I commend you, Reverend Stallings, for your Christian stand on this past Sunday, in welcoming Negroes to your worship service on a nonsegregated basis. I commend the Catholic leaders of this state for integrating Spring Hill College several years ago.

But despite these notable exceptions, I must honestly reiterate that I have been disappointed with the church. I do not say this as one of those negative critics who can always find something wrong with the church. I say this as a minister of the gospel, who loves the church; who was nurtured in its bosom; who has been sustained by its spiritual blessings and who will remain true to it as long as the cord of life shall lengthen.

When I was suddenly catapulted into the leadership of the bus protest in Montgomery, Alabama, a few years ago, I felt we would be supported by the white church. I felt that the white ministers, priests and rabbis of the South would be among our strongest allies. Instead, some have been outright opponents, refusing to understand the freedom movement and misrepresenting its leaders; all too many others have been more cautious than courageous and have remained silent behind the anesthetizing security of stained-glass windows.

In spite of my shattered dreams, I came to Birmingham with the hope that the white religious leadership of this community would see the justice of our cause and, with deep moral concern, would serve as the channel through which our just grievances could reach the power structure. I had hoped that each of you would understand. But again I have been disappointed.

I have heard numerous southern religious leaders admonish their worshipers to comply with a desegregation decision because it is the law, but I have longed to hear white ministers declare: "Follow this decree because integration is morally right and because the Negro is your brother." In the midst of blatant injustices inflicted upon the Negro, I have watched white churchmen stand on the sideline and mouth pious irrelevancies and sanctimonious trivialities. In the midst of a mighty struggle to rid our nation of racial and economic injustice, I have heard many ministers say: "Those are social issues, with which the gospel has no real concern." And I have watched many churches commit themselves to a completely other-worldly religion which makes a strange, un-Biblical distinction between body and soul, between the sacred and the secular.

I have traveled the length and breadth of Alabama, Mississippi and all the other southern states. On sweltering summer days and crisp autumn mornings I have looked at the South's beautiful churches with their lofty spires pointing heavenward. I have beheld the impressive outlines of her massive religious-education buildings. Over and over I have found myself asking: "What kind of people worship here? Who is their God? Where were their voices when the lips of Governor Barnett dripped with words of interposition and nullification? Where were they when Governor Wallace gave a clarion call for defiance and hatred? Where were their voices of support when bruised and weary Negro men and women decided to rise from the dark dungeons of complacency to the bright hills of creative protest?"

Yes, these questions are still in my mind. In deep disappointment I have wept over the laxity of the church. But be assured that my tears have been tears of love. There can be no deep disappointment where there is not deep love. Yes, I love the church. How could I do otherwise? I am in the rather unique position of being the son, the grandson and the great-grandson of preachers. Yes, I see the church as the body of Christ. But, oh! How we have blemished and scarred that body through social neglect and through fear of being nonconformists.

There was a time when the church was very powerful—in the time when the early Christians rejoiced at being deemed worthy to suffer for what they believed. In those days the church was not merely a thermometer that recorded the ideas and principles of popular opinion; it was a thermostat that transformed the mores of society. Whenever the early Christians entered a town, the people in power became disturbed and immediately sought to convict the Christians for being "disturbers of the peace" and "outside agitators." But the Christians pressed on, in the conviction that they were "a colony of heaven," called to obey God rather than man. Small in number, they were big in commitment. They were too God-intoxicated to be "astronomically intimidated." By their effort and example they brought an end to such ancient evils as infanticide and gladiatorial contests.

Things are different now. So often the contemporary church is a weak, ineffectual voice with an uncertain sound. So often it is an archdefender of the status quo. Far from being disturbed by the presence of the church, the power structure of the average community is consoled by the church's silent—and often even vocal—sanction of things as they are.

But the judgment of God is upon the church as never before. If today's church does not recapture the sacrificial spirit of the early church, it will lose its authenticity, forfeit the loyalty of millions, and be dismissed as an irrelevant social club with no meaning for the twentieth century. Every day I meet young people whose disappointment with the church has turned into outright disgust.

Perhaps I have once again been too optimistic. Is organized religion too inextricably bound to the status quo to save our nation and the world? Perhaps I must turn my faith to the inner spiritual church, the church within the church, as the true *ekklesia* and the hope of the world. But again I am thankful to God that some noble souls from the ranks of organized religion have broken loose from the paralyzing chains of conformity and joined us as active partners in the struggle for freedom. They have left their secure congregations and walked the streets of Albany, Georgia, with us. They have gone down the highways of the South on tortuous rides for freedom. Yes, they have gone to jail with us. Some have been dismissed from their churches, have lost the support of their bishops and fellow ministers. But they have acted in the faith that right defeated is stronger than evil triumphant. Their witness has been the spiritual salt that has preserved the true meaning of the gospel in these troubled times. They have carved a tunnel of hope through the dark mountain of disappointment.

I hope the church as a whole will meet the challenge of this decisive hour. But even if the church does not come to the aid of justice, I have no despair about the future. I have no fear about the outcome of our struggle in Birmingham, even if our motives are at present misunderstood. We will reach the goal of freedom in Birmingham and all over the nation, because the goal of America is freedom. Abused and scorned though we may be, our destiny is tied up with America's destiny. Before the pilgrims landed at Plymouth, we were here. Before the pen of Jefferson etched the majestic words of the Declaration of Independence across the pages of history, we were here. For more than two centuries our forebears labored in this country without wages; they made cotton king; they built the homes of their masters while suffering gross injustice and shameful humiliation—and yet out of a bottomless vitality they continued to thrive and develop. If the inexpressible cruelties of slavery could not stop us, the opposition we now face will surely fail. We will win our freedom because the sacred heritage of our nation and the eternal will of God are embodied in our echoing demands.

Before closing I feel impelled to mention one other point in your statement that has troubled me profoundly. You warmly commended the Birmingham police force for keeping "order" and "preventing violence." I doubt that you would have so warmly commended the police force if you had seen its dogs sinking their teeth into unarmed, nonviolent Negroes. I doubt that you would so quickly commend the policemen if you were to observe their ugly and inhumane treatment of Negroes here in the city jail; if you were to watch them push and curse old Negro women and young Negro girls; if you were to see them slap and kick old Negro men and young boys; if you were to observe them, as they did on two occasions, refuse to give us food because we wanted to sing our grace together. I cannot join you in your praise of the Birmingham police department.

It is true that the police have exercised a degree of discipline in handling the demonstrators. In this sense they have conducted themselves rather "nonviolently" in public. But for what purpose? To preserve the evil system of segregation. Over the past few years I have consistently preached that nonviolence demands that the means we use must be as pure as the ends we seek. I have tried to make clear that it is wrong to use immoral means to attain moral ends. But now I must affirm that it is just as wrong, or perhaps even more so, to use moral means to preserve immoral ends. Perhaps Mr. Connor and his policemen have been rather nonviolent in public, as was Chief Pritchett in Albany, Georgia, but they have used the moral means of nonviolence to maintain the immoral end of racial injustice. As T. S. Eliot has said: "The last temptation is the greatest treason: To do the right deed for the wrong reason."

I wish you had commended the Negro sit-inners and demonstrators of Birmingham for their sublime courage, their willingness to suffer and their amazing discipline in the midst of great provocation. One day the South will recognize its real heroes. They will be the James Merediths, with the noble sense of purpose that enables them to face jeering and hostile mobs, and with the agonizing loneliness that characterizes the life of the pioneer. They will be old, oppressed, battered Negro women, symbolized in a seventy-two-year-old woman in Montgomery, Alabama, who rose up with a sense of dignity and with her people decided not to ride segregated buses, and who responded with ungrammatical profundity to one who inquired about her weariness: "My feet is tired, but my soul is at rest." They will be the young high school and college students, the young ministers of the gospel and a host of their elders, courageously and nonviolently sitting in at lunch counters and willingly going to jail for conscience's sake. One day the South will know that when these disinherited children of God sat down at lunch counters, they were in reality standing up for what is best in the American dream and for the most sacred values in our Judaeo-Christian heritage, thereby bringing our nation back to those great wells of democracy which were dug by the founding fathers in their formulation of the Constitution and the Declaration of Independence.

Never before have I written so long a letter. I'm afraid it is much too long to take your precious time. I can assure you that it would have been much shorter if I had been writing from a comfortable desk, but what else can one do when he is alone in a narrow jail cell, other than write long letters, think long thoughts and pray long prayers?

If I have said anything in this letter that overstates the truth and indicates an unreasonable impatience, I beg you to forgive me. If I have said anything that understates the truth and indicates my having a patience that allows me to settle for anything less than brotherhood, I beg God to forgive me.

I hope this letter finds you strong in the faith. I also hope that circumstances will soon make it possible for me to meet each of you, not as an integrationist or a civil-rights leader but as a fellow clergyman and a Christian brother. Let us all hope that the dark clouds of racial prejudice will soon pass away and the deep fog of misunderstanding will be lifted from our fear-drenched communities, and in some not too distant tomorrow the radiant stars of love and brotherhood will shine over our great nation with all their scintillating beauty.

Yours for the cause of Peace and Brotherhood,
Martin Luther King, Jr.

Considerations

Thinking

What does King mean by "a nonviolent direct-action program"? What do you think about the necessity for "tension," which, according to King, is "necessary for growth"?

What do you think of King's claim that "privileged groups seldom give up their privileges voluntarily"? Is that still true?

How can you tell when a law is "out of harmony with the moral law"?

Connecting

Turn to King's response to the clergymen's admonition to wait. Read aloud the entire passage, beginning with the words, "But when you have seen vicious mobs lynch your mothers and fathers at will and drown your sisters and brothers at whim . . ." What do you know after reading the passage aloud that you did not know when you read it silently?

In what ways might you consider King's letter historical? What are its limitations as a historical document?

Writing

Write an essay in which you assess the extent to which you think this claim of King's rings true in your community or at your college at the turn into the twenty-first century: "Anyone who lives inside the United States can never be considered an outsider anywhere within its bounds."

Write your own letter to address an injustice in your community or in your college.

Leonard Kriegel
(b. 1933)

Leonard Kriegel, a retired professor of English from the City College of New York, is a novelist, short story writer, and essayist. His work includes *Quitting Time* (a novel), *Notes for a Two-Dollar Window* (a memoir), and *Falling into Life* (a collection of essays). His stories and essays have appeared in the *American Scholar, Dissent,* the *Sewanee Review,* the *Gettysburg Review,* the *Georgia Review, Raritan, Partisan Review, The Nation,* the *New Republic,* and the *New York Times Magazine.* He has completed a new collection of essays, *Flying Solo.*

"Falling into Life" first appeared in the *American Scholar;* it recounts a moment from Kriegel's early bout with polio and reminds us of the euphoria that accompanies our fall into life, and perhaps into death.

Falling into Life

It is not the actual death a man is doomed to die but the deaths his imagination anticipates that claim attention as one grows older. We are constantly being reminded that the prospect of death forcefully concentrates the mind. While that may be so, it is not a prospect that does very much else for the imagination—other than to make one aware of its limitations and imbalances.

Over the past five years, as I have moved into the solidity of middle age, my own most formidable imaginative limitation has turned out to be a surprising need for symmetry. I am possessed by a peculiar passion: I want to believe that my life has been balanced out. And because I once had to learn to fall in order to keep that life mine, I now seem to have convinced myself that I must also learn to fall into death.

Falling into life wasn't easy, and I suspect that is why I hunger for such awkward symmetry today. Having lost the use of my legs during the polio epidemic that swept across the eastern United States during the summer of 1944, I was soon immersed in a process of rehabilitation that was, at least when looked at in retrospect, as much spiritual as physical.

That was a full decade before the discovery of the Salk vaccine ended polio's reign as the disease most dreaded by America's parents and their children. Treatment of the disease had been standardized by 1944: following the initial onslaught of the virus, patients were kept in isolation for a period of ten days to two weeks. Following that, orthodox medical opinion was content to subject patients to as much heat as they could stand. Stiff paralyzed limbs were swathed in heated, coarse woolen towels known as "hot packs." (The towels were that same greenish brown as blankets issued to American GIs, and they reinforced a boy's sense of being at war.) As soon as the hot packs had baked enough pain and stiffness out of a patient's body so that he could be moved on and off a stretcher, the treatment was ended, and the patient faced a series of daily immersions in a heated pool.

I would ultimately spend two full years at the appropriately named New York State Reconstruction Home in West Haverstraw. But what I remember most vividly about the first three months of my stay there was being submerged in a hot pool six times a day, for periods of between fifteen and twenty minutes. I would lie on a stainless steel slab, my face alone out of water, while the wet heat rolled against my dead legs and the physical therapist was at my side working at a series of manipulations intended to bring my useless muscles back to health.

Each immersion was a baptism by fire in the water. While my mind pitched and reeled with memories of the "normal" boy I had been a few weeks earlier, I would close my eyes and focus not, as my therapist urged, on bringing dead legs back to life but on my strange fall from the childhood grace of the physical. Like all eleven-year-old boys, I had spent a good deal of time thinking about my body. Before the attack of the virus, however, I thought about it only in connection with my own lunge toward adolescence. Never before had my body seemed an object in itself. Now it was. And like the twenty-one other boys in the ward—all of us between the ages of nine and twelve—I sensed I would never move beyond the fall from grace, even as I played with memories of the way I once had been.

Each time I was removed from the hot water and placed on a stretcher by the side of the pool, there to await the next immersion, I was fed salt tablets. These were simply intended to make up for the sweat we lost, but salt tablets seemed to me the cruelest confirmation of my new status as spiritual debtor. Even today, more than four decades later, I still shiver at the mere thought of those salt tablets. Sometimes the hospital orderly would literally have to pry my mouth open to force me to swallow them. I dreaded the nausea the taste of salt inspired in me. Each time I was resubmerged in the hot pool, I would grit my teeth—not from the flush of heat sweeping over my body but from the thought of what I would have to face when I would again be taken out of the water. To be an eater of salt was far more humiliating than to endure pain. Nor was I alone in feeling this way. After lights-out had quieted the ward, we boys would furtively whisper from cubicle to cubicle of how we dreaded being forced to swallow salt tablets. It was that, rather than the pain we endured, that anchored our sense of loss and dread.

Any recovery of muscle use in a polio patient usually took place within three months of the disease's onset. We all knew that. But as time passed, every boy in the ward learned to recite stories of those who, like Lazarus, had witnessed their own bodily resurrection. Having fallen from physical grace, we also chose to fall away from the reality in front of us. Our therapists were skilled and dedicated, but they weren't wonder-working saints. Paralyzed legs and arms rarely responded to their manipulations. We could not admit to ourselves, or to them, that we were permanently crippled. But each of us knew without knowing that his future was tied to the body that floated on the stainless steel slab.

We sweated out the hot pool and we choked on the salt tablets, and through it all we looked forward to the promise of rehabilitation. For, once the stiffness and pain had been baked and boiled out of us, we would no longer be eaters of salt. We would not be what we once had been, but at least we would be candidates for re-entry into the world, admittedly made over to face its demands encased in leather and steel.

I suppose we might have been told that our fall from grace was permanent. But I am still grateful that no one—neither doctors nor nurses nor therapists, not even that sadistic orderly, himself a former polio patient, who limped through our lives and through our pain like some vengeful presence—told me that my chances of regaining the use of my legs were nonexistent. Like every other boy in the ward,

I organized my needs around whatever illusions were available. And the illusion I needed above any other was that one morning I would simply wake up and rediscover the "normal" boy of memory, once again playing baseball in French Charley's Field in Bronx Park rather than roaming the fields of his own imagination. At the age of eleven, I needed to weather reality, not face it. And to this very day, I silently thank those who were concerned enough about me, or indifferent enough to my fate, not to tell me what they knew.

Like most boys, sick or well, I was an adaptable creature—and rehabilitation demanded adaptability. The fall from bodily grace transformed each of us into acolytes of the possible, pragmatic Americans for whom survival was method and strategy. We would learn, during our days in the New York State Reconstruction Home, to confront the world that was. We would learn to survive the way we were, with whatever the virus had left intact.

I had fallen away from the body's prowess, but I was being led toward a life measured by different standards. Even as I fantasized about the past, it disappeared. Rehabilitation, I was to learn, was ahistorical, a future devoid of any significant claim on the past. Rehabilitation was a thief's primer of compensation and deception: its purpose was to teach one how to steal a touch of the normal from an existence that would be striking in its abnormality.

When I think back to those two years in the ward, the boy who made his rehabilitation most memorable was Joey Tomashevski. Joey was the son of an upstate dairy farmer, a Polish immigrant who had come to America before the Depression and whose English was even poorer than the English of my own shtetl-bred father. The virus had left both of Joey's arms so lifeless and atrophied that I could circle where his bicep should have been with pinky and thumb and still stick the forefinger of my own hand through. And yet, Joey assumed that he would make do with whatever had been left him. He accepted without question the task of making his toes and feet over into fingers and hands. With lifeless arms encased in a canvas sling that looked like the breadbasket a European peasant might carry to market, Joey would sit up in bed and demonstrate how he could maneuver fork and spoon with his toes.

I would never have dreamed of placing such confidence in my fingers, let alone my toes. I found, as most of the other boys in the ward did, Joey's unabashed pride in the flexibility and control with which he could maneuver a forkful of mashed potatoes into his mouth a continuous indictment of my sense of the world's natural order. We boys with dead legs would gather round his bed in our wheelchairs and silently watch Joey display his dexterity with a vanity so open and naked that it seemed an invitation to being struck down yet again. But Joey's was a vanity already tested by experience. For he was more than willing to accept whatever challenges the virus threw his way. For the sake of demonstrating his skill to us, he kicked a basketball from the auditorium stage through the hoop attached to a balcony some fifty feet away. When one of our number derisively called him lucky, he proceeded to kick five of seven more balls through that same hoop.

I suspect that Joey's pride in his ability to compensate for what had been taken away from him irritated me, because I knew that, before I could pursue my own rehabilitation with such singular passion, I had to surrender myself to what was being demanded of me. And that meant I had to learn to fall. It meant that I had to learn, as Joey Tomashevski had already learned, how to transform absence into opportunity. Even though I still lacked Joey's instinctive willingness to live with the legacy of the virus, I found myself being overhauled, re-created in much the same way as a car engine is rebuilt. Nine months after I arrived in the ward, a few weeks before my twelfth birthday, I was fitted for double long-legged braces bound together by a steel pelvic band circling my waist. Lifeless or not, my legs were precisely measured, the steel carefully molded to form, screws and locks and leather joined to one another for my customized benefit alone. It was technology that would hold me up—another offering on the altar of compensation. "You get what you give," said Jackie Lyons, my closest friend in the ward. For he, too, was now a novitiate of the possible. He, too, now had to learn how to choose the road back.

Falling into life was not a metaphor; it was real, a process learned only through doing, the way a baby learns to crawl, to stand, and then to walk. After the steel bands around calves and thighs and pelvis had been covered over by the rich-smelling leather, after the braces had been precisely fitted to allow my fear-ridden imagination the surety of their holding presence, I was pulled to my feet. For the first time in ten months, I stood. Two middle-aged craftsmen, the hospital bracemakers who worked in a machine shop deep in the basement, held me in place as my therapist wedged two wooden crutches beneath my shoulders.

They stepped back, first making certain that my grip on the crutches was firm. Filled with pride in their technological prowess, the three of them stood in front of me, admiring their skill. Had I been created in the laboratory of Mary Shelley's Dr. Frankenstein, I could not have felt myself any more the creature of scientific pride. I stood on the braces, crutches beneath my shoulders slanting outward like twin towers of Pisa. I flushed, swallowed hard, struggled to keep from crying, struggled not to be overwhelmed by my fear of falling.

My future had arrived. The leather had been fitted, the screws had been turned to the precise millimeter, the locks at the knees and the bushings at the ankles had been properly tested and retested. That very afternoon I was taken for the first time to a cavernous room filled with barbells and Indian clubs and crutches and walkers. I would spend an hour each day there for the next six months. In the rehab room, I would learn how to mount two large wooden steps made to the exact measure of a New York City bus's. I would swing on parallel bars from one side to the other, my arms learning how they would have to hurl me through the world. I balanced Indian clubs like a circus juggler because my therapist insisted it would help my coordination. And I was expected to learn to fall.

I was a dutiful patient. I did as I was told because I could see no advantage to doing anything else. I hungered for the approval of those in authority—doctors, nurses, therapists, the two bracemakers. Again and again, my therapist demonstrated how I was to throw my legs from the hip. Again and again, I did as I was told. Grabbing the banister with my left hand, I threw my leg from the hip while pushing off my right crutch. Like some baby elephant (despite the sweat lost in the heated pool, the months of inactivity in bed had fattened me up considerably), I dangled from side to side on the parallel bars. Grunting with effort, I did everything demanded of me. I did it with an unabashed eagerness to please those who had power over my life. I wanted to put myself at risk. I wanted to do whatever was supposed to be "good" for me. I believed as absolutely as I have ever believed in anything that rehabilitation would finally placate the hunger of the virus.

But when my therapist commanded me to fall, I cringed. For the prospect of falling terrified me. Every afternoon, as I worked through my prescribed activities, I prayed that I would be able to fall when the session ended. Falling was the most essential "good" of all the "goods" held out for my consideration by my therapist. I believed that. I believed it so intensely that the belief itself was painful. Everything else asked of me was given—and given gladly. I mounted the bus stairs, pushed across the parallel bars until my arms ached with the effort, allowed the medicine ball to pummel me, flailed away at the empty air with my fists because my therapist wanted me to rid myself of the tension within. The slightest sign of approval from those in authority was enough to make me puff with pleasure. Other boys in the ward might not have taken rehabilitation seriously, but I was an eager servant cringing before the promise of approval.

Only I couldn't fall. As each session ended, I would be led to the mats that took up a full third of the huge room. "It's time," the therapist would say. Dutifully, I would follow her, step after step. Just as dutifully, I would stand on the edge of those two-inch-thick mats, staring down at them until I could feel my body quiver. "All you have to do is let go," my therapist assured me. "The other boys do it. Just let go and fall."

But the prospect of letting go was precisely what terrified me. That the other boys in the ward had no trouble in falling added to my shame and terror. I didn't need my therapist to tell me the two-inch-thick mats would keep me from hurting myself. I knew there was virtually no chance of injury when I fell, but that knowledge simply made me more ashamed of a cowardice that was as monumental as it was unexplainable. Had it been able to rid me of my sense of my own cowardice, I would happily have settled for bodily harm. But I was being asked to surrender myself to the emptiness of space, to let go and crash down to the mats below, to feel myself suspended in air when nothing stood between me and the vacuum of the world. *That* was the prospect that overwhelmed me. *That* was what left me sweating with rage and humiliation. The contempt I felt was for my own weakness.

I tried to justify what I sensed could never be justified. Why should I be expected to throw myself into emptiness? Was this sullen terror the price of compensation, the badge of normality? Maybe my refusal to fall embodied some deeper thrust than I could then understand. Maybe I had unconsciously seized upon some fundamental resistance to the forces that threatened to overwhelm me. What did it matter that the ground was covered by the thick mats? The tremors I feared were in my heart and soul.

Shame plagued me—and shame is the older brother to disease. Flushing with shame, I would stare down at the mats. I could feel myself wanting to cry out. But I shriveled at the thought of calling more attention to my cowardice. I would finally hear myself whimper, "I'm sorry. But I can't. I can't let go."

Formless emptiness. A rush of air through which I would plummet toward obliteration. As my "normal" past grew more and more distant, I reached for it more and more desperately, recalling it like some movie whose plot has long since been forgotten but whose scenes continue to comfort through images disconnected from anything but themselves. I remembered that there had been a time when the prospect of falling evoked not terror but joy: football games on the rainsoftened autumn turf of Mosholu Parkway, belly-flopping on an American Flyer down its snow-covered slopes in winter, rolling with a pack of friends down one of the steep hills in Bronx Park. Free falls from the past, testifying not to a loss of the self but to an absence of barriers.

My therapist pleaded, ridiculed, cajoled, threatened, bullied. I was sighed over and railed at. But I couldn't let go and fall. I couldn't sell my terror off so cheaply. Ashamed as I was, I wouldn't allow myself to be bullied out of terror.

A month passed—a month of struggle between me and my therapist. Daily excursions to the rehab room, daily practice runs through the future that was awaiting me. The daily humiliation of discovering that one's own fear had been transformed into a public issue, a subject of discussion among the other boys in the ward, seemed unending.

And then, terror simply evaporated. It was as if I had served enough time in that prison. I was ready to move on. One Tuesday afternoon, as my session ended, the therapist walked resignedly alongside me toward the mats. "All right, Leonard. It's time again. All you have to do is let go and fall." Again, I stood above the mats. Only this time, it was as if something beyond my control or understanding had decided to let my body's fall from grace take me down for good. I was not seized by the usual paroxysm of fear. I didn't feel myself break out in a terrified sweat. It was over.

I don't mean that I suddenly felt myself spring into courage. That wasn't what happened at all. The truth was I had simply been worn down into letting go, like a boxer in whose eyes one recognizes not the flicker of defeat—that issue never having been in doubt—but the acceptance of defeat. Letting go no longer held my imagination captive. I found myself quite suddenly faced with a necessary fall—a fall into life.

So it was that I stood above the mat and heard myself sigh and then felt myself let go, dropping through the quiet air, crutches slipping off to the sides. What I didn't feel this time was the threat of my body slipping into emptiness, so mummified by the terror before it that the touch of air pre-empted even death. I dropped. I did not crash. I dropped. I did not collapse. I dropped. I did not plummet. I felt myself enveloped by a curiously gentle moment in my life. In that sliver of time before I hit the mat, I was kissed by space.

My body absorbed the slight shock and I rolled onto my back, braced legs swinging like unguided missiles into the free air, crutches dropping away to the sides. Even as I fell through the air, I could sense the shame and fear drain from my soul, and I knew that my sense of my own cowardice would soon follow. In falling, I had given myself a new start, a new life.

"That's it!" my therapist triumphantly shouted. "You let go! And there it is!"

You let go! And there it is! Yes, and you discover not terror but the only self you are going to be allowed to claim anyhow. You fall free, and then you learn that those padded mats hold not courage but the unclaimed self. And if it turned out to be not the most difficult of tasks, did that make my sense of jubilation any less?

From that moment, I gloried in my ability to fall. Falling became an end in itself. I lost sight of what my therapist had desperately been trying to demonstrate for me—that there was a purpose in learning how to fall. For she wanted to teach me through the fall what I would have to face in the future. She wanted to give me a wholeness I could not give myself. For she knew that mine would be a future so different from what confronts the "normal" that I had to learn to fall into life in order not to be overwhelmed.

From that day, she urged me to practice falling as if I were a religious disciple being urged by a master to practice spiritual discipline. Letting go meant allowing my body to float into space, to turn at the direction of the fall and follow the urgings of emptiness. For her, learning to fall was learning the most essential of American lessons: how to turn incapacity into capacity.

"You were afraid of hurting yourself," she explained to me. "But that's the beauty of it. When you let go, you can't hurt yourself."

An echo of the streets and playgrounds I called home until I met the virus. American slogans: go with the flow, roll with the punch, slide with the threat until it is no longer a threat. They were simply slogans, and they were all intended to create strength from weakness, a veritable world's fair of compensation.

I returned to the city a year later. By that time, I was a willing convert, one who now secretly enjoyed demonstrating his ability to fall. I enjoyed the surprise that would greet me as I got to my feet, unscathed and undamaged. However perverse it may seem, I felt a certain pleasure when, as I walked with a friend, I felt a crutch slip out of my grasp. Watching the thrust of concern darken his features, I felt myself in control of my own capacity. For falling had become the way my body sought out its proper home. It was an earthbound body, and mine would be an earthbound life. My quest would be for the solid ground beneath me. Falling with confidence, I fell away from terror and fear.

Of course, some falls took me unawares, and I found myself letting go too late or too early. Bruised in ego and sometimes in body, I would pull myself to my feet to consider what had gone wrong. Yet I was essentially untroubled. Such defeats were part of the game, even when they confined me to bed for a day or two afterward. I was an accountant of pain, and sometimes heavier payment was demanded. In my mid-thirties, I walked my two-year-old son's babysitter home, tripped on the curbstone, and broke my wrist. At forty-eight, an awkward fall triggered by a carelessly unlocked brace sent me smashing against the bathtub and into surgery for a broken femur. It took four months for me to learn to walk on the crutches all over again. But I learned. I already knew how to fall.

I knew such accidents could be handled. After all, pain was not synonymous with mortality. In fact, pain was insurance against an excessive consciousness of mortality. Pain might validate the specific moment in time, but it didn't have very much to do with the future. I did not yet believe that falling into life had anything to do with falling into death. It was simply a way for me to exercise control over my own existence.

It seems to me today that, when I first let my body fall to those mats, I was somehow giving myself the endurance I would need to survive in this world. In a curious way, falling became a way of celebrating what I had lost. My legs were lifeless, useless, but their loss had created a dancing image in whose shadowy gyrations I recognized a strange but potentially interesting new self. I would survive. I knew that now. I could let go, I could fall, and, best of all, I could get up.

To create an independent self, a man had to rid himself of both the myths that nurtured him and the myths that held him back. Learning to fall had been the first lesson in how I yet might live successfully as a cripple. Even disease had its inviolate principles. I understood that the most dangerous threat to the sense of self I needed was an inflated belief in my own capacity. Falling rid a man of excess baggage; it taught him how each of us is dependent on balance.

But what really gave falling legitimacy was the knowledge that I could get to my feet again. That was what taught me the rules of survival. As long as I could pick myself up and stand on my own two feet, brace-bound and crutch-propped as I was, the fall testified to my ability to live in the here and now, to stake my claim as an American who had turned incapacity into capacity. For such a man, falling might well be considered the language of everyday achievement.

But the day came, as I knew it must come, when I could no longer pick myself up. It was then that my passion for symmetry in endings began. On that day, spurred on by another fall, I found myself spinning into the inevitable future.

The day was actually a rainy night in November of 1983. I had just finished teaching at the City College Center for Worker Education, an off-campus degree program for working adults, and had joined some friends for dinner. All of us, I remember, were in a jovial, celebratory mood, although I no longer remember what it was we were celebrating. Perhaps it was simply the satisfaction of being good friends and colleagues at dinner together.

We ate in a Spanish restaurant on Fourteenth Street in Manhattan. It was a dinner that took on, for me at least, the intensity of a time that would assume greater and greater significance as I grew older, one of those watershed moments writers are so fond of. In the dark, rain-swept New York night, change and possibility seemed to drift like a thick fog all around us.

Our mood was still convivial when we left the restaurant around eleven. The rain had slackened off to a soft drizzle and the street glistened beneath the play of light on the wet black creosote. At night, rain in the city has a way of transforming proportion into optimism. The five of us stood around on the slicked-down sidewalk, none of us willing to be the first to break the richness of the mood by leaving.

Suddenly, the crutch in my left hand began to slip out from under me, slowly, almost deliberately, as if the crutch had a mind of its own and had not yet made the commitment that would send me down. Apparently, I had hit a slick patch of city sidewalk, some nub of concrete worn smooth as medieval stone by thousands of shoppers and panhandlers and tourists and students who daily pounded the bargain hustlings of Fourteenth Street.

Instinctively, I at first tried to fight the fall, to seek for balance by pushing off from the crutch in my right hand. But as I recognized that the fall was inevitable, I simply went slack—and for the thousandth time my body sought vindication in its ability to let go and drop. These good friends had seen me fall before. They knew my childish vanities, understood that I still thought of falling as a way to demonstrate my control of the traps and uncertainties that lay in wait for us all.

Thirty-eight years earlier, I had discovered that I could fall into life simply by letting go. Now I made a different discovery—that I could no longer get to my feet by myself. I hit the wet ground and quickly turned over and pushed up, trying to use one of the crutches as a prop to boost myself to my feet, as I had been taught to do as a boy of twelve.

But try as hard as I could, I couldn't get to my feet. It wasn't that I lacked physical strength. I knew that my arms were as powerful as ever as I pushed down on the wet concrete. It had nothing to do with the fact that the street was wet, as my friends insisted later. No, it had to do with a subtle, if mysterious, change in my own sense of rhythm and balance. My body had decided—*and decided on its own, autonomously*—that the moment had come for me to face the question of endings. It was the body that chose its time of recognition.

It was, it seems to me now, a distinctively American moment. It left me pondering limitations and endings and summations. It left me with the curiously buoyant sense that mortality had quite suddenly made itself a felt presence rather than the rhetorical strategy used by the poets and novelists I taught to my students. This was what writers had in mind when they spoke of the truly common fate, this sense of ending coming to one unbidden. This had brought with it my impassioned quest for symmetry. As I lay on the wet ground—no more than a minute or two—all I could think of was how much I wanted my life to balance out. It was as if I were staring into a future in which time itself had evaporated.

Here was a clear, simple perception, and there was nothing mystical about it. There are limitations we recognize and those that recognize us. My friends, who had nervously been standing around while I tried to get to my feet, finally asked if they could help me up. "You'll have to," I said. "I can't get up any other way."

Two of them pulled me to my feet while another jammed the crutches beneath my arms, as the therapist and the two bracemakers had done almost four decades earlier. When I was standing, they proceeded to joke about my sudden incapacity in that age-old way men of all ages have, as if words might codify loss and change and time's betrayal. I joined in the joking. But what I really wanted was to go home and contemplate this latest fall in the privacy of my apartment. The implications were clear: I would never again be an eater of salt, I would also never again get to my feet on my own. A part of my life had ended. But that didn't depress me. In fact, I felt almost as exhilarated as I had thirty-eight years earlier, when my body surrendered to the need to let go and I fell into life.

Almost four years have passed since I fell on the wet sidewalk of Fourteenth Street. I suppose it wasn't a particularly memorable fall. It wasn't even particularly significant to anyone who had not once fallen into life. But it was inevitable, the first time I had let go into a time when it would no longer even be necessary to let go.

It was a fall that left me with the knowledge that I could no longer pick myself up. That meant I now needed the help of others as I had not needed their help before. It was a fall that left me burning with this strange passion for symmetry, this desire to balance my existence out. When the day comes, I want to be able to fall into my death as nakedly as I once had to fall into my life.

Do not misunderstand me. I am not seeking a way out of mortality, for I believe in nothing more strongly than I believe in the permanency of endings. I am not looking for a way out of this life, a life I continue to find immensely enjoyable— even if I can no longer pull myself to my own two feet. Of course, a good deal in my life has changed. For one thing, I am increasingly impatient with those who claim to have no use for endings of any sort. I am also increasingly embarrassed by the thought of the harshly critical adolescent I was, self-righteously convinced that the only way for a man to go to his end was by kicking and screaming.

But these are, I suppose, the kinds of changes any man or woman of forty or fifty would feel. Middle-aged skepticism is as natural as adolescent acne. In my clearer, less passionate moments, I can even laugh at my need for symmetry in beginnings and endings as well as my desire to see my own eventual death as a line running parallel to my life. Even in mathematics, let alone life, symmetry is sometimes too neat, too closed off from the way things actually work. After all, it took me a full month before I could bring myself to let go and fall into life.

I no longer talk about how one can seize a doctrine of compensation from disease. I don't talk about it, but it still haunts me. In my heart, I believe it offers a man the only philosophy by which he can actually live. It is the only philosophy that strips away both spiritual mumbo jumbo and the procrustean weight of existential anxiety. In the final analysis, a man really is what a man does.

Believing as I do, I wonder why I so often find myself trying to frame a perspective that will prove adequate to a proper sense of ending. Perhaps that is why I find myself sitting in a bar with a friend, trying to explain to him all that I have learned from falling. "There must be a time," I hear myself tell him, "when a man has the right to stop thinking about falling."

"Sure," my friend laughs. "Four seconds before he dies."

Considerations

Thinking

What does it mean in a more normal life than that of Kriegel's boyhood to organize one's needs "around whatever illusions were available." In what ways was that necessity of Kriegel's every adolescent's necessity?

What do you think Kriegel means when he says that his friend Jackie Lyons was a "novitiate of the possible"?

Why do you suppose it was more difficult for Kriegel than for the other boys simply to "surrender [himself] to the emptiness of space," to let himself fall onto those protective mats?

What do you think of the paradox of a fortunate fall? Do you think that falls often serve as a prelude to a newfound life?

Connecting

Why do you suppose Kriegel includes the story about Joey Tomashevski, the boy who was so nimble with his toes? How does his appearance in the essay help Kriegel develop his idea about falling?

Recount some moment in your own life when you were, as Kriegel was, "kissed by space"—when you finally let go and experienced something on the other side of dread.

How do you account for Kriegel's passion for symmetry? How do you suppose the fall into death will somehow balance out that earlier fall into life?

Writing

Write an essay about rehabilitation—its meaning and its application, from your perspective.

Kriegel seems primarily concerned about telling the story of learning to fall, although he attaches to that story, almost from the outset, an evolving concern, a story if you will, about falling into death. Write a three-page account of the various ideas that grow out of those two stories, along with your sense of how those ideas about life and death fit together in this essay.

Barry Lopez
(b. 1945)

Barry Lopez—born in New York, raised in southern California, educated at the University of Notre Dame—has taught at the University of Iowa and at Carlton College and served as an editor at *Harper's* and the *North American Review*. Lopez is best known as a writer whose passionate commitment to history and preservation has brought him into touch with knowledge often hidden from those who fail to see how our ideas and our perceptions are gifts bestowed on us by a world that reveals its secrets only when we have the patience, interest, and experience to discern them. His books include *Of Wolves and Men, Artic Dreams, Crossing Open Ground, Coyote Love,* and *The Rediscovery of North America.* He has received the John Burroughs Medal and an award in literature from the American Academy and Institute of Arts and Letters.

"The Stone Horse" recounts a moment of awareness, when Lopez was able to feel intensely and then reflect on his own (our own) connection with a past that is in danger of slipping away from us; he was moved by a stone horse.

The Stone Horse

I

The deserts of southern California, the high, relatively cooler and wetter Mojave and the hotter, dryer Sonoran to the south of it, carry the signatures of many cultures. Prehistoric rock drawings in the Mojave's Coso Range, probably the greatest concentration of petroglyphs in North America, are at least three thousand years old. Big-game-hunting cultures that flourished six or seven thousand years before that are known from broken spear tips, choppers, and burins left scattered along the shores of great Pleistocene lakes, long since evaporated. Weapons and tools discovered at China Lake may be thirty thousand years old; and worked stone from a quarry in the Calico Mountains is, some argue, evidence that human beings were here more than 200,000 years ago.

Because of the long-term stability of such arid environments, much of this prehistoric stone evidence still lies exposed on the ground, accessible to anyone who passes by—the studious, the acquisitive, the indifferent, the merely curious. Archaeologists do not agree on the sequence of cultural history beyond about twelve thousand years ago, but it is clear that these broken bits of chalcedony, chert, and obsidian, like the animal drawings and geometric designs etched on walls of basalt throughout the desert, anchor the earliest threads of human history, the first record of human endeavor here.

Western man did not enter the California desert until the end of the eighteenth century, 250 years after Coronado brought his soldiers into the Zuni pueblos in a bewildered search for the cities of Cibola. The earliest appraisals of the land were cursory, hurried. People traveled *through* it, en route to Santa Fe or the California coastal settlements. Only miners tarried. In 1823 what had been Spain's became Mexico's, and in 1848 what had been Mexico's became America's; but the bare, jagged mountains and dry lake beds, the vast and uniform plains of creosote bush and yucca plants, remained as obscure as the northern Sudan until the end of the nineteenth century.

Before 1940 the tangible evidence of twentieth-century man's passage here consisted of very little—the hard tracery of travel corridors; the widely scattered, relatively insignificant evidence of mining operations; and the fair expanse of irrigated fields at the desert's periphery. In the space of a hundred years or so the wagon roads were paved, railroads were laid down, and canals and high-tension lines were built to bring water and electricity across the desert to Los Angeles from the Colorado River. The dark mouths of gold, talc, and tin mines yawned from the bony flanks of desert ranges. Dust-encrusted chemical plants stood at work on the lonely edges of dry lake beds. And crops of grapes, lettuce, dates, alfalfa, and cotton covered the Coachella and Imperial valleys, north and south of the Salton Sea, and the Palo Verde Valley along the Colorado.

These developments proceeded with little or no awareness of earlier human occupations by cultures that preceded those of the historic Indians—the Mohave, the Chemehuevi, the Quechan. (Extensive irrigation began actually to change the climate of the Sonoran Desert, and human settlements, the railroads, and farming introduced many new, successful plants into the region.)

During World War II, the American military moved into the desert in great force, to train troops and to test equipment. They found the clear weather conducive to year-round flying, the dry air and isolation very attractive. After the war, a complex of training grounds, storage facilities, and gunnery and test ranges was permanently settled on more than three million acres of military reservations. Few perceived the extent or significance of the destruction of the aboriginal sites that took place during tank maneuvers and bombing runs or in the laying out of highways, railroads, mining districts, and irrigated fields. The few who intuited that something like an American Dordogne Valley lay exposed here were (only) amateur archaeologists; even they reasoned that the desert was too vast for any of this to matter.

After World War II, people began moving out of the crowded Los Angeles basin into homes in Lucerne, Apple, and Antelope valleys in the western Mojave. They emigrated as well to a stretch of resort land at the foot of the San Jacinto Mountains that included Palm Springs, and farther out to old railroad and military towns like Twentynine Palms and Barstow. People also began exploring the desert, at first in military-surplus jeeps and then with a variety of all-terrain and off-road vehicles that became available in the 1960s. By the mid-1970s, the number of people using such vehicles for desert recreation had increased exponentially. Most came and went in innocent curiosity; the few who didn't wreaked a havoc all out of proportion to their numbers. The disturbance of previously isolated archaeological sites increased by an order of magnitude. Many sites were vandalized before archaeologists, themselves late to the desert, had any firm grasp of the bounds of human history in the desert. It was as though in the same moment an Aztec library had been discovered intact various lacunae had begun to appear.

The vandalism was of three sorts: the general disturbance usually caused by souvenir hunters and by the curious and the oblivious; the wholesale stripping of a place by professional thieves for black-market sale and trade; and outright destruction, in which vehicles were actually used to ram and trench an area. By 1980, the Bureau of Land Management estimated that probably 35 percent of the archaeological sites in the desert had been vandalized. The destruction at some places by rifles and shotguns, or by power winches mounted on vehicles, was, if one cared for history, demoralizing to behold.

In spite of public education, land closures, and stricter law enforcement in recent years, the BLM estimates that, annually, about 1 percent of the archaeological record in the desert continues to be destroyed or stolen.

II

A BLM archaeologist told me, with understandable reluctance, where to find the intaglio. I spread my Automobile Club of Southern California map of Imperial County out on his desk, and he traced the route with a pink felt-tip pen. The line crossed Interstate 8 and then turned west along the Mexican border.

"You can't drive any farther than about here," he said, marking a small X. "There's boulders in the wash. You walk up past them."

On a separate piece of paper he drew a route in a smaller scale that would take me up the arroyo to a certain point where I was to cross back east, to another arroyo. At its head, on higher ground just to the north, I would find the horse.

"It's tough to spot unless you know it's there. Once you pick it up . . ." He shook his head slowly, in a gesture of wonder at its existence.

I waited until I held his eye. I assured him I would not tell anyone else how to get there. He looked at me with stoical despair, like a man who had been robbed twice, whose belief in human beings was offered without conviction.

I did not go until the following day because I wanted to see it at dawn. I ate breakfast at four A.M. in El Centro and then drove south. The route was easy to follow, though the last section of road proved difficult, broken and drifted over with sand in some spots. I came to the barricade of boulders and parked. It was light enough by then to find my way over the ground with little trouble. The contours of the landscape were stark, without any masking vegetation. I worried only about rattlesnakes.

I traversed the stone plain as directed, but, in spite of the frankness of the land, I came on the horse unawares. In the first moment of recognition I was without feeling. I recalled later being startled, and that I held my breath. It was laid out on the ground with its head to the east, three times life size. As I took in its outline I felt a growing concentration of all my senses, as though my attentiveness to the pale rose color of the morning sky and other peripheral images had now ceased to be important. I was aware that I was straining for sound in the windless air, and I felt the uneven pressure of the earth hard against my feet. The horse, outlined in a standing profile on the dark ground, was as vivid before me as a bed of tulips.

I've come upon animals suddenly before, and felt a similar tension, a precipitate heightening of the senses. And I have felt the inexplicable but sharply boosted intensity of a wild moment in the bush, where it is not until some minutes later that you discover the source of electricity—the warm remains of a grizzly bear kill, or the still moist tracks of a wolverine.

But this was slightly different. I felt I had stepped into an unoccupied corridor. I had no familiar sense of history, the temporal structure in which to think: This horse was made by Quechan people three hundred years ago. I felt instead a headlong rush of images: people hunting wild horses with spears on the Pleistocene veld of southern California; Cortés riding across the causeway into Montezuma's Tenochtitlán; a short-legged Comanche, astride his horse like some sort of ferret, slashing through cavalry lines of young men who rode like farmers; a hood exploding past my face one morning in a corral in Wyoming. These images had the weight and silence of stone.

When I released my breath, the images softened. My initial feeling, of facing a wild animal in a remote region, was replaced with a calm sense of antiquity. It was then that I became conscious, like an ordinary tourist, of what was before me, and thought: this horse was probably laid out by Quechan people. But when? I wondered. The first horses they saw, I knew, might have been those that came north from Mexico in 1692 with Father Eusebio Kino. But Cocopa people, I recalled, also came this far north on occasion, to fight with their neighbors, the Quechan. And *they* could have seen horses with Melchior Díaz, at the mouth of the Colorado River in the fall of 1540. So, it could be four hundred years old. (No one in fact knows.)

I still had not moved. I took my eyes off the horse for a moment to look south over the desert plain into Mexico, to look east past its head at the brightening sunrise, to situate myself. Then, finally, I brought my trailing foot slowly forward and stood erect. Sunlight was running like a thin sheet of water over the stony ground and it threw the horse into relief. It looked as though no hand had ever disturbed the stones that gave it its form.

The horse had been brought to life on ground called desert pavement, a tight, flat matrix of small cobbles blasted smooth by sand-laden winds. The uniform, monochromatic blackness of the stones, a patina of iron and magnesium oxides called desert varnish, is caused by long-term exposure to the sun. To make this type of low-relief ground glyph, or intaglio, the artist either selectively turns individual stones over to their lighter side or removes areas of stone to expose the lighter soil underneath, creating a negative image. This horse, about eighteen feet from brow to rump and eight feet from withers to hoof, had been made in the latter way, and its outline was bermed at certain points with low ridges of stone a few inches high to enhance its three-dimensional qualities. (The left side of the horse was in full profile; each leg was extended at 90 degrees to the body and fully visible, as though seen in three-quarter profile.)

I was not eager to move. The moment I did I would be back in the flow of time, the horse no longer quivering in the same way before me. I did not want to feel again the sequence of quotidian events—to be drawn off into deliberation and analysis. A human being, a four-footed animal, the open land. That was all that was present—and a "thoughtless" understanding of the very old desires bearing on this particular animal: to hunt it, to render it, to fathom it, to subjugate it, to honor it, to take it as a companion.

What finally made me move was the light. The sun now filled the shallow basin of the horse's body. The weighted line of the stone berm created the illusion of a mane and the distinctive roundness of an equine belly. The change in definition impelled me. I moved to the left, circling past its rump, to see how the light might flesh the horse out from various points of view. I circled it completely before squatting on my haunches. Ten or fifteen minutes later I chose another view. The third time I moved, to a point near the rear hooves, I spotted a stone tool at my feet. I stared at it a long while, more in awe than disbelief, before reaching out to pick it up. I turned it over in my left palm and took it between my fingers to feel its cutting edge. It is always difficult, especially with something so portable, to rechannel the desire to steal.

I spent several hours with the horse. As I changed positions and as the angle of the light continued to change I noticed a number of things. The angle at which the pastern carried the hoof away from the ankle was perfect. Also, stones had been placed within the image to suggest at precisely the right spot the left shoulder above the foreleg. The line that joined thigh and hock was similarly accurate. The muzzle alone seemed distorted—but perhaps these stones had been moved by a later hand. It was an admirably accurate representation, but not what a breeder would call perfect conformation. There was the suggestion of a bowed neck and an undershot jaw, and the tail, as full as a winter coyote's, did not appear to be precisely to scale.

The more I thought about it, the more I felt I was looking at an individual horse, a unique combination of generic and specific detail. It was easy to imagine one of Kino's horses as a model, or a horse that ran off from one of Coronado's columns. What kind of horses would these have been? I wondered. In the sixteenth century the most sought-after horses in Europe were Spanish, the offspring of Arabian stock and Barbary horses that the Moors brought to Iberia and bred to the older, eastern European strains brought in by the Romans. The model for this horse, I speculated, could easily have been a palomino, or a descendant of horses trained for lion hunting in North Africa.

A few generations ago, cowboys, cavalry quartermasters, and draymen would have taken this horse before me under consideration and not let up their scrutiny until they had its heritage fixed to their satisfaction. Today, the distinction between draft and harness horses is arcane knowledge, and no image may come to mind for a blue roan or a claybank horse. The loss of such refinement in everyday conversation leaves me unsettled. People praise the Eskimo's ability to distinguish among forty types of snow but forget the skill of others who routinely differentiate between overo and tobiano pintos. Such distinctions are made for the same reason. You have to do it to be able to talk clearly about the world.

For parts of two years I worked as a horse wrangler and packer in Wyoming. It is dim knowledge now; I would have to think to remember if a buckskin was a kind of dun horse. And I couldn't throw a double-diamond hitch over a set of panniers—the packer's basic tie-down—without guidance. As I squatted there in the desert, however, these more personal memories seemed tenuous in comparison with the sweep of this animal in human time. My memories had no depth. I thought of the Hittite cavalry riding against the Syrians 3,500 years ago. And the first of the Chinese emperors, Ch'in Shih Huang, buried in Shensi Province in 210 B.C. with thousands of life-size horses and soldiers, a terra-cotta guardian army. What could I know of what was in the mind of whoever made this horse? Was there some racial memory of it as an animal that had once fed the artist's ancestors and then disappeared from North America? And then returned in this strange alliance with another race of men?

Certainly, whoever it was, the artist had observed the animal very closely. Certainly the animal's speed had impressed him. Among the first things the Quechan would have learned from an encounter with Kino's horses was that their own long-distance runners—men who could run down mule deer—were no match for this animal.

From where I squatted I could look far out over the Mexican plain. Juan Bautista de Anza passed this way in 1774, extending El Camino Real into Alta California from Sinaloa. He was followed by others, all of them astride the magical horse; *gente de razón,* the people of reason, coming into the country of *los primitivos.* The horse, like the stone animals of Egypt, urged these memories upon me. And as I drew them up from some forgotten corner of my mind—huge horses carved in the white chalk downs of southern England by an Iron Age people; Spanish horses rearing and wheeling in fear before alligators in Florida—the images seemed tethered before me. With this sense of proportion, a memory of my own—the morning I almost lost my face to a horse's hoof—now had somewhere to fit.

I rose up and began to walk slowly around the horse again. I had taken the first long measure of it and was now looking for a way to depart, a new angle of light, a fading of the image itself before the rising sun, that would break its hold on me. As I circled, feeling both heady and serene at the encounter, I realized again how strangely vivid it was. It had been created on a barren bajada between two arroyos, as nondescript a place as one could imagine. The only plant life here was a few wands of ocotillo cactus. The ground beneath my shoes was so hard it wouldn't take the print of a heavy animal even after a rain. The only sounds I heard here were the voices of quail.

The archaeologist had been correct. For all its forcefulness, the horse is inconspicuous. If you don't care to see it you can walk right past it. That pleases him, I think. Unmarked on the bleak shoulder of the plain, the site signals to no one; so he wants no protective fences here, no informative plaque, to act as beacons. He would rather take a chance that no motorcyclist, no aimless wanderer with a flair for violence and a depth of ignorance, will ever find his way here.

The archaeologist had given me something before I left his office that now seemed peculiar—an aerial photograph of the horse. It is widely believed that an aerial view of an intaglio provides a fair and accurate depiction. It does not. In the photograph the horse looks somewhat crudely constructed; from the ground it appears far more deftly rendered. The photograph is of a single moment, and in that split second the horse seems vaguely impotent. I watched light pool in the intaglio at dawn; I imagine you could watch it withdraw at dusk and sense the same animation I did. In those prolonged moments its shape and so, too, its general character changed—noticeably. The living quality of the image, its immediacy to the eye, was brought out by the light-in-time, not, at least here, in the camera's frozen instant.

Intaglios, I thought, were never meant to be seen by gods in the sky above. They were meant to be seen by people on the ground, over a long period of shifting light. This could even be true of the huge figures on the Plain of Nazca in Peru, where people could walk for the length of a day beside them. It is our own impatience that leads us to think otherwise.

This process of abstraction, almost unintentional, drew me gradually away from the horse. I came to a position of attention at the edge of the sphere of its influence. With a slight bow I paid my respects to the horse, its maker, and the history of us all, and departed.

III

A short distance away I stopped the car in the middle of the road to make a few notes. I could not write down what I was thinking when I was with the horse. It would have seemed disrespectful, and it would have required another kind of attention. So now I patiently drained my memory of the details it had fastened itself upon. The road I'd stopped on was adjacent to the All American Canal, the major source of water for the Imperial and Coachella valleys. The water flowed west placidly. A disjointed flock of coots, small, dark birds with white bills, was paddling against the current, foraging in the rushes.

I was peripherally aware of the birds as I wrote, the only movement in the desert, and of a series of sounds from a village a half-mile away. The first sounds from this collection of ramshackle houses in a grove of cottonwoods were the distracted dawn voices of dogs. I heard them intermingled with the cries of a rooster. Later, the high-pitched voices of children calling out to each other came disembodied through the dry desert air. Now, a little after seven, I could hear someone practicing on the trumpet, the same rough phrases played over and over. I suddenly remembered how as children we had tried to get the rhythm of a galloping horse with hands against our thighs, or by fluttering our tongues against the roofs of our mouths.

After the trumpet, the impatient calls of adults summoning children. Sunday morning. Wood smoke hung like a lens in the trees. The first car starts—a cold eight-cylinder engine, of Chrysler extraction perhaps, goosed to life, then throttled back to murmur through dual mufflers, the obbligato music of a shade-tree mechanic. The rote bark of mongrel dogs at dawn, the jagged outcries of men and women, an engine coming to life. Like a thousand villages from West Virginia to Guadalajara.

I finished my notes—where was I going to find a description of the horses that came north with the conquistadors? Did their manes come forward prominently over the brow, like this one's, like the forelocks of Blackfeet and Assiniboin men in nineteenth-century paintings? I set the notes on the seat beside me.

The road followed the canal for a while and then arced north, toward Interstate 8. It was slow driving and I fell to thinking how the desert had changed since Anza had come through. New plants and animals—the MacDougall cottonwood, the English house sparrow, the chukar from India—have about them now the air of the native born. Of the native species, some—no one knows how many—are extinct. The populations of many others, especially the animals, have been sharply reduced. The idea of a desert impoverished by agricultural poisons and varmint hunters, by off-road vehicles and military operations, did not seem as disturbing to me, however, as this other horror, now that I had been those hours with the horse. The vandals, the few who crowbar rock art off the desert's walls, who dig up graves, who punish the ground that holds intaglios, are people who devour history. Their self-centered scorn, their disrespect for ideas and images beyond their ken, create the awful atmosphere of loose ends in which totalitarianism thrives, in which the past is merely curious or wrong.

I thought about the horse sitting out there on the unprotected plain. I enumerated its qualities in my mind until a sense of its vulnerability receded and it became an anchor for something else. I remembered that history, a history like this one, which ran deeper than Mexico, deeper than the Spanish, was a kind of medicine. It permitted the great breadth of human expression to reverberate, and it did not urge you to locate its apotheosis in the present.

Each of us, individuals and civilizations, has been held upside down like Achilles in the River Styx. The artist mixing his colors in the dim light of Altamira; an Egyptian ruler lying still now, wrapped in his byssus, stored against time in a pyramid; the faded Dorset culture of the Arctic; the Hmong and Samburu and Walbiri of historic time; the modern nations. This great, imperfect stretch of human expression is the clarification and encouragement, the urging and the reminder, we call history. And it is inscribed everywhere in the face of the land, from the mountain passes of the Himalayas to a nameless bajada in the California desert.

Small birds rose up in the road ahead, startled, and flew off. I prayed no infidel would ever find that horse.

Considerations

Thinking

How does the horse serve as a "kind of medicine" for Lopez? How can it be medicinal for the rest of us? What is our illness?

What is an intaglio? Does Lopez manage to convince you that a photograph of an intaglio might not be good enough to give you a sense of the thing itself?

Connecting

Read the entire essay a second time, looking for what Lopez reveals about the nature and the power of images. Codify it.

How can Loren Eiseley's "The Dance of the Frogs" help you understand the relationship between Lopez and that image of the horse, or should we say, between Lopez and the horse?

Writing

Write a two- or three-page analysis of the way in which the three parts of the essay— the historical section, the actual encounter with the horse, and the reflective aftermath— work together to reveal Lopez's central idea.

Write an essay explaining how Lopez "reads" the horse, how he first pushes reflections out of the way as he stands in the presence of the horse and then, later, brings historical knowledge to bear on what he has experienced.

Nancy Mairs
(b. 1943)

Nancy Mairs is a teacher, essayist, and prize-winning poet who has also worked as a technical editor at the Smithsonian Astrophysical Observatory, the MIT Press, and the Harvard Law School. Her books include *Plaintext, Carnal Acts, Remembering the Bone House* (autobiography), and *All the Rooms of the Yellow House* (poems).

In "On Being a Cripple," Mairs describes her struggle with multiple sclerosis. She raises important questions about what those with disabling diseases wish to call themselves and how they wish others to describe them. One especially striking feature of this essay is its honesty, particularly its concern with using language that accurately characterizes Mairs's physical condition.

On Being a Cripple

To escape is nothing. Not to escape is nothing.

— LOUISE BOGAN

The other day I was thinking of writing an essay on being a cripple. I was thinking hard in one of the stalls of the women's room in my office building, as I was shoving my shirt into my jeans and tugging up my zipper. Preoccupied, I flushed, picked up my book bag, took my cane down from the hook, and unlatched the door. So many movements unbalanced me, and as I pulled the door open I fell over backward, landing fully clothed on the toilet seat with my legs splayed in front of me: the old beetle-on-its-back routine. Saturday afternoon, the building deserted, I was free to laugh aloud as I wriggled back to my feet, my voice bouncing off the yellowish tiles from all directions. Had anyone been there with me, I'd have been still and faint and hot with chagrin. I decided that it was high time to write the essay.

First, the matter of semantics. I am a cripple. I choose this word to name me. I choose from among several possibilities, the most common of which are "handicapped" and "disabled." I made the choice a number of years ago, without thinking, unaware of my motives for doing so. Even now, I'm not sure what those motives are, but I recognize that they are complex and not entirely flattering. People—crippled or not—wince at the word "cripple," as they do not at "handicapped" or "disabled." Perhaps I want them to wince. I want them to see me as a tough customer, one to whom the fates/gods/viruses have not been kind, but who can face the brutal truth of her existence squarely. As a cripple, I swagger.

But, to be fair to myself, a certain amount of honesty underlies my choice. "Cripple" seems to me a clean word, straightforward and precise. It has an honorable history, having made its first appearance in the Lindisfarne Gospel in the tenth century. As a lover of words, I like the accuracy with which it describes my condition: I have lost the full use of my limbs. "Disabled," by contrast, suggests any incapacity, physical or mental. And I certainly don't like "handicapped," which implies that I have deliberately been put at a disadvantage, by whom I can't imagine (my God is not a Handicapper General), in order to equalize chances in the great race of life. These words seem to me to be moving away from my condition, to be widening the gap between word and reality. Most remote is the recently coined euphemism "differently abled," which partakes of the same semantic hopefulness that transformed countries from "undeveloped" to "underdeveloped," then to "less developed," and finally to "developing" nations. People have continued to starve in those countries during the shift. Some realities do not obey the dictates of language.

Mine is one of them. Whatever you call me, I remain crippled. But I don't care what you call me, so long as it isn't "differently abled," which strikes me as pure verbal garbage designed, by its ability to describe anyone, to describe no one. I subscribe to George Orwell's thesis that "the slovenliness of our language makes it easier for us to have foolish thoughts." And I refuse to participate in the degeneration of the language to the extent that I deny that I have lost anything in the course of this calamitous disease; I refuse to pretend that the only differences between you and me are the various ordinary ones that distinguish any one person from another. But call me "disabled" or "handicapped" if you like. I have long since grown accustomed to them; and if they are vague, at least they hint at the truth. Moreover, I use them myself. Society is no readier to accept crippledness than to accept death, war, sex, sweat, or wrinkles. I would never refer to another person as a cripple. It is the word I use to name only myself.

I haven't always been crippled, a fact for which I am soundly grateful. To be whole of limb is, I know from experience, infinitely more pleasant and useful than to be crippled; and if that knowledge leaves me open to bitterness at my loss, the physical soundness I once enjoyed (though I did not enjoy it half enough) is well worth the occasional stab of regret. Though never any good at sports, I was a normally active child and young adult. I climbed trees, played hopscotch, jumped rope, skated, swam, rode my bicycle, sailed. I despised team sports, spending some of the wretchedest afternoons of my life, sweaty and humiliated, behind a field-hockey stick and under a basketball hoop. I tramped alone for miles along the bridle paths that webbed the woods behind the house I grew up in. I swayed through countless dim hours in the arms of one man or another under the scattered shot of light from mirrored balls, and gyrated through countless more as Tab Hunter and Johnny Mathis gave way to the Rolling Stones, Creedence Clearwater Revival, Cream. I walked down the aisle. I pushed baby carriages, changed tires in the rain, marched for peace.

When I was twenty-eight I started to trip and drop things. What at first seemed my natural clumsiness soon became too pronounced to shrug off. I consulted a neurologist, who told me that I had a brain tumor. A battery of tests, increasingly disagreeable, revealed no tumor. About a year and a half later I developed a blurred spot in one eye. I had, at last, the episodes "disseminated in space and time" requisite for a diagnosis: multiple sclerosis. I have never been sorry for the doctor's initial misdiagnosis, however. For almost a week, until the negative results of the tests were in, I thought that I was going to die right away. Every day for the past nearly ten years, then, has been a kind of gift. I accept all gifts.

Multiple sclerosis is a chronic degenerative disease of the central nervous system, in which the myelin that sheathes the nerves is somehow eaten away and scar tissue forms in its place, interrupting the nerves' signals. During its course, which is unpredictable and uncontrollable, one may lose vision, hearing, speech, the ability to walk, control of bladder and/or bowels, strength in any or all extremities, sensitivity to touch, vibration, and/or pain, potency, coordination of movements—the list of possibilities is lengthy and, yes, horrifying. One may also lose one's sense of humor. That's the easiest to lose and the hardest to survive without.

In the past ten years, I have sustained some of these losses. Characteristic of MS are sudden attacks, called exacerbations, followed by remissions, and these I have not had. Instead, my disease has been slowly progressive. My left leg is now so weak that I walk with the aid of a brace and a cane; and for distances I use an Amigo, a variation on the electric wheelchair that looks rather like an electrified kiddie car. I no longer have much use of my left hand. Now my right side is weakening as well. I still have the blurred spot in my right eye. Overall, though, I've been lucky so far. My world has, of necessity, been circumscribed by my losses, but the terrain left me has been ample enough for me to continue many of the activities that absorb me: writing, teaching, raising children and cats and plants and snakes, reading, speaking publicly about MS and depression, even playing bridge with people patient and honorable enough to let me scatter cards every which way without sneaking a peek.

Lest I begin to sound like Pollyanna, however, let me say that I don't like having MS. I hate it. My life holds realities—harsh ones, some of them—that no right-minded human being ought to accept without grumbling. One of them is fatigue. I know of no one with MS who does not complain of bone-weariness; in a disease that presents an astonishing variety of symptoms, fatigue seems to be a common factor. I wake up in the morning feeling the way most people do at the end of a bad day, and I take it from there. As a result, I spend a lot of time *in extremis* and, impatient with limitation, I tend to ignore my fatigue until my body breaks down in some way and forces rest. Then I miss picnics, dinner parties, poetry readings, the brief visits of old friends from out of town. The offspring of a puritanical tradition of exceptional venerability, I cannot view these lapses without shame. My life often seems a series of small failures to do as I ought.

I lead, on the whole, an ordinary life, probably rather like the one I would have led had I not had MS. I am lucky that my predilections were already solitary, sedentary, and bookish—unlike the world-famous French cellist I have read about, or the young woman I talked with one long afternoon who wanted only to be a jockey. I had just begun graduate school when I found out something was wrong with me, and I have remained, interminably, a graduate student. Perhaps I would not have if I'd thought I had the stamina to return to a full-time job as a technical editor; but I've enjoyed my studies.

In addition to studying, I teach writing courses. I also teach medical students how to give neurological examinations. I pick up freelance editing jobs here and there. I have raised a foster son and sent him into the world, where he has made me two grandbabies, and I am still escorting my daughter and son through adolescence. I go to Mass every Saturday. I am a superb, if messy, cook. I am also an enthusiastic laundress, capable of sorting a hamper full of clothes into five subtly differentiated piles, but a terrible housekeeper. I can do italic writing and, in an emergency, bathe an oil-soaked cat. I play a fiendish game of Scrabble. When I have the time and the money, I like to sit on my front steps with my husband, drinking Amaretto and smoking a cigar, as we imagine our counterparts in

Leningrad and make sure that the sun gets down once more behind the sharp childish scrawl of the Tucson Mountains.

This lively plenty has its bleak complement, of course, in all the things I can no longer do. I will never run again, except in dreams, and one day I may have to write that I will never walk again. I like to go camping, but I can't follow George and the children along the trails that wander out of a campsite through the desert or into the mountains. In fact, even on the level I've learned never to check the weather or try to hold a coherent conversation: I need all my attention for my wayward feet. Of late, I have begun to catch myself wondering how people can propel themselves without canes. With only one usable hand, I have to select my clothing with care not so much for style as for ease of ingress and egress, and even so, dressing can be laborious. I can no longer do fine stitchery, pick up babies, play the piano, braid my hair. I am immobilized by acute attacks of depression, which may or may not be physiologically related to MS but are certainly its logical concomitant.

These two elements, the plenty and the privation, are never pure, nor are the delight and wretchedness that accompany them. Almost every pickle that I get into as a result of my weakness and clumsiness—and I get into plenty—is funny as well as maddening and sometimes painful. I recall one May afternoon when a friend and I were going out for a drink after finishing up at school. As we were climbing into opposite sides of my car, chatting, I tripped and fell, flat and hard, onto the asphalt parking lot, my abrupt departure interrupting him in mid-sentence. "Where'd you go?" he called as he came around the back of the car to find me hauling myself up by the door frame. "Are you all right?" Yes, I told him, I was fine, just a bit rattly, and we drove off to find a shady patio and some beer. When I got home an hour or so later, my daughter greeted me with "What have you done to yourself?" I looked down. One elbow of my white turtleneck with the green froggies, one knee of my white trousers, one white kneesock were blood-soaked. We peeled off the clothes and inspected the damage, which was nasty enough but not alarming. That part wasn't funny: The abrasions took a long time to heal, and one got a little infected. Even so, when I think of my friend talking earnestly, suddenly, to the hot thin air while I dropped from his view as though through a trap door, I find the image as silly as something from a Marx Brothers movie.

I may find it easier than other cripples to amuse myself because I live propped by the acceptance and the assistance and, sometimes, the amusement of those around me. Grocery clerks tear my checks out of my checkbook for me, and sales clerks find chairs to put into dressing rooms when I want to try on clothes. The people I work with make sure I teach at times when I am least likely to be fatigued, in places I can get to, with the materials I need. My students, with one anonymous exception (in an end-of-the-semester evaluation), have been unperturbed by my disability. Some even like it. One was immensely cheered by the information that I paint my own fingernails; she decided, she told me, that if I could go to such trouble over fine details, she could keep on writing essays. I suppose I became some sort of bright-fingered muse. She wrote good essays, too.

The most important struts in the framework of my existence, of course, are my husband and children. Dismayingly few marriages survive the MS test, and why should they? Most twenty-two- and nineteen-year-olds, like George and me, can vow in clear conscience, after a childhood of chickenpox and summer colds, to keep one another in sickness and in health so long as they both shall live. Not many are equipped for catastrophe: the dismay, the depression, the extra work, the boredom that a degenerative disease can insinuate into a relationship. And our society, with its emphasis on fun and its association of fun with physical performance, offers little encouragement for a whole spouse to stay with a crippled partner. Children experience similar stresses when faced with a crippled parent, and they are more helpless, since parents and children can't usually get divorced. They hate, of course, to be different from their peers, and the child whose mother is tacking down the aisle of a school auditorium packed with proud parents like a Cape Cod dinghy in a stiff breeze jolly well stands out in a crowd. Deprived of legal divorce, the child can at least deny the mother's disability, even her existence, forgetting to tell her about recitals and PTA meetings, refusing to accompany her to stores or church or the movies, never inviting friends to the house. Many do.

But I've been limping along for ten years now, and so far George and the children are still at my left elbow, holding tight. Anne and Matthew vacuum floors and dust furniture and haul trash and rake up dog droppings and button my cuffs and bake lasagne and Toll House cookies with just enough grumbling so I know that they don't have brain fever. And far from hiding me, they're forever dragging me by racks of fancy clothes or through teeming school corridors, or welcoming gaggles of friends while I'm wandering through the house in Anne's filmy pink babydoll pajamas. George generally calls before he brings someone home, but he does just as many dumb thankless chores as the children. And they all yell at me, laugh at some of my jokes, write me funny letters when we're apart—in short, treat me as an ordinary human being for whom they have some use. I think they like me. Unless they're faking. . . .

Faking. There's the rub. Tugging at the fringes of my consciousness always is the terror that people are kind to me only because I'm a cripple. My mother almost shattered me once, with that instinct mothers have—blind, I think, in this case, but unerring nonetheless—for striking blows along the fault-lines of their children's hearts, by telling me, in an attack on my selfishness, "We all have to make allowances for you, of course, because of the way you are." From the distance of a couple of years, I have to admit that I haven't any idea just what she meant, and I'm not sure that she knew either. She was awfully angry. But at the time, as the words thudded home, I felt my worst fear, suddenly realized. I could bear being called selfish: I am. But I couldn't bear the corroboration that those around me were doing in fact what I'd always suspected them of doing, professing fondness while silently putting up with me because of the way I am. A cripple. I've been a little cracked ever since.

Along with this fear that people are secretly accepting shoddy goods comes a relentless pressure to please—to prove myself worth the burdens I impose, I guess, or to build a substantial account of goodwill against which I may write drafts in times of need. Part of the pressure arises from social expectations. In our society, anyone who deviates from the norm had better find some way to compensate. Like fat people, who are expected to be jolly, cripples must bear their lot meekly and cheerfully. A grumpy cripple isn't playing by the rules. And much of the pressure is self-generated. Early on I vowed that, if I had to have MS, by God I was going to do it well. This is a class act, ladies and gentlemen. No tears, no recriminations, no faint-heartedness.

One way and another, then, I wind up feeling like Tiny Tim, peering over the edge of the table at the Christmas goose, waving my crutch, piping down God's blessing on us all. Only sometimes I don't want to play Tiny Tim. I'd rather be Caliban, a most scurvy monster. Fortunately, at home no one much cares whether I'm a good cripple or a bad cripple as long as I make vichyssoise with fair regularity. One evening several years ago, Anne was reading at the dining-room table while I cooked dinner. As I opened a can of tomatoes, the can slipped in my left hand and juice spattered me and the counter with bloody spots. Fatigued and infuriated, I bellowed, "I'm so sick of being crippled!" Anne glanced at me over the top of her book. "There now," she said, "do you feel better?" "Yes," I said, "yes, I do." She went back to her reading. I felt better. That's about all the attention my scurviness ever gets.

Because I hate being crippled, I sometimes hate myself for being a cripple. Over the years I have come to expect—even accept—attacks of violent self-loathing. Luckily, in general our society no longer connects deformity and disease directly with evil (though a charismatic once told me that I have MS because a devil is in me) and so I'm allowed to move largely at will, even among small children. But I'm not sure that this revision of attitude has been particularly helpful. Physical imperfection, even freed of moral disapprobation, still defies and violates the ideal, especially for women, whose confinement in their bodies as objects of desire is far from over. Each age, of course, has its ideal, and I doubt that ours is any better or worse than any other. Today's ideal woman, who lives on the glossy pages of dozens of magazines, seems to be between the ages of eighteen and twenty-five; her hair has body, her teeth flash white, her breath smells minty, her underarms are dry; she has a career but is still a fabulous cook, especially of meals that take less than twenty minutes to prepare; she does not ordinarily appear to have a husband or children; she is trim and deeply tanned; she jogs, swims, plays tennis, rides a bicycle, sails, but does not bowl; she travels widely, even to out-of-the-way places like Finland and Samoa, always in the company of the ideal man, who possesses a nearly identical set of characteristics. There are a few exceptions. Though usually white and often blonde, she may be black, Hispanic, Asian, or Native American, so long as she is unusually sleek. She may be old, provided she is selling a laxative or is Lauren Bacall. If she is selling a detergent, she may be married and have a flock of strikingly messy children. But she is never a cripple.

Like many women I know, I have always had an uneasy relationship with my body. I was not a popular child, largely, I think now, because I was peculiar: intelligent, intense, moody, shy, given to unexpected actions and inexplicable notions and emotions. But as I entered adolescence, I believed myself unpopular because I was homely: my breasts too flat, my mouth too wide, my hips too narrow, my clothing never quite right in fit or style. I was not, in fact, particularly ugly, old photographs inform me, though I was well off the ideal; but I carried this sense of self-alienation with me into adulthood, where it regenerated in response to the depredations of MS. Even with my brace I walk with a limp so pronounced that, seeing myself on the videotape of a television program on the disabled, I couldn't believe that anything but an inchworm could make progress humping along like that. My shoulders droop and my pelvis thrusts forward as I try to balance myself upright, throwing my frame into a bony S. As a result of contractures, one shoulder is higher than the other and I carry one arm bent in front of me, the fingers curled into a claw. My left arm and leg have wasted into pipe-stems, and I try always to keep them covered. When I think about how my body must look to others, especially to men, to whom I have been trained to display myself, I feel ludicrous, even loathsome.

At my age, however, I don't spend much time thinking about my appearance. The burning egocentricity of adolescence, which assures one that all the world is looking all the time, has passed, thank God, and I'm generally too caught up in what I'm doing to step back, as I used to, and watch myself as though upon a stage. I'm also too old to believe in the accuracy of self-image. I know that I'm not a hideous crone, that in fact, when I'm rested, well dressed, and well made up, I look fine. The self-loathing I feel is neither physically nor intellectually substantial. What I hate is not me but a disease.

I am not a disease.

And a disease is not—at least not singlehandedly—going to determine who I am, though at first it seemed to be going to. Adjusting to a chronic incurable illness, I have moved through a process similar to that outlined by Elizabeth Kübler-Ross in *On Death and Dying*. The major difference—and it is far more significant than most people recognize—is that I can't be sure of the outcome, as the terminally ill cancer patient can. Research studies indicate that, with proper medical care, I may achieve a "normal" life span. And in our society, with its vision of death as the ultimate evil, worse even than decrepitude, the response to such news is, "Oh well, at least you're not going to *die*." Are there worse things than dying? I think that there may be.

I think of two women I know, both with MS, both enough older than I to have served me as models. One took to her bed several years ago and has been there ever since. Although she can sit in a high-backed wheelchair, because she is incontinent she refuses to go out at all, even though incontinence pants, which are readily available at any pharmacy, could protect her from embarrassment. Instead, she stays at home and insists that her husband, a small quiet man, a retired civil servant, stay there with her except for a quick weekly foray to the supermarket. The other woman, whose illness was diagnosed when she was eighteen, a nursing student engaged to a young doctor, finished her training, married her doctor, accompanied him to Germany when he was in the service, bore three sons and a daughter, now grown and gone. When she can, she travels with her husband; she plays bridge, embroiders, swims regularly; she works, like me, as a symptomatic-patient instructor of medical students in neurology. Guess which woman I hope to be.

At the beginning, I thought about having MS almost incessantly. And because of the unpredictable course of the disease, my thoughts were always terrified. Each night I'd get into bed wondering whether I'd get out again the next morning, whether I'd be able to see, to speak, to hold a pen between my fingers. Knowing that the day might come when I'd be physically incapable of killing myself, I thought perhaps I ought to do so right away, while I still had the strength. Gradually I came to understand that the Nancy who might one day lie inert under a bed-sheet, arms and legs paralyzed, unable to feed or bathe herself, unable to reach out for a gun, a bottle of pills, was not the Nancy I was at present, and that I could not presume to make decisions for that future Nancy, who might well not want in the least to die. Now the only provision I've made for the future Nancy is that when the time comes—and it is likely to come in the form of pneumonia, friend to the weak and the old—I am not to be treated with machines and medications. If she is unable to communicate by then, I hope she will be satisfied with these terms.

Thinking all the time about having MS grew tiresome and intrusive, especially in the large and tragic mode in which I was accustomed to considering my plight. Months and even years went by without catastrophe (at least without one related to MS), and really I was awfully busy, what with George and children and snakes and students and poems, and I hadn't the time, let alone the inclination, to devote myself to being a disease. Too, the richer my life became, the funnier it seemed, as though there were some connection between largesse and laughter, and so my tragic stance began to waver until, even with the aid of a brace and a cane, I couldn't hold it for very long at a time.

After several years I was satisfied with my adjustment. I had suffered my grief and fury and terror, I thought, but now I was at ease with my lot. Then one summer day I set out with George and the children across the desert for a vacation in California. Part way to Yuma I became aware that my right leg felt funny. "I think I've had an exacerbation," I told George. "What shall we do?" he asked. "I think we'd better get the hell to California," I said, "because I don't know whether I'll ever make it again." So we went on to San Diego and then to Orange, up the Pacific Coast Highway to Santa Cruz, across to Yosemite, down to Sequoia and Joshua Tree, and so back over the desert to home. It was a fine two-week trip, filled with friends and fair weather, and I wouldn't have missed it for the world, though I did in fact make it back to California two years later. Nor would there have been any point in missing it, since in MS, once the symptoms have appeared, the neurological damage has been done, and there's no way to predict or prevent that damage.

The incident spoiled my self-satisfaction, however. It renewed my grief and fury and terror, and I learned that one never finishes adjusting to MS. I don't know now why I thought one would. One does not, after all, finish adjusting to life, and MS is simply a fact of my life—not my favorite fact, of course—but as ordinary as my nose and my tropical fish and my yellow Mazda station wagon. It may at any time get worse, but no amount of worry or anticipation can prepare me for a new loss. My life is a lesson in losses. I learn one at a time.

And I had best be patient in the learning, since I'll have to do it like it or not. As any rock fan knows, you can't always get what you want. Particularly when you have MS. You can't, for example, get cured. In recent years researchers and the organizations that fund research have started to pay MS some attention even though it isn't fatal; perhaps they have begun to see that life is something other than a quantitative phenomenon, that one may be very much alive for a very long time in a life that isn't worth living. The researchers have made some progress toward understanding the mechanism of the disease: It may well be an autoimmune reaction triggered by a slow-acting virus. But they are nowhere near its prevention, control, or cure. And most of us want to be cured. Some, unable to accept incurability, grasp at one treatment after another, no matter how bizarre: megavitamin therapy, gluten-free diet, injections of cobra venom, hypothermal suits, lymphocytopharesis, hyperbaric chambers. Many treatments are probably harmless enough, but none are curative.

The absence of a cure often makes MS patients bitter toward their doctors. Doctors are, after all, the priests of modern society, the new shamans, whose business is to heal, and many an MS patient roves from one to another, searching for the "good" doctor who will make him well. Doctors too think of themselves as healers, and for this reason many have trouble dealing with MS patients, whose disease in its intransigence defeats their aims and mocks their skills. Too few doctors, it is true, treat their patients as whole human beings, but the reverse is also true. I have always tried to be gentle with my doctors, who often have more at stake in terms of ego than I do. I may be frustrated, maddened, depressed by the incurability of my disease, but I am not diminished by it, and they are. When I push myself up from my seat in the waiting room and stumble toward them, I incarnate the limitation of their powers. The least I can do is refuse to press on their tenderest spots.

This gentleness is part of the reason that I'm not sorry to be a cripple. I didn't have it before. Perhaps I'd have developed it anyway—how could I know such a thing?—and I wish I had more of it, but I'm glad of what I have. It has opened and enriched my life enormously, this sense that my frailty and need must be mirrored in others, that in searching for and shaping a stable core in a life wrenched by change and loss, change and loss, I must recognize the same process, under individual conditions, in the lives around me. I do not deprecate such knowledge, however I've come by it.

All the same, if a cure were found, would I take it? In a minute. I may be a cripple, but I'm only occasionally a loony and never a saint. Anyway, in my brand of theology God doesn't give bonus points for a limp. I'd take a cure; I just don't need one. A friend who also has MS startled me once by asking, "Do you ever say to yourself, 'Why me, Lord?'" "No, Michael, I don't," I told him, "because whenever I try, the only response I can think of is 'Why not?'" If I could make a cosmic deal, who would I put in my place? What in my life would I give up in exchange for sound limbs and a thrilling rush of energy? No one. Nothing. I might as well do the job myself. Now that I'm getting the hang of it.

Considerations

Thinking

Why does Mairs insist on referring to herself as a "cripple" rather than as "handicapped" or "disabled"? What is Mairs's objection to newly coined euphemistic terms such as "differently abled"?

What does Mairs mean by saying, "I'd take a cure; I just don't need one"? To what extent are her identity and her image of herself bound up with her disease? What can we learn about Mairs from the metaphors she uses to describe herself as a person with multiple sclerosis?

Connecting

Consider Mairs's discussion of female beauty midway through the essay. Does her description of the ideal of American female beauty seem accurate? How is it related to images of beauty presented in the media?

Compare the image of female beauty presented in Mairs's essay with that presented in Maxine Hong Kingston's "No Name Woman." Compare the way Mairs describes her relation to her multiple sclerosis with the way Alice Walker describes her scarred eye in "Beauty: When the Other Dancer Is the Self."

Writing

Write an essay about your own attempts to come to terms with some kind of imperfection—physical, social, intellectual. Try to account for the extent to which this imperfection and your efforts to deal (or live) with it affect your self-image, your attitudes, or your behavior.

Do some research on multiple sclerosis, and write an essay presenting your findings. Link your research to Mairs's descriptions of her disease.

N. Scott Momaday
(b. 1934)

N. Scott Momaday was born in Oklahoma in 1934 and was educated at New Mexico University and at Stanford, where he earned a Ph.D. and now teaches. Momaday won the 1969 Pulitzer Prize for his novel *House Made of Dawn.* He is also the author of a children's book, *Owl in the Cedar Tree,* two volumes of poetry, and an autobiographical memoir, *The Way to Rainy Mountain.* Recent work includes *The Ancient Child* (1989) and *In the Presence of the Sun* (1991).

The essay that follows was published in the popular magazine *National Geographic* in 1976. In it, Momaday describes the sacredness of the land in language that is at once simple and elegant.

A First American Views His Land

> First Man
> behold:
> the earth
> glitters
> with leaves;
> the sky
> glistens
> with rain.
> Pollen
> is borne
> on winds
> that low
> and lean
> upon
> mountains.
> Cedars
> blacken
> the slopes—
> and pines.

One hundred centuries ago. There is a wide, irregular landscape in what is now northern New Mexico. The sun is a dull white disk, low in the south; it is a perfect mystery, a deity whose coming and going are inexorable. The gray sky is curdled, and it bears very close upon the earth. A cold wind runs along the ground, dips and spins, flaking drift from a pond in the bottom of a ravine. Beyond the wind the silence is acute. A man crouches in the ravine, in the darkness there, scarcely visible. He moves not a muscle; only the wind lifts a lock of his hair and lays it back along his neck. He wears skins and carries a spear. These things in particular mark his human intelligence and distinguish him as the lord of the universe. And for him the universe is especially *this* landscape; for him the landscape is an element like the air. The vast, virgin wilderness is by and large his whole context. For him there is no possibility of existence elsewhere.

Directly there is a blowing, a rumble of breath deeper than the wind, above him, where some of the hard clay of the bank is broken off and the clods roll down into the water. At the same time there appears on the skyline the massive head of a long-horned bison, then the hump, then the whole beast, huge and black on the sky, standing to a height of seven feet at the hump, with horns that extend six feet across the shaggy crown. For a moment it is poised there; then it lumbers obliquely down the bank to the pond. Still the man does not move, though the beast is now only a few steps upwind. There is no sign of what is about to happen; the beast meanders; the man is frozen in repose.

Then the scene explodes. In one and the same instant the man springs to his feet and bolts forward, his arm cocked and the spear held high, and the huge animal lunges in panic, bellowing, its whole weight thrown violently into the bank, its hooves churning and chipping earth into the air, its eyes gone wide and wild and white. There is a moment in which its awful, frenzied motion is wasted, and it is mired and helpless in its fear, and the man hurls the spear with his whole strength, and the point is driven into the deep, vital flesh, and the bison in its agony staggers and crashes down and dies.

This ancient drama of the hunt is enacted again and again in the landscape. The man is preeminently a predator, the most dangerous of all. He hunts in order to survive; his very existence is simply, squarely established upon that basis. But he hunts also because he can, because he has the means; he has the ultimate weapon of his age, and his prey is plentiful. His relationship to the land has not yet become a moral equation.

But in time he will come to understand that there is an intimate, vital link between the earth and himself, a link that implies an intricate network of rights and responsibilities. In some unimagined future he will understand that he has the ability to devastate and perhaps destroy his environment. That moment will be one of extreme crisis in his evolution.

The weapon is deadly and efficient. The hunter has taken great care in its manufacture, especially in the shaping of the flint point, which is an extraordinary thing. A larger flake has been removed from each face, a groove that extends from the base nearly to the tip. Several hundred pounds of pressure, expertly applied, were required to make these grooves. The hunter then is an artisan, and he must know how to use rudimentary tools. His skill, manifest in the manufacture of this artifact, is unsurpassed for its time and purpose. By means of this weapon is the Paleo-Indian hunter eminently able to exploit his environment.

Thousands of years later, about the time that Columbus begins his first voyage to the New World, another man, in the region of the Great Lakes, stands in the forest shade on the edge of a sunlit brake. In a while a deer enters into the pool of light. Silently the man fits an arrow to a bow, draws aim, and shoots. The arrow zips across the distance and strikes home. The deer leaps and falls dead.

But this latter-day man, unlike his ancient predecessor, is only incidentally a hunter; he is also a fisherman, a husbandman, even a physician. He fells trees and builds canoes; he grows corn, squash, and beans, and he gathers fruits and nuts; he uses hundreds of species of wild plants for food, medicine, teas, and dyes. Instead of one animal, or two or three, he hunts many, none to extinction as the Paleo-Indian may have done. He has fitted himself far more precisely into the patterns of the wilderness than did his ancient predecessor. He lives on the land; he takes his living from it; but he does not destroy it. This distinction supports the fundamental ethic that we call conservation today. In principle, if not yet in name, this man is a conservationist.

These two hunting sketches are far less important in themselves than is that long distance between them, that whole possibility within the dimension of time. I believe that in that interim there grew up in the mind of man an idea of the land as sacred.

At dawn
eagles
lie and
hover
above
the plain
where light
gathers
in pools.
Grasses
shimmer
and shine.
Shadows
withdraw
and lie
away
like smoke.

"The earth is our mother. The sky is our father." This concept of nature, which is at the center of the Native American world view, is familiar to us all. But it may well be that we do not understand entirely what the concept is in its ethical and philosophical implications.

I tell my students that the American Indian has a unique investment in the American landscape. It is an investment that represents perhaps thirty thousand years of habitation. That tenure has to be worth something in itself—a great deal, in fact. The Indian has been here a long time; he is at home here. That simple and obvious truth is one of the most important realities of the Indian world, and it is integral in the Indian mind and spirit.

How does such a concept evolve? Where does it begin? Perhaps it begins with the recognition of beauty, the realization that the physical world *is* beautiful. We don't know much about the ancient hunter's sensibilities. It isn't likely that he had leisure in his life for the elaboration of an aesthetic ideal. And yet the weapon he made was beautiful as well as functional. It has been suggested that much of the minute chipping along the edges of his weapon served no purpose but that of aesthetic satisfaction.

A good deal more is known concerning that man of the central forests. He made beautiful boxes and dishes out of elm and birch bark, for example. His canoes were marvelous, delicate works of art. And this aesthetic perception was a principle of the whole Indian world of his time, as indeed it is of our time. The contemporary Native American is a man whose strong aesthetic perceptions are clearly evident in his arts and crafts, in his religious ceremonies, and in the stories and songs of his rich oral tradition. This, in view of the pressures that have been brought to bear upon the Indian world and the drastic changes that have been effected in its landscape, is a blessing and an irony.

Consider for example the Navajos of the Four Corners area. In recent years an extensive coal-mining operation has mutilated some of their most sacred land. A large power plant in that same region spews a contamination into the sky that is visible for many miles. And yet, as much as any people of whom I have heard, the Navajos perceive and celebrate the beauty of the physical world.

There is a Navajo ceremonial song that celebrates the sounds that are made in the natural world, the particular voices that beautify the earth:

> Voice above,
> Voice of thunder,
> Speak from the
> dark of clouds;
> Voice below,
> Grasshopper voice,
> Speak from the
> green of plants;
> So may the earth
> be beautiful.

There is in the motion and meaning of this song a comprehension of the world that is peculiarly native, I believe, that is integral in the Native American mentality. Consider: The singer stands at the center of the natural world, at the source of its sound, of its motion, of its life. Nothing of that world is inaccessible to him or lost upon him. His song is filled with reverence, with wonder and delight, and with confidence as well. He knows something about himself and about the things around him—and he knows that he knows. I am interested in what he sees and hears; I am interested in the range and force of his perception. Our immediate impression may be that his perception is narrow and deep—vertical. After all, "voice above . . . voice below," he sings. But is it vertical only? At each level of his expression there is an extension of his awareness across the whole landscape. The voice above is the voice of thunder, and thunder rolls. Moreover, it issues from the impalpable dark clouds and runs upon their horizontal range. It is a sound that integrates the whole of the atmosphere. And even so, the voice below, that of the grasshopper, issues from the broad plain and multiplicity of plants. And of course the singer is mindful of much more than thunder and insects; we are given in his song the wide angle of his vision and his hearing—and we are given the testimony of his dignity, his trust, and his deep belief.

This comprehension of the earth and air is surely a matter of morality, for it brings into account not only man's instinctive reaction to his environment but the full realization of his humanity as well, the achievement of his intellectual and spiritual development as an individual and as a race.

In my own experience I have seen numerous examples of this regard for nature. My grandfather Mammedaty was a farmer in his mature years; his grandfather was a buffalo hunter. It was not easy for Mammedaty to be a farmer; he was a Kiowa, and the Kiowas never had an agrarian tradition. Yet he had to make his living, and the old, beloved life of roaming the plains and hunting the buffalo was gone forever. Even so, as much as any man before him, he fitted his mind and will and spirit to the land; there was nothing else. He could not have conceived of living apart from the land.

In *The Way to Rainy Mountain* I set down a small narrative that belongs in the oral tradition of my family. It indicates something essential about the Native American attitude toward the land:

"East of my grandmother's house, south of the pecan grove, there is buried a woman in a beautiful dress. Mammedaty used to know where she is buried, but now no one knows. If you stand on the front porch of the house and look eastward towards Carnegie, you know that the woman is buried somewhere within the range of your vision. But her grave is unmarked. She was buried in a cabinet, and she wore a beautiful dress. How beautiful it was! It was one of those fine buckskin dresses, and it was decorated with elk's teeth and beadwork. That dress is still there, under the ground."

It seems to me that this statement is primarily a declaration of love for the land, in which the several elements—the woman, the dress, and this plain—are at last become one reality, one expression of the beautiful in nature. Moreover, it seems to me a peculiarly Native American expression in this sense: that the concentration of things that are explicitly remembered—the general landscape, the simple, almost abstract nature of the burial, above all the beautiful dress, which is wholly singular in kind (as well as in its function within the narrative)—is especially Indian in character. The things that are *not* explicitly remembered—the woman's name, the exact location of her grave—are the things that matter least in the special view of the storyteller. What matters here is the translation of the woman into the landscape, a translation particularly signified by means of the beautiful and distinctive dress, an *Indian* dress.

When I was a boy, I lived for several years at Jemez Pueblo, New Mexico. The Pueblo Indians are perhaps more obviously invested in the land than are other people. Their whole life is predicated upon a thorough perception of the physical world and its myriad aspects. When I first went there to live, the cacique, or chief, of the Pueblos was a venerable old man with long, gray hair and bright, deep-set eyes. He was entirely dignified and imposing—and rather formidable in the eyes of a boy. He excited my imagination a good deal. I was told that this old man kept the calendar of the tribe, that each morning he stood on a certain spot of ground near the center of the town and watched to see where the sun appeared on the skyline. By means of this solar calendar did he know and announce to his people when it was time to plant, to harvest, to perform this or that ceremony. This image of him in my mind's eye—the old man gazing each morning after the ranging sun—came to represent for me the epitome of that real harmony between man and the land that signifies the Indian world.

One day when I was riding my horse along the Jemez River, I looked up to see a long caravan of wagons and people on horseback and on foot. Men, women, and children were crossing the river ahead of me, moving out to the west, where most of the cultivated fields were, the farmland of the town. It was a wonderful sight to see, this long procession, and I was immediately deeply curious. I wanted to investigate, but it was not in me to do so at once, for that racial reserve, that sense of propriety that is deep-seated in Native American culture, stayed me, held me up. Then I saw someone coming toward me on horseback, galloping. It was a friend of mine, a boy of my own age. "Come on," he said. "Come with us." "Where are you going?" I asked casually. But he would not tell me. He simply laughed and urged me to come along, and of course I was very glad to do so. It was a bright spring morning, and I had a good horse under me, and the prospect of adventure was delicious. We moved far out across the eroded plain to the farthest fields at the foot of a great red mesa, and there we planted two large fields of corn. And afterward, on the edge of the fields, we sat on blankets and ate a feast in the shade of a cottonwood grove. Later I learned it was the cacique's fields we planted. And this is an ancient tradition at Jemez. The people of the town plant and tend and harvest the cacique's fields, and in the winter the hunters give to him a portion of the meat that they bring home from the mountains. It is as if the cacique is himself the translation of man, every man, into the landscape.

I have not forgotten that day, nor shall I forget it. I remember the warm earth of the fields, the smooth texture of seeds in my hands, and the brown water moving slowly and irresistibly among the rows. Above all I remember the spirit in which the procession was made, the work was done, and the feasting was enjoyed. It was a spirit of communion, of the life of each man in relation to the life of the planet and of the infinite distance and silence in which it moves. We made, in concert, an appropriate expression of that spirit.

One afternoon an old Kiowa woman talked to me, telling me of the place in Oklahoma in which she had lived for a hundred years. It was the place in which my grandparents, too, lived; and it is the place where I was born. And she told me of a time even further back, when the Kiowas came down from the north and centered their culture in the red earth of the southern plains. She told wonderful stories, and as I listened, I began to feel more and more sure that her voice proceeded from the land itself. I asked her many things concerning the Kiowas, for I wanted to understand all that I could of my heritage. I told the old woman that I had come there to learn from her and from people like her, those in whom the old ways were preserved. And she said simply: "It is good that you have come here." I believe that her word "good" meant many things; for one thing it meant *right,* or *appropriate.* And indeed it was appropriate that she should speak of the land. She was eminently qualified to do so. She had a great reverence for the land, and an ancient perception of it, a perception that it acquired only in the course of many generations.

It is this notion of the appropriate, along with that of the beautiful, that forms the Native American perspective on the land. In a sense these considerations are indivisible; Native American oral tradition is rich with songs and tales that celebrate natural beauty, the beauty of the natural world. What is more appropriate to our world than that which is beautiful:

> At noon
> turtles
> enter
> slowly
> into
> the warm
> dark loam.
> Bees hold
> the swarm.

> Meadows
> recede
> through planes
> of heat
> and pure
> distance.

Very old in the Native American world view is the conviction that the earth is vital, that there is a spiritual dimension to it, a dimension in which man rightly exists. It follows logically that there are ethical imperatives in this matter. I think: Inasmuch as I am in the land, it is appropriate that I should affirm myself in the spirit of the land. I shall celebrate my life in the world and the world in my life. In the natural order man invests himself in the landscape and at the same time incorporates the landscape into his own most fundamental experience. This trust is sacred.

The process of investment and appropriation is, I believe, preeminently a function of the imagination. It is accomplished by means of an act of the imagination that is especially ethical in kind. We are what we imagine ourselves to be. The Native American is someone who thinks of himself, imagines himself in a particular way. By virtue of his experience his idea of himself comprehends his relationship to the land.

And the quality of this imagining is determined as well by racial and cultural experience. The Native American's attitudes toward this landscape have been formulated over a long period of time, a span that reaches back to the end of the Ice Age. The land, *this* land, is secure in his racial memory.

In our society as a whole we conceive of the land in terms of ownership and use. It is a lifeless medium of exchange; it has for most of us, I suspect, no more spirituality than has an automobile, say, or a refrigerator. And our laws confirm us in this view, for we can buy and sell the land, we can exclude each other from it, and in the context of ownership we can use it as we will. Ownership implies use, and use implies consumption.

But this way of thinking of the land is alien to the Indian. His cultural intelligence is opposed to these concepts; indeed, for him they are all but inconceivable quantities. This fundamental distinction is easier to understand with respect to ownership than to use, perhaps. For obviously the Indian does use, and has always used, the land and the available resources in it. The point is that *use* does not indicate in any real way his idea of the land. "Use" is neither his word nor his idea. As an Indian I think: "You say that I *use* the land, and I reply, yes, it is true; but it is not the first truth. The first truth is that I *love* the land; I see that it is beautiful; I delight in it; I am alive in it."

In the long course of his journey from Asia and in the realization of himself in the New World, the Indian has assumed a deep ethical regard for the earth and sky, a reverence for the natural world that is antipodal to that strange tenet of modern civilization that seemingly has it that man must destroy his environment. It is this ancient ethic of the Native American that must shape our efforts to preserve the earth and the life upon and within it.

> At dusk
> the gray
> foxes

stiffen
in cold;
blackbirds
are fixed
in white
branches.
Rivers
follow
the moon,
the long
white track
of the
full moon.

Considerations

Thinking

What are some implications of Momaday's expression of the Native American world view concerning what he describes as the earth's spiritual dimension? What do you think he means by suggesting that there are "ethical imperatives" for human beings in their relationship with the earth?

What aspect of Momaday's Native American perspective does he put in counterpoint to looking at the earth in terms of "ownership and use"? Why?

Connecting

How does each of the stories Momaday introduces into his essay fit in with the ideas and cultural perspectives he develops? What does the poem he includes contribute to the essay?

Compare Momaday's discussion of the Native American perspective toward nature and the land with that of Leslie Marmon Silko in "Landscape, History, and the Pueblo Imagination."

Writing

Write an essay in which you explore the implications of what it means to "love the land" in Momaday's terms.

Write an analysis of the poem that Momaday includes in his essay. Discuss the image of nature the poem conveys.

Toni Morrison
(b. 1931)

Toni Morrison, a novelist, won the Nobel Prize in literature in 1993. Her novels include *Song of Solomon, Sula, The Bluest Eye, Jazz, Beloved,* and *Paradise.* She has an unerring instinct about the plight of African Americans and a remarkable talent for reconstructing their inner lives.

"The Site of Memory" was a talk given at the New York Public Library. In it, Morrison reveals her own process of transforming slave narratives into fiction—telling how she tracks "an image from picture to meaning to text." Her aim is also to "throw into relief the differences between self-recollection (memoir) and fiction."

The Site of Memory

My inclusion in a series of talks on autobiography and memoir is not entirely a misalliance. Although it's probably true that a fiction writer thinks of his or her work as alien in that company, what I have to say may suggest why I'm not completely out of place here. For one thing, I might throw into relief the differences between self-recollection (memoir) and fiction, and also some of the similarities—the places where those two crafts embrace and where that embrace is symbiotic.

But the authenticity of my presence here lies in the fact that a very large part of my own literary heritage is the autobiography. In this country the print origins of black literature (as distinguished from the oral origins) were slave narratives. These book-length narratives (autobiographies, recollections, memoirs), of which well over a hundred were published, are familiar texts to historians and students of black history. They range from the adventure-packed life of Olaudah Equiano's *The Interesting Narrative of the Life of Olaudah Equiano, or Gustavus Vassa, the African, Written by Himself* (1769) to the quiet desperation of *Incidents in the Life of a Slave Girl: Written by Herself* (1861), in which Harriet Jacob ("Linda Brent") records hiding for seven years in a room too small to stand up in; from the political savvy of Frederick Douglass's *Narrative of the Life of Frederick Douglass, an American Slave, Written by Himself* (1845) to the subtlety and modesty of Henry Bibb, whose voice, in *Life and Adventures of Henry Bibb, an American Slave, Written by Himself* (1849), is surrounded by ("loaded with" is a better phrase) documents attesting to its authenticity. Bibb is careful to note that his formal schooling (three weeks) was short, but that he was "educated in the school of adversity, whips, and chains." Born in Kentucky, he put aside his plans to escape in order to marry. But when he learned that he was the father of a slave and watched the degradation of his wife and child, he reactivated those plans.

Whatever the style and circumstances of these narratives, they were written to say principally two things. One: "This is my historical life—my singular, special example that is personal, but that also represents the race." Two: "I write this text to persuade other people—you, the reader, who is probably not black—that we are human beings worthy of God's grace and the immediate abandonment of slavery." With these two missions in mind, the narratives were clearly pointed.

In Equiano's account, the purpose is quite up-front. Born in 1745 near the Niger River and captured at the age of ten, he survived the Middle Passage, American plantation slavery, wars in Canada and the Mediterranean; learned navigation and clerking from a Quaker named Robert King, and bought his freedom at twenty-one. He lived as a free servant, traveling widely and living most of his latter life in England. Here he is speaking to the British without equivocation: "I hope to have the satisfaction of seeing the renovation of liberty and justice resting on the British government. . . . I hope and expect the attention of gentlemen of power. . . . May the time come—at least the speculation is to me pleasing—when the sable people shall gratefully commemorate the auspicious era of extensive freedom." With typically eighteenth-century reticence he records his singular and representative life for one purpose: to change things. In fact, he and his co-authors *did* change things. Their works gave fuel to the fires that abolitionists were setting everywhere.

More difficult was getting the fair appraisal of literary critics. The writings of church martyrs and confessors are and were read for the eloquence of their message as well as their experience of redemption, but the American slaves' autobiographical narratives were frequently scorned as "biased," "inflammatory" and "improbable." These attacks are particularly difficult to understand in view of the fact that it was extremely important, as you can imagine, for the writers of these narratives to appear as objective as possible—not to offend the reader by being too angry, or by showing too much outrage, or by calling the reader names. As recently as 1966, Paul Edwards, who edited and abridged Equiano's story, praises the narrative for its refusal to be "inflammatory."

"As a rule," Edwards writes, "he [Equiano] puts no emotional pressure on the reader other than that which the situation itself contains—his language does not strain after our sympathy, but expects it to be given naturally and at the proper time. This quiet avoidance of emotional display produces many of the best passages in the book." Similarly, an 1836 review of Charles Bell's *Life and Adventures of a Fugitive Slave*, which appeared in the "Quarterly Anti-Slavery Magazine," praised Bell's account for its objectivity. "We rejoice in the book the more, because it is not a partisan work. . . . It broaches no theory in regard to [slavery], nor proposes any mode or time of emancipation."

As determined as these black writers were to persuade the reader of the evil of slavery, they also complimented him by assuming his nobility of heart and his high-mindedness. They tried to summon up his finer nature in order to encourage him to employ it. They knew that their readers were the people who could make a difference in terminating slavery. Their stories—of brutality, adversity and deliverance—had great popularity in spite of critical hostility in many quarters and patronizing sympathy in others. There was a time when the hunger for "slave stories" was difficult to quiet, as sales figures show. Douglass's *Narrative* sold five thousand copies in four months; by 1847 it had sold eleven thousand copies. Equiano's book had thirty-six editions between 1789 and 1850. Moses Roper's book had ten editions from 1837 to 1856; William Wells Brown's was reprinted four times in its first year. Solomon Northrop's book sold twenty-seven thousand copies before two years had passed. A book by Josiah Henson (argued by some to be the model for the "Tom" of Harriet Beecher Stowe's *Uncle Tom's Cabin*) had a pre-publication sale of five thousand.

In addition to using their own lives to expose the horrors of slavery, they had a companion motive for their efforts. The prohibition against teaching a slave to read and write (which in many Southern states carried severe punishment) and against a slave's learning to read and write had to be scuttled at all costs. These writers knew that literacy was power. Voting, after all, was inextricably connected to the ability to read; literacy was a way of assuming and proving the "humanity" that the Constitution denied them. That is why the narratives carry the subtitle "written by himself," or "herself," and include introductions and prefaces by white sympathizers to authenticate them. Other narratives, "edited by" such well-known anti-slavery figures as Lydia Maria Child and John Greenleaf Whittier, contain prefaces to assure the reader how little editing was needed. A literate slave was supposed to be a contradiction in terms.

One has to remember that the climate in which they wrote reflected not only the Age of Enlightenment but its twin, born at the same time, the Age of Scientific Racism. David Hume, Immanuel Kant and Thomas Jefferson, to mention only a few, had documented their conclusions that blacks were incapable of intelligence. Frederick Douglass knew otherwise, and he wrote refutations of what Jefferson said in "Notes on the State of Virginia": "Never yet could I find that a black had uttered a thought above the level of plain narration, never see even an elementary trait of painting or sculpture." A sentence that I have always thought ought to be engraved at the door to the Rockefeller Collection of African Art. Hegel, in 1813, had said that Africans had no "history" and couldn't write in modern languages. Kant disregarded a perceptive observation by a black man by saying, "This fellow was quite black from head to foot, a clear proof that what he said was stupid."

Yet no slave society in the history of the world wrote more—or more thoughtfully—about its own enslavement. The milieu, however, dictated the purpose and the style. The narratives are instructive, moral and obviously representative. Some of them are patterned after the sentimental novel that was in vogue at the time. But whatever the level of eloquence or the form, popular taste discouraged the writers from dwelling too long or too carefully on the more sordid details of their experience. Whenever there was an unusually violent incident, or a scatological one, or something "excessive," one finds the writer taking refuge in the literary conventions of the day. ("I was left in a state of distraction not to be described" (Equiano). "But let us now leave the rough usage of the field . . . and turn our attention to the less repulsive slave life as it existed in the house of my childhood" (Douglass). "I am not about to harrow the feelings of my readers by a terrific representation of the untold horrors of that fearful system of oppression. . . . It is not my purpose to descend deeply into the dark and noisome caverns of the hell of slavery" (Henry Box Brown).)

Over and over, the writers pull the narrative up short with a phrase such as, "But let us drop a veil over these proceedings too terrible to relate." In shaping the experience to make it palatable to those who were in a position to alleviate it, they were silent about many things, and they "forgot" many other things. There was a

[handwritten marginal note:] shows their courage and ultimate success in the face of great adversity, and seems to uplift the reader

careful selection of the instances that they would record and a careful rendering of those that they chose to describe. Lydia Maria Child identified the problem in her introduction to "Linda Brent's" tale of sexual abuse: "I am well aware that many will accuse me of indecorum for presenting these pages to the public; for the experiences of this intelligent and much-injured woman belong to a class which some call delicate subjects, and others indelicate. This peculiar phase of Slavery has generally been kept veiled; but the public ought to be made acquainted with its monstrous features, and I am willing to take the responsibility of presenting them with the veil drawn [aside]."

But most importantly—at least for me—there was no mention of their interior life.

For me—a writer in the last quarter of the twentieth century, not much more than a hundred years after Emancipation, a writer who is black and a woman— the exercise is very different. My job becomes how to rip that veil drawn over "proceedings too terrible to relate." The exercise is also critical for any person who is black, or who belongs to any marginalized category, for, historically, we were seldom invited to participate in the discourse even when we were its topic.

Moving that veil aside requires, therefore, certain things. First of all, I must trust my own recollections. I must also depend on the recollections of others. Thus memory weighs heavily in what I write, in how I begin and in what I find to be significant. Zora Neale Hurston said, "Like the dead-seeming cold rocks, I have memories within that came out of the material that went to make me." These "memories within" are the subsoil of my work. But memories and recollections won't give me total access to the unwritten interior life of these people. Only the act of the imagination can help me.

If writing is thinking and discovery and selection and order and meaning, it is also awe and reverence and mystery and magic. I suppose I could dispense with the last four if I were not so deadly serious about fidelity to the milieu out of which I write and in which my ancestors actually lived. Infidelity to that milieu—the absence of the interior life, the deliberate excising of it from the records that the slaves themselves told—is precisely the problem in the discourse that proceeded without us. How I gain access to that interior life is what drives me and is the part of this talk which both distinguishes my fiction from autobiographical strategies and which also embraces certain autobiographical strategies. It's a kind of literary archeology: on the basis of some information and a little bit of guesswork you journey to a site to see what remains were left behind and to reconstruct the world that these remains imply. What makes it fiction is the nature of the imaginative act: my reliance on the image—on the remains—in addition to recollection, to yield up a kind of a truth. By "image," of course, I don't mean "symbol"; I simply mean "picture" and the feelings that accompany the picture.

Fiction, by definition, is distinct from fact. Presumably it's the product of imagination—invention—and it claims the freedom to dispense with "what really happened," or where it really happened, or when it really happened, and nothing in it needs to be publicly verifiable, although much in it can be verified. By contrast, the scholarship of the biographer and the literary critic seems to us only trustworthy when the events of fiction can be traced to some publicly verifiable fact. It's the research of the "Oh, yes, this is where he or she got it from" school, which gets its own credibility from excavating the credibility of the sources of the imagination, not the nature of the imagination.

The work that I do frequently falls, in the minds of most people, into that realm of fiction called fantastic, or mythic, or magical, or unbelievable. I'm not comfortable with these labels. I consider that my single gravest responsibility (in spite of that magic) is not to lie. When I hear someone say, "Truth is stranger than fiction," I think that old chestnut is truer than we know, because it doesn't say that truth is truer than fiction; just that it's stranger, meaning that it's odd. It may be excessive, it may be more interesting, but the important thing is that it's random— and fiction is not random. *it is not ludicrous, but has a point that can be traced, and though not "true" in accuracy, it is truth as percieved by the author — and maybe a far more believable truth than what really occurs*

Therefore the crucial distinction for me is not the difference between fact and fiction, but the distinction between fact and truth. Because facts can exist without human intelligence, but truth cannot. So if I'm looking to find and expose a truth about the interior life of people who didn't write it (which doesn't mean that they didn't have it); if I'm trying to fill in the blanks that the slave narratives left—to part the veil that was so frequently drawn, to implement the stories that I heard— then the approach that's most productive and most trustworthy for me is the recollection that moves from the image to the text. Not from the text to the image.

Simone de Beauvoir, in *A Very Easy Death,* says, "I don't know why I was so shocked by my mother's death." When she heard her mother's name being called at the funeral by the priest, she says, "Emotion seized me by the throat. . . . 'Françoise de Beauvoir': the words brought her to life; they summed up her history, from birth to marriage to widowhood to the grave. Françoise de Beauvoir—that retiring woman, so rarely named, became an *important* person." The book becomes an exploration both into her own grief and into the images in which the grief lay buried.

Unlike Mme. de Beauvoir, Frederick Douglass asks the reader's patience for spending about half a page on the death of his grandmother—easily the most profound loss he had suffered—and he apologizes by saying, in effect, "It really was very important to me. I hope you aren't bored by my indulgence." He makes no attempt to explore that death: its images or its meaning. His narrative is as close to factual as he can make it, which leaves no room for subjective speculation. James Baldwin, on the other hand, in *Notes of a Native Son,* says, in recording his father's life and his own relationship to his father, "All of my father's Biblical texts and songs, which I had decided were meaningless, were ranged before me at his death like empty bottles, waiting to hold the meaning which life would give them for me." And then his text fills those bottles. Like Simone de Beauvoir, he moves from the event to the image that it left. My route is the reverse: the image comes first and tells me what the "memory" is about.

I can't tell you how I felt when my father died. But I was able to write *Song of Solomon* and imagine, not him, and not his specific interior life, but the world that he inhabited and the private or interior life of the people in it. And I can't tell you how I felt reading to my grandmother while she was turning over and over in her bed (because she was dying, and she was not comfortable), but I could try to reconstruct the world that she lived in. And I have suspected, more often than not, that I *know* more than she did, that I *know* more than my grandfather and my great-grand-mother did, but I also know that I'm no wiser than they were. And whenever I have tried earnestly to diminish their vision and prove to myself that I know more, and when I have tried to speculate on their interior life and match it up with my own, I have been overwhelmed every time by the richness of theirs compared to my own. Like Frederick Douglass talking about his grandmother, and James Baldwin talking about his father, and Simone de Beauvoir talking about her mother, these people are my access to me; they are my entrance into my own interior life. Which is why the images that float around them—the remains, so to speak, at the archeological site—surface first, and they surface so vividly and so compellingly that I acknowledge them as my route to a reconstruction of a world, to an exploration of an interior life that was not written and to the revelation of a kind of truth.

So the nature of my research begins with something as ineffable and as flexible as a dimly recalled figure, the corner of a room, a voice. I began to write my second book, which was called *Sula*, because of my preoccupation with a picture of a woman and the way in which I heard her name pronounced. Her name was Hannah, and I think she was a friend of my mother's. I don't remember seeing her very much, but what I do remember is the color around her—a kind of violet, a suffusion of something violet—and her eyes, which appeared to be half closed. But what I remember most is how the women said her name: how they said "Hannah Peace" and smiled to themselves, and there was some secret about her that they knew, which they didn't talk about, at least not in my hearing, but it seemed *loaded* in the way in which they said her name. And I suspected that she was a little bit of an outlaw but that they approved in some way.

And then, thinking about their relationship to her and the way in which they talked about her, the way in which they articulated her name, made me think about friendship between women. What is it that they forgive each other for? And what is it that is unforgivable in the world of women? I don't want to know any more about Miss Hannah Peace, and I'm not going to ask my mother who she really was and what did she do and what were you laughing about and why were you smiling? Because my experience when I do this with my mother is so crushing: she will give you *the* most pedestrian information you ever heard, and I would like to keep all of my remains and my images intact in their mystery when I begin. Later I will get to the facts. That way I can explore two worlds—the actual and the possible.

What I want to do this evening is to track an image from picture to meaning to text—a journey which appears in the novel that I'm writing now, which is called *Beloved*.

I'm trying to write a particular kind of scene, and I see corn on the cob. To "see" corn on the cob doesn't mean that it suddenly hovers; it only means that it keeps coming back. And in trying to figure out "What is all this corn doing?" I discover what it *is* doing.

I see the house where I grew up in Lorain, Ohio. My parents had a garden some distance away from our house, and they didn't welcome me and my sister there, when we were young, because we were not able to distinguish between the things that they wanted to grow and the things that they didn't, so we were not able to hoe, or weed, until much later.

I see them walking, together, away from me. I'm looking at their backs and what they're carrying in their arms: their tools, and maybe a peck basket. Sometimes when they walk away from me they hold hands, and they go to this other place in the garden. They have to cross some railroad tracks to get there.

I also am aware that my mother and father sleep at odd hours because my father works many jobs and works at night. And these naps are times of pleasure for me and my sister because nobody's giving us chores, or telling us what to do, or nagging us in any way. In addition to which, there is some feeling of pleasure in them that I'm only vaguely aware of. They're very rested when they take these naps. *ha ha*

And later on in the summer we have an opportunity to eat corn, which is the one plant that I can distinguish from the others, and which is the harvest that I like the best; the others are the food that no child likes—the collards, the okra, the strong, violent vegetables that I would give a great deal for now. But I do like the corn because it's sweet, and because we all sit down to eat it, and it's finger food, and it's hot, and it's even good cold, and there are neighbors in, and there are uncles in, and it's easy, and it's nice.

The picture of the corn and the nimbus of emotion surrounding it became a powerful one in the manuscript I'm now completing.

Authors arrive at text and subtext in thousands of ways, learning each time they begin anew how to recognize a valuable idea and how to render the texture that accompanies, reveals or displays it to its best advantage. The process by which this is accomplished is endlessly fascinating to me. I have always thought that as an editor for twenty years I understood writers better than their most careful critics, because in examining the manuscript in each of its subsequent stages I knew the author's process, how his or her mind worked, what was effortless, what took time, where the "solution" to a problem came from. The end result—the book—was all that the critic had to go on.

Still, for me, that was the least important aspect of the work. Because, no matter how "fictional" the account of these writers, or how much it was a product of invention, the act of imagination is bound up with memory. You know, they straightened out the Mississippi River in places, to make room for houses and livable acreage. Occasionally the river floods these places. "Floods" is the word they use, but in fact it is not flooding; it is remembering. Remembering where it used to be. All water has a perfect memory and is forever trying to get back to where it was. Writers are like that: remembering where we were, what valley we ran through, what the banks were like, the light that was there and the route back to our original place. It is emotional memory—what the nerves and the skin remember as well as how it appeared. And a rush of imagination is our "flooding."

Along with personal recollection, the matrix of the work I do is the wish to extend, fill in and complement slave autobiographical narratives. But only the matrix. What comes of all that is dictated by other concerns, not least among them the novel's own integrity. Still, like water, I remember where I was before I was "straightened out."

Q. I would like to ask about your point of view as a novelist. Is it a vision, or are you taking the part of the particular characters?

A. I try sometimes to have genuinely minor characters just walk through, like a walk-on actor. But I get easily distracted by them, because a novelist's imagination goes like that: every little road looks to me like an adventure, and once you begin to claim it and describe it, it looks like more, and you invent more and more and more. I don't mind doing that in my first draft, but afterward I have to cut back. I have seen myself get distracted, and people have loomed much larger than I had planned, and minor characters have seemed a little bit more interesting than they need to be for the purposes of the book. In that case I try to endow them: if there are little pieces of information that I want to reveal, I let them do some of the work. But I try not to get carried away; I try to restrain it, so that, finally, the texture is consistent and nothing is wasted; there are no words in the final text that are unnecessary, and no people who are not absolutely necessary.

As for the point of view, there should be the illusion that it's the characters' point of view, when in fact it isn't; it's really the narrator who is there but who doesn't make herself (in my case) known in that role. I like the feeling of a *told* story, where you hear a voice but you can't identify it, and you think it's your own voice. It's a comfortable voice, and it's a guiding voice, and it's alarmed by the same things that the reader is alarmed by, and it doesn't know what's going to happen next either. So you have this sort of guide. But that guide can't have a personality; it can only have a sound, and you have to feel comfortable with this voice, and then this voice can easily abandon itself and reveal the interior dialogue of a character. So it's a combination of using the point of view of various characters but still retaining the power to slide in and out, provided that when I'm "out" the reader doesn't see little fingers pointing to what's in the text.

What I really want is that intimacy in which the reader is under the impression that he isn't really reading this; that he is participating in it as he goes along. It's unfolding, and he's always two beats ahead of the characters and right on target.

Q. You have said that writing is a solitary activity. Do you go into steady seclusion when you're writing, so that your feelings are sort of contained, or do you have to get away, and go out shopping and . . . ?

A. I do all of it. I've been at this book for three years. I go out shopping, and I stare, and I do whatever. It goes away. Sometimes it's very intense and I walk—I mean, I write a sentence and I jump up and run outside or something; it sort of beats you up. And sometimes I don't. Sometimes I write long hours every day. I get up at 5:30 and just go do it, and if I don't like it the next day, I throw it away. But I sit down and do it. By now I know how to get to that place where something is working. I didn't always know; I thought every thought I had was interesting—because it was mine. Now I know better how to throw away things that are not useful. I can stand around and do other things and think about it at the same time. I don't mind not writing every minute; I'm not so terrified.

When you first start writing—and I think it's true for a lot of beginning writers—you're scared to death that if you don't get that sentence right that minute it's never going to show up again. And it isn't. But it doesn't matter—another one will, and it'll probably be better. And I don't mind writing badly for a couple of

[handwritten margin note: builds ease and a warm relationship between reader and book — allows the active relationship to be created]

[handwritten margin note: patience]

days because I know I can fix it—and fix it again and again and again, and it will be better. I don't have the hysteria that used to accompany some of those dazzling passages that I thought the world was just dying for me to remember. I'm a little more sanguine about it now. Because the best part of it all, the absolutely most delicious part, is finishing it and then doing it over. That's the thrill of a lifetime for me: if I can just get done with that first phase and then have infinite time to fix it and change it. I rewrite a lot, over and over again, so that it looks like I never did. I try to make it look like I never touched it, and that takes a lot of time and a lot of sweat.

appearances can be deceptive

Q. In "Song of Solomon," what was the relationship between your memories and what you made up? Was it very tenuous?

A. Yes, it was tenuous. For the first time I was writing a book in which the central stage was occupied by men, and which had something to do with my loss, or my perception of loss, of a man (my father) and the world that disappeared with him. (It didn't, but I *felt* that it did.) So I was re-creating a time period that was his—not biographically his life or anything in it; I use whatever's around. But it seemed to me that there was this big void after he died, and I filled it with a book that was about men because my two previous books had had women as the central characters. So in that sense it was about my memories and the need to invent. I had to do something. I was in such a rage because my father was dead. The connections between us were threads that I either mined for a lot of strength or they were purely invention. But I created a male world and inhabited it and it had this quest—a journey from stupidity to epiphany, of a man, a complete man. It was my way of exploring all that, of trying to figure out what he may have known.

very eloquent

Considerations

Thinking

Morrison tells us that "a literate slave was supposed to be a contradiction in terms." What are the implications of such a statement—in the slaves' time and in ours? Fill in the blank to fit our present-day circumstance: "A _____ is a contradiction in terms."

What do you think about Morrison's belief that she can reach truth through fiction? Do you believe in fictional truth-telling, or would you rather just have the facts? Explain.

Connecting

When Morrison describes her job as a fiction writer, she says she has first to look at slave narratives and then "rip that veil drawn over 'proceedings too terrible to relate.'" In reconstructing what the interior life of her characters must have been like, she must also trust her "own recollections," her own memories. But none of that is enough, finally: "Only the act of the imagination can help me." How do you suppose such imaginative acts are related to what Stephen Jay Gould calls the "inferential acts" that characterize scientific thinking? Morrison, recall, speaks of her work as "a kind of literary archaeology."

Morrison says that when she does her reconstructing, she relies on the "image—on the remains" she finds at the site. How might her notion about images help you with your writing?

Writing

Write an essay in which you explore the ramifications of Morrison's claim that "facts can exist without human intelligence, but truth cannot."

Morrison tells us that the images at the archeological site "surface first, and they surface so vividly and so compellingly that I acknowledge them as my route to a reconstruction of a world, to an exploration of an interior life that was not written and to the revelation of a kind of truth." See what happens when you follow Morrison's path. Return to an archeological site in your memory; record the image, render it, and see what it reveals to you.

Tim O'Brien
(b. 1946)

Tim O'Brien was born in Austin, Minnesota. After attending Macalaster College and Harvard University, he was drafted into the Army during the Vietnam war, in which he fought and was wounded. O'Brien's work often combines elements of fiction and nonfiction, as for example, the pieces in his first book, *If I Die in a Combat Zone, Box Me Up and Ship Me Home* (1973), for which he coined the term *autofiction* to indicate their blend of fiction and autobiography.

His more recent collection, *The Things They Carried,* while largely fiction, also contains pieces such as "How to Tell a True War Story" that read more like essays. This piece, in fact, calls attention to its factuality, inviting readers to consider the way fact and fiction intersect and diverge, fade in and out of one another. The piece is noteworthy as well for the striking stories it includes and for the way it depends on the storyteller's distinctive voice.

How to Tell a True War Story

This is true.

I had a buddy in Vietnam. His name was Bob Kiley, but everybody called him Rat.

[handwritten annotation: AKA - Rat; Vietnam underlined; "Bob Kiley" circled]

A friend of his gets killed, so about a week later Rat sits down and writes a letter to the guy's sister. Rat tells her what a great brother she had, how together the guy was, a number one pal and comrade. A real soldier's soldier, Rat says. Then he tells a few stories to make the point, how her brother would always volunteer for stuff nobody else would volunteer for in a million years, dangerous stuff, like doing recon or going out on these really badass night patrols. Stainless steel balls, Rat tells her. The guy was a little crazy, for sure, but crazy in a good way, a real daredevil, because he liked the challenge of it, he liked testing himself, just man against gook. A great, great guy, Rat says.

Anyway, it's a terrific letter, very personal and touching. Rat almost bawls writing it. He gets all teary telling about the good times they had together, how her brother made the war seem almost fun, always raising hell and lighting up villes and bringing smoke to bear every which way. A great sense of humor, too. Like the time at this river when he went fishing with a whole damn crate of hand grenades. Probably the funniest thing in world history, Rat says, all that gore, about twenty zillion dead gook fish. Her brother, he had the right attitude. He knew how to have a good time. On Halloween, this real hot spooky night, the dude paints up his body all different colors and puts on this weird mask and hikes over to a ville and goes trick-or-treating almost stark naked, just boots and balls and an M-16. A tremendous human being, Rat says. Pretty nutso sometimes, but you could trust him with your life.

And then the letter gets very sad and serious. Rat pours his heart out. He says he loved the guy. He says the guy was his best friend in the world. They were like soul mates, he says, like twins or something, they had a whole lot in common. He tells the guy's sister he'll look her up when the war's over.

So what happens?

Rat mails the letter. He waits two months. The dumb cooze never writes back.

A true war story is never moral. It does not instruct, nor encourage virtue, nor suggest models of proper human behavior, nor restrain men from doing the things men have always done. If a story seems moral, do not believe it. If at the

440

end of a war story you feel uplifted, or if you feel that some small bit of rectitude has been salvaged from the larger waste, then you have been made the victim of a very old and terrible lie. There is no rectitude whatsoever. There is no virtue. As a first rule of thumb, therefore, you can tell a true war story by its absolute and uncompromising allegiance to obscenity and evil. Listen to Rat Kiley. Cooze, he says. He does not say bitch. He certainly does not say woman, or girl. He says cooze. Then he spits and stares. He's nineteen years old—it's too much for him—so he looks at you with those big sad gentle killer eyes and says *cooze,* because his friend is dead, and because it's so incredibly sad and true: she never wrote back.

You can tell a true war story if it embarrasses you. If you don't care for obscenity, you don't care for the truth; if you don't care for the truth, watch how you vote. Send guys to war, they come home talking dirty.

Listen to Rat: "Jesus Christ, man, I write this beautiful fuckin' letter, I slave over it, and what happens? The dumb cooze never writes back."

The dead guy's name was Curt Lemon. What happened was, we crossed a muddy river and marched west into the mountains, and on the third day we took a break along a trail junction in deep jungle. Right away, Lemon and Rat Kiley started goofing. They didn't understand about the spookiness. They were kids; they just didn't know. A nature hike, they thought, not even a war, so they went off into the shade of some giant trees—quadruple canopy, no sunlight at all—and they were giggling and calling each other yellow mother and playing a silly game they'd invented. The game involved smoke grenades, which were harmless unless you did stupid things, and what they did was pull out the pin and stand a few feet apart and play catch under the shade of those huge trees. Whoever chickened out was a yellow mother. And if nobody chickened out, the grenade would make a light popping sound and they'd be covered with smoke and they'd laugh and dance around and then do it again.

It's all exactly true.

It happened to *me,* nearly twenty years ago, and I still remember that trail junction and those giant trees and a soft dripping sound somewhere beyond the trees. I remember the smell of moss. Up in the canopy there were tiny white blossoms, but no sunlight at all, and I remember the shadows spreading out under the trees where Curt Lemon and Rat Kiley were playing catch with smoke grenades. Mitchell Sanders sat flipping his yo-yo. Norman Bowker and Kiowa and Dave Jensen were dozing, or half dozing, and all around us were those ragged green mountains.

Except for the laughter things were quiet.

At one point, I remember, Mitchell Sanders turned and looked at me, not quite nodding, as if to warn me about something, as if he already *knew,* then after a while he rolled up his yo-yo and moved away.

It's hard to tell you what happened next.

They were just goofing. There was a noise, I suppose, which must've been the detonator, so I glanced behind me and watched Lemon step from the shade into bright sunlight. His face was suddenly brown and shining. A handsome kid, really. Sharp gray eyes, lean and narrow-waisted, and when he died it was almost *when we die, is it accurate to say that life was sucked from us?*

beautiful, the way the sunlight came around him and lifted him up and sucked him high into a tree full of moss and vines and white blossoms.

In any war story, but especially a true one, it's difficult to separate what happened from what seemed to happen. What seems to happen becomes its own happening and has to be told that way. The angles of vision are skewed. When a booby trap explodes, you close your eyes and duck and float outside yourself. When a guy dies, like Curt Lemon, you look away and then look back for a moment and then look away again. The pictures get jumbled; you tend to miss a lot. And then afterward, when you go to tell about it, there is always that surreal seemingness, which makes the story seem untrue, but which in fact represents the hard and exact truth as it *seemed.*

* * *

In many cases a true war story cannot be believed. If you believe it, be skeptical. It's a question of credibility. Often the crazy stuff is true and the normal stuff isn't, because the normal stuff is necessary to make you believe the truly incredible craziness.

In other cases you can't even tell a true war story. Sometimes it's just beyond telling.

I heard this one, for example, from Mitchell Sanders. It was near dusk and we were sitting at my foxhole along a wide muddy river north of Quang Ngai. I remember how peaceful the twilight was. A deep pinkish red spilled out on the river, which moved without sound, and in the morning we would cross the river and march west into the mountains. The occasion was right for a good story.

"God's truth," Mitchell Sanders said. "A six-man patrol goes up into the mountains on a basic listening-post operation. The idea's to spend a week up there, just lie low and listen for enemy movement. They've got a radio along, so if they hear anything suspicious—anything—they're supposed to call in artillery or gunships, whatever it takes. Otherwise they keep strict field discipline. Absolute silence. They just listen."

Sanders glanced at me to make sure I had the scenario. He was playing with his yo-yo, dancing it with short, tight little strokes of the wrist.

His face was blank in the dusk.

"We're talking regulation, by-the-book LP. These six guys, they don't say boo for a solid week. They don't got tongues. *All* ears."

"Right," I said.

"Understand me?"

"Invisible."

Sanders nodded.

"Affirm," he said. "Invisible. So what happens is, these guys get themselves deep in the bush, all camouflaged up, and they lie down and wait and that's all they do, nothing else, they lie there for seven straight days and just listen. And man, I'll tell you—it's spooky. This is mountains. You don't *know* spooky till you been there. Jungle, sort of, except it's way up in the clouds and there's always this fog—like rain, except it's not raining—everything's all wet and swirly and tangled up and you can't see jack, you can't find your own pecker to piss with. Like you don't even have a body. Serious spooky. You just go with the vapors—the fog sort of takes you in . . . And the sounds, man. The sounds carry forever. You hear stuff nobody should *ever* hear."

Sanders was quiet for a second, just working the yo-yo, then he smiled at me.

"So after a couple days the guys start hearing this real soft, kind of wacked-out music. Weird echoes and stuff. Like a radio or something, but it's not a radio, it's this strange gook music that comes right out of the rocks. Faraway, sort of, but right up close, too. They try to ignore it. But it's a listening post, right? So they listen. And every night they keep hearing that crazyass gook concert. All kinds of chimes and xylophones. I mean, this is wilderness—no way, it can't be real—but there it *is*, like the mountains are tuned in to Radio fucking Hanoi. Naturally they get nervous. One guy sticks Juicy Fruit in his ears. Another guy almost flips. Thing is, though, they can't report music. They can't get on the horn and call back to base and say, 'Hey, listen, we need some firepower, we got to blow away this weirdo gook rock band.' They can't do that. It wouldn't go down. So they lie there in the fog and keep their mouths shut. And what makes it extra bad, see, is the poor dudes can't horse around like normal. Can't joke it away. Can't even talk to each other except maybe in whispers, all hush-hush, and that just revs up the willies. All they do is listen."

Again there was some silence as Mitchell Sanders looked out on the river. The dark was coming on hard now, and off to the west I could see the mountains rising in silhouette, all the mysteries and unknowns.

"This next part," Sanders said quietly, "you won't believe."

"Probably not," I said.

"You won't. And you know why?" He gave me a long, tired smile. "Because it happened. Because every word is absolutely dead-on true." *fore warning*

Sanders made a sound in his throat, like a sigh, as if to say he didn't care if I believed him or not. But he did care. He wanted me to feel the truth, to believe by the raw force of feeling. He seemed sad, in a way.

"These six guys," he said, "they're pretty fried out by now, and one night they start hearing voices. Like at a cocktail party. That's what it sounds like, this big swank gook cocktail party somewhere out there in the fog. Music and chitchat and stuff. It's crazy, I know, but they hear the champagne corks. They hear the actual martini glasses. Real hoity-toity, all very civilized, except this isn't civiliza-tion. This is Nam. *racism , ethnocentrism*

"Anyway, the guys try to be cool. They just lie there and groove, but after a while they start hearing—you won't believe this—they hear chamber music. They hear violins and cellos. They hear this terrific mama-san soprano. Then after a while they hear gook opera and a glee club and the Haiphong Boys Choir and a barbershop quartet and all kinds of weird chanting and Buddha-Buddha stuff. And the whole time, in the background, there's still that cocktail party going on. All these different voices. Not human voices, though. Because it's the mountains. Follow me? The rock—it's *talking*. And the fog, too, and the grass and the goddamn mongooses. Everything talks. The trees talk politics, the monkeys talk religion. The whole country. Vietnam. The place talks. It talks. Understand? Nam—it truly *talks*.

"The guys can't cope. They lose it. They get on the radio and report enemy movement—a whole army, they say—and they order up the firepower. They get arty and gunships. They call in air strikes. And I'll tell you, they fuckin' crash that cocktail party. All night long, they just smoke those mountains. They make jungle juice. They blow away trees and glee clubs and whatever else there is to blow away. Scorch time. They walk napalm up and down the ridges. They bring in the Cobras and F-4s, they use Willie Peter and HE and incendiaries. It's all fire. They make those mountains burn.

"Around dawn things finally get quiet. Like you never even *heard* quiet before. One of those real thick, real misty days—just clouds and fog, they're off in this special zone—and the mountains are absolutely dead-flat silent. Like Brigadoon—pure vapor, you know? Everything's all sucked up inside the fog. Not a single sound, except they still *hear* it.

"So they pack up and start humping. They head down the mountain, back to base camp, and when they get there they don't say diddly. They don't talk. Not a word, like they're deaf and dumb. Later on this fat bird colonel comes up and asks what the hell happened out there. What'd they hear? Why all the ordnance? The man's ragged out, he gets down tight on their case. I mean, they spent six trillion dollars on firepower, and this fatass colonel wants answers, he wants to know what the fuckin' story is.

"But the guys don't say zip. They just look at him for a while, sort of funny like, sort of amazed, and the whole war is right there in that stare. It says everything you can't ever say. It says, man, you got *wax* in your ears. It says, poor bastard, you'll never know—wrong frequency—you don't *even* want to hear this. Then they salute the fucker and walk away, because certain stories you don't ever tell."

You can tell a true war story by the way it never seems to end. Not then, not ever. Not when Mitchell Sanders stood up and moved off into the dark.

It all happened.

Even now, at this instant, I remember that yo-yo. In a way, I suppose, you had to be there, you had to hear it, but I could tell how desperately Sanders wanted me to believe him, his frustration at not quite getting the details right, not quite pinning down the final and definitive truth.

And I remember sitting at my foxhole that night, watching the shadows of Quang Ngai, thinking about the coming day and how we would cross the river and march west into the mountains, all the ways I might die, all the things I did not understand.

Late in the night Mitchell Sanders touched my shoulder.

"Just came to me," he whispered. "The moral, I mean. Nobody listens. Nobody hears nothin'. Like that fatass colonel. The politicians, all the civilian types. Your girlfriend. My girlfriend. Everybody's sweet little virgin girlfriend. What they need is to go out on LP. The vapors, man. Trees and rocks—you got to *listen* to your enemy."

And then again, in the morning, Sanders came up to me. The platoon was preparing to move out, checking weapons, going through all the little rituals that preceded a day's march. Already the lead squad had crossed the river and was filing off toward the west.

"I got a confession to make," Sanders said. "Last night, man, I had to make up a few things."

"I know that."

"The glee club. There wasn't any glee club."

"Right."

"No opera."

"Forget it, I understand."

"Yeah, but listen, it's still true. Those six guys, they heard wicked sound out there. They heard sound you just plain won't believe."

Sanders pulled on his rucksack, closed his eyes for a moment, then almost smiled at me. I knew what was coming.

"All right," I said, "what's the moral?"

"Forget it."

"No, go ahead."

For a long while he was quiet, looking away, and the silence kept stretching out until it was almost embarrassing. Then he shrugged and gave me a stare that lasted all day.

"Hear that quiet, man?" he said. "That quiet—just listen. There's your moral."

In a true war story, if there's a moral at all, it's like the thread that makes the cloth. You can't tease it out. You can't extract the meaning without unraveling the deeper meaning. And in the end, really, there's nothing much to say about a true war story, except maybe "Oh."

True war stories do not generalize. They do not indulge in abstraction or analysis.

For example: War is hell. As a moral declaration the old truism seems perfectly true, and yet because it abstracts, because it generalizes, I can't believe it with my stomach. Nothing turns inside. *need to have that inner connection*

It comes down to gut instinct. A true war story, if truly told, makes the stomach believe.

* * *

This one does it for me. I've told it before—many times, many versions—but here's what actually happened.

We crossed that river and marched west into the mountains. On the third day, Curt Lemon stepped on a booby-trapped 105 round. He was playing catch with Rat Kiley, laughing, and then he was dead. The trees were thick; it took nearly an hour to cut an LZ for the dustoff.

Later, higher in the mountains, we came across a baby VC water buffalo. What it was doing there I don't know—no farms or paddies—but we chased it down and got a rope around it and led it along to a deserted village where we set up for the night. After supper Rat Kiley went over and stroked its nose.

He opened up a can of C rations, pork and beans, but the baby buffalo wasn't interested.

Rat shrugged.

He stepped back and shot it through the right front knee. The animal did not make a sound. It went down hard, then got up again, and Rat took careful aim and shot off an ear. He shot it in the hindquarters and in the little hump at its back. He shot it twice in the flanks. It wasn't to kill; it was to hurt. He put the rifle muzzle up against the mouth and shot the mouth away. Nobody said much. The whole platoon stood there watching, feeling all kinds of things, but there wasn't a great deal of pity for the baby water buffalo. Curt Lemon was dead. Rat Kiley had lost his best friend in the world. Later in the week he would write a long personal letter to the guy's sister, who would not write back, but for now it was a question of pain. He shot off the tail. He shot away chunks of meat below the ribs. All around us there was the smell of smoke and filth and deep greenery, and the evening was humid and very hot. Rat went to automatic. He shot randomly, almost casually, quick little spurts in the belly and butt. Then he reloaded, squatted down, and shot it in the left front knee. Again the animal fell hard and tried to get up, but this time it couldn't quite make it. It wobbled and went down sideways. Rat shot it in the nose. He bent forward and whispered something, as if talking to a pet, then he shot it in the throat. All the while the baby buffalo was silent, or almost silent, just a light bubbling sound where the nose had been. It lay very still. Nothing moved except the eyes, which were enormous, the pupils shiny black and dumb.

Rat Kiley was crying. He tried to say something, but then cradled his rifle and went off by himself.

The rest of us stood in a ragged circle around the baby buffalo. For a time no one spoke. We had witnessed something essential, something brand-new and profound, a piece of the world so startling there was not yet a name for it.

Somebody kicked the baby buffalo.

It was still alive, though just barely, just in the eyes.

"Amazing," Dave Jensen said. "My whole life, I never seen anything like it."

"Never?"

"Not hardly. Not once."

Kiowa and Mitchell Sanders picked up the baby buffalo. They hauled it across the open square, hoisted it up, and dumped it in the village well.

Afterward, we sat waiting for Rat to get himself together.

"Amazing," Dave Jensen kept saying. "A new wrinkle. I never seen it before."

Mitchell Sanders took out his yo-yo. "Well, that's Nam," he said. "Garden of Evil. Over here, man, every sin's real fresh and original."

How do you generalize?

War is hell, but that's not the half of it, because war is also mystery and terror and adventure and courage and discovery and holiness and pity and despair and longing and love. War is nasty; war is fun. War is thrilling; war is drudgery. War makes you a man; war makes you dead.

The truths are contradictory. It can be argued, for instance, that war is grotesque. But in truth war is also beauty. For all its horror, you can't help but gape at the awful majesty of combat. You stare out at tracer rounds unwinding through the dark like brilliant red ribbons. You crouch in ambush as a cool, impassive moon rises over the nighttime paddies. You admire the fluid symmetries of troops on the move, the harmonies of sound and shape and proportion, the great sheets of metal-fire streaming down from a gunship, the illumination rounds, the white phosphorus, the purply orange glow of napalm, the rocket's red glare. It's not pretty, exactly. It's astonishing. It fills the eye. It commands you. You hate it, yes, but your eyes do not. Like a killer forest fire, like cancer under a microscope, any battle or bombing raid or artillery barrage has the aesthetic purity of absolute moral indifference—a powerful, implacable beauty—and a true war story will tell the truth about this, though the truth is ugly.

To generalize about war is like generalizing about peace. Almost everything is true. Almost nothing is true. At its core, perhaps, war is just another name for death, and yet any soldier will tell you, if he tells the truth, that proximity to death brings with it a corresponding proximity to life. After a firefight, there is always the immense pleasure of aliveness. The trees are alive. The grass, the soil—everything. All around you things are purely living, and you among them, and the aliveness makes you tremble. You feel an intense, out-of-the-skin awareness of your living self—your truest self, the human being you want to be and then become by the force of wanting it. In the midst of evil you want to be a good man. You want decency. You want justice and courtesy and human concord, things you never knew you wanted. There is a kind of largeness to it, a kind of godliness. Though it's odd, you're never more alive than when you're almost dead. You recognize what's valuable. Freshly, as if for the first time, you love what's best in yourself and in the world, all that might be lost. At the hour of dusk you sit at your foxhole and look out on a wide river turning pinkish red, and at the mountains beyond, and although in the morning you must cross the river and go into the mountains and do terrible things and maybe die, even so, you find yourself studying the fine colors on the river, you feel wonder and awe at the setting of the sun, and you are filled with a hard, aching love for how the world could be and always should be, but now is not.

Mitchell Sanders was right. For the common soldier, at least, war has the feel—the spiritual texture—of a great ghostly fog, thick and permanent. There is no clarity. Everything swirls. The old rules are no longer binding, the old truths no longer true. Right spills over into wrong. Order blends into chaos, love into hate, ugliness into beauty, law into anarchy, civility into savagery. The vapors suck you in. You can't tell where you are, or why you're there, and the only certainty is overwhelming ambiguity.

In war you lose your sense of the definite, hence your sense of truth itself, and therefore it's safe to say that in a true war story nothing is ever absolutely true.

Often in a true war story there is not even a point, or else the point doesn't hit you until twenty years later, in your sleep, and you wake up and shake your wife and start telling the story to her, except when you get to the end you've forgotten the point again. And then for a long time you lie there watching the story happen in your head. You listen to your wife's breathing. The war's over. You close your eyes. You smile and think, Christ, what's the *point?*

This one wakes me up.

In the mountains that day, I watched Lemon turn sideways. He laughed and said something to Rat Kiley. Then he took a peculiar half step, moving from shade into bright sunlight, and the booby-trapped 105 round blew him into a tree. The parts were just hanging there, so Dave Jensen and I were ordered to shinny up and peel him off. I remember the white bone of an arm. I remember pieces of skin and something wet and yellow that must've been the intestines. The gore was horrible, and stays with me. But what wakes me up twenty years later is Dave Jensen singing "Lemon Tree" as we threw down the parts.

You can tell a true war story by the questions you ask. Somebody tells a story, let's say, and afterward you ask, "Is it true?" and if the answer matters, you've got your answer.

For example, we've all heard this one. Four guys go down a trail. A grenade sails out. One guy jumps on it and takes the blast and saves his three buddies.

Is it true?

The answer matters.

You'd feel cheated if it never happened. Without the grounding reality, it's just a trite bit of puffery, pure Hollywood, untrue in the way all such stories are untrue. Yet even if it did happen—and maybe it did, anything's possible—even then you know it can't be true, because a true war story does not depend upon that kind of truth. Absolute occurrence is irrelevant. A thing may happen and be a total lie; another thing may not happen and be truer than the truth. For example: Four guys go down a trail. A grenade sails out. One guy jumps on it and takes the blast, but it's a killer grenade and everybody dies anyway. Before they die, though, one of the dead guys says, "The fuck you do *that* for?" and the jumper says, "Story of my life, man," and the other guy starts to smile but he's dead.

That's a true story that never happened.

Twenty years later, I can still see the sunlight on Lemon's face. I can see him turning, looking back at Rat Kiley, then he laughed and took that curious half step from shade into sunlight, his face suddenly brown and shining, and when his foot touched down, in that instant, he must've thought it was the sunlight that was killing him. It was not the sunlight. It was a rigged 105 round. But if I could ever get the story right, how the sun seemed to gather around him and pick him up and lift him high into a tree, if I could somehow re-create the fatal whiteness of that light, the quick glare, the obvious cause and effect, then you would believe the last thing Curt Lemon believed, which for him must've been the final truth.

Now and then, when I tell this story, someone will come up to me afterward and say she liked it. It's always a woman. Usually it's an older woman of kindly temperament and humane politics. She'll explain that as a rule she hates war stories; she can't understand why people want to wallow in all the blood and gore.

But this one she liked. The poor baby buffalo, it made her sad. Sometimes, even, there are little tears. What I should do, she'll say, is put it all behind me. Find new stories to tell.

I won't say it but I'll think it.

I'll picture Rat Kiley's face, his grief, and I'll think, *You dumb cooze.*

Because she wasn't listening.

It *wasn't* a war story. It was a *love* story.

But you can't say that. All you can do is tell it one more time, patiently, adding and subtracting, making up a few things to get at the real truth. No Mitchell Sanders, you tell her. No Lemon, no Rat Kiley. No trail junction. No baby buffalo. No vines or moss or white blossoms. Beginning to end, you tell her, it's all made up. Every goddamn detail—the mountains and the river and especially that poor dumb baby buffalo. None of it happened. *None* of it. And even if it did happen, it didn't happen in the mountains, it happened in this little village on the Batangan Peninsula, and it was raining like crazy, and one night a guy named Stink Harris woke up screaming with a leech on his tongue. You can tell a true war story if you just keep on telling it.

And in the end, of course, a true war story is never about war. It's about sunlight. It's about the special way that dawn spreads out on a river when you know you must cross the river and march into the mountains and do things you are afraid to do. It's about love and memory. It's about sorrow. It's about sisters who never write back and people who never listen.

[handwritten: because, in essence, a true war story is about life and all the encompasses it — it is a celebration of sorts]

Considerations

Thinking

What, according to O'Brien, are the characteristics of a true war story? What do you think might characterize untrue or false war stories? Is this a true war story? Why or why not?

What do you think of the examples of war stories O'Brien includes to illustrate the characteristics of a true war story?

Connecting

Use a few of O'Brien's characteristics of true war stories to evaluate any war story you have heard or read.

Compare the way O'Brien approaches the truth of stories with Lee K. Abbott's approach to telling stories and getting at truth in "The True Story of Why I Do What I Do."

In telling his final war story, O'Brien says, "That's a true story that never happened." What does he mean? Can a writer of true stories make up "a few things to get at the real truth"? Why or why not?

Writing

Select one passage you find especially engaging in O'Brien's piece and write a few pages reacting to and commenting upon what is said or shown there.

Discuss the extent to which the following comment from Philip Caputo's *A Rumor of War* corroborates what O'Brien suggests about war in "How to Tell a True War Story."

Writing about this kind of warfare is not a simple task. Repeatedly, I have found myself wishing that I had been the veteran of a conventional war, with dramatic campaigns and historic battles for subject matter instead of a monotonous succession of ambushes and fire-fights. But there were no Normandies or Gettysburgs for us, no epic clashes that decided the fates of armies or nations. The war was mostly a matter of enduring weeks of expectant waiting and, at random intervals, of conducting vicious manhunts through jungles and swamps where snipers harassed us constantly and booby traps cut us down one by one.

The tedium was occasionally relieved by a large-scale search-and-destroy operation, but the exhilaration of riding the lead helicopter into a landing zone was usually followed by more of the same hot walking, with the mud sucking at our boots and the sun thudding against our helmets while an invisible enemy shot at us from distant tree lines. The rare instances when the VC chose to fight a set-piece battle provided the only excitement; not ordinary excitement, but the manic ecstasy of contact. Weeks of bottled-up tensions would be released in a few minutes of orgiastic violence, men screaming and shouting obscenities above the explosions of grenades and the rapid, rippling bursts of automatic rifles.

Beyond adding a few more corpses to the weekly body count, none of these encounters achieved anything; none will ever appear in military histories or be studied by cadets at West Point. Still, they changed us and taught us, the men who fought in them; in those obscure skirmishes we learned the old lessons about fear, cowardice, courage, suffering, cruelty, and comradeship. Most of all, we learned about death at an age when it is common to think of oneself as immortal. Everyone loses that illusion eventually, but in civilian life it is lost in installments over the years. We lost it all at once and, in the span of months, passed from boyhood through manhood to a premature middle age. The knowledge of death, of the implacable limits placed on a man's existence, severed us from our youth as irrevocably as a surgeon's scissors had once severed us from the womb. And yet, few of us were past twenty-five. We left Vietnam peculiar creatures, with young shoulders that bore rather old heads.

George Orwell
(1903–1950)

George Orwell is the pen name of Eric Blair, born in 1903 to English parents in Bengal, India. Orwell was educated in England, at Crossgates School, and at Eton as a King's Scholar. After declining the university, he went to Burma, where he served as a subdivisional officer in the Indian Imperial Police.

Best known for his fictional allegories *Animal Farm* and *1984,* Orwell has also written remarkable nonfiction, including both books and essays. *Homage to Catalonia* (1938) provides an eyewitness account of the Spanish Civil War, in which Orwell served as a soldier on the Republican side. *The Road to Wigan Pier* (1937) provides an angry account of mining conditions in northern England.

In "Marrakech," Orwell presents an account of a visit to the north African city in Morocco. He organizes his essay as a series of vignettes—brief descriptions of different places around the city, each of which conveys through carefully selected details and artfully constructed incidents an idea about the people who inhabit Marrakech. In "Shooting an Elephant," Orwell presents an analysis of the evils of imperialism by recounting a memorable experience.

Marrakech

As the corpse went past the flies left the restaurant table in a cloud and rushed after it, but they came back a few minutes later.

The little crowd of mourners—all men and boys, no women—threaded their way across the market-place between the piles of pomegranates and the taxis and the camels, wailing a short chant over and over again. What really appeals to the flies is that the corpses here are never put into coffins, they are merely wrapped in a piece of rag and carried on a rough wooden bier on the shoulders of four friends. When the friends get to the burying-ground they hack an oblong hole a foot or two deep, dump the body in it and fling over it a little of the dried-up, lumpy earth, which is like broken brick. No gravestone, no name, no identifying mark of any kind. The burying-ground is merely a huge waste of hummocky earth, like a derelict building-lot. After a month or two no one can even be certain where his own relatives are buried.

When you walk through a town like this—two hundred thousand inhabitants, of whom at least twenty thousand own literally nothing except the rags they stand up in—when you see how the people live, and still more how easily they die, it is always difficult to believe that you are walking among human beings. All colonial empires are in reality founded upon that fact. The people have brown faces—besides, there are so many of them! Are they really the same flesh as yourself? Do they even have names? Or are they merely a kind of undifferentiated brown stuff, about as individual as bees or coral insects? They rise out of the earth, they sweat and starve for a few years, and then they sink back into the nameless mounds of the graveyard and nobody notices that they are gone. And even the graves themselves soon fade back into the soil. Sometimes, out for a walk, as you break your way through the prickly pear, you notice that it is rather bumpy underfoot, and only a certain regularity in the bumps tells you that you are walking over skeletons.

I was feeding one of the gazelles in the public gardens.

Gazelles are almost the only animals that look good to eat when they are still alive, in fact, one can hardly look at their hindquarters without thinking of mint sauce. The gazelle I was feeding seemed to know that this thought was in my mind, for though it took the piece of bread I was holding out it obviously did not like me. It nibbled rapidly at the bread, then lowered its head and tried to butt me, then took another nibble and then butted again. Probably its idea was that if it could drive me away the bread would somehow remain hanging in mid-air.

An Arab navvy working on the path nearby lowered his heavy hoe and sidled towards us. He looked from the gazelle to the bread and from the bread to the gazelle, with a sort of quiet amazement, as though he had never seen anything quite like this before. Finally he said shyly in French:

"I could eat some of that bread."

I tore off a piece and he stowed it gratefully in some secret place under his rags. This man is an employee of the Municipality.

When you go through the Jewish quarters you gather some idea of what the medieval ghettoes were probably like. Under their Moorish rulers the Jews were only allowed to own land in certain restricted areas, and after centuries of this kind of treatment they have ceased to bother about overcrowding. Many of the streets are a good deal less than six feet wide, the houses are completely windowless, and sore-eyed children cluster everywhere in unbelievable numbers, like clouds of flies. Down the centre of the street there is generally running a little river of urine.

In the bazaar huge families of Jews, all dressed in the long black robe and little black skull-cap, are working in dark fly-infested booths that look like caves. A carpenter sits cross-legged at a prehistoric lathe, turning chair-legs at lightning speed. He works the lathe with a bow in his right hand and guides the chisel with his left foot, and thanks to a lifetime of sitting in this position his left leg is warped out of shape. At his side his grandson, aged six, is already starting on the simpler parts of the job.

I was just passing the coppersmiths' booths when somebody noticed that I was lighting a cigarette. Instantly, from the dark holes all round, there was a frenzied rush of Jews, many of them old grandfathers with flowing grey beards, all clamouring for a cigarette. Even a blind man somewhere at the back of one of the booths heard a rumour of cigarettes and came crawling out, groping in the air with his hand. In about a minute I had used up the whole packet. None of these people, I suppose, works less than twelve hours a day, and every one of them looks on a cigarette as a more or less impossible luxury.

As the Jews live in self-contained communities they follow the same trades as the Arabs, except for agriculture. Fruit-sellers, potters, silversmiths, blacksmiths, butchers, leather-workers, tailors, water-carriers, beggars, porters—whichever way you look you see nothing but Jews. As a matter of fact there are thirteen thousand of them, all living in the space of a few acres. A good job Hitler isn't here. Perhaps he is on his way, however. You hear the usual dark rumours about the Jews, not only from the Arabs but from the poorer Europeans.

"Yes, mon vieux, they took my job away from me and gave it to a Jew. The Jews! They're the real rulers of this country, you know. They've got all the money. They control the banks, finance—everything."

"But," I said, "isn't it a fact that the average Jew is a labourer working for about a penny an hour?"

"Ah, that's only for show! They're all moneylenders really. They're cunning, the Jews."

In just the same way, a couple of hundred years ago, poor old women used to be burned for witchcraft when they could not even work enough magic to get themselves a square meal.

All people who work with their hands are partly invisible, and the more important the work they do, the less visible they are. Still, a white skin is always fairly conspicuous. In northern Europe, when you see a labourer ploughing a field, you probably give him a second glance. In a hot country, anywhere south of Gibraltar or east of Suez, the chances are that you don't even see him. I have noticed this again and again. In a tropical landscape one's eye takes in everything except the human beings. It takes in the dried-up soil, the prickly pear, the palm tree and the distant mountain, but it always misses the peasant hoeing at his patch. He is the same colour as the earth, and a great deal less interesting to look at.

It is only because of this that the starved countries of Asia and Africa are accepted as tourist resorts. No one would think of running cheap trips to the Distressed Areas. But where the human beings have brown skins their poverty is simply not noticed. What does Morocco mean to a Frenchman? An orange-grove or a job in government service. Or to an Englishman? Camels, castles, palm-trees, Foreign Legionnaires, brass trays and bandits. One could probably live here for years without noticing that for nine-tenths of the people the reality of life is an endless, back-breaking struggle to wring a little food out of an eroded soil.

Most of Morocco is so desolate that no wild animal bigger than a hare can live on it. Huge areas which were once covered with forest have turned into a treeless waste where the soil is exactly like broken-up brick. Nevertheless a good deal of it is cultivated, with frightful labour. Everything is done by hand. Long lines of women, bent double like inverted capital Ls, work their way slowly across the field, tearing up the prickly weeds with their hands, and the peasant gathering lucerne for fodder pulls it up stalk by stalk instead of reaping it, thus saving an inch or two on each stalk. The plough is a wretched wooden thing, so frail that one can easily carry it on one's shoulder, and fitted underneath with a rough iron spike which stirs the soil to a depth of about four inches. This is as much as the strength of the animals is equal to. It is usual to plough with a cow and a donkey yoked together. Two donkeys would not be quite strong enough, but on the other hand two cows would cost a little more to feed. The peasants possess no harrows, they merely plough the soil several times over in different directions, finally leaving it in rough furrows, after which the whole field has to be shaped with hoes into small oblong patches, to conserve water. Except for a day or two after the rare rainstorms there is never enough water. Along the edges of the fields channels are hacked out to a depth of thirty or forty feet to get at the tiny trickles which run through the subsoil.

Every afternoon a file of very old women passes down the road outside my house, each carrying a load of firewood. All of them are mummified with age and the sun, and all of them are tiny. It seems to be generally the case in primitive communities that the women, when they get beyond a certain age, shrink to the size of children. One day a poor old creature who could not have been more than four feet tall crept past me under a vast load of wood. I stopped her and put a five-sou piece (a little more than a farthing) into her hand. She answered with a shrill wail, almost a scream, which was partly gratitude but mainly surprise. I suppose that from her point of view, by taking any notice of her, I seemed almost to be violating a law of nature. She accepted her status as an old woman, that is to say as a beast of burden. When a family is travelling it is quite usual to see a father and a grown-up son riding ahead on donkeys, and an old woman following on foot, carrying the baggage.

But what is strange about these people is their invisibility. For several weeks, always at about the same time of day, the file of old women had hobbled past the house with their firewood, and though they had registered themselves on my eyeballs I cannot truly say that I had seen them. Firewood was passing—that was how I saw it. It was only that one day I happened to be walking behind them, and the curious up-and-down motion of a load of wood drew my attention to the human being underneath it. Then for the first time I noticed the poor old earth-coloured bodies, bodies reduced to bones and leathery skin, bent double under the crushing weight. Yet I suppose I had not been five minutes on Moroccan soil before I noticed the overloading of the donkeys and was infuriated by it. There is no question that the donkeys are damnably treated. The Moroccan donkey is hardly bigger than a St Bernard dog, it carries a load which in the British army would be considered too much for a fifteen-hands mule, and very often its pack-saddle is not taken off its back for weeks together. But what is peculiarly pitiful is that it is the most willing creature on earth, it follows its master like a dog and does not need either bridle or halter. After a dozen years of devoted work it suddenly drops dead, whereupon its master tips it into the ditch and the village dogs have torn its guts out before it is cold.

This kind of thing makes one's blood boil, whereas—on the whole—the plight of the human beings does not. I am not commenting, merely pointing to a fact. People with brown skins are next door to invisible. Anyone can be sorry for the donkey with its galled back, but it is generally owing to some kind of accident if one even notices the old woman under her load of sticks.

As the storks flew northward the Negroes were marching southward—a long, dusty column, infantry, screw-gun batteries and then more infantry, four or five thousand men in all, winding up the road with a clumping of boots and a clatter of iron wheels.

They were Senegalese, the blackest Negroes in Africa, so black that sometimes it is difficult to see whereabouts on their necks the hair begins. Their splendid bodies were hidden in reach-me-down khaki uniforms, their feet squashed into boots that looked like blocks of wood, and every tin hat seemed to be a couple of sizes too small. It was very hot and the men had marched a long way. They slumped under the weight of their packs and the curiously sensitive black faces were glistening with sweat.

As they went past a tall, very young Negro turned and caught my eye. But the look he gave me was not in the least the kind of look you might expect. Not hostile, not contemptuous, not sullen, not even inquisitive. It was the shy, wide-eyed Negro look, which actually is a look of profound respect. I saw how it was. This wretched boy, who is a French citizen and has therefore been dragged from the forest to scrub floors and catch syphilis in garrison towns, actually has feelings of reverence before a white skin. He has been taught that the white race are his masters, and he still believes it.

But there is one thought which every white man (and in this connection it doesn't matter twopence if he calls himself a Socialist) thinks when he sees a black army marching past. "How much longer can we go on kidding these people? How long before they turn their guns in the other direction?"

It was curious, really. Every white man there has this thought stowed somewhere or other in his mind. I had it, so had the other onlookers, so had the officers on their sweating chargers and the white NCOs marching in the ranks. It was a kind of secret which we all knew and were too clever to tell; only the Negroes didn't know it. And really it was almost like watching a flock of cattle to see the long column, a mile or two miles of armed men, flowing peacefully up the road, while the great white birds drifted over them in the opposite direction, glittering like scraps of paper.

Considerations

Thinking

This essay says something about Marrakech and about its people. What political point does Orwell make in describing both the place and the people?

To make his point, Orwell relies on incident, illustration, and analogy. In the gazelle episode, for example, a brief scenario is described and a bit of conversation included. What is implied by the man's remark, "I could eat some of that bread"? What is implied by his act of putting the bread in his clothes?

Connecting

In the essay overall, Orwell presents a series of scenes—the burial ground, the zoo, the ghetto, the women carrying firewood, the Senegalese troops—all to convey his view of Marrakech. What does each scene imply, and how are the scenes related?

You might think of the section that begins "When you go through the Jewish quarters" as a miniature version of the essay as a whole. This section contains a series of vignettes, each of which suggests an idea. Identify the scenes and explain what they have in common.

Writing

Write an advertisement or travel poster inviting Americans to vacation in Marrakech, either Orwell's Marrakech or the Marrakech of today. You might think of yourself as a representative for public relations for the Morrocan government. Or you might write as a member of a United Nations committee on world brotherhood.

Describe your neighborhood or campus by selecting a series of locations for brief descriptive vignettes. Try to suggest rather than explicitly state your overall view of the place the vignettes convey.

Shooting an Elephant

George Orwell

In Moulmein, in lower Burma, I was hated by large numbers of people—the only time in my life that I have been important enough for this to happen to me. I was sub-divisional police officer of the town, and in an aimless, petty kind of way anti-European feeling was very bitter. No one had the guts to raise a riot, but if a European woman went through the bazaars alone somebody would probably spit betel juice over her dress. As a police officer I was an obvious target and was baited whenever it seemed safe to do so. When a nimble Burman tripped me up on the football field and the referee (another Burman) looked the other way, the crowd yelled with hideous laughter. This happened more than once. In the end the sneering yellow faces of young men that met me everywhere, the insults hooted after me when I was at a safe distance, got badly on my nerves. The young Buddhist priests were the worst of all. There were several thousands of them in the town and none of them seemed to have anything to do except stand on street corners and jeer at Europeans.

All this was perplexing and upsetting. For at that time I had already made up my mind that imperialism was an evil thing and the sooner I chucked up my job and got out of it the better. Theoretically—and secretly, of course—I was all for the Burmese and all against their oppressors, the British. As for the job I was doing, I hated it more bitterly than I can perhaps make clear. In a job like that you see the dirty work of Empire at close quarters. The wretched prisoners huddling in the stinking cages of the lock-ups, the gray, cowed faces of the long-term convicts, the scarred buttocks of the men who had been flogged with bamboos—all these oppressed me with an intolerable sense of guilt. But I could get nothing into perspective. I was young and ill educated and I had had to think out my problems in the utter silence that is imposed on every Englishman in the East. I did not even know that the British Empire is dying, still less did I know that it is a great deal better than the younger empires that are going to supplant it. All I knew was that I was stuck between my hatred of the empire I served and my rage against the evil-spirited little beasts who tried to make my job impossible. With one part of my mind I thought of the British Raj as an unbreakable tyranny, as something clamped down, in *saecula saeculorum*, upon the will of prostrate peoples; with another part I thought that the greatest joy in the world would be to drive a bayonet into a Buddhist priest's guts. Feelings like these are the normal by-products of imperialism; ask any Anglo-Indian official, if you can catch him off duty.

One day something happened which in a roundabout way was enlightening. It was a tiny incident in itself, but it gave me a better glimpse than I had had before of the real nature of imperialism—the real motives for which despotic governments act. Early one morning the sub-inspector at a police station the other end of the town rang me up on the 'phone and said that an elephant was ravaging the bazaar. Would I please come and do something about it? I did not know what I could do, but I wanted to see what was happening and I got on to a pony and started out. I took my rifle, an old .44 Winchester and much too small to kill an elephant, but I thought the noise might be useful *in terrorem*. Various Burmans stopped me on the way and told me about the elephant's doings. It was not, of course, a wild elephant, but a tame one which had gone "must." It had been chained up, as tame elephants always are when their attack of "must" is due, but on the previous night it had broken its chain and escaped. Its mahout, the only person who could manage it when it was in that state, had set out in pursuit, but had taken the wrong direction and was now twelve hours' journey away, and in the morning the elephant had suddenly reappeared in the town. The Burmese population had no weapons and were quite helpless against it. It had already destroyed somebody's bamboo hut, killed a cow and raided some fruit-stalls and devoured the stock; also it had met the municipal rubbish van and, when the driver jumped out and took to his heels, had turned the van over and inflicted violences upon it.

The Burmese sub-inspector and some Indian constables were waiting for me in the quarter where the elephant had been seen. It was a very poor quarter, a labyrinth of squalid bamboo huts, thatched with palm-leaf, winding all over a steep hillside. I remember that it was a cloudy, stuffy morning at the beginning of the rains. We began questioning the people as to where the elephant had gone and, as usual, failed to get any definite information. That is invariably the case in the East; a story always sounds clear enough at a distance, but the nearer you get to the scene of events the vaguer it becomes. Some of the people said that the elephant had gone in one direction, some said that he had gone in another, some professed not even to have heard of any elephant. I had almost made up my mind that the whole story was a pack of lies, when we heard yells a little distance away. There was a loud, scandalized cry of "Go away, child! Go away this instant!" and an old woman with a switch in her hand came round the corner of a hut, violently shooing away a crowd of naked children. Some more women followed, clicking their tongues and exclaiming; evidently there was something that the children ought not to have seen. I rounded the hut and saw a man's dead body sprawling in the mud. He was an Indian, a black Dravidian coolie, almost naked, and he could not have been dead many minutes. The people said that the elephant had come suddenly upon him round the corner of the hut, caught him with its trunk, put its foot on his back and ground him into the earth. This was the rainy season and the ground was soft, and his face had scored a trench a foot deep and a couple of yards long. He was lying on his belly with arms crucified and head sharply twisted to one side. His face was coated with mud, the eyes wide open, the teeth bared and grinning with an expression of unendurable agony. (Never tell me, by the way, that the dead look peaceful. Most of the corpses I have seen looked devilish.) The friction of the great beast's foot had stripped the skin from his back as neatly as one skins a rabbit. As soon as I saw the dead man I sent an orderly to a friend's house nearby to borrow an elephant rifle. I had already sent back the pony, not wanting it to go mad with fright and throw me if it smelt the elephant.

The orderly came back in a few minutes with a rifle and five cartridges, and meanwhile some Burmans had arrived and told us that the elephant was in the paddy fields below only a few hundred yards away. As I started forward practically the whole population of the quarter flocked out of the houses and followed me. They had seen the rifle and were all shouting excitedly that I was going to shoot the elephant. They had not shown much interest in the elephant when he was merely ravaging their homes, but it was different now that he was going to be shot. It was a bit of fun to them, as it would be to an English crowd; besides they wanted the meat. It made me vaguely uneasy. I had no intention of shooting the elephant—I had merely sent for the rifle to defend myself if necessary—and it is always unnerving to have a crowd following you. I marched down the hill, looking and feeling a fool, with the rifle over my shoulder and an ever-growing army of people jostling at my heels. At the bottom, when you got away from the huts, there was a metalled road and beyond that a miry waste of paddy fields a thousand yards across, not yet ploughed but soggy from the first rains and dotted with coarse grass. The elephant was standing eight yards from the road, his left side toward us. He took not the slightest notice of the crowd's approach. He was tearing up bunches of grass, beating them against his knees to clean them, and stuffing them into his mouth.

I had halted on the road. As soon as I saw the elephant I knew with perfect certainty that I ought not to shoot him. It is a serious matter to shoot a working elephant—it is comparable to destroying a huge and costly piece of machinery—and obviously one ought not to do it if it can possibly be avoided. And at that distance, peacefully eating, the elephant looked no more dangerous than a cow. I thought then and I think now that his attack of "must" was already passing off; in which case he would merely wander harmlessly about until the mahout came back and caught him. Moreover, I did not in the least want to shoot him. I decided that I would watch him for a little while to make sure that he did not turn savage again, and then go home.

But at that moment I glanced round at the crowd that had followed me. It was an immense crowd, two thousand at the least and growing every minute. It blocked the road for a long distance on either side. I looked at the sea of yellow faces above the garish clothes—faces all happy and excited over this bit of fun, all certain that the elephant was going to be shot. They were watching me as they would watch a conjurer about to perform a trick. They did not like me, but with the magical rifle in my hands I was momentarily worth watching. And suddenly I realized that I should have to shoot the elephant after all. The people expected it of me and I had got to do it; I could feel their two thousand wills pressing me forward, irresistibly. And it was at this moment, as I stood there with the rifle in my hands, that I first grasped the hollowness, the futility of the white man's dominion in the East. Here was I, the white man with his gun, standing in front of the unarmed native crowd—seemingly the leading actor of the piece; but in reality I was only an absurd puppet pushed to and fro by the will of those yellow faces behind. I perceived in this moment that when the white man turns tyrant it is his own freedom that he destroys. He becomes a sort of hollow, posing dummy, the conventionalized figure of a sahib. For it is the condition of his rule that he shall spend his life in trying to impress the "natives," and so in every crisis he has got to do what the "natives" expect of him. He wears a mask, and his face grows to fit it. I had got to shoot the elephant. I had committed myself to doing it when I sent for the rifle. A sahib has got to act like a sahib; he has got to appear resolute, to know his own mind and do definite things. To come all that way, rifle in hand, with two thousand people marching at my heels, and then to trail feebly away, having done nothing—no, that was impossible. The crowd would laugh at me. And my whole life, every white man's life in the East, was one long struggle not to be laughed at.

But I did not want to shoot the elephant. I watched him beating his bunch of grass against his knees with that preoccupied grandmotherly air that elephants have. It seemed to me that it would be murder to shoot him. At that age I was not squeamish about killing animals, but I had never shot an elephant and never wanted to. (Somehow it always seems worse to kill a *large* animal.) Besides, there was the beast's owner to be considered. Alive, the elephant was worth at least a hundred pounds; dead, he would only be worth the value of his tusks, five pounds, possibly. But I had got to act quickly. I turned to some experienced-looking Burmans who had been there when we arrived, and asked them how the elephant had been behaving. They all said the same thing: he took no notice of you if you left him alone, but he might charge if you went too close to him.

It was perfectly clear to me what I ought to do. I ought to walk up to within, say, twenty-five yards of the elephant and test his behavior. If he charged, I could shoot; if he took no notice of me, it would be safe to leave him until the mahout came back. But also I knew that I was going to do no such thing. I was a poor shot with a rifle and the ground was soft mud into which one would sink at every step. If the elephant charged and I missed him, I should have about as much chance as a toad under a steam-roller. But even then I was not thinking particularly of my own skin, only of the watchful yellow faces behind. For at that moment, with the crowd watching me, I was not afraid in the ordinary sense, as I would have been if I had been alone. A white man mustn't be frightened in front of "natives," and so, in general, he isn't frightened. The sole thought in my mind was that if anything went wrong those two thousand Burmans would see me pursued, caught, trampled on, and reduced to a grinning corpse like that Indian up the hill. And if that happened it was quite probable that some of them would laugh. That would never do. There was only one alternative. I shoved the cartridges into the magazine and lay down on the road to get a better aim.

The crowd grew very still, and a deep, low, happy sigh, as of people who see the theater curtain go up at last, breathed from innumerable throats. They were going to have their bit of fun after all. The rifle was a beautiful German thing with cross-hair sights. I did not then know that in shooting an elephant one would shoot to cut an imaginary bar running from ear-hole to ear-hole. I ought, therefore, as the elephant was sideways on, to have aimed straight at his ear-hole, actually I aimed several inches in front of this, thinking the brain would be further forward.

When I pulled the trigger I did not hear the bang or feel the kick—one never does when a shot goes home—but I heard the devilish roar of glee that went up from the crowd. In that instant, in too short a time, one would have thought, even for the bullet to get there, a mysterious, terrible change had come over the elephant. He neither stirred nor fell, but every line of his body had altered. He looked suddenly stricken, shrunken, immensely old, as though the frightful impact of the bullet had paralyzed him without knocking him down. At last, after what seemed a long time—it might have been five seconds, I dare say—he sagged flabbily to his knees. His mouth slobbered. An enormous senility seemed to have settled upon him. One could have imagined him thousands of years old. I fired again into the same spot. At the second shot he did not collapse but climbed with desperate slowness to his feet and stood weakly upright, with legs sagging and head drooping. I fired a third time. That was the shot that did for him. You could see the agony of it jolt his whole body and knock the last remnant of strength from his legs. But in falling he seemed for a moment to rise, for as his hind legs collapsed beneath him he seemed to tower upward like a huge rock toppling, his trunk reaching skyward like a tree. He trumpeted, for the first and only time. And then down he came, his belly toward me with a crash that seemed to shake the ground even where I lay.

I got up. The Burmans were already racing past me across the mud. It was obvious that the elephant would never rise again, but he was not dead. He was breathing very rhythmically with long rattling gasps, his great mound of a side painfully rising and falling. His mouth was wide open—I could see far down into caverns of pale pink throat. I waited a long time for him to die, but his breathing did not weaken. Finally I fired my two remaining shots into the spot where I thought his heart must be. The thick blood welled out of him like red velvet, but still he did not die. His body did not even jerk when the shots hit him, the tortured breathing continued without a pause. He was dying, very slowly and in great agony, but in some world remote from me where not even a bullet could damage him further. I felt that I had got to put an end to that dreadful noise. It seemed dreadful to see the great beast lying powerless to move and yet powerless to die, and not even to be able to finish him. I sent back for my small rifle and poured shot after shot into his heart and down his throat. They seemed to make no impression. The tortured gasps continued as steadily as the ticking of a clock.

In the end I could not stand it any longer and went away. I heard later that it took him half an hour to die. Burmans were bringing dahs and baskets even before I left, and I was told they had stripped his body almost to the bones by the afternoon.

Afterward, of course, there were endless discussions about the shooting of the elephant. The owner was furious, but he was only an Indian and could do nothing. Besides, legally I had done the right thing, for a mad elephant has to be killed, like a mad dog, if its owner fails to control it. Among the Europeans opinion was divided. The older men said I was right, the younger men said it was a damn shame to shoot an elephant for killing a coolie, because an elephant was worth more than any damn Coringhee coolie. And afterward I was very glad that the coolie had been killed; it put me legally in the right and it gave me a sufficient pretext for shooting the elephant. I often wondered whether any of the others grasped that I had done it solely to avoid looking a fool.

Considerations

Thinking

What is Orwell's main idea in this essay, and where does he express it? What is the effect of introducing this idea in the middle of the essay rather than reserving it for the end?

Look carefully at Orwell's description of the death of the elephant. What is the effect of that description? What might the elephant represent? Why?

Connecting

In "Shooting an Elephant" as well as in "Marrakech," Orwell makes extensive use of simile and metaphor. In paragraphs 7 and 10 of "Shooting an Elephant," for example, he relies heavily on the imagery of theater and acting. Explain how this imagery serves to convey Orwell's idea.

Compare Orwell's use of such forms of comparison in "Shooting an Elephant" with his use of them in one of his other essays.

Writing

Write an essay in which you describe a time when you were pressured into doing something you didn't want to do. Explain the circumstances, what you did and why, and how you felt about it afterward.

Write an analysis of paragraphs 7–9 or of paragraphs 11–12. Explain what Orwell says, shows, and suggests in either set of paragraphs—and how he goes about it.

Cynthia Ozick
(b. 1928)

Cynthia Ozick was born in New York City, the daughter of a pharmacist. After receiving a B.A. from New York University and an M.A. from Ohio State University, she began writing fiction, publishing her first novel, *Trust,* in 1966. She has subsequently published additional novels, novellas, and short stories. In addition to her fiction, Ozick has published two collections of essays, *Art and Ardor* (1983) and *Metaphor and Memory* (1989).

In "The Seam of the Snail," her talent is amply evident—in a richness of language including a profusion of details and a persistence in working out the implications of her most important and striking images. Her essay, which celebrates the contrast between her and her mother's styles of being alive, is itself full of energy, passion, and vitality.

The Seam of the Snail

In my Depression childhood, whenever I had a new dress, my cousin Sarah would get suspicious. The nicer the dress was, and especially the more expensive it looked, the more suspicious she would get. Finally she would lift the hem and check the seams. This was to see if the dress had been bought or if my mother had sewed it. Sarah could always tell. My mother's sewing had elegant outsides, but there was something catch-as-catch-can about the insides. Sarah's sewing, by contrast, was as impeccably finished inside as out; not one stray thread dangled.

My uncle Jake built meticulous grandfather clocks out of rosewood; he was a perfectionist, and sent to England for the clockworks. My mother built serviceable radiator covers and a serviceable cabinet, with hinged doors, for the pantry. She built a pair of bookcases for the living room. Once, after I was grown and in a house of my own, she fixed the sewer pipe. She painted ceilings, and also land-scapes; she reupholstered chairs. One summer she planted a whole yard of tall corn. She thought herself capable of doing anything, and did everything she imagined. But nothing was perfect. There was always some clear flaw, never visible head-on. You had to look underneath where the seams were. The corn thrived, though not in rows. The stalks elbowed one another like gossips in a dense little village.

"Miss Brrrroooobaker," my mother used to mock, rolling her Russian rs, whenever I crossed a t she had left uncrossed, or corrected a word she had mis-spelled, or became impatient with a v that had tangled itself up with a w in her speech. ("Vvventriloquist," I would say. "Vvventriloquist," she would obediently repeat. And the next time it would come out "wiolinist.") Miss Brubaker was my high school English teacher, and my mother invoked her name as an emblem of raging finical obsession. "Miss Brrrroooobaker," my mother's voice hoots at me down the years, as I go on casting and recasting sentences in a tiny handwriting on monomaniacally uniform paper. The loops of my mother's handwriting—it was the Palmer Method—were as big as hoops, spilling generous splashy ebul-lience. She could pull off, at five minutes' notice, a satisfying dinner for 10 con-cocted out of nothing more than originality and panache. But the napkin would be folded a little off-center, and the spoon might be on the wrong side of the knife. She was an optimist who ignored trifles; for her, God was not in the details but in the intent. And all these culinary and agricultural efflorescences were extracurricular, accomplished in the crevices and niches of a 14-hour business day. When she scribbled out her family memoirs, in heaps of dog-eared notebooks, or on the backs of old bills, or on the margins of last year's calendar, I would resist typing them; in the speed of the chase she often omitted words like "the," "and," "will." The same flashing and bountiful hand fashioned and fired ceramic pots, and painted brilliant autumn views and vases of imaginary flowers and ferns, and decorated ordinary Woolworth platters with lavish enameled gardens. But bits of the painted petals would chip away.

Lavish: my mother was as lavish as nature. She woke early and saturated the hours with work and inventiveness, and read late into the night. She was all profusion, abundance, fabrication. Angry at her children, she would run after us whirling the cord of the electric iron, like a lasso or a whip; but she never caught us. When, in the seventh grade, I was afraid of failing the Music Appreciation final exam because I could not tell the difference between "To a Wild Rose" and "Barcarolle," she got the idea of sending me to school with a gauze sling rigged up on my writing arm, and an explanatory note that was purest fiction. But the sling kept slipping off. My mother gave advice like mad—she boiled over with so much passion for the predicaments of strangers that they turned into permanent cronies. She told intimate stories about people I had never heard of.

Despite the gargantuan Palmer loops (or possibly because of them), I have always known that my mother's was a life of—intricately abashing word!—excellence: insofar as excellence means ripe generosity. She burgeoned, she proliferated; she was endlessly leafy and flowering. She wore red hats, and called herself a gypsy. In her girlhood she marched with the suffragettes and for Margaret Sanger* and called herself a Red. She made me laugh, she was so varied: like a tree on which lemons, pomegranates, and prickly pears absurdly all hang together. She had the comedy of prodigality.

My own way is a thousand times more confined. I am a pinched perfectionist, the ultimate fruition of Miss Brubaker; I attend to crabbed minutiae and am self-trammeled through taking pains. I am a kind of human snail, locked in and condemned by my own nature. The ancients believed that the moist track left by the snail as it crept was the snail's own essence, depleting its body little by little; the farther the snail toiled, the smaller it became, until it finally rubbed itself out. That is how perfectionists are. Say to us Excellence, and we will show you how we use up our substance and wear ourselves away, while making scarcely any progress at all. The fact that I am an exacting perfectionist in a narrow strait only, and nowhere else, is hardly to the point, since nothing matters to me so much as a comely and muscular sentence. It is my narrow strait, this snail's road: the track of the sentence I am writing now; and when I have eked out the wet substance, ink or blood, that is its mark, I will begin the next sentence. Only in reading out sentences am I perfectionist; but then there is nothing else I know how to do, or take much interest in. I miter every pair of abutting sentences as scrupulously as Uncle Jake fitted one strip of rosewood against another. My mother's worldly and bountiful hand has escaped me. The sentence I am writing is my cabin and my shell,

*(1883–1966) American leader in the birth control movement.

compact, self-sufficient. It is the burnished horizon—a merciless planet where flawlessness is the single standard, where even the inmost seams, however hidden from a laxer eye, must meet perfection. Here "excellence" is not strewn casually from a tipped cornucopia, here disorder does not account for charm, here trifles rule like tyrants.

I measure my life in sentences, and my sentences are superior to my mother's, pressed out, line by line, like the lustrous ooze on the underside of the snail, the snail's secret open seam, its wound, leaking attar. My mother was too mettlesome to feel the force of a comma. She scorned minutiae. She measured her life according to what poured from the horn of plenty, which was her ample, cascading, elastic, susceptible, inexact heart. My narrower heart rides between the tiny horns of the snail, dwindling as it goes.

And out of this thinnest thread, this ink-wet line of words, must rise a visionary fog, a mist, a smoke, forging cities, histories, sorrows, quagmires, entanglements, lives of sinners, even the life of my furnace-hearted mother: so much wilderness, waywardness, plentitude on the head of the precise and impeccable snail, between the horns.

Considerations

Thinking

Which do you think is a better title for this essay, "The Seam of the Snail" or "Excellence"? Why? How does Ozick characterize her mother? How does she present herself in relation to her mother? To what extent does Ozick integrate or harmonize the different tendencies each embodies?

Connecting

To what extent do you share characteristics that Ozick possesses? To what extent do you share (or prefer) her mother's way of being?

Identify two metaphors or analogies Ozick uses to describe herself, her mother, or each of them. Explain what Ozick conveys with her metaphors or analogies and what she gains by employing them.

Identify the tone and temper of the following poem. Does it better suggest Ozick or her mother? Why?

A Taste of Rue Cher

Every day I wake up again
to the smell of mandarin oranges
seeping through my open window.
The jazz musician serenades me
his American muse.
My ankles give out to cobblestone streets--
Their elegant sway is not my way,
but I'll continue to practice and pretend.
Purple is the color of my memory
and red the color of my shoes
that walk me down your street.
Christine Kane Molito

Writing

Write an essay in which you define yourself by contrasting yourself with another.

Compare Ozick's depiction of her mother with June Jordan's portrayal of hers in "Many Rivers to Cross."

Roy Reed
(b. 1930)

Roy Reed was a national and then a foreign correspondent for the *New York Times* following a long stint with the *Arkansas Gazette*. Reed recently retired as a professor of journalism at the University of Arkansas and is a farmer in the hills around Fayetteville. He has completed a biography of Orval Faubus, a former governor of Arkansas.

"Spring Comes to Hogeye" is from Reed's book of essays, *Looking for Hogeye*. In this essay, Reed focuses on Ira Solenberger, an aging farmer, who is waiting for the late arrival of spring. With Solenberger's help, Reed raises some interesting questions about the mysteries of plowing and planting as he looks deep into the ebb and flow of the seasons.

Spring Comes to Hogeye

Spring was late in the Ozark Mountains. The first week of April had passed, and the oaks and maples were only then risking a few pale green shoots, tentative little leaves that would not constitute much of a loss if another frost stole in at night on the villainous northwest air.

Ira Solenberger was also late. Practically everybody else in Hogeye had braved the hazard of frost and had planted corn, onions, English peas and Irish potatoes. A few, emulating the bold dogwood and redbud trees, which for more than a week had been blooming bright white and purple against the dark hills, had gone so far as to put out beans, squash and even tender tomato plants.

But Mr. Solenberger, who was regarded as the best gardener in Washington County, had not plowed a furrow or planted a seed. Like the craggy maple in front of his house (itself one of the oldest things in Hogeye, a relic of the Butterfield Stage era), he found that his sap was slow to rise that spring. It had not occurred to him to blame it on his eighty-six years.

"It's that old flu," he said. "Got it back in the winter and can't get rid of it. First time I've had it since 19 and 18."

He opened the door of his heating stove and threw another chunk of wood on the fire. He closed it a little sharply and glanced out the window toward his empty garden.

Every April, the main thing going on in the rural South is vegetable gardening. A farmer might take an hour to talk politics or help a cow give birth, but the really urgent business for him, his wife and all of the children who are old enough to keep their feet off the onion sets is getting seeds and plants in the ground to take advantage of the warming days. With a little luck, the sweet corn planted in early April will have roasting ears ("roashnears," they are called) by the middle of June.

This is a pursuit that seeks every year to outwit the awful force that pushes the shoots from the oak's branches, and that turns Seth Timmons's meadow from brown to green, and impels swallows to build nests in weathered barns.

It was the same force, that spring, that pushed Ira Solenberger out the door in a hat and coat, hunched against the biting bright air blowing up from the Illinois River, to kick the dirt and study the sky, and then retreat to the house to throw another chunk of wood on the fire.

There is still a poet up the road at Fayetteville who, in those days, drove into the hills every April to study the hills and watch for Robert Frost's signs—the gold that is nature's first evidence, "her hardest hue to hold"—and for private signs of his own that stirred his spirit.

Ira Solenberger's mind ran less to poetry than to science. He was an amateur magician, and he performed magic with plants as well as cards.

"Summer before last, I grafted some tomatoes on some poke stalks."

Why?

"Just to see if they would grow."

But when he talked of nature and growth, he used words that Frost might have used, or Thoreau.

"Plow deep. There's one acre right under another acre. I plow both of them."

"Phosphorous makes things grow roots. If you get roots, you're going to get something else."

"I farm with a tractor. But when it gets rowed up and a-growing, I use a roan horse."

He was now in the April sun, away from the stove. His eye scanned the three and a half acres where, just a year earlier—unencumbered by the flu—he had planted rhubarb, corn, tomatoes, squash, sweet potatoes, Irish potatoes, okra, green beans, cantaloupes, radishes, onions, cucumbers and strawberries. He had harvested a bumper crop of everything. He had eaten what he wanted and sold the rest at the farmers' market on the square at Fayetteville.

He pointed to a fallow patch and said, "That's where I had my watermelons last year." He spoke in a loud, professorial voice, as if addressing the cows at the top of the hill.

"They told me I raised the biggest watermelons in Northwest Arkansas. One of them weighed eighty-three pounds.

"I've had people ask me, 'What's your secret for raising watermelons?' I tell them, 'I ain't got no secret.'"

Then, still addressing the cows, he proceeded to tell the secret. Plow the ground deep. Watermelons need more air than water, and deep plowing lets in air.

"I plow turrible deep. Eight or ten inches." He grinned with private satisfaction and moved on to a strawberry patch.

Mr. Solenberger believed in humus. He produced it by placing mulch between the rows. I once knew a Mississippi liberal who enjoyed a minor reputation as a gardener by mulching old copies of the *New York Times*. Mr. Solenberger did not take the *Times*. He used dead crab grass.

"Make sure it's rotten," he said, jabbing the air with an open pocket knife. "If you plow under something that ain't rotten, it's a detriment to you for the first season."

Many of his neighbors planted by the moon, and still do. Mr. Solenberger did not.

"I don't pay any attention to the moon, and I'll tell you why. I've got a neighbor that plants by the moon, and I asked him a question one day that he couldn't answer. I said, 'You plant a seed in dry ground, when the moon is right, and it won't come up. Then ten days later it comes a rain and that seed sprouts and comes up. But by then the sign of the moon is wrong. How do you account for that?' He couldn't answer that. I don't plant by the moon. I plant by the ground."

He was troubled, though, by another phenomenon, and he was a little reluctant to talk about it. He said the frosts seemed to come later each spring, just as the force that drove him to the plow seemed to have arrived late that year.

"The timber's awful slow a-leafing out." He cast a blue eye toward the hill across the road. "When I was a boy, we weren't bothered with frost. When spring come, it come. Our spring's almost a month later than it used to be."

I asked him what he thought the reason was. He glanced at my face to see whether I was ready to accept what he had to say. He decided to risk it.

"Well, sir, I believe the world twists a little bit. You know, everything that grows twists around to the right. Follows the sun. Even our storms that come out of the Gulf, they twist to the right. It's just nature."

Why was a man of eighty-six still involved every April with the earth's greening, as if it were his own? He passed the question off quickly. He indicated that it was merely the same motive that led him to do card tricks and tell jokes and graft tomatoes to poke weed.

"I just like to be doing things."

He returned to the question later, however, sidling up to it so as not to sound too serious. He began by confessing that spring was his favorite season. I asked him why, and he said, "Life is at a high ebb in the spring."

He leaned his chair back against the porch wall and hooked his shoe heels over the lower rung. He studied the trees on the hill across the road, and then he said, "People who are getting up in years, more of them die in the winter when the days are short, and in the hours after midnight. Life is at a low ebb after midnight and in the short days. Did you know that? And the shorter the days, the lower the ebb."

Thus it was the lengthening days that sent Ira Solenberger to the garden, and he could no more resist than the hapless oak bud could resist becoming a leaf.

He was also right about the other. He thrived for one more season of the high ebb. He made one more garden. Then he died in the winter, during the short days.

Considerations

Thinking

Why do you suppose Mr. Solenberger is impatient about the coming of spring? What are the outward signs of his impatience?

What is Reed's attitude toward Mr. Solenberger? How do you know?

Does Mr. Solenberger seem wise to you, or does he seem like a fool? How can you tell?

Connecting

What do you think this question of Reed's has to do with the rest of his essay: "Why was a man of eighty-six still involved every April with the earth's greening, as if it were his own?"

Why does Reed include the paragraph about the "poet up the road at Fayetteville"? Why are Robert Frost's words important in that paragraph?

Writing

Begin by writing a character sketch about someone you know who is interesting. Interview the person, if possible, or interview someone who knows that person well.

Use the character sketch as the basis for writing an essay like "Spring Comes to Hogeye." Bring character sketch and idea together to create the essay. If appropriate, add other stories to those about your character, stories that help you illustrate and develop your idea.

Richard Rodriguez
(b. 1944)

Richard Rodriguez, born in San Francisco, the son of Mexican immigrants, earned his B.A. from Stanford University and his Ph.D. from the University of California at Berkeley. His essays and articles have appeared in *Harper's* (where he is a contributing editor), *Saturday Review, American Scholar,* the *New York Times,* the *Los Angeles Times, Mother Jones,* and the *New Republic.* He has written two books—*Hunger of Memory: The Education of Richard Rodriguez* and *Days of Obligation: An Argument with My Mexican Father*—and two BBC documentaries.

His awards include the Frankel Medal from the National Endowment for the Humanities, a Fulbright Fellowship, and the International Journalism Award from the World Affairs Council of California. Recently, he received a George Foster Peobody Award for his *Newshour* essays on American life. He is known by some as a TV essayist. Many of his essays can be read on the Internet at http://pbs.org/newshour/ww/rodriguez.html.

"The Achievement of Desire," a chapter from *Hunger of Memory*, reveals the perils of an education founded on principles of imitation rather than on originality and creativity; it suggests how nostalgia can serve as a counterpoise for the isolating weight of such an education. "Victorian Houses" considers the metaphorical importance of the city of San Francisco to the lives of gay men.

The Achievement of Desire

I stand in the ghetto classroom—"the guest speaker"—attempting to lecture on the mystery of the sounds of our words to rows of diffident students. "Don't you hear it? Listen! The music of our words. '*Sumer is icumen in*. . . .' And songs on the car radio. We need Aretha Franklin's voice to fill plain words with music—her life." In the face of their empty stares, I try to create an enthusiasm. But the girls in the back row turn to watch some boy passing outside. There are flutters of smiles, waves. And someone's mouth elongates heavy, silent words through the barrier of glass. Silent words—the lips straining to shape each voiceless syllable: "*Meet meee late errr.*" By the door, the instructor smiles at me, apparently hoping that I will be able to spark some enthusiasm in the class. But only one student seems to be listening. A girl, maybe fourteen. In this gray room her eyes shine with ambition. She keeps nodding and nodding at all that I say; she even takes notes. And each time I ask a question, she jerks up and down in her desk like a marionette, while her hand waves over the bowed heads of her classmates. It is myself (as a boy) I see as she faces me now (a man in my thirties).

The boy who first entered a classroom barely able to speak English, twenty years later concluded his studies in the stately quiet of the reading room in the British Museum. Thus with one sentence I can summarize my academic career. It will be harder to summarize what sort of life connects the boy to the man.

With every award, each graduation from one level of education to the next, people I'd meet would congratulate me. Their refrain always the same: "Your parents must be very proud." Sometimes then they'd ask me how I managed it—my "success." (How?) After a while, I had several quick answers to give in reply. I'd admit, for one thing, that I went to an excellent grammar school. (My earliest teachers, the nuns, made my success their ambition.) And my brother and both my sisters were very good students. (They often brought home the shiny school trophies I came to want.) And my mother and father always encouraged me. (At every graduation they were behind the stunning flash of the camera when I turned to look at the crowd.)

As important as these factors were, however, they account inadequately for my academic advance. Nor do they suggest what an odd success I managed. For although I was a very good student, I was also a very bad student. I was a "scholarship boy," a certain kind of scholarship boy. Always successful, I was always unconfident. Exhilarated by my progress. Sad. I became the prized student—anxious and eager to learn. Too eager, too anxious—an imitative and unoriginal pupil. My brother and two sisters enjoyed the advantages I did, and they grew to be as successful as I, but none of them ever seemed so anxious about their schooling. A second-grade student, I was the one who came home and corrected the "simple" grammatical mistakes of our parents. ("Two negatives make a positive.") Proudly I announced—to my family's startled silence—that a teacher had said I was losing all trace of a Spanish accent. I was oddly annoyed when I was unable to get parental help with a homework assignment. The night my father tried to help me with an arithmetic exercise, he kept reading the instructions, each time more deliberately, until I pried the textbook out of his hands, saying, "I'll try to figure it out some more by myself."

When I reached the third grade, I outgrew such behavior. I became more tactful, careful to keep separate the two very different worlds of my day. But then, with ever-increasing intensity, I devoted myself to my studies. I became bookish, puzzling to all my family. Ambition set me apart. When my brother saw me struggling home with stacks of library books, he would laugh, shouting: "Hey, Four Eyes!" My father opened a closet one day and was startled to find me inside, reading a novel. My mother would find me reading when I was supposed to be asleep or helping around the house or playing outside. In a voice angry or worried or just curious, she'd ask: "What do you see in your books?" It became the family's joke. When I was called and wouldn't reply, someone would say I must be hiding under my bed with a book.

(How did I manage my success?)

What I am about to say to you has taken me more than twenty years to admit: *A primary reason for my success in the classroom was that I couldn't forget that schooling was changing me and separating me from the life I enjoyed before becoming a student.* That simple realization! For years I never spoke to anyone about it. Never mentioned a thing to my family or my teachers or classmates. From a very early age, I understood enough, just enough about my classroom experiences to keep what I knew repressed, hidden beneath layers of embarrassment. Not until my last months as a graduate student, nearly thirty years old, was it possible for me to think much about the reasons for my academic success. Only then. At the end of my schooling, I needed to determine how far I had moved from my past. The adult finally confronted, and now must publicly say, what the child shuddered from knowing and could never admit to himself or to those many faces that smiled at his every success. ("Your parents must be very proud. . . .")

I

At the end, in the British Museum (too distracted to finish my dissertation) for weeks I read, speed-read, books by modern educational theorists, only to find infrequent and slight mention of students like me. (Much more is written about the more typical case, the lower-class student who barely is helped by his schooling.) Then one day, leafing through Richard Hoggart's *The Uses of Literacy*, I found, in his description of the scholarship boy, myself. For the first time I realized that there were other students like me, and so I was able to frame the meaning of my academic success, its consequent price—the loss.

Hoggart's description is distinguished, at least initially, by deep understanding. What he grasps very well is that the scholarship boy must move between environments, his home and the classroom, which are at cultural extremes, opposed. With his family, the boy has the intense pleasure of intimacy, the family's consolation in feeling public alienation. Lavish emotions texture home life. *Then*, at school, the instruction bids him to trust lonely reason primarily. Immediate needs set the pace of his parents' lives. From his mother and father the boy learns to trust spontaneity and nonrational ways of knowing. *Then*, at school, there is mental calm. Teachers emphasize the value of a reflectiveness that opens a space between thinking and immediate action.

Years of schooling must pass before the boy will be able to sketch the cultural differences in his day as abstractly as this. But he senses those differences early. Perhaps as early as the night he brings home an assignment from school and finds the house too noisy for study.

> He has to be more and more alone, if he is going to "get on." He will have, proba-bly unconsciously, to oppose the ethos of the hearth, the intense gregariousness of the working-class family group. Since everything centres upon the living-room, there is unlikely to be a room of his own; the bedrooms are cold and inhos-pitable, and to warm them or the front room, if there is one, would not only be expensive, but would require an imaginative leap—out of the tradition—which most families are not capable of making. There is a corner of the living-room table. On the other side Mother is ironing, the wireless is on, someone is singing a snatch of song or Father says intermittently whatever comes into his head. The boy has to cut himself off mentally, so as to do his homework, as well as he can.[1]

The next day, the lesson is as apparent at school. There are even rows of desks. Discussion is ordered. The boy must rehearse his thoughts and raise his hand before speaking out in a loud voice to an audience of classmates. And there is time enough, and silence, to think about ideas (big ideas) never considered at home by his parents.

Not for the working-class child alone is adjustment to the classroom difficult. Good schooling requires that any student alter early childhood habits. But the working-class child is usually least prepared for the change. And, unlike many middle-class children, he goes home and sees in his parents a way of life not only different but starkly opposed to that of the classroom. (He enters the house and hears his parents talking in ways his teachers discourage.)

Without extraordinary determination and the great assistance of others—at home and at school—there is little chance for success. Typically most working-class children are barely changed by the classroom. The exception succeeds. The relative few become scholarship students. Of these, Richard Hoggart estimates, most manage a fairly graceful transition. Somehow they learn to live in the two very different worlds of their day. There are some others, however, those Hoggart pejoratively terms "scholarship boys," for whom success comes with special anxiety. Scholarship boy: good student, troubled son. The child is "moderately endowed," intellectually mediocre, Hoggart supposes—though it may be more pertinent to note the special qualities of temperament in the child. High-strung child. Brooding. Sensitive. Haunted by the knowledge that one *chooses* to become a student. (Education is not an inevitable or natural step in growing up.) Here is a child who cannot forget that his academic success distances him from a life he loved, even from his own memory of himself.

Initially, he wavers, balances allegiance. ("The boy is himself [until he reaches, say, the upper forms] very much of *both* the worlds of home and school. He is enormously obedient to the dictates of the world of school, but emotionally still strongly wants to continue as part of the family circle.") Gradually, necessarily, the balance is lost. The boy needs to spend more and more time studying, each night enclosing himself in the silence permitted and required by intense concentration. He takes his first step toward academic success, away from his family.

From the very first days, through the years following, it will be with his parents—the figures of lost authority, the persons toward whom he feels deepest love—that the change will be most powerfully measured. A separation will unravel between them. Advancing in his studies, the boy notices that his mother and father have not changed as much as he. Rather, when he sees them, they often remind him of the person he once was and the life he earlier shared with them. He realizes what some Romantics also know when they praise the working class for the capacity for human closeness, qualities of passion and spontaneity, that the rest of us experience in like measure only in the earliest part of our youth. For the Romantic, this doesn't make working-class life childish. Working-class life challenges precisely because it is an *adult* way of life.

The scholarship boy reaches a different conclusion. He cannot afford to admire his parents. (How could he and still pursue such a contrary life?) He permits himself embarrassment at their lack of education. And to evade nostalgia for the life he has lost, he concentrates on the benefits education will bestow upon him. He becomes especially ambitious. Without the support of old certainties and consolations, almost mechanically, he assumes the procedures and doctrines of the classroom. The kind of allegiance the young student might have given his mother and father only days earlier, he transfers to the teacher, the new figure of authority. "[The scholarship boy] tends to make a father-figure of his form-master," Hoggart observes.

But Hoggart's calm prose only makes me recall the urgency with which I came to idolize my grammar school teachers. I began by imitating their accents, using their diction, trusting their every direction. The very first facts they dispensed, I grasped with awe. Any book they told me to read, I read—then waited for them to tell me which books I enjoyed. Their every casual opinion I came to adopt and to trumpet when I returned home. I stayed after school "to help"—to get my teacher's undivided attention. It was the nun's encouragement that mattered most to me. (She understood exactly what—my parents never seemed to appraise so well—all my achievements entailed.) Memory gently caressed each word of praise bestowed in the classroom so that compliments teachers paid me years ago come quickly to mind even today.

The enthusiasm I felt in second-grade classes I flaunted before both my parents. The docile, obedient student came home a shrill and precocious son who insisted on correcting and teaching his parents with the remark: "My teacher told us. . . ."

I intended to hurt my mother and father. I was still angry at them for having encouraged me toward classroom English. But gradually this anger was exhausted, replaced by guilt as school grew more and more attractive to me. I grew increasingly successful, a talkative student. My hand was raised in the classroom; I yearned to answer any question. At home, life was less noisy than it had been. (I spoke to classmates and teachers more often each day than to family members.) Quiet at home, I sat with my papers for hours each night. I never forgot that schooling had irretrievably changed my family's life. That knowledge, however, did not weaken ambition. Instead, it strengthened resolve. Those times I remembered the loss of my past with regret, I quickly reminded myself of all the things my teachers could give me. (They could make me an educated man.) I tightened my grip on pencil and books. I evaded nostalgia. Tried hard to forget. But one does not forget by trying to forget. One only remembers. I remembered too well that education had changed my family's life. I would not have become a scholarship boy had I not so often remembered.

Once she was sure that her children knew English, my mother would tell us, "You should keep up your Spanish." Voices playfully groaned in response. "¡Pochos!" my mother would tease. I listened silently.

After a while, I grew more calm at home. I developed tact. A fourth-grade student, I was no longer the show-off in front of my parents. I became a conventionally dutiful son, politely affectionate, cheerful enough, even—for reasons beyond choosing—my father's favorite. And much about my family life was easy then, comfortable, happy in the rhythm of our living together: hearing my father getting ready for work; eating the breakfast my mother had made me; looking up from a novel to hear my brother or one of my sisters playing with friends in the backyard; in winter, coming upon the house all lighted up after dark.

But withheld from my mother and father was any mention of what most mattered to me: the extraordinary experience of first-learning. Late afternoon: in the midst of preparing dinner, my mother would come up behind me while I was trying to read. Her head just over mine, her breath warmly scented with food. "What are you reading?" Or, "Tell me all about your new courses." I would barely respond, "Just the usual things, nothing special." (A half smile, then silence. Her head moving back in the silence. Silence! Instead of the flood of intimate sounds that had once flowed smoothly between us, there was this silence.) After dinner, I would rush to a bedroom with papers and books. As often as possible, I resisted parental pleas to "save lights" by coming to the kitchen to work. I kept so much, so often, to myself. Sad. Enthusiastic. Troubled by the excitement of coming upon new ideas. Eager. Fascinated by the promising texture of a brand-new book. I hoarded the pleasures of learning. Alone for hours. Enthralled. Nervous. I rarely looked away from my books—or back on my memories. Nights when relatives visited and the front rooms were warmed by Spanish sounds, I slipped quietly out of the house.

It mattered that education was changing me. It never ceased to matter. My brother and sisters would giggle at our mother's mispronounced words. They'd correct her gently. My mother laughed girlishly one night, trying not to pronounce *sheep* as *ship*. From a distance I listened sullenly. From that distance, pretending not to notice on another occasion, I saw my father looking at the title pages of my library books. That was the scene on my mind when I walked home with a fourth-grade companion and heard him say that his parents read to him every night. (A strange-sounding book—*Winnie the Pooh*.) Immediately, I wanted to know, "What is it like?" My companion, however, thought I wanted to know about the plot of the book. Another day, my mother surprised me by asking for a "nice" book to read. "Something not too hard you think I might like." Carefully I chose one, Willa Cather's *My Ántonia*. But when, several weeks later, I happened to see it next to her bed unread except for the first few pages, I was furious and suddenly wanted to cry. I grabbed up the book and took it back to my room and placed it in its place, alphabetically on my shelf.

"Your parents must be very proud of you." People began to say that to me about the time I was in sixth grade. To answer affirmatively, I'd smile. Shyly I'd smile, never betraying my sense of the irony: I was not proud of my mother and father. I was embarrassed by their lack of education. It was not that I ever thought they were stupid, though stupidly I took for granted their enormous native intelligence. Simply, what mattered to me was that they were not like my teachers.

But, "Why didn't you tell us about the award?" my mother demanded, her frown weakened by pride. At the grammar school ceremony several weeks after, her eyes were brighter than the trophy I'd won. Pushing back the hair from my forehead, she whispered that I had "shown" the *gringos*. A few minutes later, I heard my father speak to my teacher and felt ashamed of his labored, accented words. Then guilty for the shame. I felt such contrary feelings. (There is no simple road-map through the heart of the scholarship boy.) My teacher was so soft-spoken and her words were edged sharp and clean. I admired her until it seemed to me that she spoke too carefully. Sensing that she was condescending to them, I became nervous. Resentful. Protective. I tried to move my parents away. "You both must be very proud of Richard," the nun said. They responded quickly. (They were proud.) "We are proud of all our children." Then this afterthought: "They sure didn't get their brains from us." They all laughed. I smiled.

Tightening the irony into a knot was the knowledge that my parents were always behind me. They made success possible. They evened the path. They sent their children to parochial schools because the nuns "teach better." They paid a tuition they couldn't afford. They spoke English to us.

For their children my parents wanted chances they never had—an easier way. It saddened my mother to learn that some relatives forced their children to start working right after high school. To *her* children she would say, "Get all the education you can." In schooling she recognized the key to job advancement. And with the remark she remembered her past.

As a girl new to America my mother had been awarded a high school diploma by teachers too careless or busy to notice that she hardly spoke English. On her own, she determined to learn how to type. That skill got her jobs typing envelopes in letter shops, and it encouraged in her an optimism about the possibility of advancement. (Each morning when her sisters put on uniforms, she chose a bright-colored dress.) The years of young womanhood passed, and her typing speed increased. She also became an excellent speller of words she mispronounced. "And I've never been to college," she'd say, smiling, when her children asked her to spell words they were too lazy to look up in a dictionary.

Typing, however, was dead-end work. Finally frustrating. When her youngest child started high school, my mother got a full-time office job once again. (Her paycheck combined with my father's to make us—in fact—what we had already become in our imagination of ourselves—middle class.) She worked then for the (California) state government in numbered civil service positions secured by examinations. The old ambition of her youth was rekindled. During the lunch hour, she consulted bulletin boards for announcements of openings. One day she saw mention of something called an "anti-poverty agency." A typing job. A glamorous job, part of the governor's staff. "A knowledge of Spanish required." Without hesitation she applied and became nervous only when the job was suddenly hers.

"Everyone comes to work all dressed up," she reported at night. And didn't need to say more than that her co-workers wouldn't let her answer the phones. She was only a typist, after all, albeit a very fast typist. And an excellent speller. One morning there was a letter to be sent to a Washington cabinet officer. On the dictating tape, a voice referred to urban guerrillas. My mother typed (the wrong word, correctly): "gorillas." The mistake horrified the anti-poverty bureaucrats who shortly after arranged to have her returned to her previous position. She would go no further. So she willed her ambition to her children. "Get all the education you can; with an education you can do anything." (With a good education *she* could have done anything.)

When I was in high school, I admitted to my mother that I planned to become a teacher someday. That seemed to please her. But I never tried to explain that it was not the occupation of teaching I yearned for as much as it was something more elusive: I wanted to *be* like my teachers, to possess their knowledge, to assume their authority, their confidence, even to assume a teacher's persona.

In contrast to my mother, my father never verbally encouraged his children's academic success. Nor did he often praise us. My mother had to remind him to "say something" to one of his children who scored some academic success. But whereas my mother saw in education the opportunity for job advancement, my father recognized that education provided an even more startling possibility: it could enable a person to escape from a life of mere labor.

In Mexico, orphaned when he was eight, my father left school to work as an "apprentice" for an uncle. Twelve years later, he left Mexico in frustration and arrived in America. He had great expectations then of becoming an engineer. ("Work for my hands and my head.") He knew a Catholic priest who promised to get him money enough to study full time for a high school diploma. But the promises came to nothing. Instead there was a dark succession of warehouse, cannery, and factory jobs. After work he went to night school along with my mother. A year, two passed. Nothing much changed, except that fatigue worked its way into the bone; then everything changed. He didn't talk anymore of becoming an engineer. He stayed outside on the steps of the school while my mother went inside to learn typing and shorthand.

By the time I was born, my father worked at "clean" jobs. For a time he was a janitor at a fancy department store. ("Easy work; the machines do it all.") Later he became a dental technician. ("Simple.") But by then he was pessimistic about the ultimate meaning of work and the possibility of ever escaping its claims. In some of my earliest memories of him, my father already seems aged by fatigue. (He has never really grown old like my mother.) From boyhood to manhood, I have remembered him in a single image: seated, asleep on the sofa, his head thrown back in a hideous corpselike grin, the evening newspaper spread out before him. "But look at all you've accomplished," his best friend said to him once. My father said nothing. Only smiled.

It was my father who laughed when I claimed to be tired by reading and writing. It was he who teased me for having soft hands. (He seemed to sense that some great achievement of leisure was implied by my papers and books.) It was my father who became angry while watching on television some woman at the Miss America contest tell the announcer that she was going to college. ("Majoring in fine arts.") "College!" he snarled. He despised the trivialization of higher education, the inflated grades and cheapened diplomas, the half education that so often passed as mass education in my generation.

It was my father again who wondered why I didn't display my awards on the wall of my bedroom. He said he liked to go to doctors' offices and see their certificates and degrees on the wall. ("Nice.") My citations from school got left in closets at home. The gleaming figure astride one of my trophies was broken, wingless, after hitting the ground. My medals were placed in a jar of loose change. And when I lost my high school diploma, my father found it as it was about to be thrown out with the trash. Without telling me, he put it away with his own things for safekeeping.

These memories slammed together at the instant of hearing that refrain familiar to all scholarship students: "Your parents must be proud. . . ." Yes, my parents were proud. I knew it. But my parents regarded my progress with more than mere pride. They endured my early precocious behavior—but with what private anger and humiliation? As their children got older and would come home to challenge ideas both of them held, they argued before submitting to the force of logic or superior factual evidence with the disclaimer, "It's what we were taught in our time to believe." These discussions ended abruptly, though my mother remembered them on other occasions when she complained that our "big ideas" were going to our heads. More acute was her complaint that the family wasn't close anymore, like some others she knew. Why weren't we close, "more in the Mexican style"? Everyone is so private, she added. And she mimicked the yes and no answers she got in reply to her questions. Why didn't we talk more? (My father never asked.) I never said.

I was the first in my family who asked to leave home when it came time to go to college. I had been admitted to Stanford, one hundred miles away. My departure would only make physically apparent the separation that had occurred long before. But it was going too far. In the months preceding my leaving, I heard the question my mother never asked except indirectly. In the hot kitchen, tired at the end of her workday, she demanded to know, "Why aren't the colleges here in Sacramento good enough for you? They are for your brother and sister." In the middle of a car ride, not turning to face me, she wondered, "Why do you need to go so far away?" Late at night, ironing, she said with disgust, "Why do you have to put us through this big expense? You know your scholarship will never cover it all." But when September came there was a rush to get everything ready. In a bedroom that last night I packed the big brown valise, and my mother sat nearby sewing initials onto the clothes I would take. And she said no more about my leaving.

Months later, two weeks of Christmas vacation: the first hours home were the hardest. ("What's new?") My parents and I sat in the kitchen for a conversation. (But, lacking the same words to develop our sentences and to shape our interests, what was there to say? What could I tell them of the term paper I had just finished on the "universality of Shakespeare's appeal"?) I mentioned only small, obvious things: my dormitory life; weekend trips I had taken; random events. They responded with news of their own. (One was almost grateful for a family crisis about which there was much to discuss.) We tried to make our conversation seem like more than an interview.

II

From an early age I knew that my mother and father could read and write both Spanish and English. I had observed my father making his way through what, I now suppose, must have been income tax forms. On other occasions I waited apprehensively while my mother read onion-paper letters airmailed from Mexico with news of a relative's illness or death. For both my parents, however, reading was something done out of necessity and as quickly as possible. Never did I see either of them read an entire book. Nor did I see them read for pleasure. Their reading consisted of work manuals, prayer books, newspaper, recipes.

Richard Hoggart imagines how, at home,

> . . . [the scholarship boy] sees strewn around, and reads regularly himself, maga-
> zines which are never mentioned at school, which seem not to belong to the
> world to which the school introduces him; at school he hears about and reads
> books never mentioned at home. When he brings those books into the house
> they do not take their place with other books which the family are reading, for
> often there are none or almost none; his books look, rather, like strange tools.

In our house each school year would begin with my mother's careful instruc-tion: "Don't write in your books so we can sell them at the end of the year." The remark was echoed in public by my teachers, but only in part: "Boys and girls, don't write in your books. You must learn to treat them with great care and respect."

OPEN THE DOORS OF YOUR MIND WITH BOOKS, read the red and white poster over the nun's desk in early September. It soon was apparent to me that reading was the classroom's central activity. Each course had its own book. And the information gathered from a book was unquestioned. READ TO LEARN, the sign on the wall advised in December. I privately wondered: What was the connection between reading and learning? Did one learn something only by reading it? Was an idea only an idea if it could be written down? In June, CONSIDER BOOKS YOUR BEST FRIENDS. Friends? Reading was, at best, only a chore. I needed to look up whole paragraphs of words in a dictionary. Lines of type were dizzying, the eye having to move slowly across the page, then down, and across. . . . The sentences of the first books I read were coolly impersonal. Toned hard. What most bothered me, however, was the isolation reading required. To console myself for the loneliness I'd feel when I read, I tried reading in a very soft voice. Until: "Who is doing all that talking to his neighbor?" Shortly after, remedial reading classes were arranged for me with a very old nun.

At the end of each school day, for nearly six months, I would meet with her in the tiny room that served as the school's library but was actually only a storeroom for used textbooks and a vast collection of *National Geographics.* Everything about our sessions pleased me: the smallness of the room; the noise of the janitor's broom hitting the edge of the long hallway outside the door; the green of the sun, lighting the wall; and the old woman's face blurred white with a beard. Most of the time we took turns. I began with my elementary text. Sentences of astonishing simplicity seemed to me lifeless and drab: "The boys ran from the rain . . . She wanted to sing . . . The kite rose in the blue." Then the old nun would read from her favorite books, usually biographies of early American presidents. Playfully she ran through complex sentences, calling the words alive with her voice, making it seem that the author somehow was speaking directly to me. I smiled just to listen to her. I sat there and sensed for the very first time some possibility of fellowship between a reader and a writer, a communication, never *intimate* like that I heard spoken words at home convey, but one nonetheless *personal.*

One day the nun concluded a session by asking me why I was so reluctant to read by myself. I tried to explain; said something about the way written words made me feel all alone—almost, I wanted to add but didn't, as when I spoke to myself in a room just emptied of furniture. She studied my face as I spoke; she seemed to be watching more than listening. In an uneventful voice she replied that I had nothing to fear. Didn't I realize that reading would open up whole new worlds? A book could open doors for me. It could introduce me to people and show me places I never imagined existed. She gestured toward the bookshelves. (Bare-breasted African women danced, and the shiny hubcaps of automobiles on the back covers of the *Geographic* gleamed in my mind.) I listened with respect. But her words were not very influential. I was thinking then of another consequence of literacy, one I was too shy to admit but nonetheless trusted. Books were going to make me "educated." *That* confidence enabled me, several months later, to overcome my fear of the silence.

In fourth grade I embarked upon a grandiose reading program. "Give me the names of important books," I would say to startled teachers. They soon found out that I had in mind "adult books." I ignored their suggestion of anything I suspected was written for children. (Not until I was in college, as a result, did I read

Huckleberry Finn or *Alice's Adventures in Wonderland.*) Instead, I read *The Scarlet Letter* and Franklin's *Autobiography.* And whatever I read I read for extra credit. Each time I finished a book, I reported the achievement to a teacher and basked in the praise my effort earned. Despite my best efforts, however, there seemed to be more and more books I needed to read. At the library I would literally tremble as I came upon whole shelves of books I hadn't read. So I read and I read and I read: *Great Expectations;* all the short stories of Kipling; *The Babe Ruth Story;* the entire first volume of the *Encyclopedia Britannica* (A–ANSTEY); the *Iliad; Moby Dick; Gone with the Wind; The Good Earth; Ramona; Forever Amber; The Lives of the Saints; Crime and Punishment; The Pearl.* . . . Librarians who initially frowned when I checked out the maximum ten books at a time started saving books they thought I might like. Teachers would say to the rest of the class, "I only wish the rest of you took reading as seriously as Richard obviously does."

But at home I would hear my mother wondering, "What do you see in your books?" (Was reading a hobby like her knitting? Was so much reading even healthy for a boy? Was it the sign of "brains"? Or was it just a convenient excuse for not helping about the house on Saturday mornings?) Always, "What do you see . . .?"

What *did* I see in my books? I had the idea that they were crucial for my academic success, though I couldn't have said exactly how or why. In the sixth grade I simply concluded that what gave a book its value was some major idea or theme it contained. If that core essence could be mined and memorized, I would become learned like my teachers. I decided to record in a notebook the themes of the books that I read. After reading *Robinson Crusoe,* I wrote that its theme was "the value of learning to live by oneself." When I completed *Wuthering Heights,* I noted the danger of "letting emotions get out of control." Rereading these brief moralistic appraisals usually left me disheartened. I couldn't believe that they were really the source of reading's value. But for many more years, they constituted the only means I had of describing to myself the educational value of books.

In spite of my earnestness, I found reading a pleasurable activity. I came to enjoy the lonely good company of books. Early on weekday mornings, I'd read in my bed. I'd feel a mysterious comfort then, reading in the dawn quiet—the blue-gray silence interrupted by the occasional churning of the refrigerator motor a few rooms away or the more distant sounds of a city bus beginning its run. On weekends I'd go to the public library to read, surrounded by old men and women. Or, if the weather was fine, I would take my books to the park and read in the shade of a tree. A warm summer evening was my favorite reading time. Neighbors would leave for vacation and I would water their lawns. I would sit through the twilight on the front porches or in backyards, reading to the cool, whirling sounds of the sprinklers.

I also had favorite writers. But often those writers I enjoyed most I was least able to value. When I read William Saroyan's *The Human Comedy*, I was immediately pleased by the narrator's warmth and the charm of his story. But as quickly I became suspicious. A book so enjoyable to read couldn't be very "important." Another summer I determined to read all the novels of Dickens. Reading his fat novels, I loved the feeling I got—after the first hundred pages—of being at home in a fictional world where I knew the names of the characters and cared about what was going to happen to them. And it bothered me that I was forced away at the conclusion, when the fiction closed tight, like a fortune-teller's fist—the futures of all the major characters neatly resolved. I never knew how to take such feelings seriously, however. Nor did I suspect that these experiences could be part of a novel's meaning. Still, there were pleasures to sustain me after I'd finish my books. Carrying a volume back to the library, I would be pleased by its weight. I'd run my fingers along the edge of the pages and marvel at the breadth of my achievement. Around my room, growing stacks of paperback books reenforced my assurance.

I entered high school having read hundreds of books. My habit of reading made me a confident speaker and writer of English. Reading also enabled me to sense something of the shape, the major concerns, of Western thought. (I was able to say something about Dante and Descartes and Engels and James Baldwin in my high school term papers.) In these various ways, books brought me academic success as I hoped that they would. But I was not a good reader. Merely bookish, I lacked a point of view when I read. Rather, I read in order to acquire a point of view. I vacuumed books for epigrams, scraps of information, ideas, themes—anything to fill the hollow within me and make me feel educated. When one of my teachers suggested to his drowsy tenth-grade English class that a person could not have a "complicated idea" until he had read at least two thousand books, I heard the remark without detecting either its irony or its very complicated truth. I merely determined to compile a list of all the books I had ever read. Harsh with myself, I included only once a title I might have read several times. (How, after all, could one read a book more than once?) And I included only those books over a hundred pages in length. (Could anything shorter be a book?)

There was yet another high school list I compiled. One day I came across a newspaper article about the retirement of an English professor at a nearby state college. The article was accompanied by a list of the "hundred most important books of Western Civilization." "More than anything else in my life," the professor told the reporter with finality, "these books have made me all that I am." That was the kind of remark I couldn't ignore. I clipped out the list and kept it for the several months it took me to read all of the titles. Most books, of course, I barely understood. While reading Plato's *Republic,* for instance, I needed to keep looking at the book jacket comments to remind myself what the text was about. Nevertheless, with the special patience and superstition of a scholarship boy, I looked at every word of the text. And by the time I reached the last word, relieved, I convinced myself that I had read *The Republic.* In a ceremony of great pride, I solemnly crossed Plato off my list.

III

The scholarship boy pleases most when he is young—the working-class child struggling for academic success. To his teachers, he offers great satisfaction; his success is their proudest achievement. Many other persons offer to help him. A businessman learns the boy's story and promises to underwrite part of the cost of his college education. A woman leaves him her entire library of several hundred books when she moves. His progress is featured in a newspaper article. Many people seem happy for him. They marvel. "How did you manage so fast?" From all sides, there is lavish praise and encouragement.

In his grammar school classroom, however, the boy already makes students around him uneasy. They scorn his desire to succeed. They scorn him for constantly wanting the teacher's attention and praise. "Kiss Ass," they call him when his hand swings up in response to every question he hears. Later, when he makes it to college, no one will mock him aloud. But he detects annoyance on the faces of some students and even some teachers who watch him. It puzzles him often. In college, then in graduate school, he behaves much as he always has. If anything is different about him it is that he dares to anticipate the successful conclusion of his studies. At last he feels that he belongs in the classroom, and this is exactly the source of the dissatisfaction he causes. To many persons around him, he appears too much the academic. There may be some things about him that recall his beginnings—his shabby clothes; his persistent poverty; or his dark skin (in those cases when it symbolizes his parents' disadvantaged condition)—but they only make clear how far he has moved from his past. He has used education to remake himself.

It bothers his fellow academics to face this. They will not say why exactly. (They sneer.) But their expectations become obvious when they are disappointed. They expect—they want—a student less changed by his schooling. If the scholarship boy, from a past so distant from the classroom, could remain in some basic way unchanged, he would be able to prove that it is possible for anyone to become educated without basically changing from the person one was.

Here is no fabulous hero, no idealized scholar-worker. The scholarship boy does not straddle, cannot reconcile, the two great opposing cultures of his life. His success is unromantic and plain. He sits in the classroom and offers those sitting beside him no calming reassurance about their own lives. He sits in the seminar room—a man with brown skin, the son of working-class Mexican immigrant parents. (Addressing the professor at the head of the table, his voice catches with nervousness.) There is no trace of his parents' in his speech. Instead he approximates the accents of teachers and classmates. Coming from *him* those sounds seem suddenly odd. Odd too is the effect produced when *he* uses academic jargon—bubbles at the tip of his tongue: "*Topos* . . . negative capability . . . vegetation imagery in Shakespearean comedy." He lifts an opinion from Coleridge, takes something else from Frye or Empson or Leavis. He even repeats exactly his professor's earlier comment. All his ideas are clearly borrowed. He seems to have no thought of his own. He chatters while his listeners smile—their look one of disdain.

When he is older and thus when so little of the person he was survives, the scholarship boy makes only too apparent his profound lack of *self*-confidence. This is the conventional assessment that even Richard Hoggart repeats:

> [The scholarship boy] tends to over-stress the importance of examinations, of the piling-up of knowledge and of received opinions. He discovers a technique of

apparent learning, of the acquiring of facts rather than of the handling and use of facts. He learns how to receive a purely literate education, one using only a small part of the personality and challenging only a limited area of his being. He begins to see life as a ladder, as permanent examination with some praise and some further exhortation at each stage. He becomes an expert imbiber and doler-out; his competence will vary, but will rarely be accompanied by genuine enthusiasms. He rarely feels the reality of knowledge, of other men's thoughts and imaginings, on his own pulses. . . . He has something of the blinkered pony about him.

But this is criticism more accurate than fair. The scholarship boy is a very bad student. He is the great mimic; a collector of thoughts, not a thinker; the very last person in class who ever feels obliged to have an opinion of his own. In large part, however, the reason he is such a bad student is because he realizes more often and more acutely than most other students—than Hoggart himself—that education requires radical self-reformation. As a very young boy, regarding his parents, as he struggles with an early homework assignment, he knows this too well. That is why he lacks self-assurance. He does not forget that the classroom is responsible for remaking him. He relies on his teacher, depends on all that he hears in the classroom and reads in his books. He becomes in every obvious way the worst student, a dummy mouthing the opinions of others. But he would not be so bad—nor would he become so successful, a *scholarship* boy—if he did not accurately perceive that the best synonym for primary "education" is "imitation."

Those who would take seriously the boy's success—and his failure—would be forced to realize how great is the change any academic undergoes, how far one must move from one's past. It is easiest to ignore such considerations. So little is said about the scholarship boy in pages and pages of educational literature. Nothing is said of the silence that comes to separate the boy from his parents. Instead, one hears proposals for increasing the self-esteem of students and encouraging early intellectual independence. Paragraphs glitter with a constellation of terms like *creativity* and *originality*. (Ignored altogether is the function of imitation in a student's life.) Radical educationalists meanwhile complain that ghetto schools "oppress" students by trying to mold them, stifling native characteristics. The truer critique would be just the reverse: not that schools change ghetto students too much, but that while they might promote the occasional scholarship student, they change most students barely at all.

From the story of the scholarship boy there is no specific pedagogy to glean. There is, however, a much larger lesson. His story makes clear that education is a long, unglamorous, even demeaning process—*a nurturing never natural to the person one was before one entered a classroom.* At once different from most other students, the scholarship boy is also the archetypal "good student." He exaggerates the difficulty of being a student, but his exaggeration reveals a general predicament. Others are changed by their schooling as much as he. They too must re-form themselves. They must develop the skill of memory long before they become truly critical thinkers. And when they read Plato for the first several times, it will be with awe more than deep comprehension.

The impact of schooling on the scholarship boy is only more apparent to the boy himself and to others. Finally, although he may be laughable—a blinkered pony—the boy will not let his critics forget their own change. He ends up too much like them. When he speaks, they hear themselves echoed. In his pedantry, they trace their own. His ambitions are theirs. If his failure were singular, they might readily pity him. But he is more troubling than that. They would not scorn him if this were not so.

IV

Like me, Hoggart's imagined scholarship boy spends most of his years in the classroom afraid to long for his past. Only at the very end of his schooling does the boy-man become nostalgic. In this sudden change of heart, Richard Hoggart notes:

> He longs for the membership he lost, "he pines for some Nameless Eden where he never was." The nostalgia is the stronger and the more ambiguous because he is really "in quest of his own absconded self yet scared to find it." He both wants to go back and yet thinks he has gone beyond his class, feels himself weighted with knowledge of his own and their situation, which hereafter forbids him the simpler pleasures of his father and mother.

According to Hoggart, the scholarship boy grows nostalgic because he remains the uncertain scholar, bright enough to have moved from his past, yet unable to feel easy, a part of a community of academics.

This analysis, however, only partially suggests what happened to me in my last year as a graduate student. When I traveled to London to write a dissertation on English Renaissance literature, I was finally confident of membership in a "community of scholars." But the pleasure that confidence gave me faded rapidly. After only two or three months in the reading room of the British Museum, it became clear that I had joined a lonely community. Around me each day were dour faces eclipsed by large piles of books. There were the regulars, like the old couple who arrived every morning, each holding a loop of the shopping bag which contained all their notes. And there was the historian who chattered madly to herself. ("Oh dear! Oh! Now, what's this? What? Oh, my!") There were also the faces of young men and women worn by long study. And everywhere eyes turned away the moment our glance accidentally met. Some persons I sat beside day after day, yet we passed silently at the end of the day, strangers. Still, we were united by a common respect for the written word and for scholarship. We did form a union, though one in which we remained distant from one another.

More profound and unsettling was the bond I recognized with those writers whose books I consulted. Whenever I opened a text that hadn't been used for years, I realized that my special interests and skills united me to a mere handful of academics. We formed an exclusive—eccentric!—society, separated from others who would never care or be able to share our concerns. (The pages I turned were stiff like layers of dead skin.) I began to wonder: Who, besides my dissertation director and a few faculty members, would ever read what I wrote? And: Was my dissertation much more than an act of social withdrawal? These questions went unanswered in the silence of the Museum reading room. They remained to trouble me after I'd leave the library each afternoon and feel myself shy—unsteady, speaking simple sentences at the grocer's or the butcher's on my way back to my bed-sitter.

Meanwhile my file cards accumulated. A professional, I knew exactly how to search a book for pertinent information. I could quickly assess and summarize the usability of the many books I consulted. But whenever I started to write, I knew too much (and not enough) to be able to write anything but sentences that were overly cautious, timid, strained brittle under the heavy weight of footnotes and qualifications. I seemed unable to dare a passionate statement. I felt drawn by professionalism to the edge of sterility, capable of no more than pedantic, lifeless, unassailable prose.

Then nostalgia began.

After years spent unwilling to admit its attractions, I gestured nostalgically toward the past. I yearned for that time when I had not been so alone. I became impatient with books. I wanted experience more immediate. I feared the library's silence. I silently scorned the gray, timid faces around me. I grew to hate the growing pages of my dissertation on genre and Renaissance literature. (In my mind I heard relatives laughing as they tried to make sense of its title.) I wanted something—I couldn't say exactly what. I told myself that I wanted a more passionate life. And a life less thoughtful. And above all, I wanted to be less alone. One day I heard some Spanish academics whispering back and forth to each other, and their sounds seemed ghostly voices recalling my life. Yearning became preoccupation then. Boyhood memories beckoned, flooded my mind. (Laughing intimate voices. Bounding up the front steps of the porch. A sudden embrace inside the door.)

For weeks after, I turned to books by educational experts. I needed to learn how far I had moved from my past—to determine how fast I would be able to recover something of it once again. But I found little. Only a chapter in a book by Richard Hoggart. . . . I left the reading room and the circle of faces.

I came home. After the year in England, I spent three summer months living with my mother and father, relieved by how easy it was to be home. It no longer seemed very important to me that we had little to say. I felt easy sitting and eating and walking with them. I watched them, nevertheless, looking for evidence of those elastic, sturdy strands that bind generations in a web of inheritance. I thought as I watched my mother one night: Of course a friend had been right when she told me that I gestured and laughed just like my mother. Another time I saw for myself: my father's eyes were much like my own, constantly watchful.

But after the early relief, this return, came suspicion, nagging until I realized that I had not neatly sidestepped the impact of schooling. My desire to do so was precisely the measure of how much I remained an academic. *Negatively* (for that is how this idea first occurred to me): my need to think so much and so abstractly about my parents and our relationship was in itself an indication of my long education. My father and mother did not pass their thinking about the cultural meanings of their experience. It was I who described their daily lives with airy ideas. And yet, *positively:* the ability to consider experience so abstractly allowed me to shape into desire what would otherwise have remained indefinite, meaningless longing in the British Museum. If, because of my schooling, I had grown culturally separated from my parents, my education finally had given me ways of speaking and caring about that fact.

My best teachers in college and graduate school, years before, had tried to prepare me for this conclusion, I think, when they discussed texts of aristocratic pastoral literature. Faithfully, I wrote down all that they said. I memorized it: "The praise of the unlettered by the highly educated is one of the primary themes of 'elitist' literature." But, "the importance of the praise given the unsolitary, richly passionate and spontaneous life is that it simultaneously reflects the value of a reflective life." I heard it all. But there was no way for any of it to mean very much to me. I was a scholarship boy at the time, busily laddering my way up the rungs of education. To pass an examination, I copied down exactly what my teachers told me. It would require many more years of schooling (an inevitable miseducation) in which I came to trust the silence of reading and the habit of abstracting from immediate experience—moving away from a life of closeness and immediacy I remembered with my parents, growing older—before I turned unafraid to desire the past, and thereby achieved what had eluded me for so long—the end of education.

NOTES

[1]All quotations in this essay are from Richard Hoggart, *The Uses of Literacy* (London: Chatto and Windus, 1957), chapter 10. [Author's note]

Considerations

Thinking

There is a feeling throughout this essay that Rodriguez is not pleased with being a "scholarship boy." Where do you first detect that uneasiness? Where do you begin to understand it?

What do you suppose Rodriguez has in mind when he talks about "some possibility of fellowship between a reader and a writer"?

What do you imagine Rodriguez means in the last sentence of the essay when he speaks of "the end of education"?

Connecting

Are you a "good reader"? Or do you, too, "read in order to acquire a point of view"? What comes first, an idea to guide your reading or reading itself? Explain.

Distinguish two of your own college experiences—one that involved creativity and originality and one that was nothing more than imitation. What do you make of those two experiences?

What happens, according to Rodriguez, when finally you can connect nostalgia with your accumulated reading and imitating?

Is a scholarship boy a product only of working-class families?

Writing

Write an essay that tries to answer Rodriguez's questions: "What was the connection between reading and learning? Did one learn something only by reading it? Was an idea only an idea if it could be written down?"

Write an essay on what you consider to be the "consequences of literacy," as you know them.

Late Victorians

Richard Rodriguez

Saint Augustine writes from his cope of dust that we are restless hearts, for earth is not our true home. Human unhappiness is evidence of our immortality. Intuition tells us we are meant for some other city.

Elizabeth Taylor, quoted in a magazine article of twenty years ago, spoke of cerulean Richard Burton days on her yacht, days that were nevertheless undermined by the elemental private reflection: This must end.

On a Sunday in summer, ten years ago, I was walking home from the Latin mass at Saint Patrick's, the old Irish parish downtown, when I saw thousands of people on Market Street. It was San Francisco's Gay Freedom Day parade—not the first, but the first I ever saw. Private lives were becoming public. There were marching bands. There were floats. Banners blocked single lives thematically into a processional mass, not unlike the consortiums of the blessed in Renaissance paintings, each saint cherishing the apparatus of his martyrdom: GAY DENTISTS. BLACK AND WHITE LOVERS. GAYS FROM BAKERSFIELD. LATINA LESBIANS. From the foot of Market Street they marched, east to west, following the mythic American path toward optimism.

I followed the parade to Civic Center Plaza, where flags of routine nations yielded sovereignty to a multitude. Pastel billows flowed over all.

Five years later, another parade. Politicians waved from white convertibles. Dykes on Bikes revved up, thumbs upped. But now banners bore the acronyms of death. AIDS. ARC. Drums were muffled as passing, plum-spotted young men slid by on motorized cable cars

Though I am alive now, I do not believe that an old man's pessimism is truer than a young man's optimism simply because it comes after. There are things a young man knows that are true and are not yet in the old man's power to recollect. Spring has its sappy wisdom. Lonely teenagers still arrive in San Francisco aboard Greyhound buses. The city can still seem, I imagine, by comparison to where they came from, paradise.

Four years ago, on a Sunday in winter, a brilliant spring afternoon, I was jogging near Fort Point while overhead a young woman was, with difficulty, climbing over the railing of the Golden Gate Bridge. Holding down her skirt with one hand, with the other she waved to a startled spectator (the newspaper next day quoted a workman who was painting the bridge) before she stepped onto the sky.

To land like a spilled purse at my feet.

Serendipity has an eschatological tang here. Always has. Few American cities have had the experience, as we have had, of watching the civic body burn even as we stood, out of body, on a hillside, in a movie theater. Jeanette MacDonald's loony scatting of "San Francisco" has become our go-to-hell anthem. San Francisco has taken some heightened pleasure from the circus of final things. To Atlantis, to Pompeii, to the Pillar of Salt, we add the Golden Gate Bridge, not golden at all but rust red. San Francisco toys with the tragic conclusion.

For most of its brief life, San Francisco has entertained an idea of itself as heaven on earth, whether as Cold Town or City Beautiful or Treasure Island or Haight-Ashbury.

San Francisco can support both comic and tragic conclusions because the city is geographically *in extremis*, a metaphor for the farthest-flung possibility, a metaphor for the end of the line. Land's end.

To speak of San Francisco as land's end is to read the map from one direction only—as Europeans would read or as the East Coast has always read it. In my lifetime, San Francisco has become an Asian city. To speak, therefore, of San Francisco as land's end is to betray parochialism. Before my parents came to California from Mexico, they saw San Francisco as the North. The West was not west for them.

I cannot claim for myself the memory of a skyline such as the one César saw. César came to San Francisco in middle age; César came here as to some final place. He was born in South America; he had grown up in Paris; he had been everywhere, done everything; he assumed the world. Yet César was not condescending toward San Francisco, not at all. Here César saw revolution, and he embraced it.

Whereas I live here because I was born here. I grew up ninety miles away, in Sacramento. San Francisco was the nearest, the easiest, the inevitable city, since I needed a city. And yet I live here surrounded by people for whom San Francisco is a quest.

I have never looked for utopia on a map. Of course, I believe in human advancement. I believe in medicine, in astrophysics, in washing machines. But my compass takes its cardinal point from tragedy. If I respond to the metaphor of spring, I nevertheless learned, years ago, from my Mexican parents, from my Irish nuns, to count on winter. The point of Eden for me, for us, is not approach but expulsion.

After I met César in 1984, our friendly debate concerning the halcyon properties of San Francisco ranged from restaurant to restaurant. I spoke of limits. César boasted of freedoms.

It was César's conceit to add to the gates of Jerusalem, to add to the soccer fields of Tijuana, one other dreamscape hoped for the world over. It was the view from a hill, through a mesh of electrical tram wires, of an urban neighborhood in a valley. The vision took its name from the protruding wedge of a theater marquee. Here César raised his glass without discretion: To the Castro.

There were times, dear César, when you tried to switch sides if only to scorn American optimism, which, I remind you, had already become your own. At the high school where César taught, teachers and parents had organized a campaign to keep kids from driving themselves to the junior prom in an attempt to forestall liquor and death. Such a scheme momentarily reawakened César's Latin skepticism.

Didn't the Americans know? (His tone exaggerated incredulity.) Teenagers will crash into lampposts on their way home from proms, and there is nothing to be done about it. You cannot forbid tragedy.

By California standards I live in an old house. But not haunted. There are too many tall windows, there is too much salty light, especially in winter, though the windows rattle, rattle in summer when the fog lies overhead, and the house creaks and prowls at night. I feel myself immune to any confidence it seeks to tell.

To grow up homosexual is to live with secrets and within secrets. In no other place are those secrets more closely guarded than within the family home. The grammar of the gay city borrows metaphors from the nineteenth-century house. "Coming out of the closet" is predicated upon family laundry, dirty linen, skeletons.

I live in a tall Victorian house that has been converted to four apartments; four single men.

Neighborhood streets are named to honor nineteenth-century men of action, men of distant fame. Clay. Jackson. Scott. Pierce. Many Victorians in the neighborhood date from before the 1906 earthquake and fire.

Architectural historians credit the gay movement of the 1970s with the urban restoration of San Francisco. Twenty years ago this was a borderline neighborhood. This room, like all the rooms of the house, was painted headache green, apple green, boardinghouse green. In the 1970s homosexuals moved into black and working-class parts of the city, where they were perceived as pioneers or as blockbusters, depending.

Two decades ago some of the least expensive sections of San Francisco were wooden Victorian sections. It was thus a coincidence of the market that gay men found themselves living with the architectural metaphor for family. No other architecture in the American imagination is more evocative of family than the Victorian house. In those same years, the 1970s, and within those same Victorian houses, homosexuals were living rebellious lives to challenge the foundations of domesticity.

Was "queer bashing" as much a manifestation of homophobia as a reaction against gentrification? One heard the complaint often enough that gay men were as promiscuous with their capital as otherwise, buying, fixing up, then selling and moving on. Two incomes, no children, described an unfair advantage. No sooner would flower boxes begin to appear than an anonymous reply was smeared on the sidewalk out front: KILL FAGGOTS.

The three- or four-story Victorian house, like the Victorian novel, was built to contain several generations and several classes under one roof, behind a single oaken door. What strikes me is the confidence of Victorian architecture. Stairs, connecting one story with another, describe the confidence that bound generations together through time, confidence that the family would inherit the earth.

If Victorian houses exude a sturdy optimism by day, they are also associated in our imaginations with the Gothic—with shadows and cobwebby gimcrack, long corridors. The nineteenth century was remarkable for escalating optimism even as it excavated the back stairs, the descending architecture of nightmare— Freud's labor and Engels's.

I live on the second story, in rooms that have been rendered as empty as Yorick's skull—gutted, unrattled, in various ways unlocked, added skylights and new windows, new doors. The hallway remains the darkest part of the house.

This winter the hallway and lobby are being repainted to resemble an eighteenth-century French foyer. Of late we had walls and carpet of Sienese red; a baroque mirror hung in an alcove by the stairwell. Now we are to have enlightened austerity of an expensive sort—black-and-white marble floors and faux masonry. A man comes in the afternoons to texture the walls with a sponge and a rag and to paint white mortar lines that create an illusion of permanence, of stone.

The renovation of Victorian San Francisco into dollhouses for libertines may have seemed, in the 1970s, an evasion of what the city was actually becoming. San Francisco's rows of storied houses proclaimed a multigenerational orthodoxy, all the while masking the city's unconventional soul. Elsewhere, meanwhile, domestic America was coming undone.

Suburban Los Angeles, the prototype for a new America, was characterized by a more apparently radical residential architecture. There was, for example, the work of Frank Gehry. In the 1970s Gehry exploded the nuclear-family house, turning it inside out intellectually and in fact. Though, in a way, Gehry merely completed the logic of the postwar suburban tract house with its one story, its sliding glass doors, Formica kitchen, two-car garage. The tract house exchanged privacy for mobility. Heterosexuals opted for the one-lifetime house, the freeway, the birth-control pill, minimalist fiction.

The age-old description of homosexuality is of a sin against nature. Moralistic society has always judged emotion literally. The homosexual was sinful because he had no kosher place to stick it. In attempting to drape the architecture of sodomy with art, homosexuals have lived for thousands of years against the expectations of nature. Barren as Shakers and, interestingly, as concerned with the small effect, homosexuals have made a covenant against nature. Homosexual survival lay in artifice, in plumage, in lampshades, sonnets, musical comedy, couture, syntax, religious ceremony, opera, lacquer, irony.

I once asked Enrique, an interior decorator, if he had many homosexual clients. "*Mais non,*" said he, flexing his eyelids. "Queers don't need decorators. They were born knowing how. All this A.S.I.D. stuff—tests and regulations—as if you can confer a homosexual diploma on a suburban housewife by granting her a discount card."

A knack? The genius, we are beginning to fear in an age of AIDS, is irreplaceable—but does it exist? The question is whether the darling affinities are innate to homosexuality or whether they are compensatory. Why have so many homosexuals retired into the small effect, the ineffectual career, the stereotype, the card shop, the florist? *Be gentle with me?* Or do homosexuals know things others do not?

This way power lay: Once upon a time the homosexual appropriated to himself a mystical province, that of taste. Taste, which is, after all, the insecurity of the middle class, became the homosexual's licentiate to challenge the rule of nature. (The fairy in his blood, he intimated.)

Deciding how best to stick it may be only an architectural problem or a question of physics or of engineering or of cabinetry. Nevertheless, society's condemnation forced the homosexual to find his redemption outside nature. *We'll put a little skirt here.* The impulse is not to create but to re-create, to sham, to convert to sauce, to rouge, to fragrance, to prettify. No effect is too small or too ephemeral to be snatched away from nature, to be ushered toward the perfection of artificiality. *We'll bring out the highlights there.* The homosexual has marshaled the architecture of the straight world to the very gates of Versailles—that great Vatican of fairyland—beyond which power is converted to leisure. In San Francisco in the 1980s the highest form of art became interior decoration. The glory hole was thus converted to an eighteenth-century French foyer.

I live away from the street, in a back apartment, in two rooms. I use my bedroom as a visitor's room—the sleigh bed tricked up with shams into a sofa—whereas I rarely invite anyone into my library, the public room, where I write, the public gesture.

I read in my bedroom in the afternoon because the light is good there, especially now, in winter, when the sun recedes from the earth.

There is a door in the south wall that leads to a balcony. The door was once a window. Inside the door, inside my bedroom, are twin green shutters. They are false shutters, of no function beyond wit. The shutters open into the room; they have the effect of turning my apartment inside out.

A few months ago I hired a man to paint the shutters green. I wanted the green shutters of Manet—you know the ones I mean—I wanted a weathered look, as of verdigris. For several days the painter labored, rubbing his paints into the wood and then wiping them off again. In this way he rehearsed for me decades of the ravages of weather. Yellow enough? Black?

The painter left one afternoon, saying he would return the next day, leaving behind his tubes, his brushes, his sponges and rags. He never returned. Someone told me he has AIDS.

Repainted façades extend now from Jackson Street south into what was once the heart of the black "Mo"—black Fillmore Street. Today there are watercress sandwiches at three o'clock where recently there had been loudmouthed kids, hole-in-the-wall bars, pimps. Now there are tweeds and perambulators, matrons and nannies. Yuppies. And gays.

The gay male revolution had greater influence on San Francisco in the 1970s than did the feminist revolution. Feminists, with whom I include lesbians—such was the inclusiveness of the feminist movement—were preoccupied with career, with escape from the house in order to create a sexually democratic city. Homosexual men sought to reclaim the house, the house that traditionally had been the reward for heterosexuality, with all its selfless tasks and burdens.

Leisure defined the gay male revolution. The gay political movement began, by most accounts, in 1969, with the Stonewall riots in New York City, whereby gay men fought to defend the nonconformity of their leisure.

It was no coincidence that homosexuals migrated to San Francisco in the 1970s, for the city was famed as a playful place, more Catholic than Protestant in its eschatological intuition. In 1975 the state of California legalized consensual homosexuality, and about that same time Castro Street, southwest of downtown, began to eclipse Polk Street as the homosexual address in San Francisco. Polk Street was a string of bars. The Castro was an entire district. The Castro had Victorian houses and churches, bookstores and restaurants, gyms, dry cleaners, supermarkets, and an elected member of the Board of Supervisors. The Castro supported baths and bars, but there was nothing furtive about them. On Castro Street the light of day penetrated gay life through clear plate-glass windows. The light of day discovered a new confidence, a new politics. Also a new look—a noncosmopolitan, Burt Reynolds, butch-kid style: beer, ball games, Levi's, short hair, muscles.

Gay men who lived elsewhere in the city, in Pacific Heights or in the Richmond, often spoke with derision of "Castro Street clones," describing the look, or scorned what they called the ghettoization of homosexuality. To an older generation of homosexuals, the blatancy of sexuality on Castro Street threatened the discreet compromise they had negotiated with a tolerant city.

As the Castro district thrived, Folsom Street, south of Market, also began to thrive, as if in counterdistinction to the utopian Castro. The Folsom Street area was a warehouse district of puddled alleys and deserted streets. Folsom Street offered an assortment of leather bars, an evening's regress to the outlaw sexuality of the fifties, the forties, the nineteenth century, and so on—an eroticism of the dark, of the Reeperbahn, or of the guardsman's barracks.

The Castro district implied that sexuality was more crucial, that homosexuality was the central fact of identity. The Castro district, with its ice cream parlors and hardware stores, was the revolutionary place.

Into which carloads of vacant-eyed teenagers from other districts or from middle-class suburbs would drive after dark, cruising the neighborhood for solitary victims.

The ultimate gay basher was a city supervisor named Dan White, ex-cop, ex-boxer, ex-fireman, ex–altar boy. Dan White had grown up in the Castro district; he recognized the Castro revolution for what it was. Gays had achieved power over him. He murdered the mayor and he murdered the homosexual member of the Board of Supervisors.

Katherine, a sophisticate if ever there was one, nevertheless dismisses the two men descending the aisle at the opera house: "All so sleek and smooth-jowled and silver-haired—they don't seem real, poor darlings. It must be because they don't have children."

Lodged within Katherine's complaint is the perennial heterosexual annoyance with the homosexual's freedom from child rearing, which places the homosexual not so much beyond the pale as it relegates the homosexual outside "responsible" life.

It was the glamour of gay life, after all, as much as it was the feminist call to career, that encouraged heterosexuals in the 1970s to excuse themselves from nature, to swallow the birth-control pill. Who needs children? The gay bar became the paradigm for the singles bar. The gay couple became the paradigm for the selfish couple—all dressed up and everywhere to go. And there was the example of the gay house in illustrated life-style magazines. At the same time that suburban housewives were looking outside the home for fulfillment, gay men were reintroducing a new generation in the city—heterosexual men and women—to the complacencies of the barren house.

Puritanical America dismissed gay camp followers as yuppies; the term means to suggest infantility. Yuppies were obsessive and awkward in their materialism. Whereas gays arranged a decorative life against a barren state, yuppies sought early returns, lives that were not to be all toil and spin. Yuppies, trained to careerism from the cradle, wavered in their pursuit of the northern European ethic—indeed, we might now call it the pan-Pacific ethic—in favor of the Mediterranean, the Latin, the Catholic, the Castro, the Gay .

The international architectural idioms of Skidmore, Owings & Merrill, which defined the city's skyline in the 1970s, betrayed no awareness of any street-level debate concerning the primacy of play in San Francisco nor of any human dramas resulting from urban redevelopment. The repellent office tower was a fortress raised against the sky, against the street, against the idea of a city. Offices were hives where money was made, and damn all.

In the 1970s San Francisco was divided between the interests of downtown and the pleasures of the neighborhoods. Neighborhoods asserted idiosyncrasy, human scale, light. San Francisco neighborhoods perceived downtown as working against their influence in determining what the city should be. Thus neighborhoods seceded from the idea of a city.

The gay movement rejected downtown as representing "straight" conformity. But was it possible that heterosexual Union Street was related to Castro Street? Was it possible that either was related to the Latino Mission district? Or to the Sino-Russian Richmond? San Francisco, though complimented worldwide for holding its center, was in fact without a vision of itself entire.

In the 1980s, in deference to the neighborhoods, City Hall would attempt a counterreformation of downtown, forbidding "Manhattanization." Shadows were legislated away from parks and playgrounds. Height restrictions were lowered beneath an existing skyline. Design, too, fell under the retrojurisdiction of the city planner's office. The Victorian house was presented to architects as a model of what the city wanted to uphold and to become. In heterosexual neighborhoods, one saw newly built Victorians. Downtown, postmodernist prescriptions for playfulness advised skyscrapers to wear party hats, buttons, comic mustaches. Philip

Johnson yielded to the dollhouse impulse to perch angels atop one of his sky-scrapers.

In the 1970s, like a lot of men and women in this city, I joined a gym. My club, I've even caught myself calling it.

In the gay city of the 1970s, bodybuilding became an architectural preoccupation of the upper middle class. Bodybuilding is a parody of labor, a useless accumulation of the laborer's bulk and strength. No useful task is accomplished. And yet there is something businesslike about the habitués, and the gym is filled with the punch-clock logic of the workplace. Machines clank and hum. Needles on gauges toll spent calories.

The gym is at once a closet of privacy and an exhibition gallery. All four walls are mirrored.

I study my body in the mirror. Physical revelation—nakedness—is no longer possible, cannot be desired, for the body is shrouded in meat and wears itself.

The intent is some merciless press of body against a standard, perfect mold. Bodies are "cut" or "pumped" or "buffed" as on an assembly line in Turin. A body becomes so many extrovert parts. Delts, pecs, lats.

I harness myself in a Nautilus cage.

Lats become wings. For the gym is nothing if not the occasion for transcendence. From homosexual to autosexual . . .

I lift weights over my head, baring my teeth like an animal with the strain.

. . . to nonsexual. The effect of the overdeveloped body is the miniaturization of the sexual organs—of no function beyond wit. Behold the ape become Blakean angel, revolving in an empyrean of mirrors.

The nineteenth-century mirror over the fireplace in my bedroom was purchased by a decorator from the estate of a man who died last year of AIDS. It is a top-heavy piece, confusing styles. Two ebony-painted columns support a frieze of painted glass above the mirror. The frieze depicts three bourgeois Graces and a couple of free-range cherubs. The lake of the mirror has formed a cataract, and at its edges it is beginning to corrode.

Thus the mirror that now draws upon my room owns some bright curse, maybe—some memory not mine.

As I regard this mirror, I imagine Saint Augustine's meditation slowly hardening into syllogism, passing down through centuries to confound us: Evil is the absence of good.

We have become accustomed to figures disappearing from our landscape. Does this not lead us to interrogate the landscape?

With reason do we invest mirrors with the superstition of memory, for they, though glass, though liquid captured in a bay, are so often less fragile than we are. They—bright ovals or rectangles or rounds—bump down unscathed, unspilled through centuries, whereas we . . .

The man in the red baseball cap used to jog so religiously on Marina Green. By the time it occurs to me that I have not seen him for months, I realize he may be dead—not lapsed, not moved away. People come and go in the city, it's true.

But in San Francisco in 1990, death has become as routine an explanation for disappearance as Allied Van Lines.

AIDS, it has been discovered, is a plague of absence. Absence opened in the
blood. Absence condensed into the fluid of passing emotion. Absence shot
through opalescent tugs of semen to deflower the city.

And then AIDS, it was discovered, is a nonmetaphorical disease, a disease like
any other. Absence sprang from substance—a virus, a hairy bubble perched upon
a needle, a platter of no intention served round: fever, blisters, a death sentence.

At first I heard only a few names, names connected, perhaps with the right
faces, perhaps not. People vaguely remembered, as through the cataract of this
mirror, from dinner parties or from intermissions. A few articles in the press. The
rumored celebrities. But within months the slow beating of the blood had found
its bay.

One of San Francisco's gay newspapers, the *Bay Area Reporter*, began to
accept advertisements from funeral parlors and casket makers, inserting them
between the randy ads for leather bars and tanning salons. The *Reporter* invited
homemade obituaries—lovers writing of lovers, friends remembering friends and
the blessings of unexceptional life.

Peter. Carlos. Gary. Asel. Perry. Nikos.

Healthy snapshots accompany each annal. At the Russian River. By the
Christmas tree. Lifting a beer. In uniform. A dinner jacket. A satin gown.

He was born in Puerto La Libertad, El Salvador.

He attended Apple Valley High School, where he was their first male cheerleader.

From El Paso. From Medford. From Germany. From Long Island.

I moved back to San Francisco in 1979. Oh, I had had some salad days elsewhere, but by 1979 I was a wintry man. I came here in order not to be distracted by
the ambitions or, for that matter, the pleasures of others but to pursue my own
ambition. Once here, though, I found the company of men who pursued an earthly
paradise charming. Skepticism became my demeanor toward them—I was the
dinner-party skeptic, a firm believer in Original Sin and in the limits of possibility.

Which charmed them.

He was a dancer.

*He settled into the interior-design department of Gump's, where he worked until his
illness.*

He was a teacher.

César, for example.

César could shave the rind from any assertion to expose its pulp and jelly. But
César was otherwise ruled by pulp. César loved everything that ripened in time.
Freshmen. Bordeaux. César could fashion liturgy from an artichoke. Yesterday it
was not ready (cocking his head, rotating the artichoke in his hand over a pot of
cold water). Tomorrow will be too late (Yorick's skull). Today it is perfect (as he lit
the fire beneath the pot). We will eat it now.

If he's lucky, he's got a year, a doctor told me. If not, he's got two.

The phone rang. AIDS had tagged a friend. And then the phone rang again.
And then the phone rang again. Michael had tested positive. Adrian, well, what he

had assumed were shingles . . . Paul was back in the hospital. And César, dammit, César, even César, especially César.

That winter before his death César traveled back to South America. On his return to San Francisco he described to me how he had walked with his mother in her garden—his mother chafing her hands as if she were cold. But it was not cold, he said. They moved slowly. Her summer garden was prolonging itself this year, she said. The cicadas will not stop singing.

When he lay on his deathbed, César said everyone else he knew might get AIDS and die. He said I would be the only one spared—"spared" was supposed to have been chased with irony, I knew, but his voice was too weak to do the job. "You are too circumspect," he said then, wagging his finger upon the coverlet.

So I was going to live to see that the garden of earthly delights was, after all, only wallpaper—was that it, César? Hadn't I always said so? It was then I saw that the greater sin against heaven was my unwillingness to embrace life.

It was not as in some Victorian novel—the curtains drawn, the pillows plumped, the streets strewn with sawdust. It was not to be a matter of custards in covered dishes, steaming possess, *Try a little of this, my dear.* Or gathering up the issues of *Architectural Digest* strewn about the bed. Closing the biography of Diana Cooper and marking its place. Or the unfolding of discretionary screens, morphine, parrots, pavilions.

César experienced agony.

Four of his high school students sawed through a Vivaldi quartet in the corridor outside his hospital room, prolonging the hideous garden.

In the presence of his lover Gregory and friends, Scott passed from this life . . .

He died peacefully at home in his lover Ron's arms.

Immediately after a friend led a prayer for him to be taken home and while his dear mother was reciting the Twenty-third Psalm, Bill peacefully took his last breath.

I stood aloof at César's memorial, the kind of party he would enjoy, everyone said. And so for a time César lay improperly buried, unconvincingly resurrected in the conditional: would enjoy. What else could they say? César had no religion beyond aesthetic bravery.

Sunlight remains. Traffic remains. Nocturnal chic attaches to some discovered restaurant. A new novel is reviewed in the *New York Times.* And the mirror rasps on its hook. The mirror is lifted down.

A priest friend, a good friend, who out of naivete plays the cynic, tells me—this is on a bright, billowy day; we are standing outside—"It's not as sad as you may think. There is at least spectacle in the death of the young. Come to the funeral of an old lady sometime if you want to feel an empty church."

I will grant my priest friend this much: that it is easier, easier on me, to sit with gay men in hospitals than with the staring old. Young men talk as much as they are able.

But those who gather around the young man's bed do not see spectacle. This doll is Death. I have seen people caressing it, staring Death down. I have seen people wipe its tears, wipe its ass; I have seen people kiss Death on his lips, where once there were lips.

Chris was inspired after his own diagnosis in July 1987 with the truth and reality of how such a terrible disease could bring out the love, warmth, and support of so many friends and family.

Sometimes no family came. If there was family, it was usually mother. Mom. With her suitcase and with the torn flap of an envelope in her hand.

Brenda. Pat. Connie. Toni. Soledad.

Or parents came but then left without reconciliation, some preferring to say cancer.

But others came. Sissies were not, after all, afraid of Death. They walked his dog. They washed his dishes. They bought his groceries. They massaged his poor back. They changed his bandages. They emptied his bedpan.

Men who sought the aesthetic ordering of existence were recalled to nature. Men who aspired to the mock-angelic settled for the shirt of hair. The gay community of San Francisco, having found freedom, consented to necessity—to all that the proud world had for so long held up to them, withheld from them, as "real humanity."

And if gays took care of their own, they were not alone. AIDS was a disease of the entire city; its victims were as often black, Hispanic, straight. Neither were Charity and Mercy only white, only male, only gay. Others came. There were nurses and nuns and the couple from next door, co-workers, strangers, teenagers, corporations, pensioners. A community was forming over the city.

Cary and Rick's friends and family wish to thank the many people who provided both small and great kindnesses.

He was attended to and lovingly cared for by the staff at Coming Home Hospice.

And the saints of this city have names listed in the phone book, names I heard called through a microphone one cold Sunday in Advent as I sat in Most Holy Redeemer Church. It might have been any of the churches or community centers in the Castro district, but it happened at Most Holy Redeemer at a time in the history of the world when the Roman Catholic Church still pronounced the homosexual a sinner.

A woman at the microphone called upon volunteers from the AIDS Support Group to come forward. One by one, in twos and threes, throughout the church, people stood up, young men and women, and middle-aged and old, straight, gay, and all of them shy at being called. Yet they came forward and assembled in the sanctuary, facing the congregation, grinning self-consciously at one another, their hands hidden behind them.

I am preoccupied by the fussing of a man sitting in the pew directly in front of me—in his seventies, frail, his iodine-colored hair combed forward and pasted upon his forehead. Fingers of porcelain clutch the pearly beads of what must have been his mother's rosary. He is not the sort of man any gay man would have chosen to become in the 1970s. He is probably not what he himself expected to become. Something of the old dear about him, wizened butterfly, powdered old pour. Certainly he is what I fear becoming. And then he rises, this old monkey, with the most beatific dignity, in answer to the microphone, and he strides into the sanctuary to take his place in the company of the Blessed.

So this is it—this, what looks like a Christmas party in an insurance office and not as in Renaissance paintings, and not as we had always thought, not some flower-strewn, some sequined curtain call of grease-painted heroes gesturing to the stalls. A lady with a plastic candy cane pinned to her lapel. A Castro clone with a red bandanna exploding from his hip pocket. A perfume-counter lady with an Hermès scarf mantled upon her left shoulder. A black man in a checkered sports coat. The pink-haired punkess with a jewel in her nose. Here, too, is the gay couple in middle age, wearing interchangeable plaid shirts and corduroy pants. Blood and shit and Mr. Happy Face. These know the weight of bodies.

Bill died.

. . . Passed on to heaven.

. . . Turning over in his bed one night and then gone.

These learned to love what is corruptible, while I, barren skeptic, reader of Saint Augustine, curator of the earthly paradise, inheritor of the empty mirror, I shift my tailbone upon the cold, hard pew.

Considerations

Thinking

After reading the entire essay, go back to reconsider Rodriguez's beginning. Why do you suppose he begins with Saint Augustine and a sense of "our true home"? What "other city" do you believe that Rodriguez considers us "meant for"? Why does he think so?

As you read the essay a second time, highlight the religious allusions or religious images throughout the essay. How do they contribute to the essay's overarching idea?

What are the implications of Rodriguez's claim that "Taste, which is, after all, the insecurity of the middle class, became the homosexual's licentiate to challenge the rule of nature"?

Connecting

What does Rodriguez make of the relationship between yuppies and homosexuals? Do you consider his analysis of that relationship sound? Are matters more complex than he suggests? Explain.

The last section of Rodriguez's essay begins "The nineteenth-century mirror over the fireplace in my bedroom . . ." and contains within its early paragraphs a return to Saint Augustine (with whom he began his essay). How does this last section connect with the rest of the essay? What is its purpose? How does it complicate and clarify Rodriguez's central idea?

Writing

Write a paragraph explaining what you think Rodriguez means by these statements: "There are things a young man knows that are true and are not yet in the old man's power to recollect. Spring has its sappy wisdom"? In a second paragraph, try to imagine things that you already know that are not yet in the old man's or the old woman's power to recollect.

Write a short account of what you think Rodriguez means by "the grammar of the gay city." Why are houses so important to that grammar? Why, especially, Victorian houses?

Phyllis Rose
(b. 1942)

Phyllis Rose, a professor of English at Wesleyan University, has written essays and reviews for a wide variety of periodicals, including *Vogue,* the *Atlantic Monthly,* the *Washington Post,* and the *New York Times.* She has published biographies of Josephine Baker and Virginia Woolf, written a study of five Victorian marriages *(Parallel Lives),* and published two collections of essays—*Writing About Women* (1985) and *Never Say Goodbye* (1990).

In "Tools of Torture," Rose explores some surprising connections between beauty and pain. The essay is noteworthy for its striking comparisons and its easy and casual manner.

Tools of Torture: An Essay on Beauty and Pain

In a gallery off the rue Dauphine, near the *parfumerie* where I get my massage, I happened upon an exhibit of medieval torture instruments. It made me think that pain must be as great a challenge to the human imagination as pleasure. Otherwise there's no accounting for the number of torture instruments. One would be quite enough. The simple pincer, let's say, which rips out flesh. Or the head crusher, which breaks first your tooth sockets, then your skull. But in addition I saw tongs, thumbscrews, a rack, a ladder, ropes and pulleys, a grill, a garrote, a Spanish horse, a Judas cradle, an iron maiden, a cage, a gag, a strappado, a stretching table, a saw, a wheel, a twisting stork, an inquisitor's chair, a breast breaker, and a scourge. You don't need complicated machinery to cause incredible pain. If you want to saw your victim down the middle, for example, all you need is a slightly bigger than usual saw. If you hold the victim upside down so the blood stays in his head, hold his legs apart and start sawing at the groin, you can get as far as the navel before he loses consciousness.

Even in the Middle Ages, before electricity, there were many things you could do to torment a person. You could tie him up in an iron belt that held the arms and legs up to the chest and left no point of rest, so that all his muscles went into spasm within minutes and he was driven mad within hours. This was the twisting stork, a benign-looking object. You could stretch him out backward over a thin piece of wood so that his whole body weight rested on his spine, which pressed against the sharp wood. Then you could stop up his nostrils and force water into his stomach through his mouth. Then, if you wanted to finish him off, you and your helper could jump on his stomach, causing internal hemorrhage. This torture was called the rack. If you wanted to burn someone to death without hearing him scream, you could use a tongue lock, a metal rod between the jaw and collarbone that prevented him from opening his mouth. You could put a person in a chair with spikes on the seat and arms, tie him down against the spikes, and beat him, so that every time he flinched from the beating he drove his own flesh deeper onto the spikes. This was the inquisitor's chair. If you wanted to make it worse, you could heat the spikes. You could suspend a person over a pointed wooden pyramid and whenever he started to fall asleep, you could drop him onto the point. If you were Ippolito Marsili, the inventor of this torture, known as the

Judas cradle, you could tell yourself you had invented something humane, a torture that worked without burning flesh or breaking bones. For the torture here was supposed to be sleep deprivation.

The secret of torture, like the secret of French cuisine, is that nothing is unthinkable. The human body is like a foodstuff, to be grilled, pounded, filleted. Every opening exists to be stuffed, all flesh to be carved off the bone. You take an ordinary wheel, a heavy wooden wheel with spokes. You lay the victim on the ground with blocks of wood at strategic points under his shoulders, legs, and arms. You use the wheel to break every bone in his body. Next you tie his body onto the wheel. With all its bones broken, it will be pliable. However, the victim will not be dead. If you want to kill him, you hoist the wheel aloft on the end of a pole and leave him to starve. Who would have thought to do this with a man and a wheel? But, then, who would have thought to take the disgusting snail, force it to render its ooze, stuff it in its own shell with garlic butter, bake it, and eat it?

Not long ago I had a facial—only in part because I thought I needed one. It was research into the nature and function of pleasure. In a dark booth at the back of the beauty salon, the aesthetician put me on a table and applied a series of ointments to my face, some cool, some warmed. After a while she put something into my hand, cold and metallic. "Don't be afraid, madame," she said. "It is an electrode. It will not hurt you. The other end is attached to two metal cylinders, which I roll over your face. They break down the electricity barrier on your skin and allow the moisturizers to penetrate deeply." I didn't believe this hocus-pocus. I didn't believe in the electricity barrier or in the ability of these rollers to break it down. But it all felt very good. The cold metal on my face was a pleasant change from the soft warmth of the aesthetician's fingers. Still, since Algeria it's hard to hear the word "electrode" without fear. So when she left me for a few minutes with a moist, refreshing cheesecloth over my face, I thought, What if the goal of her expertise had been pain, not moisture? What if the electrodes had been electrodes in the Algerian sense? What if the cheesecloth mask were dipped in acid?

In Paris, where the body is so pampered, torture seems particularly sinister, not because it's hard to understand but because—as the dark side of sensuality—it seems so easy. Beauty care is among the glories of Paris. *Soins esthétiques* include makeup, facials, massages (both relaxing and reducing), depilations (partial and complete), manicures, pedicures, and tanning, in addition to the usual run of *soins* for the hair: cutting, brushing, setting, waving, styling, blowing, coloring, and streaking. In Paris the state of your skin, hair, and nerves is taken seriously, and there is little of the puritanical thinking that tries to persuade us that beauty comes from within. Nor do the French think, as Americans do, that beauty should be offhand and low-maintenance. Spending time and money on *soins esthétiques* is appropriate and necessary, not self-indulgent. Should that loving attention to the body turn malevolent, you have torture. You have the procedure—the aesthetic, as it were—of torture, the explanation for the rich diversity of torture instruments, but you do not have the cause.

Historically torture has been a tool of legal systems, used to get information needed for a trial or, more directly, to determine guilt or innocence. In the Middle

Ages confession was considered the best of all proofs, and torture was the way to produce a confession. In other words, torture didn't come into existence to give vent to human sadism. It is not always private and perverse but sometimes social and institutional, vetted by the government and, of course, the Church. (There have been few bigger fans of torture than Christianity and Islam.) Righteousness, as much as viciousness, produces torture. There aren't squads of sadists beating down the doors to the torture chambers begging for jobs. Rather, as a recent book on torture by Edward Peters says, the institution of torture creates sadists; the weight of a culture, Peters suggests, is necessary to recruit torturers. You have to convince people that they are working for a great goal in order to get them to overcome their repugnance to the task of causing physical pain to another person. Usually the great goal is the preservation of society, and the victim is presented to the torturer as being in some way out to destroy it.

From another point of view, what's horrifying is how easily you can persuade someone that he is working for the common good. Perhaps the most appalling psychological experiment of modern times, by Stanley Milgram, showed that ordinary, decent people in New Haven, Connecticut, could be brought to the point of inflicting (as they thought) severe electric shocks on other people in obedience to an authority and in pursuit of a goal, the advancement of knowledge, of which they approved. Milgram used—some would say abused—the prestige of science and the university to make his point, but his point is chilling nonetheless. We can cluck over torture, but the evidence at least suggests that with intelligent handling most of us could be brought to do it ourselves.

In the Middle Ages, Milgram's experiment would have had no point. It would have shocked no one that people were capable of cruelty in the interest of something they believed in. That was as it should be. Only recently in the history of human thought has the avoidance of cruelty moved to the forefront of ethics. "Putting cruelty first," as Judith Shklar says in *Ordinary Vices*, is comparatively new. The belief that the "pursuit of happiness" is one of man's inalienable rights, the idea that "cruel and unusual punishment" is an evil in itself, the Benthamite notion that behavior should be guided by what will produce the greatest happiness for the greatest number—all these principles are only two centuries old. They were born with the eighteenth-century democratic revolutions. And in two hundred years they have not been universally accepted. Wherever people believe strongly in some cause, they will justify torture—not just the Nazis, but the French in Algeria.

Many people who wouldn't hurt a fly have annexed to fashion the imagery of torture—the thongs and spikes and metal studs—hence reducing it to the frivolous and transitory. Because torture has been in the mainstream and not on the margins of history, nothing could be healthier. For torture to be merely kinky would be a big advance. Exhibitions like the one I saw in Paris, which presented itself as educational, may be guilty of pandering to the tastes they deplore. Solemnity may be the wrong tone. If taking one's goals too seriously is the danger, the best discouragement of torture may be a radical hedonism that denies that any goal is worth the means, that refuses to allow the nobly abstract to seduce us from the sweetness of the concrete. Give people a good croissant and a good cup of coffee in the morning. Give them an occasional facial and a plate of escargots. Marie Antoinette picked a bad moment to say "Let them eat cake," but I've often thought she was on the right track.

All of which brings me back to Paris, for Paris exists in the imagination of much of the world as the capital of pleasure—of fun, food, art, folly, seduction, gallantry, and beauty. Paris is civilization's reminder to itself that nothing leads you less wrong than your awareness of your own pleasure and a genial desire to spread it around. In that sense the myth of Paris constitutes a moral touchstone, standing for the selfish frivolity that helps keep priorities straight.

Considerations

Thinking

Do you think Rose is correct in her assertion that "wherever people believe strongly in some cause, they will justify torture"? Why or why not? Do you think torture is ever justified?

Do you agree with Rose that the Milgram experiment she refers to is "perhaps the most appalling psychological experiment of modern times"? Why or why not?

Connecting

Summarize the connections Rose identifies between torture and French cuisine. What is your reaction to the analogies she draws between torture and cooking?

What connections does Rose make between the beauty parlor and the torture chamber?

Can Rose's speculations and analogies be further extended to the health and fitness club? Why or why not?

Writing

Write a letter to Phyllis Rose responding to those parts of her essay that struck you more forcibly—whether you like or dislike what she has to say.

Track down Stanley Milgram's description of his experiment on obedience to authority. Discuss your response to Milgram's experiment and his results.

Sharman Apt Russell
(b. 1945)

Sharman Apt Russell teaches writing at Western New Mexico University. Her work has appeared in The *Missouri Review,* The *Threepenny Review,* and *Quarterly West.* "Homebirth" is from her collection of essays, *Songs of the Fluteplayer: Seasons of Life in the Southwest.*

In "Homebirth," Russell looks closely at the practice of giving birth at home in the company of family and midwives, and contrasts it with delivery in a hospital under the charge of paternalistic male physicians.

Homebirth

Her clinic is a tiny whitewashed adobe blazoned with turquoise paint on the door and window sills. Turquoise is a popular color here in Silver City; in Mexican folklore, it has the power to ward off witches. Outside, posted on the minuscule lawn, a neat hand-lettered sign reads Licensed Midwife and then again, underneath, *Partera Registrada.* Inside is a waiting room with three chairs, a box of children's toys, and a decor that leans toward primitive art. A large bulletin board shows a collage of colorful snapshots: euphoric mothers holding newborn babies, euphoric fathers holding newborn babies, babies themselves with eyes squeezed shut and hands upraised in gestures of peace. In a number of photos is the midwife herself, looking tired and pleased.

I am here to pick up a friend, a fellow teacher, who is six months pregnant. A former student of mine, Angelica Gutierrez, waits on the chair beside me. I have been teaching writing skills at the nearby university for nine years, and I see my former students everywhere: at the bank, at the grocery store, at the park with our mutual children. I am not surprised now to see Angelica, and instead of flipping through the magazines provided, we talk about her births.

In 1984 Angelica was sixteen when she had her first baby in the hospital. "Awful, awful, awful," she says of that. They didn't let her husband be with her during labor. They shaved her pubic hair. They took the baby away afterwards. When she was nineteen and pregnant again, Angelica couldn't afford to go to the hospital and so approached, with trepidation, a local midwife. Today Angelica is having her third child. Her husband's new insurance would cover a team of specialists. But Angelica is in love with the homebirth experience. Her friends think she is crazy. "Aren't you scared?" they ask. "No, I'm happy," she says. "Listen to me. This is wonderful."

Angelica's children are being born in the same house that their grandfather and great-uncles and great-aunts were born in. Up into the 1950s, most babies in Grant County were born at home, attended by a registered and licensed midwife. Thirty years later, homebirth accounts for only two percent of national births, a figure true for this area as well. In this clinic, the midwife averages two births a month, although she would like to do more. Her clients range from teenagers to thirty-five-year-old "teacher types." Forty percent are Hispanic, an ethnic group that makes up over 60 percent of the county's population. About half of her customers are on Medicaid. Of these, those who are having a homebirth only to save money almost always, the midwife says, find some last minute, last ditch way to the hospital.

In any discussion of homebirth, ideas of safety—"Aren't you afraid?"—usually come up. In New Mexico, the statistics of midwives and their homebirths are consistently better or similar to hospital births. Indeed, studies across the country and across the world confirm the reasonableness of having a baby at home; the World Health Organization has even urged the United States to support midwives as a way of reducing our high infant mortality rate. For people in the homebirth movement, this is all very old news. Safety is a priority. It is not, necessarily, the heart of the matter.

In 1984, the year Angelica went to the hospital for her first child, I was having my first child in an adobe house thirty miles from town. Like Angelica, I did not choose homebirth intuitively. In truth, I probably would not have had one if most of my friends had not. More bluntly, I did it because they did. Peer pressure may not seem a good reason for this or any decision of importance. In reality, it is exactly why we do so many important things, from getting married to wearing clothes on a hot summer's day. Normalcy is defined by what people are normally doing around you, and the majority of my friends—teacher types, ex-hippies, and one computer consultant—were birthing at home.

My acceptance of a homebirth was also influenced by my husband. Together, we had sweated and strained to build a single adobe room, fifteen-by-twenty feet large. We had made each brick, hammered in each nail, and rolled up the vigas onto the roof by the brute strength of our arms. Although the choice was mine to make, it was clear that a birth in this, our home, followed truly and cleanly from the vision that had brought us here. A homebirth was another way of claiming this house and land as our own. It was a root sinking into the ground. It appealed to my husband's imagination, and in our constructed lives, imagination was a potent force.

Finally, not least, there was my midwife. As she had impressed Angelica on their first meeting, so she impressed me. She is a beautiful Anglo woman, with long golden hair and green eyes, who at the age of twenty-eight projected the authority of someone much older. Those who do not find beauty powerful are possibly around it too much or have never seen it at all. I don't know what this gift did to or for my midwife. I know only that she appeared tremendously competent, forthright, and self-assured. In her presence I felt it would be too gauche, too life-denying, to feel anything but trust in whatever she believed in. (I would realize, years later, that I had obscurely and pre-adolescently fallen in love with her.)

My midwife's assumption that I was also forthright, competent, and self-assured more or less corresponded with my own self-image. At the same time, I had doubts that I never revealed in our biweekly and then weekly sessions. There were moments in which I hoped for some physical problem that would rule out homebirth at the last minute. Under a licensed midwife, the list of these is long, for the integrity of homebirth lies in its restriction to a low-risk pregnancy. If, for example, my baby was too large, too small, too late, too early—then I would go to the hospital.

I had never stayed overnight in a hospital before. Now, suddenly, my picture of that experience grew increasingly benign. Hospital beds seemed so cool and inviting. Hospital white was such a clean color. I knew that such whiteness had its price. The most respected obstetrician in town had once smirked at me and let loose the Freudian slip, "I'd love to have your baby for you, Sharman." Still, secretly, I yearned to lay down the burden of having a child and to lay it precisely in the hands of someone who *was* paternal and overbearing. Let an obstetrician take the credit of birth, as long as he also took the blame. Let him lead me blind-folded through this valley of uncertainty. Let the drugs contract my uterus and the forceps extract the child. If the unspeakable happened, if horror struck and the baby died or was damaged, I believed—I rationalized—that I would be safer in the hospital. I did not mean physically. I meant emotionally. I would not have to feel as much there. A passive figure, wheeled on a metal table, strapped in, drugged, catheterized, fed through an IV, hooked to a machine: I would not be myself. I would not be responsible.

With inverse psychology, these feelings also led me home. The more I yearned for an outside authority, the more I guessed what was to be gained in not relinquishing my own. Something messy, bloody, and intensely personal lay ahead. It must be important if I was afraid of it. It must be, I reasoned, too impor-tant to give away.

Desired and even orchestrated, my first pregnancy had its share of inauspi-cious omens. As I drove home with the good news, a truck turning left accor-dioned my fender into the passenger's seat. Three days later, a doctor gave me Progesterone to "prevent miscarriage." In my vulnerable state, I still roused myself to protest. "Don't take it," the man said classically, "if you don't care about your baby." Soon after I learned that Progesterone was a known cause of birth defects. When I rushed to confirm this with another doctor, he spoke of "heart holes" and "limb reductions" and noted, in a kindly way, that his office did abortions. My third appointment was with a specialist who dismissed the whole affair. In his opinion, if my husband and I were not willing to risk this pregnancy, we were not willing to risk pregnancy at all.

At this point, four weeks after conception, I settled into being an expectant mother. My initiation was fairly typical. Most pregnant women I know have either had a true scare or have concocted one. Growing a baby is the most exotic of lands, bordered by joy, fraught with a sense of danger, and beset by internal poli-tics. Nine months is barely enough time for us to drain these emotions to their last bittersweet dregs. By the end, discomfort compels us. Like adventurers cast on some Pacific isle, we are ready to sail back to civilization.

Thirty-year-old women often have a long first labor, and I was no exception. The amniotic sac ruptured at four o'clock Tuesday morning and as I jumped from the bed to let the water gush from my body, I felt very young, like a child who had gotten up too early on Christmas. For two weeks, I had kept prepared the bag of things my midwife required of me. These included disposable surgical gloves, a bottle of Betadine, a suction for the baby's nose, a thermometer, a large pan, sani-tary napkins, three towels, three sheets, and a dozen clean rags. The last three items had to be sterilized, a feat accomplished by placing them in a brown paper bag in a hot oven for two hours. The "sterilization" lasted two weeks, and I had re-sterilized everything a few days ago. Smugly, a good girl, I returned to bed and a fitful sleep.

In the morning, I called my midwife. By late afternoon she had arrived with her assistant, also a licensed midwife, in a big red van. As the summer evening darkened our south-facing wall of windows, my contractions began seriously. By nine o'clock, they lasted a minute and were two to three minutes apart. My husband set out dinner, a friend came over to help, music was played, and happy talk eddied about the room. I began to pace up and down from the bed to the table to the rocking chair that symbolized our future. My route followed no particular pattern but traced the cement grouting of a floor covered with yellow and orange Mexican tile. As each contraction heightened, my steps slowed, and I counted the tiles, and counted my steps.

By midnight, people were taking shifts. My midwife was herself seven months pregnant and had fallen asleep in the big red van. Her assistant lay on a cot outside, under the dramatic sweep of the Milky Way. Earlier she had impressed us by picking out constellations like Perseus and Lacerta. For three hours, my friend stayed with me and then woke my husband who, for the rest of the night, read aloud *The Yearling* by Marjorie Kinnan Rawlings. I listened to his voice, not the words, and continued to pace the floor, slowly, slavishly, like some ancient Chinese woman with bound feet.

Tedium is a word to describe that labor. The contractions went on, and on, a kneading and cramping meant to stretch and pull open the circular muscles around the cervix. This dilation, measured in centimeters, is complete at the magical number of ten: at that point, the baby is ready to be pushed down the birth canal. Periodically through the night, the midwife or her assistant would check the baby's heartbeat with a stethoscope on my belly. They also checked inside me for an update on the cervix, and for most of that interminable Wednesday, the update was disappointing. At 1:00 A.M., I was three centimeters. At 7:00 A.M., I was four.

At that time, our little adobe had no hot water, and as a way of "making it happen" we all trooped over to a neighbor's house so that I could take a shower and enema. Now, in the few minutes between contractions, I dozed in the hallucinatory way that causes the head to snap upright just as the soul touches the coastline of sleep. There in the shower I saw the pink porcelain tile come alarmingly close. I snapped awake and did not fall. A few hours later, back home again, I had dilated to five.

It was a bold bright afternoon and the southern glass wall of which we were so proud framed the lengthening shadows of yuccas on grama grass. My water had broken a day and a half before, and I had been in moderate to hard labor for fifteen hours. I asked my midwife why it was taking so long. She may have replied that a mother can lengthen labor out of fear or rejection of the child. More probably, she did not say this at all. More probably, it was only an idea rattling about in my head, and I suspected, in the heads of those around me. It was an idea that made me angry. I wasn't afraid! I wanted the baby! I asked my midwife if there was something I could do.

"Get mad," she suggested. "Tell your body you're ready."

That fit my mood well and so I began to mutter, "I'm mad! I'm ready!" as I wandered in my slow and crazy way about the room.

Next I asked the midwife if crying ever helped.

"Oh yes," she assured me, brightening a little. We were both lovers of strategy—of scientific reasoning, technique, and causation. Who knew what chemicals a good cry might stimulate?

Strategically then, my husband and I went off for a car ride on the bumpy road that leads from our house to the black-topped highway. When we reached its flat expanse, we went on driving and in the car, between contractions, as the scenery unrolled, I cried.

In hindsight, the comic moment occurred when we stopped at a trailhead into the Gila National Forest and Gila Wilderness Area. The path follows the sparkling Sapillo Creek, and my husband thought that a short hike along this creek, in the beauty of the woods, would be a good idea. Protesting, I stumbled from the car and leaned heavily on his arm. As we hobbled a few steps down the path, a backpacker emerged from what must have been a first trip or a long one. Spying us, he broke into a grin. We were the first human beings he had seen for days, and eagerly he began the hail-well-met exchange that hikers luxuriate in. He did not get the expected reply. Instead, a huge woman moaned in his face, turned her husband around, and labored back to the car before ever reaching the scenic Sapillo. The backpacker's face remains with me today: young, acne marked, shocked at my inappropriateness.

An hour later, at the house, the midwife's assistant lay tanning on her cot and flipping the last pages of a murder mystery. The midwife sat inside, doing nothing, in a straight-backed chair. She had circles under her eyes, and her own pregnant stomach bloomed uncomfortably beneath her folded hands. "You know," she said, as I began once more to whine and pace the floor. "The pains are only going to get worse."

I stared at her, devastated. They were? At that moment they felt pretty bad. Was this a hint? A move to the hospital? The latter had not occurred to me, for my doubts about homebirth had vanished at the onset of a labor that was long and tedious but never fearful. Now I felt admonished and betrayed. "I'm really mad now," I muttered to my body, to my uterus, to the baby itself. "I'm really ready!"

Later still, we checked my dilation. By this time, I think, I was too tired to feel hopeful. "Oh, you're going to love this," the midwife said. The room's ceiling of pine vigas glowed with the golden light of freshly cut wood. In fact, the ceiling always glowed like this but I rarely noticed it. "You're at nine centimeters. You're almost there!" She laughed, I laughed, and suddenly everyone but me began to move with a bustle and wonderful sense of purpose. Water started boiling. I heard the joyful clink of instruments. I got up from the bed, but no. For the first time, after twenty hours of walking, I wanted only to lie down. From the windows I could see the tip of Cooke's Peak turning to lavender. The hills below were silhouetted against a royal blue in which a single planet shone. Another evening, another night, was at hand.

It took an hour more of waiting and three of pushing before anyone was born. In that time, I learned a lot. As a child, I had never been an athlete in competitive sports, had never understood about concentration or team effort. Once in the sixth grade I did make the "B" team, where my idea of playing baseball was to daydream in the outfield until the ball came to me, by which time it was almost always too late to catch it. In my twenties, for exercise, I became a runner and let my mind and body go their separate ways. Now, here, lying naked in a quilted bed, was what I imagined the best kind of athleticism to be about—about pushing yourself to the limit, about believing in yourself, trying again, moving through the pain, listening to your coach, and trying again.

You can do it! The baby was posterior, lying against my back, and that made it harder. You can do it! I had no urge to push, I didn't know how, and that made it harder. You can do it! My squad of cheerleaders—midwife, assistant, husband, friend—rallied me again and again with that cry. You can do it, they said, and when they forgot to cheer me on, I reminded them to, for I depended on their enthusiasm. I followed their instructions. I used their energy. This was a group effort and, for the first time in my life, I was at the center of it. I was the focal point, concentrating, intent, working, only sometimes scared. Can I do it? I asked them. You can, they said. And I did. It felt great. (My husband has his own story to tell. The pine vigas glowed. Darkness lapped at the window. He had never felt so connected to his life.)

As seven pounds of newborn spilled into the world, I heard the assistant say "It's a blondie!" and then, in a moment, "Oh, what a temper." Gently, they put the amazingly solid baby on my stomach. My husband and I drew close together and stared: our daughter looked floppy, distracted, radiantly pink. It was one minute past midnight, slightly chilly, and someone bundled her into a blanket. My husband cut the cord and we squabbled briefly over who would hold her first. "Maria!" I breathed into her tiny ear. She turned to me, dazed and uncomprehending. Then she held still and took my breast.

As the placenta slithered out, the midwife kneaded my stomach. When I continued to bleed, she gave me a shot of Pitocin to control hemorrhage. By then, the baby had already been given its one and five minute rating on the Apgar scale, where she scored high. As in a hospital, silver nitrate would be applied to her eyes to prevent infection and she would be given a dose of Vitamin K. Because I am Rh negative, a sample of the cord blood would be sent to the hospital. Meanwhile the midwife was sewing up a small tear in my perineum, and my friend, as she is wont to do, went quietly about the business of washing dishes and cleaning house. My husband sat and rocked his child. Outside, the darkness had the eerie expectant sheen of early morning. The birds were still asleep. The birth was over. I felt tremendously energized.

The word *midwife* literally means "with woman" and this quality of witness is perhaps the midwife's greatest virtue. Witness implies empathy, equality, and, in practical terms, a willingness to stay with a laboring mother for as long as it takes. During Hippocrates' time, in Western society, midwives were an honored class. But in the Dark Ages, this feminine profession became increasingly devalued. The idea that witches, acting as midwives, killed unbaptized babies and used them in Satanic rites seemed logical to the Church. As potential sources of birth control and abortion techniques, midwives were doubly damned—and occasionally burned.

By the sixteenth century, tradesmen called barber-surgeons were being brought in for cases of obstructed childbirth. These men brought a bag of perforators and metal hooks used to drag a child from the womb whole or piecemeal. The later refinement of forceps was a major breakthrough in obstetrics. But like other tools of science they were seen as distinctly masculine. At this point, the use of instruments in delivery can be seen as a rough dividing line, with women on one side and men on the other.

The rest of Western midwifery is marked by a struggle between the sexes to gain control of the birth process. By 1850, a part of life historically dominated by women was being successfully usurped. At first, midwives fought back, accusing doctors even then of using instruments unnecessarily to avoid "the onerous chore of staying up throughout the night." Playing hardball, they also brought in the specter of lust: what other motive could explain such "frequent examinations with the finger and the hand"? In response, physicians encouraged the idea that even a normal delivery was so dangerous as to override any embarrassment, suspicion, or pain on the part of the patient. By the twentieth century, pregnancy had evolved, philosophically, into a life-threatening disease.

Starting in the 1920s with the beatific-sounding Twilight Sleep—morphine followed by a hallucinogen coupled with ether or chloroform—mothers could be completely removed from the birth of their children. In 1950, my mother fondly remembers being given a shot, blankness, and then waiting in bed while the nurses took care of my sister. For other women, the hospital experience was anything but beatific, and the horror stories of these years are well known: the isolation of labor, the leather straps, the high metal stirrups. In this setting, the woman was seen, from a technician's point of view, as a birthing machine that required service. Usually the machine also required tinkering. Oxytocyn to start up a "slow" uterus, pain relievers to ease the artificial and unnaturally strong contractions, synthetic hormones again as the drugs impaired the mother's ability to push. Babies were born "blue" from a drug-induced lack of oxygen. The Cesarean rate skyrocketed. And in 1980, American hospitals had more infant deaths due to birth injuries and respiratory diseases than almost any other industrialized nation.

There was opposition. As we learned about the dangers of drugs, both mothers and doctors came to see them as less desirable. Husbands and family members were allowed in the delivery room. Certain medical routines—induced labor, intravenous feeding, and the episiotomy—became less routine. In remote areas, progress, as usual, moved in fits and starts. Still, in 1987 when I was pregnant with my second child, a progressive family-care doctor had just opened her office, nurse-midwives worked at the hospital, and the hospital itself touted a "birthing room" with homey atmosphere and wooden cradle for the baby. Even the most respected obstetrician in town had adopted a different, if still paternal, stance. One friend reported with dismay that he would not let her have the painkiller she requested. "Wait it out," he cajoled her cheerfully. "Just a few more minutes. You can do it."

In part because my options were greater, my decision to have a second home-birth was not automatic. In some ways I felt more conservative than before and, to my surprise, so did my midwife. After three more years of catching babies, she had a greater respect for her relationship to statistics. If only 1 percent of mothers hemorrhage dangerously after labor, the midwife who sees a hundred mothers will see the one who does. If only a fraction of cords are looped too tightly about the baby's neck, it's still a significant number; in one year my midwife had three such babies. That she could handle these emergencies was not in question. But her natural optimism had tempered, and she no longer did births more than twenty minutes from the hospital. For my husband and me, she would make an exception. But she also suggested we have the birth in town, at a friend's house, say, or—as one couple did—at a nearby hotel.

This time, my husband and I even visited the hospital's new birthing room. There was nothing wrong with it, exactly. The pink pillows matched the pink coverlet, the baby's cradle had been varnished to a shine, and a poster of trees covered one entire wall. Best of all, as the nurse showed us, was the mechanical bed that rose up and down and let the woman actually sit up during delivery. In the tour, we went on to examine the traditional labor room next door. Here was the flat white table with its heavy stirrups, surrounded by the decor of machinery and plastic. Of course, our guide said, there was no guarantee I would get the birthing room. I would get on a list, and it was first-come, first-served. There was no guarantee I would not wind up flat on my back on the white table, a position which, short of being hanged upside down, is perhaps the worst one for delivery. There was no guarantee I would get the pink coverlet.

In the end, as I went home and thought about it, the pink coverlet didn't even look that good. Naturally I would come to the hospital if I needed to. I would even have the birth in town so as to be closer to its services. But as for the bed that rose up and down—as though I couldn't rise up and down by myself! as though the privilege of being able to sit up was the best I could hope for, a privilege granted by the pulleys of a mechanical bed—as for first-come, first-served and stirrups to place my feet, no, I thought, not for me. I was grateful for the hospital. It was an important aid to birth. But it was not a replacement.

My intuition, at long last, had started to kick in.

In retrospect, it seems my ambiguity concerning homebirth vanished for the rest of that pregnancy. In truth, I don't think it did until the beginning of labor. Then, as before, all my doubts disappeared and I was where I needed to be, focusing on the task at hand.

In this birth, events moved so rapidly that my focus blurred a little. Labor started with strong contractions at 12:30 A.M. and ended with a ten-pound baby boy six hours later. In this birth, I didn't try to be stoic. This one hurt more. This time, too, my husband's and midwife's reassurances rang a bit perfunctory. We were all surprised at the speed of dilation. We were all a bit more businesslike and a bit less magical. No golden *vigas* glowed over our heads, for we were at a friend's house, in a modern room with walls made of sheetrock. This time, when the baby's large head began to crown, I screamed in outrage. I hollered out my midwife's name, not caring who heard me or what they might think. My friend, her husband, their two young sons, and my three-year-old daughter were sitting in the middle of the room, watching me with considerable interest. Something in their position, crosslegged on the floor, made me feel like a television set. In a small but well-lit clearing of my mind, I realized that I had a choice. I could grit my teeth or scream unbecomingly. What does it matter? I remember thinking. Perhaps in this instance, screaming was the better strategy.

After all the fuss, our son emerged with a headful of brown hair and a mouth screwed only slightly in irritation. His Apgar scores were nearly perfect, his wrists and ankles rolled with fat. Flopped on my stomach, he stared up at me peacefully in the morning light. For a few minutes, the assistant took the baby and busied herself verifying his patently healthy condition. Peacefully I delivered the placenta and continued to bleed. My midwife gave me a dose of Pitocin and then another. Because large babies are associated with diabetes, she also telephoned our pediatrician. Outside the window, the sky trailed banners of celebratory pink. Relieved and euphoric, I submitted to the medical procedures: my blood pressure taken, some slight stitching up. Because I had hemorrhaged, the midwife measured the iron in my blood with a small hand-held device, and my husband was impressed with this bit of gadgetry. Within an hour, a friend came by and took pictures. In all of these, my daughter holds her new brother. While the rest of us look obediently at the camera, she and he gaze with complete concentration into each other's eyes.

My daughter is nearly five now. Recently, in a seminar at work, I was asked to remember a time when I had felt powerful. Instantly I saw Maria's birth. I did not, of course, see a baby's head crowning. Instead I saw my own naked thighs and knees spread unnaturally apart. I saw, at the periphery of vision, the blurred hands and faces of my husband and friends. I saw the colors of my grandmother's quilt glowing intensely. It seemed that one of my legs was streaked with blood. It would seem that I had never been so vulnerable, so dependent in all my life. Yet I remember this, a physical memory, lodged deep in the body, as a moment of power. In my second homebirth, I remember as well the unabashed decision to shriek. I remember, still, feeling at the center.

As my friend emerges from her appointment with the midwife, I say goodbye to Angelica Gutierrez. I also say hello to the midwife, who stops to tell me about a homebirth-related case headed for the Supreme Court. This class action suit will determine if women have a constitutional right to choose their place of giving birth and if midwives have a constitutional right to practice their profession. My midwife is passionate about the subject. So am I. It appalls me that homebirth is illegal in some states. I am aghast that Arizona midwives cannot carry Pitocin. All of us, all the women in this room, feel the flare of anger. It dies quickly and, eager to start their private communion, the midwife and Angelica disappear into the office.

On my way out, I touch the door and tell my friend that turquoise is the color to ward off witches. "Oh," she says, lulled and euphoric by her visit to the midwife, "it's my favorite color too."

Her big belly, taut and firm, pushes out into the late afternoon air. Life is swimming inside her. A child dreams beneath the skin. Briefly she rests a hand on the highest point of her curved stomach, where I would like, very much, to put my hand as well.

Considerations

Thinking

At the beginning of her essay, Russell tells us that "safety is a priority" for those involved with homebirth but that "it is not, necessarily, the heart of the matter." What do you think Russell sees as the heart of the matter?

What do you consider the essential difference between Russell's husband and the other men mentioned in this essay?

If you were having a baby or attending a birth, where would you want to be, in a home or in a hospital? How does Russell's essay affect your decision?

Connecting

How does the competitive sports analogy help Russell render her account of the birth of her first child? What do you learn about homebirth from that analogy?

What connections does Russell make in her essay to suggest how "pregnancy had evolved, philosophically, into a life-threatening disease" by the twentieth century?

What is the relationship between witches and male doctors in this essay?

Writing

When Russell speaks of the beautiful Anglo woman who was her midwife, she tells us, "Those who do not find beauty powerful are possibly around it too much or have never seen it at all." Write an essay in which you deepen our understanding of Russell's claim. Use your own experience—including your reading—to help you clarify your thoughts.

Recall a moment when you felt powerful. Write an essay that reveals the meaning and significance of that moment—and of any other moments that you include in your essay to help you with your revelation.

Scott Russell Sanders
(b. 1945)

Scott Russell Sanders's many books include *The Paradise of Bombs, In Limestone Country, Secrets of the Universe, Staying Put,* and *Writing from the Center.* His essays have appeared in literary and popular magazines such as *North American Review, Georgia Review, Sewanee Review, Omni,* and *New Dimensions.* He has been a Woodrow Wilson Fellow, a Marshall Scholar, a Bennett Fellow in creative writing, and a National Endowment for the Arts Fellow.

In "Wayland," Sanders traces a voyage he made back to his childhood home after a twenty-five-year absence; it was a journey back to bedrock values.

Wayland

Two blacktop roads, broken by frost and mended with tar, running from nowhere to nowhere, cross at right angles in the rumpled farm country of northeastern Ohio. The neighborhood where they intersect is called Wayland—not a village, not even a hamlet, only a cluster of barns and silos and frame houses and a white steepled Methodist church. Just north of Wayland, the Army fenced in fifty square miles of ground for a bomb factory, and just to the south the Corps of Engineers built a dam and flooded even more square miles for a reservoir. I grew up behind those government fences in the shadows of bunkers, and on farms that have since vanished beneath those government waters. Family visits to church began carrying me to Wayland when I was five, romance was carrying me there still at seventeen, and in the years between I was drawn there often by duty or desire. Thus it happened that within shouting distance of the Wayland crossroads I met seven of the great mysteries.

Even as a boy, oblivious much of the time to all save my own sensations, I knew by the tingle in my spine when I had bumped into something utterly new. I groped for words to describe what I had felt, as I grope still. Since we give labels to all that puzzles us, as we name every blank space on the map, I could say that what I stumbled into in Wayland were the mysteries of death, life, beasts, food, mind, sex, and God. But these seven words are only tokens, worn coins that I drop onto the page, hoping to bribe you, coins I finger as reminders of those awful encounters.

The roads that cross at Wayland are too humble to show on the Ohio map, too small even to wear numbers. And yet, without maps or mistakes, without quite meaning to, I recently found my way back there from half a thousand miles away, after an absence of twenty-five years, led along the grooves of memory.

The grooves are deep, and they set me vibrating well before I reached the place, as the spiral cuts in phonograph records will shake music from a needle. I was heading toward Cleveland when I took a notion to veer off the interstate and see what had become of Akron, which led me to see what had become of Kent, which led me to Ravenna, the seat of Portage County. Nothing aside from stoplights made me pause. Not sure what I was looking for, I drove east from the county seat along a highway hurtling with trucks. Soon the rusted chain link fence of the Ravenna Arsenal came whipping by on my left and the raised bed of the Baltimore & Ohio tracks surged by on the right. Then I realized where I was going. My knuckles whitened on the steering wheel as I turned from the highway, put my back toward the trucks and bombs, and passed under the railroad through a concrete arch. Beyond the arch, the woods and fields and houses of Wayland shimmered in the October sunlight, appearing to my jealous eye scarcely changed after a quarter of a century.

I knew the place had changed, of course, if only because in the years since I had come here last—drawn in those days like a moth to the flame of a girl—the population of the earth had nearly doubled. Every crossroads, every woods, every field on the planet is warping under the pressure of our terrible hunger. So I knew that Wayland had changed, for all its pastoral shimmer in the autumn light. Yet I was grateful that on the surface it so much resembled my childhood memories, for in my effort to live adequately in the present, I had come here to conduct some business with the past. What had brought me back to Wayland was a need to dig through the fluff and debris of ordinary life, down to some bedrock of feeling and belief.

I left my car in the graveled parking lot of the church and set out walking. Without planning my steps, I meandered where memory led, and where it led was from station to station of my childhood astonishment. Not yet ready for the church, I went next door to the parsonage, where I had first caught a whiff of death. The white clapboard house, a two-story box with a porch across the front and a green hipped roof, could have belonged to any of the neighboring farms. That was appropriate, for the ministers who succeeded one another in the house often preached as though they were farmers, weeding out sins, harvesting souls.

The minister whom I knew first was the Reverend Mr. Knipe, a bulky man sunken with age, his hair as white as the clapboards on the parsonage, his voice like the cooing of pigeons in the barn. Much in life amused him. Whenever he told you something that struck him as funny, he would cover his mouth with a hand to hide his smile. Despite the raised hand, often his laugh burst free and rolled over you. I began listening to him preach and pray and lead hymns when I was five, and for the next two years I heard Reverend Knipe every Sunday, until his voice became for me that of the Bible itself, even the voice of God. Then one Sunday when I was seven, I shook his great hand after the service as usual, suffering him to bend down and pat my head, and I went home to my dinner and he went home to his. While his wife set the table in the parsonage, Reverend Knipe rested on the front porch in his caned rocking chair, drifted off to sleep, and never woke up.

When Mother told me of this, the skin prickled on my neck. To sleep and never wake! To be a white-haired man with a voice like a barnful of pigeons, and the next minute to be nothing at all! Since my parents considered me too young to attend the funeral, I could only imagine what had become of his body, and I imagined not decay but evaporation—the flesh dispersing into thin air like morning mist from a pond.

The following Sunday, while a visitor preached, I stole from church and crept over to the parsonage. I drew to the edge of the porch, wrapped my fingers around the spindles of the railing, and stared at the empty rocker. Reverend Knipe will never sit in that chair again, I told myself. Never, never, never. I tried to imagine how long forever would last. I tried to imagine how it would feel to be nothing. No thing. Suddenly chair and house and daylight vanished, and I was gazing into a dark hole, I was falling, I was gone. I caught a whiff of death, the damp earthy smell seeping from beneath the porch. It was also the smell of mud, of leaping grass, of spring. Clinging to that sensation, I pulled myself up out of the hole. There was the house again, the chair. I let go of the railing, swung away, and ran back to the church, chanting to myself: *He was old and I am young. He was old and I am young.*

Nights, often, and sometimes in the broad light of day, I still have to scrabble up out of that hole. We all do. Sometime in childhood, each of us bangs head-on into the blank fact we call death. Once that collision takes place, the shock of it never wears off. We may find ourselves returning to the spot where it occurred as to the scene of an accident, the way I found myself drawn, half a lifetime later, to the front steps of this parsonage. I was a stranger to the family who lived there now. Not wishing to intrude on them, I paused by the steps and surveyed the porch. Vinyl siding had covered the clapboard. An aluminum folding chair had replaced the rocker. I squatted by the railing, lowering my face to the height of a seven-year-old, closed my eyes against the shadows, and sniffed. From below the sill of the porch came the earth's dank perennial breath, fetid and fertile. Yes, I thought, filling myself with the smell: this abides, this is real; no matter the name we give it, life or death, it is a fact as rough and solid as a stone squeezed in the palm of the hand.

A dog yapped inside the parsonage. I stood up hurriedly and backed away, before anyone could appear at the door to ask me what in tarnation I was looking for under that porch.

Still following the grooves of memory, I crossed the road to stand in the driveway of another white frame house. It was not so much the house that drew me as it was the side yard, where, about this time each fall, we brought our apples for pressing. The old press with its wooden vat and iron gears used to balance on concrete blocks in the shade of a willow. We would pick apples in the military reservation, from orchards that had been allowed to go wild after the government bulldozed the farmsteads. Unsprayed, blotched and wormy, these apples were also wonderfully sweet. We kept them in bushel baskets and cardboard boxes in the cellar, their fragrance filling the house, until we had accumulated enough to load our station wagon. Then we drove here, parked beside the willow, and fed our fruit into the press.

On this mild October day, the willow looked as I remembered it, thick in the trunk and gold in the leaves. There was no sign of a press, but that did not keep me from remembering what it was like to squeeze apples. First we pulped them in a mill, then we wrapped them in cheesecloth and tamped them down, layer by layer, into the slotted wooden vat. To mash them, we spun a cast iron wheel. It was easy to begin with, so easy that my brother and sister and I could make the spokes whirl. Later, the cranking would become too hard for us, and our mother would take her turn, then our father, then both of them together. The moment that set me trembling, however, came early on, while my hand was still on the iron wheel, the moment when cider began to ooze through the cheesecloth, between the slats, and down the spout into a waiting bucket. Out of the dirt, out of the gnarled trunks and wide-flung branches, out of the ripe red fruit had come this tawny juice. When my arms grew tired, I held a Mason jar under the spout, caught a glassful, and drank it down. It was as though we had squeezed the planet and out had poured sweetness.

What came back to me, musing there by the willow all these years later, was the sound of cider trickling into the bucket, the honeyed taste of it, and my bewilderment that rain and wood and dirt and sun had yielded this juice. Amazing, that we can drink the earth! Amazing, that it quenches our thirst, answers our hunger! Who would have predicted such an outlandish thing? Who, having sipped, can forget that it is the earth we swallow?

Well, I had forgotten; or at least I had buried under the habits of casual eating that primal awareness of the meaning of food. And so here was another fundamental perception, renewed for me by my sojourn in Wayland. This image of cider gushing from a spout was my cornucopia, proof of the dazzling abundance that sustains us.

From the cider house I walked downhill to the crossroads. One corner was still a pasture, browsed by three horses, another was a scrubby field grown up in brush and weeds, and the other two corners were expansive lawns. Through the brushy field meandered a creek where I used to hunt frogs with a flashlight and bucket. As in all the Octobers I could remember, the maples in the yards were scarlet, the pasture oaks were butterscotch, and the sycamores along the creek were stripped down to their voluptuous white limbs. Yellow mums and bright red pokers of salvia were still thriving in flowerbeds. A portly older man on a riding mower was cutting one of the lawns, while from a stump beside the driveway an older woman observed his progress, a hand shading her eyes. I knew them from childhood, but their names would not come. I waved, and they waved back. That was conversation enough. I had no desire to speak with them or with anyone in Wayland, since I would have been hard put to explain who I was or why I had come back. Maybe I also wanted to keep the past pure, unmixed with the present.

Because the crossroads are laid out on the grid of survey lines, the blacktop runs due north and south, east and west. The roads were so little traveled that I could stand in the intersection, the tar gummy beneath my boots, and gaze along the pavement in each of the cardinal directions. I had just come from the south, where the church gleamed on its hill. My view to the north was cut off by the railroad, except for the arched opening of the underpass, through which I could see the rusted fence of the Arsenal. Memories of a girl I had courted were beckoning from the west; but less feverish memories beckoned from the opposite direction, and that is where I chose to go next.

A quarter mile east of the crossroads I came to a farm where the Richards family used to breed and board and train horses. Although the name on the mailbox had changed, ten or twelve horses were grazing, as before, in a paddock beside the barn. I leaned against the fence and admired them.

In boyhood I had raised and ridden horses of my own, a stocky mixture of Shetland pony and the high-stepping carriage breed known as hackney. They all came out of a single ornery mare called Belle, and they all had her color, a sorrel coat that grew sleek in summer and shaggy in winter. We used to bring Belle here to the Richards place for mating with a hackney stallion. Years before the voltage of sex began to make my own limbs jerk, I had been amazed by the stallion's urgency and the mare's skittishness. He nipped and nuzzled and pursued her; she danced and wheeled. Their energy seemed too great for the paddock to hold. Surely the fence would give way, the barn itself would fall! Then at length Belle shivered to a standstill and allowed the stallion to lift his forelegs onto her rump, his back legs jigging, hoofs scrambling for purchase, her legs opening to his dark pizzle, the two of them momentarily one great plunging beast. And then, if luck held, twelve months later Belle would open her legs once more and drop a foal. Within minutes of entering the world, the foal would be tottering about on its wobbly stilts, drunk on air, and it would be ramming its muzzle into Belle's belly in search of milk. What a world, that the shivering union of mare and stallion in the barnyard should lead to this new urgency!

Musing there by the paddock on this October afternoon, I felt toward the grazing horses a huge affection. Each filled its hide so gloriously. I gave a low whistle. Several massive heads bobbed up and swung toward me, jaws working on grass, ears pricked forward. Their black eyes regarded me soberly, then all but one of the heads returned to grazing. The exception was a palomino gelding, who tossed his white mane, switched his white tail, and started ambling in my direction. As he drew near, I stretched my right arm toward him, palm open. Had I known I would be coming here, I would have brought apples or sugar cubes. My father would have pulled a cigarette from his pocket and offered that. But all I had to offer was the salt on my skin. The palomino lowered his muzzle to my palm, sniffed cautiously, then curled out his rasping red tongue and licked.

I knew that sandpapery stroke on my hand as I knew few other sensations. Just so, my own horses had nibbled oats and sugar and sweat from my palm. The pressure of their tongues made my whole body sway. There by the fence, past and present merged, and I was boy and man, swaying. I reveled in the muscular touch, animal to animal. Contact! It assured me that I was not alone in the world. I was a creature among creatures.

When the palomino lost interest in my right hand, I offered my left. He sniffed idly, and, finding it empty, turned back to the greater temptation of grass. But the rasp of his tongue on my palm stayed with me, another clean, hard fact, another piece of bedrock on which to build a life.

*   *   *

The field across the road from the Richards place was grown up into a young woods, mostly staghorn sumac and cedar and oak. When I had seen it last, twenty-five years earlier, this had been a meadow luxuriant with grasses and wild-flowers. Back where the far edge of the field ran up against the sinuous line of willows bordering the creek, there had been a cottage, low and brown, moss growing on the roof, weeds lapping at the windows, a place that looked from a distance more like a forgotten woodpile than a house. Today, no cottage showed above the vigorous trees. But near my feet I could see the twin ruts of the dirt track that used to lead back to the place. I followed them, my boots knocking seeds from thistle and wild rye.

I knew the meadow and the cottage because the woman who used to live here was my science teacher in high school. Fay Givens must have been in her early sixties when I met her in my freshman year. Many students mocked her for being so unthinkably old, for looking like a schoolmarm, for loving science, for trembling when she spoke about nature. She would gaze fervently into a beaker as though an entire galaxy spun before her. She grew so excited while recounting the habits of molecules that she would skip about the lab and clap her spotted hands. She would weep for joy over what swam before her in a microscope. Mrs. Givens wept easily, more often than not because of a wisecrack or prank from one of the students. Our cruelty was a defense against the claim she made on us. For she was inviting us to share her passionate curiosity. She called us to hunger and thirst after knowledge of the universe.

I would not join the others in mocking her. I supposed it was pity that held me back, or an ingrained respect for my elders. Only in the fall of my freshman year, on a day when Mrs. Givens brought us here to this field for a botany class, did I realize that I could not mock her because I loved her. She led us through her meadow, naming every plant, twirling the bright fallen leaves, telling which birds ate which berries, opening milkweed pods, disclosing the burrows of ground-hogs, parting the weeds to reveal caterpillars and crickets, showing where mice had severed blades of grass. Much of the meadow she had planted, with seeds carried in her pockets from the neighboring countryside. Every few years she burned it, as the Indians had burned the prairies, to keep the woods from reclaiming it.

While Mrs. Givens told us these things in her quavery voice, students kept sidling away to smoke or joke or dabble their hands in the creek, until there were only three of us following her. I stayed with her not from a sense of obedience but from wonder. To know this patch of land, I dimly realized, would be the work of a lifetime. But in knowing it deeply, right down to the foundations, you would comprehend a great deal more, perhaps everything. As she touched the feathery plants of her meadow, as she murmured the names and histories of the creatures who shared the place with her, I came to feel that this was holy ground. And if the meadow was holy, why not the entire earth?

At one point, Mrs. Givens knelt amid the bristly spikes of a tall russet grass. "You see why it's called foxtail, don't you?" she said. "Livestock won't eat it, but you can twist the stalks together and make a fair rope. Farmers used to bind up corn fodder with hanks of foxtail." She grasped one of the spikes, and, with a rake of her thumb, brushed seeds into her palm. She poured a few seeds into my hand and a few into the hands of the other two students who had remained with her. "Now what do you have there?" she asked us.

We stared at the barbed grains in our palms. "Seeds," one of us replied.

"That's the universe unfolding," she told us, "right there in your hands. The same as in every cell of our bodies. Now *why?* That's the question I can't ever get behind. Why should the universe be alive? Why does it obey laws? And why these particular laws? For that matter, why is there a universe at all?" She gave a rollicking laugh. "And isn't it curious that there should be creatures like us who can walk in this beautiful field and puzzle over things?"

She asked her questions gaily, and I have carried them with me all these years in the same spirit. They rose in me again on this October afternoon as I followed the dirt track to the spot where her cottage used to be. Stones marked the cellar hole and the front stoop. Brush grew up through the space left by her death. The woods had reclaimed her meadow. Yet the ground still felt holy. Her marveling gaze had disclosed for me the force and shapeliness of things, and that power survived her passing. She taught me that genius is not in our looking but in what we see. If only we could be adequate to the given world, we need not dream of paradise.

Reversing my steps, I walked back to the crossroads and kept going west for a hundred yards or so, until I fetched up before the house where, as a simmering teenager, I had wooed a girl. Let me call her Veronica. She and her family moved from Wayland soon after the Army Corps of Engineers built that needless dam, and so on this October day her house was for me another shell filled only with memory. The present kept abrading the past, however, because during the few minutes while I stood there a grown man in a go-cart kept zooming around the yard, following a deeply gouged path. Every time he roared past, he peered at me from beneath his crash helmet. I nodded, assuming the look of one who is infatuated with loud machines, and that appeared to satisfy him.

Veronica had the face of a queen on the deck of cards with which I learned to play poker, a face I considered perfect. Words tumbled from her lush lips, impulsively, like rabbits fleeing a burrow. Black wavy hair tumbled down her back, twitching nearly to her slender hips. Having learned in marriage what it means to love a woman, I cannot say that what I felt for Veronica was quite love. Nor was it simply lust, although for much of my seventeenth year the mere thought of her set me aching. At that age, I would have been reluctant to see myself as the urgent stallion and Veronica as the skittish mare. Later, I would realize that horseflesh and humanflesh dance to the same ardent music, even though our human dance is constrained by rules that horses never know. During the season of our affection, Veronica was a chased girl but also a chaste one, and I was a polite boy, both of us keenly aware of boundaries.

In her backyard there was a sycamore tree that loomed high over the house, its fat trunk a patchwork of peeling bark and its crooked upper branches as creamy as whole milk. Wooden crossbars nailed to the trunk formed a ladder up to a treehouse. Veronica and I often sat beneath the sycamore on a stone bench, talking and falling silent, aware of parental eyes watching us from the kitchen. With our backs to the house, our sides pressed together, I could risk brushing a hand over her knee, she could run a fingernail under my chin. But even a kiss, our mouths so visibly meeting, would have prompted a visit from the kitchen.

One October day, a day very like this one of my return to Wayland, Veronica and I were sitting on the bench, hunting for words to shape our confusion, when suddenly she leapt to her feet and said, "Let's go up to the treehouse."

"We'll get filthy," I said. I glanced with misgiving at my white knit shirt and chino pants, so carefully pressed. Her lemony blouse was protected by a green corduroy jumper.

"It'll wash out," she said, tugging me by the hand.

I stood. Without waiting for me, she kicked off her shoes and clambered up the wooden rungs, but instead of halting at the rickety platform of the treehouse, she kept on, swaying from limb to limb. I watched until the flashing of her bare legs made me look away. When she had gone as high as she dared, high enough to escape the view from the kitchen, she balanced on a branch and called to me, "Come on up! Are you afraid?"

I was afraid—but not of the tree. I stepped onto a crossbrace and started climbing, and as I climbed there was nowhere else to look but up, and there was nothing else to see above me except those white legs parted within the green hoop of her skirt. Her creamy forked limbs and the creamy forked limbs of the sycamore merged in my sight, as they merge now in memory, and I was drawn upward into the pale shadows between her thighs. My knowledge of what I was climbing toward would remain abstract for a number of years. I understood only that where her legs joined there was an opening, a gateway for life coming and going. When I reached Veronica I put my hand, briefly, where my gaze had gone, just far enough to feel the surprising warmth of that secret, satiny place. Then I withdrew my hand and she smoothed her skirt, neither of us risking a word, and we teetered there for a hundred heartbeats on those swaying branches, shaken by inner as well as outer winds. Then the kitchen door creaked open and her mother's voice inquired as to our sanity, and we climbed down. I went first, as though to catch Veronica should she fall, my eyes toward the ground.

The buzzing of the go-cart eventually wore through the husk of memory, and my lungs filled with the present. I became again what I was, a man long married, a man with a daughter the age Veronica had been on that day of our climb into the tree. The sycamore still rose behind the house, twenty-five years taller, crisp brown leaves rattling in the wind, the pale upper limbs as pale and silky as ever.

I had a choice of returning to the church by the road or across the stubble of a cornfield. I chose the field. All the way, I could see the white steepled box gleaming on its rise. The only car in the parking lot was mine. Beyond a treeline to the southwest, beyond the annihilating waters of the reservoir that I could not bear to look at, the sun wallowed down toward dusk. The church might already be locked, I thought, so late on a weekday afternoon. Still I did not hurry. My boots scuffed the ridges where corn had stood. Raccoons and crows would find little to feast on in this stubble, for the harvester had plucked it clean. I recalled the biblical injunction to farmers, that they leave the margins of their fields unpicked, for the poor and the beasts. I thought of the margins in a life, in my life, the untended zones beyond the borders of clarity, the encircling wilderness out of which new powers and visions come.

A cornfield is a good approach to a church, for you arrive with dirt on your boots, the smell of greenery in your nostrils, dust on your tongue. The door would be locked, I figured, and the main door was, the broad entrance through which the Methodist women carried their piety and their pies, through which men carried mortgages and mortality, through which children like myself carried headfuls of questions. But the rear door was unlocked. I left my boots on the stoop and went inside.

The back room I entered had the familiarity of a place one returns to in dream: the squeaky pine boards of the floor, the dwarf tables where children would sit on Sundays to color pictures of Jesus, the brass hooks where the choir would hang their robes and the minister his hat, the folding chairs collapsed into a corner, the asthmatic furnace, and on a counter the stack of lathe-turned walnut plates for the offering.

Every few paces I halted, listening. The joints of the church cricked as the sun let go. Birds fussed beyond the windows. But no one else was about; this relieved me, for here least of all was I prepared to explain myself. I had moved too long in circles where to confess an interest in religious things marked one as a charlatan, a sentimentalist, or a fool. No doubt I have all three qualities in my character. But I also have another quality, and that is an unshakable hunger to know who I am, where I am, and into what sort of cosmos I have been so briefly and astonishingly sprung. Whatever combination of shady motives might have led me here, the impulse that shook me right then was a craving to glimpse the very source and circumference of things.

I made my way out through the choir door into the sanctuary. Cushionless pews in somber ranks, uncarpeted floor, exposed beams in the vault overhead and whitewashed plaster on the walls: it was a room fashioned by men and women who knew barns, for preachers who lived out of saddlebags, in honor of a God who cares nothing for ornament. No tapestries, no shrines, no racks of candles, no gold on the altar, no bragging memorials to vanished patrons. The window glass, unstained, let in the plain light of day.

I sat in a pew midway along the central aisle and looked out through those clear windows. My reasons for coming here were entwined with that sky full of light. As a boy I had looked out, Sunday after Sunday, to see corn grow and clouds blow, to watch crows bustle among the tops of trees, to follow hawks, unmindful of the Sabbath, on their spiraling hunts, and to sense in all this radiant surge the same rush I felt under my fingers when I pressed a hand to my throat. There was no gulf between outside and inside. We gathered in this room not to withdraw, but more fully to enter the world.

On this day of my return, I kept watching the sky as the light thinned and the darkness thickened. I became afraid. Afraid of dying, yes, but even more of not having lived, afraid of passing my days in a stupor, afraid of squandering my moment in the light. I gripped the pew in front of me to still my trembling. I wanted to dive down to the center of being, touch bedrock, open my eyes and truly, finally, unmistakably see. I shifted my gaze from the darkening window to the altar, to the wooden cross, to the black lip of the Bible showing from the pulpit. But those were only props for a play that was forever in rehearsal, the actors clumsy, the script obscure. I was myself one of the actors, sustained in my own clumsy efforts by the hope that one day the performance would be perfect, and everything would at last come clear.

One cannot summon grace with a whistle. The pew beneath me, the air around me, the darkening windows did not turn to fire. The clouds of unknowing did not part. I sat there for a long while, and then I rose and made my way down the aisle, past the organ, through the choir door and back room, out into the freshening night. On the stoop I drew on my boots and laced them up. The chrome latch of my car was already cool. I drove back through the crossroads with headlights glaring, alert for animals that might dash before me in the confusion of dusk.

There is more to be seen at any crossroads than one can see in a lifetime of looking. My return visit to Wayland was less than two hours long. Once again half a thousand miles distant from that place, making this model from slippery words, I cannot be sure where the pressure of mind has warped the surface of things. If you were to go there, you would not find every detail exactly as I have described it. How could you, bearing as you do a past quite different from mine? No doubt my memory, welling up through these lines, has played tricks with time and space.

What memory is made of I cannot say; my body, at least, is made of atoms on loan from the earth. How implausible, that these atoms should have gathered to form this *I*, this envelope of skin that walks about and strokes horses and tastes apples and trembles with desire in the branches of a sycamore and gazes through the windows of a church at the ordinary sky. Certain moments in one's life cast their influence forward over all the moments that follow. My encounters in Wayland shaped me first as I lived through them, then again as I recalled them during my visit, and now as I write them down. That is of course why I write them down. The self is a fiction. I make up the story of myself with scraps of memory, sensation, reading, and hearsay. It is a tale I whisper against the dark. Only in rare moments of luck or courage do I hush, forget myself entirely, and listen to the silence that precedes and surrounds and follows all speech.

If you have been keeping count, you may have toted up seven mysteries, or maybe seven times seven, or maybe seven to the seventh power. My hunch is that, however we count, there is only one mystery. In our nearsightedness, we merely glimpse the light scintillating off the numberless scales of Leviathan, and we take each spark for a separate wonder.

Could we bear to see all the light at once? Could we bear the roar of infinite silence? I sympathize with science, where, in order to answer a question, you limit the variables. You draw a circle within which everything can be measured, and you shut out the rest of the universe. But every enclosure is a makeshift, every boundary an illusion. With great ingenuity, we decipher some of the rules that govern this vast shining dance, but all our efforts could not change the least of them.

Nothing less than the undivided universe can be our true home. Yet how can one speak or even think about the whole of things? Language is of only modest help. Every sentence is a wispy net, capturing a few flecks of meaning. The sun shines without vocabulary. The salmon has no name for the desire that drives it upstream. The newborn groping for the nipple knows hunger long before it knows a single word. Even with an entire dictionary in one's head, one eventually comes to the end of words. Then what? Then drink deep like the baby, swim like the salmon, burn like any brief star.

Considerations

Thinking

Early in the essay, Sanders uses seven words to, as he says, "bribe you" to follow him into his stumble into "the mysteries of death, life, beasts, food, mind, sex, and God." To what extent do you think he succeeds in communicating his experience of those mysteries?

Toward the end of "Wayland," Sanders says that if you visit the place described you would not find it just as he has described it—not so much because it has changed but because of how memory plays "tricks with time and space." What does Sanders mean, and how is what he says about memory related to his comment, "The self is a fiction. I make up the story of myself . . . "?

Connecting

Compare what Sanders says about returning to a place after you have been away for a while with your experience of returning to places you have moved away from. Consider, for example, your experience of returning to an old neighborhood or a school you once attended.

Compare the way Sanders writes about returning to Wayland with the way James Baldwin writes about his experience living abroad and coming home again.

Writing

Write an essay about your return to a place after being away for some time. Try to show your readers how the place differed and how it remained the same. Explain how your perceptions of it at the different times may have been affected by who you were at those times.

Write Sanders a letter responding to this claim of his: "With great ingenuity, we decipher some of the rules that govern this vast shining dance [of ours through life], but all our efforts could not change the least of them." Do you agree with Sanders? Do you think he believes what he says? Explain.

Richard Selzer
(b. 1928)

Richard Selzer was born in Troy, New York, and educated at Union College, Albany Medical College, and Yale University. Selzer began writing at age forty, amid the rigors of medical responsibilities as a surgeon and a professor of surgery at Yale; he recently retired to devote himself full time to writing. Throughout his medical career, Selzer led a second life as an essayist and storyteller, publishing six books, beginning with *Rituals of Surgery* (1974). His most recent books are *Down from Troy* (1992), an autobiography, and *Raising the Dead* (1993), a work that blends history, autobiography and fiction, and *The Doctor Stories* (1998), a collection of tales, new and old.

In "A Mask on the Face of Death," which appeared in *Best American Essays 1988*, Selzer describes the AIDS situation in Haiti. His essay is notable for its precise rendering of place and for its distinctive presentation of character, as Selzer employs techniques of the fiction writer in conveying ideas and perspectives.

A Mask on the Face of Death

It is ten o'clock at night as we drive up to the Copacabana, a dilapidated brothel on the rue Dessalines in the red-light district of Port-au-Prince. My guide is a young Haitian, Jean-Bernard. Ten years before, J-B tells me, at the age of fourteen, "like every good Haitian boy" he had been brought here by his older cousins for his *rite de passage*. From the car to the entrance, we are accosted by a half dozen men and women for sex. We enter, go down a long hall that breaks upon a cavernous room with a stone floor. The cubicles of the prostitutes, I am told, are in an attached wing of the building. Save for a red-purple glow from small lights on the walls, the place is unlit. Dark shapes float by, each with a blindingly white stripe of teeth. Latin music is blaring. We take seats at the table farthest from the door. Just outside, there is the rhythmic lapping of the Caribbean Sea. About twenty men are seated at the tables or lean against the walls. Brightly dressed women, singly or in twos or threes, stroll about, now and then exchanging banter with the men. It is as though we have been deposited in act two of Bizet's *Carmen*. If this place isn't Lillas Pastia's tavern, what is it?

Within minutes, three light-skinned young women arrive at our table. They are very beautiful and young and lively. Let them be Carmen, Mercedes and Frasquita.

"I want the old one," says Frasquita, ruffling my hair. The women laugh uproariously.

"Don't bother looking any further," says Mercedes. "We are the prettiest ones."

"We only want to talk," I tell her.

"Aaah, aaah," she crows. "*Massissi*. You are *massissi*." It is the contemptuous Creole term for homosexual. If we want only to talk, we must be gay. Mercedes and Carmen are slender, each weighing one hundred pounds or less. Frasquita is tall and hefty. They are dressed for work: red taffeta, purple chiffon and black sequins. Among them a thousand gold bracelets and earrings multiply every speck of light. Their bare shoulders are like animated lamps gleaming in the shadowy room. Since there is as yet no business, the women agree to sit with us. J-B orders beer and cigarettes. We pay each woman $10.

"Where are you from?" I begin.

"We are Dominican."

"Do you miss your country?"

"Oh, yes, we do." Six eyes go muzzy with longing. "Our country is the most beautiful in the world. No country is like the Dominican. And it doesn't stink like this one."

"Then why don't you work there? Why come to Haiti?"

"Santo Domingo has too many whores. All beautiful, like us. All light-skinned. The Haitian men like to sleep with light women."

"Why is that?"

"Because always, the whites have all the power and the money. The black men can imagine they do, too, when they have us in bed."

Eleven o'clock. I looked around the room that is still sparsely peopled with men.

"It isn't getting any busier," I say. Frasquita glances over her shoulder. Her eyes drill the darkness.

"It is still early," she says.

"Could it be that the men are afraid of getting sick?" Frasquita is offended.

"Sick! They do not get sick from us. We are healthy, strong. Every week we go for a checkup. Besides, we know how to tell if we are getting sick."

"I mean sick with AIDS." The word sets off a hurricane of taffeta, chiffon and gold jewelry. They are all gesticulation and fury. It is Carmen who speaks.

"AIDS!" Her lips curl about the syllable. "There is no such thing. It is a false disease invented by the American government to take advantage of the poor countries. The American President hates poor people, so now he makes up AIDS to take away the little we have." The others nod vehemently.

"*Mira, mon cher.* Look, my dear," Carmen continues. "One day the police came here. Believe me, they are worse than the *tonton macoutes* with their subma-chine guns. They rounded up one hundred and five of us and they took our blood. That was a year ago. None of us have died, you see? We are all still here. *Mira,* we sleep with all the men and we are not sick."

"But aren't there some of you who have lost weight and have diarrhea?"

"One or two, maybe. But they don't eat. That is why they are weak."

"Only the men die," says Mercedes. "They stop eating, so they die. It is hard to kill a woman."

"Do you eat well?"

"Oh, yes, don't worry, we do. We eat like poor people, but we eat." There is a sudden scream from Frasquita. She points to a large rat that has emerged from beneath our table.

"My God!" she exclaims. "It is big like a pig." They burst into laughter. For a moment the women fall silent. There is only the restlessness of their many bracelets. I give them each another $10.

"Are many of the men here bisexual?"

"Too many. They do it for money. Afterward, they come to us." Carmen lights a cigarette and looks down at the small lace handkerchief she has been folding and unfolding with immense precision on the table. All at once she turns it over as though it were the ace of spades.

"*Mira, blanc* . . . look, white man," she says in a voice suddenly full of fore-boding. Her skin too seems to darken to coincide with the tone of her voice.

"*Mira*, soon many Dominican women will die in Haiti!"

"Die of what?"

She shrugs. "It is what they do to us."

"Carmen," I say, "if you knew that you had AIDS, that your blood was bad, would you still sleep with men?" Abruptly, she throws back her head and laughs. It is the same laughter with which Frasquita had greeted the rat at our feet. She stands and the others follow.

"*Méchant!* You wicked man," she says. Then, with terrible solemnity, "You don't know anything."

"But you are killing the Haitian men," I say.

"As for that," she says, "everyone is killing everyone else." All at once, I want to know everything about these three—their childhood, their dreams, what they do in the afternoon, what they eat for lunch.

"Don't leave," I say. "Stay a little more." Again, I reach for my wallet. But they are gone, taking all the light in the room with them—Mercedes and Carmen to sit at another table where three men have been waiting. Frasquita is strolling about the room. Now and then, as if captured by the music, she breaks into a few dance steps, snapping her fingers, singing to herself.

Midnight. And the Copacabana is filling up. Now it is like any other seedy nightclub where men and women go hunting. We get up to leave. In the center a couple are dancing a *méringue*. He is the most graceful dancer I have ever watched; she, the most voluptuous. Together they seem to be riding the back of the music as it gallops to a precisely sexual beat. Closer up, I see that the man is short of breath, sweating. All at once, he collapses into a chair. The woman bends over him, coaxing, teasing, but he is through. A young man with a long polished stick blocks my way.

"I come with you?" he asks. "Very good time. You say yes? Ten dollars? Five?"

I have been invited by Dr. Jean William Pape to attend the AIDS clinic of which he is the director. Nothing from the outside of the low whitewashed structure would suggest it as a medical facility. Inside, it is divided into many small cubicles and a labyrinth of corridors. At nine A.M. the hallways are already full of emaciated silent men and women, some sitting on the few benches, the rest leaning against the walls. The only sounds are subdued moans of discomfort interspersed with coughs. How they eat us with their eyes as we pass.

The room where Pape and I work is perhaps ten feet by ten. It contains a desk, two chairs and a narrow wooden table that is covered with a sheet that will not be changed during the day. The patients are called in one at a time, asked how they feel and whether there is any change in their symptoms, then examined on the table. If the patient is new to the clinic, he or she is questioned about sexual activities.

A twenty-seven-year-old man whose given name is Miracle enters. He is wobbly, panting, like a groggy boxer who has let down his arms and is waiting for the last punch. He is neatly dressed and wears, despite the heat, a heavy woolen cap. When he removes it, I see that his hair is thin, dull reddish and straight. It is one of the signs of AIDS in Haiti, Pape tells me. The man's skin is covered with a dry itchy rash. Throughout the interview and examination he scratches himself slowly, absentmindedly. The rash is called prurigo. It is another symptom of AIDS in Haiti. This man has had diarrhea for six months. The laboratory reports that the diarrhea is due to an organism called cryptosporidium, for which there is no treatment. The telltale rattling of the tuberculous moisture in his chest is audible without a stethoscope. He is like a leaky cistern that bubbles and froths. And, clearly, exhausted.

"Where do you live?" I ask.

"Kenscoff." A village in the hills above Port-au-Prince.

"How did you come here today?"

"I came on the *tap-tap*." It is the name given to the small buses that swarm the city, each one extravagantly decorated with religious slogans, icons, flowers, animals, all painted in psychedelic colors. I have never seen a *tap-tap* that was not covered with passengers as well, riding outside and hanging on. The vehicles are little masterpieces of contagion, if not of AIDS then of the multitude of germs which Haitian flesh is heir to. Miracle is given a prescription for a supply of Sera, which is something like Gatorade, and told to return in a month.

"Mangé kou bêf," says the doctor in farewell. "Eat like an ox." What can he mean? The man has no food or money to buy any. Even had he food, he has not the appetite to eat or the ability to retain it. To each departing patient the doctor will say the same words—*"Mangé kou bêf."* I see that it is his way of offering a hopeful goodbye.

"Will he live until his next appointment?" I ask.

"No." Miracle leaves to catch the *tap-tap* for Kenscoff.

Next is a woman of twenty-six who enters holding her right hand to her forehead in a kind of permanent salute. In fact, she is shielding her eye from view. This is her third visit to the clinic. I see that she is still quite well nourished.

"Now, you'll see something beautiful, tremendous," the doctor says. Once seated upon the table, she is told to lower her hand. When she does, I see that her right eye and its eyelid are replaced by a huge fungating ulcerated tumor, a side product of her AIDS. As she turns her head, the cluster of lymph glands in her neck to which the tumor has spread is thrown into relief. Two years ago she received a blood transfusion at a time when the country's main blood bank was grossly contaminated with AIDS. It has since been closed down. The only blood available in Haiti is a small supply procured from the Red Cross.

"Can you give me medicine?" the woman wails.

"No."

"Can you cut it away?"

"No."

"Is there radiation therapy?" I ask.

"No."

"Chemotherapy?" The doctor looks at me in what some might call weary amusement. I see that there is nothing to do. She has come here because there is nowhere else to go.

"What will she do?"

"Tomorrow or the next day or the day after that she will climb up into the mountains to seek relief from the *houngan,* the voodoo priest, just as her slave ancestors did two hundred years ago."

Then comes a frail man in his thirties, with a strangely spiritualized face, like a child's. Pus runs from one ear onto his cheek, where it has dried and caked. He has trouble remembering, he tells us. In fact, he seems confused. It is from toxoplasmosis of the brain, an effect of his AIDS. This man is bisexual. Two years ago he engaged in oral sex with foreign men for money. As I palpate the swollen glands of his neck, a mosquito flies between our faces. I swat at it, miss. Just before coming to Haiti I had read that the AIDS virus had been isolated from a certain mosquito. The doctor senses my thought.

"Not to worry," he says. "So far as we know there has never been a case transmitted by insects."

"Yes," I say. "I see."

And so it goes until the last, the thirty-sixth AIDS patient has been seen. At the end of the day I am invited to wash my hands before leaving. I go down a long hall to a sink. I turn on the faucets but there is no water.

"But what about *you?*" I ask the doctor. "You are at great personal risk here—the tuberculosis, the other infections, no water to wash . . ." He shrugs, smiles faintly and lifts his hands palm upward.

We are driving up a serpiginous steep road into the barren mountains above Port-au-Prince. Even in the bright sunshine the countryside has the bloodless color of exhaustion and indifference. Our destination is the Baptist Mission Hospital, where many cases of AIDS have been reported. Along the road there are slow straggles of schoolchildren in blue uniforms who stretch out their hands as we pass and call out, "Give me something." Already a crowd of outpatients has gathered at the entrance to the mission compound. A tour of the premises reveals that in contrast to the aridity outside the gates, this is an enclave of productivity, lush with fruit trees and poinsettia.

The hospital is clean and smells of creosote. Of the forty beds, less than a third are occupied. In one male ward of twelve beds, there are two patients. The chief physician tells us that last year he saw ten cases of AIDS each week. Lately the number has decreased to four or five.

"Why is that?" we want to know.

"Because we do not admit them to the hospital, so they have learned not to come here."

"Why don't you admit them?"

"Because we would have nothing but AIDS here then. So we send them away."

"But I see that you have very few patients in bed."

"That is also true."

"Where do the AIDS patients go?"

"Some go to the clinic in Port-au-Prince or the general hospital in the city. Others go home to die or to the voodoo priest."

"Do the people with AIDS know what they have before they come here?"

"Oh, yes, they know very well, and they know there is nothing to be done for them."

Outside, the crowd of people is dispersing toward the gate. The clinic has been canceled for the day. No one knows why. We are conducted to the office of the reigning American pastor. He is a tall, handsome Midwesterner with an ecclesiastical smile.

"It is voodoo that is the devil here." He warms to his subject. "It is a demonic religion, a cancer on Haiti. Voodoo is worse than AIDS. And it is one of the reasons for the epidemic. Did you know that in order for a man to become a *houngan* he must perform anal sodomy on another man? No, of course you didn't. And it doesn't stop there. The *houngans* tell the men that in order to appease the spirits they too must do the same thing. So you have ritualized homosexuality. That's what is spreading the AIDS." The pastor tells us of a nun who witnessed two acts of sodomy in a provincial hospital where she came upon a man sexually assaulting a houseboy and another man mounting a male patient in his bed.

"Fornication," he says. "It is Sodom and Gomorrah all over again, so what can you expect from these people?" Outside his office we are shown a cage of terrified, cowering monkeys to whom he coos affectionately. It is clear that he loves them. At the car, we shake hands.

"By the way," the pastor says, "what is your religion? Perhaps I am a kinsman?"

"While I am in Haiti," I tell him, "it will be voodoo or it will be nothing at all."

Abruptly, the smile breaks. It is as though a crack had suddenly appeared in the face of an idol.

From the mission we go to the general hospital. In the heart of Port-au-Prince, it is the exact antithesis of the immaculate facility we have just left—filthy, crowded, hectic and staffed entirely by young interns and residents. Though it is associated with a medical school, I do not see any members of the faculty. We are shown around by Jocelyne, a young intern in a scrub suit. Each bed in three large wards is occupied. On the floor about the beds, hunkered in the posture of the innocent poor, are family members of the patients. In the corridor that constitutes the emergency room, someone lies on a stretcher receiving an intravenous infusion. She is hardly more than a cadaver.

"Where are the doctors in charge?" I ask Jocelyne. She looks at me questioningly.

"We are in charge."

"I mean your teachers, the faculty."

"They do not come here."

"What is wrong with that woman?"

"She has had diarrhea for three months. Now she is dehydrated." I ask the woman to open her mouth. Her throat is covered with the white plaques of thrush, a fungus infection associated with AIDS.

"How many AIDS patients do you see here?"

"Three or four a day. We send them home. Sometimes the families abandon them, then we must admit them to the hospital. Every day, then, a relative comes to see if the patient has died. They want to take the body. That is important to them. But they know very well that AIDS is contagious and they are afraid to keep them at home. Even so, once or twice a week the truck comes to take away the bodies. Many are children. They are buried in mass graves."

"Where do the wealthy patients go?"

"There is a private hospital called Canapé Vert. Or else they go to Miami. Most of them, rich and poor, do not go to the hospital. Most are never diagnosed."

"How do you know these people have AIDS?"

"We don't know sometimes. The blood test is inaccurate. There are many false positives and false negatives. Fifteen percent of those with the disease have negative blood tests. We go by their infections—tuberculosis, diarrhea, fungi, herpes, skin rashes. It is not hard to tell."

"Do they know what they have?"

"Yes. They understand at once and they are prepared to die."

"Do the patients know how AIDS is transmitted?"

"They know, but they do not like to talk about it. It is taboo. Their memories do not seem to reach back to the true origins of their disaster. It is understandable, is it not?"

"Whatever you write, don't hurt us any more than we have already been hurt." It is a young Haitian journalist with whom I am drinking a rum punch. He means that any further linkage of AIDS and Haiti in the media would complete the economic destruction of the country. The damage was done early in the epidemic when the Centers for Disease Control in Atlanta added Haitians to the three other high-risk groups—hemophiliacs, intravenous drug users and homosexual and bisexual men. In fact, Haitians are no more susceptible to AIDS than anyone else. Although the CDC removed Haitians from special scrutiny in 1985, the lucrative tourism on which so much of the country's economy was based was crippled. Along with tourism went much of the foreign business investment. Worst of all was the injury to the national pride. Suddenly Haiti was indicted as the source of AIDS in the western hemisphere.

What caused the misunderstanding was the discovery of a large number of Haitian men living in Miami with AIDS antibodies in their blood. They denied absolutely they were homosexuals. But the CDC investigators did not know that homosexuality is the strongest taboo in Haiti and that no man would ever admit to it. Bisexuality, however, is not uncommon. Many married men and heterosexually oriented males will occasionally seek out other men for sex. Further, many, if not most, Haitian men visit female prostitutes from time to time. It is not difficult to see that once the virus was set loose in Haiti, the spread would be swift through both genders.

Exactly how the virus of AIDS arrived is not known. Could it have been brought home by the Cuban soldiers stationed in Angola and thence to Haiti, about fifty miles away? Could it have been passed on by the thousands of Haitians living in exile in Zaire, who later returned home or immigrated to the United States? Could it have come from the American and Canadian homosexual tourists, and, yes, even some U.S. diplomats who have traveled to the island to have sex with impoverished Haitian men all too willing to sell themselves to feed their families? Throughout the international gay community Haiti was known as a good place to go for sex.

On a private tip from an official at the Ministry of Tourism, J-B and I drive to a town some fifty miles from Port-au-Prince. The hotel is owned by two Frenchmen who are out of the country, one of the staff tells us. He is a man of about thirty and clearly he is desperately ill. Tottering, short of breath, he shows us about the empty hotel. The furnishings are opulent and extreme—tiger skins on the wall, a live leopard in the garden, a bedroom containing a giant bathtub with gold faucets. Is it the heat of the day or the heat of my imagination that makes these walls echo with the painful cries of pederasty?

The hotel where we are staying is in Pétionville, the fashionable suburb of Port-au-Prince. It is the height of the season but there are no tourists, only a dozen or so French and American businessmen. The swimming pool is used once or twice a day by a single person. Otherwise, the water remains undisturbed until dusk, when the fruit bats come down to drink in midswoop. The hotel keeper is an American. He is eager to set me straight on Haiti.

"What did and should attract foreign investment is a combination of reliable weather, an honest and friendly populace, low wages and multilingual managers."

"What spoiled it?"

"Political instability and a bad American press about AIDS." He pauses, then adds: "To which I hope you won't be contributing."

"What about just telling the truth?" I suggest.

"Look," he says, "there is no more danger of catching AIDS in Haiti than in New York or Santo Domingo. It is not where you are but what you do that counts." Agreeing, I ask if he had any idea that much of the tourism in Haiti during the past few decades was based on sex.

"No idea whatsoever. It was only recently that we discovered that that was the case."

"How is it that you hoteliers, restaurant owners and the Ministry of Tourism did not know what *tout* Haiti knew?"

"Look. All I know is that this is a middle-class, family-oriented hotel. We don't allow guests to bring women, or for that matter men, into their rooms. If they did, we'd ask them to leave immediately."

At five A.M. the next day the telephone rings in my room. A Creole-accented male voice.

"Is the lady still with you, sir?"

"There is no lady here."

"In your room, sir, the lady I allowed to go up with a package?"

"There is no lady here, I tell you."

At seven A.M. I stop at the front desk. The clerk is a young man.

"Was it you who called my room at five o'clock?"

"Sorry," he says with a smile. "It was a mistake, sir. I meant to ring the room next door to yours." Still smiling, he holds up his shushing finger.

Next to Dr. Pape, director of the AIDS clinic, Bernard Liautaud, a dermatologist, is the most knowledgeable Haitian physician on the subject of the epidemic. Together, the two men have published a dozen articles on AIDS in international medical journals. In our meeting they present me with statistics:

- There are more than one thousand documented cases of AIDS in Haiti, and as many as one hundred thousand carriers of the virus.
- Eighty-seven percent of AIDS is now transmitted heterosexually. While it is true that the virus was introduced via the bisexual community, that route has decreased to 10 percent or less.
- Sixty percent of the wives or husbands of AIDS patients tested positive for the antibody.
- Fifty percent of the prostitutes tested in the Port-au-Prince area are infected.
- Eighty percent of the men with AIDS have had contact with prostitutes.
- The projected number of active cases in four years is ten thousand. (Since my last visit, the Haitian Medical Association broke its silence on the epidemic by warning that one million of the country's six million people could be carriers by 1992.)

The two doctors have more to tell. "The crossing over of the plague from the homosexual to the heterosexual community will follow in the United States within two years. This, despite the hesitation to say so by those who fear to sow panic among your population. In Haiti, because bisexuality is more common, there was an early crossover into the general population. The trend, inevitably, is the same in the two countries."

"What is there to do, then?"

"Only education, just as in America. But here the Haitians reject the use of condoms. Only the men who are too sick to have sex are celibate."

"What is to be the end of it?"

"When enough heterosexuals of the middle and upper classes die, perhaps there will be the panic necessary for the people to change their sexual lifestyles."

This evening I leave Haiti. For two weeks I have fastened myself to this lovely fragile land like an ear pressed to the ground. It is a country to break a traveler's heart. It occurs to me that I have not seen a single jogger. Such a public expenditure of energy while everywhere else strength is ebbing—it would be obscene. In my final hours, I go to the Cathédral of Sainte Trinité, the inner walls of which are covered with murals by Haiti's most renowned artists. Here are all the familiar Bible stories depicted in naïveté and piety, and all in such an exuberance of color as to tax the capacity of the retina to receive it, as though all the vitality of Haiti had been turned to paint and brushed upon these walls. How to explain its efflorescence at a time when all else is lassitude and inertia? Perhaps one day the plague will be rendered in poetry, music, painting, but not now. Not now.

Considerations

Thinking

What images of AIDS does Selzer present? Taken together, what do those images suggest about the disease?

What attitudes about AIDS are conveyed by the people Selzer talks with—the prostitutes, the pastor, the journalist, the hotel manager, the doctors?

Connecting

Examine each of the essay's six scenes. Identify the focus of each and consider how the scenes are related.

Consider what Selzer shows about AIDS in light of what Susan Sontag and Randy Shilts say about it in "AIDS and Its Metaphors" and "Talking AIDS to Death."

Writing

Analyze Selzer's essay to identify and explain the techniques he uses to convey the essay's idea. You might consider Selzer's use of dialogue, details, imagery, metaphor and analogy, and scene.

Compare Selzer's technique of scenic description with that of George Orwell in "Marrakech" and Alice Walker in "Beauty: When the Other Dancer Is the Self."

Randy Shilts
(1951–1994)

When Randy Shilts died in 1994, he was national correspondent of the *San Francisco Chronicle* and the author of three best-selling books: *The Mayor of Castro Street: The Life and Times of Harvey Milk,* about gay political power in San Francisco; *And the Band Played On: Politics, People, and the AIDS Epidemic,* an international best-seller naming the government and the public health and scientific establishments as culprits in the AIDS crisis; and *Conduct Unbecoming,* a searching inquiry into gay life, frustration, and torment in the military. Shilts was named Outstanding Author of 1988 by the American Society of Authors and Journalists for *And the Band Played On.*

"Talking AIDS to Death" is a provocative familiar essay in which Shilts reveals his frustration over being an AIDS celebrity and still being unable to effect significant change at the national level to combat the crisis that was killing his friends . . . and that eventually killed him as well.

Talking AIDS to Death

I'm talking to my friend Kit Herman when I notice a barely perceptible spot on the left side of his face. Slowly, it grows up his cheekbone, down to his chin, and forward to his mouth. He talks on cheerfully, as if nothing is wrong, and I'm amazed that I'm able to smile and chat on, too, as if nothing were there. His eyes become sunken; his hair turns gray; his ear is turning purple now, swelling into a carcinomatous cauliflower, and still we talk on. He's dying in front of me. He'll be dead soon if nothing is done.

Dead soon if nothing is done.

"Excuse me, Mr. Shilts, I asked if you are absolutely sure, if you can categorically state that you definitely can*not* get AIDS from a mosquito."

I forget the early-morning nightmare and shift into my canned response. All my responses are canned now. I'm an AIDS talk-show jukebox. Press the button, any button on the AIDS question list, and I have my canned answer ready. Is this Chicago or Detroit?

"Of course you can get AIDS from a mosquito," I begin.

Here I pause for dramatic effect. In that brief moment, I can almost hear the caller murmur, "I *knew* it."

"If you have unprotected anal intercourse with an infected mosquito, you'll get AIDS," I continue. "Anything short of that and you won't."

The talk-show host likes the answer. All the talk-show hosts like my answers because they're short, punchy, and to the point. Not like those boring doctors with long recitations of scientific studies so overwritten with maybes and qualifiers that they frighten more than they reassure an AIDS-hysteric public. I give good interviews, talk-show producers agree. It's amazing, they say, how I always stay so cool and never lose my temper.

"Mr. Shilts, has there ever been a case of anyone getting AIDS from a gay waiter?"

"In San Francisco, I don't think they allow heterosexuals to be waiters. This fact proves absolutely that if you could get AIDS from a gay waiter, all northern California would be dead by now."

I gave that same answer once on a Bay Area talk show, and my caller, by the sound of her a little old lady, quickly rejoined, "What if that gay waiter took my salad back into the kitchen and ejaculated into my salad dressing? Couldn't I get AIDS then?"

I didn't have a pat answer for that one, and I still wonder at what this elderly caller thought went on in the kitchens of San Francisco restaurants.

546

Fortunately, this morning's phone-in—in Chicago, it turned out—is not as imaginative.

"You know, your question reminds me of a joke we had in California a couple of years back," I told the caller. "How many heterosexual waiters in San Francisco does it take to screw in a light bulb? The answer is both of them."

The host laughs, the caller is silent. Next comes the obligatory question about whether AIDS can be spread through coughing.

I had written a book to change the world, and here I was on talk shows throughout America, answering questions about mosquitoes and gay waiters.

This wasn't exactly what I had envisioned when I began writing *And the Band Played On*. I had hoped to effect some fundamental changes. I really believed I could alter the performance of the institutions that had allowed AIDS to sweep through America unchecked.

AIDS had spread, my book attested, because politicians, particularly those in charge of federal-level response, had viewed the disease as a political issue, not an issue of public health—they deprived researchers of anything near the resources that were needed to fight it. AIDS had spread because government health officials consistently lied to the American people about the need for more funds, being more concerned with satisfying their political bosses and protecting their own jobs than with telling the truth and protecting the public health. And AIDS had spread because indolent news organizations shunned their responsibility to provide tough, adversarial reportage, instead basing stories largely on the Official Truth of government press releases. The response to AIDS was never even remotely commensurate with the scope of the problem.

I figured the federal government, finally exposed, would stumble over itself to accelerate the pace of AIDS research and put AIDS prevention programs on an emergency footing. Once publicly embarrassed by the revelations of its years of shameful neglect, the media would launch serious investigative reporting on the epidemic. Health officials would step forward and finally lay bare the truth about how official disregard had cost this country hundreds of thousands of lives. And it would never happen again.

I was stunned by the "success" of my book. I quickly acquired all the trappings of bestsellerdom: *60 Minutes* coverage of my "startling" revelations, a Book-of-the-Month Club contract, a miniseries deal with NBC, translation into six languages, book tours on three continents, featured roles in movie-star-studded AIDS fund raisers, regular appearances on network news shows, and hefty fees on the college lecture circuit. A central figure in my book became one of *People* magazine's "25 Most Intriguing People of 1987," even though he had been dead for nearly four years, and the *Los Angeles Herald Examiner* pronounced me one of the "in" authors of 1988. The mayor of San Francisco even proclaimed my birthday last year "Randy Shilts Day."

And one warm summer day as I was sunning at a gay resort in the redwoods north of San Francisco, a well-toned, perfectly tanned young man slid into a chaise next to me and offered the ultimate testimony to my fifteen minutes of fame. His dark eyelashes rising and falling shyly, he whispered, "When I saw you on *Good Morning America* a couple weeks ago, I wondered what it would be like to go to bed with you."

"You're the world's first AIDS celebrity," enthused a friend at the World Health Organization, after hearing one of WHO's most eminent AIDS authorities say he would grant me an interview on one condition—that I autograph his copy of my book. "It must be great," he said.

It's not so great.

The bitter irony is, my role as an AIDS celebrity just gives me a more elevated promontory from which to watch the world make the same mistakes in the handling of the AIDS epidemic that I had hoped my work would help to change. When I return from network tapings and celebrity glad-handing, I come back to my home in San Francisco's gay community and see friends dying. The lesions spread from their cheeks to cover their faces, their hair falls out, they die slowly, horribly, and sometimes suddenly, before anybody has a chance to know they're sick. They die in my arms and in my dreams, and nothing at all has changed.

Never before have I succeeded so well; never before have I failed so miserably.

I gave my first speech on the college lecture circuit at the University of California at Los Angeles in January 1988. I told the audience that there were 50,000 diagnosed AIDS cases in the United States as of that week and that within a few months there would be more people suffering from this deadly disease in the United States than there were Americans killed during the Vietnam War. There were audible gasps. During the question-and-answer session, several students explained that they had heard that the number of AIDS cases in America was leveling off.

In the next speech, at the University of Tennessee, I decided to correct such misapprehension by adding the federal government's projections—the 270,000 expected to be dead or dying from AIDS in 1991, when the disease would kill more people than any single form of cancer, more than car accidents. When I spoke at St. Cloud State University in Minnesota three months later, I noted that the number of American AIDS cases had that week surpassed the Vietnam benchmark. The reaction was more a troubled murmur than a gasp.

By the time I spoke at New York City's New School for Social Research in June and there were 65,000 AIDS cases nationally, the numbers were changing so fast that the constant editing made my notes difficult to read. By then as many as 1,000 Americans a week were learning that they, too, had AIDS, or on the average, about one every fourteen minutes. There were new government projections to report, too: by 1993, some 450,000 Americans would be diagnosed with AIDS. In that year, one American will be diagnosed with the disease every thirty-six seconds. Again, I heard the gasps.

For my talk at a hospital administrators' conference in Washington in August, I started using little yellow stick-ons to update the numbers on my outline. That made it easier to read; there were now 72,000 AIDS cases. Probably this month, or next, I'll tell another college audience that the nation's AIDS case load has topped 100,000, and there will be gasps again.

The gasps always amaze me. Why are they surprised? In epidemics, people get sick and die. That's what epidemics do to people and that's why epidemics are bad.

When Kit Herman was diagnosed with AIDS on May 13, 1986, his doctor leaned over his hospital bed, took his hand, and assured him, "Don't worry, you're in time for AZT." The drug worked so well that all Kit's friends let themselves think he might make it. And we were bolstered by the National Institutes of Health's assurance that AZT was only the first generation of AIDS drugs, and that the hundreds of millions of federal dollars going into AIDS treatment research meant there would soon be a second and third generation of treatments to sustain life beyond AZT's effectiveness. Surely nothing was more important, considering the federal government's own estimates that between 1 and 1.5 million Americans were infected with the Human Immunodeficiency Virus (HIV), and virtually all would die within the next decade if nothing was done. The new drugs, the NIH assured everyone, were "in the pipeline," and government scientists were working as fast as they possibly could.

Despite my nagging, not one of dozens of public-affairs-show producers chose to look seriously into the development of those long-sought second and third generations of AIDS drugs. In fact, clinical trials of AIDS drugs were hopelessly stalled in the morass of bureaucracy at the NIH, but this story tip never seemed to cut it with producers. Clinical trials were not sexy. Clinical trials were boring.

I made my third *Nightline* appearance in January 1988 because new estimates had been released revealing that one in sixty-one babies born in New York City carried antibodies to the AIDS virus. And the link between those babies and the disease was intravenous drug use by one or both parents. Suddenly, junkies had become the group most likely to catch and spread AIDS through the heterosexual community. Free needles to junkies—now there was a sizzling television topic. I told the show's producers I'd talk about that, but that I was much more interested in the issue of AIDS treatments—which seemed most relevant to the night's program, since Ted Koppel's other guest was Dr. Anthony Fauci, associate NIH director for AIDS, and the Reagan administration's most visible AIDS official.

After fifteen minutes of talk on the ins and outs and pros and cons of free needles for intravenous drug users, I raised the subject of the pressing need for AIDS treatments. Koppel asked Fauci what was happening. The doctor launched into a discussion of treatments "in the pipeline" and how government scientists were working as fast as they possibly could.

I'd heard the same words from NIH officials for three years: drugs were in the pipeline. Maybe it was true, but when were they going to come out of their goddamn pipeline? Before I could formulate a polite retort to Fauci's stall, however, the segment was over, Ted was thanking us, and the red light on the camera had blipped off. Everyone seemed satisfied that the government was doing everything it possibly could to develop AIDS treatments.

Three months later, I was reading a week-old *New York Times* in Kit's room in the AIDS ward at San Francisco General Hospital. It was April, nearly two years after my friend's AIDS diagnosis. AZT had given him two years of nearly perfect health, but now its effect was wearing off, and Kit had suffered his first major AIDS-related infection since his original bout with pneumonia—cryptococcal meningitis. The meningitis could be treated, we all knew, but the discovery of this insidious brain infection meant more diseases were likely to follow. And the long-promised second and third generations of AIDS drugs were still nowhere on the horizon.

While perusing the worn copy of the *Times,* I saw a story about Dr. Fauci's testimony at a congressional hearing. After making Fauci swear an oath to tell the truth, a subcommittee headed by Congressman Ted Weiss of New York City asked why it was taking so long to get new AIDS treatments into testing at a time when Congress was putting hundreds of millions of dollars into NIH budgets for just such purposes. At first Fauci talked about unavoidable delays. He claimed government scientists were working as fast as they could. Pressed harder, he finally admitted that the problem stemmed "almost exclusively" from the lack of staffing in his agency. Congress had allocated funds, it was true, but the Reagan administration had gotten around spending the money by stingily refusing to let Fauci hire anybody. Fauci had requested 127 positions to speed the development of AIDS treatments; the administration had granted him eleven. And for a year, he had not told anyone. For a year, this spokesman for the public health answered reporters that AIDS drugs were in the pipeline and that government scientists had all the money they needed. It seemed that only when faced with the penalty of perjury would one of the administration's top AIDS officials tell the truth. That was the real story, I thought, but for some reason nobody else had picked up on it.

At the international AIDS conference in Stockholm two months later, the other reporters in "the AIDS pack" congratulated me on my success and asked what I was working on now. I admitted that I was too busy promoting the British and German release of my book to do much writing myself, and next month I had the Australian tour. But if I *were* reporting, I added with a vaguely conspiratorial tone, I'd look at the *scandal* in the NIH. Nobody had picked up that *New York Times* story from a few months ago about staffing shortages on AIDS clinical trials. The lives of 1.5 million HIV-infected Americans hung in the balance, and the only way you could get a straight answer out of an administration AIDS official was to put him under oath and make him face the charge of perjury. Where I went to journalism school, *that* was a news story.

One reporter responded to my tip with the question "But who's going to play *you* in the miniseries?"

A few minutes later, when Dr. Fauci came into the press room, the world's leading AIDS journalists got back to the serious business of transcribing his remarks. Nobody asked him if he was actually telling the truth, or whether they should put him under oath to ensure a candid response to questions about when we'd get AIDS treatments. Most of the subsequent news accounts of Dr. Fauci's comments faithfully reported that many AIDS treatments were in the pipeline. Government scientists, he said once more, were doing all they possibly could.

The producer assured my publisher that Morton Downey, Jr., would be "serious" about AIDS. "He's not going to play games on this issue," the producer said, adding solemnly, "His brother has AIDS. He understands the need for compassion." The abundance of Mr. Downey's compassion was implicit in the night's call-in poll question: "Should all people with AIDS be quarantined?"

Downey's first question to me was, "You *are* a homosexual, aren't you?"

He wasn't ready for my canned answer: "Why do you ask? Do you want a date or something?"

The show shifted into an earnest discussion of quarantine. In his television studio, Clearasil-addled high school students from suburban New Jersey held up MORTON DOWNEY FAN CLUB signs and cheered aggressively when the truculent, chain-smoking host appeared to favor a kind of homespun AIDS Auschwitz. The youths shouted down any audience member who stepped forward to defend the rights of AIDS sufferers, their howls growing particularly vitriolic if the speakers were gay. These kids were the ilk from which Hitler drew his Nazi youth. In the first commercial break, the other guest, an AIDS activist, and I told Downey we would walk off the show if he didn't tone down his gay-baiting rhetoric. Smiling amiably, Downey took a long drag on his cigarette and assured us, "Don't worry, I have a fallback position."

That comment provided one of the most lucid moments in my year as an AIDS celebrity. Downey's "fallback position," it was clear, was the opposite of what he was promoting on the air. Of course, he didn't *really* believe that people with AIDS, people like his brother, should all be locked up. This was merely a deliciously provocative posture to exploit the working-class resentments of people who needed someone to hate. AIDS sufferers and gays would do for this week. Next week, if viewership dropped and Downey needed a new whipping boy, maybe he'd move on to Arabs, maybe Jews. It didn't seem to matter much to him, since he didn't believe what he was saying anyway. For Morton Downey, Jr., talking about AIDS was not an act of conscience; it was a ratings ploy. He knew it, he let his guests know it, his producers certainly knew it, and his television station knew it. The only people left out of the joke were his audience.

The organizers of the Desert AIDS Project had enlisted actor Kirk Douglas and CBS morning anchor Kathleen Sullivan to be honorary co-chairs of the Palm Springs fund raiser. The main events would include a celebrity tennis match pitting Douglas against Mayor Sonny Bono, and a $1,500-a-head dinner at which I would receive a Lucite plaque for my contributions to the fight against AIDS. The next morning I would fly to L.A. to speak at still another event, this one with Shirley MacLaine, Valerie Harper, and Susan Dey of *L.A. Law*.

The desert night was exquisite. There were 130 dinner guests, the personification of elegance and confidence, who gathered on a magnificent patio of chocolate-brown Arizona flagstone at the home of one of Palm Springs's most celebrated interior designers. A lot of people had come simply to see what was regarded as one of the most sumptuous dwellings in this sumptuous town.

When I was called to accept my reward, I began with the same lineup of jokes I use on talk shows and on the college lecture circuit. They work every time.

I told the crowd about how you get AIDS from a mosquito.

Kirk Douglas laughed; everybody laughed.

Next, I did the how-many-gay-waiters joke.

Kirk Douglas laughed; everybody laughed.

Then I mentioned the woman who asked whether she could get AIDS from a waiter ejaculating in her salad dressing.

That one always has my college audiences rolling in the aisles, so I paused for the expected hilarity.

But in the utter stillness of the desert night air, all that could be heard was the sound of Kirk Douglas's steel jaw dropping to the magnificent patio of chocolate-brown Arizona flagstone. The rest was silence.

"You've got to remember that most of these people came because they're my clients," the host confided later. "You said that, and all I could think was how I'd have to go back to stitching slipcovers when this was done."

It turned out that there was more to my lead-balloon remark than a mis-judged audience. Local AIDS organizers told me that a year earlier, a rumor that one of Palm Springs's most popular restaurants was owned by a homosexual, and that most of its waiters were gay, had terrified the elite community. Patronage at the eatery quickly plummeted, and it had nearly gone out of business. Fears that I dismissed as laughable were the genuine concerns of my audience, I realized. My San Francisco joke was a Palm Springs fable.

As I watched the busboys clear the tables later that night, I made a mental note not to tell that joke before dinner again. Never had I seen so many uneaten salads, so much wasted iceberg lettuce.

A friend had just tested antibody positive, and I was doing my best to cheer him up as we ambled down the sidewalk toward a Castro Street restaurant a few blocks from where I live in San Francisco. It seems most of my conversations now have to do with who has tested positive or lucked out and turned up negative, or who is too afraid to be tested. We had parked our car near Coming Home, the local hospice for AIDS patients and others suffering from terminal illnesses, and as we stepped around a nondescript, powder-blue van that blocked our path, two men in white uniforms emerged from the hospice's side door. They carried a stretcher, and on the stretcher was a corpse, neatly wrapped in a royal-blue blan-ket and secured with navy-blue straps. My friend and I stopped walking. The men quickly guided the stretcher into the back of the van, climbed in the front doors, and drove away. We continued our walk but didn't say anything.

I wondered if the corpse was someone I had known. I'd find out Thursday when the weekly gay paper came out. Every week there are at least two pages filled with obituaries of the previous week's departed. Each week, when I turn to those pages, I hold my breath, wondering whose picture I'll see. It's the only way to keep track, what with so many people dying.

Sometimes I wonder if an aberrant mother or two going to mass at the Most Holy Redeemer Church across the street from Coming Home Hospice has ever warned a child, "That's where you'll end up it you don't obey God's law." Or whether some youngster, feeling that first awareness of a different sexuality, has looked at the doorway of this modern charnel house with an awesome, gnawing dread of annihilation.

"Is the limousine here? Where are the dancers?"

The room fell silent. Blake Rothaus had sounded coherent until that moment, but he was near death now and his brain was going. We were gathered around his bed in a small frame house on a dusty street in Oklahoma City. The twenty-four-year-old was frail and connected to life through a web of clear plastic tubing. He stared up at us and seemed to recognize from our looks that he had lapsed into dementia. A friend broke the uncomfortable silence.

"Of course, we all brought our dancing shoes," he said. "Nice fashionable pumps at that. I wouldn't go out without them."

Everyone laughed and Blake Rothaus was lucid again.

Blake had gone to high school in a San Francisco suburb. When he was a sophomore, he told us, he and his best friend sometimes skipped school, sneaking to the city to spend their afternoons in the gay neighborhood around Castro Street.

It's a common sight, suburban teenagers playing hooky on Castro Street. I could easily imagine him standing on a corner not far from my house. But back in 1982, when he was eighteen, I was already writing about a mysterious, unnamed disease that had claimed 330 victims in the United States.

Blake moved back to Oklahoma City with his family after he graduated from high school. When he fell ill with AIDS, he didn't mope. Instead, he started pestering Oklahoma health officials with demands to educate people about this disease and to provide services for the sick. The state health department didn't recoil. At the age of twenty-two, Blake Rothaus had become the one-man nucleus for Oklahoma's first AIDS patient services. He was the hero of the Sooner State's AIDS movement and something of a local legend.

Though the state had reported only 250 AIDS cases, Oklahoma City had a well-coordinated network of religious leaders, social workers, health-care providers, gay-rights advocates, state legislators, and businessmen, all committed to providing a sane and humane response to this frightening new disease.

"I think it's the old Dust Bowl mentality," suggested one AIDS organizer. "When the hard times come, people pull together."

My past year's travels to twenty-nine states and talks with literally thousands of people have convinced me of one thing about this country and AIDS: most Americans want to do the right thing about this epidemic. Some might worry about mosquitoes and a few may be suspicious of their salad dressing. But beyond these fears is a reservoir of compassion and concern that goes vastly underreported by a media that needs conflict and heartlessness to fashion a good news hook.

In Kalamazoo, Michigan, when I visited my stepmother, I was buttonholed by a dozen middle-aged women who wondered anxiously whether we were any closer to a vaccine or a long-term treatment. One mentioned a hemophiliac nephew. Another had a gay brother in Chicago. A third went to a gay hairdresser who, she quickly added, was one of the finest people you'd ever meet. When I returned to my conservative hometown of Aurora, Illinois, nestled among endless fields of corn and soy, the local health department told me they receive more calls than they know what to do with from women's groups, parishes, and community organizations that want to do something to help. In New Orleans, the archconservative, pro-nuke, anti-gay bishop had taken up the founding of an AIDS hospice as a personal mission because, he said, when people are sick, you've got to help them out.

Scientists, reporters, and politicians privately tell me that of course *they* want to do more about AIDS, but they have to think about the Morton Downeys of the world, who argue that too much research or too much news space or too much official sympathy is being meted out to a bunch of miscreants. They do as much as they can, they insist; more would rile the resentments of the masses. So the institutions fumble along, convinced they must pander to the lowest common denominator, while the women and men of America's heartland pull me aside to fret about a dying cousin or co-worker and to plead, "When will there be a cure? When will this be over?"

"I think I'll make it through this time," Kit said to me, "but I don't have it in me to go through it again."

We were in room 3 in San Francisco General Hospital's ward 5A, the AIDS ward. The poplar trees outside Kit's window were losing their leaves, and the first winter's chill was settling over the city. I was preparing to leave for my fourth and, I hoped, final media tour, this time for release of the book in paperback and on audiocassette; Kit was preparing to die.

The seizures had started a week earlier, indicating he was suffering either from toxoplasmosis, caused by a gluttonous protozoa that sets up housekeeping in the brain; or perhaps it was a relapse of cryptococcal meningitis; or, another specialist guessed, it could be one of those other nasty brain infections that nobody had seen much of until the past year. Now that AIDS patients were living longer, they fell victim to even more exotic infections than in the early days. But the seizures were only part of it. Kit had slowly been losing the sight in his left eye to a herpes infection. And the Kaposi's sarcoma lesions that had scarred his face were beginning to coat the inside of his lungs. When Kit mentioned he'd like to live until Christmas, the doctors said he might want to consider having an early celebration this year, because he wasn't going to be alive in December.

"I can't take another infection," Kit said.

"What does that mean?"

"Morphine," Kit answered, adding mischievously, "lots of it."

We talked briefly about the mechanics of suicide. We both knew people who'd made a mess of it, and people who had done it right. It was hardly the first time the subject had come up in conversation for either of us. Gay men facing AIDS now exchange formulas for suicide as casually as housewives swap recipes for chocolate-chip cookies.

Kit was released from the hospital a few days later. He had decided to take his life on a Tuesday morning. I had to give my first round of interviews in Los Angeles that day, so I stopped on the way to the airport to say goodbye on Monday. All day Tuesday, while I gave my perfectly formed sound bites in a round of network radio appearances, I wondered: Is this the moment he's slipping out of consciousness and into that perfect darkness? When I called that night, it turned out he'd delayed his suicide until Thursday to talk to a few more relatives. I had to give a speech in Portland that day, so on the way to the airport I stopped again. He showed me the amber-brown bottle with the bubble-gum-pink morphine syrup, and we said another goodbye.

The next morning, Kit drank his morphine and fell into a deep sleep. That afternoon, he awoke and drowsily asked what time it was. When told it was five hours later, he murmured, "That's amazing. I should have been dead hours ago."

And then he went back to sleep.

That night, Kit woke up again.

"You know what they say about near-death experiences?" he asked. "Going toward the light?"

Shaking his head, he sighed. "No light. Nothing."

His suicide attempt a failure, Kit decided the timing of his death would now be up to God. I kept up on the bizarre sequence of events by phone and called as soon as I got back to San Francisco. I was going to tell Kit that his theme song should be "Never Can Say Goodbye," but then the person on the other end of the phone told me that Kit had lapsed into a coma.

The next morning, he died.

Kit's death was like everything about AIDS—anticlimactic. By the time he actually did die, I was almost beyond feeling.

The next day, I flew to Boston for the start of the paperback tour, my heart torn between rage and sorrow. All week, as I was chauffeured to my appearances on *Good Morning America, Larry King Live,* and various CNN shows, I kept thinking, It's all going to break. I'm going to be on a TV show with some officious government health spokesman lying to protect his job, and I'm going to start shouting, "You lying son of a bitch. Don't you know there are people, real people, people I love out there dying?" Or I'll be on a call-in show and another mother will phone about her thirty-seven-year-old son who just died and it will hit me all at once, and I'll start weeping.

But day after day as the tour went on, no matter how many official lies I heard and how many grieving mothers I talked to, the crack-up never occurred. All my answers came out rationally in tight little sound bites about institutional barriers to AIDS treatments and projections about 1993 case loads.

By the last day of the tour, when a limousine picked me up at my Beverly Hills hotel for my last round of satellite TV interviews, I knew I had to stop. In a few weeks I'd return to being national correspondent for the *Chronicle,* and it was time to get off the AIDS celebrity circuit, end the interviews and decline the invitations to the star-studded fund raisers, and get back to work as a newspaper reporter. That afternoon, there was just one last radio interview to a call-in show in the San Fernando Valley, and then it would be over.

The first caller asked why his tax money should go toward funding an AIDS cure when people got the disease through their own misdeeds.

I used my standard jukebox answer about how most cancer cases are linked to people's behavior but that nobody ever suggested we stop trying to find a cure for cancer.

A second caller phoned to ask why her tax money should go to finding an AIDS cure when these people clearly deserved what they got.

I calmly put a new spin on the same answer, saying in America you usually don't sentence people to die for having a different lifestyle from yours.

Then a third caller phoned in to say that he didn't care if all those queers and junkies died, as did a fourth and fifth and sixth caller. By then I was shouting, "You stupid bigot. You just want to kill off everybody you don't like. You goddamn Nazi."

The talk-show host sat in stunned silence. She'd heard I was so *reasonable*. My anger baited the audience further, and the seventh and eighth callers began talking about "you guys," as if only a faggot like myself could give a shit about whether AIDS patients all dropped dead tomorrow.

In their voices, I heard the reporters asking polite questions of NIH officials. Of course, they had to be polite to the government doctors; dying queers weren't anything to lose your temper over. I heard the dissembling NIH researchers go home to their wives at night, complain about the lack of personnel, and shrug; this was just how it was going to have to be for a while. They'd excuse their inaction by telling themselves that if they went public and lost their jobs, worse people would replace them. It was best to go along. But how would they feel if *their* friends, *their* daughters, were dying of this disease? Would they be silent—or would they shout? Maybe they'll forgive me for suspecting they believed that ultimately a bunch of fags weren't worth losing a job over. And when I got home, I was going to have to watch my friends get shoved into powder-blue vans, and it wasn't going to change.

The history of the AIDS epidemic, of yesterday and of today, was echoing in the voices of those callers. And I was screaming at them, and the show host just sat there stunned, and I realized I had rendered myself utterly and completely inarticulate.

I stopped, took a deep breath, and returned to compound-complex sentences about the American tradition of compassion and the overriding need to overcome institutional barriers to AIDS treatments.

When I got home to San Francisco that night, I looked over some notes I had taken from a conversation I'd had with Kit during his last stay in the hospital. I was carping about how frustrated I was at the prospect of returning to my reporting job. If an internationally acclaimed best seller hadn't done shit to change the world, what good would mere newspaper stories do?

"The limits of information," Kit said. "There's been a lot written on it."

"Oh," I said.

Kit closed his eyes briefly and faded into sleep while plastic tubes fed him a cornucopia of antibiotics. After five minutes, he stirred, looked up, and added, as if we had never stopped talking, "But you don't really have a choice. You've got to keep on doing it. What else are you going to do?"

Considerations

Thinking

At the beginning and at the end of his essay, Shilts sounds a note of deep concern about what happens in the AIDS epidemic "if nothing is done." How does he make you respond to that concern?

How would you characterize Shilts' sense of humor? How does he use it to further his cause? Does he ever misuse it?

What happened when, during a radio interview to a call-in show, Shilts stopped talking "rationally in tight little sound bites"? What are the broader implications of losing control while waging a frustrating war against indifference, ignorance, and an epidemic?

Connecting

What does the evidence in this essay suggest about the relationship between death, laughter, and courage in the gay community?

In what ways does Richard Selzer's essay "A Mask on the Face of Death" help you understand the magnitude of the problems Shilts writes about?

Writing

Write a couple of paragraphs about the ironic implications of the essay's title: "Talking AIDS to Death." What do you think Shilts had in mind when he chose that title?

Write an essay about "the limits of information," that phrase Shilts' friend Kit mentions near the end of the essay. Your essay need not focus on AIDS; choose any subject area that interests you. Develop your essay through research or through anecdote and recollected experience, or through both research and experience.

Leslie Marmon Silko
(b. 1948)

Leslie Marmon Silko, poet, essayist, and storyteller, was born in New Mexico of Laguna parentage. Silko spent her childhood on the Laguna Pueblo Indian Reservation. She has published a volume of poetry, *Laguna Woman* (1974); a collection of short stories, *Storyteller* (1981); and two novels, *Ceremony* (1977) and *Almanac of the Dead* (1991). She has been the recipient of a MacArthur Fellowship as well as other awards.

In "Landscape, History, and the Pueblo Imagination," Silko explains the relationship between nature and people. She also explains the significance of Pueblo burial customs, and she encourages people to develop an attitude toward the land based on harmony, respect, and connectedness.

Landscape, History, and the Pueblo Imagination

From a High Arid Plateau in New Mexico

You see that after a thing is dead, it dries up. It might take weeks or years, but eventually if you touch the thing, it crumbles under your fingers. It goes back to dust. The soul of the thing has long since departed. With the plants and wild game the soul may have already been borne back into bones and blood or thick green stalk and leaves. Nothing is wasted. What cannot be eaten by people or in some way used must then be left where other living creatures may benefit. What domestic animals or wild scavengers can't eat will be fed to the plants. The plants feed on the dust of these few remains.

The ancient Pueblo people buried the dead in vacant rooms or partially collapsed rooms adjacent to the main living quarters. Sand and clay used to construct the roof make layers many inches deep once the roof has collapsed. The layers of sand and clay make for easy gravedigging. The vacant room fills with cast-off objects and debris. When a vacant room has filled deep enough, a shallow but adequate grave can be scooped in a far corner. Archaeologists have remarked over formal burials complete with elaborate funerary objects excavated in trash middens of abandoned rooms. But the rocks and adobe mortar of collapsed walls were valued by the ancient people. Because each rock had been carefully selected for size and shape, then chiseled to an even face. Even the pink clay adobe melting with each rainstorm had to be prayed over, then dug and carried some distance. Corn cobs and husks, the rinds and stalks and animal bones were not regarded by the ancient people as filth or garbage. The remains were merely resting at a midpoint in their journey back to dust. Human remains are not so different. They should rest with the bones and rinds where they all may benefit living creatures— small rodents and insects—until their return is completed. The remains of things—animals and plants, the clay and the stones—were treated with respect. Because for the ancient people all these things had spirit and being.

The antelope merely consents to return home with the hunter. All phases of the hunt are conducted with love. The love the hunter and the people have for the Antelope People. And the love of the antelope who agree to give up their meat and blood so that human beings will not starve. Waste of meat or even the thoughtless handling of bones cooked bare will offend the antelope spirits. Next year the hunters will vainly search the dry plains for antelope. Thus it is necessary to return carefully the bones and hair, and the stalks and leaves to the earth who first created them. The spirits remain close by. They do not leave us.

The dead become dust, and in this becoming they are once more joined with the Mother. The ancient Pueblo people called the earth the Mother Creator of all things in this world. Her sister, the Corn Mother, occasionally merges with her because all succulent green life rises out of the depths of the earth.

Rocks and clay are part of the Mother. They emerge in various forms, but at some time before, they were smaller particles or great boulders. At a later time they may again become what they once were. Dust.

A rock shares this fate with us and with animals and plants as well. A rock has being or spirit, although we may not understand it. The spirit may differ from the spirit we know in animals or plants or in ourselves. In the end we all originate from the depths of the earth. Perhaps this is how all beings share in the spirit of the Creator. We do not know.

From the Emergence Place

Pueblo potters, the creators of petroglyphs and oral narratives, never conceived of removing themselves from the earth and sky. So long as the human consciousness remains *within* the hills, canyons, cliffs, and the plants, clouds, and sky, the term *landscape,* as it has entered the English language, is misleading. "A portion of territory the eye can comprehend in a single view" does not correctly describe the relationship between the human being and his or her surroundings. This assumes the viewer is somehow *outside* or *separate from* the territory he or she surveys. Viewers are as much a part of the landscape as the boulders they stand on. There is no high mesa edge or mountain peak where one can stand and not immediately be part of all that surrounds. Human identity is linked with all the elements of Creation through the clan: you might belong to the Sun Clan or the Lizard Clan or the Corn Clan or the Clay Clan.[1] Standing deep within the natural world, the ancient Pueblo understood the thing as it was—the squash blossom, grasshopper, or rabbit itself could never be created by the human hand. Ancient Pueblos took the modest view that the thing itself (the landscape) could not be improved upon. The ancients did not presume to tamper with what had already been created. Thus *realism,* as we now recognize it in painting and sculpture, did not catch the imaginations of Pueblo people until recently.

The squash blossom itself is *one thing:* itself. So the ancient Pueblo potter abstracted what she saw to be the key elements of the squash blossom—the four symmetrical petals, with four symmetrical stamens in the center. These key elements, while suggesting the squash flower, also link it with the four cardinal directions. By representing only its intrinsic form, the squash flower is released from a limited meaning or restricted identity. Even in the most sophisticated abstract form, a squash flower or a cloud or a lightning bolt became intricately connected with a complex system of relationships which the ancient Pueblo people maintained with each other, and with the populous natural world they lived within. A bolt of lightning is itself, but at the same time it may mean much more. It may be a messenger of good fortune when summer rains are needed. It may deliver death, perhaps the result of manipulations by the Gunnadeyahs, destructive necromancers. Lightning may strike down an evil-doer. Or lightning may strike a person of good will. If the person survives, lightning endows him or her with heightened power.

Pictographs and petroglyphs of constellations or elk or antelope draw their magic in part from the process wherein the focus of all prayer and concentration is upon the thing itself, which, in its turn, guides the hunter's hand. Connection with the spirit dimensions requires a figure or form which is all-inclusive. A "life-like" rendering of an elk is too restrictive. Only the elk *is* itself. A *realistic* rendering of an elk would be only one particular elk anyway. The purpose of the hunt rituals and magic is to make contact with *all* the spirits of the Elk.

The land, the sky, and all that is within them—the landscape—includes human beings. Interrelationships in the Pueblo landscape are complex and fragile. The unpredictability of the weather, the aridity and harshness of much of the terrain in the high plateau country explain in large part the relentless attention the ancient Pueblo people gave the sky and the earth around them. Survival depended upon harmony and cooperation not only among human beings, but among all things—the animate and the less animate, since rocks and mountains were known to move, to travel occasionally.

The ancient Pueblos believed the Earth and the Sky were sisters (or sister and brother in the post-Christian version). As long as good family relations are maintained, then the Sky will continue to bless her sister, the Earth, with rain, and the Earth's children will continue to survive. But the old stories recall incidents in which troublesome spirits or beings threaten the earth. In one story, a malicious ka'tsina, called the Gambler, seizes the Shiwana, or Rainclouds, the Sun's beloved children.[2] The Shiwana are snared in magical power late one afternoon on a high mountain top. The Gambler takes the Rainclouds to his mountain stronghold where he locks them in the north room of his house. What was his idea? The Shiwana were beyond value. They brought life to all things on earth. The Gambler wanted a big stake to wager in his games of chance. But such greed, even on the part of only one being, had the effect of threatening the survival of all life on earth.

Sun Youth, aided by old Grandmother Spider, outsmarts the Gambler and the rigged game, and the Rainclouds are set free. The drought ends, and once more life thrives on earth.

Through the Stories We Hear Who We Are

All summer the people watch the west horizon, scanning the sky from south to north for rain clouds. Corn must have moisture at the time the tassels form. Otherwise pollination will be incomplete, and the ears will be stunted and shriveled. An inadequate harvest may bring disaster. Stories told at Hopi, Zuni, and at Acoma and Laguna describe drought and starvation as recently as 1900. Precipitation in west-central New Mexico averages fourteen inches annually. The western Pueblos are located at altitudes over 5,600 feet above sea level, where winter temperatures at night fall below freezing. Yet evidence of their presence in the high desert plateau country goes back ten thousand years. The ancient Pueblo people not only survived in this environment, but many years they thrived. In A.D. 1100 the people at Chaco Canyon had built cities with apartment buildings of stone five stories high. Their sophistication as sky-watchers was surpassed only by Mayan and Inca astronomers. Yet this vast complex of knowledge and belief, amassed for thousands of years, was never recorded in writing.

Instead, the ancient Pueblo people depended upon collective memory through successive generations to maintain and transmit an entire culture, a world view complete with proven strategies for survival. The oral narrative, or "story," became the medium in which the complex of Pueblo knowledge and belief was maintained. Whatever the event or the subject, the ancient people perceived the world and themselves within that world as part of an ancient continuous story composed of innumerable bundles of other stories.

The ancient Pueblo vision of the world was inclusive. The impulse was to leave nothing out. Pueblo oral tradition necessarily embraced all levels of human experience. Otherwise, the collective knowledge and beliefs comprising ancient Pueblo culture would have been incomplete. Thus stories about the Creation and Emergence of human beings and animals into this World continue to be retold each year for four days and four nights during the winter solstice. The "humma-hah" stories related events from the time long ago when human beings were still able to communicate with animals and other living things. But, beyond these two preceding categories, the Pueblo oral tradition knew no boundaries. Accounts of the appearance of the first Europeans in Pueblo country or of the tragic encounters between Pueblo people and Apache raiders were no more and no less important than stories about the biggest mule deer ever taken or adulterous couples surprised in cornfields and chicken coops. Whatever happened, the ancient people instinctively sorted events and details into a loose narrative structure. Everything became a story.

Traditionally everyone, from the youngest child to the oldest person, was expected to listen and to be able to recall or tell a portion, if only a small detail, from a narrative account or story. Thus the remembering and retelling were a communal process. Even if a key figure, an elder who knew much more than others, were to die unexpectedly, the system would remain intact. Through the efforts of a great many people, the community was able to piece together valuable accounts and crucial information that might otherwise have died with an individual.

Communal storytelling was a self-correcting process in which listeners were encouraged to speak up if they noted an important fact or detail omitted. The people were happy to listen to two or three different versions of the same event or the same humma-hah story. Even conflicting versions of an incident were welcomed for the entertainment they provided. Defenders of each version might joke and tease one another, but seldom were there any direct confrontations. Implicit in the Pueblo oral tradition was the awareness that loyalties, grudges, and kinship must always influence the narrator's choices as she emphasizes to listeners this is the way *she* has always heard the story told. The ancient Pueblo people sought a communal truth, not an absolute. For them this truth lived somewhere within the web of differing versions, disputes over minor points, outright contradictions tangling with old feuds and village rivalries.

A dinner-table conversation, recalling a deer hunt forty years ago when the largest mule deer ever was taken, inevitably stimulates similar memories in listeners. But hunting stories were not merely after-dinner entertainment. These accounts contained information of critical importance about behavior and migration patterns of mule deer. Hunting stories carefully described key landmarks and locations of fresh water. Thus a deer-hunt story might also serve as a "map." Lost travelers, and lost piñon-nut gatherers, have been saved by sighting a rock formation they recognize only because they once heard a hunting story describing this rock formation.

The importance of cliff formations and water holes does not end with hunting stories. As offspring of the Mother Earth, the ancient Pueblo people could not conceive of themselves within a specific landscape. Location, or "place," nearly always plays a central role in the Pueblo oral narratives. Indeed, stories are most frequently recalled as people are passing by a specific geographical feature or the exact place where a story takes place. The precise date of the incident often is less important than the place or location of the happening. "Long, long ago," "a long time ago," "not too long ago," and "recently" are usually how stories are classified in terms of time. But the places where the stories occur are precisely located, and prominent geographical details recalled, even if the landscape is well-known to listeners. Often because the turning point in the narrative involved a peculiarity or special quality of a rock or tree or plant found only at that place. Thus, in the case of many of the Pueblo narratives, it is impossible to determine which came first: the incident or the geographical feature which begs to be brought alive in a story that features some unusual aspect of this location.

There is a giant sandstone boulder about a mile north of Old Laguna, on the road to Paguate. It is ten feet tall and twenty feet in circumference. When I was a child, and we would pass this boulder driving to Paguate village, someone usually made reference to the story about Kochininako, Yellow Woman, and the Estrucuyo, a monstrous giant who nearly ate her. The Twin Hero Brothers saved Kochininako, who had been out hunting rabbits to take home to feed her mother and sisters. The Hero Brothers had heard her cries just in time. The Estrucuyo had cornered her in a cave too small to fit its monstrous head. Kochininako had already thrown to the Estrucuyo all her rabbits, as well as her moccasins and most of her clothing. Still the creature had not been satisfied. After killing the Estrucuyo with their bows and arrows, the Twin Hero Brothers slit open the Estrucuyo and cut out its heart. They threw the heart as far as they could. The monster's heart landed there, beside the old trail to Paguate village, where the sandstone boulder rests now.

It may be argued that the existence of the boulder precipitated the creation of a story to explain it. But sandstone boulders and sandstone formations of strange shapes abound in the Laguna Pueblo area. Yet most of them do not have stories. Often the crucial element in a narrative is the terrain—some specific detail of the setting.

A high dark mesa rises dramatically from a grassy plain fifteen miles southeast of Laguna, in an area known as Swanee. On the grassy plain one hundred and forty years ago, my great-grandmother's uncle and his brother-in-law were grazing their herd of sheep. Because visibility on the plain extends for over twenty miles, it wasn't until the two sheepherders came near the high dark mesa that the Apaches were able to stalk them. Using the mesa to obscure their approach, the raiders swept around from both ends of the mesa. My great-grandmother's relatives were killed, and the herd lost. The high dark mesa played a critical role: the mesa had compromised the safety which the openness of the plains had seemed to assure. Pueblo and Apache alike relied upon the terrain, the very earth herself, to give them protection and aid. Human activities or needs were maneuvered to fit the existing surroundings and conditions. I imagine the last afternoon of my distant ancestors as warm and sunny for late September. They might have been traveling slowly, bringing the sheep closer to Laguna in preparation for the approach of colder weather. The grass was tall and only beginning to change from green to a yellow which matched the late-afternoon sun shining off it. There might have been comfort in the warmth and the sight of the sheep fattening on good pasture which lulled my ancestors into their fatal inattention. They might have had a rifle whereas the Apaches had only bows and arrows. But there would have been four or five Apache raiders, and the surprise attack would have canceled any advantage the rifles gave them.

Survival in any landscape comes down to making the best use of all available resources. On that particular September afternoon, the raiders made better use of the Swanee terrain than my poor ancestors did. Thus the high dark mesa and the story of the two lost Laguna herders became inextricably linked. The memory of them and their story resides in part with the high black mesa. For as long as the mesa stands, people within the family and clan will be reminded of the story of that afternoon long ago. Thus the continuity and accuracy of the oral narratives are reinforced by the landscape—and the Pueblo interpretation of that landscape is *maintained.*

The Migration Story: An Interior Journey

The Laguna Pueblo migration stories refer to specific places—mesas, springs, or cottonwood trees—not only locations which can be visited still, but also locations which lie directly on the state highway route linking Paguate village with Laguna village. In traveling this road as a child with older Laguna people I first heard a few of the stories from that much larger body of stories linked with the Emergence and Migration.[3] It may be coincidental that Laguna people continue to follow the same route which, according to the Migration story, the ancestors followed south from the Emergence Place. It may be that the route is merely the shortest and best route for car, horse, or foot traffic between Laguna and Paguate villages. But if the stories about boulders, springs, and hills are actually remnants from a ritual that retraces the creation and emergence of the Laguna Pueblo people as a culture, as the people they became, then continued use of that route creates a unique relationship between the ritual-mythic world and the actual, everyday world. A journey from Paguate to Laguna down the long incline of Paguate Hill retraces the original journey from the Emergence Place, which is located slightly north of the Paguate village. Thus the landscape between Paguate and Laguna takes on a deeper significance: the landscape resonates the spiritual or mythic dimension of the Pueblo world even today.

Although each Pueblo culture designates a specific Emergence Place—usually a small natural spring edged with mossy sandstone and full of cattails and wild watercress—it is clear that they do not agree on any single location or natural spring as the one and only true Emergence Place. Each Pueblo group recounts its own stories about Creation, Emergence, and Migration, although they all believe that all human beings, with all the animals and plants, emerged at the same place and at the same time.[4]

Natural springs are crucial sources of water for all life in the high desert plateau country. So the small spring near Paguate village is literally the source and continuance of life for the people in the area. The spring also functions on a spiritual level, recalling the original Emergence Place and linking the people and the spring water to all other people and to that moment when the Pueblo people became aware of themselves as they are even now. The Emergence was an emergence into a precise cultural identity. Thus the Pueblo stories about the Emergence and Migration are not to be taken as literally as the anthropologists might wish. Prominent geographical features and landmarks which are mentioned in the narratives exist for ritual purposes, not because the Laguna people actually journeyed south for hundreds of years from Chaco Canyon or Mesa Verde, as the archaeologists say, or eight miles from the site of the natural springs at Paguate to the sandstone hilltop at Laguna.

The eight miles, marked with boulders, mesas, springs, and river crossings, are actually a ritual circuit or path which marks the interior journey the Laguna people made: a journey of awareness and imagination in which they emerged from being within the earth and from everything included in earth to the culture and people they became, differentiating themselves for the first time from all that had surrounded them, always aware that interior distances cannot be reckoned in physical miles or in calendar years.

The narratives linked with prominent features of the landscape between Paguate and Laguna delineate the complexities of the relationship which human beings must maintain with the surrounding natural world if they hope to survive in this place. Thus the journey was an interior process of the imagination, a growing awareness that being human is somehow different from all other life—animal, plant, and inanimate. Yet we are all from the same source: the awareness never deteriorated into Cartesian duality, cutting off the human from the natural world.

The people found the opening into the Fifth World too small to allow them or any of the animals to escape. They had sent a fly out through the small hole to tell them if it was the world which the Mother Creator had promised. It was, but there was the problem of getting out. The antelope tried to butt the opening to enlarge it, but the antelope enlarged it only a little. It was necessary for the badger with her long claws to assist the antelope, and at last the opening was enlarged enough so that all the people and animals were able to emerge up into the Fifth World. The human beings could not have emerged without the aid of antelope and badger. The human beings depended upon the aid and charity of the animals. Only through interdependence could the human beings survive. Families belonged to clans, and it was by clan that the human being joined with the animal and plant world. Life on the high arid plateau became viable when the human beings were able to imagine themselves as sisters and brothers to the badger, antelope, clay, yucca, and sun. Not until they could find a viable relationship to the terrain, the landscape they found themselves in, could they *emerge*. Only at the moment the requisite balance between human and *other* was realized could the

Pueblo people become a culture, a distinct group whose population and survival remained stable despite the vicissitudes of climate and terrain.

Landscape thus has similarities with dreams. Both have the power to seize terrifying feelings and deep instincts and translate them into images—visual, aural, tactile—into the concrete where human beings may more readily confront and channel the terrifying instincts or powerful emotions into rituals and narratives which reassure the individual while reaffirming cherished values of the group. The identity of the individual as a part of the group and the greater Whole is strengthened, and the terror of facing the world alone is extinguished.

Even now, the people at Laguna Pueblo spend the greater portion of social occasions recounting recent incidents or events which have occurred in the Laguna area. Nearly always, the discussion will precipitate the retelling of older stories about similar incidents or other stories connected with a specific place. The stories often contain disturbing or provocative material, but are nonetheless told in the presence of children and women. The effect of these inter-family or inter-clan exchanges is the reassurance for each person that she or he will never be separated or apart from the clan, no matter what might happen. Neither the worst blunders or disasters nor the greatest financial prosperity and joy will ever be permitted to isolate anyone from the rest of the group. In the ancient times, cohesiveness was all that stood between extinction and survival, and, while the individual certainly was recognized, it was always as an individual simultaneously bonded to family and clan by a complex bundle of custom and ritual. You are never the first to suffer a grave loss or profound humiliation. You are never the first, and you understand that you will probably not be the last to commit or be victimized by a repugnant act. Your family and clan are able to go on at length about others now passed on, others older or more experienced than you who suffered similar losses.

The wide deep arroyo near the Kings Bar (located across the reservation borderline) has over the years claimed many vehicles. A few years ago, when a Viet Nam veteran's new red Volkswagen rolled backwards into the arroyo while he was inside buying a six-pack of beer, the story of his loss joined the lively and large collection of stories already connected with that big arroyo. I do not know whether the Viet Nam veteran was consoled when he was told the stories about the other cars claimed by the ravenous arroyo. All his savings of combat pay had gone for the red Volkswagen. But this man could not have felt any worse than the man who, some years before, had left his children and mother-in-law in his station wagon with the engine running. When he came out of the liquor store his station wagon was gone. He found it and its passengers upside down in the big arroyo. Broken bones, cuts and bruises, and a total wreck of the car. The big arroyo has a wide mouth. Its existence needs no explanation. People in the area regard the arroyo much as they might regard a living being, which has a certain character and personality. I seldom drive past that wide deep arroyo without feeling a familiarity with and even a strange affection for this arroyo. Because as treacherous as it may be, the arroyo maintains a strong connection between human beings and the earth. The arroyo demands from us the caution and attention that constitute respect. It is this sort of respect the old believers have in mind when they tell us we must respect and love the earth.

Hopi Pueblo elders have said that the austere and, to some eyes, barren plains and hills surrounding their mesa-top villages actually help to nurture the spirituality of the Hopi *way*. The Hopi elders say the Hopi people might have settled in locations far more lush where daily life would not have been so grueling. But there on the high silent sandstone mesas that overlook the sandy arid expanses stretching to all horizons, the Hopi elders say the Hopi people must "live by their prayers" if they are to survive. The Hopi way cherishes the intangible: the riches realized from interaction and interrelationships with all beings above all else. Great abundances of material things, even food, the Hopi elders believe, tend to lure human attention away from what is most valuable and important. The views of the Hopi elders are not much different from those elders in all the Pueblos.

The bare vastness of the Hopi landscape emphasizes the visual impact of every plant, every rock, every arroyo. Nothing is overlooked or taken for granted. Each ant, each lizard, each lark is imbued with great value simply because the creature is there, simply because the creature is alive in a place where any life at all is precious. Stand on the mesa edge at Walpai and look west over the bare distances toward the pale blue outlines of the San Francisco peaks where the ka'tsina spirits reside. So little lies between you and the sky. So little lies between you and the earth. One look and you know that simply to survive is a great triumph, that every possible resource is needed, every possible ally—even the most humble insect or reptile. You realize you will be speaking with all of them if you intend to last out the year. Thus it is that the Hopi elders are grateful to the landscape for aiding them in their quest as spiritual people.

Out Under the Sky

My earliest memories are of being outside, under the sky. I remember climbing the fence when I was three years old, and heading for the plaza in the center of Laguna village because other children passing by had told me there were ka'tsinas there dancing with pieces of wood in their mouths. A neighbor woman retrieved me before I ever saw the wood-swallowing ka'tsinas, but from an early age I knew that I wanted to be outside. Outside walls and fences.

My father had wandered all the hills and mesas around Laguna when he was a child. Because the Indian School and the taunts of the other children did not set well with him. It had been difficult in those days to be part Laguna and part white, or *amedicana*. It was still difficult when I attended the Indian School at Laguna.

Our full-blooded relatives and clanspeople assured us we were theirs and that we belonged there because we had been born and reared there. But the racism of the wider world we call America had begun to make itself felt years before. My father's response was to head for the mesas and hills with his older brother, their dog, and .22 rifles. They retreated to the sandstone cliffs and juniper forests. Out in the hills they were not lonely because they had all the living creatures of the hills around them, and, whatever the ambiguities of racial heritage, my father and my uncle understood what the old folks had taught them: the earth loves all of us regardlessly, because we are her children.

I started roaming those same mesas and hills when I was nine years old. At eleven I rode away on my horse, and explored places my father and uncle could not have reached on foot. I was never afraid or lonely, although I was high in the hills, many miles from home. Because I carried with me the feeling I'd acquired from listening to the old stories, that the land all around me was teeming with creatures that were related to human beings and to me. The stories had also left me with a feeling of familiarity and warmth for the mesas and hills and boulders where the incidents or action in the stories had taken place. I felt as if I had actually been to those places, although I had only heard stories about them. Somehow the stories had given a kind of being to the mesas and hills, just as the stories had left me with the sense of having spent time with the people in the stories, although they had long since passed on.

It is unremarkable to sense the presence of those long passed at the locations where their adventures took place. Spirits range without boundaries of any sort. Spirits may be called back in any number of ways. The method used in the calling also determines how the spirit manifests itself. I think a spirit may or may not choose to remain at the site of its passing or death. I think they might be in a number of places at the same time. Storytelling can procure fleeting moments to experience who they were and how life felt long ago. What I enjoyed most as a child was standing at the site of an incident recounted in one of the ancient stories Aunt Susie had told us as girls. What excited me was listening to old Aunt Susie tell us an old-time story and then for me to realize that I was familiar with a certain mesa or cave that figured as the central location of the story she was telling. That was when the stories worked best. Because then I could sit there listening and be able to visualize myself as being located *within* the story being told, within the landscape. Because the storytellers did not just tell the stories, they would in their way act them out. The storyteller would imitate voices for vast dialogues between the various figures in the story. So we sometimes say the moment is alive again within us, within our imaginations and our memory, as we listen.

Aunt Susie once told me how it had been when she was a child and her grandmother agreed to tell the children stories. The old woman would always ask the youngest child in the room to go open the door. "Go open the door," her grandmother would say. "Go open the door so our esteemed ancestors may bring us the precious gift of their stories." Two points seem clear: the spirits could be present and the stories were valuable because they taught us how we were the people we believed we were. The myth, the web of memories and ideas that create an identity, a part of oneself. This sense of identity was intimately linked with the surrounding terrain, to the landscape which has often played a significant role in a story or in the outcome of a conflict.

The landscape sits in the center of Pueblo belief and identity. Any narratives about the Pueblo people necessarily give a great deal of attention and detail to all aspects of a landscape. For this reason, the Pueblo people have always been extremely reluctant to relinquish their land for dams or highways. For this reason, Taos Pueblo fought from 1906 until 1973 to win back their sacred Blue Lake, which was illegally taken from them by the creation of Taos National Forest. For this reason, the decision in the early 1950s to begin open-pit mining of the huge uranium deposits north of Laguna, near Paguate village, has had a powerful psychological impact upon the Laguna people. Already a large body of stories has grown up around the subject of what happens to people who disturb or destroy the earth. I was a child when the mining began and the apocalyptic warning stories were being told. And I have lived long enough to begin hearing the stories which verify the earlier warnings.

All that remains of the gardens and orchards that used to grow in the sandy flats southeast of Paguate village are the stories of the lovely big peaches and apricots the people used to grow. The Jackpile Mine is an open pit that has been blasted out of the many hundreds of acres where the orchards and melon patches once grew. The Laguna people have not witnessed changes to the land without strong reactions. Descriptions of the landscape *before* the mine are as vivid as any description of the present-day destruction by the open-pit mining. By its very ugliness and by the violence it does to the land, the Jackpile Mine insures that from now on it, too, will be included in the vast body of narratives which make up the history of the Laguna people and the Pueblo landscape. And the description of what that landscape looked like *before* the uranium mining began will always carry considerable impact.

Landscape as a Character in Fiction

Drought or the disappearance of game animals may signal disharmony or even witchcraft. When the rain clouds fail to appear in time to help the corn plants, or the deer are suddenly scarce, then we know the very sky and earth are telling human beings that all is not well. A deep arroyo continues to claim victims.

When I began writing I found that the plots of my short stories very often featured the presence of elements out of the landscape, elements which directly influenced the outcome of events. Nowhere is landscape more crucial to the outcome than in my short story, "Storyteller." The site is southwest Alaska, near the village of Bethel, on the Kushokwim River. Tundra country. Here the winter landscape can suddenly metamorphize into a seamless blank white so solid that pilots in aircraft without electronic instruments lose their bearings and crash their planes straight into the frozen tundra, believing down to be up. Here on the Alaska tundra, in mid-February, not all the space-age fabrics, electronics, or engines can ransom human beings from the restless shifting forces of the winter sky and winter earth.

The young Yupik Eskimo woman works out an elaborate yet subconscious plan to avenge the deaths of her parents. After months of baiting the trap, she lures the murderer onto the river ice where he falls through to his death. The murderer is a white man who operates the village trading post. For years the murderer has existed like a parasite, exploiting not only the fur-bearing animals and the fish, but the Yupik people themselves. When the Yupik woman kills him, the white trader has just finished cashing in on the influx of workers for the petroleum exploration and pipeline who have suddenly come to the tiny village. For the Yupik people, souls deserving punishment spend varying lengths of time in a place of freezing. The Yupik see the world's end coming with ice, not fire. Although the white trader possesses every possible garment, insulation, heating fuel, and gadget ever devised to protect him from the frozen tundra environment, he still dies, drowning under the freezing river ice. Because the white man had not reckoned with the true power of that landscape, especially not the power which the Yupik woman understood instinctively and which she used so swiftly and efficiently. The white man had reckoned with the young woman and determined he could overpower her. But the white man failed to account for the conjunction of the landscape with the woman. The Yupik woman had never seen herself as anything but a part of that sky, that frozen river, that tundra. The river ice and the blinding white are her accomplices, and yet the Yupik woman never for a moment misunderstands her own relationship with that landscape. After the white trader has crashed through the river ice, the young woman finds herself a great distance from either shore of the treacherous frozen river. She can see nothing but the whiteness of the sky swallowing the earth. But far away in the distance, on the side of her log and tundra sod cabin, she is able to see the spot of bright red. A bright red marker she had nailed up weeks earlier because she was intrigued by the contrast between all that white and the spot of brilliant red. The Yupik woman knows the appetite of the frozen river. She realizes that the ice and the fog, the tundra and the snow seek constantly to be reunited with the living beings which skitter across it. The Yupik woman knows that inevitably she and all things will one day lie in those depths. But the woman is young and her instinct is to live. The Yupik woman knows how to do this.

Inside the small cabin of logs and tundra sod, the old Storyteller is mumbling the last story he will ever tell. It is the story of the hunter stalking a giant polar bear the color of blue glacier ice. It is a story which the old Storyteller has been telling since the young Yupik woman began to arrange the white trader's death.

But a sudden storm develops. The hunter finds himself on an ice floe off shore. Visibility is zero, and the scream of the wind blots out all sound. Quickly the hunter realizes he is being stalked. Hunted by all the forces, by all the elements of the sky and earth around him. When at last the hunter's own muscles spasm and cause the jade knife to fall and shatter the ice, the hunter's death in the embrace of the giant ice blue bear is the foretelling of the world's end. When humans have blasted and burned the last bit of life from the earth, an immeasurable freezing will descend with a darkness that obliterates the sun.

Notes

[1]Clan—A social unit composed of families sharing common ancestors who trace their lineage back to the Emergence where their ancestors allied themselves with certain plants or animals or elements.

[2]Ka'tsina—Ka'tsinas are spirit beings who roam the earth and who inhabit kachina masks worn in Pueblo ceremonial dances.

[3]The Emergence—All human beings, animals, and life which had been created emerged from the four worlds below when the earth became habitable. The Migration—The Pueblo people emerged in the Fifth World, but they had already been warned they would have to travel and search before they found the place they were meant to live.

[4]Creation—Tse'itsi'nako, Thought Woman, the Spider, thought about it, and everything she thought came into being. First she thought of three sisters for herself, and they helped her think of the rest of the Universe, including the Fifth World and the four worlds below. The Fifth World is the world we are living in today. There are four previous worlds below this world.

Considerations

Thinking

What is the relationship between a Pueblo and the landscape?

How do stories incorporate features of the landscape? To what end do they do so? In what way do Pueblo stories become mythic?

What do you suppose is Silko's sense of the spiritual?

Connecting

Compare the images of the house and the earth at the beginning and ending of Silko's essay. What do those images have to do with Silko's central ideas?

What do you think is the central idea that Silko associates with the creation story she tells, the story about coming out of the earth into the Fifth World?

Writing

Analyze how Silko uses various images of the gaping hole to develop her ideas about the Pueblo people.

Compare Silko's treatment of Native Americans with that of Diana Hume George in "Wounded Chevy at Wounded Knee." As a coda to your comparison, give your readers a sense of what you think these two women might have to say to one another about the plight of Native Americans.

Susan Sontag
(b. 1933)

One of America's foremost intellectuals, Susan Sontag has been intimately involved in the world of ideas all her life. After studying at the University of California at Berkeley, she earned a B.A. in philosophy from the University of Chicago at the age of eighteen. After studying religion at Union Theological Seminary in New York, she studied philosophy and literature at Harvard, receiving master's degrees in both fields. She has also studied at Oxford and the Sorbonne. From the other side of the desk, Sontag has taught and lectured extensively at many universities, but especially at Rutgers and Columbia.

The subjects of Sontag's books and essays range widely, though two of her books explore ways of thinking about disease—*Illness as Metaphor* (1978) and *AIDS and Its Metaphors* (1989), from which the selection reprinted here has been taken. This piece reveals Sontag's erudition as well as here capacity for incisive analysis. These intellectual qualities Sontag puts in the service of understanding, especially of understanding how our ways of talking about AIDS reflect our deepest fears.

AIDS and Its Metaphors

"Plague" is the principal metaphor by which the AIDS epidemic is understood. And because of AIDS, the popular misidentification of cancer as an epidemic, even a plague, seems to be receding: AIDS has banalized cancer.

Plague, from the Latin *plaga* (stroke, wound), has long been used metaphorically as the highest standard of collective calamity, evil, scourge—Procopius, in his masterpiece of calumny, *The Secret History,* called the Emperor Justinian worse than the plague ("fewer escaped")—as well as being a general name for many frightening diseases. Although the disease to which the word is permanently affixed produced the most lethal of recorded epidemics, being experienced as a pitiless slayer is not necessary for a disease to be regarded as plague-like. Leprosy, very rarely fatal now, was not much more so when at its greatest epidemic strength, between about 1050 and 1350. And syphilis has been regarded as a plague—Blake speaks of "the youthful Harlot's curse" that "blights with plagues the Marriage hearse"—not because it killed often, but because it was disgracing, disempowering, disgusting.

It is usually epidemics that are thought of as plagues. And these mass incidences of illness are understood as inflicted, not just endured. Considering illness as a punishment is the oldest idea of what causes illness, and an idea opposed by all attention to the ill that deserves the noble name of medicine. Hippocrates, who wrote several treatises on epidemics, specifically ruled out "the wrath of God" as a cause of bubonic plague. But the illnesses interpreted in antiquity as punishments, like the plague in *Oedipus,* were not thought to be shameful, as leprosy and subsequently syphilis were to be. Diseases, insofar as they acquired meaning, were collective calamities, and judgments on a community. Only injuries and disabilities, not diseases, were thought of as individually merited. For an analogy in the literature of antiquity to the modern sense of a shaming, isolating disease, one would have to turn to Philoctetes and his stinking wound.

The most feared diseases, those that are not simply fatal but transform the body into something alienating, like leprosy and syphilis and cholera and (in the imagination of many) cancer, are the ones that seem particularly susceptible to promotion to "plague." Leprosy and syphilis were the first illnesses to be consistently described as repulsive. It was syphilis that, in the earliest descriptions by doctors at the end of the fifteenth century, generated a version of the metaphors that flourish around AIDS: of a disease that was not only repulsive and retributive but collectively invasive. Although Erasmus, the most influential European pedagogue of the early sixteenth century, described syphilis as "nothing but a kind of leprosy" (by 1529 he called it "something worse than leprosy"), it had already been understood as something different, because sexually transmitted. Paracelsus speaks (in Donne's paraphrase) of "that foule contagious disease which then had invaded mankind in a few places, and since overflowes in all, that for punishment of generall licentiousnes God first inflicted that disease." Thinking of syphilis as a punishment for an individual's transgression was for a long time, virtually until the disease became easily curable, not really distinct from regarding it as retribution for the licentiousness of a community—as with AIDS now, in the rich industrial countries. In contrast to cancer, understood in a modern way as a disease incurred by (and revealing of) individuals, AIDS is understood in a premodern way, as a disease incurred by people both as individuals and as members of a "risk group"—that neutral-sounding, bureaucratic category which also revives the archaic idea of a tainted community that illness has judged.

Not every account of plague or plague-like diseases, of course, is a vehicle for lurid stereotypes about illness and the ill. The effort to think critically, historically, about illness (about disaster generally) was attempted throughout the eighteenth century: say, from Defoe's *A Journal of the Plague Year* (1722) to Alessandro Manzoni's *The Betrothed* (1827). Defoe's historical fiction, purporting to be an eyewitness account of bubonic plague in London in 1665, does not further any understanding of the plague as punishment or, a later part of the script, as a transforming experience. And Manzoni, in his lengthy account of the passage of plague through the duchy of Milan in 1630, is avowedly committed to presenting a more accurate, less reductive view than his historical sources. But even these two complex narratives reinforce some of the perennial, simplifying ideas about plague.

One feature of the usual script for plague: The disease invariably comes from somewhere else. The names for syphilis, when it began its epidemic sweep through Europe in the last decade of the fifteenth century, are an exemplary illustration of the need to make a dreaded disease foreign.[1] It was the "French pox" to the English, *morbus Germanicus* to the Parisians, the Naples sickness to the Florentines, the Chinese disease to the Japanese. But what may seem like a joke about the inevitability of chauvinism reveals a more important truth: that there is a link between imagining disease and imagining foreignness. It lies perhaps in the very concept of wrong, which is archaically identical with the non-us, the alien. A polluting person is always wrong, as Mary Douglas has observed. The inverse is also true: A person judged to be wrong is regarded as, at least potentially, a source of pollution.

The foreign place of origin of important illnesses, as of drastic changes in the weather, may be no more remote than a neighboring country. Illness is a species of invasion, and indeed is often carried by soldiers. Manzoni's account of the plague of 1630 (chapters 31 to 37) begins:

> The plague which the Tribunal of Health had feared might enter the Milanese provinces with the German troops had in fact entered, as is well known; and it is also well known that it did not stop there, but went on to invade and depopulate a large part of Italy.

Defoe's chronicle of the plague of 1665 begins similarly, with a flurry of ostentatiously scrupulous speculation about its foreign origin:

> It was about the beginning of September, 1664, that I, among the rest of my neighbours, heard in ordinary discourse that the plague was returned again in Holland; for it had been very violent there, and particularly at Amsterdam and Rotterdam, in the year 1663, whither, they say, it was brought, some said from Italy, others from the Levant, among some goods which were brought home by their Turkey fleet; others said it was brought from Candia; others from Cyprus. It mattered not from whence it came; but all agreed it was come into Holland again.

The bubonic plague that reappeared in London in the 1720s had arrived from Marseilles, which was where plague in the eighteenth century was usually thought to enter Western Europe: brought by seamen, then transported by soldiers and merchants. By the nineteenth century the foreign origin was usually more exotic, the means of transport less specifically imagined, and the illness itself had become phantasmagorical, symbolic.

At the end of *Crime and Punishment* Raskolnikov dreams of plague: "He dreamt that the whole world was condemned to a terrible new strange plague that had come to Europe from the depths of Asia." At the beginning of the sentence it is "the whole world," which turns out by the end of the sentence to be "Europe," afflicted by a lethal visitation from Asia. Dostoevsky's model is undoubtedly cholera, called Asiatic cholera, long endemic in Bengal, which had rapidly become and remained through most of the nineteenth century a worldwide epidemic disease. Part of the centuries-old conception of Europe as a privileged cultural entity is that it is a place which is colonized by lethal diseases coming from elsewhere. Europe is assumed to be by rights free of disease. (And Europeans have been astoundingly callous about the far more devastating extent to which they—as invaders, as colonists—have introduced *their* lethal diseases to the exotic, "primitive" world: Think of the ravages of smallpox, influenza, and cholera on the aboriginal populations of the Americas and Australia.) The tenacity of the connection of exotic origin with dreaded disease is one reason why cholera, of which there were four great outbreaks in Europe in the nineteenth century, each with a lower death toll than the preceding one, has continued to be more memorable than smallpox, whose ravages increased as the century went on (half a million died in the European smallpox pandemic of the early 1870s) but which could not be construed as, plague-like, a disease with a non-European origin.

Plagues are no longer "sent," as in Biblical and Greek antiquity, for the question of agency has blurred. Instead, peoples are "visited" by plagues. And the visitations recur, as is taken for granted in the subtitle of Defoe's narrative, which explains that it is about that "which happened in London during the Last Great Visitation in 1665." Even for non-Europeans, lethal disease may be called a visitation. But a visitation on "them" is invariably described as different from one on "us." "I believe that about one half of the whole people was carried off by this visitation," wrote the English traveler Alexander Kinglake, reaching Cairo at a time of the bubonic plague (sometimes called "oriental plague"). "The Orientals, however, have more quiet fortitude than Europeans under afflictions of this sort." Kinglake's influential book *Eothen* (1844)—suggestively subtitled "Traces of Travel Brought Home from the East"—illustrates many of the enduring Eurocentric presumptions about others, starting from the fantasy that peoples with little reason to expect exemption from misfortune have a lessened capacity to *feel* misfortune. Thus it is believed that Asians (or the poor, or blacks, or Africans, or Moslems) don't suffer or don't grieve as Europeans (or whites) do. The fact that illness is associated with the poor—who are, from the perspective of the privileged, aliens in one's midst—reinforces the association of illness with the foreign: with an exotic, often primitive place.

Thus, illustrating the classic script for plague, AIDS is thought to have started in the "dark continent," then spread to Haiti, then to the United States and to Europe, then . . . It is understood as a tropical disease: another infestation from the so-called Third World, which is after all where most people in the world live, as well as a scourge of the *tristes tropiques*. Africans who detect racist stereotypes in much of the speculation about the geographical origin of AIDS are not wrong. (Nor are they wrong in thinking that depictions of Africa as the cradle of AIDS must feed anti-African prejudices in Europe and Asia.) The subliminal connection made to notions about a primitive past and the many hypotheses that have been fielded about possible transmission from animals (a disease of green monkeys? African swine fever?) cannot help but activate a familiar set of stereotypes about animality, sexual license, and blacks. In Zaire and other countries in Central Africa where AIDS is killing tens of thousands, the counterreaction has begun. Many doctors, academics, journalists, government officials, and other educated people believe that the virus was sent to Africa from the United States, an act of bacteriological warfare (whose aim was to decrease the African birth rate) which got out of hand and has returned to afflict its perpetrators. A common African version of this belief about the disease's provenance has the virus fabricated in a CIA-Army laboratory in Maryland, sent from there to Africa, and brought back to its country of origin by American homosexual missionaries returning from Africa to Maryland.[2]

At first it was assumed that AIDS must become widespread elsewhere in the same catastrophic form in which it has emerged in Africa, and those who still think this will eventually happen invariably invoke the Black Death. The plague metaphor is an essential vehicle of the most pessimistic reading of the epidemiological prospects. From classic fiction to the latest journalism, the standard plague story is of inexorability, inescapability. The unprepared are taken by surprise; those observing the recommended precautions are struck down as well. *All* succumb when the story is told by an omniscient narrator, as in Poe's parable "The Masque of the Red Death" (1842), inspired by an account of a ball held in Paris during the cholera epidemic of 1832. Almost all—if the story is told from the point of view of a traumatized witness, who will be a benumbed survivor, as in Jean Giono's Stendhalian novel *Horseman on the Roof* (1951), in which a young Italian nobleman in exile wanders through cholera-stricken southern France in the 1830s.

Plagues are invariably regarded as judgments on society, and the metaphoric inflation of AIDS into such a judgment also accustoms people to the inevitability of global spread. This is a traditional use of sexually transmitted diseases: to be described as punishments not just of individuals but of a group ("generall licentiousnes"). Not only venereal diseases have been used in this way, to identify transgressing or vicious populations. Interpreting any catastrophic epidemic as a sign of moral laxity or political decline was as common until the later part of the last century as associating dreaded diseases with foreignness. (Or with despised and feared minorities.) And the assignment of fault is not contradicted by cases that do not fit. The Methodist preachers in England who connected the cholera epidemic of 1832 with drunkenness (the temperance movement was just starting) were not understood to be claiming that *everybody* who got cholera was a drunkard: There is always room for "innocent victims" (children, young women). Tuberculosis, in its identity as a disease of the poor (rather than of the "sensitive"), was also linked by late-nineteenth-century reformers to alcoholism. Responses to illnesses associated with sinners and the poor invariably recommended the adoption of middle-class values: the regular habits, productivity, and emotional self-control to which drunkenness was thought the chief impediment.[3] Health itself was eventually identified with these values, which were religious as well as mercantile, health being evidence of virtue as disease was of depravity. The dictum that cleanliness is next to godliness is to be taken quite literally. The succession of cholera epidemics in the nineteenth century shows a steady waning of religious interpretations of the disease; more precisely, these increasingly coexisted with other explanations. Although, by the time of the epidemic of 1866, cholera was commonly understood not simply as a divine punishment but as the consequence of remediable defects of sanitation, it was still regarded as the scourge of the sinful. A writer in the *New York Times* declared (April 22, 1866): "Cholera is especially the punishment of neglect of sanitary laws; it is the curse of the dirty, the intemperate, and the degraded."[4]

That it now seems unimaginable for cholera or a similar disease to be regarded in this way signifies not a lessened capacity to moralize about diseases but only a change in the kind of illnesses that are used didactically. Cholera was perhaps the last major epidemic disease fully qualifying for plague status for almost a century. (I mean cholera as a European and American, therefore a nineteenth-century, disease; until 1817 there had never been a cholera epidemic outside the Far East.) Influenza, which would seem more plague-like than any other epidemic in this century if loss of life were the main criterion, and which struck as suddenly as cholera and killed as quickly, usually in a few days, was never viewed metaphorically as a plague. Nor was a more recent epidemic, polio. One reason why plague notions were not invoked is that these epidemics did not have enough of the attributes perenially ascribed to plagues. (For instance, polio was construed as typically a disease of children—of the innocent.) The more important reason is that there has been a shift in the focus of the moralistic exploitation of illness. This shift, to diseases that can be interpreted as judgments on the individual, makes it harder to use epidemic disease as such. For a long time cancer was the illness that best fitted this secular culture's need to blame and punish and censor through the imagery of disease. Cancer was a disease of an individual, and understood as the result not of an action but rather of a failure to act (to be prudent, to exert proper self-control, or to be properly expressive). In the twentieth century it has become almost impossible to moralize about epidemics—except those which are transmitted sexually.

The persistence of the belief that illness reveals, and is a punishment for, moral laxity or turpitude can be seen in another way, by noting the persistence of descriptions of disorder or corruption as a disease. So indispensable has been the plague metaphor in bringing summary judgments about social crisis that its use hardly abated during the era when collective diseases were no longer treated so moralistically—the time between the influenza and encephalitis pandemics of the early and mid-1920s and the acknowledgment of a new, mysterious epidemic illness in the early 1980s—and when great infectious epidemics were so often and confidently proclaimed a thing of the past.[5] The plague metaphor was common in the 1930s as a synonym for social and psychic catastrophe. Evocations of plague of this type usually go with rant, with antiliberal attitudes: Think of Artaud on theater and plague, of Wilhelm Reich on "emotional plague." And such a generic "diagnosis" necessarily promotes antihistorical thinking. A theodicy as well as a demonology, it not only stipulates something emblematic of evil but makes this the bearer of a rough, terrible justice. In Karel Čapek's *The White Plague* (1937), the loathsome pestilence that has appeared in a state where fascism has come to power afflicts only those over the age of forty, those who could be held morally responsible.

Written on the eve of the Nazi takeover of Czechoslovakia, Čapek's allegorical play is something of an anomaly—the use of the plague metaphor to convey
the menace of what is defined as barbaric by a mainstream European liberal. The
play's mysterious, grisly malady is something like leprosy, a rapid, invariably fatal
leprosy that is supposed to have come, of course, from Asia. But Čapek is not
interested in identifying political evil with the incursion of the foreign. He scores
his didactic points by focusing not on the disease itself but on the management of
information about it by scientists, journalists, and politicians. The most famous
specialist in the disease harangues a reporter ("The disease of the hour, you might
say. A good five million have died of it to date, twenty million have it and at least
three times as many are going about their business, blithely unaware of the
marble-like, marble-sized spots on their bodies"); chides a fellow doctor for using
the popular terms, "the white plague" and "Peking leprosy," instead of the scientific name, "the Cheng Syndrome"; fantasizes about how his clinic's work on identifying the new virus and finding a cure ("every clinic in the world has an intensive
research program") will add to the prestige of science and win a Nobel Prize for its
discoverer; revels in hyperbole when it is thought a cure has been found ("it was
the most dangerous disease in all history, worse than the bubonic plague"); and
outlines plans for sending those with symptoms to well-guarded detention camps
("Given that every carrier of the disease is a potential spreader of the disease, we
must protect the uncontaminated from the contaminated. All sentimentality in
this regard is fatal and therefore criminal"). However cartoonish Čapek's ironies
may seem, they are a not improbable sketch of catastrophe (medical, ecological)
as a managed public event in modern mass society. And however conventionally
he deploys the plague metaphor, as an agency of retribution (in the end the plague
strikes down the dictator himself), Čapek's feel for public relations leads him to
make explicit in the play the understanding of disease *as* a metaphor. The eminent
doctor declares the accomplishments of science to be as nothing compared with
the merits of the dictator, about to launch a war, "who has averted a far worse
scourge: the scourge of anarchy, the leprosy of corruption, the epidemic of barbaric liberty, the plague of social disintegration fatally sapping the organism of our
nation."

Camus's *The Plague,* which appeared a decade later, is a far less literal use of
plague by another great European liberal, as subtle as Čapek's *The White Plague* is
schematic. Camus's novel is not, as is sometimes said, a political allegory in which
the outbreak of bubonic plague in a Mediterranean port city represents the Nazi
occupation. This plague is not retributive. Camus is not protesting anything, not
corruption or tyranny, not even mortality. The plague is no more or less than an
exemplary event, the irruption of death that gives life its seriousness. His use of
plague, more epitome than metaphor, is detached, stoic, aware—it is not about
bringing judgment. But, as in Čapek's play, characters in Camus's novel declare
how unthinkable it is to have a plague in the twentieth century . . . as if the belief
that such a calamity could not happen, could not happen *anymore,* means that it
must.

NOTES

1. As noted in the first accounts of the disease: "This malady received from different peoples whom it affected different names," writes Giovanni di Vigo in 1514. Like earlier treatises on syphilis, written in Latin—by Nicolo Leoniceno (1497) and by Juan Almenar (1502)—the one by di Vigo calls it *morbus Gallicus,* the French disease. (Excerpts from this and other accounts of the period, including *Syphilis: Or a Poetical History of the French Disease* [1530] by Girolamo Fracastoro, who coined the name that prevailed, are in *Classic Descriptions of Disease,* edited by Ralph H. Major [1932].) Moralistic explanations abounded from the beginning. In 1495, a year after the epidemic started, the Emperor Maximilian issued an edict declaring syphilis to be an affliction from God for the sins of men.

   The theory that syphilis came from even farther than a neighboring country, that it was an entirely new disease in Europe, a disease of the New World brought back to the Old by sailors of Columbus who had contracted it in America, became the accepted explanation of the origin of syphilis in the sixteenth century and is still widely credited. It is worth noting that the earliest medical writers on syphilis did not accept the dubious theory. Leoniceno's *Libellus de Epidemia, quam vulgo morbum Gallicum vocant* starts by taking up the question of whether "the French disease under another name was common to the ancients," and says he believes firmly that it was.

2. The rumor may not have originated as a KGB-sponsored "disinformation" campaign, but it received a crucial push from Soviet propaganda specialists. In October 1985 the Soviet weekly *Literaturnaya Gazeta* published an article alleging that the AIDS virus had been engineered by the U.S. government during biological-warfare research at Fort Detrick, Maryland, and was being spread abroad by U.S. servicemen who had been used as guinea pigs. The source cited was an article in the Indian newspaper *Patriot.* Repeated on Moscow's "Radio Peace and Progress" in English, the story was taken up by newspapers and magazines throughout the world. A year later it was featured on the front page of London's conservative, mass-circulation *Sunday Express.* ("The killer AIDS virus was artificially created by American scientists during laboratory experiments which went disastrously wrong—and a massive cover-up has kept the secret from the world until today.") Though ignored by most American newspapers, the *Sunday Express* story was recycled in virtually every other country. As recently as the summer of 1987, it appeared in newspapers in Kenya, Peru, Sudan, Nigeria, Senegal, and Mexico. Gorbachev-era policies have since produced an official denial of the allegations by two eminent members of the Soviet Academy of Sciences, which was published in *Izvestia* in late October 1987. But the story is still being repeated—from Mexico to Zaire, from Australia to Greece.

3. According to the more comprehensive diagnosis favored by secular reformers, cholera was the result of poor diet and "indulgence in irregular habits." Officials of the Central Board of Health in London warned that there were no specific treatments for the disease, and advised paying attention to fresh air and cleanliness, though "the true preventatives are a healthy body and a cheerful, unruffled mind." Quoted in R. J. Morris, *Cholera 1832* (1976).

4. Quoted in Charles E. Rosenberg, *The Cholera Years: The United States in 1832, 1849, and 1866* (1962).

5. As recently as 1983, the historian William H. McNeill, author of *Plagues and Peoples,* started his review of a new history of the Black Death by asserting: "One of the things that separate us from our ancestors and make contemporary experience profoundly different from that of other ages is the disappearance of epidemic disease as a serious factor in human life" (*New York Review of Books,* July 21, 1983). The Eurocentric presumption of this and many similar statements hardly needs pointing out.

Considerations

Thinking

What are the connotations of the word *plague?* To what extent, according to Sontag, is AIDS viewed as a plague by the general population? Why do you think Sontag focuses on the causes of plague, on who or what is seen as ultimately responsible for its spreading?

Why do you think Sontag spends time discussing literary representations of plague such as Daniel Defoe's *A Journal of the Plague Year?* What do her literary and historical references and discussion add to her argument about AIDS?

Connecting

What connections between medieval bubonic plague and AIDS does Sontag consider? What is her view of the comparisons made between the two diseases?

Consider Sontag's view of AIDS in terms of what Randy Shilts says about the disease in his essay "Talking AIDS to Death," and of what Richard Selzer says in "A Mask on the Face of Death."

Writing

Write an essay in which you identify three or four essential facets of Sontag's argument about AIDS and what an understanding of the disease in her terms would mean for how we should think about AIDS and respond to it.

Identify and explore the most prominent and pervasive metaphors that have been used to characterize AIDS. Follow Sontag's lead in thinking about the implications of those metaphors for national health policy and for the responses of those who do not have the disease to those who do.

Brent Staples
(b. 1951)

Brent Staples is a journalist who earned his B.A. from Widener University and his Ph.D. from the University of Chicago. His work has appeared in *Harpers, New York Woman,* the *New York Times Magazine, Chicago Magazine,* and *Down Beat.* He has recently published his autobiography, *Parallel Time: Growing Up in Black and White.*

"Just Walk On By" first appeared in 1986. In this essay, Staples examines his "unwieldy inheritance . . . the ability to alter public space in ugly ways." In the essay, he is a "youngish black man."

Just Walk On By: A Black Man Ponders His Power to Alter Public Space

My first victim was a woman—white, well dressed, probably in her early twenties. I came upon her late one evening on a deserted street in Hyde Park, a relatively affluent neighborhood in an otherwise mean, impoverished section of Chicago. As I swung onto the avenue behind her, there seemed to be a discreet, uninflammatory distance between us. Not so. She cast back a worried glance. To her, the youngish black man—a broad six feet two inches with a beard and billowing hair, both hands shoved into the pockets of a bulky military jacket—seemed menacingly close. After a few more quick glimpses, she picked up her pace and was soon running in earnest. Within seconds she disappeared into a cross street.

That was more than a decade ago. I was twenty-two years old, a graduate student newly arrived at the University of Chicago. It was in the echo of that terrified woman's footfalls that I first began to know the unwieldy inheritance I'd come into—the ability to alter public space in ugly ways. It was clear that she thought herself the quarry of a mugger, a rapist, or worse. Suffering a bout of insomnia, however, I was stalking sleep, not defenseless wayfarers. As a softy who is scarcely able to take a knife to a raw chicken—let alone hold it to a person's throat—I was surprised, embarrassed, and dismayed all at once. Her flight made me feel like an accomplice in tyranny. It also made it clear that I was indistinguishable from the muggers who occasionally seeped into the area from the surrounding ghetto. That first encounter, and those that followed, signified that a vast, unnerving gulf lay between nighttime pedestrians—particularly women—and me. And I soon gathered that being perceived as dangerous is a hazard in itself. I only needed to turn a corner into a dicey situation, or crowd some frightened, armed person in a foyer somewhere, or make an errant move after being pulled over by a policeman. Where fear and weapons meet—and they often do in urban America—there is always the possibility of death.

In that first year, my first away from my hometown, I was to become thoroughly familiar with the language of fear. At dark, shadowy intersections in Chicago, I could cross in front of a car stopped at a traffic light and elicit the *thunk, thunk, thunk* of the driver—black, white, male, or female—hammering down the door locks. On less traveled streets after dark, I grew accustomed to but never comfortable with people who crossed to the other side of the street rather than pass me. Then there were the standard unpleasantries with police, doormen, bouncers, cabdrivers, and others whose business is to screen out troublesome individuals *before* there is any nastiness.

I moved to New York nearly two years ago and I have remained an avid night walker. In central Manhattan, the near-constant crowd cover minimizes tense one-on-one street encounters. Elsewhere—visiting friends in SoHo, where sidewalks are narrow and tightly spaced buildings shut out the sky—things can get very taut indeed.

Black men have a firm place in New York mugging literature. Norman Podhoretz in his famed (or infamous) 1963 essay, "My Negro Problem—And Ours," recalls growing up in terror of black males; they "were tougher than we were, more ruthless," he writes—and as an adult on the Upper West Side of Manhattan, he continues, he cannot constrain his nervousness when he meets black men on certain streets. Similarly, a decade later, the essayist and novelist Edward Hoagland extols a New York where once "Negro bitterness bore down mainly on other Negroes." Where some see mere panhandlers, Hoagland sees "a mugger who is clearly screwing up his nerve to do more than just *ask* for money." But Hoagland has "the New Yorker's quick-hunch posture for broken-field maneuvering," and the bad guy swerves away.

I often witness that "hunch posture," from women after dark on the warren-like streets of Brooklyn where I live. They seem to set their faces on neutral and, with their purse straps strung across their chests bandolier style, they forge ahead as though bracing themselves against being tackled. I understand, of course, that the danger they perceive is not a hallucination. Women are particularly vulnerable to street violence, and young black males are drastically overrepresented among the perpetrators of that violence. Yet these truths are no solace against the kind of alienation that comes of being ever the suspect, against being set apart, a fearsome entity with whom pedestrians avoid making eye contact.

It is not altogether clear to me how I reached the ripe old age of twenty-two without being conscious of the lethality nighttime pedestrians attributed to me. Perhaps it was because in Chester, Pennsylvania, the small, angry industrial town where I came of age in the 1960s, I was scarcely noticeable against a backdrop of gang warfare, street knifings, and murders. I grew up one of the good boys, had perhaps a half-dozen fistfights. In retrospect, my shyness of combat has clear sources.

Many things go into the making of a young thug. One of those things is the consummation of the male romance with the power to intimidate. An infant discovers that random flailings send the baby bottle flying out of the crib and crashing to the floor. Delighted, the joyful babe repeats those motions again and again, seeking to duplicate the feat. Just so, I recall the points at which some of my boyhood friends were finally seduced by the perception of themselves as tough guys. When a mark cowered and surrendered his money without resistance, myth and reality merged—and paid off. It is, after all, only manly to embrace the power to frighten and intimidate. We, as men, are not supposed to give an inch of our lane on the highway; we are to seize the fighter's edge in work and in play and even in love; we are to be valiant in the face of hostile forces.

Unfortunately, poor and powerless young men seem to take all this nonsense literally. As a boy, I saw countless tough guys locked away; I have since buried several, too. They were babies, really—a teenage cousin, a brother of twenty-two, a childhood friend in his midtwenties—all gone down in episodes of bravado played out in the streets. I came to doubt the virtues of intimidation early on. I chose, perhaps even unconsciously, to remain a shadow—timid, but a survivor.

The fearsomeness mistakenly attributed to me in public places often has a perilous flavor. The most frightening of these confusions occurred in the late 1970s and early 1980s when I worked as a journalist in Chicago. One day, rushing into the office of a magazine I was writing for with a deadline story in hand, I was mistaken for a burglar. The office manager called security and, with an ad hoc posse, pursued me through the labyrinthine halls, nearly to my editor's door. I had no way of proving who I was. I could only move briskly toward the company of someone who knew me.

Another time I was on assignment for a local paper and killing time before an interview. I entered a jewelry store on the city's affluent Near North Side. The proprietor excused herself and returned with an enormous red Doberman pinscher straining at the end of a leash. She stood, the dog extended toward me, silent to my questions, her eyes bulging nearly out of her head. I took a cursory look around, nodded, and bade her good night. Relatively speaking, however, I never fared as badly as another black male journalist. He went to nearby Waukegan, Illinois, a couple of summers ago to work on a story about a murderer who was born there. Mistaking the reporter for the killer, police hauled him from his car at gunpoint and but for his press credentials would probably have tried to book him. Such episodes are not uncommon. Black men trade tales like this all the time.

In "My Negro Problem—And Ours," Podhoretz writes that the hatred he feels for blacks makes itself known to him through a variety of avenues—one being his discomfort with that "special brand of paranoid touchiness" to which he says blacks are prone. No doubt he is speaking here of black men. In time, I learned to smother the rage I felt at so often being taken for a criminal. Not to do so would surely have led to madness—via that special "paranoid touchiness" that so annoyed Podhoretz at the time he wrote the essay.

I began to take precautions to make myself less threatening. I move about with care, particularly late in the evening. I give a wide berth to nervous people on subway platforms during the wee hours, particularly when I have exchanged business clothes for jeans. If I happen to be entering a building behind some people who appear skittish, I may walk by, letting them clear the lobby before I return, so as not to seem to be following them. I have been calm and extremely congenial on those rare occasions when I've been pulled over by the police.

And on late-evening constitutionals along streets less traveled by, I employ what has proved to be an excellent tension-reducing measure: I whistle melodies from Beethoven and Vivaldi and the more popular classical composers. Even steely New Yorkers hunching toward nighttime destinations seem to relax, and occasionally they even join in the tune. Virtually everybody seems to sense that a mugger wouldn't be warbling bright, sunny selections from Vivaldi's *Four Seasons*. It is my equivalent of the cowbell that hikers wear when they know they are in bear country.

Considerations

Thinking

What is the chief way that Staples wins your confidence in this essay? Why might he not be able to win your confidence the same way on the street? Think of reasons other than appearance.

What do you think of the precautions Staples takes to "make [himself] less threatening"? Should he have to take such precautions?

Connecting

Staples writes about two white men—Norman Podhoretz and Edward Hoagland—who write about black men. What use does Staples make of those two writers and their ideas? What is his attitude about them? How can you tell?

Go to the library and read Norman Mailer's essay "The White Negro" in *Advertisements for Myself*. What do you think Staples would have to say about the effect that essay might have on his ability to walk serenely down the streets of New York minding his own business? In what other ways might Mailer's attempt to romanticize the "Negro" complicate the lives of African Americans?

Writing

Tell a story of your own that illustrates what Staples calls "the male romance with the power to intimidate." Let that story serve as a departure for a closer examination of your attitude toward such a romance.

Write Staples a letter exploring the complications involved in taking him or any other man at face value on the streets of an American city, late at night when you are alone.

Margaret Talbot
(b. 1946)

Margaret Talbot is a Senior Editor at the *New Republic* magazine in Washington, D.C. She was formerly editor of *Lingua Franca,* and has written for a number of publications, including the *Washington Post, Slate,* and *Vogue.* Her essay "Les Très Riches Heures de Martha Stewart" was published in the *New Republic.* In it, Talbot examines the cultural relevance of the recent phenomenon of Martha Stewart and the kind of lifestyle associated with her.

Les Très Riches Heures de Martha Stewart

Every age gets the household goddess it deserves. The '60s had Julia Child, the sophisticated French chef who proved as permissive as Dr. Spock. She may have proselytized for a refined foreign cuisine from her perch at a Boston PBS station, but she was always an anti-snob, vowing to "take a lot of the la dee dah out of French cooking." With her madras shirts and her penumbra of curls, her 6'2″ frame and her whinny of a voice, she exuded an air of Cambridge eccentricity— faintly bohemian and a little tatty, like a yellowing travel poster. She was messy and forgiving. When Julia dropped an egg or collapsed a soufflé, she shrugged and laughed. "You are alone in the kitchen, nobody can see you, and cooking is meant to be fun," she reminded her viewers. She wielded lethal-looking kitchen knives with campy abandon, dipped her fingers into crème anglaise and wiped her chocolate-smeared hands on an apron tied carelessly at her waist. For Child was also something of a sensualist, a celebrant of appetite as much as a pedant of cooking.

In the '90s, and probably well into the next century, we have Martha Stewart, corporate overachiever turned domestic superachiever, Mildred Pierce in earth-toned Armani. Martha is the anti-Julia. Consider the extent of their respective powers. At the height of her success, Child could boast a clutch of bestselling cookbooks and a *gemütlich* TV show shot on a single set. At what may or may not be the height of her success, here's what Stewart can claim: a 5-year-old magazine, *Martha Stewart Living,* with a circulation that has leapt to 1.5 million; a popular cable TV show, also called "Martha Stewart Living" and filmed at her luscious Connecticut and East Hampton estates; a dozen wildly successful gardening, cooking and lifestyle books; a mail-order business, Martha-by-Mail; a nationally syndicated newspaper column, "Ask Martha"; a regular Wednesday slot on the "Today" show; a line of $110-a-gallon paints in colors inspired by the eggs her Araucana hens lay; plans to invade cyberspace—in short, an empire.

Julia limited herself to cooking lessons, with the quiet implication that cooking was a kind of synecdoche for the rest of bourgeois existence; but Martha's parish is vaster, her field is all of life. Her expertise, as she recently explained to *Mediaweek* magazine, covers, quite simply, "Beautiful soups and how to make them, beautiful houses and how to build them, beautiful children and how to raise them." (From soups to little nuts.) She presides, in fact, over a phenomenon that, in other realms, is quite familiar in American society and culture: a cult, devoted to her name and image.

In the distance between these two cynosures of domestic life lies a question: What does the cult of Martha mean? Or, to put it another way, what have we done, exactly, to deserve her?

If you have read the paper or turned on the television in the last year or so, you have probably caught a glimpse of the WASPy good looks, the affectless demeanor, the nacreous perfection of her world. You may even know the outlines of her story. Middle-class girl from a Polish-American family in Nutley, New Jersey, works her way through Barnard in the early '60s, modeling on the side. She becomes a stockbroker, a self-described workaholic and insomniac who by the '70s is making six figures on Wall Street, and who then boldly trades it all in . . . for life as a workaholic, insomniac evangelist for domesticity whose business now generates some $200 million in profits a year. (She herself, according to the *Wall Street Journal*, makes a salary of $400,000 a year from Time, Inc., which generously supplements this figure with a $40,000 a year clothing allowance and other candies.) You may even have admired her magazine, with its art-book production values and spare design, every kitchen utensil photographed like an Imogen Cunningham nude, every plum or pepper rendered with the loving detail of an eighteenth-century botanical drawing, every page a gentle exhalation of High Class.

What you may not quite realize, if you have not delved deeper into Stewart's oeuvre, is the ambition of her design for living—the absurd, self-parodic dream of it. To read Martha Stewart is to know that there is no corner of your domestic life that cannot be beautified or improved under careful tutelage, none that should not be colonized by the rhetoric and the discipline of quality control. Work full time though you may, care for your family though you must, convenience should never be your watchword in what Stewart likes to call, in her own twee coinage, "homekeeping." Convenience is the enemy of excellence. "We do not pretend that these are 'convenience' foods," she writes loftily of the bread and preserves recipes in a 1991 issue of the magazine. "Some take days to make. But they are recipes that will produce the very best results, and we know that is what you want." Martha is a kitchen-sink idealist. She scorns utility in the name of beauty. But her idealism, of course, extends no further than surface appearances, which makes it a very particular form of idealism indeed.

To spend any length of time in Martha-land is to realize that it is not enough to serve your guests homemade pumpkin soup as a first course. You must present it in hollowed-out, hand-gilded pumpkins as well. It will not do to serve an Easter ham unless you have baked it in a roasting pan lined with, of all things, "tender, young, organically-grown grass that has not yet been cut." And, when serving a "casual" lobster and corn dinner al fresco, you really ought to fashion dozens of cunning little bamboo brushes tied with raffia and adorned with a chive so that each of your guests may butter their corn with something pretty.

To be a Martha fan (or more precisely, a Martha adept) is to understand that a terracotta pot is just a terracotta pot until you have "aged" it, painstakingly rubbing yogurt into its dampened sides, then smearing it with plant food or "something you found in the woods" and patiently standing by while the mold sprouts. It is to think that maybe you could do this *kind* of thing, anyway—start a garden, say, in your scruffy backyard—and then to be brought up short by Martha's enumeration, in *Martha Stewart's Gardening,* of forty-nine "essential" gardening tools. These range from a "polesaw" to a "corn fiber broom" to three different kinds of pruning shears, one of which—the "loppers"—Martha says she has in three different sizes. You have, perhaps, a trowel. But then Martha's garden is a daunting thing to contemplate, what with its topiary mazes and state-of-the-art chicken coop; its "antique" flowers and geometric herb garden. It's half USDA station, half Sigginghurst. And you cannot imagine making anything remotely like it at your own house, not without legions of artisans and laborers and graduate students in landscape design, and a pot of money that perhaps you'll unearth when you dig up the yard.

In *The Culture of Narcissism,* Christopher Lasch describes the ways in which pleasure, in our age, has taken on "the qualities of work," allowing our leisure-time activities to be measured by the same standards of accomplishment that rule the workplace. It is a phenomenon that he memorably characterizes as "the invasion of play by the rhetoric of achievement." For Lasch, writing in the early '70s, the proliferation of sex-advice manuals offered a particularly poignant example. Today, though, you might just as easily point to the hundreds of products and texts, from unctious home-furnishings catalogs to upscale "shelter" magazines to self-help books like *Meditations for Women Who Do Too Much,* that tell us exactly how to "nest" and "cocoon" and "nurture," how to "center" and "retreat," and how to measure our success at these eminently private pursuits. Just as late-nineteenth-century marketers and experts promised to bring Americans back in touch with the nature from which modern industrial life had alienated them, so today's "shelter" experts—the word is revealingly primal—promise to reconnect us with a similarly mystified home. The bourgeois home as lost paradise, retrievable through careful instruction.

Martha Stewart is the apotheosis of this particular cult of expertise, and its most resourceful entrepreneur. She imagines projects of which we would never have thought—gathering dewy grass for our Easter ham, say—and makes us feel the pressing need for training in them. And she exploits, brilliantly, a certain estrangement from home that many working women feel these days. For women who are working longer and longer hours at more and more demanding jobs, it's easy to think of home as the place where chaos reigns and their own competence is called into doubt: easy to regard the office, by comparison, as the bulwark of order. It is a reversal, of course, of the hoary concept of home as a refuge from the tempests of the marketplace. But these days, as the female executives in a recent study attested, the priority they most often let slide is housekeeping: they'll abide disorder at home that they wouldn't or couldn't abide at the office. No working couple's home is the oasis of tranquility and Italian marble countertops that Marthaism seems to promise. But could it be? Should it be? Stewart plucks expertly at that chord of doubt.

In an era when it is not at all uncommon to be cut off from the traditional sources of motherwit and household lore—when many of us live far from the families into which we were born and have started our own families too late to benefit from the guidance of living parents or grandparents—domestic pedants like Martha Stewart rightly sense a big vacuum to fill. Stewart's books are saturated with nostalgia for lost tradition and old moldings, for her childhood in Nutley and for her mother's homemade preserves. In the magazine, her "Remembering" column pines moralistically for a simpler era, when beach vacations meant no television or video games, just digging for clams and napping in hammocks. Yet Stewart's message is that such simplicity can only be achieved now through strenuous effort and a flood of advice. We might be able to put on a picnic or a dinner party without her help, she seems to tell us, but we wouldn't do it properly, beautifully, in the spirit of excellence that we expect of ourselves at work.

It may be that Stewart's special appeal is to women who wouldn't want to take their mother's word anyway, to babyboomer daughters who figure that their sensibilities are just too different from their stay-at-home moms', who can't throw themselves into housekeeping without thinking of their kitchen as a catering business and their backyards as a garden show. In fact, relatively few of Martha's fans are housewives—72 percent of the subscribers to *Martha Stewart Living* are employed outside the home as managers or professionals—and many of them profess to admire her precisely because she isn't one, either. As one such Martha acolyte, an account executive at a Christian radio station, effused on the Internet: "[Stewart] is my favorite independent woman and what an entrepreneur! She's got her own television show, magazine, books and even her own brand of latex paint. . . . Martha is a feisty woman who settles for nothing less than perfection."

For women such as these, the didactic faux-maternalism of Martha Stewart seems the perfect answer. She may dispense the kind of homekeeping advice that a mother would, but she does so in tones too chill and exacting to sound "maternal," singling out, for example, those "who will always be too lazy" to do her projects. She makes housekeeping safe for the professional woman by professionalizing housekeeping. And you never forget that Stewart is herself a mogul, even when she's baking rhubarb crisp and telling you, in her Shakeresque mantra, that "It's a Good Thing."

It is tempting to see the Martha cult purely as a symptom of anti-feminist backlash. Though she may not directly admonish women to abandon careers for hearth and home. Stewart certainly exalts a way of life that puts hearth and home at its center, one that would be virtually impossible to achieve without *somebody's* full-time devotion. (Camille Paglia has praised her as "someone who has done a tremendous service for ordinary women—women who identify with the roles of wife, mother, and homemaker.") Besides, in those alarming moments when Stewart slips into the social critic's mode, she can sound a wee bit like Phyllis Schlafly—less punitive and more patrician, maybe, but just as smug about the moral uplift of a well-ordered home. Her philosophy of cultivating your own walled garden while the world outside is condemned to squalor bears the hallmarks of Reagan's America—it would not be overreading to call it a variety of conservatism. "Amid the horrors of genocidal war in Bosnia and Rwanda, the AIDS epidemic and increasing crime in many cities," Stewart writes in a recent column, "there are those of us who desire positive reinforcement of some very basic tenets of good living." And those would be? "Good food, gardening, crafts, entertaining and home improvement." (Hollow out the pumpkins, they're starving in Rwanda.)

Yet it would, in the end, be too simplistic to regard her as a tool of the feminine mystique, or as some sort of spokesmodel for full-time mommies. For one thing, there is nothing especially June Cleaverish, or even motherly, about Stewart. She has taken a drubbing, in fact, for looking more convincing as a businesswoman than a dispenser of milk and cookies. (Remember the apocryphal tale that had Martha flattening a crate of baby chicks while backing out of a driveway in her Mercedes?) Her habitual prickliness and Scotchguard perfectionism are more like the badges of the striving good girl, still cut to the quick by her classmates' razzing when she asked for extra homework.

Despite the ritual obeisance that Martha pays to Family, moreover, she is not remotely interested in the messy contingencies of family life. In the enchanted world of Turkey Hill, there are no husbands (Stewart was divorced from hers in 1990), only loyal craftsmen, who clip hedges and force dogwood with self-effacing dedication. Children she makes use of as accessories, much like Parisian women deploy little dogs. The books and especially the magazine are often graced with photographic spreads of parties and teas where children pale as waxen angels somberly disport themselves, their fair hair shaped into tasteful blunt cuts, their slight figures clad in storybook velvet or lace. "If I had to choose one essential element for the success of an Easter brunch," she writes rather menacingly in her 1994 *Menus for Entertaining,* "it would be children." The homemade Halloween costumes modeled by wee lads and lasses in an October 1991 issue of *Martha Stewart Living* do look gorgeous—the Caravaggio colors, the themes drawn from nature. But it's kind of hard to imagine a 5-year-old boy happily agreeing to go as an acorn this year, instead of say, Batman. And why should he? In Marthaland, his boyhood would almost certainly be overridden in the name of taste.

If Stewart is a throwback, it's not so much to the 1950s as to the 1850s, when the doctrine of separate spheres did allow married or widowed women of the upper classes a kind of power—unchallenged dominion over the day-to-day functioning of the home and its servants, in exchange for ceding the public realm to men. At Turkey Hill, Stewart is the undisputed chatelaine, micromanaging her estate in splendid isolation. (This hermetic pastoral is slightly marred, of course, by the presence of cameras.) Here the domestic arts have become ends in themselves, unmoored from family values and indeed from family.

Stewart's peculiar brand of didacticism as another nineteenth-century precedent—in the domestic science or home economics movement. The domestic scientists' favorite recipes—"wholesome" concoctions of condensed milk and canned fruit, rivers of white sauce—would never have passed Martha's muster; but their commitment to painstakingly elegant presentation, their concern with the look of food even more than its taste, sound a lot like Stewart's. And, more importantly, so does their underlying philosophy. They emerged out of a tradition: the American preference for food writing of the prescriptive, not the descriptive, kind, for food books that told you, in M. F. K. Fisher's formulation, not about eating but about what to eat. But they took this spirit much further. Like Stewart, these brisk professional women of the 1880s and '90s believed that true culinary literacy could not be handed down or casually absorbed; it had to be carefully taught. (One of the movement's accomplishments, if it can be called that, was the home ec curriculum.)

Like Stewart, the domestic scientists were not bent on liberating intelligent women from housework. Their objective was to raise housework to a level worthy of intelligent women. They wished to apply rational method to the chaos and the drudgery of housework and, in so doing, to earn it the respect accorded men's stuff like science and business. Neither instinct, nor intuition, nor mother's rough-hewn words of advice would have a place in the scientifically managed home of the future. As Laura Shapiro observes in *Perfection Salad,* her lively and perceptive history of domestic science, the ideal new housewife was supposed to project, above all, "self-sufficiency, self-control, and a perfectly bland façade." Sound familiar?

It is in their understanding of gender roles, however, that the doyennes of home ec most closely prefigure Marthaism. Like Stewart, they cannot be classified either as feminists or traditionalists. Their model housewife was a pseudo-professional with little time for sublimating her ego to her husband's or tenderly ministering to his needs. She was more like a factory supervisor than either the Victorian angel of the home or what Shapiro calls the courtesan type, the postwar housewife who was supposed to zip through her chores so she could gussy herself up for her husband. In Martha's world, too, the managerial and aesthetic challenges of "homekeeping" always take priority, and their intricacy and ambition command a respect that mere wifely duties never could. Her husbandless hauteur is rich with the self-satisfaction of financial and emotional independence.

* * *

In the end, Stewart's fantasies have as much to do with class as with gender. The professional women who read her books might find themselves longing for a breadwinner, but a lifestyle this beautiful is easier to come by if you've never needed a breadwinner in the first place. Stewart's books are a dreamy advertisement for independent wealth—or, more accurately, for its facsimile. You may not have a posh pedigree, but with a little effort (okay, a lot) you can adopt its trappings. After all, Martha wasn't born to wealth either, but now she attends the weddings of people with names like Charles Booth-Cliborn (she sent to his in London, the magazine tells us) and caters them for couples named Sissy and Kelsey (see her *Wedding Planner,* in which their yacht is decorated with a "Just Married" sign).

She is not an American aristocrat, but she plays one on TV. And you can play one, too, at least in your own home. Insist on cultivating only those particular yellow plums you tasted in the Dordogne, buy your copper cleaner only at Delherin in Paris, host lawn parties where guests come "attired in the garden dress of the Victorian era," and you begin to simulate the luster of lineage. Some of Stewart's status-augmenting suggestion must strike even her most faithful fans as ridiculous. For showers held after the baby is born, Martha "likes presenting the infant with engraved calling cards that the child can then slip into thank you notes and such for years to come." What a great idea. Maybe your baby can gum them for a while first, thoughtfully imprinting them with his signature drool.

The book that best exemplifies her class-consciousness is *Martha Stewart's New Old House,* a step-by-step account of refurbishing a Federal-style farmhouse in Westport, Connecticut. Like all her books, it contains many, many pictures of Martha; here she's frequently shown supervising the work of plasterers, carpenters and other "seemingly taciturn men." *New Old House* establishes Stewart's ideal audience: a demographic niche occupied by the kind of people who, like her, can afford to do their kitchen countertops in "mottled, gray-green, hand-honed slate from New York state, especially cut" for them. The cost of all this (and believe me, countertops are only the beginning) goes unmentioned. If you have to ask, maybe you're not a Martha kind of person after all.

In fact, Stewart never seems all that concerned with reassuring her readers of their ability to afford such luxuries or their right to enjoy them. She's more concerned with establishing her own claims. Her reasoning seems to go something like this: the houses that she buys and renovates belong to wealthy families who passed them down through generations. But these families did not properly care for their patrimony. The widowed Bulkeley sisters, erstwhile owners of Turkey Hill, had let the estate fall "into great disrepair. All the farms and outbuildings were gone. . . . The fields around had been sold off by the sisters in 2-acre building lots; suburbia encroached." The owner of the eponymous New Old House was a retired librarian named Miss Adams who "had little interest in the house other than as a roof over her head. Clearly a frugal spirit, she had no plans to restore the house, and she lived there until she could no longer cope with the maintenance and upkeep of the place. The house was in dire need of attention, and since no other family member wanted to assume responsibility, Miss Adams reluctantly decided to sell her family home. I wanted very much to save the

Adams house, to put it to rights, to return its history to it, to make it livable once again."

It's a saga with overtones of Jamesian comedy: a family with bloodlines but no money is simultaneously rescued and eclipsed by an energetic upstart with money but no bloodlines. The important difference—besides the fact that Martha is marrying the house, not the son—is that she also has taste. And it's taste, far more than money, she implies, that gives her the right to these splendid, neglected piles of brick. Unlike the "frugal" Misses Bulkeley, she will keep suburbia at bay; unlike the careless Miss Adams, she would never resort to "hideous rugs" in (yuck) shades of brown. They don't understand their own houses; she does, and so she *deserves* to own their houses. But leave it to Martha to get all snippy about these people's aesthetic oversights while quietly celebrating their reversion to type. They're useful to her, and not only because their indifference to decor bolsters her claim to their property. Like the pumpkin pine floors and original fixtures, these quaintly cheeseparing New Englanders denote the property's authenticity.

The fantasy of vaulting into the upper crust that Martha Stewart fulfilled, and now piques in her readers, is about more than just money, of course. Among other things, it's about time, and the luxurious plenitude of it. Living the Martha way would mean enjoying a surfeit of that scarce commodity, cooking and crafting at the artisanal pace her projects require. Trouble is, none of us overworked Americans has time to spare these days—and least of all the upscale professional women whom Stewart targets. Martha herself seemed to acknowledge this when she told *Inside Media* that she attracts at least two classes of true believers: the "Be-Marthas," who have enough money and manic devotion to follow many of her lifestyle techniques, and the "Do-Marthas," who "are a little bit envious" and "don't have as much money as the Be-Marthas."

To those fulsome categories, you could surely add the "watch Marthas" or the "read Marthas," people who might consider, say, making their own rabbit-shaped wire topiary forms, but only consider it, who mostly just indulge in the fantasy of doing so, if only they had the time. There is something undeniably soothing about watching Martha at her absurdly time-consuming labors. A female "media executive" explained the appeal to Barbara Lippert in *New York* magazine: "I never liked Martha Stewart until I started watching her on Sunday mornings. I turn on the TV, and I'm in my pajamas, still in this place between sleep and reality. And she's showing you how to roll your tablecloths in parchment paper. She's like a character when she does her crafts. It reminds me of watching Mr. Green Jeans on Captain Kangaroo. I remember he had a shoebox he took out that was filled with craft things. There would be a close-up on his hands with his buffed nails. And then he would show you how to cut an oaktag with a scissor, or when he folded paper, he'd say: 'There you go, boys and girls,' and it was very quiet. It's like she brings out this great meditative focus and calm."

The show does seem strikingly unfrenetic. Unlike just about everything else on TV, including the "Our Home" show, which follows it on Lifetime, it eschews

Kathy Lee–type banter, perky music, swooping studio shots and jittery handheld cameras. Instead there's just Martha, alone in her garden or kitchen, her teacherly tones blending with birdsong, her recipes cued to the seasons. Whimsical recorder music pipes along over the credits. Martha's crisply ironed denim shirts, pearl earrings, and honey-toned highlights bespeak the fabulousness of Connecticut. Her hands move slowly, deliberately over her yellow roses or her Depression glasses. Martha is a Puritan who prepares "sinful" foods—few of her recipes are low-fat or especially health-conscious—that are redeemed by the prodigious labors, the molasses afternoons, involved in serving them. (She preys upon our guilt about overindulgence, then hints at how to assuage it.) Here at Turkey Hill, time is as logy as a honey-sated bumblebee. Here on Lifetime, the cable channel aimed at baby-boom women, Martha's stately show floats along in a sea of stalker movies. Thighmaster commercials and "Weddings of a Lifetime" segments, and by comparison, I have to say, she looks rather dignified. Would that we all had these *très riches heures.*

But if we had the hours, if we had the circumstances, wouldn't we want to fill them with something of our own, with a domestic grace of our own devising? Well, maybe not anymore. For taste is no longer an expression of individuality. It is, more often, an instrument of conformism, a way to assure ourselves that we're living by the right codes, dictated or sanctioned by experts. Martha Stewart's "expertise" is really nothing but another name for the perplexity of her cowed consumers. A lifestyle cult as all-encompassing as hers could thrive only at a time when large numbers of Americans have lost confidence in their own judgment about the most ordinary things. For this reason, *Martha Stewart Living* isn't really living at all.

Considerations

Thinking

Explain what Talbot means when she says, "Every age gets the household goddess it deserves." What is a "household goddess," and how does Martha Stewart exemplify the epitome of a particular type and style of household fashion?

What question does Talbot's essay raise and answer? How well does Talbot explain the significance of the Martha Stewart cult? What does the author mean by saying, "*Martha Stewart Living* isn't really living at all"?

Connecting

Talbot's essay analyzes a social phenomenon as does William Cronon's essay "The Trouble with Wilderness." Compare the writers' approaches to their subjects.

What does Talbot gain from introducing Julia Child, the cooking expert, into her essay? What, for Talbot, does Julia Child represent? How does Julia Child help Talbot explain the significance of Martha Stewart?

Writing

Write an essay that analyzes a social phenomenon, perhaps the success of a particular type of music or dance, or the popularity of a singer, filmmaker, or other currently fashionable aspect of culture.

Write an analysis of Talbot's essay, first dividing it into introduction, body, and conclusion, then further dividing the middle into sections. Explain what Talbot says in each part.

Amy Tan
(b. 1952)

Amy Tan was born and raised in Stockton, California. After her father's death, she moved with her mother to Switzerland, where she attended high school. She attended college in Oregon before taking a job with IBM as a writer of computer manuals. A few years later, having been inspired by Louise Erdrich's interlocked stories about Native American (Chippewa) life in her book *Love Medicine*, Tan began writing the interlocking stories that soon became her best-selling novel, *The Joy Luck Club* (1989).

Like the stories in *The Joy Luck Club* and those in her later novel, *The Kitchen God's Wife*, the essay that follows concerns Tan's exploration of cultural difference and cultural connectedness through language. Tan conveys through description and example how using different kinds of English leads to widely differing results.

Mother Tongue

I am not a scholar of English or literature. I cannot give you much more than personal opinions on the English language and its variations in this country or others.

I am a writer. And by that definition, I am someone who has always loved language. I am fascinated by language in daily life. I spend a great deal of my time thinking about the power of language—the way it can evoke an emotion, a visual image, a complex idea, or a simple truth. Language is the tool of my trade. And I use them all—all the Englishes I grew up with.

Recently, I was made keenly aware of the different Englishes I do use. I was giving a talk to a large group of people, the same talk I had already given to half a dozen other groups. The nature of the talk was about my writing, my life, and my book, *The Joy Luck Club*. The talk was going along well enough, until I remembered one major difference that made the whole talk sound wrong. My mother was in the room. And it was perhaps the first time she had heard me give a lengthy speech, using the kind of English I have never used with her. I was saying things like "The intersection of memory upon imagination" and "There is an aspect of my fiction that relates to thus-and-thus"—a speech filled with carefully wrought grammatical phrases, burdened, it suddenly seemed to me, with nominalized forms, past perfect tenses, conditional phrases, all the forms of standard English that I had learned in school and through books, the forms of English I did not use at home with my mother.

Just last week, I was walking down the street with my mother, and I again found myself conscious of the English I was using, the English I do use with her. We were talking about the price of new and used furniture and I heard myself saying this: "Not waste money that way." My husband was with us as well, and he didn't notice any switch in my English. And then I realized why. It's because over the twenty years we've been together I've often used that same kind of English with him, and sometimes he even uses it with me. It has become our language of intimacy, a different sort of English that relates to family talk, the language I grew up with.

So you'll have some idea of what this family talk I heard sounds like, I'll quote what my mother said during a recent conversation which I videotaped and then transcribed. During this conversation, my mother was talking about a political gangster in Shanghai who had the same last name as her family's, Du, and how the gangster in his early years wanted to be adopted by her family, which was rich by comparison. Later, the gangster became more powerful, far richer than my mother's family, and one day showed up at my mother's wedding to pay his respects. Here's what she said in part:

"Du Yusong having business like fruit stand. Like off the street kind. He is Du like Du Zong—but not Tsung-ming Island people. The local people call putong, the river east side, he belong to that side local people. That man want to ask Du Zong father take him in like become own family. Du Zong father wasn't look down on him, but didn't take seriously, until that man big like become a mafia. Now important person, very hard to inviting him. Chinese way, came only to show respect, don't stay for dinner. Respect for making big celebration, he shows up. Mean gives lots of respect. Chinese custom. Chinese social life that way. If too important won't have to stay too long. He come to my wedding. I didn't see, I heard it. I gone to boy's side, they have YMCA dinner. Chinese age I was nineteen."

You should know that my mother's expressive command of English belies how much she actually understands. She reads the *Forbes* report, listens to *Wall Street Week,* converses daily with her stockbroker, reads all of Shirley MacLaine's books with ease—all kinds of things I can't begin to understand. Yet some of my friends tell me they understand 50 percent of what my mother says. Some say they understand 80 to 90 percent. Some say they understand none of it, as if she were speaking pure Chinese. But to me, my mother's English is perfectly clear, perfectly natural. It's my mother tongue. Her language, as I hear it, is vivid, direct, full of observation and imagery. That was the language that helped shape the way I saw things, expressed things, made sense of the world.

Lately, I've been giving more thought to the kind of English my mother speaks. Like others, I have described it to people as "broken" or "fractured" English. But I wince when I say that. It has always bothered me that I can think of no other way to describe it other than "broken," as if it were damaged and needed to be fixed, as if it lacked a certain wholeness and soundness. I've heard other terms used, "limited English," for example. But they seem just as bad, as if everything is limited, including people's perceptions of the limited English speaker.

I know this for a fact, because when I was growing up, my mother's "limited" English limited *my* perception of her. I was ashamed of her English. I believed that her English reflected the quality of what she had to say. That is, because she expressed them imperfectly her thoughts were imperfect. And I had plenty of empirical evidence to support me: the fact that people in department stores, at banks, and at restaurants did not take her seriously, did not give her good service, pretended not to understand her, or even acted as if they did not hear her.

My mother has long realized the limitations of her English as well. When I was fifteen, she used to have me call people on the phone to pretend I was she. In this guise, I was forced to ask for information or even to complain and yell at people who had been rude to her. One time it was a call to her stockbroker in New York. She had cashed out her small portfolio and it just so happened we were going to go to New York the next week, our very first trip outside California. I had to get on the phone and say in an adolescent voice that was not very convincing, "This is Mrs. Tan."

And my mother was standing in the back whispering loudly, "Why he don't send me check, already two weeks late. So mad he lie to me, losing me money."

And then I said in perfect English, "Yes, I'm getting rather concerned. You had agreed to send the check two weeks ago, but it hasn't arrived."

Then she began to talk more loudly. "What he want, I come to New York tell him front of his boss, you cheating me?" And I was trying to calm her down, make her be quiet, while telling the stockbroker, "I can't tolerate any more excuses. If I don't receive the check immediately, I am going to have to speak to your manager when I'm in New York next week." And sure enough, the following week there we were in front of this astonished stockbroker, and I was sitting there red-faced and quiet, and my mother, the real Mrs. Tan, was shouting at his boss in her impeccable broken English.

We used a similar routine just five days ago, for a situation that was far less humorous. My mother had gone to the hospital for an appointment, to find out about a benign brain tumor a CAT scan had revealed a month ago. She said she had spoken very good English, her best English, no mistakes. Still, she said, the hospital did not apologize when they said they had lost the CAT scan and she had come for nothing. She said they did not seem to have any sympathy when she told them she was anxious to know the exact diagnosis, since her husband and son had both died of brain tumors. She said they would not give her any more information until the next time and she would have to make another appointment for that. So she said she would not leave until the doctor called her daughter. She wouldn't budge. And when the doctor finally called her daughter, me, who spoke in perfect English—lo and behold—we had assurances the CAT scan would be found, promises that a conference call on Monday would be held, and apologies for any suffering my mother had gone through for a most regrettable mistake.

I think my mother's English almost had an effect on limiting my possibilities in life as well. Sociologists and linguists probably will tell you that a person's developing language skills are more influenced by peers. But I do think that the language spoken in the family, especially in immigrant families which are more insular, plays a large role in shaping the language of the child. And I believe that it affected my results on achievement tests, IQ tests, and the SAT. While my English skills were never judged as poor, compared to math, English could not be considered my strong suit. In grade school I did moderately well, getting perhaps B's, sometimes B-pluses, in English and scoring perhaps in the sixtieth or seventieth percentile on achievement tests. But those scores were not good enough to override the opinion that my true abilities lay in math and science, because in those areas I achieved A's and scored in the ninetieth percentile or higher.

This was understandable. Math is precise; there is only one correct answer. Whereas, for me at least, the answers on English tests were always a judgment call, a matter of opinion and personal experience. Those tests were constructed around items like fill-in-the-blank sentence completion, such as "Even though Tom was ____, Mary thought he was ____." And the correct answer always seemed to be the most bland combinations of thoughts, for example, "Even though Tom was shy, Mary thought he was charming," with the grammatical structure "even though" limiting the correct answer to some sort of semantic opposites, so you wouldn't get answers like, "Even though Tom was foolish, Mary thought he was ridiculous." Well, according to my mother, there were very few limitations as to what Tom could have been and what Mary might have thought of him. So I never did well on tests like that.

The same was true with word analogies, pairs of words in which you were supposed to find some sort of logical, semantic relationship—for example, "*Sunset* is to *nightfall* as ____ is to ____." And here you would be presented with a list of four possible pairs, one of which showed the same kind of relationship: *red* is to *stoplight, bus* is to *arrival, chills* is to *fever, yawn* is to *boring.* Well, I could never think that way. I knew what the tests were asking, but I could not block out of my mind the images already created by the first pair, "*sunset* is to *nightfall*"—and I would see a burst of colors against a darkening sky, the moon rising, the lowering of a curtain of stars. And all the other pairs of words—red, bus, stoplight, boring—just threw up a mass of confusing images, making it impossible for me to sort out something as logical as saying: "A sunset precedes nightfall" is the same as "a chill precedes a fever." The only way I would have gotten that answer right would have been to imagine an associative situation, for example, my being disobedient and staying out past sunset, catching a chill at night, which turns into feverish pneumonia as punishment, which indeed did happen to me.

I have been thinking about all this lately, about my mother's English, about achievement tests. Because lately I've been asked, as a writer, why there are not more Asian Americans represented in American literature. Why are there few Asian Americans enrolled in creative writing programs? Why do so many Chinese students go into engineering? Well, these are broad sociological questions I can't begin to answer. But I have noticed in surveys—in fact, just last week—that Asian students, as a whole, always do significantly better on math achievement tests than in English. And this makes me think that there are other Asian-American students whose English spoken in the home might also be described as "broken" or "limited." And perhaps they also have teachers who are steering them away from writing and into math and science, which is what happened to me.

Fortunately, I happen to be rebellious in nature and enjoy the challenge of disproving assumptions made about me. I became an English major my first year in college, after being enrolled as pre-med. I started writing nonfiction as a freelancer the week after I was told by my former boss that writing was my worst skill and I should hone my talents toward account management.

But it wasn't until 1985 that I finally began to write fiction. And at first I wrote using what I thought to be wittily crafted sentences, sentences that would finally prove I had mastery over the English language. Here's an example from the first draft of a story that later made its way into *The Joy Luck Club,* but without this line: "That was my mental quandary in its nascent state." A terrible line, which I can barely pronounce.

Fortunately, for reasons I won't get into today, I later decided I should envision a reader for the stories I would write. And the reader I decided upon was my mother, because these were stories about mothers. So with this reader in mind— and in fact she did read my early drafts—I began to write stories using all the Englishes I grew up with: the English I spoke to my mother, which for lack of a better term might be described as "simple"; the English she used with me, which for lack of a better term might be described as "broken"; my translation of her Chinese, which could certainly be described as "watered down"; and what I imagined to be her translation of her Chinese if she could speak in perfect English, her internal language, and for that I sought to preserve the essence, but neither an English nor a Chinese structure. I wanted to capture what language ability tests can never reveal: her intent, her passion, her imagery, the rhythms of her speech, and the nature of her thoughts.

Apart from what any critic had to say about my writing, I knew I had succeeded where it counted when my mother finished reading my book and gave me her verdict: "So easy to read."

Considerations

Thinking

Why does Tan reject terms such as *limited, broken,* or *fractured* to describe her mother's spoken English? Do you agree with her? Why or why not?

Why is Tan's mother's English so important to Amy Tan herself?

Connecting

Tan describes how the English she uses with her mother and her husband differs from the language she uses with others in public. To what extent do you use language differently with different people or different groups?

Have you ever been ashamed of your own use of English or of another's? Why or why not?

Compare Tan's attitude toward her mother's English with that of Richard Rodriguez toward his parents' English in "The Achievement of Desire."

Compare your response to Tan's ideas with your response to David Reich's ideas in "'Mother Tongue' and Standard English."

Writing

Write an essay about an occasion (or occasions) when your use of language had a significant effect on something that happened to you or that affected someone else's feelings.

Discuss Tan's contention that "language spoken in the family, especially in immigrant families . . . plays a large role in shaping the language of the child."

Lewis Thomas
(1913–1993)

Lewis Thomas, born in New York, was educated at Princeton and Harvard. He served as president of Memorial Sloan-Kettering Cancer Center from 1973 to 1980. Earlier, he had worked as a research pathologist and as a medical administrator in the South Pacific during World War II, at the Rockefeller Institute, Tulane University, the University of Minnesota, New York University, and the Yale University School of Medicine. He is the author of a number of collections of essays, including *The Youngest Science, The Medusa and the Snail, The Lives of a Cell* (National Book Award winner), and *Late Night Thoughts on Listening to Mahler's Ninth Symphony.*

"The Corner of the Eye" suggests that much of importance lies just on the periphery of our vision, or barely audible in the corners of our minds. The essay also speaks of the earth's secrets, an aspect of which Thomas takes up in another essay, *The Lives of a Cell,* where he reflects on our symbiotic relation to nature.

The Corner of the Eye

There are some things that human beings can see only out of the corner of the eye. The niftiest examples of this gift, familiar to all children, are small, faint stars. When you look straight at one such star, it vanishes; when you move your eyes to stare into the space nearby, it reappears. If you pick two faint stars, side by side, and focus on one of the pair, it disappears and now you can see the other in the corner of your eye, and you can move your eyes back and forth, turning off the star in the center of your retina and switching the other one on. There is a physiological explanation for the phenomenon: we have more rods, the cells we use for light perception, at the periphery of our retinas, more cones, for perceiving color, at the center.

Something like this happens in music. You cannot really hear certain sequences of notes in a Bach fugue unless at the same time there are other notes being sounded, dominating the field. The real meaning in music comes from tones only audible in the corner of the mind.

I used to worry that computers would become so powerful and sophisticated as to take the place of human minds. The notion of Artificial Intelligence used to scare me half to death. Already, a large enough machine can do all sorts of intelligent things beyond our capacities: calculate in a split second the answers to mathematical problems requiring years for a human brain, draw accurate pictures from memory, even manufacture successions of sounds with a disarming resemblance to real music. Computers can translate textbooks, write dissertations of their own for doctorates, even speak in machine-tooled, inhuman phonemes any words read off from a printed page. They can communicate with one another, holding consultations and committee meetings of their own in networks around the earth.

Computers can make errors, of course, and do so all the time in small, irritating ways, but the mistakes can be fixed and nearly always are. In this respect they are fundamentally inhuman, and here is the relaxing thought: computers will not take over the world, they cannot replace us, because they are not designed, as we are, for ambiguity.

Imagine the predicament faced by a computer programmed to make language, not the interesting communication in sounds made by vervets or in symbols by brilliant chimpanzee prodigies, but real human talk. The grammar would not be too difficult, and there would be no problem in constructing a vocabulary of etymons, the original, pure, unambiguous words used to name real things. The impossibility would come in making the necessary mistakes we humans make with words instinctively, intuitively, as we build our kinds of language, changing the meanings to imply quite different things, constructing and elaborating the varieties of ambiguity without which speech can never become human speech.

Look at the record of language if you want to glimpse the special qualities of the human mind that lie beyond the reach of any machine. Take, for example, the metaphors we use in everyday speech to tell ourselves who we are, where we live, and where we come from.

The earth is a good place to begin. The word "earth" is used to name the ground we walk on, the soil in which we grow plants or dig clams, and the planet itself; we also use it to describe all of humanity ("the whole earth responds to the beauty of a child," we say to each other).

The earliest word for earth in our language was the Indo-European root *dhghem,* and look what we did with it. We turned it, by adding suffixes, into *humus* in Latin; today we call the complex polymers that hold fertile soil together "humic" acids, and somehow or other the same root became "humility." With another suffix the word became "human." Did the earth become human, or did the human emerge from the earth? One answer may lie in that nice cognate word "humble." "Humane" was built on, extending the meaning of both the earth and ourselves. In ancient Hebrew, *adamha* was the word for earth, *adam* for man. What computer could run itself through such manipulations as those?

We came at the same system of defining ourselves from the other direction. The word *wiros* was the first root for man; it took us in our vanity on to "virile" and "virtue," but also turned itself into the Germanic word *weraldh,* meaning the life of man, and thence in English to our word "world."

There is a deep hunch in this kind of etymology. The world of man derives from this planet, shares origin with the life of the soil, lives in humility with all the rest of life. I cannot imagine programming a computer to think up an idea like that, not a twentieth-century computer, anyway.

The world began with what it is now the fashion to call the "Big Bang." Characteristically, we have assigned the wrong words for the very beginning of the earth and ourselves, in order to evade another term that would cause this century embarrassment. It could not, of course, have been a bang of any sort, with no atmosphere to conduct the waves of sound, and no ears. It was something else, occurring in the most absolute silence we can imagine. It was the Great Light.

We say it had been chaos before, but it was not the kind of place we use the word "chaos" for today, things tumbling over each other and bumping around. Chaos did not have that meaning in Greek; it simply meant empty.

We took it, in our words, from chaos to cosmos, a word that simply meant order, cosmetic. We perceived the order in surprise, and our cosmologists and physicists continue to find new and astonishing aspects of the order. We made up the word "universe" from the whole affair, meaning literally turning everything into one thing. We used to say it was a miracle, and we still permit ourselves to refer to the whole universe as a marvel, holding in our unconscious minds the original root meaning of these two words, miracle and marvel—from the ancient root word *smei,* signifying a smile. It immensely pleases a human being to see something never seen before, even more to learn something never known before, most of all to think something never thought before. The rings of Saturn are the latest surprise. All my physicist friends are enchanted by this phenomenon, marveling at the small violations of the laws of planetary mechanics, shocked by the unaccountable braids and spokes stuck there among the rings like graffiti. It is nice for physicists to see something new and inexplicable; it means that the laws of nature are once again about to be amended by a new footnote.

The greatest surprise of all lies within our own local, suburban solar system. It is not Mars; Mars was surprising in its way but not flabbergasting; it was a disappointment not to find evidences of life, and there was some sadness in the pictures sent back to earth from the Mars Lander, that lonely long-legged apparatus poking about with its jointed arm, picking up sample after sample of the barren Mars soil, looking for any flicker of life and finding none; the only sign of life on Mars was the Lander itself, an extension of the human mind all the way from earth to Mars, totally alone.

Nor is Saturn the great surprise, nor Jupiter, nor Venus, nor Mercury, nor any of the glimpses of the others.

The overwhelming astonishment, the queerest structure we know about so far in the whole universe, the greatest of all cosmological scientific puzzles, confounding all our efforts to comprehend it, is the earth. We are only now beginning to appreciate how strange and splendid it is, how it catches the breath, the loveliest object afloat around the sun, enclosed in its own blue bubble of atmosphere, manufacturing and breathing its own oxygen, fixing its own nitrogen from the air into its own soil, generating its own weather at the surface of its rain forests, constructing its own carapace from living parts: chalk cliffs, coral reefs, old fossils from earlier forms of life now covered by layers of new life meshed together around the globe, Troy upon Troy.

Seen from the right distance, from the corner of the eye of an extraterrestrial visitor, it must surely seem a single creature, clinging to the round warm stone, turning in the sun.

Considerations

Thinking

Why is the title—"The Corner of the Eye"—so important to Thomas?

What is Thomas really trying to tell us about the earth? Where does he make that point most clearly?

Connecting

Why do you suppose Thomas tells us that he used to worry about computers' becoming too powerful? Why are "ambiguity" and "surprise" so crucial to our understanding of Thomas' idea?

What is hidden in the "record of language" that interests Thomas so much?

Writing

Select and describe one instance of seeing something out of the corner of your eye or detecting something out of the corner of your mind. Is there some logical explanation for what you saw or heard? Explain.

Go to the library and read two more essays from Thomas' books of essays. On the basis of those two essays and the two in this anthology, try to characterize what you think of as a preoccupation, central to Thomas' way of thinking.

The Lives of a Cell

Lewis Thomas

We are told that the trouble with Modern Man is that he has been trying to detach himself from nature. He sits in the topmost tiers of polymer, glass, and steel, dangling hi pulsing legs, surveying at a distance the writhing life of the planet. In this scenario, Man comes on as a stupendous lethal force, and the earth is pictured as something delicate, like rising bubbles at the surface of a country pond, or flights of fragile birds.

But it is illusion to think that there is anything fragile about the life of the earth; surely this is the toughest membrane imaginable in the universe, opaque to probability, impermeable to death. We are the delicate part, transient and vulnerable as cilia. Nor is it a new thing for man to invent an existence that he imagines to be above the rest of life, this has been his most consistent intellectual exertion down the millennia. As illusion, it has never worked out to his satisfaction in the past, any more than it does today. Man is embedded in nature.

The biologic science of recent years has been making this a more urgent fact of life. The new, hard problem will be to cope with the dawning, intensifying realization of just how interlocked we are. The old, clung-to notions most of us have held about our special lordship are being deeply undermined.

Item. A good case can be made for our nonexistence as entities. We are not made up, as we had always supposed, of successively enriched packets of our own parts. We are shared, rented, occupied. At the interior of our cells, driving them, providing the oxidative energy that sends us out for the improvement of each shining day, are the mitochondria, and in a strict sense they are not ours. They turn out to be little separate creatures, the colonial posterity of migrant prokaryocytes, probably primitive bacteria that swam into ancestral precursors of our eukaryotic cells and stayed here. Ever since, they have maintained themselves and their ways, replicating in their own fashion, privately, with their own DNA and RNA quite different from ours. They are as much symbionts as the rhizobial bacteria in the roots of beans. Without them, we would not move a muscle, drum a finger, think a thought.

Mitochondria are stable and responsible lodgers, and I choose to trust them. But what of the other little animals, similarly established in my cells, sorting and balancing me, clustering me together? My centrioles, basal bodies, and probably a good many other more obscure tiny beings at work inside my cells, each with its own special genome, are as foreign, and as essential, as aphids in anthills. My cells are no longer the pure line entities I was raised with; they are ecosystems more complex than Jamaica Bay.

I like to think that they work in my interest, that each breath they draw for me, but perhaps it is they who walk through the local park in the early morning, sensing my senses, listening to my music, thinking my thoughts.

I am consoled, somewhat, by the thought that the green plants are in the same fix. They could not be plants, or green, without their chloroplasts, which run the photosynthetic enterprise and generate oxygen for the rest of us. As it turns out, chloroplasts are also separate creatures with their own genomes, speaking their own language.

We carry stores of DNA in our nuclei that may have come in, at one time or another, from the fusion of ancestral cells and the linking of ancestral organisms in symbiosis. Our genomes are catalogues of instructions from all kinds of sources in nature, filed for all kinds of contingencies. As for me, I am grateful for differentiation and speciation, but I cannot feel as separate an entity as I did a few years ago, before I was told these things, nor, I should think, can anyone else.

Item. The uniformity of the earth's life, more astonishing than its diversity, is accountable by the high probability that we derived, originally, from some single cell, fertilized in a bolt of lightning as the earth cooled. It is from the progeny of this parent cell that we take our looks; we still share genes around, and the resemblance of the enzymes of grasses to those of whales is a family resemblance.

The viruses, instead of being single-minded agents of disease and death, now begin to look more like mobile genes. Evolution is still an infinitely long and tedious biologic game, with only the winners staying at the table, but the rules are beginning to look more flexible. We live in a dancing matrix of viruses; they dart, rather like bees, from organism to organism, from plant to insect to mammal to me and back again, and into the sea, tugging along pieces of this genome, strings of genes from that, transplanting grafts of DNA, passing around heredity as though at a great party. They may be a mechanism for keeping new, mutant kinds of DNA in the widest circulation among us. If this is true, the odd virus disease, on which we must focus so much of our attention in medicine, may be looked on as an accident, something dropped.

Item. I have been trying to think of the earth as a kind of organism, but it is no go. I cannot think of it this way. It is too big, too complex, with too many working parts lacking visible connections. The other night, driving through a hilly, wooded part of southern New England, I wondered about this. If not like an organism, what is it like what is it *most* like? Then, satisfactorily for that moment, it came to me: it is *most* like a single cell.

Considerations

Thinking

To what extent do you agree with Thomas that we have been trying to detach ourselves from nature?

Does Thomas's revised scenario seem more or less optimistic than the conventional one he corrects? What do you think of his claim that we humans are the delicate part?

Does it matter whether or not we accept Thomas's analogy that the earth is a single cell?

Connecting

How do Thomas's strategies as a science writer for a popular audience compare with those of Stephen Jay Gould in his essay "Women's Brains"?

Identify two comparisons Thomas employs in "Lives of a Cell" and comment on their purpose, significance, and effectiveness.

Writing

Consider a scientific or technical subject that interests or concerns you, such as pollution, cloning, gene therapy, or chemical food additives.

Write an essay about it that begins or at least includes some popular misconception that you correct. Try to use comparison and possibly anecdote as well as description, explanation, and argument in your essay.

Alice Walker
(b. 1944)

Alice Walker has written poetry, fiction, and essays. Her novel *The Color Purple,* which won both a Pulitzer Prize and an American Book Award, was made into a feature film. Her essays and speeches have been collected in two volumes—*Living by the Word* (1988) and *In Search of Our Mothers' Gardens* (1983), from which the following selection has been taken.

In "Beauty: When the Other Dancer Is the Self," Walker describes a childhood incident that left her blind in one eye. The essay is remarkable for the images Walker uses to convey the complexity of her feelings and the richness of her experience. The essay is also noteworthy for its handling of the passage of time and for the way Walker dramatizes the immediacy of her experience.

Beauty: When the Other Dancer Is the Self

It is a bright summer day in 1947. My father, a fat, funny man with beautiful eyes and a subversive wit, is trying to decide which of his eight children he will take with him to the county fair. My mother, of course, will not go. She is knocked out from getting most of us ready: I hold my neck stiff against the pressure of her knuckles as she hastily completes the braiding and the beribboning of my hair.

My father is the driver for the rich old white lady up the road. Her name is Miss Mey. She owns all the land for miles around, as well as the house in which we live. All I remember about her is that she once offered to pay my mother thirty-five cents for cleaning her house, raking up piles of her magnolia leaves, and washing her family's clothes, and that my mother—she of no money, eight children, and a chronic earache—refused it. But I do not think of this in 1947. I am two-and-a-half years old. I want to go everywhere my daddy goes. I am excited at the prospect of riding in a car. Someone has told me fairs are fun. That there is room in the car for only three of us doesn't faze me at all. Whirling happily in my starchy frock, showing off my biscuit-polished patent-leather shoes and lavender socks, tossing my head in a way that makes my ribbons bounce, I stand, hands on hips, before my father. "Take me, Daddy," I say with assurance; "I'm the prettiest!"

Later, it does not surprise me to find myself in Miss Mey's shiny black car, sharing the back seat with the other lucky ones. Does not surprise me that I thoroughly enjoy the fair. At home that night I tell the unlucky ones all I can remember about the merry-go-round, the man who eats live chickens, and the teddy bears, until they say: that's enough, baby Alice. Shut up now, and go to sleep.

It is Easter Sunday, 1950. I am dressed in a green, flocked, scalloped-hem dress (handmade by my adoring sister, Ruth) that has its own smooth satin petticoat and tiny hot-pink roses tucked into each scallop. My shoes, new T-strap patent leather, again highly biscuit-polished. I am six years old and have learned one of the longest Easter speeches to be heard that day, totally unlike the speech I said when I was two: "Easter lilies/pure and white/blossom in/the morning light." When I rise to give my speech I do so on a great wave of love and pride and expectation. People in the church stop rustling their new crinolines. They seem to hold their breath. I can tell they admire my dress, but it is my spirit, bordering on sassiness (womanishness), they secretly applaud.

"That girl's a little *mess*," they whisper to each other, pleased.

Naturally I say my speech without stammer or pause, unlike those who stutter, stammer, or, worst of all, forget. This is before the word "beautiful" exists in people's vocabulary, but "Oh, isn't she the *cutest* thing!" frequently floats my way. "And got so much sense!" they gratefully add . . . for which thoughtful addition I thank them to this day.

It was great fun being cute. But then, one day, it ended.

I am eight years old and a tomboy. I have a cowboy hat, cowboy boots, checkered shirt and pants, all red. My playmates are my brothers, two and four years older than I. Their colors are black and green, the only difference in the way we are dressed. On Saturday nights we all go to the picture show, even my mother; Westerns are her favorite kind of movie. Back home, "on the ranch," we pretend we are Tom Mix, Hopalong Cassidy, Lash LaRue (we've even named one of our dogs Lash LaRue); we chase each other for hours rustling cattle, being outlaws, delivering damsels from distress. Then my parents decide to buy my brothers guns. These are not "real" guns. They shoot BBs, copper pellets my brothers say will kill birds. Because I am a girl, I do not get a gun. Instantly I am relegated to the position of Indian. Now there appears a great distance between us. They shoot and shoot at everything with their new guns. I try to keep up with my bow and arrows.

One day while I am standing on top of our makeshift "garage"—pieces of tin nailed across some poles—holding my bow and arrow and looking out toward the fields, I feel an incredible blow in my right eye. I look down just in time to see my brother lower his gun.

Both brothers rush to my side. My eye stings, and I cover it with my hand. "If you tell," they say, "we will get a whipping. You don't want that to happen, do you?" I do not. "Here is a piece of wire," says the older brother, picking it up from the roof; "say you stepped on one end of it and the other flew up and hit you." The pain is beginning to start. "Yes," I say. "Yes, I will say that is what happened." If I do not say this is what happened, I know my brothers will find ways to make me wish I had. But now I will say anything that gets me to my mother.

Confronted by our parents we stick to the lie agreed upon. They place me on a bench on the porch and I close my left eye while they examine the right. There is a tree growing from underneath the porch that climbs past the railing to the roof. It is the last thing my right eye sees. I watch as its trunk, its branches, and then its leaves are blotted out by the rising blood.

I am in shock. First there is intense fever, which my father tries to break using lily leaves bound around my head. Then there are chills: my mother tries to get me to eat soup. Eventually, I do not know how, my parents learn what has happened. A week after the "accident" they take me to see a doctor. "Why did you wait so long to come?" he asks, looking into my eye and shaking his head. "Eyes are sympathetic," he says. "If one is blind, the other will likely become blind too."

This comment of the doctor's terrifies me. But it is really how I look that bothers me most. Where the BB pellet struck there is a glob of whitish scar tissue, a hideous cataract, on my eye. Now when I stare at people—a favorite pastime, up to now—they will stare back. Not at the "cute" little girl, but at her scar. For six years I do not stare at anyone, because I do not raise my head.

Years later, in the throes of a mid-life crisis, I ask my mother and sister whether I changed after the "accident." "No," they say, puzzled. "What do you mean?"

What do I mean?

I am eight, and, for the first time, doing poorly in school, where I have been something of a whiz since I was four. We have just moved to the place where the "accident" occurred. We do not know any of the people around us because this is a different county. The only time I see the friends I knew is when we go back to our old church. The new school is the former state penitentiary. It is a large stone building, cold and drafty, crammed to overflowing with boisterous, ill-disciplined children. On the third floor there is a huge circular imprint of some partition that has been torn out.

"What used to be here?" I ask a sullen girl next to me on our way past it to lunch.

"The electric chair," says she.

At night I have nightmares about the electric chair, and about all the people reputedly "fried" in it. I am afraid of the school, where all the students seem to be budding criminals.

"What's the matter with your eye?" they ask, critically.

When I don't answer (I cannot decide whether it was an "accident" or not), they shove me, insist on a fight.

My brother, the one who created the story about the wire, comes to my rescue. But then brags so much about "protecting" me, I become sick.

After months of torture at the school, my parents decide to send me back to our old community, to my old school. I live with my grandparents and the teacher they board. But there is no room for Phoebe, my cat. By the time my grandparents decide there is room, and I ask for my cat, she cannot be found. Miss Yarborough, the boarding teacher, takes me under her wing, and begins to teach me to play the piano. But soon she marries an African—a "prince," she says—and is whisked away to his continent.

At my old school there is at least one teacher who loves me. She is the teacher who "knew me before I was born" and bought my first baby clothes. It is she who makes life bearable. It is her presence that finally helps me turn on the one child at the school who continually calls me "one-eyed bitch." One day I simply grab him by his coat and beat him until I am satisfied. It is my teacher who tells me my mother is ill.

My mother is lying in bed in the middle of the day, something I have never seen. She is in too much pain to speak. She has an abscess in her ear. I stand looking down on her, knowing that if she dies, I cannot live. She is being treated with warm oils and hot bricks held against her cheek. Finally a doctor comes. But I must go back to my grandparents' house. The weeks pass but I am hardly aware of it. All I know is that my mother might die, my father is not so jolly, my brothers still have their guns, and I am the one sent away from home.

"You did not change," they say.

Did I imagine the anguish of never looking up?

I am twelve. When relatives come to visit I hide in my room. My cousin Brenda, just my age, whose father works in the post office and whose mother is a nurse, comes to find me. "Hello," she says. And then she asks, looking at my recent school picture, which I did not want taken, and on which the "glob," as I think of it, is clearly visible, "You still can't see out of that eye?"

"No," I say, and flop back on the bed over my book.

That night, as I do almost every night, I abuse my eye. I rant and rave at it, in front of the mirror. I plead with it to clear up before morning. I tell it I hate and despise it. I do not pray for sight. I pray for beauty.

"You did not change," they say.

I am fourteen and baby-sitting for my brother Bill, who lives in Boston. He is my favorite brother and there is a strong bond between us. Understanding my feelings of shame and ugliness he and his wife take me to a local hospital, where the "glob" is removed by a doctor named O. Henry. There is still a small bluish crater where the scar tissue was, but the ugly white stuff is gone. Almost immediately I become a different person from the girl who does not raise her head. Or so I think. Now that I've raised my head I win the boyfriend of my dreams. Now that I've raised my head I have plenty of friends. Now that I've raised my head classwork comes from my lips as faultlessly as Easter speeches did, and I leave high school as valedictorian, most popular student, and *queen,* hardly believing my luck. Ironically, the girl who was voted most beautiful in our class (and was) was later shot twice through the chest by a male companion, using a "real" gun, while she was pregnant. But that's another story in itself. Or is it?

"You did not change," they say.

It is now thirty years since the "accident." A beautiful journalist comes to visit and to interview me. She is going to write a cover story for her magazine that focuses on my latest book. "Decide how you want to look on the cover," she says. "Glamorous, or whatever."

Never mind "glamorous," it is the "whatever" that I hear. Suddenly all I can think of is whether I will get enough sleep the night before the photography session: If I don't, my eye will be tired and wander, as blind eyes will.

At night in bed with my lover I think up reasons why I should not appear on the cover of a magazine. "My meanest critics will say I've sold out," I say. "My family will now realize I write scandalous books."

"But what's the real reason you don't want to do this?" he asks.

"Because in all probability," I say in a rush, "my eye won't be straight."

"It will be straight enough," he says. Then, "Besides, I thought you'd made your peace with that."

And I suddenly remember that I have.

I remember:

I am talking to my brother Jimmy, asking if he remembers anything unusual about the day I was shot. He does not know I consider that day the last time my father, with his sweet home remedy of cool lily leaves, chose me, and that I suffered and raged inside because of this. "Well," he says, "all I remember is standing by the side of the highway with Daddy, trying to flag down a car. A white man stopped, but when Daddy said he needed somebody to take his little girl to the doctor, he drove off."

I remember:

I am in the desert for the first time. I fall totally in love with it. I am so overwhelmed by its beauty, I confront for the first time, consciously, the meaning of the doctor's words years ago: "Eyes are sympathetic. If one is blind, the other will likely become blind too." I realize I have dashed about the world madly, looking at this, looking at that, storing up images against the fading of the light. *But I might have missed seeing the desert!* The shock of that possibility—and gratitude for over twenty-five years of sight—sends me literally to my knees. Poem after poem comes—which is perhaps how poets pray.

On Sight

I am so thankful I have seen
The Desert
And the creatures in the desert
And the desert Itself.

The desert has its own moon
Which I have seen
With my own eye.
There is no flag on it.

Trees of the desert have arms
All of which are always up
That is because the moon is up
The sun is up
Also the sky
The Stars
Clouds
None with flags.

If there were flags, I doubt
the trees would point.
Would you?

But mostly, I remember this:

I am twenty-seven, and my baby daughter is almost three. Since her birth I have worried about her discovery that her mother's eyes are different from other people's. Will she be embarrassed? I think. What will she say? Every day she watches a television program called *Big Blue Marble.* It begins with a picture of the earth as it appears from the moon. It is bluish, a little battered-looking, but full of light, with whitish clouds swirling around it. Every time I see it I weep with love, as if it is a picture of Grandma's house. One day when I am putting Rebecca down for her nap, she suddenly focuses on my eye. Something inside me cringes, gets ready to try to protect myself. All children are cruel about physical differences, I know from experience, and that they don't always mean to be is another matter. I assume Rebecca will be the same.

But no-o-o-o. She studies my face intently as we stand, her inside and me outside her crib. She even holds my face maternally between her dimpled little hands. Then, looking every bit as serious and lawyerlike as her father, she says, as if it may just possibly have slipped my attention: "Mommy, there's a *world* in your eye." (As in, "Don't be alarmed, or do anything crazy.") And then, gently, but with great interest: "Mommy, where did you *get* that world in your eye?"

For the most part, the pain left then. (So what, if my brothers grew up to buy even more powerful pellet guns for their sons and to carry real guns themselves. So what, if a young "Morehouse man" once nearly fell off the steps of Trevor Arnett Library because he thought my eyes were blue.) Crying and laughing I ran to the bathroom, while Rebecca mumbled and sang herself to sleep. Yes indeed, I realized, looking into the mirror. There *was* a world in my eye. And I saw that it was possible to love it: that in fact, for all it had taught me of shame and anger and inner vision, I *did* love it. Even to see it drifting out of orbit in boredom, or rolling up out of fatigue, not to mention floating back at attention in excitement (bearing witness, a friend has called it), deeply suitable to my personality, and even characteristic of me.

That night I dream I am dancing to Stevie Wonder's song "Always" (the name of the song is really "As," but I hear it as "Always"). As I dance, whirling and joyous, happier than I've ever been in my life, another bright-faced dancer joins me. We dance and kiss each other and hold each other through the night. The other dancer has obviously come through all right, as I have done. She is beautiful, whole, and free. And she is also me.

Considerations

Thinking

Consider the extent to which Walker's injury affected her self-image. How important is it that Walker's injury was facial? Why?

Why does Walker's attitude toward her old injury and its consequences change? Explain what Walker learns during her trip to the desert and as a result of her daughter's observation, "Mommy, there's a *world* in your eye."

Connecting

Relate Walker's presentation of herself as a young girl with her self-presentation as a young woman.

Consider the extent to which Walker's essay illustrates familiar conventional attitudes about women's beauty.

Compare Walker's essay in this respect with Meloy's "Voice of the Looking-Glass."

Writing

Describe a time when an accident or other turn of events damaged your self-image, made you feel insecure or unhappy with yourself. Explain how you came to terms with your situation and what the consequences for your later life have been—or might yet be.

Analyze Walker's use of imagery to convey the meaning and feeling of her experience.

Compare Walker's description of her injury and response to it with Leonard Kriegel's in "Falling into Life."

Cornel West
(b. 1953)

Cornel West grew up in Tulsa, Oklahoma. He graduated from Harvard and Princeton Universities and taught at Union Theological Seminary and the Yale University Divinity School. He has also taught at Harvard and the University of Paris, and, most recently at Harvard University.

His many books include *Breaking Bread: Insurgent Black Intellectual Life* (1991) and *Race Matters* (1993), for which the following essay serves as an introduction. West urges his readers to understand the causes of racism. He appeals to their sense of justice and wisdom to resolve the hitherto intractable problems that could destroy American society. His tone is measured and his language carefully balanced to avoid excessive passion.

Race Matters

Since the beginning of the nation, white Americans have
suffered from a deep inner uncertainty as to who they really are.
One of the ways that has been used to simplify the answer has
been to seize upon the presence of black Americans and use
them as a marker, a symbol of limits, a metaphor for the
"outsider." Many whites could look at the social position of
blacks and feel that color formed an easy and reliable gauge for
determining to what extent one was or was not American.
Perhaps that is why one of the first epithets that many European
immigrants learned when they got off the boat was the term
"nigger"—it made them feel instantly American. But this is
tricky magic. Despite his racial difference and social status,
something indisputably American about Negroes not only raised
doubts about the white man's value system but aroused the
troubling suspicion that whatever else the true American is, he
is also somehow black.

–RALPH ELLISON
"WHAT AMERICA WOULD BE LIKE WITHOUT BLACKS" (1970)

What happened in Los Angeles in April of 1992 was neither a race riot nor a
class rebellion. Rather, this monumental upheaval was a multiracial, trans-class,
and largely male display of justified social rage. For all its ugly, xenophobic
resentment, its air of adolescent carnival, and its downright barbaric behavior, it
signified the sense of powerlessness in American society. Glib attempts to reduce
its meaning to the pathologies of the black underclass, the criminal actions of
hoodlums, or the political revolt of the oppressed urban masses miss the mark.
Of those arrested, only 36 percent were black, more than a third had full-time
jobs, and most claimed to shun political affiliation. What we witnessed in Los
Angeles was the consequence of a lethal linkage of economic decline, cultural
decay, and political lethargy in American life. Race was the visible catalyst, not
the underlying cause.

626

The meaning of the earthshaking events in Los Angeles is difficult to grasp because most of us remain trapped in the narrow framework of the dominant liberal and conservative views of race in America, which with its worn-out vocabulary leaves us intellectually debilitated, morally disempowered, and personally depressed. The astonishing disappearance of the event from public dialogue is testimony to just how painful and distressing a serious engagement with race is. Our truncated public discussions of race suppress the best of who and what we are as a people because they fail to confront the complexity of the issue in a candid and critical manner. The predictable pitting of liberals against conservatives, Great Society Democrats against self-help Republicans, reinforces intellectual parochialism and political paralysis.

The liberal notion that more government programs can solve racial problems is simplistic—precisely because it focuses *solely* on the economic dimension. And the conservative idea that what is needed is a change in the moral behavior of poor black urban dwellers (especially poor black men, who, they say, should stay married, support their children, and stop committing so much crime) highlights immoral actions while ignoring public responsibility for the immoral circumstances that haunt our fellow citizens.

The common denominator of these views of race is that each still sees black people as a "problem people," in the words of Dorothy I. Height, president of the National Council of Negro Women, rather than as fellow American citizens with problems. Her words echo the poignant "unasked question" of W. E. B. Du Bois, who, in *The Souls of Black Folk* (1903), wrote:

> They approach me in a half-hesitant sort of way, eye me curiously or compassionately, and then instead of saying directly, How does it feel to be a problem? they say, I know an excellent colored man in my town . . . . Do not these Southern outrages make your blood boil? At these I smile, or am interested, or reduce the boiling to a simmer, as the occasion may require. To the real question, How does it feel to be a problem? I answer seldom a word.

Nearly a century later, we confine discussions about race in America to the "problems" black people pose for whites rather than consider what this way of viewing black people reveals about us as a nation.

This paralyzing framework encourages liberals to relieve their guilty consciences by supporting public funds directed at "the problems"; but at the same time, reluctant to exercise principled criticism of black people, liberals deny them the freedom to err. Similarly, conservatives blame the "problems" on black people themselves—and thereby render black social misery invisible or unworthy of public attention.

Hence, for liberals, black people are to be "included" and "integrated" into "our" society and culture, while for conservatives they are to be "well behaved" and "worthy of acceptance" by "our" way of life. Both fail to see that the presence and predicaments of black people are neither additions to nor defections from American life, but rather *constitutive elements of that life*.

To engage in a serious discussion of race in America, we must begin not with the problems of black people but with the flaws of American society—flaws rooted in historic inequalities and longstanding cultural stereotypes. How we set up the terms for discussing racial issues shapes our perception and response to these issues. As long as black people are viewed as a "them," the burden falls on blacks to do all the "cultural" and "moral" work necessary for healthy race relations. The implication is that only certain Americans can define what it means to be American—and the rest must simply "fit in."

The emergence of strong black-nationalist sentiments among blacks, especially among young people, is a revolt against this sense of having to "fit in." The variety of black-nationalist ideologies, from the moderate views of Supreme Court Justice Clarence Thomas in his youth to those of Louis Farrakhan today, rest upon a fundamental truth: White America has been historically weak-willed in ensuring racial justice and has continued to resist fully accepting the humanity of blacks. As long as double standards and differential treatment abound—as long as the rap performer Ice-T is harshly condemned while former Los Angeles Police Chief Daryl F. Gates's antiblack comments are received in polite silence, as long as Dr. Leonard Jeffries's anti-Semitic statements are met with vitriolic outrage while presidential candidate Patrick J. Buchanan's anti-Semitism receives a genteel response—black nationalisms will thrive.

Afrocentrism, a contemporary species of black nationalism, is a gallant yet misguided attempt to define an African identity in a white society perceived to be hostile. It is gallant because it puts black doings and sufferings, not white anxieties and fears, at the center of discussion. It is misguided because—out of fear of cultural hybridization and through silence on the issue of class, retrograde views on black women, gay men, and lesbians, and a reluctance to link race to the common good—it reinforces the narrow discussions about race.

To establish a new framework, we need to begin with a frank acknowledgment of the basic humanness and Americanness of each of us. And we must acknowledge that as a people—*E Pluribus Unum*—we are on a slippery slope toward economic strife, social turmoil, and cultural chaos. If we go down, we go down together. The Los Angeles upheaval forced us to see not only that we are not connected in ways we would like to be but also, in a more profound sense, that this failure to connect binds us even more tightly together. The paradox of race in America is that our common destiny is more pronounced and imperiled precisely when our divisions are deeper. The Civil War and its legacy speak loudly here. And our divisions are growing deeper. Today, eighty-six percent of white suburban Americans live in neighborhoods that are less than one percent black, meaning that the prospects for the country depend largely on how its cities fare in the hands of a suburban electorate. There is no escape from our interracial interdependence, yet enforced racial hierarchy dooms us as a nation to collective paranoia and hysteria—the unmaking of any democratic order.

The verdict in the Rodney King case which sparked the incidents in Los Angeles was perceived to be wrong by the vast majority of Americans. But whites have often failed to acknowledge the widespread mistreatment of black people, especially black men, by law enforcement agencies, which helped ignite the spark. The verdict was merely the occasion for deep-seated rage to come to the surface. This rage is fed by the "silent" depression ravaging the country—in which real weekly wages of all American workers since 1973 have declined nearly twenty percent, while at the same time wealth has been upwardly distributed.

The exodus of stable industrial jobs from urban centers to cheaper labor markets here and abroad, housing policies that have created "chocolate cities and vanilla suburbs" (to use the popular musical artist George Clinton's memorable phrase), white fear of black crime, and the urban influx of poor Spanish-speaking and Asian immigrants—all have helped erode the tax base of American cities just as the federal government has cut its supports and programs. The result is unemployment, hunger, homelessness, and sickness for millions.

And a pervasive spiritual impoverishment grows. The collapse of meaning in life—the eclipse of hope and absence of love of self and others, the breakdown of family and neighborhood bonds—leads to the social deracination and cultural denudement of urban dwellers, especially children. We have created rootless, dangling people with little link to the supportive networks—family, friends, school—that sustain some sense of purpose in life. We have witnessed the collapse of the spiritual communities that in the past helped Americans face despair, disease, and death and that transmit through the generations dignity and decency, excellence and elegance.

The result is lives of what we might call "random nows," of fortuitous and fleeting moments preoccupied with "getting over"—with acquiring pleasure, property, and power by any means necessary. (This is not what Malcolm X meant by this famous phrase.) Post-modern culture is more and more a market culture dominated by gangster mentalities and self-destructive wantonness. This culture engulfs all of us—yet its impact on the disadvantaged is devastating, resulting in extreme violence in everyday life. Sexual violence against women and homicidal assaults by young black men on one another are only the most obvious signs of this empty quest for pleasure, property, and power.

Last, this rage is fueled by a political atmosphere in which images, not ideas, dominate, where politicians spend more time raising money than debating issues. The functions of parties have been displaced by public polls, and politicians behave less as thermostats that determine the climate of opinion than as thermometers registering the public mood. American politics has been rocked by an unleashing of greed among opportunistic public officials—who have followed the lead of their counterparts in the private sphere, where, as of 1989, one percent of the population owned thirty-seven percent of the wealth and ten percent of the population owned eighty-six percent of the wealth—leading to a profound cynicism and pessimism among the citizenry.

And given the way in which the Republican Party since 1968 has appealed to popular xenophobic images—playing the black, female, and homophobic cards to realign the electorate along race, sex, and sexual-orientation lines—it is no surprise that the notion that we are all part of one garment of destiny is discredited. Appeals to special interests rather than to public interests reinforce this polarization. The Los Angeles upheaval was an expression of utter fragmentation by a powerless citizenry that includes not just the poor but all of us.

What is to be done? How do we capture a new spirit and vision to meet the challenges of the post-industrial city, post-modern culture, and post-party politics?

First, we must admit that the most valuable sources for help, hope, and power consist of ourselves and our common history. As in the ages of Lincoln, Roosevelt, and King, we must look to new frameworks and languages to understand our multilayered crisis and overcome our deep malaise.

Second, we must focus our attention on the public square—the common good that undergirds our national and global destinies. The vitality of any public square ultimately depends on how much we *care* about the quality of our lives together. The neglect of our public infrastructure, for example—our water and sewage systems, bridges, tunnels, highways, subways, and streets—reflects not only our myopic economic policies, which impede productivity, but also the low priority we place on our common life.

The tragic plight of our children clearly reveals our deep disregard for public well-being. About one out of every five children in this country lives in poverty, including one out of every two black children and two out of every five Hispanic children. Most of our children—neglected by overburdened parents and bombarded by the market values of profit-hungry corporations—are ill-equipped to live lives of spiritual and cultural quality. Faced with these facts, how do we expect ever to constitute a vibrant society?

One essential step is some form of large-scale public intervention to ensure access to basic social goods—housing, food, health care, education, child care, and jobs. We must invigorate the common good with a mixture of government, business, and labor that does not follow any existing blueprint. After a period in which the private sphere has been sacralized and the public square gutted, the temptation is to make a fetish of the public square. We need to resist such dogmatic swings.

Last, the major challenge is to meet the need to generate new leadership. The paucity of courageous leaders—so apparent in the response to the events in Los Angeles—requires that we look beyond the same elites and voices that recycle the older frameworks. We need leaders—neither saints nor sparkling television personalities—who can situate themselves within a larger historical narrative of this country and our world, who can grasp the complex dynamics of our peoplehood and imagine a future grounded in the best of our past, yet who are attuned to the frightening obstacles that now perplex us. Our ideals of freedom, democracy, and equality must be invoked to invigorate all of us, especially the landless, propertyless, and luckless. Only a visionary leadership that can motivate "the better angels of our nature," as Lincoln said, and activate possibilities for a freer, more efficient, and stable America—only that leadership deserves cultivation and support.

This new leadership must be grounded in grass-roots organizing that highlights democratic accountability. Whoever *our* leaders will be as we approach the twenty-first century, their challenge will be to help Americans determine whether a genuine multiracial democracy can be created and sustained in an era of global economy and a moment of xenophobic frenzy.

Let us hope and pray that the vast intelligence, imagination, humor, and courage of Americans will not fail us. Either we learn a new language of empathy and compassion, or the fire this time will consume us all.

Considerations

Thinking

What, according to West, is "the paradox of race in America"? What does he believe is required for the problems of racial tension to be resolved? Has he omitted anything of importance? What cultural values animate his argument?

Connecting

West begins by referring to the Los Angeles riots of April 1992. How did you respond to learning about those riots in the media? Why?

Compare the argument West makes here—especially what he says about the inadequacies of liberal and conservative positions—with the argument Martin Luther King, Jr., makes in "Letter from Birmingham Jail."

Writing

Write an essay in which you explore your own thoughts and feelings about race in America. You may wish to tell a personal story (or more than one). You may prefer to refer to events such as the Los Angeles riots, civil rights marches or demonstrations of an earlier time, or some other significant public events.

Compare what West says about race in America with what Ralph Ellison suggests about racial difference in the epigraph to West's essay.

Virginia Woolf
(1882–1941)

Virginia Woolf was a brilliant novelist, a distinguished essayist, and an astute critic of literature and of British culture. Her novels include *Jacob's Room, Mrs. Dalloway, To the Lighthouse,* and *The Waves.* There are also five volumes of essays. *Roger Fry: A Biography; Moments of Being,* a collection of autobiographical writings; and *A Room of One's Own,* an expansive exploration about women, writing, and dire circumstance, attest to Woolf's interest in other genres and confirm her genius.

"Old Mrs. Grey" takes us into the land of terror and gives us glimpses of the possibility of peace in death. It conveys its idea through a single story replete with poignant images that inform the idea. "Craftsmanship" entertains us as only a talk can do, teasing us to understand the power of a language that Woolf considers useless for all practical purposes.

Craftsmanship

The title of this series is "Words Fail Me," and this particular talk is called "Craftsmanship." We must suppose, therefore, that the talker is meant to discuss the craft of words—the craftsmanship of the writer. But there is something incongruous, unfitting, about the term "craftsmanship" when applied to words. The English dictionary, to which we always turn in moments of dilemma, confirms us in our doubts. It says that the word "craft" has two meanings; it means in the first place making useful objects out of solid matter—for example, a pot, a chair, a table. In the second place, the word "craft" means cajolery, cunning, deceit. Now we know little that is certain about words, but this we do know—words never make anything that is useful; and words are the only things that tell the truth and nothing but the truth. Therefore, to talk of craft in connexion with words is to bring together two incongruous ideas, which if they mate can only give birth to some monster fit for a glass case in a museum. Instantly, therefore, the title of the talk must be changed, and for its substituted another—A Ramble round Words, perhaps. For when you cut off the head of a talk it behaves like a hen that has been decapitated. It runs round in a circle till it drops dead—so people say who have killed hens. And that must be the course, or circle, of this decapitated talk. Let us then take for our starting point the statement that words are not useful. This happily needs little proving, for we are all aware of it. When we travel on the Tube, for example, when we wait on the platform for a train, there, hung up in front of us, on an illuminated signboard, are the words "Passing Russell Square." We look at those words; we repeat them; we try to impress that useful fact upon our minds; the next train will pass Russell Square. We say over and over again as we pace. "Passing Russell Square, passing Russell Square." And then as we say them, the words shuffle and change, and we find ourselves saying "Passing away saith the world, passing away . . . The leaves decay and fall, the vapours weep their burthen to the ground. Man comes . . ." And then we wake up and find ourselves at King's Cross.

Take another example. Written up opposite us in the railway carriage are the words: "Do not lean out of the window." At the first reading the useful meaning, the surface meaning, is conveyed; but soon, as we sit looking at the words, they shuffle, they change; and we begin saying, "Windows, yes windows—casements opening on the foam of perilous seas in faery lands forlorn." And before we know what we are doing, we have leant out of the window; we are looking for Ruth in tears amid the alien corn. The penalty for that is twenty pounds or a broken neck.

This proves, if it needs proving, how very little natural gift words have for being useful. If we insist on forcing them against their nature to be useful, we see to our cost how they mislead us, how they fool us, how they land us a crack on the head. We have been so often fooled in this way by words, they have so often proved that they hate being useful, that it is their nature not to express one simple statement but a thousand possibilities—they have done this so often that at last, happily, we are beginning to face the fact. We are beginning to invent another language—a language perfectly and beautifully adapted to express useful statements, a language of signs. There is one great living master of this language to whom we are all indebted, that anonymous writer—whether man, woman or disembodied spirit nobody knows—who describes hotels in the Michelin Guide. He wants to tell us that one hotel is moderate, another good, and a third the best in the place. How does he do it? Not with words; words would at once bring into being shrubberies and billiard tables, men and women, the moon rising and the long splash of the summer sea—all good things, but all here beside the point. He sticks to signs; one gable; two gables; three gables. That is all he says and all he needs to say. Baedeker carries the sign language still further into the sublime realms of art. When he wishes to say that a picture is good, he uses one star; if very good, two stars; when, in his opinion, it is a work of transcendent genius, three black stars shine on the page, and that is all. So with a handful of stars and daggers the whole of art criticism, the whole of literary criticism could be reduced to the size of a sixpenny bit—there are moments when one could wish it. But this suggests that in time to come writers will have two languages at their service; one for fact, one for fiction. When the biographer has to convey a useful and necessary fact, as, for example, that Oliver Smith went to college and took a third in the year 1892, he will say so with a hollow O on top of the figure five. When the novelist is forced to inform us that John rang the bell; after a pause the door was opened by a parlourmaid who said, "Mrs. Jones is not at home," he will to our great pain and his own comfort convey that repulsive statement not in words, but in signs—say, a capital H on top of the figure three. Thus we may look forward to the day when our biographies and novels will be slim and muscular; and a railway company that says: "Do not lean out of the window" in words will be fined a penalty not exceeding five pounds for the improper use of language.

Words, then, are not useful. Let us now inquire into their other quality, their positive quality, that is, their power to tell the truth. According once more to the dictionary there are at least three kinds of truth: God's or gospel truth; literary truth; and home truth (generally unflattering). But to consider each separately would take too long. Let us then simplify and assert that since the only test of truth is length of life, and since words survive the chops and changes of time longer than any other substance, therefore they are the truest. Buildings fall; even the earth perishes. What was yesterday a cornfield is today a bungalow. But words, if properly used, seems able to live for ever. What, then, we may ask next, is the proper use of words? Not, so we have said, to make a useful statement; for a useful statement is a statement that can mean only one thing. And it is the nature of words to mean many things. Take the simple sentence "Passing Russell Square." That proved useless because besides the surface meaning it contained so many sunken meanings. The word "passing" suggested the transiency of things, the passing of time and the changes of human life. Then the word "Russell" suggested the rustling of leaves and the skirt on a polished floor; also the ducal house of Bedford and half the history of England. Finally the word "Square" brings in the sight, the shape of an actual square combined with some visual suggestion of the stark angularity of stucco. Thus one sentence of the simplest kind rouses the imagination, the memory, the eye and the ear—all combine in reading it.

But they combine—they combine unconsciously together. The moment we single out and emphasize the suggestions as we have done here they become unreal; and we, too, become unreal—specialists, word mongers, phrase findings, not readers. In reading we have to allow the sunken meanings to remain sunken, suggested, not stated; lapsing and flowing into each other like reeds on the bed of a river. But the words in that sentence—Passing Russell Square—are of course very rudimentary words. They show no trace of the strange, of the diabolical power which words possess when they are not tapped out by a typewriter but comes fresh from a human brain—the power that is to suggest the writer; his character, his appearance, his wife, his family, his house—even the cat on the hearthrug. Why words do this, how they do it, how to prevent them from doing it nobody knows. They do it without the writer's will; often against his will. No writer presumably wishes to impose his own miserable character, his own private secrets and vices upon the reader. But has any writer, who is not a typewriter, succeeded in being wholly impersonal? Always, inevitably, we know them as well as their books. Such is the suggestive power of words that they will often make a bag book into a very lovable human being, and a good book into a man whom we can hardly tolerate in the room. Even words that are hundreds of years old have this power; when they are new they have it so strongly that they deafen us to the writer's meaning—it is them we see, them we hear. That is one reason why our judgments of living writers are so wildly erratic. Only after the writer is dead do his words to some extent become disinfected, purified of the accidents of the living body.

Now, this power of suggestion is one of the most mysterious properties of words. Everyone who has ever written a sentence must be conscious or half-conscious of it. Words, English words, are full of echoes, of memories, of associations—naturally. They have been out and about, on people's lips, in their houses, in the streets, in the fields, for so many centuries. And that is one of the chief difficulties in writing them to-day—that they are so stored with meanings, with memories, that they have contracted so many famous marriages. The splendid word "incarnadine," for example—who can use it without remembering also "multitudinous seas"? In the old days, of course, when English was a new language, writers could invent new words and use them. Nowadays it is easy enough to invent new words—they spring to the lips whenever we see a new sight or feel a new sensation—but we cannot use them because the language is old. You cannot use a brand new word in an old language because of the very obvious yet mysterious fact that a word is not a single and separate entity, but part of other words. It is not a word indeed until it is part of a sentence. Words belong to each other, although, of course, only a great writer knows that the word "incarnadine" belongs to "multitudinous seas." To combine new words with old words is fatal to the constitution of the sentence. In order to use new words properly you would have to invent a new language; and that, though no doubt we shall come to it, is not at the moment our business. Our business is to see what we can do with the English language as it is. How can we combine the old words in new orders so that they survive, so that they create beauty, so that they tell the truth? That is the question.

And the person who could answer that question would deserve whatever crown of glory the world has to offer. Think what it would mean if you could teach, if you could learn, the art of writing. Why, every book, every newspaper would tell the truth, would create beauty. But there is, it would appear, some obstacle in the way, some hindrance to the teaching of words. For though at this moment at least a hundred professors are lecturing upon the literature of the past, at least a thousand critics are reviewing the literature of the present, and hundreds upon hundreds of young men and women are passing examinations in English literature with the utmost credit, still—do we write better, do we read better than we read and wrote four hundred years ago when we were unlectured, uncriticized, untaught? Is our Georgian literature a patch on the Elizabethan? Where then are we to lay the blame? Not on our professors; not on our reviewers; not on our writers; but on words. It is words that are to blame. They are the wildest, freest, most irresponsible, most unteachable of all things. Of course, you can catch them and sort them and place them in alphabetical order in dictionaries. But words do not live in dictionaries; they live in the mind. If you want proof of this, consider how often in moments of emotion when we most need words we find none. Yet there is the dictionary; there at our disposal are some half a million words all in alphabetical order. But can we use them? No, because words do not live in dictionaries; they live in the mind. Look again at the dictionary. There beyond a doubt lie plays more splendid than *Antony and Cleopatra;* poems more lovely than the *Ode to a Nightingale;* novels beside which *Pride and Prejudice* or *David Copperfield* are the crude bunglings of amateurs. It is only a question of finding the right words and putting them in the right order. But we cannot do it because they do not live in dictionaries; they live in the mind. And how do they live in the mind? Variously and strangely, much as human beings live, by ranging hither and thither, by falling in love, and mating together., It is true that they are much less bound by ceremony and convention than we are. Royal words mate with commoners. English words marry French words, German words, Indian words, Negro words, if they have a fancy. Indeed, the less we inquire into the past of our dear Mother English the better it will be for that lady's reputation. For she has gone a-roving, a-roving fair maid.

Thus to lay down any laws for such irreclaimable vagabonds is worse than useless. A few trifling rules of grammar and spelling are all the constraint we can put on them. All we can say about them, as we peer at them over the edge of that deep, dark and fitfully illuminated cavern in which they live—the mind—all we can say about them is that they seem to like people to think and to feel before they use them, but to think and to feel not about then, but about something different. They are highly sensitive, easily made self-conscious. They do not like to have their purity or their impurity discussed. If you start a Society for Pure English, they will show their resentment by starting another for impure English—hence the unnatural violence of much modern speech; it is a protest against the puritans. They are highly democratic, too; they believe that one word is as good as another; uneducated words are as good as educated words, uncultivated words as cultivated words, there are no ranks or titles in their society. Nor do they like being lifted out on the point of a pen and examined separately. They hang together, in sentences, in paragraphs, sometimes for whole pages at a time. They hate being useful; they hate making money; they hate being lectured about in public. In short, they hate anything that stamps them with one meaning or confines them to one attitude, for it is their nature to change.

Perhaps that is their most striking peculiarity—their need of change. It is because the truth they try to catch is many-sided, and they convey it by being themselves many-sided, flashing this way, then that. Thus they mean one thing to one person, another thing to another person; they are unintelligible to one generation, plain as a pikestaff to the next. And it is because of this complexity that they survive. Perhaps then one reason why we have no great poet, novelist, or critic writing today is that we refuse words their liberty. We pin them down to one meaning, their useful meaning, the meaning which makes us catch the train, the meaning which makes us pass the examination. And when words are pinned down they fold their wings and die. Finally, and most emphatically, words, like ourselves, in order to live at their ease, need privacy. Undoubtedly they like us to think, and they like us to feel, before we use them; but they also like us to pause; to become unconscious. Our unconsciousness is their privacy; our darkness is their light . . . That pause was made, that veil of darkness was dropped, to tempt words to come together in one of those swift marriages which are perfect images and create everlasting beauty. But no—nothing of that sort is going to happen tonight. The little wretches are out of temper; disobliging; disobedient; dumb. What is it that they are muttering? "Time's up! Silence!"

Considerations

Thinking

In your own words, explain why Woolf changed the title of her talk from "Craftsmanship" to "A Ramble round Words." Do you think Woolf is telling the truth, or do you think she's just charming her listeners? Why?

What is the difference between "the useful meaning, the surface meaning" and those other meanings Woolf teases us with, what she later calls "sunken meanings"?

What do you think is Woolf's attitude about the "power of suggestion" that words have? Show us how that attitude is reflected in her own words.

Connecting

Look at either of Gretel Ehrlich's essays in this anthology and consider how Woolf's idea about "sunken meanings" might apply to Ehrlich's use of language.

Go out into your community and investigate the language of signs. Does the language behave, proving itself utilitarian, or does it set your mind off on alien trips? Explain, being as specific as possible.

Writing

Consider these three questions? What lessons can you as a writer learn from Woolf's playful discussion about the life that words live in the mind? What do you make of Woolf's final consideration of "unconsciousness?" What do we as writers have to give up momentarily to let words have their play in the unconscious? Write a short response to each of these questions. Wait a day, then see if you can condense and combine your responses into one paragraph that *reveals* what you think Woolf means about the value of language.

"Craftsmanship" was written to be read aloud, over the radio. Read next "Old Mrs. Grey" to see how it differs from "Craftsmanship." Prepare a short analysis for the class accounting for your findings.

Write a paragraph or two about the relationship between Woolf's ideas in paragraphs 4 and 5 of "Craftsmanship" and the idea Didion expresses in "Georgia O'Keeffe" relating to style as character (pp. 200–202).

Old Mrs. Grey

Virginia Woolf

There are moments even in England, now, when even the busiest, most contented suddenly let fall what they hold—it may be the week's washing. Sheets and pyjamas crumble and dissolve in their hands, because, though they do not state this in so many words, it seems silly to take the washing round to Mrs. Peel when out there over the fields over the hills, there is no washing; no pinning of clotheslines; mangling and ironing; no work at all, but boundless rest. Stainless and boundless rest; space unlimited; untrodden grass; wild birds flying; hills whose smooth uprise continues that wild flight.

Of all this however only seven foot by four could be seen from Mrs. Grey's corner. That was the size of her front door which stood wide open, though there was a fire burning in the grate. The fire looked like a small spot of dusty light feebly trying to escape from the embarrassing pressure of the pouring sunshine.

Mrs. Grey sat on a hard chair in the corner looking—but at what? Apparently at nothing. She did not change the focus of her eyes when visitors came in. Her eyes had ceased to focus themselves; it may be that they had lost the power. They were aged eyes, blue, unspectacled. They could see, but without looking. She had never used her eyes on anything minute and difficult; merely upon faces, and dishes and fields. And now at the age of ninety-two they saw nothing but a zigzag of pain wriggling across the door, pain that twisted her legs as it wriggled; jerked her body to and fro like a marionette. Her body was wrapped round the pain as a damp sheet is folded over a wire. The wire was spasmodically jerked by a cruel invisible hand. She flung out a foot, a hand. Then it stopped. She sat still for a moment.

In that pause she saw herself in the past at ten, at twenty, at twenty-five. She was running in and out of a cottage with eleven brothers and sisters. The line jerked. She was thrown forward in her chair.

"All dead. All dead," she mumbled. "My brothers and sisters. And my husband gone. My daughter too. But I go on. Every morning I pray God to let me pass."

The morning spread seven foot by four green and sunny. Like a fling of grain the birds settled on the land. She was jerked again by another tweak of the tormenting hand.

"I'm an ignorant old woman. I can't read or write, and every morning when I crawls downstairs, I say I wish it were night; and every night, when I crawls up to bed, I say I wish it were day. I'm only an ignorant old woman. But I prays to God: O let me pass. I'm an ignorant old woman—I can't read or write."

So when the colour went out of the doorway, she could not see the other page which is then lit up; or hear the voices that have argued, sung, talked for hundreds of years.

The jerked limbs were still again.

"The doctor comes every week. The parish doctor now. Since my daughter went, we can't afford Dr. Nicholls. But he's a good man. He says he wonders I don't go. He says my heart's nothing but wind and water. Yet I don't seem able to die."

So we—humanity—insist that the body shall still cling to the wire. We put out the eyes and the ears; but we pinion it there, with a bottle of medicine, a cup of tea, a dying fire, like a rook on a barn door; but a rook that still lives, even with a nail through it.

Considerations

Thinking

What is this essay's implicit argument?

Why do you suppose Woolf lets us hear Mrs. Grey talk?

Why does Woolf take us inside Mrs. Grey's house and let us see the "morning spread seven foot by four green and sunny"?

Connecting

Make a list of the images in the essay. How do those images help you understand Woolf's idea?

Go to the library and find a reproduction of René Magritte's painting *The Human Condition I*. How does that painting help you understand Mrs. Grey's condition?

Writing

Write a short, speculative account of what you think Woolf would have "us" do about the Mrs. Greys of the world.

Visit someone in the hospital or in a nursing home; then write an essay about that person's predicament.

Write an essay in which you argue for or against euthanasia.

Jeanette Winterson
(b. 1959)

Jeanette Winterson, adopted as a child, was raised in an evangelical atmosphere in Manchester, England. She graduated from St. Catherine's College, Oxford. Later, she won the 1985 Whitbread Prize for best first fiction (*Oranges Are Not the Only Fruit*). Her third novel, *The Passion,* won the John Llewelyn Rhys Prize, and *Sexing the Cherry* won the American Academy of Arts and Letters' E. M. Forster Award. Other works include *Written on the Body, Art & Lies, The World and Other Places, Gut Symmetries,* and *Art Objects: Essays on Ecstasy and Effrontery.* She lives in the English countryside outside London.

In "The Semiotics of Sex," from *Art Objects,* Winterson raises serious questions about the relationship between a writer's life and her art, as she develops interesting ideas about what constitutes art.

The Semiotics of Sex

I was in a bookshop recently when a young woman approached me.
She told me she was writing an essay on my work and that of Radclyffe Hall.
Could I help?
"Yes," I said. "Our work has nothing in common."
"I thought you were a lesbian," she said.

I have become aware that the chosen sexual difference of one writer is, in itself, thought sufficient to bind her in semiotic sisterhood with any other writer, also lesbian, dead or alive.

I am, after all, a pervert, so I will not mind sharing a bed with a dead body. This bed in the shape of a book, this book in the shape of a bed, must accommodate us every one, because, whatever our style, philosophy, class, age, preoccupations and talent, we are lesbians and isn't that the golden key to the single door of our work?

In any discussion of art and the artist, heterosexuality is backgrounded, whilst homosexuality is foregrounded. What you fuck is much more important than how you write. This may be because reading takes more effort than sex. It may be because the word "sex" is more exciting than the word "book." Or is it? Surely that depends on what kind of sex and what kind of book? I can only assume that straight sex is so dull that even a book makes better reportage. No one asks Iris Murdoch about her sex life. Every interviewer I meet asks me about mine and what they do not ask they invent. I am a writer who happens to love women. I am not a lesbian who happens to write.

What is it about? Prurience? Stupidity? And as Descartes didn't say, "I fuck therefore I am."? The straight world is wilful in its pursuit of queers and it seems to me that to continually ask someone about their homosexuality, when the reason to talk is a book, a picture, a play, is harassment by the back door.

The Queer world has colluded in the misreading of art as sexuality. Art is difference, but not necessarily sexual difference, and while to be outside of the mainstream of imposed choice is likely to make someone more conscious, it does not automatically make that someone an artist. A great deal of gay writing, especially gay writing around the Aids crisis, is therapy, is release, is not art. It is its subject matter and no more and I hope by now that I have convinced my readers in these essays, that all art, including literature, is much more than its subject matter. It is true that a number of gay and lesbian writers have attracted an audience and some attention simply because they are queer. Lesbians and gays do need their own culture, as any sub-group does, including the sub-group of heterosexuality, but the problems start when we assume that the fact of our queerness bestows on us special powers. It might make for certain advantages (it is helpful for a woman artist not to have a husband) but it cannot, of itself, guarantee art. Lesbians and gay men, who have to examine so much of what the straight world takes for granted, must keep on examining their own standards in all things, and especially the standards we set for our own work.

I think this is particularly urgent where fiction and poetry are concerned and where it is most tempting to assume that the autobiography of Difference will be enough.

Let me put it another way: if I am in love with Peggy and I am a composer I can express that love in an ensemble or a symphony. If I am in love with Peggy and I am a painter, I need not paint her portrait, I am free to express my passion in splendid harmonies of colour and line. If I am a writer, I will have to be careful, I must not fall into the trap of believing that my passion, of itself, is art. As a composer or a painter I know that it is not. I know that I shall have to find a translation of form to make myself clear. I know that the language of my passion and the language of my art are not the same thing.

Of course there is a paradox here; the most powerful written work often masquerades as autobiography. It offers itself as raw when in fact it is sophisticated. It presents itself as a kind of diary when really it is an oration. The best work speaks intimately to you even though it has been consciously made to speak intimately to thousands of others. The bad writer believes that sincerity of feeling will be enough, and pins her faith on the power of experience. The true writer knows that feeling must give way to form. It is through the form, not in spite of, or accidental to it, that the most powerful emotions are let loose over the greatest number of people.

Art must resist autobiography if it hopes to cross boundaries of class, culture . . . and . . . sexuality. Literature is not a lecture delivered to a special interest group, it is a force that unites its audience. The sub-groups are broken down.

How each artist learns to translate autobiography into art is a problem that each artist solves for themselves. When solved, unpicking is impossible, we cannot work backwards from the finished text into its raw material. The commonest mistake of critics and biographers is to assume that what holds significance for them necessarily held significance for the writer. Forcing the work back into autobiography is a way of trying to contain it, of making what has become unlike anything else into what is just like everything else. It may be that in the modern world, afraid of feeling, it is more comfortable to turn the critical gaze away from a fully realised piece of work. It is always easier to focus on sex. The sexuality of the writer is a wonderful diversion.

If Queer culture is now working against assumptions of identity as sexuality, art goes there first, by implicitly or explicitly creating emotion around the forbidden. Some of the early feminist arguments surrounding the wrongfulness of men painting provocative female nudes seem to me to have overlooked the possibility or the fact of another female as the viewer. Why should she identify with the nude? What deep taboos make her unable to desire the nude?

Opera, before and after the nineteenth century, but not during, enjoyed serious games of sexual ambiguity, and opera fans will know the delicious and disturbing pleasure of watching a woman disguised as a man and hearing her woo another woman with a voice unmistakably female. Our opera ancestors knew the now forbidden pleasure of listening to a man sing as a woman; in his diary, Casanova writes of the fascination and desire felt for these compromising creatures by otherwise heterosexual men. Music is androgynously sexy and with the same sensuous determination penetrates male and female alike. Unless of course one resists it, and how much sex-resistance goes on under the lie of "I don't like opera"?

Similarly, I am sure that a lot of the coyness and silliness that accompanies productions of Shakespeare that include cross-dressing roles, is an attempt to steer them clear of Queer. As long as we all know that a pretence is happening; the pretence of Principal Boy or music-hall camp, we are safe in our het-suits. Too many directors overlook the obvious fact that in Shakespeare, the disguises are meant to convince. They are not a comedian's joke. We too must fall in love. We too must know what it is to find that we have desired another woman, desired another man. And should we really take at face value those fifth acts where everyone simply swops their partner to the proper sex and goes home to live happily ever after?

I am not suggesting that we should all part with our husbands and live Queer.

I am not suggesting that a lesbian who recognises desire for a man sleep with him. We need not be so crude. What we do need is to accept in ourselves, with pleasure, the subtle and various emotions that are the infinity of a human being. More, not less, is the capacity of the heart. More not less is the capacity of art.

Art coaxes out of us emotions we normally do not feel. It is not that art sets out to shock (that is rare), it is rather that art occupies ground unconquered by social niceties. Seeking neither to please nor to displease, art works to enlarge emotional possibility. In a dead society that inevitably puts it on the side of the rebels. Do not mistake me, I am not of the voting party of bohemians and bad boys, and the rebelliousness of art does not make every rebel an artist. The rebellion of art is a daily rebellion against the state of living death routinely called real life.

Where every public decision has to be justified in the scale of corporate profit, poetry unsettles these apparently self-evident propositions, not through ideology, but by its very presence and ways of being, its embodiment of states of longing and desire.

ADRIENNE RICH, *WHAT IS FOUND THERE:*
NOTEBOOKS ON POETRY AND POLITICS (1993)

And not only public decisions but also private compromises. Calculations of the heart that should never be made. It is through the acceptance of breakdown; breakdown of fellowship, of trust, of community, of communication, of language, of love, that we begin to break down ourselves, a fragmented society afraid of feeling.

Against this fear, art is fresh healing and fresh pain. The rebel writer who brings healing and pain, need not be a Marxist or a Socialist, need not be political in the journalistic sense and may fail the shifting tests of Correctness, while standing as a rebuke to the hollowed out days and as a refuge for our stray hearts. Communist and People's Man, Stephen Spender, had the right credentials, but Catholic and cultural reactionary T. S. Eliot made the poetry. It is not always so paradoxical but it can be, and the above example should be reason enough not to judge the work by the writer. Judge the writer by the work.

When I read Adrienne Rich or Oscar Wilde, rebels of very different types, the fact of their homosexuality should not be uppermost. I am not reading their work to get at their private lives. I am reading their work because I need the depth-charge it carries.

Their formal significance, the strength of their images, their fidelity to language makes it possible for them to reach me across distance and time. If each were not an exceptional writer, neither would be able to reach beyond the interests of their own sub-group. The truth is that both have an audience who do not share the sexuality of the subversiveness of playwright and poet but who cannot fail to be affected by those elements when they read Rich and Wilde. Art succeeds where polemic fails.

Nevertheless, there are plenty of heterosexual readers who won't touch books by Queers and plenty of Queer readers who are only out to scan a bent kiss. We all know of men who won't read books by women and in spite of the backlash that dresses this up in high sounding notions of creativity, it is ordinary terror of difference. Men do not feel comfortable looking at the world through eyes that are not male. It has nothing to do with sentences or syntax, it is sexism by any other name. It would be a pity if lesbians and gay men retreated into the same kind of cultural separatism. We learn early how to live in two words; our own and that of the dominant model, why not learn how to live in multiple worlds? The strange prismatic worlds that art offers? I do not want to read only books by women, only books by Queers, I want all that there is, so long as it is genuine and it seems to me that to choose our reading matter according to the sex and/or sexuality of the writer is a dismal way to read. For lesbians and gay men it has been vital to create our own counter-culture but that does not mean that there is nothing in straight culture that we can use. We are more sophisticated than that and it is worth remembering that the conventional mind is its own prison.

The man who won't read Virginia Woolf, the lesbian who won't touch T. S. Eliot, are both putting subjective concerns in between themselves and the work. Literature, whether made by heterosexuals or homosexuals, whether to do with lives gay or straight, packs in it supplies of energy and emotion that all of us need. Obviously if a thing is not art, we will not get any artistic pleasure out of it and we will find it void of the kind of energy and emotion we can draw on indefinitely. It is difficult, when we are surrounded by trivia makers and trivia merchants, all claiming for themselves the power of art, not to fall for the lie that there is no such thing or that it is anything. The smallness of it all is depressing and it is inevitable that we will have to whip out the magnifying glass of our own interests to bring the thing up to size. "Is it about me?" "Is it amusing?" "Is it dirty?" "What about the sex?" are not aesthetic questions but they are the questions asked by most reviewers and by most readers most of the time. Unless we setup criteria of judgement that are relevant to literature, and not to sociology, entertainment, topicality etc., we are going to find it harder and harder to know what it is that separates art from everything else.

Learning to read is more than learning to group the letters on a page. Learning to read is a skill that marshals the entire resources of body and mind. I do not mean the endless dross-skimming that passes for literacy, I mean the ability to engage with a text as you would another human being. To recognise it in its own right, separate, particular, to let it speak in its own voice, not in a ventriloquism of yours. To find its relationship to you that is not its relationship to anyone else. To recognise, at the same time, that you are neither the means nor the method of its existence and that the love between you is not a mutual suicide. The love between you offers an alternative paradigm; a complete and fully realised vision in a chaotic unrealised world. Art is not amnesia, and the popular idea of books as escapism or diversion, misses altogether what art is. There is plenty of escapism and diversion to be had, but it cannot be had from real books, real pictures, real music, real theatre. Art is the realisation of complex emotion.

We value sensitive machines. We spend billions of pounds to make them more sensitive yet, so that they detect minerals deep in the earth's crust, radioactivity thousands of miles away. We don't value sensitive human beings and we spend no money on their priority. As machines become more delicate and human beings coarser, will antennae and fibreoptic claim for themselves what was uniquely human? Not rationality, not logic, but that strange network of fragile perception, that means I can imagine, that teaches me to love, a lodging of recognition and tenderness where I sometimes know the essential beat that rhythms life.

The artist as radar can help me. The artist who combines an exceptional sensibility with an exceptional control over her material. This equipment, unfunded, unregarded, gift and discipline kept tuned to untapped frequencies, will bring home signals otherwise lost to me. Will make for my ears and eyes what was the proper of the hawk. This sharpness and stretch of wings has not in it the comfort of escape. It has in it warnings and chances and painful beauty. It is not what I know and it is not what I am. The mirror turns out to be a through looking-glass, and beyond are places I have never reached. Once reached there is no need to leave them again. Art is not tourism it is an ever-expanding territory. Art is not Capitalism, what I find in it, I may keep. The title takes my name.

The realisation of complex emotion.

Complex emotion is pivoted around the forbidden. When I feel the complexities of a situation I am feeling the many-sidedness of it, not the obvious smooth shape, grasped at once and easily forgotten. Complexity leads to perplexity. I do not know my place. There is a clash between what I feel and what I had expected to feel. My logical self fails me, and no matter how I try to pace it out, there is still something left over that will not be accounted for. All of us have felt like this, all of us have tried to make the rough places smooth; to reason our way out of a gathering storm. Usually dishonesty is our best guide. We call inner turbulence "blowing things up out of all proportion." We call it "seven-year itch." We call it "over-tiredness." Like Adam we name our beasts, but not well, and we find they do not come when called.

Complex emotion often follows some major event in our lives; sex, falling in love, birth, death, are the commonest and in each of these potencies are strong taboos. The striking loneliness of the individual when confronted with these large happenings that we all share, is a loneliness of displacement. The person is thrown out of the normal groove of their life and whilst they stumble, they also have to carry a new weight of feeling, feeling that threatens to overwhelm them. Consequences of misery and breakdown are typical and in a repressive society that pretends to be liberal, misery and breakdown can be used as subtle punishments for what we no longer dare legislate against. Inability to cope is defined as a serious weakness in a macho culture like ours, but what is inability to cope, except a spasmodic, faint and fainter protest against a closed-in drugged-up life where suburban values are touted as the greatest good? A newborn child, the moment of falling in love, can cause in us seismic shocks that will, if we let them, help to re-evaluate what things matter, what things we take for granted. This is frightening, and as we get older it is harder to face such risks to the deadness that we are. Art offers the challenge we desire but also the shape we need when our own world seems most shapeless. The formal beauty of art is threat and relief to the formless neutrality of unrealised life.

"Ah" you will say, "She means Art as Consolation. The lonely romantic who reads Jane Eyre. The computer misfit wandering with Wordsworth."

I do not think of art as Consolation. I think of it as Creation. I think of it as an energetic space that begets energetic space. Works of art do not reproduce themselves, they re-create themselves and have at the same time sufficient permanent power to create rooms for us, the dispossessed. In other words, art makes it possible to live in energetic space.

When I talk about creating emotion around the forbidden, I do not mean disgust around the well known. Forget the lowlife, tourist, squeaky clean middle-class bad boys who call their sex-depravity in blunt prose, fine writing. Forget the copycat girls who wouldn't know the end of a dildo from a vacuum rod. They are only chintz dipped in mud and we are after real material. What is forbidden is scarier, sexier, unnightmared by the white-collar cataloguers of crap. "Don't do that" makes for easy revolt. What is forbidden is hidden. To worm into the heart and mind until what one truly desires has been encased in dark walls of what one ought to desire, is the success of the serpent. Serpents of state, serpents of religion, serpents in the service of education, monied serpents, mythic serpents, weaving their lies backwards into history. Two myths out of many: the first, Hebrew: Eve in the garden persuaded to eat that which she has never desired to eat ("The serpent bade me eat"). The second, Greek: Medusa, the Gorgon, whose serpent hair turns all who look on her to stone.

There are many ways of reading these myths, that is the way with myths, but for the purposes of this argument, I want us to be wary of bodies insinuated to desire what they do not desire and of hearts turned to stone.

How can I know what I feel? When a writer asks herself that question she will have to find the words to answer it, even if the answer is another question. The writer will have to make her words into a true equivalent of her heart. If she cannot, if she can only hazard at the heart, arbitrarily temporarily, she may be a psychologist but she will not be a poet.

It is the poet who goes further than any human scientist. The poet who with her dredging net must haul up difficult things and return them to the present. As she does this, the reader will begin to recognise parts of herself so neatly buried that they seem to have been buried from birth. She will be able to hear clearly the voices that have whispered at her for so many years. Some of those voices will prove false, she will perhaps learn to fear her own fears. The attendant personalities that are clinically labelled as schizophrenia, can be brought into a harmonious balance. It is not necessary to be shut up in one self, to grind through life like an ox at a mill, always treading the same ground. Human beings are capable of powered flight; we can travel across ourselves and find that self multiple and vast. The artist knows this; at the same time that art is prising away old dead structures that have rusted almost unnoticed into our flesh, art is pushing at the boundaries we thought were fixed. The convenient lies fall; the only boundaries are the boundaries of our imagination.

How much can we imagine? The artist is an imaginer. The artist imagines the forbidden because to her it is not forbidden. If she is freer than other people it is the freedom of her single allegiance to her work. Most of us have divided loyalties, most of us have sold ourselves. The artist is not divided and she is not for sale. Her clarity of purpose protects her although it is her clarity of purpose that is most likely to irritate most people. We are not happy with obsessives, visionaries, which means, in effect, that we are not happy with artists. Why do we flee from feeling? Why do we celebrate those who lower us in the mire of their own making while we hound those who come to us with hands full of difficult beauty?

If we could imagine ourselves out of despair?

If we could imagine ourselves out of helplessness?

What would happen if we could imagine in ourselves authentic desire?

What would happen if one woman told the truth about herself? The world would split open.

MURIEL RUKEYSER

In search of this truth, beyond the fear of the consequences of this truth, are the flight-maps of art. When truth is at stake, and in a society that desperately needs truth, we have to be wary of those side-tracks to nowhere that mislead us from the journey we need to make. There are plenty of Last Days signposts to persuade us that nothing is worth doing and that each one of us lives in a private nightmare occasionally relieved by temporary pleasure.

Art is not a private nightmare, not even a private dream, it is a shared human connection that traces the possibilities of past and future in the whorl of now. It is a construct, like science, like religion, like the world itself. It is as artificial as you and me and as natural too. We have never been able to live without it, we have never been able to live with it. We claim it makes no difference whilst nervously barring it out of our lives. Part of this barring is to gender it, to sex it, to find ways of containing and reducing this fascinating fear. But to what are our efforts directed? What is it that we seek to mock and discourage? It is the human spirit free.

I was in a bookshop recently and a young man came up to me and said "Is *Sexing the Cherry* a reading of *Four Quartets*?"
"Yes," I said, and he kissed me.

Considerations

Thinking

What do you suppose Winterson means when she urges us to "learn how to live in multiple worlds"?

What is the problem with too great a reliance on "rationality" as Winterson sees it?

Is it true that only music can be "androgynously sexy"? Or can other forms of art have it both ways, perhaps with more difficulty? Explain.

Connecting

What do you think Winterson would make of the ideas E. M. Forster expresses about art in "Not Looking at Pictures"?

Compare Winterson's ideas about truth with those expressed by Virginia Woolf in "Craftsmanship." Begin by looking at the lines Winterson quotes from Muriel Rukeyser: "What would happen if one woman told the truth about herself? The world would split open." Then consider whether Winterson and Woolf are pointing toward the same kind of truth. Taking up your journal, try to explain your findings to yourself.

Writing

Go through Winterson's essay and make a catalog of what she might be willing to call "Aspects of Art"—qualities that distinguish art from other things. After compiling your list, write a short essay about what you consider art to be. Use Winterson to help you make your case, but use as well whatever knowledge you have or acquire about art (art of your choosing) just by looking at it and thinking about it.

Imagine and construct a short exchange among Winterson, Virginia Woolf, and Sven Birkerts on the subject of "reading." You can make up the language of exchange if you wish, but it should be based on your own careful reading of the three essayists.

Consider these sentences of Winterson's:

The bad writer believes that sincerity of feeling will be enough, and pins her faith on the power of experience. The true writer knows that feeling must give way to form. It is through the form, not in spite of, or accidental to it, that the most powerful emotions are let loose over the greatest number of people.

What do you think Winterson means by *form,* and how does form let "loose" those "powerful emotions"? Write a page or two of speculation about these questions that Winterson doesn't answer.

STUDENTS RESPOND TO THREE PROFESSIONAL WRITERS IN DEPTH

One advantage of reading more than a single essay by a writer is that you can see how a writer approaches different subjects and how that writer varies his or her approach to the same subject. We have selected three essays each by Maxine Hong Kingston, Richard Selzer, and E. B. White, all of whom write about their experiences. Kingston describes her cultural experience as an Asian American woman of Chinese ancestry. Relevant also is the fact that she is a woman writing about women. Richard Selzer writes about his experiences as a surgeon. E. B. White describes episodes from his life that lead him to reflect on issues of time and change and mortality. All three writers use personal experience as evidence in developing their ideas.

Kingston, Selzer, and White explore in their essays issues and questions that haunt them. Even though Kingston's three pieces have different topics, their concern with race, gender, and culture overlap. Selzer's three pieces focus on matters related to surgery, mystery, coincidence, compassion. White's essays seem completely different from one another at first glance, but they too contain overlapping ideas and concerns that echo and reverberate from one essay to another. One way of reading the work of each writer is to look to see how each piece echoes and speaks to other pieces.

For each writer, we have included an introduction that sets their essays in the context of their lives and their writing. Student essays follow the work of these professional writers—three analytical essays based on Maxine Hong Kingston's "On Discovery," two based on Richard Selzer's essays, and three research essays based on the writings of E. B. White.

Maxine Hong Kingston
(b. 1940)

Although she had a novel published in 1989 (*Tripmaster Monkey: His Fake Book*), Maxine Hong Kingston is best known for her earlier mixed-genre works, *The Woman Warrior* (1976) and *China Men* (1980), winner of the American Book Award. Kingston has described the earlier work as the book of her mother since it is filled with stories her mother told her, stories about Chinese women, her Asian ancestors whom Kingston describes as the ghosts of her girlhood. *China Men,* by contrast, is her father's book since it tells the stories of her male ancestors, including her father and grandfathers—though she learned these male stories too from women, especially from her mother. Both books are filled with stories. Both mix fact and fiction, autobiography and legend, combining in imaginative ways family history with fictional invention.

Kingston's books are, thus, difficult to classify. They refuse to sit still and accept the tidy categories we devise for prose narrative. The selections excerpted here from these two family chronicles reflect the curious and striking effects Kingston achieves throughout them with her blending of myth and legend with autobiography and family history. Moreover, in addition to their provocative combinations of fact and fiction, the two books possess another striking quality: their compelling voices. Kingston's narratives retell heard stories, stories told *by* her and stories told *to* her. Her stories derive from an oral tradition—the "talk story"—sustained largely by Chinese women. Kingston thus simultaneously inherits this oral narrative tradition and participates in it. Perhaps even more importantly, however, by inscribing her mother's stories and imagining her own variants of them, Kingston marks that tradition with her own distinctive imaginative imprint. In doing so, she demonstrates the power of these stories to enthrall readers outside the Chinese cultural tradition.

Maxine Hong Kingston was born and raised in Stockton, California, where her immigrant parents operated a laundry. She graduated from the University of California at Berkeley in 1962, and she has taught high school and college English, primarily in Hawaii, where she lived for seventeen years before moving to Oakland, California.

Kingston's autobiographical impulse appears strongly in "Silence," an excerpt from *The Woman Warrior.* In "Silence," we see Kingston begin to negotiate the struggle between the Chinese culture she inherited and the American culture she was born into. Her silence powerfully illustrates her uncertainty about how to invoke one cultural perspective without revoking or violating the other.

Kingston's versatility in letting the voices of others speak through her is powerfully manifested in "No Name Woman," the opening section of *The Woman Warrior.* As Esther Schor has pointed out in *Women's Voices,* the first voice we hear in "No Name Woman" is the voice of her mother, who "ironically . . . admonishes the daughter to silence even as she nourishes her with stories." Kingston's instincts as a writer are revealed not only in the stories she chooses to tell, but in the voices she creates to tell them. This is as true for the multiple voices we hear in "No Name Woman" as for the singularly different voices that sound in the other tales Kingston narrates in both books, including the brief parable, "On Discovery," which turns gender role and power inside out.

To some extent, Kingston is a woman's writer precisely because she gives public voice to what women had spoken only in private or what they had to keep silent. To some extent, she is also an ethnic writer, one who transmits stories of her Cantonese heritage. Her artistry and imaginative sympathy, however, transcend the limits of both gender and culture, as Kingston invents a world and constructs a self that appear both strange and familiar, at once "other" and recognizably our own.

No Name Woman

"You must not tell anyone," my mother said, "what I am about to tell you. In China your father had a sister who killed herself. She jumped into the family well. We say that your father has all brothers because it is as if she had never been born.

"In 1924 just a few days after our village celebrated seventeen hurry-up weddings—to make sure that every young man who went 'out on the road' would responsibly come home—your father and his brothers and your grandfather and his brothers and your aunt's new husband sailed for America, the Gold Mountain. It was your grandfather's last trip. Those lucky enough to get contracts waved good-bye from the decks. They fed and guarded the stowaways and helped them off in Cuba, New York, Bali, Hawaii. 'We'll meet in California next year,' they said. All of them sent money home.

"I remember looking at your aunt one day when she and I were dressing; I had not noticed before that she had such a protruding melon of a stomach. But I did not think, 'She's pregnant,' until she began to look like other pregnant women, her shirt pulling and the white tops of her black pants showing. She could not have been pregnant, you see, because her husband had been gone for years. No one said anything. We did not discuss it. In early summer she was ready to have the child, long after the time when it could have been possible.

"The village had also been counting. On the night the baby was to be born the villagers raided our house. Some were crying. Like a great saw, teeth strung with lights, files of people walked zigzag across our land, tearing the rice. Their lanterns doubled in the disturbed black water, which drained away through the broken bunds. As the villagers closed in, we could see that some of them, probably men and women we knew well, wore white masks. The people with long hair hung it over their faces. Women with short hair made it stand up on end. Some had tied white bands around their foreheads, arms, and legs.

"At first they threw mud and rocks at the house. Then they threw eggs and began slaughtering our stock. We could hear the animals scream their deaths—the roosters, the pigs, a last great roar from the ox. Familiar wild heads flared in our night windows; the villagers encircled us. Some of the faces stopped to peer at us, their eyes rushing like searchlights. The hands flattened against the panes, framed heads, and left red prints.

"The villagers broke in the front and the back doors at the same time, even though we had not locked the doors against them. Their knives dripped with the blood of our animals. They smeared blood on the doors and walls. One woman swung a chicken, whose throat she had slit, splattering blood in red arcs about her. We stood together in the middle of our house, in the family hall with the pictures and tables of the ancestors around us, and looked straight ahead.

"At that time the house had only two wings. When the men came back we would build two more to enclose our courtyard and a third one to begin a second courtyard. The villagers pushed through both wings, even your grandparents' rooms, to find your aunt's, which was also mine until the men returned. From this room a new wing for one of the younger families would grow. They ripped up her clothes and shoes and broke her combs, grinding them underfoot. They tore her work from the loom. They scattered the cooking fire and rolled the new weaving in it. We could hear them in the kitchen breaking our bowls and banging the pots. They overturned the great waist-high earthenware jugs; duck eggs, pickled fruits, vegetables burst out and mixed in acrid torrents. The old woman from the next field swept a broom through the air and loosed the spirits-of-the-broom over our heads. 'Pig.' 'Ghost.' 'Pig,' they sobbed and scolded while they ruined our house.

"When they left, they took sugar and oranges to bless themselves. They cut pieces from the dead animals. Some of them took bowls that were not broken and clothes that were not torn. Afterward we swept up the rice and sewed it back up into sacks. But the smells from the spilled preserves lasted. Your aunt gave birth in the pigsty that night. The next morning when I went up for the water, I found her and the baby plugging up the family well.

"Don't let your father know that I told you. He denies her. Now that you have started to menstruate, what happened to her could happen to you. Don't humiliate us. You wouldn't like to be forgotten as if you had never been born. The villagers are watchful."

Whenever she had to warn us about life, my mother told stories that ran like this one, a story to grow up on. She tested our strength to establish realities. Those in the emigrant generations who could not reassert brute survival died young and far from home. Those of us in the first American generations have had to figure out how the invisible world the emigrants built around our childhoods fit in solid America.

The emigrants confused the gods by diverting their curses, misleading them with crooked streets and false names. They must try to confuse their offspring as well, who, I suppose, threaten them in similar ways—always trying to get things straight, always trying to name the unspeakable. The Chinese I know hide their names; sojourners take new names when their lives change and guard their real names with silence.

Chinese-Americans, when you try to understand what things in you are Chinese, how do you separate what is peculiar to childhood, to poverty, insanities, one family, your mother who marked your growing with stories, from what is Chinese? What is Chinese tradition and what is the movies?

If I want to learn what clothes my aunt wore, whether flashy or ordinary, I would have to begin, "Remember Father's drowned-in-the-well sister?" I cannot ask that. My mother has told me once and for all the useful parts. She will add nothing unless powered by Necessity, a riverbank that guides her life. She plants vegetable gardens rather than lawns; she carries the odd-shaped tomatoes home from the fields and eats food left for the gods.

Whenever we did frivolous things, we used up energy; we flew high kites. We children came up off the ground over the melting cones our parents brought home from work and the American movie on New Year's Day—*Oh, You Beautiful Doll* with Betty Grable one year, and *She Wore a Yellow Ribbon* with John Wayne another year. After the one carnival ride each, we paid in guilt; our tired father counted his change on the dark walk home.

Adultery is extravagance. Could people who hatch their own chicks and eat the embryos and the heads for delicacies and boil the feet in vinegar for party food, leaving only the gravel, eating even the gizzard lining—could such people engender a prodigal aunt? To be a woman, to have a daughter in starvation time was a waste enough. My aunt could not have been the lone romantic who gave up everything for sex. Women in the old China did not choose. Some man had commanded her to lie with him and be his secret evil. I wonder whether he masked himself when he joined the raid on her family.

Perhaps she encountered him in the fields or on the mountain where the daughters-in-law collected fuel. Or perhaps he first noticed her in the marketplace. He was not a stranger because the village housed no strangers. She had to have dealings with him other than sex. Perhaps he worked an adjoining field, or he sold her the cloth for the dress she sewed and wore. His demand must have surprised, then terrified her. She obeyed him; she always did as she was told.

When the family found a young man in the next village to be her husband, she stood tractably beside the best rooster, his proxy, and promised before they met that she would be his forever. She was lucky that he was her age and she would be the first wife, an advantage secure now. The night she first saw him, he had sex with her. Then he left for America. She had almost forgotten what he looked like. When she tried to envision him, she only saw the black and white face in the group photograph the men had had taken before leaving.

The other man was not, after all, much different from her husband. They both gave orders: she followed. "If you tell your family, I'll beat you. I'll kill you. Be here again next week." No one talked sex, ever. And she might have separated the rapes from the rest of living if only she did not have to buy her oil from him or gather wood in the same forest. I want her fear to have lasted just as long as rape lasted so that the fear could have been contained. No drawn-out fear. But women at sex hazarded birth and hence lifetimes. The fear did not stop but permeated everywhere. She told the man, "I think I'm pregnant." He organized the raid against her.

On nights when my mother and father talked about their life back home, sometimes they mentioned an "outcast table" whose business they still seemed to be settling, their voices tight. In a commensal tradition, where food is precious, the powerful older people made wrongdoers eat alone. Instead of letting them start separate new lives like the Japanese, who could become samurais and geishas, the Chinese family, faces averted but eyes glowering sideways, hung on to the offenders and fed them leftovers. My aunt must have lived in the same house as my parents and eaten at an outcast table. My mother spoke about the raid as if she had seen it, when she and my aunt, a daughter-in-law to a different household, should not have been living together at all. Daughters-in-law lived with their husbands' parents, not their own; a synonym for marriage in Chinese is "taking a daughter-in-law." Her husband's parents could have sold her, mortgaged her, stoned her. But they had sent her back to her own mother and father, a mysterious act hinting at disgraces not told me. Perhaps they had thrown her out to deflect the avengers.

She was the only daughter; her four brothers went with her father, husband, and uncles "out on the road" and for some years became western men. When the goods were divided among the family, three of the brothers took land, and the youngest, my father, chose an education. After my grandparents gave their daughter away to her husband's family, they had dispensed all the adventure and all the property. They expected her alone to keep the traditional ways, which her brothers, now among the barbarians, could fumble without detection. The heavy, deep-rooted women were to maintain the past against the flood, safe for returning. But the rare urge west had fixed upon our family, and so my aunt crossed boundaries not delineated in space.

The work of preservation demands that the feelings playing about in one's guts not be turned into action. Just watch their passing like cherry blossoms. But perhaps my aunt, my forerunner, caught in a slow life, let dreams grow and fade and after some months or years went toward what persisted. Fear at the enormities of the forbidden kept her desires delicate, wire and bone. She looked at a man because she liked the way the hair was tucked behind his ears, or she liked the question-mark line of a long torso curving at the shoulder and straight at the hip. For warm eyes or a soft voice or a slow walk—that's all—a few hairs, a line, a brightness, a sound, a pace, she gave up family. She offered us up for a charm that vanished with tiredness, a pigtail that didn't toss when the wind died. Why, the wrong lighting could erase the dearest thing about him.

It could very well have been, however, that my aunt did not take subtle enjoyment of her friend, but, a wild woman, kept rollicking company. Imagining her free with sex doesn't fit, though. I don't know any women like that, or men either. Unless I see her life branching into mine, she gives me no ancestral help.

To sustain her being in love, she often worked at herself in the mirror, guessing at the colors and shapes that would interest him, changing them frequently in order to hit on the right combination. She wanted to look back.

On a farm near the sea, a woman who tended her appearance reaped a reputation for eccentricity. All the married women blunt-cut their hair in flaps about their ears or pulled it back in tight buns. No nonsense. Neither style blew easily into heart-catching tangles. And at their weddings they displayed themselves in their long hair for the last time. "It brushed the backs of my knees," my mother tells me. "It was braided, and even so, it brushed the backs of my knees."

At the mirror my aunt combed individuality into her bob. A bun could have been contrived to escape into black streamers blowing in the wind or in quiet wisps about her face, but only the older women in our picture album wear buns. She brushed her hair back from her forehead, tucking the flaps behind her ears. She looped a piece of thread, knotted into a circle between her index fingers and thumbs, and ran the double strand across her forehead. When she closed her fingers as if she were making a pair of shadow geese bite, the string twisted together catching the little hairs. Then she pulled the thread away from her skin, ripping the hairs out neatly, her eyes watering from the needles of pain. Opening her fingers, she cleaned the thread, then rolled it along her hairline and the tops of the eyebrows. My mother did the same to me and my sisters and herself. I used to believe that the expression "caught by the short hairs" meant a captive held with a depilatory string. It especially hurt at the temples, but my mother said we were lucky we didn't have to have our feet bound when we were seven. Sisters used to sit on their beds and cry together, she said, as their mothers or their slave removed the bandages for a few minutes each night and let the blood gush back into their veins. I hope that the man my aunt loved appreciated a smooth brow, that he wasn't just a tits-and-ass man.

Once my aunt found a freckle on her chin, at a spot that the almanac said predestined her for unhappiness. She dug it out with a hot needle and washed the wound with peroxide.

More attention to her looks than these pullings of hairs and pickings at spots would have caused gossip among the villagers. They owned work clothes and good clothes, and they wore good clothes for feasting the new seasons. But since a woman combing her hair hexes beginnings, my aunt rarely found an occasion to look her best. Women looked like great sea snails—the corded wood, babies, and laundry they carried were the whorls on their backs. The Chinese did not admire a bent back; goddesses and warriors stood straight. Still there must have been a marvelous freeing of beauty when a worker laid down her burden and stretched and arched.

Such commonplace loveliness, however, was not enough for my aunt. She dreamed of a lover for the fifteen days of New Year's, the time for families to exchange visits, money, and food. She plied her secret comb. And sure enough she cursed the year, the family, the village, and herself.

Even as her hair lured her imminent lover, many other men looked at her. Uncles, cousins, nephews, brothers would have looked, too, had they been home between journeys. Perhaps they had already been restraining their curiosity, and they left, fearful that their glances, like a field of nesting birds, might be startled and caught. Poverty hurt, and that was their first reason for leaving. But another, final reason for leaving the crowded house was the never-said.

She may have been unusually beloved, the precious only daughter, spoiled and mirror-gazing because of the affection the family lavished on her. When her husband left, they welcomed the chance to take her back from the in-laws; she could live like the little daughter for just a while longer. There are stories that my grandfather was different from other people, "crazy ever since the little Jap bayoneted him in the head." He used to put his naked penis on the dinner table, laughing. And one day he brought home a baby girl, wrapped up inside his brown western-style greatcoat. He had traded one of his sons, probably my father, the youngest, for her. My grandmother made him trade back. When he finally got a daughter of his own, he doted on her. They must have all loved her, except perhaps my father, the only brother who never went back to China, having once been traded for a girl.

Brothers and sisters, newly men and women, had to efface their sexual color and present plain miens. Disturbing hair and eyes, a smile like no other, threatened the ideal of five generations living under one roof. To focus blurs, people shouted face to face and yelled from room to room. The immigrants I know have loud voices, unmodulated to American tones even after years away from the village where they called their friendships out across the fields. I have not been able to stop my mother's screams in public libraries or over telephones. Walking erect (knees straight, toes pointed forward, not pigeon-toed, which is Chinese-feminine) and speaking in an inaudible voice, I have tried to turn myself American-feminine. Chinese communication was loud, public. Only sick people had to whisper. But at the dinner table, where the family members came nearest one another, no one could talk, not the outcasts nor any eaters. Every word that falls from the mouth is a coin lost. Silently they gave and accepted food with both hands. A preoccupied child who took his bowl with one hand got a sideways glare. A complete moment of total attention is due everyone alike. Children and lovers have no singularity here, but my aunt used a secret voice, a separate attentiveness.

She kept the man's name to herself throughout her labor and dying; she did not accuse him that he be punished with her. To save her inseminator's name she gave silent birth.

He may have been somebody in her own household, but intercourse with a man outside the family would have been no less abhorrent. All the village were kinsmen, and the titles shouted in loud country voices never let kinship be forgotten. Any man within visiting distance would have been neutralized as a lover—"brother," "younger brother," "older brother"—115 relationship titles. Parents researched birth charts probably not so much to assure good fortune as to circumvent incest in a population that has but one hundred surnames. Everybody has eight million relatives. How useless then sexual mannerisms, how dangerous.

As if it came from an atavism deeper than fear, I used to add "brother" silently to boys' names. It hexed the boys, who would or would not ask me to dance, and made them less scary and as familiar and deserving of benevolence as girls.

But, of course, I hexed myself also—no dates. I should have stood up, both arms waving, and shouted out across libraries, "Hey, you! Love me back." I had no idea, though, how to make attraction selective, how to control its direction and magnitude. If I made myself American-pretty so that the five or six Chinese boys in the class fell in love with me, everyone else—the Caucasian, Negro, and Japanese boys—would too. Sisterliness, dignified and honorable, made much more sense.

Attraction eludes control so stubbornly that whole societies designed to organize relationships among people cannot keep order, not even when they bind people to one another from childhood and raise them together. Among the very poor and the wealthy, brothers married their adopted sisters, like doves. Our family allowed some romance, paying adult brides' prices and providing dowries so that their sons and daughters could marry strangers. Marriage promises to turn strangers into friendly relatives—a nation of siblings.

In the village structure, spirits shimmered among the live creatures, balanced and held in equilibrium by time and land. But one human being flaring up into violence could open up a black hole, a maelstrom that pulled in the sky. The frightened villagers, who depended on one another to maintain the real, went to my aunt to show her a personal, physical representation of the break she made in the "roundness." Misallying couples snapped off the future, which was to be embodied in true offspring. The villagers punished her for acting as if she could have a private life, secret and apart from them.

If my aunt had betrayed the family at a time of large grain yields and peace, when many boys were born, and wings were being built on many houses, perhaps she might have escaped such severe punishment. But the men—hungry, greedy, tired of planting in dry soil, cuckolded—had been forced to leave the village in order to send food-money home. There were ghost plagues, bandit plagues, wars with the Japanese, floods. My Chinese brother and sister had died of an unknown sickness. Adultery, perhaps only a mistake during good times, became a crime when the village needed food.

The round moon cakes and round doorways, the round tables of graduated size that fit one roundness inside another, round windows and rice bowls—these talismans had lost their power to warn this family of the law: A family must be whole, faithfully keeping the descent line by having sons to feed the old and the dead who in turn look after the family. The villagers came to show my aunt and lover-in-hiding a broken house. The villagers were speeding up the circling of events because she was too shortsighted to see that her infidelity had already harmed the village, that waves of consequences would return unpredictably, sometimes in disguise, as now, to hurt her. This roundness had to be made coin-sized so that she would see its circumference: Punish her at the birth of her baby. Awaken her to the inexorable. People who refused fatalism because they could invent small resources insisted on culpability. Deny accidents and wrest fault from the stars.

After the villagers left, their lanterns now scattering in various directions toward home, the family broke their silence and cursed her. "Aiaa, we're going to die. Death is coming. Death is coming. Look what you've done. You've killed us. Ghost! Dead Ghost! Ghost! You've never been born." She ran out into the fields, far enough from the house so that she could no longer hear their voices, and pressed herself against the earth, her own land no more. When she felt the birth coming, she thought that she had been hurt. Her body seized together. "They've hurt me too much," she thought. "This is gall, and it will kill me." With forehead and knees against the earth, her body convulsed and then relaxed. She turned on her back, lay on the ground. The black well of sky and stars went out and out for-ever; her body and her complexity seemed to disappear. She was one of the stars, a bright dot in blackness, without home, without a companion, in eternal cold and silence. An agoraphobia rose in her, speeding higher and higher, bigger and bigger; she would not be able to contain it; there would be no end to fear.

Flayed, unprotected against space, she felt pain return, focusing her body. This pain chilled her—a cold, steady kind of surface pain. Inside, spasmodically, the other pain, the pain of the child, heated her. For hours she lay on the ground, alternately body and space. Sometimes a vision of normal comfort obliterated reality: She saw the family in the evening gambling at the dinner table, the young people massaging their elders' backs. She saw them congratulating one another, high joy on the mornings the rice shoots came up. When these pictures burst, the stars drew yet further apart. Black space opened.

She got to her feet to fight better and remembered that old-fashioned women gave birth in their pigsties to fool the jealous, pain-dealing gods, who do not snatch piglets. Before the next spasms could stop her, she ran to the pigsty, each step a rushing out into emptiness. She climbed over the fence and knelt in the dirt. It was good to have a fence enclosing her, a tribal person alone.

Laboring, this woman who had carried her child as a foreign growth that sickened her every day, expelled it at last. She reached down to touch the hot, wet, moving mass, surely smaller than anything human, and could feel that it was human after all—fingers, toes, nails, nose. She pulled it up on to her belly, and it lay curled there, butt in the air, feet precisely tucked one under the other. She opened her loose shirt and buttoned the child inside. After resting, it squirmed and thrashed and she pushed it up to her breast. It turned its head this way and that until it found her nipple. There, it made little snuffling noises. She clenched her teeth at its preciousness, lovely as a young calf, a piglet, a little dog.

She may have gone to the pigsty as a last act of responsibility: She would protect this child as she had protected its father. It would look after her soul, leaving supplies on her grave. But how would this tiny child without family find her grave when there would be no marker for her anywhere, neither in the earth nor the family hall? No one would give her a family hall name. She had taken the child with her into the wastes. At its birth the two of them had felt the same raw pain of separation, a wound that only the family pressing tight could close. A child with no descent line would not soften her life but only trail after her, ghostlike, begging her to give it purpose. At dawn the villagers on their way to the fields would stand around the fence and look.

Full of milk, the little ghost slept. When it awoke, she hardened her breasts against the milk that crying loosens. Toward morning she picked up the baby and walked to the well.

Carrying the baby to the well shows loving. Otherwise abandon it. Turn its face into the mud. Mothers who love their children take them along. It was probably a girl; there is some hope of forgiveness for boys.

"Don't tell anyone you had an aunt. Your father does not want to hear her name. She has never been born." I have believed that sex was unspeakable and words so strong and fathers so frail that "aunt" would do my father mysterious harm. I have thought that my family, having settled among immigrants who had also been their neighbors in the ancestral land, needed to clean their name, and a wrong word would incite the kinspeople even here. But there is more to this silence: They want me to participate in her punishment. And I have.

In the twenty years since I heard this story I have not asked for details nor said my aunt's name; I do not know it. People who comfort the dead can also chase after them to hurt them further—a reverse ancestor worship. The real punishment was not the raid swiftly inflicted by the villagers, but the family's deliberately forgetting her. Her betrayal so maddened them, they saw to it that she would suffer forever, even after death. Always hungry, always needing, she would have to beg food from other ghosts, snatch and steal it from those whose living descendants give them gifts. She would have to fight the ghosts massed at crossroads for the buns a few thoughtful citizens leave to decoy her away from village and home so that the ancestral spirits could feast unharassed. At peace, they could act like gods, not ghosts, their descent lines providing them with paper suits and dresses, spirit money, paper houses, paper automobiles, chicken, meat, and rice into eternity—essences delivered up in smoke and flames, steam and incense rising from each rice bowl. In an attempt to make the Chinese care for people outside the family, Chairman Mao encourages us now to give our paper replicas to the spirits of outstanding soldiers and workers, no matter whose ancestors they may be. My aunt remains forever hungry. Goods are not distributed evenly among the dead.

My aunt haunts me—her ghost drawn to me because now, after fifty years of neglect, I alone devote pages of paper to her, though not origamied into houses and clothes. I do not think she always means me well. I am telling on her, and she was a spite suicide, drowning herself in the drinking water. The Chinese are always very frightened of the drowned one, whose weeping ghost, wet hair hanging and skin bloated, waits silently by the water to pull down a substitute.

Considerations

Thinking

What ideas about cultural origins appear in "No Name Woman"? Which cultural attitudes does Kingston feature most prominently? Why?

What significance does Kingston give to the Chinese family "circle" and the "roundness" of family life? In what ways are secrecy and silence determining factors in the cultural experience Kingston describes?

Connecting

Consider ways in which your own family uses family stories as vehicles of instruction, as forms of entertainment, or as bonds of social solidarity.

Compare the way Kingston blends fact and fiction in "No Name Woman" with the way Loren Eiseley seems to combine fact and fiction in "The Dance of the Frogs."

Writing

Tell a story that has been part of your family lore. Be sure to account for the story's significance—for what it reveals (or conceals) about family values and attitudes.

Tell a series of family stories that reveal significant ideals of the race, culture, or ethnicity to which your family belongs.

Discuss the ways Kingston's essay and Amy Tan's "Mother Tongue" reflect and resolve differences between Chinese and American cultural practices.

Silence

When I went to kindergarten and had to speak English for the first time, I became silent. A dumbness—a shame—still cracks my voice in two, even when I want to say "hello" casually, or ask an easy question in front of the check-out counter, or ask directions of a bus driver. I stand frozen, or I hold up the line with the complete, grammatical sentence that comes squeaking out at impossible length. "What did you say?" says the cab driver, or "Speak up," so I have to perform again, only weaker the second time. A telephone call makes my throat bleed and takes up that day's courage. It spoils my day with self-disgust when I hear my broken voice come skittering out into the open. It makes people wince to hear it. I'm getting better, though. Recently I asked the postman for special-issue stamps; I've waited since childhood for postmen to give me some of their own accord. I am making progress, a little every day.

My silence was thickest—total—during the three years that I covered my school paintings with black paint. I painted layers of black over houses and flowers and suns, and when I drew on the blackboard, I put a layer of chalk on top. I was making a stage curtain, and it was the moment before the curtain parted or rose. The teachers called my parents to school, and I saw they had been saving my pictures, curling and cracking, all alike and black. The teachers pointed to the pictures and looked serious, talked seriously too, but my parents did not understand English. ("The parents and teachers of criminals were executed," said my father.) My parents took the pictures home. I spread them out (so black and full of possibilities) and pretended the curtains were swinging open, flying up, one after another, sunlight underneath, mighty operas.

During the first silent year I spoke to no one at school, did not ask before going to the lavatory, and flunked kindergarten. My sister also said nothing for three years, silent in the playground and silent at lunch. There were other quiet Chinese girls not of our family, but most of them got over it sooner than we did. I enjoyed the silence. At first it did not occur to me I was supposed to talk or to pass kindergarten. I talked at home and to one or two of the Chinese kids in class. I made motions and even made some jokes. I drank out of a toy saucer when the water spilled out of the cup, and everybody laughed, pointing at me, so I did it some more. I didn't know that Americans don't drink out of saucers.

I liked the Negro students (Black Ghosts) best because they laughed the loudest and talked to me as if I were a daring talker too. One of the Negro girls had her mother coil braids over her ears Shanghai-style like mine; we were Shanghai twins except that she was covered with black like my paintings. Two Negro kids enrolled in Chinese school, and the teachers gave them Chinese names. Some Negro kids walked me to school and home, protecting me from the Japanese kids, who hit me and chased me and stuck gum in my ears. The Japanese kids were noisy and tough. They appeared one day in kindergarten, released from concentration camp, which was a tic-tac-toe mark, like barbed wire, on the map.

It was when I found out I had to talk that school become a misery, that the silence became a misery. I did not speak and felt bad each time that I did not speak. I read aloud in first grade, though, and heard the barest whisper with little squeaks come out of my throat. "Louder," said the teacher, who scared the voice away again. The other Chinese girls did not talk either, so I knew the silence had to do with being a Chinese girl.

Reading out loud was easier than speaking because we did not have to make up what to say, but I stopped often, and the teacher would think I'd gone quiet again. I could not understand "I." The Chinese "I" has seven strokes, intricacies. How could the American "I," assuredly wearing a hat like the Chinese, have only three strokes, the middle so straight? Was it out of politeness that this writer left off the strokes the way a Chinese has to write her own name small and crooked? No, it was not politeness; "I" is a capital and "you" is lower-case. I stared at that middle line and waited so long for its black center to resolve into tight strokes and dots that I forgot to pronounce it. The other troublesome word was "here," no strong consonant to hang on to, and so flat, when "here" is two mountainous ideographs. The teacher, who had already told me every day how to read "I" and "here," put me in the low corner under the stairs again, where the noisy boys usually sat.

When my second grade class did a play, the whole class went to the auditorium except the Chinese girls. The teacher, lovely and Hawaiian, should have understood about us, but instead left us behind in the classroom. Our voices were too soft or nonexistent, and our parents never signed the permission slips anyway. They never signed anything unnecessary. We opened the door a crack and peeked out, but closed it again quickly. One of us (not me) won every spelling bee, though.

I remember telling the Hawaiian teacher, "We Chinese can't sing 'land where our fathers died.'" She argued with me about politics, while I meant because of curses. But how can I have that memory when I couldn't talk? My mother says that we, like the ghosts, have no memories.

After American school, we picked up our cigar boxes, in which we had arranged books, brushes, and an inkbox neatly, and went to Chinese school, from 5:00 to 7:30 P.M. There we chanted together, voices rising and falling, loud and soft, some boys shouting, everybody reading together, reciting together and not alone with one voice. When we had a memorization test, the teacher let each of us come to his desk and say the lesson to him privately, while the rest of the class practiced copying or tracing. Most of the teachers were men. The boys who were so well behaved in the American school played tricks on them and talked back to them. The girls were not mute. They screamed and yelled during recess, when there were no rules; they had fistfights. Nobody was afraid of children hurting themselves or of children hurting school property. The glass doors to the red and green balconies with the gold joy symbols were left wide open so that we could run out and climb the fire escapes. We played capture-the-flag in the auditorium, where Sun Yat-sen and Chiang Kai-shek's pictures hung at the back of the stage, the Chinese flag on their left and the American flag on their right. We climbed the teak ceremonial chairs and made flying leaps off the stage. One flag headquarters was behind the glass door and the other on stage right. Our feet drummed on the hollow stage. During recess the teachers locked themselves up in their office with the shelves of books, copybooks, inks from China. They drank tea and warmed their hands at a stove. There was no play supervision. At recess we had the school to ourselves, and also we could roam as far as we could go—downtown, China-town stores, home—as long as we returned before the bell rang.

At exactly 7:30 the teacher again picked up the brass bell that sat on his desk and swung it over our heads, while we charged down the stairs, our cheering magnified in the stairwell. Nobody had to line up.

Not all of the children who were silent at American school found voice at Chinese school. One new teacher said each of us had to get up and recite in front of the class, who was to listen. My sister and I had memorized the lesson perfectly. We said it to each other at home, one chanting, one listening. The teacher called on my sister to recite first. It was the first time a teacher had called on the second-born to go first. My sister was scared. She glanced at me and looked away; I looked down at my desk. I hoped that she could do it because if she could, then I would have to. She opened her mouth and a voice came out that wasn't a whisper, but it wasn't a proper voice either. I hoped that she would not cry, fear breaking up her voice like twigs underfoot. She sounded as if she were trying to sing through weeping and strangling. She did not pause or stop to end the embarrass-ment. She kept going until she said the last word, and then she sat down. When it was my turn, the same voice came out, a crippled animal running on broken legs. You could hear splinters in my voice, bones rubbing jagged against one another. I was loud, though. I was glad I didn't whisper.

How strange that the emigrant villagers are shouters, hollering face to face. My father asks, "Why is it I can hear Chinese from blocks away? Is it that I under-stand the language? Or is it they talk loud?" They turn the radio up full blast to hear the operas, which do not seem to hurt their ears. And they yell over the singers that wail over the drums, everybody talking at once, big arm gestures, spit flying. You can see the disgust on American faces looking at women like that. It isn't just the loudness. It is the way Chinese sounds, ching-chong ugly, to Ameri-can ears, not beautiful like Japanese sayonara words with the consonants and vowels as regular as Italian. We make guttural peasant noise and have Ton Duc Thang names you can't remember. And the Chinese can't hear Americans at all; the language is too soft and western music unhearable. I've watched a Chinese audience laugh, visit, talk-story, and holler during a piano recital, as if the musician could not hear them. A Chinese-American, somebody's son, was playing Chopin, which has no punctuation, no cymbals, no gongs. Chinese piano music is five black keys. Normal Chinese women's voices are strong and bossy. We American-Chinese girls had to whisper to make ourselves American-feminine. Apparently we whispered even more softly than the Americans. Once a year the teachers referred my sister and me to speech therapy, but our voices would straighten out, unpredictably normal, for the therapists. Some of us gave up, shook our heads, and said nothing, not one word. Some of us could not even shake our heads. At times shaking my head no is more self-assertion than I can manage. Most of us eventually found some voice, however faltering. We invented an American-feminine speaking personality.

Considerations

Thinking

Kingston suggests that her silence was not peculiar to her, that instead, "the silence had to do with being a Chinese girl." Do you think her gender or her race and ethnicity were more important? Why?

What do you think about the "American-feminine speaking personality" she and her friends invented?

Connecting

Have there been times in your own life when you preferred silence to speech? On what occasions might you have wished to avoid speaking? Why?

Consider to what extent silence is encouraged or valued in different social situations and cultural contexts.

Writing

Discuss how attitudes toward language and ways of using it differ among racial, cultural, and ethnic groups. Focus on two or perhaps three groups.

Or explain the major differences Kingston identifies between Chinese and American ways of speaking.

On Discovery

Once upon a time, a man, named Tang Ao, looking for the Gold Mountain, crossed an ocean, and came upon the Land of Women. The women immediately captured him, not on guard against ladies. When they asked Tang Ao to come along, he followed; if he had had male companions, he would've winked over his shoulder.

"We have to prepare you to meet the queen," the women said. They locked him in a canopied apartment equipped with pots of makeup, mirrors, and a woman's clothes. "Let us help you off with your armor and boots," said the women. They slipped his coat off his shoulders, pulled it down his arms, and shackled his wrists behind him. The women who kneeled to take off his shoes chained his ankles together.

A door opened, and he expected to meet his match, but it was only two old women with sewing boxes in their hands. "The less you struggle, the less it'll hurt," one said, squinting a bright eye as she threaded her needle. Two captors sat on him while another held his head. He felt an old woman's dry fingers trace his ear; the long nail on her little finger scraped his neck. "What are you doing?" he asked. "Sewing your lips together," she joked, blackening needles in a candle flame. The ones who sat on him bounced with laughter. But the old woman did not sew his lips together. They pulled his earlobes taut and jabbed a needle through each of them. They had to poke and probe before puncturing the layers of skin correctly, the hole in the front of the lobe in line with the one in back, the layers of skin sliding about so. They worked the needle through—a last jerk for the needle's wide eye ("needle's nose" in Chinese). They strung his raw flesh with silk threads; he could feel the fibers.

The women who sat on him turned to direct their attention to his feet. They bent his toes so far backward that his arched foot cracked. The old ladies squeezed each foot and broke many tiny bones along the sides. They gathered his toes, toes over and under one another like a knot of ginger root. Tang Ao wept with pain. As they wound the bandages tight and tighter around his feet, the women sang foot-binding songs to distract him: "Use aloe for binding feet and not for scholars."

During the months of a season, they fed him on women's food: the tea was thick with white chrysanthemums and stirred the cool female winds inside his body; chicken wings made his hair shine; vinegar soup improved his womb. They drew the loops of thread through the scabs that grew daily over the holes in his earlobes. One day they inserted gold hoops. Every night they unbound his feet, but his veins had shrunk, and the blood pumping through them hurt so much, he begged to have his feet rewrapped tight. They forced him to wash his used bandages, which were embroidered with flowers and smelled of rot and cheese. He hung the bandages up to dry, streamers that drooped and draped wall to wall. He felt embarrassed; the wrappings were like underwear, and they were his.

One day his attendants changed his gold hoops to jade studs and strapped his feet to shoes that curved like bridges. They plucked out each hair on his face, powdered him white, painted his eyebrows like a moth's wings, painted his cheeks and lips red. He served a meal at the queen's court. His hips swayed and his shoulders swiveled because of his shaped feet. "She's pretty, don't you agree?" the diners said, smacking their lips at his dainty feet as he bent to put dishes before them.

In the Women's Land there are no taxes and no wars. Some scholars say that that country was discovered during the reign of Empress Wu (A.D. 694–705), and some say earlier than that, A.D. 441, and it was in North America.

Considerations

Thinking

Kingston's "On Discovery" is a parable—a story with an implied "moral." What do you think the moral or point of "On Discovery" might be?

What do you think of Kingston's title? Why "Discovery"? What is discovered and by whom?

Why do you think Kingston includes the final paragraph? What would be gained and lost if it were omitted?

Connecting

How can this piece be related to "Silence" and "No Name Woman"? What connections do you see among these three selections?

To what extent does "On Discovery" transcend its cultural context? That is, how far are its specifically Chinese elements relevant in the United States today?

Writing

Write a short essay analyzing and interpreting "On Discovery." Write Kingston a letter telling her what you think of "On Discovery" and asking her a couple of questions about the piece.

STUDENT ESSAYS BASED ON MAXINE HONG KINGSTON'S "ON DISCOVERY"

Maxine Hong Kingston's "On Discovery" comes from her book *China Men*, which, along with *The Woman Warrior*, explores Kingston's view of the cultural roles of men and women in China. Although brief, "On Discovery" is thought-provoking, as the three student essays presented in this section demonstrate.

Each of the three essays about "On Discovery" offers a different analysis and interpretation of Kingston's essay. Each of the student essays offers a valid and interesting way to interpret and understand Kingston's piece, even though the students' views, focuses, and analyses differ. The student writers cite some of the same details. Occasionally, one writer overlaps an idea or perspective suggested by one or both of the others. Overall, the three student pieces reveal how a variety of analytical essays can be written about a single text without agreeing on every point, and indeed, by offering quite different ways of interpreting the text.

Gender Switching

Michelle Bowman

Society has often used the Asian woman as an example of sexual mystery but also of docility and subservience, which are often considered "second nature" to her. Ironically, Kingston's "Land of Women" in "On Discovery" is inhabited by Asian women. Much like the matriarchal society in the Amazon, women also rule on the "Gold Mountain." By accident, Tang Ao is unfortunate to find himself among them. Kingston shows us in "On Discovery" that in any society, there is a hierarchy of authority. Kingston uses the classic tale of pre-wedding preparations as a symbolic reference to domination and subservience.

Through a series of steps, we see Tang Ao emasculated by the same steps that a traditional Asian woman might take to become feminized, beautiful. Without these steps she would be considered an anomaly in her culture. For the sake of beauty, Tang Ao's feet are broken and bound tightly: "they bent his toes so far backward that his arched foot cracked." His ears are pierced daily with hot needles: "they strung his raw flesh with silk threads; he could feel the fibers." These pains, which the older women must inflict on Tang Ao, are not intentionally malicious; rather, they are part of womanly traditions handed down for generations of women, who also comfort him in traditional ways: "the women sang footbinding songs to distract him."

Kingston's demonstration of these careful preparations before Tang Ao's first meeting with the queen suggests something grander, perhaps a wedding. Delicate foods are given to Tang Ao, such as vinegar soup, which "improved his womb" or tea "thick with white chrysanthemums," which "stirred the cool female winds inside his body." There are several other foods given to him to smooth his skin or gloss his hair, but I would like to focus on the vinegar soup and chrysanthemum tea. The desired effects from either of these two foods would suggest that Tang Ao could produce a child or is being made ready to bear children. This beautification process alludes to the pre-wedding rituals. The older knowledgeable women constantly surround him, poking and probing at him. As in all cultures, these women already know what will befall the bride on her wedding night. They may joke with him, nurture him, or even torture him, only to postpone his inevitable encounter or to alleviate his fright. The jokes and sly nudges of the women before the bride meets her groom exclude her because she doesn't know yet that her life will be as theirs, the other married women. Tang Ao is the bride awaiting her wedding night.

Tang Ao accepts their behavior with only one question, "What are you doing?" And this is spoken before his features have been altered. Why does Tang Ao allow the women to mummify him? At the introduction Tang Ao is discovered searching for the Gold Mountain, Kingston's allusion to North America or the United States. Tang Ao has "crossed an ocean" and landed here. Before his crossing, perhaps he thought the Gold Mountain to be an oasis of opportunity. Possibly he is married in his land and seeking fortune to send to his wife. Perhaps his journeys have tired him and he would gladly go with the women who capture him. Or perhaps his interest has been piqued when the women tell him, "we have to prepare you to meet the queen." Regardless of his reasons, Tang Ao seals his fate by accompanying the women.

However, Kingston writes, "if he had had male companions, he would've winked over his shoulder." This makes Tang Ao's capture impure. His thoughts are lewd and lecherous; already his inner feelings for women are of debasement. Suddenly, he has found something better than the Gold Mountain, and it looks good. His next impression of the castle is of "a canopied apartment equipped with pots of makeup, mirrors, and a woman's clothes." With the removal of his clothes, he experiences more sexual feelings. Kingston sets up the first part of this essay with subtle sexual nuances. First, a man alone searching for fortune suddenly encounters a band of women who capture him. The women do not use any violent measures to apprehend him; he comes along gladly. Next, he is in a feminine boudoir and his clothes are being taken from him. With an abrupt twist, his wrists are "shackled" and his ankles "chained." Expecting a fight, instead he is met by "two old women with sewing boxes in their hands."

The stripping of Tang Ao's identity is a slow process of emasculation. Tang Ao loses a little bit of himself each day with the alterations being made to his body. There are people who, when lost in the wilderness, exist like the animals in their own environment. They revert to a prehuman state: hunting and eating from the land, their voices becoming thick with disuse, their memories of human life fading. As identity becomes stifled, Tang Ao's voice is muted, and he reverts to sounds and gestures: he cries, weeps, and begs. His role in society becomes increasingly dehumanized. Adding to his physical changes is the degrading shame to his dignity: "They forced him to wash his used bandages, which were embroidered with flowers and smelled of rot and cheese." He suffers with embarrassment because he has to hang the bandages out to dry, "streamers that drooped and draped wall to wall." Although this daily shame promotes cleanliness and serves a general purpose that his feet will not become infected and gangrenous, to perform this task is to admit to the world his body is producing something rank and foul that he cannot control. Tang Ao no longer has any power over his own bodily functions.

"On Discovery" is a disturbing account of gender role reversal. Both male and female audiences might agree that Tang Ao's physical transformation is both painful and revolting. However, the binding of Tang Ao's feet and consequent breaking of bones is perhaps the most vivid illustration of a vanity which goes too far: "The old ladies squeezed each foot and broke many tiny bones along the sides." The fact that he must wash out his dirty bandages nightly is also a distasteful image. Initially, it may seem that Kingston is merely relating this image to vanity. Perhaps we can also dismiss it as such until the next to last paragraph, where we read that "his hips swayed and his shoulders swiveled because of his shaped feet." This image of weakness created through self-mutilation could hardly be considered beautiful.

Or could it? One of the most attractive images of being feminine is weakness. Ironically, Tang Ao is in the Land of Women ruled by women, but made appealing because of his physical weaknesses created by their feminine standards of self-mutilation. Kingston plays with this image of culturized feminine weakness throughout "On Discovery." The binding can also be compared with other symbols of feminine vanity, such as the tight elastic of a brassiere, the metal wire inside corsets, or even hot sticky nylon pantyhose, which bring women no pleasure. These objects were designed to alter a woman's appearance and disguise her physical flaws to make her more sexually alluring.

Kingston's essay opens with sexual innuendo and moves to the nurturing of the virgin bride awaiting her wedding night. Sometimes the bride is apprehensive, and other times she is quite excited. Lastly we see Tang Ao as female servant to the queen, as Kingston returns once again to the bride metaphor. In most cultures when a woman marries she becomes the property of her husband and his family. Most often in translation, she becomes a domestic slave with few of the privileges granted to men. The married wife becomes a second-rate person, her worth no better than the family cow. She is not allowed to dine with the family; she must clean the house and work the fields. Whereas men in other countries may dress in western attire with shirt, tie, and pants, women are still confined to traditional garb in many cultures. Kingston grapples with one feminine image throughout "On Discovery," that of the slave. The woman is slave to fashion, to culture, and to her dominator. The anticipatory bridal image ironically contrasts with the dominating husband symbol represented by the queen.

"Smacking their lips at his dainty feet," the queen's court comment on Tang Ao's physical attributes. This demonstration of the beautification process for women in preparation for final inspection or the symbolic marriage and its subsequent slavery plays on the culturized lowly feminine status of women, which has taken place for centuries. Kingston breaks it down from the beginning much like the women break down Tang Ao's individuality. The women are seen as charming or inviting to Tang Ao, and he enters their world readily. Although the beautification process seems barbarous, consider the results: smooth skin, glossy hair, and shapely dainty feet. But then, Kingston delivers her punch line: all this preparation is only for Tang Ao to become a weak slave.

While Kingston's essay may be seen as an allegorical diatribe on the evils of men against women, it is not enough for Kingston to merely suggest that women are subjugated into slavery everyday. She suggests that it is inevitable for any group of people. In any society, there will always be a dominating group that sets the standards for everyone else. Perhaps the discovery in "On Discovery" suggests that when there is a dominating group, there too must be a servant underclass. Moreover, just because the Land of Women is a matriarchal society does not exclude class and gender prejudices among the women.

Kingston ends her essay by noting that "in the Women's Land there are no taxes and no wars . . . and it was in North America." She makes the reader believe she is narrating historical facts. There are several ways to look at this final paragraph: It is true that Asian people did populate North America in the early eighth century. It is also true that there have been several matriarchal societies. However, with this final observation, Kingston reminds the reader that oppression exists between both genders and races, and it has so for ages. Because of her ethnic background, she has an innate sense of ethnocentrism and because of her gender, she has an innate sense of feminism. However, she neither places blame nor allies herself with either group.

In Essence

Han N. Pham

When I was little, meaning too little to argue, too little to know better, I would always hear my mother telling me certain things with a stern face, old and worried even then, staring into mine: You can't go there. You're a girl. You can't ride the bus alone. You're a girl. The list ran on through my childhood, never seeming to stop, even when my mother told me I could do anything, be anything. But she forgot to tell me what girls could do, when rattling off that list of what we couldn't. The world seemed a place where little boys could run wild and free, the door to the world's secret pleasures flung wide open, while their female counterparts could only sit at home and stare out the window. So when I was little, too little to argue, too little to know better, I was taught that the world was a man's world, seemingly, with no place for me.

Maxine Hong Kingston turns these notions upside down with a rebellious and (for some) disturbing twist in her piece "On Discovery," a brief parable from *China Men*.

"On Discovery" describes the wayward fortunes of one man, Tang Ao, who carelessly wanders into the women's land to be caught and brought to a "canopied apartment equipped with pots of makeup, mirrors, and a woman's clothes," where he would stay while the servants of the queen, old women who bounced with laughter as they sat on him, broke his feet, pierced his ears, and stripped away every ounce of his masculinity, which they peeled off and discarded like the dirty bandages wrapped about his feet, bandages which smelled of "rot and cheese."

Perhaps this was one of the most stirring images of the story, one of feet "squeezed" in order to break "many tiny bones along the sides" and toes gathered "over and under one another like a knot of ginger root." I have seen people cringe while reading the description; Kingston's words, while innocent, take on a macabre aspect. Readers know that with each crack of bone, every tear of pain, the man that is—was—Tang Ao is dying, to be replaced by the woman within, who begged to have his feet rebound when the bandages were taken off for cleaning, because the pain that coursed through shrunken veins was too much for him to bear. I have watched faces soften with sympathy as they read the passage where

Tang Ao is forced to wash his own bandages, "streamers that drooped and draped wall to wall." Like Tang Ao, they too are embarrassed, feeling, perhaps as Tang Ao did, that the "wrappings were like underwear, and they were his."

I did not soften with sympathy.

I read the passage over, rereading and finding new insights, new images that whispered and teased my mind. When I felt that I understood, when all traces of understanding of what Tang Ao had to experience left me, hardened, I read the passage out loud to a male friend, laughing at the look on his face.

Kingston does not tell this story because it is the "classic fairy tale of the modern feminist," as my male friend declared; rather she tells it to show the gender roles that men and women played in China, and still play today. She describes the foot binding realistically, knowing that generations of young Chinese girls had to go through the same ordeal, male counterparts looking on with dispassion. Indeed, the girls' feet were bound and their cries of pain and tears went unheard for the pleasures of men. Where small waists and big bosoms and backsides are the Western ideal for women, small feet made male Chinese hearts patter with desire. Moreover, broken feet lent another attractive aspect to women, in the eyes of men—with feet so small, so broken, women could not walk without aid. Their fidelity was ensured; they could not run off to meet their lovers. So men received a double pleasure—small feet that warmed their hearts and loins and an assurance that their wives were forever their own, at their mercy, like caged birds with clipped wings.

So I did not cringe at the thought of feet being bound, of a man's ability to walk taken away. It has happened before, I tell myself, and it will happen again. One more promise of fidelity. One more pair of feet for diners to smack their lips at.

Yet, as much as I may sound like a rampant feminist, demanding justice for generations of young girls crippled in their youth, I understand that the point of Kingston's essay lies deeper than a cruel story wrought for the simple pleasure of a literary revenge. "On Discovery" is an artful illustration of Chinese talk-story, one in which Kingston, with a simple and direct language so characteristic of her style, allows for no musings about her characters, their actions, their motives. Instead, she tells the story as an onlooker might, recalling the experience. "Tang Ao wept with pain," she says, speaking of his footbinding. Not "he wailed in anger and frustration and humiliation as they bound his feet, breaking his male spirit, taking away from him his freedom." Simply, "[he] wept with pain," those few words giving the reader a glimpse of a man, once so confident, weeping softly, powerlessly, accepting, his male spirit, as it were, draining away with every tear. Kingston does not try to humiliate Tang Ao by revealing his distress; she does not use him as an object upon which to vent her anger and frustration at the roles Chinese women have been forced into through the centuries. Instead, she plays the facts as they are, the roles remaining the same, only taking on a more drastic coloration because a man has now slipped into a woman's dress, her bridge-like shoes.

Grasping this idea firmly, of a switch of roles, of power, Kingston weaves it through her story. She is not obvious, elaborate, overwhelmingly dramatic in what she has to say. Rather, she tells the story, perhaps as it was handed down to her, and allows the reader to make the connections, to find the ideas that emerge, some hitting with a blinding force, others with a subtle coyness: "What are you doing?" Tang Ao asks of the woman who scratches his ear thoughtfully, a needle in her hand, searching for a place to pierce and loop the string that will become gold hoops then, finally, jade studs, signaling the final transformation of Tang Ao from man into woman. "Sewing your lips together," she jokes, throwing her companions into cackling laughter. The irony and symbolism of this statement are lost on the reader until later, when Tang Ao is seen with broken feet, swaying gently as he bends to serve the Queen's court. His masculine lips have been metaphorically sewn together; his masculinity is bound and held captive by the bandages about his feet, the earrings in his ears.

Kingston throws us another curve, almost whizzing by us in its seeming innocence, the allure with which it passes us by before we recognize it, and pull it gently back to analyze it.

She says that there is a woman in every man.

"During the months of a season," she says, "they fed [Tang Ao] . . . tea [that] was thick with white chrysanthemums [that] stirred the cool female winds inside his body." With this small statement, Kingston lays the foundation for the theory that crowns the story of Tang Ao with a stunning blow to the senses, something that may have sent, more than all the images of broken feet and humiliating acts, past readers of this essay cringing with the impact of its significance: that men, within, are inherently women, and, consistently, that women, within, could be men. "On Discovery," along this line of thought, is no longer a cruel story of a man degraded to the status of a woman, but rather a story of role "reversal" and fate realized. Kingston tells the story "objectively," with acceptance, as one might have if this were just another story of a woman forced into a subservient social role, not to maintain her omniscient narrator status, but rather to show that Tang Ao's fate was no more poignant, no more significant, simply because he was a man. Silently, she tells us, there is man and woman. We are the same. What separates us is the fact that there are essentially two roles, one of which will fall to each of us. The fact that men, historically, have had the "more powerful" and "superior" role is irrelevant. Chance, she whispers, fate, a luck of the draw. Tang Ao's fate was one of the two roles that, unfortunately, he drew. It has happened before, and it will happen again, regardless of whether the "victim" is a man or a woman.

In a final gesture Kingston teases us into thought with her statement that "In the Women's Land there are . . . no wars," and ends by stating the various dates and places that scholars say the land was discovered. The fact remains that there is no such land, that never in the known history of the world has there been evidence that any such Women's Land ever existed. Why, then, does Kingston tack it onto the story in such an awkward yet prominent fashion? She does it to remind us, as my mother tried to remind me, that women *can* do anything, even turn the world upside down to show that a *man* can be anything—even a woman.

Men at the Mercy of Women

Dennis Son

Many say that finding a significant other is one of the greatest things that can happen to a man. A man needs someone to care about, someone to listen to, someone to love. But everything comes at a price, and, oftentimes, the price is exorbitantly high. Things happen to a man when he finds a woman, but he is unfortunately unaware of these changes most of the time. Indeed, a female can alter a man from the inside out, affecting every aspect of his essence and soul.

In her essay "On Discovery," Maxine Hong Kingston writes about a man named Tang Ao who, searching for his dream of "the Gold Mountain," came upon a "Land of Women." Because they were women, he did not have his guard up when he encountered them. It was possibly the greatest mistake of his life. They captured him and told him he was going to see their queen. What he saw instead were two old women who began the painful process of turning him into a woman. Eventually, after months of their treatment, they finished with him, and no one could tell that under all of the makeup and clothing there were the remnants of what had once been a man.

The parallels between Tang Ao's situation and a man's situation with a woman are painfully evident. Like many young men, Tang is looking for a Gold Mountain, the greatness that a man seeks to achieve throughout his life, before he is distracted. He is ambitious and courageous, willing to do almost anything to bring his goals to fruition. But his search is cut off while he is still far short of his objective. He stumbles upon a Land of Women whose inhabitants represent a girlfriend and her friends and what they can do to a man. He is distracted by these females, and before anyone knows what is going on, he has been "captured," unable to continue on his quest. Men, of course, are not literally captured, but they are in a sense enslaved by their masters, the women with whom they fall in love.

Tang also notices that this new land he has stumbled upon has no male inhabitants, only females. Such is the fate of someone who has been "whipped" by his master. Undoubtedly, he will spend most of his free time with his special friend, occasionally seeing her friends when they visit, leaving little time to acknowledge the existence of his other male friends. In essence, he is being confined to a world of females.

Tang's hell began when he was shackled and told he was going to be taken to see the queen. He was, understandably, excited. "A door opened, and he expected to meet his match, but it was only two old women with sewing boxes in their hands." But they added insult to injury. Two women sat on him and another held his head in place while the two old women jabbed needles through his earlobes to pierce them. At the same time, the women sitting on him broke several bones in his feet and wrapped them tight with bandages. He wept in pain, while the women sang songs to distract him.

The choice of details at this point in the story reflects the author's desire to reveal how painful Tang's ordeal is. Kingston describes graphically the manner in which they put holes in his ears and then break his toes: "They worked the needle through—a last jerk for the needle's wide eye. . . . They strung his raw flesh with silk threads. . . . They bent his toes so far backward that his arched foot cracked. . . . [They] broke many tiny bones along the sides. They gathered his toes . . . like a knot of ginger root." She describes his misery as accurately as possible to illustrate vividly what women can figuratively do to a man.

A man's hell begins in a very similar fashion. A man is socially shackled by his new woman. The shackles represent what men like to refer to as the "ball and chain" or being whipped. Just as the women all cooperated like a well-oiled machine to work on Tang in the story, a hapless man's woman and her friends will make sure that he does not do anything that he should not. Soon, after all the pretenses have been dropped, the doors of truth open. But he does not see a lovely queen before him. He sees someone wrought with imperfections, just like any other person. Women might as well be "old women with sewing boxes" saying, "The less you struggle, the less it'll hurt." Nothing makes her any more special than anyone else. But soon this woman begins to change her new slave, making him give up anything that takes him away for any amount of time.

The two women sitting on top of Tang Ao are symbolic of the burden a man soon begins to feel. And it is not only the burden of his woman, but also of her friends. They gang up on him until the point that he is powerless even to stand up on his own two feet. Their watchful eyes are everywhere, ready to report back to his master about any wrongdoing. The process of a man losing his freedom, which his parents have tried to instill in him since birth, is as painful as Tang's being tortured by the women working on him.

As time progressed, Tang came closer and closer to becoming a woman. The women inserted gold hoops in the holes they had made in his ears and "fed him on women's food: the tea was thick with white chrysanthemums and stirred the cool female winds inside his body; chicken wings made his hair shine; vinegar soup improved his womb." This was a key sentence in the essay. He is now being referred to as a woman. Kingston still employs the use of the pronoun "he," but he has now been given distinctly female characteristics, including a womb.

The clincher is the wrappings around his feet. His feet had been wound so tightly for so long that the veins in his feet had shrunk, and it was agonizing to have the wrappings off. They "hurt so much, he begged to have his feet rewrapped tight." So now he asked, begged even, to have them back. He took care of them and washed them every night. Now things had changed and a crucial turning point had been reached. This is another important moment. What once had to be forced upon him, what once put him through excruciating pain, what once was something that he never would have dreamed would be a part of his life, he now actively sought. He had passed the point of no return. They had succeeded. He now asked, of his own volition, for the things that they gave and did to him.

All that the women had to do now was implement the final touches. They replaced the gold hoops in his ears with jade studs and gave him shoes that curved like bridges. "They plucked out each hair on his face, powdered him white, painted his eyebrows like a moth's wings, painted his cheeks and lips red." He was now ready to be their servant as a woman. He served food at the queen's court and "his hips swayed and his shoulders swiveled" as he walked. So perfect was Tang Ao's transformation that the people he served commented on her beauty.

Such is the fate of any man who falls in love with a woman. Tang Ao's plight is symbolic of a female's impact on an unwary man. Before much time has passed, a man will grow so accustomed to having his woman around and having her love and attention that he will find it difficult to adjust to life alone. The changes she imposes on him will be sought after, even begged for, just as Tang wanted the bandages. And a life without the love and attention he is receiving becomes an unbearable possibility.

Kingston's choice of verbs is reflected in Tang Ao's position. After his capture by the women, he is always having things done to him. Whether the women are shackling him, singing to him, or feeding him, his passive position is evident. Rarely does he do anything. He just has those things done to him that the women decide to do.

Throughout the piece, Kingston's tone of cool acceptance induces a feeling of acceptance in the reader as well. Even the dialogue contributes to this feeling. Whenever anything is said, it is something that might be said if what was happening was nothing special, and merely another occurrence in the daily course of events. When Tang Ao is taken to the old women with sewing kits, they calmly joke with him. There are no specific points in the story that the reader would find particularly shocking or offensive. In this way Kingston delivers her message all the more effectively.

Kingston can also be ironic. "On Discovery" concentrates on Tang Ao's capture and transformation into a woman by women. Is it not ironic that a brave explorer, one who has reached the pinnacle of machismo, is completely conquered both physically and mentally by females? The strong is now helpless against the weak. He ends up serving women their food as some kind of waitress in the queen's court. And worse yet, he does not even make an attempt to struggle, losing his manliness altogether.

There is also irony in the fact that the things that the women do to him are the things that women do to themselves in real life to make themselves more attractive to men, so that they may have the power to control them. What Tang Ao undoubtedly liked to see females do to themselves was now being done to him. It goes to the point that the women now look at him in ways men look at women in the real world. Men are apt to make comments about women's appearances and are very blunt about it many times. But the tables have been turned. The diners at the end of the story smacked "their lips at his dainty feet as he bent" over and commented, "She's pretty, don't you agree?" They said this right in front of him and without hesitation.

In addition to being changed, Tang loses his will. Tang was put through many things that most would consider torture, but he never resists. He accepts anything that the women do to him. Not once does he attempt to free himself or bother asking them to stop, even when what they do causes him to weep in pain. The one time that he does speak up, he only asks a question, which demonstrates his passivity. His silence represents a man's willingness to submit to a woman's wishes and desires, despite any amount of pain it may cause him. If a man cannot make up his own mind, what good is he? The individuality that makes a person and defines his character is no more. He is nothing more than an automaton with a woman at the controls. Just as Tang Ao becomes a woman, the man has essentially become one as well, allowing her to run his life and define who he is. Kingston's choice of turning him into a woman instead of something else reflects this fact.

Kingston also makes a forceful statement about power in her essay. Men are put into a superior position by society. In almost every professional field men dominate. Men on average make more money. Even in social settings, it is customary that a man approaches a woman and asks her out on a date. So, by that token, men possess greater power. But who really controls this power and makes the decisions? If a woman can get a stranglehold on a man and control him, then she possesses the power. Not directly of course, but she has the ability to get what she wants nonetheless.

Kingston's final paragraph suggests some differences that would exist if women controlled the world. "In the Women's Land," Kingston writes, "there are no taxes and no wars." In their world, things that we see as necessarily evils do not exist. Maybe women are kinder and should rule the world. But in our world these are two very grim realities, implying that women are not in control. Kingston realizes that not all women control their men, and this is the reason that we are taxed and kill our fellow human beings. It is also a statement, though, of the fact that the men who are in power have not been oppressed by their women. The powerful politicians and leaders who have reached considerable heights would not be making these decisions if they were at the mercy of their women. Kingston may be trying to say that these men who climb to greatness have not been affected to nearly as great a degree as other men who may be wallowing in their mediocrity, making the unpleasant but possibly true implication that women make men complacent and lazy. These people have not been distracted from their search for the Gold Mountain.

The last sentence also makes an interesting suggestion about the uncertainty of the whole topic. The entire thing is so subjective that there are no absolutes. There are no applicable equations. Nothing is certain, and there are as many variables in individual relationships as there are quirks of peoples' personalities. In like manner, Kingston makes no definitive statements about the location and time this land was discovered. "Some scholars say that that country was discovered during the reign of Empress Wu . . . and some say earlier than that . . . and it was in North America," but no one is sure, and it will remain that way.

To an outside observer, a man in love is a sick puppy. He is a manifestation from the deepest reaches of his soul of what every man fears that he may one day become. He accepts what was previously unacceptable. But to the man who is being affected, nothing else matters.

Richard Selzer
(b. 1928)

Richard Selzer for many years was both a doctor and a writer. Like the American poet and pediatrician, William Carlos Williams, Selzer combined practicing medicine with writing about it. His books include two collections of stories, *Rituals of Surgery* (1974) and *Imagine a Woman* (1991), and four collections of essays—*Mortal Lessons* (1977), *Confessions of a Knife* (1979), *Letters to a Young Doctor* (1982), and *Taking the World in for Repairs* (1986). Throughout his work, Selzer explores the role and image of the physician, the relations between doctor and patient, and the workings of the diseased and healthy body in all its splendor. He has also written an autobiography, *Down From Troy,* and a memoir about a near-death experience, *Resurrecting the Dead.*

Born in Troy, New York, in 1928, Selzer was educated at Union College, Albany Medical College, and Yale University. Since 1960 he has lived in New Haven, where, until his retirement, he taught at the Yale Medical School and conducted a private practice in surgery, his father's medical specialty.

Selzer did not begin his writing career until he was nearly forty, when he experienced a restless urgency to do something besides practice medicine. When he realized that he possessed the talent and the desire to be a writer. Selzer dedicated himself to learning the craft of writing as he had earlier devoted himself to the art of surgery. He began, as he put it, "suturing words together," a suturing he had to teach himself. His major preparation for this writerly work was reading. Among the writers Selzer cites as formative influences were the English essayists, particularly Chesterton, Lamb, and Hazlitt. Important also were the fiction writers, Poe and Patrick White, and the Catholic mystics, especially Saint Catherine of Siena and Saint John of the Cross. To these Selzer adds the French symbolist poets, Rimbaud, Verlaine, Baudelaire, and Mallarmé. From these writers Selzer derived a sense of linguistic precision and artistic passion. His own writing combines these elements in striking ways.

Selzer has spoken in an interview with Charles Shuster about the process of writing, which for him is a solitary one. He writes in longhand, which he says possesses "a special kind of magic" in which "the manual work of fashioning the words . . . flows out of your hand as though it were a secretion from your own body." The energy of writing carries Selzer along as he goes on line by line "to get it down as the burst comes." Following this "initial fever" of writing comes what Selzer describes as the work of the "sly fox" who calculates and manipulates the draft, tinkering with it, reconstructing and polishing it. And Selzer enjoys both these stages—the impetuous commitment to paper of words recording thoughts and feelings and the disciplined reining in of revision and editing.

Selzer has calculated that he writes sixty to seventy polished, publishable pages a year—and hundreds more from which he distills those. In his published prose he aims to accomplish a number of things: to evoke experience, to amuse, to inform. Amid his lyric outpourings of language, his sometimes sensational subjects and details, Selzer aims to establish, as he points out, "a kinship with the reader," as if to say, "we're both in this together." (And by "this" Selzer means both this life about which the writing centers and also the writing itself.)

Beneath these purposes lie two others: to come to terms with his vocation and identity as doctor and writer; to make out of his experiences works of literary art. Selzer himself put it clearly and forcefully: "I am writing," he says, "to make art. That's the whole thing. To write the best I can." And when he is writing to this high standard, Selzer's words perform a double function: they teach and they heal. They heal the writer, who makes himself whole in finding language to express his sense of self and the world; and they heal the reader, who experiences the power and pleasure of art. In the act of writing, Selzer the surgeon of the body becomes a doctor of the soul.

The Knife

One holds the knife as one holds the bow of a cello or a tulip—by the stem. Not palmed nor gripped nor grasped, but lightly, with the tips of the fingers. The knife is not for pressing. It is for drawing across the field of skin. Like a slender fish, it waits, at the ready, then, go! It darts, followed by a fine wake of red. The flesh parts, falling away to yellow globules of fat. Even now, after so many times, I still marvel at its power—cold, gleaming, silent. More, I am still struck with a kind of dread that it is I in whose hand the blade travels, that my hand is its vehicle, that yet again this terrible steel-bellied thing and I have conspired for a most unnatural purpose, the laying open of the body of a human being.

A stillness settles in my heart and is carried to my hand. It is the quietude of resolve layered over fear. And it is this resolve that lowers us, my knife and me, deeper and deeper into the person beneath. It is an entry into the body that is nothing like a caress; still, it is among the gentlest of acts. Then stroke and stroke again, and we are joined by other instruments, hemostats and forceps, until the wound blooms with strange flowers whose looped handles fall to the sides in steely array.

There is sound, the tight click of clamps fixing teeth into severed blood vessels, the snuffle and gargle of the suction machine clearing the field of blood for the next stroke, the litany of monosyllables with which one prays his way down and in: *clamp, sponge, suture, tie, cut.* And there is color. The green of the cloth, the white of the sponges, the red and yellow of the body. Beneath the fat lies the fascia, the tough fibrous sheet encasing the muscles. It must be sliced and the red beef of the muscles separated. Now there are retractors to hold apart the wound. Hands move together, part, weave. We are fully engaged, like children absorbed in a game or the craftsmen of some place like Damascus.

Deeper still. The peritoneum, pink and gleaming and membranous, bulges into the wound. It is grasped with forceps, and opened. For the first time we can see into the cavity of the abdomen. Such a primitive place. One expects to find drawings of buffalo on the walls. The sense of trespassing is keener now, heightened by the world's light illuminating the organs, their secret colors revealed—maroon and salmon and yellow. The vista is sweetly vulnerable at this moment, a kind of welcoming. An arc of the liver shines high and on the right, like a dark sun. It laps over the pink sweep of the stomach, from whose lower border the gauzy momentum is draped, and through which veil one sees, sinuous, slow as just-fed snakes, the indolent coils of the intestine.

You turn aside to wash your gloves. It is a ritual cleansing. One enters this temple doubly washed. Here is man as microcosm, representing in all his parts the earth, perhaps the universe.

I must confess that the priestliness of my profession has ever been impressed on me. In the beginning there are vows, taken with all solemnity. Then there is the endless harsh novitiate of training, much fatigue, much sacrifice. At last one emerges as celebrant, standing close to the truth lying curtained in the Ark of the body. Not surplice and cassock but mask and gown are your regalia. You hold no chalice, but a knife. There is no wine, no wafer. There are only the facts of blood and flesh.

In the room the instruments lie on trays and tables. They are arranged precisely by the scrub nurse, in an order that never changes, so that you can reach blindly for a forceps or hemostat without looking away from the operating field. The instruments lie *thus!* Even at the beginning, when all is clean and tidy and no blood has been spilled, it is the scalpel that dominates. It has a figure the others do not have, the retractors and the scissors. The scalpel is all grace and line, a fierceness. It grins. It is like a cat—to be respected, deferred to, but which returns no amiability. To hold it above a belly is to know the knife's force—as though were you to give it slightest rein, it would pursue an intent of its own, driving into the flesh, a wild energy.

In a story by Borges, a deadly knife fight between two rivals is depicted. It is not, however, the men who are fighting. It is the knives themselves that are settling their own old score. The men who hold the knives are mere adjuncts to the weapons. The unguarded knife is like the unbridled war-horse that not only carries its helpless rider to his death, but tramples all beneath its hooves. The hand of the surgeon must tame this savage thing. He is a rider reining to capture a pace.

So close is the joining of knife and surgeon that they are like the Centaur—the knife, below, all equine energy, the surgeon, above, with his delicate art. One holds the knife back as much as advances it to purpose. One is master of the scissors. One is partner, sometimes rival, to the knife. In a moment it is like the long red fingernail of the Dragon Lady. Thus does the surgeon curb in order to create, restraining the scalpel, governing it shrewdly, setting the action of the operation into a pattern, giving it form and purpose.

It is the nature of creatures to live within a tight cuirass that is both their constriction and their protection. The carapace of the turtle is his fortress and retreat, yet keeps him writhing on his back in the sand. So is the surgeon rendered impotent by his own empathy and compassion. The surgeon cannot weep. When he cuts the flesh, his own must not bleed. Here it is all work. Like an asthmatic hungering for air, longing to take just one deep breath, the surgeon struggles not to feel. It is suffocating to press the feeling out. It would be easier to weep or mourn—for you know that the lovely precise world of proportion contains, just beneath, *there,* all disaster, all disorder. In a surgical operation, a risk may flash into reality: the patient dies . . . of *complication.* The patient knows this too, in a more direct and personal way, and he is afraid.

And what of that *other,* the patient, you, who are brought to the operating room on a stretcher, having been washed and purged and dressed in a white gown? Fluid drips from a bottle into your arm, diluting you, leaching your body of its personal brine. As you wait in the corridor, you hear from behind the closed door the angry clang of steel upon steel, as though a battle were being waged. There is the odor of antiseptic and ether, and masked women hurry up and down the halls, in and out of rooms. There is the watery sound of strange machinery, the tinny beeping that is the transmitted heartbeat of yet another *human being.* And all the while the dreadful knowledge that soon you will be taken, laid beneath great lamps that will reveal the secret linings of your body. In the very act of lying down, you have made a declaration of surrender. One lies down gladly for sleep or for love. But to give over one's body and will for surgery, to *lie down* for it, is a yielding of more than we can bear.

Soon a man will stand over you, gowned and hooded. In time the man will take up a knife and crack open your flesh like a ripe melon. Fingers will rummage among your viscera. Parts of you will be cut out. Blood will run free. Your blood. All the night before you have turned with the presentiment of death upon you. You have attended your funeral, wept with your mourners. You think, "I should never have had surgery in the springtime." It is too cruel. Or on a Thursday. It is an unlucky day.

Now it is time. You are wheeled in and moved to the table. An injection is given. "Let yourself go," I say. "It's a pleasant sensation," I say. "Give in," I say.

Let go? Give in? When you know that you are being tricked into the hereafter, that you will end when consciousness ends? As the monstrous silence of anesthesia falls discourteously across your brain, you watch your soul drift off.

Later, in the recovery room, you awaken and gaze through the thickness of drugs at the world returning, and you guess, at first dimly, then surely, that you have not died. In pain and nausea you will know the exultation of death averted, of life restored.

What is it, then, this thing, the knife, whose shape is virtually the same as it was three thousand years ago, but now with its head grown detachable? Before steel, it was bronze. Before bronze, stone—then back into unremembered time. Did man invent it or did the knife precede him here, hidden under ages of vegetation and hoofprints, lying in wait to be discovered, picked up, used?

The scalpel is in two parts, the handle and the blade. Joined, it is six inches from tip to tip. At one end of the handle is a narrow notched prong upon which the blade is slid, then snapped into place. Without the blade, the handle has a blind, decapitated look. It is helpless as a trussed maniac. But slide on the blade, click it home, and the knife springs instantly to life. It is headed now, edgy, leaping to mount the fingers for the gallop to its feast.

Now is the moment from which you have turned aside, from which you have averted your gaze, yet toward which you have been hastened. Now the scalpel sings along the flesh again, its brute run unimpeded by germs or other frictions. It is a slick slide home, a barracuda spurt, a rip of embedded talon. One listens, and almost hears the whine—nasal, high, delivered through that gleaming metallic snout. The flesh splits with its own kind of moan. It is like the penetration of rape.

The breasts of women are cut off, arms and legs sliced to the bone to make ready for the saw, eyes freed from sockets, intestines lopped. The hand of the surgeon rebels. Tension boils through his pores, like sweat. The flesh of the patient retaliates with hemorrhage, and the blood chases the knife wherever it is withdrawn.

Within the belly a tumor squats, toadish, fungoid. A gray mother and her brood. The only thing it does not do is croak. It too is hacked from its bed as the carnivore knife lips the blood, turning in it in a kind of ecstasy of plenty, a gluttony after the long fast. It is just for this that the knife was created, tempered, heated, its violence beaten into paper-thin force.

At last a little thread is passed into the wound and tied. The monstrous booming fury is stilled by a tiny thread. The tempest is silenced. The operation is over. On the table, the knife lies spent, on its side, the bloody meal smear-dried upon its blanks. The knife rests.

And waits.

Considerations

Thinking

What does Selzer suggest about the surgeon's scalpel?

What images of the knife does he present? That is, to what does Selzer compare the scalpel? With what effects?

What image of the doctor emerges from this essay?

Connecting

What is the relationship between Selzer's account in paragraph 8 of the story by the Argentinian writer Borges and Selzer's discussion of the surgeon's knife?

Compare Selzer's presentation of the doctor in this essay with the image of the doctor conveyed in another of his essays included in this book, or with the image of the doctor in the work of another writer.

Writing

Describe an object that is important in your work or play: a musical instrument, a tool, a vehicle, a piece of equipment. Try to see it as possessing a life of its own and a corresponding set of intentions. Explain what this object is and does, and why it is important.

Write a letter to Selzer commenting on his view of the surgeon. Ask him a few questions about his characterization of the surgeon and the scalpel.

The Masked Marvel's Last Toehold

On the fifth floor of the hospital, in the west wing, I know that a man is sitting up in his bed, waiting for me. Elihu Koontz is seventy-five, and he is diabetic. It is two weeks since I amputated his left leg just below the knee. I walk down the corridor, but I do not go straight into his room. Instead, I pause in the doorway. He is not yet aware of my presence, but gazes down at the place in the bed where his leg used to be, and where now there is the collapsed leg of his pajamas. He is totally absorbed, like an athlete appraising the details of his body. What is he thinking, I wonder. Is he dreaming the outline of his toes? Does he see there his foot's incandescent ghost? Could he be angry? Feel that I have taken from him something for which he yearns now with all his heart? Has he forgotten so soon the pain? It was pain so great as to set him apart from all other men, in a red-hot place where he had no kith or kin. What of those black gorilla toes and the soupy mess that was his heel? I watch him from the doorway. It is a kind of spying, I know.

Save for a white fringe open at the front, Elihu Koontz is bald. The hair has grown too long and is wilted. He wears it as one would wear a day-old laurel wreath. He is naked to the waist, so that I can see his breasts. They are the breasts of Buddha, inverted triangles from which the nipples swing, dark as garnets.

I have seen enough. I step into the room, and he sees that I am there.

"How did the night go, Elihu?"

He looks at me for a long moment. "Shut the door," he says.

I do, and move to the side of the bed. He takes my left hand in both of his, gazes at it, turns it over, then back, fondling, at last holding it up to his cheek. I do not withdraw from this loving. After a while he relinquishes my hand, and looks up at me.

"How is the pain?" I ask.

He does not answer, but continues to look at me in silence. I know at once that he has made a decision.

"Ever hear of The Masked Marvel?" He says this in a low voice, almost a whisper.

"What?"

692

"The Masked Marvel," he says. "You never heard of him?"

"No."

He clucks his tongue. he is exasperated.

All at once there is a recollection. It is dim, distant, but coming near.

"Do you mean the wrestler?"

Eagerly, he nods, and the breasts bob. How gnomish he looks, oval as the huge helpless egg of some outlandish lizard. He has very long arms, which, now and then, he unfurls to reach for things—a carafe of water, a get-well card. He gazes up at me, urging. He *wants* me to remember.

"Well . . . yes," I say. I am straining backward in time. "I saw him wrestle in Toronto long ago."

"Ha!" He smiles. "You saw *me*." And his index finger, held rigid and upright, bounces in the air.

The man has said something shocking, unacceptable. It must be challenged.

"You?" I am trying to smile.

Again that jab of the finger. "You saw *me*."

"No," I say. But even then, something about Elihu Koontz, those prolonged arms, the shape of his head, the sudden agility with which he leans from his bed to get a large brown envelope from his nightstand, something is forcing me toward a memory. He rummages through his papers, old newspaper clippings, photographs, and I remember . . .

It is almost forty years ago. I am ten years old. I have been sent to Toronto to spend the summer with relatives. Uncle Max has brought two tickets to the wrestling match. He is taking me that night.

"He isn't allowed," says Aunt Sarah to me. Uncle Max has angina.

"He gets too excited," she says.

"I wish you wouldn't go, Max," she says.

"You mind your own business," he says.

And we go. Out into the warm Canadian evening. I am not only abroad, I am abroad in the *evening!* I have never been taken out in the evening. I am terribly excited. The trolleys, the lights, the horns. It is a bazaar. At the Maple Leaf Gardens, we sit high and near the center. The vast arena is dark except for the brilliance of the ring at the bottom.

It begins.

The wrestlers circle. They grapple. They are all haunch and paunch. I am shocked by their ugliness, but I do not show it. Uncle Max is exhilarated. He leans forward, his eyes unblinking, on his face a look of enormous happiness. One after the other, a pair of wrestlers enter the ring. The two men join, twist, jerk, tug, bend, yank, and throw. Then they leave and are replaced by another pair. At last it is the main event. "The Angel vs. The Masked Marvel."

On the cover of the program notes, there is a picture of The Angel hanging from the limb of a tree, a noose of thick rope around his neck. The Angel hangs just so for an hour every day, it is explained, to strengthen his neck. The Masked

Marvel's trademark is a black stocking cap with holes for the eyes and mouth. He is never seen without it, states the program. No one knows who The Masked Marvel really is!

"Good," says Uncle Max. "Now you'll see something." He is fidgeting, waiting for them to appear. They come down separate aisles, climb into the ring from opposite sides. I have never seen anything like them. It is The Angel's neck that first captures the eye. The shaved nape rises in twin columns to puff into the white hood of a sloped and bosselated skull that is too small. As though, strangled by the sinews of that neck, the skull had long since withered and shrunk. The thing about The Angel is the absence of any mystery in his body. It is simply *there*. A monosyllabic announcement. A grunt. One looks and knows everything at once, the fat thighs, the gigantic buttocks, the great spine from which hang knotted ropes and pale aprons of beef. And that prehistoric head. He is all of a single hideous piece. The Angel is. No detachables.

The Masked Marvel seems dwarfish. His fingers dangle kneeward. His short legs are slightly bowed as if under the weight of the cask they are forced to heft about. He has breasts that swing when he moves! I have never seen such breasts on a man before.

There is a sudden ungraceful movement, and they close upon one another. The Angel stoops and hugs The Marvel about the waist, locking his hands behind The Marvel's back. Now he straightens and lifts The Marvel as though he were uprooting a tree. Thus he holds him, then stoops again, thrusts one hand through The Marvel's crotch, and with the other grabs him by the neck. He rears and . . . The Marvel is aloft! For a long moment, The Angel stands as though deciding where to make the toss. Then throws. Was that board or bone that splintered there? Again and again, The Angel hurls himself upon the body of The Masked Marvel.

Now The Angel rises over the fallen Marvel, picks up one foot in both of his hands, and twists the toes downward. It is far beyond the tensile strength of mere ligament, mere cartilage. The Masked Marvel does not hide his agony, but pounds and slaps the floor with his hand, now and then reaching up toward The Angel in an attitude of supplication. I have never seen such suffering. And all the while his black mask rolls from side to side, the mouth pulled to a tight slit through which issues an endless hiss that I can hear from where I sit. All at once, I hear a shouting close by.

"Break it off! Tear off a leg and throw it up here!"

It is Uncle Max. Even in the darkness I can see that he is gray. A band of sweat stands upon his upper lip. He is on his feet now, panting, one fist pressed at his chest, the other raised warlike toward the ring. For the first time I begin to think that something terrible might happen here. Aunt Sarah was right.

"Sit down, Uncle Max," I say. "Take a pill, please."

He reaches for the pillbox, gropes, and swallows without taking his gaze from the wrestlers. I wait for him to sit down.

"That's not fair," I say, "twisting his toes like that."

"It's the toehold," he explains.

"But it's not *fair*," I say again. The whole of the evil is laid open for me to perceive. I am trembling.

And now The Angel does something unspeakable. Holding the foot of The Marvel at full twist with one hand, he bends and grasps the mask where it clings to the back of The Marvel's head. And he pulls. He is going to strip it off! Lay bare an ultimate carnal mystery! Suddenly it is beyond mere physical violence. Now I am on my feet, shouting into the Maple Leaf Gardens.

"Watch out," I scream. "Stop him. Please, somebody, stop him."

Next to me, Uncle Max is chuckling.

Yet The Masked Marvel hears me, I know it. And rallies from his bed of pain. Thrusting with his free heel, he strikes The Angel at the back of the knee. The Angel falls. The Masked Marvel is on top of him, pinning his shoulders to the mat. One! Two! Three! And it is over. Uncle Max is strangely still. I am gasping for breath. All this I remember as I stand at the bedside of Elihu Koontz.

Once again, I am in the operating room. It is two years since I amputated the left leg of Elihu Koontz. Now it is his right leg which is gangrenous. I have already scrubbed. I stand to one side wearing my gown and gloves. And . . . *I am masked.* Upon the table lies Elihu Koontz, pinned in a fierce white light. Spinal anesthesia has been administered. One of his arms is taped to a board placed at a right angle to his body. Into this arm, a needle has been placed. Fluid drips here from a bottle overhead. With his other hand, Elihu Koontz beats feebly at the side of the operating table. His head rolls from side to side. His mouth is pulled into weeping. It seems to me that I have never seen such misery.

An orderly stands at the foot of the table, holding Elihu Koontz's leg aloft by the toes so that the intern can scrub the limb with antiseptic solutions. The intern paints the foot, ankle, leg, and thigh, both front and back, three times. From a corner of the room where I wait, I look down as from an amphitheater. Then I think of Uncle Max yelling, "Tear off a leg. Throw it up here." And I think that forty years later I am making the catch.

"It's not fair," I say aloud. But no one hears me. I step forward to break The Masked Marvel's last toehold.

Considerations

Thinking

Why do you think Selzer may have written this essay? Does it have a clear thesis or idea? If so, what is it, and where do you find it expressed or suggested?

In what ways does the surgeon break the Masked Marvel's toehold? Consider various meanings of the word "break."

Explain the reactions of the young boy and his uncle Max to the performance of The Masked Marvel.

Connections

Explain the relationships between and among the three parts of Selzer's essay. Consider how time is presented.

What details from the second section parallel those of the first? What parallels exist between second and third parts?

Identify two forms of comparison Selzer uses and explain their importance.

Writing

Describe a climactic moment (or parallel climactic moments) in an event you experienced. You may write about a sports event, a musical performance, an experience at work or at school. Try to recapture your experience of the event; explain its significance not only for yourself, but in a larger sense.

Write an essay that interprets the meaning and significance of "The Masked Marvel's Last Toehold." Use evidence from the essay to support your interpretation.

Imelda

I

I heard the other day that Hugh Franciscus had died. I knew him once. He was the Chief of Plastic Surgery when I was a medical student at Albany Medical College. Dr. Franciscus was the archetype of the professor of surgery—tall, vigorous, muscular, as precise in his technique as he was impeccable in his dress. Each day a clean lab coat monkishly starched, that sort of thing. I doubt that he ever read books. One book only, that of the human body, took the place of all others. He never raised his eyes from it. He read it like a printed page as though he knew that in the calligraphy there just beneath the skin were all the secrets of the world. Long before it became visible to anyone else, he could detect the first sign of granulation at the base of a wound, the first blue line of new epithelium at the periphery that would tell him that a wound would heal, or the barest hint of necrosis that presaged failure. This gave him the appearance of a prophet. "This skin graft will take," he would say, and you must believe beyond all cyanosis, exudation and inflammation that it would.

He had enemies, of course, who said he was arrogant, that he exalted activity for its own sake. Perhaps. But perhaps it was no more than the honesty of one who knows his own worth. Just look at a scalpel, after all. What a feeling of sovereignty, megalomania even, when you know that it is you and you alone who will make certain use of it. It was said, too, that he was a ladies' man. I don't know about that. It was all rumor. Besides, I think he had other things in mind than mere living. Hugh Franciscus was a zealous hunter. Every fall during the season he drove upstate to hunt deer. There was a glass-front case in his office where he showed his guns. How could he shoot a deer? we asked. But he knew better. To us medical students he was someone heroic, someone made up of several gods, beheld at a distance, and always from a lesser height. If he had grown accustomed to his miracles, we had not. He had no close friends on the staff. There was something a little sad in that. As though once long ago he had been flayed by friendship and now the slightest breeze would hurt. Confidences resulted in dishonor. Perhaps the person in whom one confided would scorn him, betray. Even though he spent his days among those less fortunate, weaker than he—the sick, after all—Franciscus seemed aware of an air of personal harshness in his environment to which he reacted by keeping his own counsel, by a certain remoteness. It was what gave him the appearance of being haughty. With the patients he was forthright. All the facts laid out, every question anticipated and answered with specific information. He delivered good news and bad with the same dispassion.

I was a third-year student, just turned onto the wards for the first time, and clerking on Surgery. Everything—the operating room, the morgue, the emergency room, the patients, professors, even the nurses—was terrifying. One picked one's way among the mines and booby traps of the hospital, hoping only to avoid the hemorrhage and perforation of disgrace. The opportunity for humiliation was everywhere.

It all began on Ward Rounds. Dr. Franciscus was demonstrating a cross-leg flap graft he had constructed to cover a large fleshy defect in the leg of a merchant seaman who had injured himself in a fall. The man was from Spain and spoke no English. There had been a comminuted fracture of the femur, much soft tissue damage, necrosis. After weeks of débridement and dressings, the wound had been made ready for grafting. Now the patient was in his fifth postoperative day. What we saw was a thick web of pale blue flesh arising from the man's left thigh, and which had been sutured to the open wound on the right thigh. When the surgeon pressed the pedicle with his finger, it blanched; when he let up, there was a slow return of the violaceous color.

"The circulation is good," Franciscus announced. "It will get better." In several weeks, we were told, he would divide the tube of flesh at its site of origin, and tailor it to fit the defect to which, by then, it would have grown more solidly. All at once, the webbed man in the bed reached out, and gripping Franciscus by the arm, began to speak rapidly, pointing to his groin and hip. Franciscus stepped back at once to disengage his arm from the patient's grasp.

"Anyone here know Spanish? I didn't get a word of that."

"The cast is digging into him up above," I said. "The edges of the plaster are rough. When he moves, they hurt."

Without acknowledging my assistance, Dr. Franciscus took a plaster shears from the dressing cart and with several large snips cut away the rough edges of the cast.

"*Gracias, gracias.*" The man in the bed smiled. But Franciscus had already moved on to the next bed. He seemed to me a man of immense strength and ability, yet without affection for the patients. He did not want to be touched by them. It was less kindness that he showed them than a reassurance that he would never give up, that he would bend every effort. If anyone could, he would solve the problems of their flesh.

Ward Rounds had disbanded and I was halfway down the corridor when I head Dr. Franciscus' voice behind me.

"You speak Spanish." It seemed a command.

"I lived in Spain for two years," I told him.

"I'm taking a surgical team to Honduras next week to operate on the natives down there. I do it every year for three weeks, somewhere. This year, Honduras. I can arrange the time away from your duties here if you'd like to come along. You will act as interpreter. I'll show you how to use the clinical camera. What you'd see would make it worthwhile."

So it was that, a week later, the envy of my classmates, I joined the mobile surgical unit—surgeons, anesthetists, nurses and equipment—aboard a Military Air Transport plane to spend three weeks performing plastic surgery on people who had been previously selected by an advance team. Honduras. I don't suppose I shall ever see it again. Nor do I especially want to. From the plane it seemed a country made of clay—burnt umber, raw sienna, dry. It had a deadweight quality, as though the ground had no buoyancy, no air sacs through which a breeze might wander. Our destination was Comayagua, a town in the Central Highlands. The town itself was situated on the edge of one of the flatlands that were linked in a network between the granite mountains. Above, all was brown, with only an occasional Spanish cedar tree; below, patches of luxuriant tropical growth. It was a day's bus ride from the airport. For hours, the town kept appearing and disappearing with the convolutions of the road. At last, there it lay before us, panting and exhausted at the bottom of the mountain.

That was all I was to see of the countryside. From then on, there was only the derelict hospital of Comayagua, with the smell of spoiling bananas and the accumulated odors of everyone who had been sick there for the last hundred years. Of the two, I much preferred the frank smell of the sick. The heat of the place was incendiary. So hot that, as we stepped from the bus, our own words did not carry through the air, but hung limply at our lips and chins. Just in front of the hospital was a thirsty courtyard where mobs of waiting people squatted or lay in the meager shade, and where, on dry days, a fine dust rose through which untethered goats shouldered. Against the walls of this courtyard, gaunt, dejected men stood, their faces, like their country, preternaturally solemn, leaden. Here no one looked up at the sky. Every head was bent beneath a wide-brimmed straw hat. In the days that followed, from the doorway of the dispensary, I would watch the brown mountains sliding about, drinking the hospital into their shadow as the afternoon grew later and later, flattening us by their very altitude.

The people were mestizos, of mixed Spanish and Indian blood. They had flat, broad, dumb museum feet. At first they seemed to me indistinguishable the one from the other, without animation. All the vitality, the hidden sexuality, was in their black hair. Soon I was to know them by the fissures with which each face was graven. But, even so, compared to us, they were masked, shut away. My job was to follow Dr. Franciscus around, photograph the patients before and after surgery, interpret and generally act as aide-de-camp. It was exhilarating. Within days I had decided that I was not just useful, but essential. Despite that we spent all day in each other's company, there were no overtures of friendship from Dr. Franciscus. He knew my place, and I knew it, too. In the afternoon he examined the patients scheduled for the next day's surgery. I would call out a name from the doorway to the examining room. In the courtyard someone would rise. I would usher the patient in, and nudge him to the examining table where Franciscus stood, always, I thought, on the verge of irritability. I would read aloud the case history, then wait while he carried out his examination. While I took the "before" photographs, Dr. Franciscus would dictate into a tape recorder:

"Ulcerating basal cell carcinoma of the right orbit—six by eight centimeters—involving the right eye and extending into the floor of the orbit. Operative plan: wide excision with enucleation of the eye. Later, bone and skin grafting." The next morning we would be in the operating room where the procedure would be carried out.

We were more than two weeks into our tour of duty—a few days to go—when it happened. Earlier in the day I had caught sight of her through the window of the dispensary. A thin, dark Indian girl about fourteen years old. A figurine, orange-brown, terra-cotta, and still attached to the unshaped clay from which she had been carved. An older, sun-weathered woman stood behind and somewhat to the left of the girl. The mother was short and dumpy. She wore a broad-brimmed hat with a high crown, and a shapeless dress like a cassock. The girl had long, loose black hair. There were tiny gold hoops in her ears. The dress she wore could have been her mother's. Far too big, it hung from her thin shoulders at some risk of slipping down her arms. Even with her in it, the dress was empty, something hanging on the back of a door. Her breasts made only the smallest imprint in the cloth, her hips none at all. All the while, she pressed to her mouth a filthy, pink, balled-up rag as though to stanch a flow or buttress against pain. I knew that what she had come to show us, what we were there to see, was hidden beneath that pink cloth. As I watched, the woman handed down to her a gourd from which the girl drank, lapping like a dog. She was the last patient of the day. They had been waiting in the courtyard for hours.

"Imelda Valdez," I called out. Slowly she rose to her feet, the cloth never leaving her mouth, and followed her mother to the examining-room door. I shooed them in.

"You sit up there on the table," I told her. "Mother, you stand over there, please." I read from the chart:

"This is a fourteen-year-old girl with a complete, unilateral, left-sided cleft lip and cleft palate. No other diseases or congenital defects. Laboratory tests, chest X ray—negative."

"Tell her to take the rag away," said Dr. Franciscus. I did, and the girl shrank back, pressing the cloth all the more firmly.

"Listen, this is silly," said Franciscus. "Tell her I've got to see it. Either she behaves, or send her away."

"Please give me the cloth," I said to the girl as gently as possible. She did not. She could not. Just then, Franciscus reached up and, taking the hand that held the rag, pulled it away with a hard jerk. For an instant the girl's head followed the cloth as it left her face, one arm still upflung against showing. Against all hope, she would hide herself. A moment later, she relaxed and sat still. She seemed to me then like an animal that looks outward at the infinite, at death, without fear, with recognition only.

Set as it was in the center of the girl's face, the defect was utterly hideous—a nude rubbery insect that had fastened there. The upper lip was widely split all the way to the nose. One white tooth perched upon the protruding upper jaw projected through the hole. Some of the bone seemed to have been gnawed away as well. Above the thing, clear almond eyes and long black hair reflected the light. Below, a slender neck where the pulse trilled visibly. Under our gaze the girl's eyes fell to her lap where her hands lay palms upward, half open. She was a beautiful bird with a crushed beak. And tense with the expectation of more shame.

"Open your mouth," said the surgeon. I translated. She did so, and the surgeon tipped back her head to see inside.

"The palate, too. Complete," he said. There was a long silence. At last he spoke.

"What is your name?" The margins of the wound melted until she herself was being sucked into it.

"Imelda." The syllables leaked through the hole with a sloth and a whistle.

"Tomorrow," said the surgeon, "I will fix your lip. *Mañana.*"

It seemed to me that Hugh Franciscus, in spite of his years of experience, in spite of all the dreadful things he had seen, must have been awed by the sight of this girl. I could see it flit across his face for an instant. Perhaps it was her small act of concealment, that he had had to demand that she show him the lip, that he had had to force her to show it to him. Perhaps it was her resistance that intensified the disfigurement. Had she brought her mouth to him willingly, without shame, she would have been for him neither more nor less than any other patient.

He measured the defect with calipers, studied it from different angles, turning her head with a finger at her chin.

"How can it ever be put back together?" I asked.

"Take her picture," he said. And to her, "Look straight ahead." Through the eye of the camera she seemed more pitiful than ever, her humiliation more complete.

"Wait!" The surgeon stopped me. I lowered the camera. A strand of her hair had fallen across her face and found its way to her mouth, becoming stuck there by saliva. He removed the hair and secured it behind her ear.

"Go ahead," he ordered. There was the click of the camera. The girl winced.

"Take three more, just in case."

When the girl and her mother had left, he took paper and pen and with a few lines drew a remarkable likeness of the girl's face.

"Look," he said. "If this dot is *A,* and this one *B,* this, *C* and this, *D,* the incisions are made to *A* to *B,* then *C* to *D. CD* must equal *AB.* It is all equilateral triangles." All well and good, but then came *X* and *Y* and rotation flaps and the rest.

"Do you see?" he asked.

"It is confusing," I told him.

"It is simply a matter of dropping the upper lip into a normal position, then crossing the gap with two triangular flaps. It is geometry," he said.

"Yes," I said. "Geometry." And relinquished all hope of becoming a plastic surgeon.

II

In the operating room the next morning the anesthesia had already been administered when we arrived from Ward Rounds. The tube emerging from the girl's mouth was pressed against her lower lip to be kept out of the field of surgery. Already, a nurse was scrubbing the face which swam in a reddish-brown lather. The tiny gold earrings were included in the scrub. Now and then, one of them gave a brave flash. The face was washed for the last time, and dried. Green towels were placed over the face to hide everything but the mouth and nose. The drapes were applied.

"Calipers!" The surgeon measured, locating the peak of the distorted Cupid's bow.

"Marking pen!" He placed the first blue dot at the apex of the bow. The nasal sills were dotted; next, the inferior philtral dimple, the vermilion line. The *A* flap and the *B* flap were outlined. On he worked, peppering the lip and nose, making sense out of chaos, realizing the lip that lay waiting in that deep essential pink, that only he could see. The last dot and line were placed. He was ready.

"Scalpel!" He held the knife above the girl's mouth.

"O.K. to go ahead?" he asked the anesthetist.

"Yes."

He lowered the knife.

"No! Wait!" The anesthetist's voice was tense, staccato. "Hold it!"

The surgeon's hand was motionless.

"What's the matter?"

"Something's wrong. I'm not sure. God, she's hot as a pistol. Blood pressure is way up. Pulse one eighty. Get a rectal temperature." A nurse fumbled beneath the drapes. We waited. The nurse retrieved the thermometer.

"One hundred seven . . . no . . . eight." There was disbelief in her voice.

"Malignant hyperthermia," said the anesthetist. "Ice! Ice! Get lots of ice!" I raced out the door, accosted the first nurse I saw.

"Ice!" I shouted. "*Hielo!* Quickly! *Hielo!*" The woman's expression was blank. I ran to another. "*Hielo! Hielo!* For the love of God, ice."

"*Hielo?*" She shrugged. "*Nada.*" I ran back to the operating room.

"There isn't any ice," I reported. Dr. Franciscus had ripped off his rubber gloves and was feeling the skin of the girl's abdomen. Above the mask his eyes were the eyes of a horse in battle.

"The EKG is wild . . ."

"I can't get a pulse . . ."

"What the hell . . ."

The surgeon reached for the girl's groin. No femoral pulse.

"EKG flat. My God! She's dead!"

"She can't be."

"She is."

The surgeon's fingers pressed the groin where there was no pulse to be felt, only his own pulse hammering at the girl's flesh to be let in.

III

It was noon, four hours later, when we left the operating room. It was a day so hot and humid I felt steamed open like an envelope. The woman was sitting on a bench in the courtyard in her dress like a cassock. In one hand she held the piece of cloth the girl had used to conceal her mouth. As we watched, she folded it once neatly, and then again, smoothing it, cleaning the cloth which might have been the head of the girl in her lap that she stroked and consoled.

"I'll do the talking here," he said. He would tell her himself, in whatever Spanish he could find. Only if she did not understand was I to speak for him. I watched him brace himself, set his shoulders. How could he tell her? I wondered. What? But I knew he would tell her everything, exactly as it had happened. As much for himself as for her, he needed to explain. But suppose she screamed, fell to the ground, attacked him, even? All that hope of love . . . gone. Even in his discomfort I knew that he was teaching me. The way to do it was professionally. Now he was standing above her. When the woman saw that he did not speak, she lifted her eyes and saw what he held crammed in his mouth to tell her. She knew, and rose to her feet.

"Señora," he began, "I am sorry." All at once he seemed to me shorter than he was, scarcely taller than she. There was a place at the crown of his head where the hair had grown thin. His lips were stones. He could hardly move them. The voice dry, dusty.

"No one could have known. Some bad reaction to the medicine for sleeping. It poisoned her. High fever. She did not wake up." The last, a whisper. The woman studied his lips as though she were deaf. He tried, but could not control a twitching at the corner of his mouth. He raised a thumb and forefinger to press something back into his eyes.

"Muerte," the woman announced to herself. Her eyes were human, deadly.

"Si, muerte." At that moment he was like someone cast, still alive, as an effigy for his own tomb. He closed his eyes. Nor did he open them until he felt the touch of the woman's hand on his arm, a touch from which he did not withdraw. Then he looked and saw the grief corroding her face, breaking it down, melting the features so that eyes, nose, mouth ran together in a distortion, like the girl's. For a long time they stood in silence. It seemed to me that minutes passed. At last her face cleared, the features rearranged themselves. She spoke, the words coming slowly to make certain that he understood her. She would go home now. The next day her sons would come for the girl, to take her home for burial. The doctor must not be sad. God has decided. And she was happy now that the harelip had been fixed so that her daughter might go to Heaven without it. Her bare feet retreating were the felted pads of a great bereft animal.

IV

The next morning I did not go to the wards, but stood at the gate leading from the courtyard to the road outside. Two young men in striped ponchos lifted the girl's body wrapped in a straw mat onto the back of a wooden cart. A donkey waited. I had been drawn to this place as one is drawn, inexplicably, to certain scenes of desolation—executions, battlefields. All at once, the woman looked up and saw me. She had taken off her hat. The heavy-hanging coil of her hair made her head seem larger, darker, noble. I pressed some money into her hand.

"For flowers," I said. "A priest." Her cheeks shook as though minutes ago a stone had been dropped into her naval and the ripples were just now reaching her head. I regretted having come to that place.

"*Si, si,*" the woman said. Her own face was stitched with flies. "The doctor is one of the angels. He has finished the work of God. My daughter is beautiful."

What could she mean! The lip had not been fixed. The girl had died before he would have done it.

"Only a fine line that God will erase in time," she said.

I reached into the cart and lifted a corner of the mat in which the girl had been rolled. Where the cleft had been there was now a fresh line of tiny sutures. The Cupid's bow was delicately shaped, the vermilion border aligned. The flattened nostril had now the same rounded shape as the other one. I let the mat fall over the face of the dead girl, but not before I had seen the touching place where the finest black hairs sprang from the temple.

'*Adiós, adiós* . . .'" And the cart creaked away to the sound of hooves, a tinkling bell.

V

There are events in a doctor's life that seem to mark the boundary between youth and age, seeing and perceiving. Like certain dreams, they illuminate a whole lifetime of past behavior. After such an event, a doctor is not the same as he was before. It had seemed to me then to have been the act of someone demented, or at least insanely arrogant. An attempt to reorder events. Her death had come to him out of order. It should have come after the lip had been repaired, not before. He could have told the mother that, no, the lip had not been fixed. But he did not. He said nothing. It had been an act of omission, one of those strange lapses to which all of us are subject and which we live to regret. It must have been then, at that moment, that the knowledge of what he would do appeared to him. The words of the mother had not consoled him; they had hunted him down. He had not done it for her. The dire necessity was his. He would not accept that Imelda had died before he could repair her lip. People who do such things break free from society. They follow their own lonely path. They have a secret which they can never reveal. I must never let on that I knew.

VI

How often I have imagined it. Ten o'clock at night. The hospital of Comayagua is all but dark. Here and there lanterns tilt and skitter up and down the corridors. One of these lamps breaks free from the others and descends the stone steps to the underground room that is the morgue of the hospital. This room wears the expression as if it had waited all night for someone to come. No silence so deep as this place with its cargo of newly dead. Only the slow drip of water over stone. The door closes gassily and clicks shut. The lock is turned. There are four tables, each with a body encased in a paper shroud. There is no mistaking her. She is the smallest. The surgeon takes a knife from his pocket and slits open the paper shroud, that part in which the girl's head is enclosed. The wound seems to be living on long after she has died. Waves of heat emanate from it, blurring his vision. All at once, he turns to peer over his shoulder. He sees nothing, only a wooden crucifix on the wall.

He removes a package of instruments from a satchel and arranges them on a tray. Scalpel, scissors, forceps, needle holder. Sutures and gauze sponges are produced. Stealthy, hunched, engaged, he begins. The dots of blue dye are still there upon her mouth. He raises the scalpel, pauses. A second glance into the darkness. From the wall a small lizard watches and accepts. The first cut is made. A sluggish flow of dark blood appears. He wipes it away with a sponge. No new blood comes to take its place. Again and again he cuts, connecting each of the blue dots until the whole of the zigzag slice is made, first on one side of the cleft, then on the other. Now the edges of the cleft are lined with fresh tissue. He sets down the scalpel and takes up scissors and forceps, undermining the little flaps until each triangle is attached only at one side. He rotates each flap into its new position. He must be certain that they can be swung without tension. They can. He is ready to suture. He fits the tiny curved needle into the jaws of the needle holder. Each suture is placed precisely the same number of millimeters from the cut edge, and the same distance apart. He ties each knot down until the edges are apposed. Not too tightly. These are the most meticulous sutures of his life. He cuts each thread close to the knot. It goes well. The vermilion border with its white skin roll is exactly aligned. One more stitch and the Cupid's bow appears as if by magic. The man's face shines with moisture. Now the nostril is incised around the margin, released, and sutured into a round shape to match its mate. He wipes the blood from the face of the girl with gauze that he has dipped in water. Crumbs of light are scattered on the girl's face. The shroud is folded once more about her. The instruments are handed into the satchel. In a moment the morgue is dark and a lone lantern ascends the stairs and is extinguished.

VII

Six weeks later I was in the darkened amphitheater of the Medical School. Tiers of seats rose in a semicircle above the small stage where Hugh Franciscus stood presenting the case material he had encountered in Honduras. It was the highlight of the year. The hall was filled. The night before he had arranged the slides in the order in which they were to be shown. I was at the controls of the slide projector.

"Next slide!" he would order from time to time in that military voice which had called forth blind obedience from generations of medical students, interns, residents and patients.

"This is a fifty-seven-year-old man with a severe burn contracture of the neck. You will notice the rigid webbing that has fused the chin to the presternal tissues. No motion of the head on the torso is possible. . . . Next slide!"

"Click," went the projector.

"Here he is after the excision of the scar tissue and with the head in full extension for the first time. The defect was then covered. . . . Next slide!"

"Click."

" . . . with full-thickness drums of skin taken from the abdomen with the Padgett dermatome. Next slide!"

"Click."

And suddenly there she was, extracted from the shadows, suspended above and beyond all of us like a resurrection. There was the oval face, the long black hair unbraided, the tiny gold hoops in her ears. And that luminous gnawed mouth. The whole of her life seemed to have been summed up in this photograph. A long silence followed that was the surgeon's alone to break. Almost at once, like the anesthetist in the operating room in Comayagua, I knew that something was wrong. It was not that the man would not speak as that he could not. The audience of doctors, nurses and students seemed to have been infected by the black, limitless silence. My own pulse doubled. It was hard to breathe. Why did he not call out for the next slide? Why did he not save himself? Why had he not removed this slide from the ones to be shown? All at once I knew that he had used his camera on her again. I could see the long black shadows of her hair flowing into the darker shadows of the morgue. The sudden blinding flash . . . The next slide would be the one taken in the morgue. He would be exposed.

In the dim light reflected from the slide, I saw him gazing up at her, seeing not the colored photograph, I thought, but the negative of it where the ghost of the girl was. For me, the amphitheater had become Honduras. I saw again that courtyard littered with patients. I could see the dust in the beam of light from the projector. It was then that I knew that she was his measure of perfection and pain—the one lost, the other gained. He, too, had heard the click of the camera, had seen her wince and felt his mercy enlarge. At last he spoke.

"Imelda." It was the one word he had heard her say. At the sound of his voice I removed the next slide from the projector. "Click" . . . and she was gone. "Click" again, and in her place the man with the orbital cancer. For a long moment Franciscus looked up in my direction, on his face an expression that I have given up trying to interpret. Gratitude? Sorrow? It made me think of the gaze of the girl when at last she understood that she must hand over to him the evidence of her body.

"This is a sixty-two-year-old man with a basal cell carcinoma of the temple eroding into the bony orbit . . ." he began as though nothing had happened.

At the end of the hour, even before the lights went on, there was loud applause. I hurried to find him among the departing crowd. I could not. Some weeks went by before I caught sight of him. He seemed vaguely convalescent, as though a fever had taken its toll before burning out.

Hugh Franciscus continued to teach for fifteen years, although he operated a good deal less, then gave it up entirely. It was as though he had grown tired of blood, of always having to be involved with blood, of having to draw it, spill it, wipe it away, stanch it. He was a quieter, softer man, I heard, the ferocity diminished. There were no more expeditions to Honduras or anywhere else.

I, too, have not been entirely free of her. Now and then, in the years that have passed, I see that donkey-cart cortège, or his face bent over hers in the morgue. I would like to have told him what I now know, that his unrealistic act was one of goodness, one of those small, persevering acts done, perhaps, to ward off madness. Like lighting a lamp, boiling water for tea, washing a shirt. But, of course, it's too late now.

Considerations

Thinking

What is Selzer's purpose (or purposes) in this essay? What, that is, do you think might be his designs on his readers?

What does Selzer suggest about how Dr. Franciscus is affected by the experience in Honduras? How is the young Dr. Selzer affected—by both the Honduran experience and by Dr. Franciscus?

Connecting

"Imelda" is arranged in seven sections. Provide a title for and explain the purpose of each section.

Consider how the sections might be grouped to form a three- or four-part essay. On what basis might the sections be combined?

Compare the image of the doctor and/or patient presented in "Imelda" with the image of the doctor and/or patient reflected in another essay, whether by Selzer or by another writer in *Encounters*.

Writing

Write an essay in which you describe and explain your relationship to an older mentor. Identify a scene or situation that led you to see your mentor in a new way and perhaps to understand something about yourself as well as him or her in the process.

STUDENT ESSAYS ON
RICHARD SELZER'S WORK

The two student essays that appear in this section are quite different in scope, and yet each focuses in its own way on Selzer's deep interest in the human body.

Neeraj Gupta investigates the sexual imagery in one of Selzer's essays—"The Knife"—and quotes liberally from that essay to establish the relationship between the imagery and Selzer's ideas about the power of a surgeon's knife.

Zack Whyte was given a broader task by his instructor. He was asked to read several of Selzer's essays and to identify what he considered to be a central preoccupation of Selzer's—a concern that works its way into a number of essays, no matter how different those essays might seem from one another. Eventually, following his analysis of a selected group of essays, Zack's task was to formulate a claim or an idea about Selzer's central preoccupation and to substantiate that claim in an essay of his own. Zack "fastens" onto what he calls Selzer's "welling love for the body." He sees that preoccupation as a revealing "undercurrent" of Selzer's imagination. To substantiate his claim, Zack quotes sparingly but effectively from thirteen of Selzer's essays, giving readers a clear understanding of Selzer and of his own idea.

Both student essays show signs of careful, analytical reading; thoughtful selection of evidence; and effective use of evidence to substantiate and develop ideas.

Sexual Imagery in Selzer's "The Knife"

Neeraj Gupta

In his essay "The Knife," Richard Selzer describes the tremendous power of the surgeon's scalpel. Specifically, he manifests the knife's awesome capacity to bring either life or death to the patient, and the terrifyingly fine line between the two. Intrinsic to the knife's power is its symbiotic relationship with the surgeon, as well as the quasi-independent will it often seems to exercise in his hands. Selzer focuses his essay on the necessity for the surgeon to learn to control his tool, and the damage that could otherwise be caused. To this end, Selzer utilizes a lengthy metaphor likening the knife to a man's penis, and the surgical operation to an act of sex. Central to this comparison is the power of both the instruments, and the difficult yet necessary task of controlling them.

Selzer opens his essay by immediately developing this metaphor. Describing the knife, "marvel[ling] at its power," he wonders at the blade's ability to "dart" into the body, "flesh part[ing]" behind it. As if the image of the knife, a phallic symbol, poking its way into the fleshy, red, physical opening of the patient wasn't enough to begin establishing his connection, Selzer goes on. He speaks of "resolve that lowers us, my knife and me, deeper and deeper into the person beneath. It is an entry into the body that is . . . among the gentlest of acts. Then stroke and stroke again, . . . until the wound blooms with strange flowers." Selzer very graphically details this metaphorical intercourse with his patient, firmly and indelibly fixing the relationship in his reader's mind.

Selzer has several motives in drawing this comparison. Most obviously, he calls attention to the fact that surgery and sex are both acts of renewal, ushering new life into the world. Just as his patient's "wound" soon "blooms with strange flowers" of health, so too does a new baby eventually burgeon from a woman's vagina; each miracle bringing rebirth where before there was only disease or age. Similarly, Selzer stresses the power inherent in both the acts of sex and surgery. In the one, he enters another person and plants a seed that will soon blossom into another life; in the other, he "unnatural[ly]" slices open a human being in an attempt to save a life. His respect for this power is palpable in his emotional ambivalence. Even as he thrills with the feeling of having the knife's ability under his guidance, he is "struck with a kind of dread that it is [he] in whose hand the blade travels," and experiences "the quietude of resolve layered over fear." This nervousness highlights the anxiety Selzer feels over his power, and emphasizes his need to be able to control the knife's actions.

Meanwhile, Selzer continues to delve deeper into his metaphor. He recounts "the litany of monosyllables with which one prays his way down and into the body," very much like a series of the grunts and moans of passion. Similarly, he paints a picture of the knife slicing into the "peritoneum, pink and gleaming and membranous, bulg[ing] into the wound" hiding the abdomen and womb. This membrane can easily be likened to the hymen sheltering the vagina of virgins. These sexual details are not evidence of any perversion on Dr. Selzer's part, nor are they meant to be crude or pornographic. Rather, they are intended to combat the "green" "clean and tidy" sterility of surgery. Selzer strives to go past the "precisely . . . arranged," well-orchestrated, automatic indifference of modern operations. The patient's body is more than just a machine in need of repair, and the surgeon more than a mechanic who can fix it. The sexual imagery replaces impersonality with intimacy, and makes the doctor's act of dealing with the "temple" of the body much more significant. The surgeon is truly devoted to what he is doing, even if at the very least, it is the purely physical appreciation of casual sex. This meaningful attachment has far-reaching consequences, for the surgical experience has the power to be the extreme good of love for the body and life for the patient, or its polar opposite, of the rape of the body's health and its death.

In Selzer's opinion, the distinctive difference between these two outcomes is the presence or lack of control. He writes, "To hold it above a belly is to know the knife's [/penis's] force." The knife has a will and power of its own, which must be kept in check. If one doesn't bind the instrument back, and stay in control of it, then one's ardor and passion will overcome all restraint, and make the object seemingly "pursue an intent of its own, driving into the flesh, a wild energy." Selzer strives to prevent this from happening. Losing control of the scalpel in a delicate surgical procedure would be ruinous; as would be excessive force in a sexual act; both would jeopardize the operation and very likely make all the efforts fruitless. As Selzer writes in his first paragraph: "The knife is not for pressing. It is for drawing across the field of skin." And yet, in each circumstance, the compulsion to relinquish the necessary control remains, and must be defeated. The strength and the power of the object needs to be responsibly "curb[ed] in order to create," for only then can one manipulate its energy to serve the more meaningful purpose of saving or starting a life.

However, the objective of control is a very difficult one to accomplish. The knife itself is said to be alive. Indeed, the connection between the scalpel and its surgeon is compared to the body of the Centaur, two different parts of a distinct whole, each different, yet alive. "The knife, below, all equine energy, the surgeon, above, with his delicate art." It is the surgeon's task to be master of the wild horse joined beneath him, to govern its power and use it responsibly. Yet Selzer gives the knife its own will, its own life. He talks about the instrument being composed of "two parts, the handle and the blade . . . At one end of the handle is a narrow notched prong upon which the blade is slid, then snapped into place . . . [S]lide on the blade, click it home, and the knife springs instantly to life. It is headed now, edgy, leaping to mount the fingers for the gallop to the feast." The knife itself is thus described in terms of a sexual act, and when the blade is finally slid into the handle's "notched prong," signaling the culmination of that act, the knife comes alive, metaphorically growing into an erection. This phallus has emotions and urges of its own that often dominate the mind above, and now eager to be carried to the woman, its wild horse–like energy is unharnessed and chomping at the bit.

In contrast to the savage desire of the knife, the surgeon must initially struggle to work towards the completion of the act. The pain and suffering that he inflicts does not escape touching him. He brings life and death, but the life is not provided painlessly. He is aware that the damage he is causing is beneficial in the long run, and yet he remains only human in continuing to recoil from the more vicious aspects of his profession. Still, he "cannot weep. When he cuts the flesh, his own must not bleed." Similarly, the sexual male could also be "rendered impotent by his own empathy and compassion." Sex may hurt the woman, while the agony of childbirth looms ahead, and all of this may make the man reluctant to continue. However, this cannot be allowed to happen. When the man hurts with his penetration, he must necessarily go on. It signifies no less love, because the acts of sex and surgery are necessary for the long-term fulfillment of both parties involved. It may bleed, it may be a little scary, but it's how the procedure goes.

Nevertheless, one is still allowed to empathize with the patient. Selzer provides images of the anxious patient on a bed in an operating room, "washed and purged and dressed in a white gown." This description is strongly evocative of a woman's wedding night, as she waits nervously in her bed with her wedding dress still on. The word patient originally meant "one who suffers." This description is certainly apt when one takes into account the dreadful fear and anticipation that the young virginal girl no doubt experiences. It is, as Selzer writes, especially difficult, because "In the very act of lying down, you have made a declaration of surrender." Indeed, he goes on to say that "to give over one's body and will for surgery, to *lie down* for it, is a yielding of more than we can bear." This symbolic submission is extremely important. The woman is giving herself up to intimacy, an experience described as where "a man will stand over you, gowned and hooded. In time the man will take up a knife and crack open your flesh like a ripe melon. Fingers will rummage . . . Blood will run free." This is obviously a terrifying vision, of a man staring at your naked form, possessing you, roughly taking your virginity. Selzer even allows that this gift of intimacy may be excessively scary, that perhaps a woman might find it too difficult to give up her body, her will, her self to a man. In these circumstances, a man must try to seduce the girl, just as the anesthesiologist lures the unwilling surgical patient to sleep. "Let yourself go," he says. "It's a pleasant sensation." "Give in." Eventually, inevitably, the patient capitulates, going through the pain and discomfort of the experience, then living to awaken with a feeling of "nausea," or morning sickness: the metaphorical sign of pregnancy and a fruitful night, or life and a successful operation.

In the final part of his essay, Selzer more particularly depicts this issue of sexual consummation. He calls it only "the moment," the time that the participants have timidly avoided confronting, but which they have steadily been travel-ing towards. Selzer writes of an "unimpeded" "brute" knife, and a "slick slide home" into the body. "The flesh," he details, "splits with its own kind of moan. It is like the penetration of rape." This passage suggests that ultimately, at the high climax of the entire operation, the phallus/knife is gaining control, and things are becoming destructively vicious. To support the notion, Selzer begins writing about the more horrific aspects of surgery: "breasts of women . . . cut off, arms and legs sliced to the bone to make ready for the saw, eyes freed from sockets, intestines lopped." Having firmly established the connection between sex and surgery, Selzer can now illustrate the negative ramifications of the sexual lack of control with terrifying surgical images. Selzer leaves it up to his readers to imagine for themselves the sight of the frenzied man, standing over the woman in the sur-geon's position of power, thrusting "wildly" in a fog of "sweat" and semen, and then, to picture the time when he has relieved his physical impulse, and the horror his mind will experience when it reasserts control. The reader is forced to face for himself the vision of the male/surgeon, "rebel[ling]" at the terrible thing he has done, the tragic rape and the destruction that are the ramifications of the loss of restraint, and the surrender to the violent impulses of the penis and the knife.

This second passage dealing with the penetration of the body finally fully explores the duality of the knife's power. In the initial entering of the body, at the essay's opening. Selzer's mind is consumed with wonder at the beauty and magnif-icence of the body, and he devotes a lot of praise to its incredible structure and complexity. However, by the piece's end, he becomes selfishly absorbed in his own penis and his own pleasure, and focuses his writing's attention on the knife, and on himself. In the first act of intercourse, he is in control; in the other, he allows himself to lose restraint and to metaphorically rape his patient, consumed as he is with his own well-being, and not his victim's. Whatever its final result, the surgery has been irrevocably tainted by its practitioner's selfish motives. Selzer himself determines the consequences of this behavior. Rather than "flowers" "bloom[ing]" this second time, he writes "Within the belly a tumor squats, toadish, fungoid," as if to point out the relative ease of ending up at either of these two extremes, of rape and love, of a tumor and blossoming flowers. Selzer ends with an image of the knife lying "spent, on its side, the bloody meal smear-dried upon its flanks." Just like the exhausted penis, it has focused its power, and now, again in control of itself, it "waits." This is an allusion back to the beginning of the essay, where the penis "waits, at the ready," to spring up, to be used again.

Once more, Selzer offers the power of the knife to be used for life or death, dependent only upon our ability to control it. Similarly, this can be said of all the important things in life. All of these objects or ideas, these metaphorical knives, are double-edged. They can be easily utilized either for good or for bad. Selzer allows us to make our own choices; he has merely detailed two extremes and examined their consequences. It is up to each of us to develop the strength of will and the courage to harness our knives and use them for the good, and to try to succeed with them the best that we can.

Sacrificing Passion

Zack Whyte

First the slice: a neat incision. The surgeon's fingers fumble inside, searching, searching. There! And with a sickening plop the liver is ripped dripping from the body, a sacrifice perhaps. Blood spews from the organ and the hole from which it appeared. The priest places the liver gingerly, guiltily maybe, on a blank page, a relic now, an object of reverence. But it is on a piece of paper, caught in the realm of the pen, and can thus be touched and examined with words. The poet takes over and starts exploring, searching for the holiness, the truth, the fire he knows is there, that must be there. He takes us with him. Nouns widen narrow arteries that we may enter, verbs smooth out the way and adjectives shine into hidden recesses. It is beautiful to go spelunking thus in the human body. Yet with the poet guiding us the roads of blood are not the only paths to take. He takes us also down the avenues of time, points out long dead people, landmarks, milestones, and through his eyes we stare directly at their innards as they dance to their own particular forgotten tune.

In Richard Selzer's skilled hands, the liver comes alive, receives a history, a personality, a divine purpose. He revels in the body, dignifies ill-thought-of organs with grand metaphor and describes in painful yet sympathetic detail the calamities that befall them. "But why?" you may well ask. "What sort of person would write lyrically about livers? What motivates such a man?" If we search for the sources of these questions, we will end up at Selzer's welling love for the body. But, please, do not think that there are no tributaries, no other sources affecting his writing. Please do not think I am reducing his essays to mere paeans to the human corpus. Each essay seems to expose another side of him, another tributary to the massive river that is his imagination. And they are layered, their waters blended in colorful confusion. I fasten on to his love of the body merely because it seems present in most all of his essays, an undercurrent of his imagination if you will.

And it is no mean swirler of eddies this current; like Vasalius, his love "is a passion, not a romance" (*Lessons* 24). But it is no Greek exuberance over perfect shapes and dimensions, no revelling in youthful strength and health. In "Skin," Selzer writes: "I hold no brief for rosy, turgid youth. It does but stir envy and leave compassion unaroused" (113). The people who touch his love are the imperfect ones, "those in whom the difference from homely to comely is but a single freckle, one wart, a crease. . . . Like imperfect postage stamps, they are the collector's items of the human race" (113). And finally he comes right out and says it: "Yes, my sympathies lie with *us*" (113). Selzer cares not for Platonic ideals, his love reaches not for the wispy clouds of perfection, but rather for that maimed, crumpled and broken human body lying there on the operating table, waiting for his knife.

At times the intensity of this love becomes overpowering, and it clings like the heavy scent of rotting flesh to the pages of his essays. At times, as in "The Knife," it inclines to lust, and with his knife he all but rapes the body. He stabs, he thrusts the knife into the unconscious body of his patient, doing his business with a feverish intensity, and then when all is done he and his knife lie spent, waiting. At other times, though, his love is of a much gentler nature. At other times he softly caresses the body with his knife, lovingly wiping away budding tumors and rotting appendages. At other times he romances his way inside his patient. In whatever form, the love is always there, moving him and us through his essays.

So there is love. But how is it there? In what language does he speak it? He loves with a religious fervor, and often lapses into that particular metaphoric, sacred space when he tries to communicate his feelings. In "The Knife," he says, "the priestliness of my profession has ever been impressed on me" (94). And in other essays he goes on to develop the themes of the operation as a sacrifice, perhaps most explicitly in "Amazons." In this essay Selzer reworks in his dreaming imagination a mastectomy performed by a female surgeon and a group of female nurses. It becomes a cultic sacrifice performed by a robed, entranced priestess upon an altar in a great, marble temple. What for some is a simple act of cut and paste, is to him a religious endeavor. It is a giving in, a giving up of actual pieces of the holy body. Imagine offering up pieces of the Ark; it is a sublime gesture of love, a supreme sacrifice. Thus does the sterile act of surgery bear oddly wondrous fruit in Selzer's imagination.

But what is the locus of his religious fervor? If he is sacrificing, he must be sacrificing to someone or something. In "Why I Left the Church," Selzer lays bare his agnosticism, but also admits his love of "the sheer pomp and procession" of the church (*Confessions* 87). The ritual holds him though God doesn't. This may in fact help explain why he is a surgeon and not a priest, for in his surgery there is ritual, there is pomp and procession, but God is relegated to the outside, to his heaven, away. But it is more complicated than that. In "An Absence of Windows," Selzer wonders at the wisdom of the utter sterility and godlessness of surgery, and perhaps of science as a whole. He wonders whether the removal of the windows in the operating room, and thereby the removal of surgery from under the eye of the divine, was such a good idea. "It did no patient a disservice to have Heaven looking over his doctor's shoulder. I very much fear that having bricked up our windows, we have lost more than the breeze; we have severed a celestial connection" (15). Selzer wants there to be some higher force than that of his surgeon's knife. He wants something looking over his shoulder, judging him. But he cannot really accept God as a single unified divinity. He wants something else, something that can make "sparks fly up from the dry husks of the human body" (16). He wants something more personal but with less personality. I would say he wants the divine, but cannot accept a God.

At the very end of "Why I Left the Church," Selzer speaks of "Love" (90). Its capitalization seems to imply that it somehow transcends love of the normal, everyday variety; it is somehow greater, more divine. This Love will neither pass nor fade; it is forever. And to Selzer, I believe, it is also immanent in the body. It is the soul of man.

It is to this Love that Selzer offers his sacrifices. It is this love that receives him, but it also is guiding him and, through him, the patient. Thus Love takes on all three roles in the sacrifice; it is God, priest and sacrificial lamb all in one. Let me elaborate. Since it is Love that guides him to commit his surgery, it is within him. Now at the very moment of sacrifice something happens, a union is achieved, as if the divinity he makes his offering to hears him and reaches out, touching him fleetingly. In "The Knife," he writes, "I said no love is made here, but love happens" (*Lessons* 98). Love happens in the house of surgery, of a sudden it is there, and it suffuses Selzer and his knife.

And Love binds Selzer to his patient. "A doctor gazes at his patient and he sees himself; joined, they are one pilgrim in search of health" (*Confessions* 63). But it is a unity that the surgeon must be wary of. He cannot work upon himself. "When he cuts the flesh, his own must not bleed" (*Lessons* 101). It is a constant threat for Selzer, this comparison of his, this Love that binds him to his patient. It is a constant fight for the priest to stay unwavering and pure of thought while performing the sacrifice, to stay as cold as his knife.

So Love then is taking on a peculiar triple role in the little play enacted in the operating theater. Rather like Odin nailed to Yggdrasil, the Tree of Life, he is sacrificing himself to himself by himself. But why? Odin did it to get the runes; he snatched them up with a roar. Odin did it to gain knowledge, wisdom, power. What does Selzer seek? Is it merely gratification of the desire to "touch the incandescent center of the human body (*Confessions* 40)?" He writes

> I have become receptive to the possibilities of love (for it is love, this thing that happens in the operating room), and each day I wait, trembling in the busy air. Perhaps today it will come. Perhaps today I will find it, take part in it, this love that blooms in the stoniest desert.   (*Lessons* 18)

Perhaps, then, he seeks ecstasy, some transcendent experience to fill his soul to the brim with the waters of belief. But not Christian belief. Selzer's ark is the living body not some dusty, mummified object of yore.

And in other essays the body is precisely where he searches for the metaphysicality he needs: "Yes, it is the exact location of the soul that I am after. The smell of it is in my nostrils, I have caught glimpses of it in the body diseased" (19). In the body diseased? Why not in perfect bodies? He knows that "it is the marred and scarred and faulty that are subject to grace" (19). Perhaps this is why they are the ones with whom his sympathies lie. But he cannot cut his way into the soul with his knife; he realizes its limitations. His pen is the only instrument delicate enough for this operation, and with it he makes his way in to look for that spark of a soul that must be there: "in the recesses of the body I search for the philosopher's stone. I know it is there, hidden in the deepest, dampest cul-de-sac. It awaits discovery. To find it would be like the harnessing of fire. It would illuminate the world" (16).

Selzer the mystic covers his beloved body in veils of living metaphor. He envisions wondrous sparks of life in each organ, even, or perhaps especially, in those diseased. In "The Twelve Spheres," Selzer presents a defense of sorts of Chinese mystical healing, especially acupuncture. He feels kindred in spirit with those ancient Chinese healers. He longs to write out prescription such as "deer-horn velvet for convulsions and anemia, or dried venom of Chinese toads for the common cold" (167). He is no straight-laced, dispassionate surgeon who operates in the sterile glare of the lamps and forgets his patient moments after the knife leaves the body. He rails against those "specimen collectors," those people who fail to see the body as "spirit thickened" (*Confession* 184). For him, surgery is an art not a science. He holds his love, his reverence for the body back so as not to interfere with his knife, but passion will assert itself. The shackles of science cannot hold it, nor his imagination.

In a race of surgeons Selzer might well bring up the rear. Doctors who invest nothing, who never break through the sterile barriers of hospital that separate them from their patients, have no fear, and it is fearlessness that makes them better doctors. Patients die, and the most efficient doctor is he who feels least at their deaths. Measured along those lines Selzer is not much of a surgeon. His compassion blurs his vision and dulls his knife. He can subvert it for a bit, but it lies in wait. In "An Absence of Windows," he has to perform surgery on a mailman, a friend. Before he knows it he has spoken the man's name aloud with some words of comfort. It is a mistake. "I should not have spoken his name aloud! No good will come of it. The syllable has peeled from me something, a skin that I need" (18). Selzer's passion for the body frees him to care but endangers his performance, making him vulnerable just when he needs protection.

Selzer is thus left in the odd position of being a doctor at the mercy of his patients. His shielding carapace gone, he feels every touch they bestow upon him. For they too have knives, and they cut him open as easily and as deftly as he cuts them. But their operations are not of a physical nature. "When the patient becomes the surgeon, he goes straight for the soul" (*Lessons* 46). In "Lessons from the Art," Selzer chronicles some of these double operations, laying open his patients as the patients calmly carve their way into his soul. And this is what sets him apart from his fellow physicians, this willingness to be operated on by his patients. He writes of looking at a particular young man kissing the crooked mouth of his wife, a mouth warped by Selzer's knife while removing a tumor in her cheek. And as the young man "twists his lips to accommodate to hers, to show her that their kiss still works" Selzer feels the knife of the two young people in him: "I hold my breath and let the wonder in," he writes, as they lay bare his soul (46).

The returned touch of the patient triggers Selzer's ecstasy, just as a lover finds happiness in a returned caress. The thrill of simply having healed finally crystallizes his love. After the cutting and ripping and patching of organs, after all the pruning of limbs and toenails, comes this elation. In "Pages from a Wound-Dresser's Diary," after having fished out a miné ball from an old soldier's wound, Selzer the Wound-Dresser writes: "All at once a strange feeling comes over me. It is happiness. I cannot resist it. And I know that if love came once, it may come again. If love should not come, still I know why I am alive" (*Confessions* 148).

'Tis thus Selzer achieves his passion. Surgeondom, priesthood, poetry, contain his *raison d'être*. But all is not so grand; there is always something disturbing the neat, surgical precision of Selzer's account of himself. In "The Knife," he writes that "one can count on absurdity. There, in the midst of our solemnities, appears, small and black and crawling, an insect: The Ant of the Absurd" (*Lessons* 99). This Ant scurries toward the altar of the body with defilement in mind. Is the body then defiled? Its holiness soiled? I think not. The Ant provides a wisdom of its own. Its own source of truth, it helps combat the stiff pretentiousness of the determined seeker of truth. The Ant of the Absurd does not defile, it only underscores the truth to be found in the passionate romance Selzer has with the body. It helps us laugh at him and with him about his own holy pretentions.

And so, finally, he sacrifices to heal his own wounds, for they too hurt and bleed; and they are not of such a physical nature that they can easily be dealt with using his steel knife and sutures. Selzer the Wound-Dresser applies the truth he finds in healing as a bandage to himself, cleansing and closing the wounds of others as well as his own wounds. The wonder he lets in while watching the young couple's crooked kiss washes away his ills, and restores his faith. The losses deepen his pain. Finally, I say, he writes about livers to heal himself.

WORKS CITED

Selzer, Richard, "The Exact Location of the Soul," "The Surgeon as a Priest," "Lessons From the Art," "The Knife," "Skin," and "The Twelve Spheres." *Mortal Lessons: Notes on the Art of Surgery.* New York: Touchstone, 1987.
———. "An Absence of Windows," "Amazons," "In the Shadow of the Winch," "The Spoils of Troy," "Why I Left the Church," "Pages from a Wound-Dresser's Diary," "The Specimen Collectors," and "Travels in Rhineland." *Confessions of a Knife.* New York: William Morrow, 1979.

E. B. White
(1899–1985)

E. B. White is generally recognized as one of America's finest writers. Long associated with the *New Yorker,* for which he wrote stories, sketches, essays, and editorials, White also contributed to another prominent magazine, Harper's, writing a monthly column, "One Man's Meat," from 1938 to 1943. These columns were collected and published with a few additional pieces from the *New Yorker* as *One Man's Meat* (1944). This book was followed by two other collections of miscellany, *The Second Tree from the Corner* (1954) and *The Points of My Compass* (1962). Besides these collections, White published, over a slightly longer span of years, three children's books: *Stuart Little* (1945), *Charlotte's Web* (1952), and *The Trumpet of the Swan* (1970). In 1976, White published a selection of his best essays, those, as he says, which had "an odor of durability clinging to them." *The Essays of E. B. White* (1977) was followed a year later by a selection of White's letters, titled simply enough, *Letters of E. B. White. Poems and Sketches of E. B. White* appeared in 1981.

Although not a complete bibliography of White's published work, this list does suggest something of White's range and versatility, as well as something about the way writing has been for him steady work over a long stretch of time. And the steadiest of White's work, in both senses of the word, has been his essays. In fact, it is as an essayist that White is best known and most highly acclaimed. And it is as an essayist that he identifies himself, defining an essayist as "a self-liberated man sustained by the childish belief that everything he thinks about, everything that happens to him, is of general interest." And again, as one who is "content with living a free life and enjoying the satisfactions of a somewhat undisciplined existence."

Edward Hoagland has noted that White's name has become almost synonymous with *essay.* And for good reason, we might add, since it is the form most congenial to his temperament, a form that allows him the latitude he needs to roam freely in thought, a form that he has been able to stamp with his own imprint. This imprint is reflected in the following elements: a scrupulous respect for his readers; an uncanny accuracy in the use of language; and an uncommon delight in common, everyday things. White sees the extraordinary in the ordinary, noticing and valuing what most of us either overlook or take for granted. And from his repeated and respectful acts of attention flow reminiscences, speculations, explorations, and questions about our common humanity, about our relationships with one another, with the past, with the worlds of technology and nature.

White is a writer whose insights derive directly from his literal observations, from what he sees. Thoreau, one of White's favorite writers—and one with whom White has much in common—once remarked that "you can't say more than you can see." White's writing bears this out. The relationship between sight and insight, between observation and speculation, is evident in essays such as "The Ring of Time," which begins with a description of a circus act and ends with speculations about time and change, and "Once More to the Lake," in which White reminisces about his boyhood summer holidays in Maine, both describing the place with startling vividness and offering unsettling speculations about the meaning of his memories. In these and in other essays, White's writing is rooted in the crucial act of vision, a vision which sees into and beyond the surface of his subjects.

White's best writing, however, is more than a record of what he has seen and thought. It is also art, literature. His best work is crafted, shaped, formed with the same attention to details of structure, texture, image, and tone that poets or painters, sculptors or novelists give their work. In "The Ring of Time," "Once More to the Lake," and "The Geese," matters of fact, details of time, place, and circumstance give way to larger concerns. The circus is more than a circus ring: it becomes an emblem of time and change; the lake is more than a summer vacation place: it becomes an image of serenity and a reminder of time, change, even death; the old gander's plight becomes White's. The images of light and water, the symbolism of circus ring and lake, along with a concern for understanding the present in relation to the past and the future, the emblematic nature of the geese—these emphases lift their respective essays beyond the merely personal and reminiscent, beyond the ordinary and the everyday into the extraordinary universality of art.

About writing itself, White has said a good deal, and said it well. In the chapter he contributed to the now famous *Elements of Style,* White notes that when we speak of a writer's style we mean "the sound his words make on paper." The voice that we hear is what distinguishes one writer from another; and it is one good reason why, to get a good sense of a writer's style, we should read his or her work aloud. Beyond this concern for hearing what language can do, White notes that a writer's style "reveals something of his spirit, his habits, his capacities, his bias . . . it is the Self escaping into the open." And, as White suggests, this Self cannot be hidden, for a writer's style "reveals his identity as surely as would his fingerprints."

Recognizing that writing is hard work requiring endurance, thought, and revision ("revising is part of writing"), White advises that beginning writers let their ears be their guide, that they avoid all tricks and mannerisms, that they see writing as "one way to go about thinking," and, finally, that they achieve style both by affecting none and by believing "in the truth and worth of the scrawl."

Throughout his years as a writer, White has often been asked for advice about writing. To one seeker he wrote: "Remember that writing is translation, and the opus to be translated is yourself." On another occasion he responded to a seventeen-year-old girl this way:

> You asked me about writing—how I did it. There is no trick to it. If you like to write and want to write, you write, no matter where you are or what else you are doing or whether anyone pays any heed. . . . If you want to write about feelings, about the end of summer, about growing, write about it. A great deal of writing is not "plotted"—most of my essays have no plot structure, they are a ramble in the woods, or a ramble in the basement of my mind.

There is a naturalness, an ease about White's writing, both in these off-hand remarks from his letters and in his more elaborately plotted essays. It is an ease that derives in part from a refusal to be either pompous or pedantic; it is an ease that derives also from a consistent attempt to be honest, to achieve the candor he admires in Montaigne; and it is a naturalness that is reflected in his style, a style that mingles the high subject and the low, the big word and the small, without flamboyance or ostentation. White's style, in short, is a badge of his character—intelligent, honest, witty, exact, and fundamentally endearing.

Once More to the Lake

One summer, along about 1904, my father rented a camp on a lake in Maine and took us all there for the month of August. We all got ringworm from some kittens and had to rub Pond's Extract on our arms and legs night and morning, and my father rolled over in a canoe with all his clothes on; but outside of that the vacation was a success and from then on none of us ever thought there was any place in the world like that lake in Maine. We returned summer after summer—always on August 1st for one month. I have since become a salt-water man, but sometimes in summer there are days when the restlessness of the tides and the fearful cold of the sea water and the incessant wind that blows across the afternoon and into the evening make me wish for the placidity of a lake in the woods. A few weeks ago this feeling got so strong I bought myself a couple of bass hooks and a spinner and returned to the lake where we used to go, for a week's fishing and to revisit old haunts.

I took along my son, who had never had any fresh water up his nose and who had seen lily pads only from train windows. On the journey over to the lake I began to wonder what it would be like. I wondered how time would have marred this unique, this holy spot—the coves and streams, the hills that the sun set behind, the camps and the paths behind the camps. I was sure that the tarred road would have found it out and I wondered in what other ways it would be desolated. It is strange how much you can remember about places like that once you allow your mind to return into the grooves that lead back. You remember one thing, and that suddenly reminds you of another thing. I guess I remembered clearest of all the early mornings, when the lake was cool and motionless, remembered how the bedroom smelled of the lumber it was made of and the wet woods whose scent entered through the screen. The partitions in the camp were thin and did not extend clear to the top of the rooms, and as I was always the first up I would dress softly so as not to wake the others, and sneak out into the sweet outdoors and start out in the canoe, keeping close along the shore in the long shadows of the pines. I remembered being very careful never to rub my paddle against the gunwale for fear of disturbing the stillness of the cathedral.

The lake had never been what you would call a wild lake. There were cottages sprinkled about the shores, and it was in farming country although the shores of the lake were quite heavily wooded. Some of the cottages were owned by nearby farmers, and you would live at the shore and eat your meals at the farmhouse. That's what our family did. But although it wasn't wild, it was a fairly large and undisturbed lake and there were places in it which, to a child at least, seemed infinitely remote and primeval.

I was right about the tar: It led to within half a mile of the shore. But when I got back there, with my boy, and we settled into a camp near a farmhouse and into the kind of summertime I had known, I could tell that it was going to be pretty much the same as it had been before—I knew it, lying in bed the first morning, smelling the bedroom, and hearing the boy sneak quietly out and go off along the shore in a boat. I began to sustain the illusion that he was I, and therefore, by simple transposition, that I was my father. This sensation persisted, kept cropping up all the time we were there. It was not an entirely new feeling, but in this setting it grew much stronger. I seemed to be living a dual existence. I would be in the middle of some simple act, I would be picking up a bait box or laying down a table fork, or I would be saying something, and suddenly it would be not I but my father who was saying the words or making the gesture. It gave me a creepy sensation.

We went fishing the first morning. I felt the same damp moss covering the worms in the bait can, and saw the dragonfly alight on the tip of my rod as it hovered a few inches from the surface of the water. It was the arrival of this fly that convinced me beyond any doubt that everything was as it always had been, that the years were a mirage and there had been no years. The small waves were the same, chucking the rowboat under the chin as we fished at anchor, and the boat was the same boat, the same color green and the ribs broken in the same places, and under the floor-boards the same fresh-water leavings and debris—the dead hellgrammite, the wisps of moss, the rusty discarded fishhook, the dried blood from yesterday's catch. We stared silently at the tips of our rods, at the dragonflies that came and went. I lowered the tip of mine into the water, tentatively, pensively dislodging the fly, which darted two feet away, poised, darted two feet back, and came to rest again a little farther up the rod. There had been no years between the ducking of this dragonfly and the other one—the one that was part of memory. I looked at the boy, who was silently watching his fly, and it was my hands that held his rod, my eyes watching. I felt dizzy and didn't know which rod I was at the end of.

We caught two bass, hauling them in briskly as though they were mackerel, pulling them over the side of the boat in a businesslike manner without any landing net, and stunning them with a blow on the back of the head. When we got back for a swim before lunch, the lake was exactly where we had left it, the same number of inches from the dock, and there was only the merest suggestion of a breeze. This seemed an utterly enchanted sea, this lake you could leave to its own devices for a few hours and come back to, and find that it had not stirred, this constant and trustworthy body of water. In the shallows, the dark, watersoaked sticks and twigs, smooth and old, were undulating in clusters on the bottom against the clean ribbed sand, and the track of the mussel was plain. A school of minnows swam by, each minnow with its small individual shadow, doubling the attendance, so clear and sharp in the sunlight. Some of the other campers were in swimming, along the shore, one of them with a cake of soap, and the water felt thin and clear and unsubstantial. Over the years there had been this person with the cake of soap, this cultist, and here he was. There had been no years.

Up to the farmhouse to dinner through the teeming, dusty field, the road under our sneakers was only a two-track road. The middle track was missing, the one with the marks of the hooves and splotches of dried, flaky manure. There had always been three tracks to choose from in choosing which track to walk in; now the choice was narrowed down to two. For a moment I missed terribly the middle alternative. But the way led past the tennis court, and something about the way it lay there in the sun reassured me; the tape had loosened along the backline, the alleys were green with plantains and other weeds, and the net (installed in June and removed in September) sagged in the dry noon, and the whole place steamed with midday heat and hunger and emptiness. There was a choice of pie for dessert, and one was blueberry and one was apple, and the waitresses were the same country girls, there having been no passage of time, only the illusion of it as in a dropped curtain—the waitresses were still fifteen; their hair had been washed, that was the only difference—they had been to the movies and seen the pretty girls with the clean hair.

Summertime, oh summertime, pattern of life indelible, the fade-proof lake, the woods unshatterable, the pasture with the sweetfern and the juniper forever and ever, summer without end; this was the background, and the life along the shore was the design, the cottages with their innocent and tranquil design, their tiny docks with the flagpole and the American flag floating against the white clouds in the blue sky, the little paths over the roots of the trees leading from camp to camp and the paths leading back to the outhouses and the can of lime for sprinkling, and at the souvenir counters at the store the miniature birch-bark canoes and the post cards that showed things looking a little better than they looked. This was the American family at play, escaping the city heat, wondering whether the newcomers in the camp at the head of the cove were "common" or "nice," wondering whether it was true that the people who drove up for Sunday dinner at the farmhouse were turned away because there wasn't enough chicken.

It seemed to me, as I kept remembering all this, that those times and those summers had been infinitely precious and worth saving. There had been jollity and peace and goodness. The arriving (at the beginning of August) had been so big a business in itself, at the railway station the farm wagon drawn up, the first smell of the pine-laden air, the first glimpse of the smiling farmer, and the great importance of the trunks and your father's enormous authority in such matters, and the feel of the wagon under you for the long ten-mile haul, and at the top of the last long hill catching the first view of the lake after eleven months of not seeing this cherished body of water. The shouts and cries of the other campers when they saw you, and the trunks to be unpacked, to give up their rich burden. (Arriving was less exciting nowadays, when you sneaked up in your car and parked it under a tree near the camp and took out the bags and in five minutes it was all over, no fuss, no loud wonderful fuss about trunks.)

Peace and goodness and jollity. The only thing that was wrong now, really, was the sound of the place, an unfamiliar nervous sound of the outboard motors. This was the note that jarred, the one thing that would sometimes break the illusion and set the years moving. In those other summertimes all motors were inboard; and when they were at a little distance, the noise they made was a sedative, an ingredient of summer sleep. They were one-cylinder and two-cylinder engines, and some were make-and-break and some were jump-spark, but they all made a sleepy sound across the lake. The one-lungers throbbed and fluttered, and the twin-cylinder ones purred and purred, and that was a quiet sound too. But now the campers all had outboards. In the daytime, in the hot mornings, these motors made a petulant, irritable sound; at night, in the still evening when the afterglow lit the water, they whined about one's ears like mosquitoes. My boy loved our rented outboard, and his great desire was to achieve singlehanded mastery over it, and authority, and he soon learned the trick of choking it a little (but not too much), and the adjustment of the needle valve. Watching him I would remember the things you could do with the old one-cylinder engines with the heavy flywheel, how you could have it eating out of your hand if you got really close to it spiritually. Motor boats in those days didn't have clutches, and you would make a landing by shutting off the motor at the proper time and coasting in with a dead rudder. But there was a way of reversing them, if you learned the trick, by cutting the switch and putting it on again exactly on the final dying revolution of the flywheel, so that it would kick back against compression and begin reversing. Approaching a dock in a strong following breeze, it was difficult to slow up sufficiently by the ordinary coasting method, and if a boy felt he had complete mastery over his motor, he was tempted to keep it running beyond its time and then reverse it a few feet from the dock. It took a cool nerve, because if you threw the switch a twentieth of a second too soon you could catch the flywheel when it still had speed enough to go up past center, and the boat would leap ahead, charging bull-fashion at the dock.

We had a good week at the camp. The bass were biting well and the sun shone endlessly, day after day. We would be tired at night and lie down in the accumulated heat of the little bedrooms after the long hot day and the breeze would stir almost imperceptibly outside and the smell of the swamp drift in through the rusty screens. Sleep would come easily and in the morning the red squirrel would be on the roof, tapping out his gay routine. I kept remembering everything, lying in bed in the mornings—the small steamboat that had a long rounded stern like the lip of a Ubangi, and how quietly she ran on the moonlight sails, when the older boys played their mandolins and the girls sang and we ate doughnuts dipped in sugar, and how sweet the music was on the water in the shining night, and what it had felt like to think about girls then. After breakfast we would go up to the store and the things were in the same place—the minnows in a bottle, the plugs and spinners disarranged and pawed over by the youngsters from the boys' camp, the Fig Newtons and the Beeman's gum. Outside, the road was tarred and cars stood in front of the store. Inside, all was just as it had always been, except there was more Coca-Cola and not so much Moxie and root beer and birch beer and sarsaparilla. We would walk out with a bottle of pop apiece and sometimes the pop would backfire up our noses and hurt. We explored the streams, quietly, where the turtles slid off the sunny logs and dug their way into the soft bottom; and we lay on the town wharf and fed worms to the tame bass. Everywhere we went I had trouble making out which was I, the one walking at my side, the one walking in my pants.

One afternoon while we were there at that lake a thunderstorm came up. It was like the revival of an old melodrama that I had seen long ago with childish awe. The second-act climax of the drama of the electrical disturbance over a lake in America had not changed in any important respect. This was the big scene, still the big scene. The whole thing was so familiar, the first feeling of oppression and heat and a general air around camp of not wanting to go very far away. In midafternoon (it was all the same) a curious darkening of the sky, and a lull in everything that had made life tick; and then the way the boats suddenly swung the other way at their moorings with the coming of a breeze out of the new quarter, and the premonitory rumble. Then the kettle drum, then the snare, then the bass drum and cymbals, then crackling light against the dark, and the gods grinning and licking their chops in the hills. Afterward the calm, the rain steadily rustling in the calm lake, the return of light and hope and spirits, and the campers running out in joy and relief to go swimming in the rain, their bright cries perpetuating the deathless joke about how they were getting simply drenched, and the children screaming with delight at the new sensation of bathing in the rain, and the joke about getting drenched linking the generations in a strong indestructible chain. And the comedian who waded in carrying an umbrella.

When the others went swimming my son said he was going in too. He pulled his dripping trunks from the line where they had hung all through the shower, and wrung them out. Languidly, and with no thought of going in, I watched him, his hard little body, skinny and bare, saw him wince slightly as he pulled up around his vitals the small, soggy, icy garment. As he buckled the swollen belt suddenly my groin felt the chill of death.

Considerations

Thinking

White's essay is, in part, a meditation on time. What ideas about time do you find White exploring? What do you think he means by saying that he "seemed to be living a dual existence"? Why is this statement important?

In what sense is White's essay about a trip to a place—a trip into his past, a projection into his future?

Connecting

To what extent can you share in the experience White describes? Why? Identify another work you have read (or viewed) that can be linked with the experience White describes or the ideas he explores.

Or consider how and why the world White describes is alien to you, how it makes assumptions or expresses values at odds with or perhaps different from your own.

Writing

Develop your own essay about time and change, perhaps using White's as a jumping-off point. You may wish to ground your essay in your experience, or you may wish to draw upon your reading of other works to develop your thinking, or you may wish to do both.

Or analyze how White's choices of language, image, and organization convey his meaning.

Or discuss the implications of the images White uses to convey a sense of what the world was like for him in the period of time spanned by the essay.

The Ring of Time

Fiddler Bayou, March 22, 1956

After the lions had returned to their cages, creeping angrily through the chutes, a little bunch of us drifted away and into an open doorway nearby, where we stood for a while in semidarkness, watching a big brown circus horse go harumphing around the practice ring. His trainer was a woman of about forty, and the two of them, horse and woman, seemed caught up in one of those desultory treadmills of afternoon from which there is no apparent escape. The day was hot, and we kibitzers were grateful to be briefly out of the sun's glare. The long rein, or tape, by which the woman guided her charge counterclockwise in his dull career formed the radius of their private circle, of which she was the revolving center; and she, too, stepped a tiny circumference of her own, in order to accommodate the horse and allow him his maximum scope. She had on a short-skirted costume and a conical straw hat. Her legs were bare and she wore high heels, which probed deep into the loose tanbark and kept her ankles in a state of constant turmoil. The great size and meekness of the horse, the repetitious exercise, the heat of the afternoon, all exerted a hypnotic charm that invited boredom; we spectators were experiencing a languor—we neither expected relief nor felt entitled to any. We had paid a dollar to get into the grounds, to be sure, but we had got our dollar's worth a few minutes before, when the lion trainer's whiplash had got caught around a toe of one of the lions. What more did we want for a dollar?

Behind me I heard someone say, "Excuse me, please," in a low voice. She was halfway into the building when I turned and saw her—a girl of sixteen or seventeen, politely threading her way through us onlookers who blocked the entrance. As she emerged in front of us, I saw that she was barefoot, her dirty little feet fighting the uneven ground. In most respects she was like any of two or three dozen showgirls you encounter if you wander about the winter quarters of Mr. John Ringling North's circus, in Sarasota—cleverly proportioned, deeply browned by the sun, dusty, eager, and almost naked. But her grave face and the naturalness of her manner gave her a sort of quick distinction and brought a new note into the gloomy octagonal building where we had all cast our lot for a few moments. As soon as she had squeezed through the crowd, she spoke a word or two to the older woman, whom I took to be her mother, stepped to the ring, and waited while the horse coasted to a stop in front of her. She gave the animal a couple of affectionate swipes on his enormous neck and then swung herself aboard. The horse immediately resumed his rocking canter, the woman goading him on, chanting something that sounded like "Hop! Hop!"

In attempting to recapture this mild spectacle, I am merely acting as recording secretary for one of the oldest of societies—the society of those who, at one time or another, have surrendered, without even a show of resistance, to the bedazzlement of a circus rider. As a writing man, or secretary, I have always felt charged with the safekeeping of all unexpected items of worldly or unworldly enchantment, as though I might be held personally responsible if even a small one were to be lost. But it is not easy to communicate anything of this nature. The circus comes as close to being the world in microcosm as anything I know; in a way, it puts all the rest of show business in the shade. Its magic is universal and complex. Out of its wild disorder comes order; from its rank smell rises the good aroma of courage and daring; out of its preliminary shabbiness comes the final splendor. And buried in the familiar boasts of its advance agents lies the modesty of most of its people. For me the circus is at its best before it has been put together. It is at its best at certain moments when it comes to a point, as through a burning glass, in the activity and destiny of a single performer out of so many. One ring is always bigger than three. One rider, one aerialist, is always greater than six. In short, a man has to catch the circus unawares to experience its full impact and share its gaudy dream.

The ten-minute ride the girl took achieved—as far as I was concerned, who wasn't looking for it, and quite unbeknownst to her, who wasn't even striving for it—the thing that is sought by performers everywhere, on whatever stage, whether struggling in the tidal currents of Shakespeare or bucking the difficult motion of a horse. I somehow got the idea she was just cadging a ride, improving a shining ten minutes in the diligent way all serious artists seize free moments to hone the blade of their talent and keep themselves in trim. Her brief tour included only elementary postures and tricks, perhaps because they were all she was capable of, perhaps because her warmup at this hour was unscheduled and the ring was not rigged for a real practice session. She swung herself off and on the horse several times, gripping his mane. She did a few knee-stands—or whatever they are called—dropping to her knees and quickly bouncing back up on her feet again. Most of the time she simply rode in a standing position, well aft on the beast, her hands hanging easily at her sides, her head erect, her straw-colored ponytail lightly brushing her shoulders, the blood of exertion showing faintly through the tan of her skin. Twice she managed a one-foot stance—a sort of ballet pose, with arms outstretched. At one point the neck strap of her bathing suit broke and she went twice around the ring in the classic attitude of a woman making minor repairs to a garment. The fact that she was standing on the back of a moving horse while doing this invested the matter with a clownish significance that perfectly fitted the spirit of the circus—jocund, yet charming. She just rolled the strap into a neat ball and stowed it inside her bodice while the horse rocked and rolled beneath her in dutiful innocence. The bathing suit proved as self-reliant as its owner and stood up well enough without benefit of strap.

The richness of the scene was in its plainness, its natural condition—of horse, of ring, of girl, even to the girl's bare feet that gripped the bare back of her proud and ridiculous mount. The enchantment grew not out of anything that happened or was performed but out of something that seemed to go round and around and around with the girl, attending her, a steady gleam in the shape of a circle—a ring of ambition, of happiness, of youth. (And the positive pleasures of equilibrium under difficulties.) In a week or two, all would be changed, all (or almost all) lost: the girl would wear makeup, the horse would wear gold, the ring would be painted, the bark would be clean for the feet of the horse, the girl's feet would be clean for the slippers that she'd wear. All, all would be lost.

As I watched with the others, our jaws adroop, our eyes alight, I became painfully conscious of the element of time. Everything in the hideous old building seemed to take the shape of a circle, conforming to the course of the horse. The rider's gaze, as she peered straight ahead, seemed to be circular, as though bent by force of circumstance; then time itself began running in circles, and so the beginning was where the end was, and the two were the same, and one thing ran into the next and time went round and around and got nowhere. The girl wasn't so young that she did not know the delicious satisfaction of having a perfectly behaved body and the fun of using it to do a trick most people can't do, but she was too young to know that time does not really move in a circle at all. I thought: "She will never be as beautiful as this again"—a thought that made me acutely unhappy—and in a flash my mind (which is too much of a busybody to suit me) had projected her twenty-five years ahead, and she was now in the center of the ring, on foot, wearing a conical hat and high-heeled shoes, the image of the older woman, holding the long rein, caught in the treadmill of an afternoon long in the future. "She is at that enviable moment in life [I thought] when she believes she can go once around the ring, make one complete circuit, and at the end be exactly the same age as at the start." Everything in her movements, her expression, told you that for her the ring of time was perfectly formed, changeless, predictable, without beginning or end, like the ring in which she was traveling at this moment with the horse that wallowed under her. And then I slipped back into my trance, and time was circular again—time, pausing quietly with the rest of us, so as not to disturb the balance of a performer.

Her ride ended as casually as it had begun. The older woman stopped the horse, and the girl slid to the ground. As she walked toward us to leave, there was a quick, small burst of applause. She smiled broadly, in surprise and pleasure; then her face suddenly regained its gravity and she disappeared through the door.

It has been ambitious and plucky of me to attempt to describe what is indescribable, and I have failed, as I knew I would. But I have discharged my duty to my society; and besides, a writer, like an acrobat, must occasionally try a stunt that is too much for him. At any rate, it is worth reporting that long before the circus comes to town, its most notable performances have already been given.

Under the bright lights of the finished show, a performer need only reflect the electric candle power that is directed upon him; but in the dark and dirty old training rings and in the makeshift cages, whatever light is generated, whatever excitement, whatever beauty, must come from original sources—from internal fires of professional hunger and delight, from the exuberance and gravity of youth. It is the difference between planetary light and the combustion of stars.

The South is the land of the sustained sibilant. Everywhere, for the appreciative visitor, the letter "s" insinuates itself in the scene: in the sound of sea and sand, in the singing shell, in the heat of sun and sky, in the sultriness of the gentle hours, in the siesta, in the stir of birds and insects. In contrast to the softness of its music, the South is also cruel and hard and prickly. A little striped lizard, flattened along the sharp green bayonet of a yucca, wears in its tiny face and watchful eye the pure look of death and violence. And all over the place, hidden at the bottom of their small sandy craters, the ant lions lie in wait for the ant that will stumble into their trap. (There are three kinds of lions in this region: the lions of the circus, the ant lions, and the Lions of the Tampa Lions Club, who roared their approval of segregation at a meeting the other day—all except one, a Lion named Monty Gurwit, who declined to roar and thereby got his picture in the paper.)

The day starts on a note of despair: the sorrowing dove, alone on its telephone wire, mourns the loss of night, weeps at the bright perils of the unfolding day. But soon the mockingbird wakes and begins an early rehearsal, setting the dove down by force of character, running through a few slick imitations, and trying a couple of original numbers into the bargain. The redbird takes it from there. Despair gives way to good humor. The Southern dawn is a pale affair, usually, quite different from our northern daybreak. It is a triumph of gradualism; night turns to day imperceptibly, softly, with no theatrics. It is subtle and undisturbing. As the first light seeps in through the blinds I lie in bed half awake, despairing with the dove, sounding the A for the brothers Alsop. All seems lost, all seems sorrowful. Then a mullet jumps in the bayou outside the bedroom window. It falls back into the water with a smart smack. I have asked several people why the mullet incessantly jump and I have received a variety of answers. Some say the mullet jump to shake off a parasite that annoys them. Some say they jump for the love of jumping—as the girl on the horse seemed to ride for the love of riding (although she, too, like all artists, may have been shaking off some parasite that fastens itself to the creative spirit and can be got rid of only by fifty turns around a ring while standing on a horse).

In Florida at this time of year, the sun does not take command of the day until a couple of hours after it has appeared in the east. It seems to carry no authority at first. The sun and the lizard keep the same schedule; they bide their time until the morning has advanced a good long way before they come fully forth and strike. The cold lizard waits astride his warming leaf for the perfect moment; the cold sun waits in his nest of clouds for the crucial time.

On many days, the dampness of the air pervades all life, all living. Matches refuse to strike. The towel, hung to dry, grows wetter by the hour. The newspaper, with its headlines about integration, wilts in your hand and falls limply into the coffee and the egg. Envelopes seal themselves. Postage stamps mate with one another as shamelessly as grasshoppers. But most of the time the days are models of beauty and wonder and comfort, with the kind sea stroking the back of the warm sand. At evening there are great flights of birds over the sea, where the light lingers; the gulls, the pelicans, the terns, the herons stay aloft for half an hour after land birds have gone to roost. They hold their ancient formations, wheel and fish over the Pass, enjoying the last of day like children playing outdoors after supper-time.

To a beachcomber from the North, which is my present status, the race problem has no pertinence, no immediacy. Here in Florida I am a guest in two houses—the house of the sun, the house of the State of Florida. As a guest, I mind my manners and do not criticize the customs of my hosts. It gives me a queer feeling, though, to be at the center of the greatest social crisis of my time and see hardly a sign of it. Yet the very absence of signs seems to increase one's awareness. Colored people do not come to the public beach to bathe, because they would not be made welcome there; and they don't fritter away their time visiting the circus, because they have other things to do. A few of them turn up at the ballpark, where they occupy a separate but equal section of the left-field bleachers and watch Negro players on the visiting Braves team using the same bases as the white players, instead of separate (but equal) bases. I have had only two small encounters with "color." A colored woman named Viola, who had been a friend of my wife's sister years ago, showed up one day with some laundry of ours that she had consented to do for us, and with the bundle she brought a bunch of nasturtiums, as a sort of natural accompaniment to the delivery of clean clothes. The flowers seemed a very acceptable thing and I was touched by them. We asked Viola about her daughter, and she said she was at Kentucky State College, studying voice.

The other encounter was when I was explaining to our cook, who is from Finland, the mysteries of bus travel in the American Southland. I showed her the bus stop, armed her with a timetable, and then, as a matter of duty, mentioned the customs of the Romans. "When you get on the bus," I said, "I think you'd better sit in one of the front seats—the seats in back are for colored people." A look of great weariness came into her face, as it does when we use too many dishes, and she replied, "Oh, I know—isn't it silly!"

Her remark, coming as it did all the way from Finland and landing on this sandbar with a plunk, impressed me. The Supreme Court said nothing about silliness, but I suspect it may play more of a role than one might suppose. People are, if anything, more touchy about being thought silly than they are about being thought unjust. I note that one of the arguments in the recent manifesto of Southern Congressmen in support of the doctrine of "separate but equal" was that it had been founded on "common sense." The sense that is common to one generation is uncommon to the next. Probably the first slave ship, with Negroes lying in chains on its decks, seemed commonsensical to the owners who operated it and to the planters who patronized it. But such a vessel would not be in the realm of common sense today. The only sense that is common, in the long run, is the sense of change—and we all instinctively avoid it, and object to the passage of time, and would rather have none of it.

The Supreme Court decision is like the Southern sun, laggard in its early stages, biding its time. It has been the law in Florida for two years now, and the years have been like the hours of the morning before the sun has gathered its strength. I think the decision is as incontrovertible and warming as the sun, and, like the sun, will eventually take charge.

But there is certainly a great temptation in Florida to duck the passage of time. Lying in warm comfort by the sea, you receive gratefully the gift of the sun, the gift of the South. This is true seduction. The day is a circle—morning, afternoon, and night. After a few days I was clearly enjoying the same delusion as the girl on the horse—that I could ride clear around the ring of day, guarded by wind and sun and sea and sand, and be not a moment older.

P.S. (April, 1962). When I first laid eyes on Fiddler Bayou, it was wild land, populated chiefly by the little crabs that gave it its name, visited by wading birds and by an occasional fisherman. Today, houses ring the bayou, and part of the mangrove shore has been bulkheaded with a concrete wall. Green lawns stretch from patio to water's edge, and sprinklers make rainbows in the light. But despite man's encroachment, Nature manages to hold her own and assert her authority: high tides and high winds in the gulf sometimes send the sea crashing across the sand barrier, depositing its wrack on lawns and ringing everyone's front door bell. The birds and the crabs accommodate themselves quite readily to the changes that have taken place; every day brings herons to hunt around among the roots of the mangroves, and I have discovered that I can approach to within about eight feet of a Little Blue Heron simply by entering the water and swimming slowly toward him. Apparently he has decided that when I'm in the water, I am without guile—possibly even desirable, like a fish.

The Ringling circus has quit Sarasota and gone elsewhere for its hibernation. A few circus families still own homes in the town, and every spring the students at the high school put on a circus, to let off steam, work off physical requirements, and provide a promotional spectacle for Sarasota. At the drugstore you can buy a postcard showing the bed John Ringling slept in. Time has not stood still for anybody but the dead, and even the dead must be able to hear the acceleration of little sports cars and know that things have changed.

From the all-wise New York Times, which has the animal kingdom ever in mind, I have learned that one of the creatures most acutely aware of the passing of time is the fiddler crab himself. Tiny spots on his body enlarge during daytime hours, giving him the same color as the mudbank he explores and thus protecting him from his enemies. At night the spots shrink, his color fades, and he is almost invisible in the light of the moon. These changes are synchronized with the tides, so that each day they occur at a different hour. A scientist who experimented with the crabs to learn more about the phenomenon discovered that even when they are removed from their natural environment and held in confinement, the rhythm of their bodily change continues uninterrupted, and they mark the passage of time in their laboratory prison, faithful to the tides in their fashion.

Considerations

Thinking

What ideas about time emerge in this essay? Why does White visualize time as running both in a straight line and in circles?

What do the three parts of White's essay have in common? What does the second part contribute to your understanding of the first part? How does it alter or otherwise modify your understanding of the first part? Why?

Connecting

Relate what White describes in either part of "The Ring of Time" to your own experience. Explain how your experience links up (or doesn't link up) with something White mentions in his essay.

Relate the ideas that emerge in your reading of "The Ring of Time" to ideas that animate White's "Once More to the Lake" or "The Geese," or both essays.

Consider Martin Luther King, Jr.'s "Letter from Birmingham Jail" in conjunction with the second part of "The Ring of Time."

Writing

Write your own essay about a ring of time of which you are a part. Consider how your own family exemplifies (or doesn't exemplify) the ideas White conveys in "The Ring of Time." You may wish to focus on one of your parents or perhaps one of your grandparents in developing your essay.

Or compare White's treatment of the subject of time and change in "The Ring of Time" with his handling of that subject in "The Geese" or "Once More to the Lake."

The Geese

Allen Cove, July 9, 1971

To give a clear account of what took place in the barnyard early in the morning on that last Sunday in June, I will have to go back more than a year in time, but a year is nothing to me these days. Besides, I intend to be quick about it, and not dawdle.

I have had a pair of elderly gray geese—a goose and a gander—living on this place for a number of years, and they have been my friends. "Companions" would be a better word; geese are friends with no one, they badmouth everybody and everything. But they are companionable once you get used to their ingratitude and their false accusations. Early in the spring, a year ago, as soon as the ice went out of the pond, my goose started to lay. She laid three eggs in about a week's time and then died. I found her halfway down the lane that connects the barnyard with the pasture. There were no marks on her—she lay with wings partly outspread, and with her neck forward in the grass, pointing downhill. Geese are rarely sick, and I think this goose's time had come and she had simply died of old age. I had noticed that her step had slowed on her trips back from the pond to the barn where her nest was. I had never known her age, and so had nothing else to go on. We buried her in our private graveyard, and I felt sad at losing an acquaintance of such long standing—long standing and loud shouting.

Her legacy, of course, was the three eggs. I knew they were good eggs and did not like to pitch them out. It seemed to me that the least I could do for my departed companion was to see that the eggs she had left in my care were hatched. I checked my hen pen to find out whether we had a broody, but there was none. During the next few days, I scoured the neighborhood for a broody hen, with no success. Years ago, if you needed a broody hen, almost any barn or henhouse would yield one. But today broodiness is considered unacceptable in a hen; the modern hen is an egg-laying machine, and her natural tendency to sit on eggs in springtime has been bred out of her. Besides, not many people keep hens anymore—when they want a dozen eggs, they don't go to the barn, they go to the First National.

Days went by. My gander, the widower, lived a solitary life—nobody to swap gossip with, nobody to protect. He seemed dazed. The three eggs were not getting any younger, and I myself felt dazed—restless and unfulfilled. I had stored the eggs down cellar in the arch where it is cool, and every time I went down there for something they seemed silently to reproach me. My plight had become known around town, and one day a friend phoned and said he would lend me an incubator designed for hatching the eggs of waterfowl. I brought the thing home, cleaned it up, plugged it in, and sat down to read the directions. After studying them, I realized that if I were to tend eggs in that incubator, I would have to withdraw from the world for thirty days—give up everything, just as a broody goose does. Obsessed though I was with the notion of bringing life into three eggs, I wasn't quite prepared to pay the price.

Instead, I abandoned the idea of incubation and decided to settle the matter by acquiring three ready-made goslings, as a memorial to the goose and a gift for the lonely gander. I drove up the road about five miles and dropped in on Irving Closson. I knew Irving had geese; he has everything—even a sawmill. I found him shoeing a very old horse in the doorway of his barn, and I stood and watched for while. Hens and geese wandered about the yard, and a turkey tom circled me, wings adroop, strutting. The horse, with one forefoot between the man's knees, seemed to have difficulty balancing himself on three legs but was quiet and sober, almost asleep. When I asked Irving if he planned to put shoes on the horse's hind feet, too, he said, "No, it's hard work for me, and he doesn't use those hind legs much anyway." Then I brought up the question of goslings, and he took me into the barn and showed me a sitting goose. He said he thought she was covering more than twenty eggs and should bring off her goslings in a couple of weeks and I could buy a few if I wanted. I said I would like three.

I took to calling at Irving's every few days—it is about the pleasantest place to visit anywhere around. At last, I was rewarded: I pulled into the driveway one morning and saw a goose surrounded by green goslings. She had been staked out like a cow. Irving had simply tied a piece of string to one leg and fastened the other end to a peg in the ground. She was a pretty goose—not as large as my old one had been, and with a more slender neck. She appeared to be a cross-bred bird, two-toned gray, with white markings—a sort of particolored goose. The goslings had the cheerful, bright, innocent look that all baby geese have. We scooped up three and tossed them into a box, and I paid Irving and carried them home.

My next concern was how to introduce these small creatures to their foster father, my old gander. I thought about this all the way home. I've had just enough experience with domesticated animals and birds to know that they are a bundle of eccentricities and crotchets, and I was not at all sure what sort of reception three strange youngsters would get from a gander who was full of sorrows and suspicions. (I once saw a gander, taken by surprise, seize a newly hatched gosling and hurl it the length of the barn floor.) I had an uneasy feeling that my three little charges might be dead within the hour, victims of a grief-crazed old fool. I decided to go slow. I fixed a makeshift pen for the goslings in the barn, arranged so that they would be separated from the gander but visible to him, and he would be visible to them. The old fellow, when he heard youthful voices, hustled right in to find out what was going on. He studied the scene in silence and with the greatest attention. I could not tell whether the look in his eye was one of malice or affection—a goose's eye is a small round enigma. After observing this introductory scene for a while, I left and went into the house.

Half an hour later, I heard a commotion in the barnyard: the gander was in full cry. I hustled out. The goslings, impatient with life indoors, had escaped from their hastily constructed enclosure in the barn and had joined their foster father in the barnyard. The cries I had heard were his screams of welcome—the old bird was delighted with the turn that events had taken. His period of mourning was over, he now had interesting and useful work to do, and he threw himself into the role of father with immense satisfaction and zeal, hissing at me with renewed malevolence, shepherding the three children here and there, and running interference against real and imaginary enemies. My fears were laid to rest. In the rush of emotion that seized him at finding himself the head of a family, his thoughts turned immediately to the pond, and I watched admiringly as he guided the goslings down the long, tortuous course through the weedy land and on down across the rough pasture between blueberry knolls and granite boulders. It was a sight to see him hold the heifers at bay so the procession could pass safely. Summer was upon us, the pond was alive again. I brought the three eggs up from the cellar and dispatched them to the town dump.

At first, I did not know the sex of my three goslings. But nothing on two legs grows any faster than a young goose, and by early fall it was obvious that I had drawn one male and two females. You tell the sex of a goose by its demeanor and its stance—the way it holds itself, its general approach to life. A gander carries his head high and affects a threatening attitude. Females go about with necks in a graceful arch and are less aggressive. My two young females looked like their mother, particolored. The young male was quite different. He feathered out white all over except for his wings, which were a very light, pearly gray. Afloat on the pond, he looked almost like a swan, with his tall, thin white neck and his cocked-up white tail—a real dandy, full of pompous thoughts and surly gestures.

Winter is a time of waiting, for man and goose. Last winter was a long wait, the pasture deep in drifts, the lane barricaded, the pond inaccessible and frozen. Life centered in the barn and the barnyard. When the time for mating came, conditions were unfavorable, and this was upsetting to the old gander. Geese like a body of water for their coupling; it doesn't have to be a large body of water—just any wet place in which a goose can become partly submerged. My old gander, studying the calendar, inflamed by passion, unable to get to the pond, showed signs of desperation. On several occasions, he tried to manage with a ten-quart pail of water that stood in the barnyard. He would chivvy one of his young foster daughters over to the pail, seize her by the nape, and hold her head under water while he made his attempt. It was never a success and usually ended up looking more like a comedy tumbling act than like coitus. One got the feeling during the water-pail routine that the gander had been consulting one of the modern sex manuals describing peculiar positions. Anyway, I noticed two things: the old fellow confined his attentions to one of the two young geese and let the other alone, and he never allowed his foster son to approach either of the girls—he was very strict about that, and the handsome young male lived all spring in a state of ostracism.

Eventually, the pond opened up, the happy band wended its way down across the melting snows, and the breeding season was officially opened. My pond is visible from the house, but it is at quite a distance. I am not a voyeur and do not spend my time watching the sex antics of geese or anything else. But I try to keep reasonably well posted on all the creatures around the place, and it was apparent that the young gander was not allowed by his foster father to enjoy the privileges of the pond and that the old gander's attentions continued to be directed to just one of the young geese. I shall call her Liz to make this tale easier to tell.

Both geese were soon laying. Liz made her nest in the barn cellar; her sister, Apathy, made hers in the tie-ups on the main floor of the barn. It was the end of April or the beginning of May. Still awfully cold—a reluctant spring.

Apathy laid three eggs, then quit. I marked them with a pencil and left them for the time being in the nest she had constructed. I made a mental note that they were infertile. Liz, unlike her sister, went right on laying, and became a laying fool. She dallied each morning at the pond with her foster father, and she laid and laid and laid, like a commercial hen. I dutifully marked the eggs as they arrived— 1, 2, 3, and so on. When she had accumulated a clutch of fifteen, I decided she had all she could cover. From then on, I took to removing the oldest egg from the nest each time a new egg was deposited. I also removed Apathy's three eggs from *her* nest, discarded them, and began substituting the purloined eggs from the barn cellar—the ones that rightfully belonged to Liz. Thus I gradually contrived to assemble a nest of fertile eggs for each bird, all of them laid by the fanatical Liz.

During the last week in May, Apathy, having produced only three eggs of her own but having acquired ten through the kind offices of her sister and me, became broody and began to sit. Liz, with a tally of twenty-five eggs, ten of them stolen, showed not the slightest desire to sit. Laying was her thing. She laid and laid, while the other goose sat and sat. The old gander, marveling at what he had wrought, showed a great deal of interest in both nests. The young gander was impressed but subdued. I continued to remove the early eggs from Liz's nest, holding her to a clutch of fifteen and discarding the extras. In late June, having produced forty-one eggs, ten of which were under Apathy, she at last sat down.

I had marked Apathy's hatching date on my desk calendar. On the night before the goslings were due to arrive, when I made my rounds before going to bed, I looked in on her. She hissed, as usual, and ran her neck out. When I shone my light at her, two tiny green heads were visible, thrusting their way through her feathers. The goslings were here—a few hours ahead of schedule. My heart leapt up. Outside, in the barnyard, both ganders stood vigil. They knew very well what was up: ganders take an enormous interest in family affairs and are deeply impressed by the miracle of the egg-that-becomes-goose. I shut the door against them and went to bed.

Next morning, Sunday, I rose early and went straight to the barn to see what the night had brought. Apathy was sitting quietly while five goslings teetered about on the slopes of the nest. One of them, as I watched, strayed from the others, and, not being able to find his way back, began sending out cries for help. They were the kind of distress signal any anxious father would instantly respond to. Suddenly, I heard sounds of a rumble outside in the barnyard where the ganders were—loud sounds of scuffling. I ran out. A fierce fight was in progress—it was no mere skirmish, it was the real thing. The young gander had grabbed the old one by the stern, his white head buried in feathers right where it would hurt the most, and was running him around the yard, punishing him at every turn—thrusting him on ahead and beating him unmercifully with his wings. It was an awesome sight, these two great male birds locked in combat, slugging it out—not for the favors of a female but for the dubious privilege of assuming the responsibilities of parenthood. The young male had suffered all spring the indignities of a restricted life at the pond; now he had turned, at last, against the old one, as though to get even. Round and round, over rocks and through weeds, they raced, struggling and tripping, the old one in full retreat and in apparent pain. It was a beautiful late-June morning, with fair-weather clouds and a light wind going, the grasses long in the orchard—the kind of morning that always carries for me overtones of summer sadness, I don't know why. Overhead, three swallows circled at low altitude, pursuing one white feather, the coveted trophy of nesting time. They were like three tiny fighter planes giving air support to the battle that raged below. For a moment, I thought of climbing the fence and trying to separate the combatants, but instead I just watched. The engagement was soon over. Plunging desperately down the lane, the old gander sank to the ground. The young one let go, turned, and walked back, screaming in triumph, to the door behind which his newly won family were waiting: a strange family indeed—the sister who was not even the mother of the babies, and the babies who were not even his own get.

When I was sure the fight was over, I climbed the fence and closed the barnyard gate, effectively separating victor from vanquished. The old gander had risen to his feet. He was in almost the same spot in the lane where his first wife had died mysteriously more than a year ago. I watched as he threaded his way slowly down the narrow path between clumps of thistles and daisies. His head was barely visible above the grasses, but his broken spirit was plain to any eye. When he reached the pasture bars, he hesitated, then painfully squatted and eased himself under the bottom bar and into the pasture, where he sat down on the cropped sward in the bright sun. I felt very deeply his sorrow and his defeat. As things go in the animal kingdom, he is about my age, and when he lowered himself to creep under the bar, I could feel in my own bones his pain at bending down so far. Two hours later, he was still sitting there, the sun by this time quite hot. I had seen his likes often enough on the benches of the treeless main street of a Florida city—spent old males, motionless in the glare of the day.

Toward the end of the morning, he walked back up the lane as far as the gate, and there he stood all afternoon, his head and orange bill looking like the head of a great snake. The goose and her goslings had emerged into the barnyard. Through the space between the boards of the gate, the old fellow watched the enchanting scene: the goslings taking their frequent drinks of water, climbing in and out of the shallow pan for their first swim, closely guarded by the handsome young gander, shepherded by the pretty young goose.

After supper, I went into the tie-ups and pulled the five remaining, unhatched eggs from the nest and thought about the five lifeless chicks inside the eggs—the unlucky ones, the ones that lacked what it takes to break out of an egg into the light of a fine June morning. I put the eggs in a basket and set the basket with some other miscellany consigned to the dump. I don't know anything sadder than a summer's day.

Considerations

Thinking

One way to think of White's essay is in terms of a fable whose animal characters reveal human characteristics and qualities. What is the moral of White's essay, as revealed by the fable?

What feelings does White express in the course of telling his story? What does the expression of his sympathies reveal about him?

Connecting

Relate the situation of "The Geese" to another work you have read (or viewed). How are the two works similar? How are they different? What might we observe by considering them together?

Compare White's presentation and portrayal of the geese with Annie Dillard's presentation of the weasel in "Living Like Weasels."

Writing

Write your own animal fable; that is, tell a story with animals as characters. Be sure that your animals can be interpreted in human terms—that their actions can be explained in terms of human motivation.

Analyze the way White writes about animals in "The Geese" with the way he or another writer does so in another work.

STUDENT RESEARCH ESSAYS BASED ON THE WORK OF E. B. WHITE

The students whose essays appear in this section were asked to write about the work of a single author but not to restrict their discussion to a single piece by that author. Christian D'Andrea's "The Human Atlas: Locating E. B. White" identifies time as an important topic in White's work.

Christian looks at White's ideas about time as they are explored in nearly a dozen of White's essays. He develops his idea about White's concern with time by looking at its appearance in White's essays, taking them up one after another.

Radhika Jones does something a bit different. She too refers to a dozen or so of White's essays and other prose pieces. But instead of discussing each in turn, Radhika weaves back and forth between White's works, referring to some of them in half a dozen places in her essay.

Both Christian D'Andrea and Radhika Jones use passages from White's work to illustrate and clarify their own ideas. Both student writers reveal White's accomplishments as a writer, and both offer thoughtful analyses and interpretations that integrate and connect different pieces of White's work that span many years, including letters and children's fiction as well as essays.

As you read these students' research essays, notice how they cite White's texts, documenting their references carefully. Notice, too, how Radhika Jones cites secondary sources, references to books and articles written by others about White's work.

The Human Atlas: Locating E. B. White

Christian D'Andrea

E.B. White lived in all but the last sixteen years of this century, and those years of experience are still alive in his sparkling, compact essays. But to capture life he shows his subjects—a pig or a goose, a man or a car—deteriorating under a pressure they cannot escape: time. White is just as hungry to relive the decay of beauty as he is to preserve it. Things are falling apart, losing their worth. In light of this, White discovers himself. Married to words and pitted against time, he turns his work into a study of himself and his opponent, of the power of corrosive time and its agents, and of his own power.

At face value, White is a humble chronicler of a charming America that no longer exists. No shroud of modern angst, yearning, or sadness surrounds his writing. And indeed, at times, the raw celebration of a memory takes over. He can be jubilant and nothing else, as he is when writing about the era of the Model T in "Farewell, My Lovely!" Out of the fusion of parts powering the car, on the basis of nothing more than a "dull rapport" between them, comes a strange, idiosyncratic harmony (*Second Tree* 33). All the efforts of a man—his placebos, his showering the car with trinkets and gizmos—not only kept the metaphysical functions in order, they also turned him into the king of all this magic, a man on par with the mystery. White knows the glory of the Model T. Not only was a man bound to his car—each stage of deterioration now a glorious dilemma for "both man and machine" (37)—man was also bound to other men. Being a "Ford owner" gave you friends across the country. A man had allies, kindred spirits, everywhere. But White was more than a part-time mechanic and comrade. While most men only swapped stories, White could recognize a Ford owner by the "hunger in (a man's) eyes that set him off from other men" (39). Rather than just acknowledging that there is a camaraderie of memory, he looks into it. He sees that the awkward charm and simple brotherhood spawned by a Model T are as obsolete in 1936 as its parts are absent from the pages of a Sears Roebuck catalogue. Value has decayed.

Although a response to the perfidious decay of the mystical will take White many years to formulate, he identifies the problem, as a thirty-year-old. The decaying metal of the Ford was endearing; the decay of America's vitality is a horror. So he exposes this horror's symptoms in hints and allegories. As he lies in bed in "A Weekend with the Angels," recovering from a nose operation during World War II, White imagines the hot-water bottle as having "to be exhumed from its cold grave at the foot of the bed" (*Second Tree* 7). The bottle is dead, without power, without the heat that gives it its purpose, and so is life dead in the modern era. Cars zoom today, they do not sputter and buck you like the Model T, and that is the tragedy. Even words are eulogized in White's short piece on grammar, "English Usage." "People are afraid of words" these days White claims (151). They are blinded and cannot see that the usage of words is sometimes "sheer luck, like getting across a street." Just as the language, White's true love, has been corralled and bereft of its spirit by the worshippers of so-called "taste" and "education," so has life itself slowly been enervated by the much more neutral but ubiquitous, powerful force of time.

But time and its partner change are not themselves horrors. After all, White declares, the sense of time is the only sense "that is common" to man ("Ring" 155). Time alone is too huge and invisible to be a foe, but it seems to bring with it states of mind that can erase the universal charm of a Model T and breed a hunger for perfection. World War II and the Industrial Revolution brought a hunger for mechanical perfection, encouraged America to let its wily spark die. Those consorts of time are the evils against which White writes.

The problem of how to fight them is the crux of White's personal search; it shapes all his scenarios and gives employment to all his characters. In "The Departure of Eustace Tilley," a genteel old man, presumably a thinker of some kind, is about to leave his anonymous town. White is the fictitious reporter for the local gab rag, ludicrous in his prying and ignorance, employing the editorial "we" that he hates so much in reality. When prodded by the reporter, Tilley reveals his poisonous predicament. "We live in a new world," he says, one from which he must escape (*Second Tree* 152). Ancient trees that "shelter the graves and throw their umbrage upon the imponderable dead" are now alive with loudspeakers. Tilley will think on "the faces of motorists drawn up for the red light," because "in their look of discontent is the answer to the industrial revolution" (153). And in this concern is Tilley's identity with White. The unwanted interview yields an admission: "I have certain macabre pilgrimages to make" (153). Indeed, this is White's calling. As Tilley pulls away from the hubbub, a single vision remains. The ground on which Tilley stood while he put his yearning into words is now nothing but a pool of tears.

But the tormented Tilley only helped clarify White's subject and quest; he only named the decay that White himself must engage in the world of his essays. White does indeed leave town and embark on strange pilgrimages, and he converts his journeys into lasting weapons against time. But White is not cocky; he even seems to question whether writing is the right mode of action. But it is his only hope, his talent, and he turns it against those consorts in the oddest ways. "The Decline of Sport" paints a not-so-farfetched picture of sports worship and statistics hoarding run amok. Out of the comedy White creates there emerges a tragic hero. Mr. Parkinson, overcome by the bad news of defeat from four simultaneous contests, draws a gun and shoots the wide receiver, the disinterested symbol of this chaos, on the field. Panic ensues; 20,003 are killed. Yet the effects are salutary. "Sport waned" and motorists "rediscovered the charms of old twisty roads . . . and barnyards" (*Second Tree* 45). White vanquishes sport, the farcical brother of Industry and War. But can he fight foe after foe with only words as his weapon, without the brute force of a gun? Yes, he seems to think, words are enough, but the search over time for the right words is exhausting.

Must a fighter against War and Industry fight alone? White looks for help in "A Weekend with the Angels," the story of his wartime convalescence. Back home in the United States, recovering, he gets a double dosage of second-hand war: a vicarious taste of combat and the grim sobriety of the hospital staffers. Overreacting to his window's "sticky transom," White enjoys the "nonsensical sensation of being in contact with the enemy" (*Second Tree* 6). But he is really not at war. Nor is he allied with the people around him. He reads the mysteriously anonymous early morning visits of a nurse as the "beauty and lunacy of which life is so subtly blended" (9). He speaks, calls her "Cousin," tries to cement their bond, and gets this reply: "There's a war on, Bud . . . so just for the heck of it I start with you." White is to have no partner in the mysteries of life's madness and beauty, no human partner in the non-fiction stories of his prose. He must fight his fictive war alone.

But even in childhood White was a loner. "Afternoon of an American Boy" is the story of his monumental first date. Having witnessed the spectacle of tea-dancing at the New York Plaza Hotel with his sister, he decides to return with a girl of special interest. Proposing to Eileen Parnell required the defeat of his "bashfulness and backwardness" (*Second Tree* 18). It looked to be an "expedition of unparalleled worldliness" (20). But in this hope for some unparalleled and yet tethered world we see White's problem. No one can match the meteoric quality of his wishes, the dazzling goals of his mind. He is looking for accompaniment, even in this date, that he will never find. Time blurs all things, and in the face of loss, even imagined loss, White's feelings go internal. Afterward, this "journey into ineptitude" with the girl leaves him stunned but inwardly "happy" (23). Later in life, as he writes, his senses yearn back to his teens, when the drumbeat of the dance melded with cinnamon on his tongue and gave the wild spirit of such moments a taste and sound, much like later moments in his life. In journeying back to his youth, White is re-discovering life's nuggets of worth, but he still is not beating down oppressive War and Industry. The recoveries are always temporary. Nothing lasts, and White laments.

Ultimately for White the wisdom, the potent attitude or aphorism from experience, that can refute the War-and-machine state of mind and hold it at bay, must lurk outside the city, where Tilley wanted to go. White makes the farm his home and attempts to ally himself with the animals. Despite the awe he feels for the mysteries of birth and creation on a farm, decay seems as evident in rural America as it is in the city. Mixed in with the seasonal progressions and their accompanying decay is the blessing of solitude; White can struggle with both practical problems and metaphysical quandaries on his own with the animals. Or so he thinks.

In "The Geese," White tends to a burgeoning family of geese, a family built up from a single widowed gander. In searching for foster children, White realizes that the dead mother goose's eggs will go without a broody hen, because "today broodiness is considered unacceptable" (*Prose Pieces* 145). This convention, a touch of the modern allegiance to efficiency, infiltrates his secluded barnyard, but White hardly notices it. With the widowed gander's acceptance of the foster goslings, White's previously sporadic understanding of the birds is sealed as he throws his lot in with the goose family. "Summer was upon us, the pond was alive again" (147), and White is riding the crest of this experience—one of those natural spontaneous combinations that constitute life's rich moments.

But War and Industry are not to be beaten by some rural commune. Everything quickly comes to a head—geese, White, and philosophy ride the course of nature and are dropped at the truth. The intensity of the farm scene peaks with the sudden fight between father and son for "the dubious privilege of . . . parenthood" (148). Bubbling within White is his lifelong respect for the miracle of incubation, the "strange calm of broodiness," and birth itself (*Second Tree* 239). Yet while the birds fought for supremacy, White "just watched" (149). In this, a deed as nondescript as the half sentence that houses it, White understands his place on the farm and his place in the world. His only soul brother is the beaten gander; the gander's sorrow, defeat, and "broken spirit" are White's own. The goose is cast off by his own family, and the man is not a part of his society. Both are "spent old males" (149). White has trouble going it alone, or with humans or animals; he watches, reports, broods on the human condition.

In "The Ring of Time" White again leaps back to a happier day. As if he is a boy enraptured by the barefoot circles of a practicing horseback acrobat, White's sense for genuine beauty and charm strikes gold in the girl's expression and concentration—wherein is seen the ambition, happiness, and youth that turn with the acrobat in suspended loops of time that began just where they had ended. Even as a young boy, White could tell she would "never be as beautiful as this again" (*Prose Pieces* 152). The circus is best raw, "before it has been put together," when rank smells and original sources exude real courage and sincerity. But as an adult writing the essay, White harps on the passive nature of his role. He declares he is "merely acting as recording secretary for one of the oldest of societies—the society of those who . . . have surrendered . . . to the bedazzlement of a circus rider" (151). He knows the raw stuff of life when he sees it throughout his life, but he is rarely active in making it. When young, he could surrender himself to the moment, enter a trance. Older, he implies, he must be rational and systematic and astute; as a middle-aged man his time is already up.

White tries to ward off the retreat of his youth—that time of the elemental America before it has been put together and bastardized—but he still faces the modern day and age. The geese told an allegorical story of alienation and profound anachronism, of beings out of time, but the death of a pig, in an essay of that name that seems strictly elegiac on the surface, is restorative on a deeper level. But it too leaves White wispy.

White quips that he was lucky it was the pig who died and not himself, otherwise there would be "none left to do the accounting" (*Second Tree* 243)—a distinct role that has become White's own. In dealing with the pig's frightening lack of hunger, White gets to know the animal intimately. He realizes that just as he had felt healthy in feeding a healthy pig, the "pig's imbalance becomes the man's, vicariously" (247). The pig's earlier struggle between the satisfaction of being scratched and the indignity of the enema parallel White's predicament: his recollections of happiness jar with his attempts to deal with the modern dilemma. With their lots "inextricably bound" (248), White reacts strongly to the veterinarian's diagnosis. "Deep hemorrhagic infarcts" are a vague concept. He does not know the name, but he knows the sickness. But this deeper world of confounded pig and man bubbles up into the narrative. At the pig's passing, White weeps "deep hemorrhagic intears" (251). What was once a horrifying, unknown specter becomes the palpable tears of a man who knows "what could be true of my pig could be true of the rest of my tidy world" (249). The injustice is that White is responsible for both himself and the pig, and possibly more. Whether his particular brand of salve is the proper one becomes an important question. White, a man who, in his own words, felt a sense of "personal deterioration" (243) in his recurring uncertainty of dates, at the end concludes he is "a man who failed to raise his pig" (253). But, in the deeper sense, White has not failed. Burial is the deserved right of things past; their memory is best preserved when their flesh is safe. The grave takes care of the flesh; White takes care of the spirit. The pig's life deteriorated, but White's work as a writer does not. Thirty years later after the events, at age eighty, he understands.

In the introduction to *The Second Tree from the Corner,* a collection of pieces that includes "Death of a Pig," White remarks that for all the farewells he bade the world in these essays written during the fifties, he has "failed to disappear" (xi). He is very much alive and has reached a state of modest control over his adversaries. The "flagless memorial days of our own choosing" ("Pig" 253) that commemorate the pig not only keep him alive but they also apply to the men and women of the war—remembered, yet allowed to lie in their graves in peace. Time has illuminated for White the best weapon against itself.

White recognizes the power of words that can satisfy the humdrum while tickling the cosmic. For this he celebrates Don Marquis, whose book, "the lives and times of archy and mehitabel," conveys his thoughts through the fictional cockroach Archy, a literary bug eager in all things but unable to use the shift key on his typewriter. Just as there was much more to White's relationship with the pig than the "slapstick" (*Second Tree* 244) of their shared medical exploits, the stories of Archy are much more than simply gaudy and irreverent. In Marquis, White sees a genuine ally. Both Marquis and White have the skill of deep vision born of awareness of deaths. Archy's falling to the floor exhausted and his creeping "feebly into a nest of . . . poems" after one draining session with his column is actually Marquis' "own obituary notice" (*Second Tree* 182).

Archy's prose has the "unmistakable whiff of the tavern" (186), the humid stickiness of originality—much like the musky air of the circus tent. This feel is a product of Marquis' unique perspective. He saw the world from its underside, as did White. Using the voice of a cockroach, Marquis could shun the constrictions of editing as well as open himself up to the loose power of free verse and get away with both. Marquis' discussions of the Almost Perfect State in his daily columns reverberate in White's mind because White knew that era. It was a time when purchasing the daily paper was "quietly exciting" (189), a nearly perfect act itself. Those days are gone. But although the savvy writer and the joy of purchasing papers have both faded, something vital is still alive, still selling copies thirty-four years after its first publication. The magic is in the book; Marquis left his energy and his song masquerading forever as the works of a wily cockroach—masked, they still live. White and his book still live, too, without the preservative quirk of a cockroach ghostwriter.

White's essays are not the armor of an embittered man. His works stand as quietly defiant acts, as bursts of value in the face of technological progress. As we survey the modes of writing and thought in White's essays, we see that as he thinks, searches, and celebrates in his prose, he looks slant at the specters of World War II and the Industrial Revolution. Nostalgic, he nevertheless confronts chaos and decay. Natural decay is sad, but it is not to be struggled against. Artificial decay—the oppressive, mechanized deterioration induced by War and Industry—is too big finally to be vanquished, but can be held at bay, kept at a safer distance from life. The secret is to trust the folly of grammar, a date, the Model T, and the geese.

WORKS CITED

White, E. B. *The Second Tree from the Corner.* New York: Harper and Row, 1984.
———. "The Geese" and "The Ring of Time." *Prose Pieces.* Ed. Pat C. Hoy II and Robert DiYanni. New York: Random House, 1988.

Essentially Egg-Shaped:
E. B. White's Image of Life

Radhika A. Jones

> I don't know of anything in the entire world more wonderful to look at than a nest with eggs in it. An egg, because it contains life, is the most perfect thing there is. It is beautiful and mysterious. An egg is a far finer thing than a tennis ball or a cake of soap. A tennis ball will always be just a tennis ball. A cake of soap will always be just a cake of soap—until it gets so small nobody wants it and they throw it away. But an egg will someday be a living creature.
>
> E. B. WHITE
> THE TRUMPET OF THE SWAN

The reverent admiration that Sam Beaver, young hero of *The Trumpet of the Swan,* has for eggs can only be rivaled by that of his creator. E. B. White's work, from his essays to his children's literature, is replete with eggs—as objects of natural beauty and as sources of life. A relatively small and simple object with an infinite number of thematic associations, the egg as subject matter perfectly reflects White's ability to transform concrete observations into clear, universal conclusions. White's eggs are rich with meaning; they are links in a never-ending cycle of life; they are sources of continuity in a world fragmented by passing time. And even in those essays that do not figure literal eggs, the sanctity, the beauty, and the fragility of life that they represent pervades White's work.

Perhaps only a writer so attuned to simplicity and detail could write an essay that is just about brown and white eggs, as is White's "Riposte." In this essay he takes issue with an Englishman who believes that Americans prefer white eggs to brown because white eggs seem more hygienic and brown eggs more countrified. "My goodness" is White's comment (*Essays* 60); "there is no such thing as an unnatural egg" (*Essays* 61). Mr. Priestley (the Englishman) has missed the point altogether—an egg is an egg; its color is irrelevant to its identity. That White would devote an entire essay to discussing this topic is a testimonial to his interest in the egg. He would not have it misjudged.

In and of themselves eggs—oval shells of calcium carbonate—are not terribly exciting, but as sources of new life they hold magical and exhilarating properties. In the spectrum of White's work, eggs hatch right and left, and White revels in each birth. One pictures White as his own character Sam Beaver, sitting awed and motionless as he witnesses the miracle of the cygnets' birth (*Trumpet* 29–30). Or as Charlotte the spider, offering her "sincere congratulations" on the occasion of the newly hatched barnyard goslings (*Web* 44). In "The Geese" White appoints himself caretaker of three goslings and meticulously looks after their eggs as a tribute to a goose acquaintance who had died of old age (*Prose* 145–49). "Spring" finds him caring for "254 little innocents"—chicks for whom he and his stove act as mother-hen (*Meat* 234–37). In short, White hails eggs as producers of life; in his writing and in his life they are objects to be revered and tended appropriately.

It would not be enough, however, simply to say that White is a writer with a healthy respect for the wonder of an egg; to do so would be to take the egg out of context. White's eggs remain very much in context; they are part of the natural cycle of life, of development. The hatching of eggs is not a once-in-a-lifetime occurrence. It happens every spring, and every spring it brings the renewal of youth and hope. "Each spring," writes White in *Charlotte's Web*, "there were new little spiders hatching out to take the place of the old" (183). Likewise, the three new goslings and their offspring in "The Geese" continue the tradition of the original pair of geese with whom White had "an acquaintance of such long standing—long standing and loud shouting" (*Prose* 145). Eggs come as dependably as the seasons; they are at once sources of stability and continuity; they are links in a natural chain.

Indeed, if White can be said to have a central preoccupation, then it is certainly the mystery of time's cyclic nature, and the precarious yet precious relationships that ensue. His literal tales of hatching eggs are only a few of his many essays and stories that address the topic of passing time and chronicle the natural cycles of life. Such is clearly the case in *Charlotte's Web*, which begins with the birth of Wilbur the pig and follows him into old age, while also telling the story of his spider friend Charlotte and her descendants. Wilbur is saved from an untimely, unnatural death by the resourceful and clever Charlotte; he lives out his life as Nature intended, as does she (White, *Web*). But *Charlotte's Web* is more than a story of animal progeny; it is a tale of how the love between two friends enriched both of their lives. White has taken us beyond the simple hatching of eggs to life outside the eggshell, where we can see his joy for life reflected in the relationships he creates among living things.

"Once More to the Lake" and "The Ring of Time" move to the realm of human relationships and life cycles, away from literal eggs. "Once More to the Lake" involves the time lapse between being a son and then becoming a father of one's own son, and depicts the change in temperament that naturally accompanies those passing years. White so vividly remembers the summers when he was a boy that he is lulled into thinking "there had been no years," but as he gradually notices subtle changes in the lake and in himself—the cacophonous sounds of the new outboard motors, his reluctance to swim in the rain as he would have done long ago—he realizes that life may be cyclic but it spirals ever forward: he has aged and there have undeniably been years (*Essays* 191–202).

"The Ring of Time" addresses the illusion of the young that time has no ramifications. "She is at that enviable moment in life," White writes of a young circus performer who is riding her horse around the ring, "when she believes she can go once around the ring, make one complete circuit, and at the end be exactly the same age as at the start" (*Essays* 145). Later in the essay he refers to this feeling as "true seduction" and a "delusion," for "time has not stood still for anybody but the dead, and even the dead must be able to hear the acceleration of little sports cars and know that things have changed" (*Essays* 148–49).

Eggs may come every spring, in other words, but they are not the same eggs; Charlotte's children and grandchildren cannot really replace Charlotte in Wilbur's eyes. White recognizes the new eggs each spring for what they are worth—sources of continuity yet also subtle change. Life is not merely seasonal repetition, even though this spring may be reminiscent of the last.

The egg is a tiny microcosm of life, and as such it is a perfect example of White's tendency to look to the smaller things in order to facilitate a better understanding of the larger issues of his day. "Who has the longer view of things, anyway, a prime minister in a closet or a man on a barn roof?" he asks in "Clear Days" (*Meat* 20), written slightly before the outbreak of World War II. Later, in 1941, he writes, "I sometimes think I am crazy—everybody else fighting and dying or working for a cause or writing to his senator, and me looking after some Barred Rock chickens" (*Meat* 236). White is clearly concerned with the topic of war, but he continues to write about it in the context of his experiences on his farm.

In his review of *One Man's Meat*, Benjamin DeMott dismisses White's subjects because they are so ordinary: he lists them as "Maine, progress as disaster, frustrations of urban life, and so on" (63) as if it bores him to include them at all. But I am more inclined to agree with the reviewer who wrote, "It is the gift of the poetic imagination to shape commonplace things into conclusions of considerable weight" (DeVane 164). To the attentive artist no place does not lend itself to observation, no topic is too mundane. White commits himself to reporting what he sees and thinking about what meaning he can derive from his observations, not to merely musing on grandiose abstractions. Likewise, he commits himself to preserving and protecting what life there is around him, instead of lamenting the lives he cannot save in Europe.

> I soon knew that the remaining warmth in this stubborn stove was all I had to pit against the Nazi idea of *Frühling*. . . . Countries are ransacked, valleys drenched with blood. Though it seems untimely I still publish my belief in the egg, the contents of the egg, the warm coal, and the necessity for pursuing whatever fire delights and sustains you. (*Meat* 237)

White invests in the egg the ultimate sanctity of human life, and he will go to great lengths to uphold it. He works within his sphere of influence to comment on more universal themes; his sight and his actions lead to insight and speculation (Hoy and DiYanni, *Prose* 144).

> "Look," he [Templeton] began in his sharp voice, "you say you have seven goslings. There were eight eggs. What happened to the other egg? Why didn't it hatch?"
> "It's a dud, I guess," said the goose. (White, *Web* 45)

E. B. White does not write fairy tales; not all of his eggs hatch. White's world has a dual nature, where happiness and sorrow co-exist peacefully, naturally. Perhaps this co-existence is the reason children recognize him as a wonderful writer, for he does not hide from them what well-meaning adults would. White has the ability to gently exploit the contradictions in life; his essays and stories probe the reality of not-so-happy endings.

When I was eight I cried for Charlotte, who died alone at the Fair Grounds (White, *Web* 171). I felt that it was grossly unfair that she who had worked so hard should perish so soon after her triumph—felt that she should at least be able to return home with Wilbur. Now I realize that White has too much respect for Nature to have permitted me that miracle. Charlotte was a spider with a spider's life span; such things cannot be altered, and certainly not by a writer as familiar with and respectful of life cycles as E. B. White.

However much White might want to promote life among his fellow creatures, he is not idealistic enough to suppose that he can always be successful. In "The Geese" he expresses a desire to hatch the old goose's three eggs as a tribute to her, but he finds himself not obsessed enough to devote himself to an incubator for the necessary thirty days. Instead, he purchases three newborn goslings from a neighbor (*Prose* 145–46). Where there is life, there is also, so to speak, non-life, and White presents this contrast directly: "Summer was upon us, the pond was alive again. I brought the three eggs up from the cellar and dispatched them to the town dump" (*Prose* 147). We are not told what to make of this incongruence, we are merely given it, and we know by the startling juxtaposition of those two sentences that White is thinking about it himself. His closing sentence is along similar lines: "I don't know anything sadder than a summer's day" (*Prose* 149). Summer days in "Once More to the Lake" are tinged with sadness as well, as the son prepares to bathe in the rain, the father feels "the chill of death" (*Essays* 202). But on the other hand, those same summer days are also replete with the joy of new life—the three goslings nurtured by White, the son who feels no chill of death. White's world is by no means pessimistic, nor is it idealistically optimistic. It is a depiction of reality as seen through the eyes of a man who acknowledges the unfortunate, yet is always willing to "publish his belief in the egg" (White, *Meat* 237). . . .

> The world White loves is more than a collection of things, natural and man-made, or a fascinating organization of reassuring cyclical, ongoing processes: it is a world in which the motive for creating, nurturing, teaching, encouraging, singing, and celebrating is love. (Elledge 303)

This love pervades White's works: it is implicit in all of his essays, all of his children's stories. It motivates him to take his son to visit his old haunt in "Once More to the Lake"; it motivates him to keep a vigil by the stove that warms the chicks in "Spring"; it motivates him to raise three goslings in memory of the old goose in "The Geese." In short, it motivates him to cherish life, and to cherish the eggs, symbolic and literal, that bring life into the world. In White's world, life is nothing short of a miracle, and "to him a miracle was essentially egg-shaped" (qtd. in Elledge 25).

WORKS CITED

DeMott, Benjamin. "Books: Pick of the List." Rev. of *Essays of E. B. White,* by E. B. White. *Saturday Review* 20 Aug. 1977: 63.

DeVane, William C. "A Celebration of Life." Rev. of *One Man's Meat,* by E. B. White. *The Yale Review* 1942: 163–165.

Elledge, Scott. *E. B. White: A Biography.* New York: W. W. Norton & Company, 1984.

Hoy, Pat C. II, and Robert DiYanni. Headnote: "E. B. White." *Prose Pieces: Essays and Stories, Sixteen Modern Writers.* New York: Random House, 1988. 143–145.

White, E. B. *Charlotte's Web.* New York: Harper & Brothers, 1952.

———. *Essays of E. B. White.* New York: Harper & Row, 1977.

———. "The Geese." *Prose Pieces: Essays and Stories, Sixteen Modern Writers.* Ed. Pat C. Hoy II and Robert DiYanni. New York: Random House, 1988. 145–149.

———. *One Man's Meat.* 2nd ed. New York: Harper & Row, 1944.

———. *The Trumpet of the Swan.* New York: Harper & Row, 1970.

THINKING AND WRITING ABOUT PAINTINGS AND PHOTOGRAPHS

PAINTINGS AND PHOTOGRAPHS FOR THINKING AND WRITING

Photographs

MATTHEW BRADY, *Gettysburg Battlefield*

KEITH CARTER, *Garlic, Starball*

ANNA NORRIS, *Financial District 1998; Spectators at the African-American Day Parade, Harlem, 1998*

ALFRED STIEGLITZ, 1918, platinum print (31); 1931, gelatin silver print (50); *Flatiron Building*

ARTHUR C. DANTO "Gettysburg"

ROSELLEN BROWN "Mojo"

ANNA NORRIS "How to Read Photographs"

JOAN DIDION "Georgia O'Keeffe"

MICHAEL COHEN "You Can Shave the Beast, but Will the Fur Grow Back?"

Discovering Ideas from Art:
Reading Sources

Discovering and formulating ideas will more than likely turn out to be the most interesting thing you have to do to become a better writer. You cannot complete an essay without an idea. Developing and substantiating that idea is the essayist's primary business.

Ideas often come to us from the *sources* that we learn to read critically and intelligently. But when we initially encounter those sources—whether books or articles or images—they often seem inert. They do not automatically tell us what we need to know. But there are ideas lurking around in the sources, and we writers have to be able to spot them. We have to read and study the sources, letting our minds play over the material until we spy an idea of our own that interests us. That idea (which will surely be revised and refined during our drafting) represents our initial attempt to make sense of the sources, whatever they might be.

You are familiar with the traditional sources of evidence: written texts of all kinds—books, essays, journals, magazines, newspapers. But there are many other valuable sources that can be read and considered as you become an accomplished researcher and writer. This book emphasizes the importance of visual images, especially paintings and photographs. It also encourages you to make use of your own experiences, to think about them, analyze them, see what they reveal to you, and, finally, use them selectively as evidence (in the form of stories) in your own essays. Like paintings and photographs, those images of experience need to be studied, need to be *read* just as if they were written texts containing significant information that can help you develop your essays.

Images can reveal things to us. But they do not reveal what they contain any more readily than the books we read. We have to stay with them. We have to look at them and then look again and again to discover what is there.

Looking at and Thinking about
Paintings and Photographs

Writing about art encourages us to concentrate on seeing what is before our eyes. Writing about a painting or photograph encourages us to slow down and observe more carefully. And writing about art also allows us to express our feelings and develop our thinking about what the work of art says to us, why it says what it does, and perhaps also how it conveys whatever it conveys.

Let's consider briefly a few things about paintings and photographs that can make your consideration of them more fruitful.

Paintings

Before writing about a painting look carefully at it (or a reproduction of it). Doing so, you might begin by thinking about some of these elements: genre, medium, composition, perspective, texture, contour or shape, line, space, color, light. Let's consider a few of these elements briefly, to suggest how you might begin to see more when you look at a painting or photograph.

Genre suggests the type or category of the painting: portrait, still life, landscape. Some paintings contain elements of two or more genres, as for example, Leonardo da Vinci's *Mona Lisa*, which though primarily a portrait, also contains a background landscape. When viewing such a painting, focus on what seems most important to you as a viewer. If there is action, ask what is happening. If there are multiple figures in the painting, ask what is their relationship one to the other. If still-life objects are portrayed along with figures, what are their relationships to one another?

If you are looking at a *portrait*, consider the surface features of the sitter: clothing, expression, setting. See if those surface features taken together suggest something about the figure's personality or character. Getting to character will require interpretation. You have to think about the features of the painting to get at something deeper.

In viewing a *still life*, you should try to identify its general characteristics while also trying to acquire a sense of the social and material conditions surrounding it. Consider these questions:

- What objects are portrayed? How realistic are they?
- Do any of the represented objects seem symbolic, pointing toward some deeper meaning? (A skull in a painting, for example, can be seen as a "momento mori" or remembrance of human mortality, with accompanying echoes of spirituality, death, afterlife.)
- Look for patterns or motifs and think about what they might suggest.
- Is everything in the painting painted the same way—same texture, degree of color, specificity of detail? Or are the contours, textures, colors of some objects rendered in different ways, calling attention to themselves by their difference?

Landscapes, too, can be approached with some common questions in mind. If there are no human figures, focus on the artist's rendering of the natural scene. Consider what the artist seems to be emphasizing.

- What does the landscape suggest about the natural world?
- What relationship exists between human figures depicted and nature? In looking at a painting like van Gogh's well-known *Starry Night*, you notice that the stars and sky occupy about three-quarters of the canvas with the village

much smaller in scale. What do you think those proportions might tell you about what van Gogh has in mind, what he is most concerned about?

- Does the landscape itself suggest something symbolic, something psychological, spiritual, economic, or political?
- To what extent might the painting's origin or cultural context help you understand it?

You need not overly concern yourself with the technical, compositional qualities of paintings, but it is important that you not overlook such things as the medium (oil, watercolor), whether the painting is on canvas, paper, wood, or silk and what effects are thereby achieved, how light plays within the painting, how the colors suggest moods. As a general aid to understanding, pay particular attention to the artist's title.

All of this is to say that your primary task is not to be an art critic, but to develop a general appreciation for looking at paintings and discovering what they can suggest to you. Turn to E. M. Forster's whimsical little essay "Not Looking at Pictures" for additional information about the excitement that can accompany a trip to a gallery.

Photographs

We are so familiar with photographs that it may be difficult to think of them as works of art that can suggest interesting ideas. And, in fact, many photographs are literally snapshots taken without conscious artistic intent or design. Nonetheless, it is worth looking closely at the kinds of photographs that have been taken with thought and care—with a concern for what the photograph expresses as well as for its surface image.

What a photographer sees when taking a photograph is more than and often quite different from the resulting photographic image. That is, any photograph is a selection from a wealth of details that are not included in the finished picture. Moreover, photographers often edit their photographs, cropping and otherwise altering the image that was originally captured by the camera.

Photographers control and select, arrange, and shape the images that we observers finally see, just as painters do with their finished canvases. Photographs, therefore, repay the same careful observation that paintings do. Here are a few guiding questions to help you slow down the process of looking so that you can see more:

- What seems to be the subject of the photograph?
- What are the relationships among the things depicted?
- What might lie behind the decision to photograph in color or in black and white? What does that choice suggest about the image itself?
- What does the title help you see? Does it limit or enhance your seeing?

- What about size, focus (sharp, fuzzy, combination), light?
- Can you discern what process was used to develop the image?

These general considerations should guide you as you go about making your own discoveries. They will move you into the process of understanding.

[We are indebted to Sylvan Barnet's *Writing about Art*, 5th ed., for many of these questions about painting and photography.]

Writing about Paintings and Photographs

Often within this anthology, in the questions that accompany essays, we will ask you to select and consider an image (a painting, photograph, sculpture, building, experience) as a way of finding an idea. To help you understand the value of such image work, we have included a number of essays by students and professionals whose persuasive work depends heavily on visual evidence. Many of the student essays began with image work.

Elizabeth MacDonald's essay, "Odalisque," began with an informal writing exercise assigned by her teacher, who asked the class to select a painting and create a word picture of that painting so that others could see it. The teacher then asked students to think about their own relationship to the painting they had selected and to write about that relationship. Those two exercises led Elizabeth to Ingres's painting *Odalisque* (end of book) and a meditation of her own on beauty and suffering. She saw in that painting a woman's body made beautiful by distortion, and she eventually wrote an essay whose central idea (that women must suffer to be beautiful) came out of her initial work with Ingres's image (see pp. 55–59).

Elizabeth MacDonald went to Ingres's painting looking for an idea of her own. The painting was not to be the focus of her essay; it was to serve, simply, as a source for her ideas. Other students go to paintings not as a source of ideas but as a subject for research and analysis. Jessica Underwood's essay "Georges de la Tour's *The Penitent Magdalen*" (pp. 77–83) develops an idea about the relationship between Georges de la Tour and his painting *The Penitent Magdalen*. Jessica's specific assigned task was to figure out the relationship between an artist's painting(s) that artist's life, and the culture out of which the painting(s) evolved. Such an essay necessarily requires a great deal of research, signs of which you can readily see in Jessica's essay.

Anna Norris's essay, "How to Read Photographs," evolved from her college work that involved photographing and writing social commentary about various welfare projects in the city of New York. We asked Anna, whose work we had seen over the last few years, to write a short essay for this anthology that would help her fellow students know more about how to read photographs. She chose to illustrate that essay with two photographs of her own (p. 72). You can see in that essay how she encourages a way of reading that should help you discover ideas of your own in the photographs that interest you.

If you turn back to the Table of Contents at the beginning of the book (p. vii), you can see at a glance that many more writers in this anthology, both student and professional, make use of paintings and photographs in their essays. You will see too in this section of the anthology reproductions of the images that served those writers. We encourage you to make use of those images for your own purposes or, after studying what other writers have done with images, to go out and select your own images as a source for your ideas and essays.

You will have ample time to read and study the images and essays in this anthology. The selections herein suggest many ways that you can make effective use of visual images, and our questions at the end of essay selections often encourage you to do your own creative work with selected images. That work with paintings, photographs, and other art objects can—like your work with written sources—lead you to fresh ideas and eventually enrich your writing.

Mary Cassatt. *The Family.* c. 1892. Oil on canvas, $32\frac{1}{4}'' \times 26\frac{1}{8}''$. Chrysler Museum of Art, Norfolk, VA. Gift of Walter P. Chrysler , Jr. 71.498.

Chrysler Museum of Art, Norfolk, VA. Gift of Walter P. Chrysler, Jr. 71.498.

EDGAR DEGAS. *THE BELLELLI FAMILY*. 1859. OIL ON CANVAS, 78$\frac{3}{4}$″ × 99$\frac{1}{2}$″.
MUSÉE DU LOUVRE, PARIS.
© Photo RMN/Gerard Blot.

LISA A. FIFIELD. *RUNNING ELK.*
1993. WATERCOLOR, GOUACHE,
AND ACRYLIC ON PAPER,
22″ × 30″. PRIVATE
COLLECTION PAT HOY.
© 1993 Lisa A. Fifield. Courtesy
of the artist.

CHARLES WILLSON PEALE. *THE PEALE FAMILY.* 1773 AND 1809. OIL ON CANVAS,
56¹/₂″ × 88³/₄″. THE NEW-YORK HISTORICAL SOCIETY, NEW YORK CITY.
Photo: The New-York Historical Society.

HENRI MATISSE. *ODALISQUE IN RED TROUSERS*. 1922. 26³/₁₆″ × 33¹/₁₆.″ MUSÉE
NATIONAL D'ARTE MODERNE/CCI CENTRE GEORGES POMPIDOU, PARIS.

© Succession H. Matisse, Paris / Artists Rights Society (ARS), New York.
Cliché du Photothéque des collections du MNAM / Cci, Paris.

GEORGIA O'KEEFFE. *SKY ABOVE CLOUDS IV.* 1965. OIL ON CANVAS, 243.8 × 731.5 CM. RESTRICTED GIFT OF THE PAUL AND GABRIELLA ROSENBAUM FOUNDATION; GIFT OF GEORGIA O'KEEFFE. THE ART INSTITUTE OF CHICAGO.
Photo: The Art Institute of Chicago.

JEAN AUGUSTE DOMINIQUE INGRES. *LA GRANDE ODALISQUE.* 1814. OIL ON CANVAS, 2′ 11¼″ × 5′ 3¾.″ MUSÉE DU LOUVRE, PARIS.
Erich Lessing/Art Resource, NY.

PABLO PICASSO. *GUERNICA*. 1937. OIL ON CANVAS, 11′ 5½″ × 25′ 5¾″.
MUSEO NACIONAL CENTRO DE ARTE REINA SOFIA, MADRID.
Giraudon/Art Resource NY. © Copyright ARS.

GIORGIO DE CHIRICO. *THE
MYSTERY AND MELANCHOLY
OF A STREET.* 1914.
OIL ON CANVAS, $34^{1}/_{4}'' \times 28^{1}/_{2}''$.
PRIVATE COLLECTION.
© SIAE/VAGA, New York.
Photograph© Allan Mitchell.

GEORGES DE LA TOUR. *THE
PENITENT MAGDALEN.*" THE
METROPOLITAN MUSEUM OF
ART. GIFT OF MR. AND MRS.
CHARLES WRIGHTSMAN.
Reprinted by permission of the Met-
ropolitan Museum of Art 1978..517.

FELIX TRUTAT. *RECLINING BACCHANTE*. 1845. MUSÉE DES BEAUX-ARTS, DIJON.
Musée des Beaux-Arts de Dijon.

TIMOTHY O'SULLIVAN. *BATTLE OF GETTYSBURG*, 1863.
FEDERAL SOLDIERS, KILLED ON JULY 1, 1863, NEAR THE
MCPHERSON WOODS, GETTYSBURG, PENNSYLVANIA.
The Granger Collection, New York.

KEITH CARTER. *GARLIC, 1991.* PHOTOGRAPH.
© Keith Carter.

KEITH CARTER. *STARBALL, 1990.* PHOTOGRAPH.
© Keith Carter.

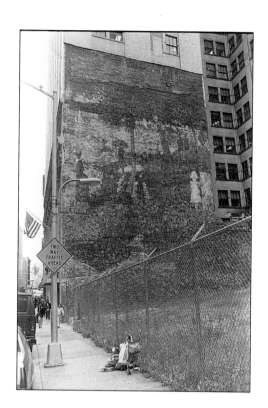

ANNA K. NORRIS.
FINANCIAL DISTRICT. 1998.
Anna K. Norris.

ANNA K. NORRIS. *SPECTATORS AT THE
AFRICAN-AMERICAN DAY PARADE.* HARLEM. 1998.
Anna K. Norris.

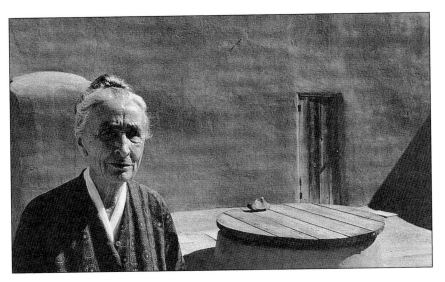

BASIL LANGTON. *GEORGIA O'KEEFFE.* 1971. IN PATIO
OF HER HOME, ABIQUIU, NEW MEXICO.

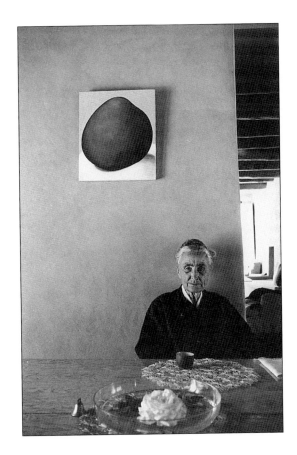

BASIL LANGTON.
GEORGIA O'KEEFFE. 1971.
AT HER HOME, ABIQUIU,
NEW MEXICO.

FLATIRON BUILDING. NEW YORK CITY.
Culver Pictures.

ACKNOWLEDGMENTS

Student essays are reprinted by permission of the authors.

Abbott, Lee K., "The True Story of Why I Do What I Do." Copyright © 1987 by Lee K. Abbott. Reprinted with permission of the author.

Anzaldua, Gloria, "How to Tame a Wild Tongue," from *Borderlands/LaFrontera: The New Mestiza* © 1987 by Gloria Anzaldua. Reprinted with permission from Aunt Lute Books.

Baldwin, James, "The Discovery of What It Means to Be an American," from *Nobody Knows My Name.* Beacon Press. Copyright © 1955, renewed 1983, by James Baldwin. Reprinted by permission of Beacon Press.

Berger, John, "Ways of Seeing: Men Looking at Women," chapter 3 from *Ways of Seeing* by John Berger. Copyright © 1972 by Penguin Books, Ltd. Used by permission of Viking Penguin, a division of Penguin Books, USA.

Brown, Rosellen, "Mojo," from *Mojo.* Rice University Press.

Brox, Jane, "Influenza 1918," from *Five Thousand Days Like This One* by Jane Brox. Copyright © 1999 by Jane Brox. Reprinted by permission of Beacon Press, Boston.

Canaday, John, "The Peale and Bellelli Families," from *What Is Art?: An Introduction to Painting, Sculpture, and Architecture.* Copyright © 1985. Reprinted by permission of McGraw-Hill College.

Cofer, Judith Ortiz, "Silent Dancing," from *Silent Dancing: A Partial Remembrance of a Puerto Rican Childhood,* by Judith Ortiz Cofer. Copyright © 1990 by Arte Publico Press. Reprinted with permission of the publisher.

Cooper, Bernard, "Burl's," from *Truth-Serum.* Copyright © 1996 by Bernard Cooper. Reprinted by permission of Houghton Mifflin Company and the author. All rights reserved.

Cronon, William, "The Trouble With Wilderness; or, Getting Back to the Wrong Nature" by William Cronon, from *Uncommon Ground: Toward Reinventing Nature,* edited by William Cronon. Copyright © 1995 by William Cronon. Reprinted by permission of W. W. Norton & Company, Inc.

Danto, Arthur C., "Gettysburg," copyright © 1988 by Arthur C. Danto. Reprinted by permission of Georges Borchardt, Inc. for the author. This essay originally appeared in *Grand Street.*

Didion, Joan, "Georgia O'Keefe," from *The White Album* by Joan Didion. Copyright © 1979 by Joan Didion. Reprinted by permission of the author.

Dillard, Annie, "Living Like Weasels," from *Teaching a Stone to Talk* by Annie Dillard. Copyright © 1982 by Annie Dillard. Reprinted by permission of HarperCollins Publishers, Inc.

Ehrlich, Gretel, "Looking for a Lost Dog," Copyright © 1995 by Gretel Ehrlich. Reprinted by permission of the author.

Eiseley, Loren, "The Dance of the Frogs," from *The Star Throwers*, by Loren Eiseley. Copyright © 1978 by the Estate of Loren C. Eiseley, Mabel L. Eiseley, Executrix. Reprinted by permission of Times Books, a division of Random House, Inc.

Forster, E.M., "Not Looking at Pictures," from *Two Cheers for Democracy*. Copyright © 1939 and renewed 1967 by E.M. Forster. Reprinted by permission of Harcourt Inc.

Fussell, Paul, "Indy," from *Thank God for the Atom Bomb and Other Essays*, by Paul Fussell, Summit Books. Reprinted by permission of the publisher.

Geller, Jaclyn, "The Celebrity Bride as Cultural Icon," from *On the Issues*: Summer, 1997. Reprinted by permission of the author.

George, Diana Hume, "Wounded Chevy at Wounded Knee," Copyright © 1996 Diane Hume George. Originally appeared in *The Missouri Review*. Reprinted in *The Lonely Other: A Woman Watching America (Essays)*, Diane Hume George, University of Illinois Press, 1996.

Gordon, Mary, "Mary Cassatt," from *Good Boys and Dead Girls*. Copyright © 1991 by Mary Gordon. Used by permission of Viking Penguin, a division of Penguin Books, USA.

Gould, Stephen Jay, "Women's Brains," reprinted from *The Panda's Thumb: More Reflections in Natural History* by Stephen Jay Gould, with the permission of W.W. Norton & Company, Inc. Copyright © 1980 by Stephen Jay Gould.

Grice, Gordon, "The Black Widow," from *High Plains Literary Review*. Copyright © 1996. Reprinted by permission of the author.

Hoy, Pat C., "War Elegy," from *The Sewanee Review*. Copyright © 1998. Reprinted by permission of the author.

Hughes, Langston, "Salvation," from *The Big Sea* by Langston Hughes. Copyright © 1940 by Langston Hughes. Copyright renewed © 1968 by Arna Bontemps and George Houston Bass. Reprinted by permission of Hill and Wang, a division of Farrar, Straus & Giroux, LLC.

Hurston, Zora Neale, "How It Feels to Be Colored Me," originally appeared in *The World Tomorrow*, in 1928. Copyright © Zora Neale Hurston. Reprinted by permission of Edgar Hurston.

Hynes, Samuel, "Flights of Fancy," quoted in Pat Hoy's *War Elegy*.

Jordan, June, "Many Rivers to Cross," from *On Call*. Copyright © 1985. Reprinted by permission of the author.

Kincaid, Jamaica, "On Seeing England for the First Time," originally published in *Transition*. Copyright © 1991. Reprinted by permission of Oxford University Press.

King, Martin Luther, Jr., "Letter from Birmingham Jail," reprinted by arrangement with The Heirs to the Estate of Martin Luther King, Jr., c/o Writers House, Inc. as agent for the proprietor. Copyright © 1963 by Martin Luther King, Jr., copyright renewed 1991 by Coretta Scott King.

Kingston, Maxine Hong, "No Name Woman," from *The Woman Warrior* by Maxine Hong Kingston. Copyright © 1976 by Maxine Hong Kingston. Reprinted by permission of Alfred A. Knopf, Inc.

Kingston, Maxine Hong, "Silence," from *The Woman Warrior* by Maxine Hong Kingston. Copyright © 1976 by Maxine Hong Kingston. Reprinted by permission of Alfred A. Knopf, Inc.

Kingston, Maxine Hong, "On Discovery," from *China Men* by Maxine Hong Kingston. Copyright © 1980 by Maxine Hong Kingston. Reprinted by permission of Alfred A. Knopf, Inc.

Kriegel, Leonard, "Falling into Life," from *Falling into Life* by Leonard Kriegel, 1991 North Point Press. Reprinted by permission of Leonard Kriegel. Copyright © 1988. This essay was originally published in *The American Scholar.*

Lopez, Barry, "The Stone Horse," reprinted by permission of Sterling Lord Literistic, Inc. Copyright by Barry Holstun Lopez, 1978, *Crossing Open Ground.*

Mairs, Nancy, "On Being a Cripple," from Nancy Mairs, "On Being a Cripple," in *Plaintext.* Reprinted by permission of The University of Arizona Press.

Morrison, Toni, "The Site of Memory," from *Inventing the Truth: The Art and Craft of Memoir,* edited by Zinsser. Copyright © 1994 by Toni Morrison. Permission granted by International Creative Management.

O'Brien, Tim, "How to Tell a True War Story," from *The Things They Carried.* Copyright © 1990 by Tim O'Brien. Reprinted by permission of Houghton Mifflin Co./Seymour Lawrence. All rights reserved.

Orwell, George, "Marrakech," from *Such, Such Were the Joys,* by George Orwell, copyright © 1953 by Sonia Brownwell Orwell and renewed 1981 by Mrs. George K. Perutz, Mrs. Miriam Gross, and Dr. Michael Dickson, Executors of the Estate of Sonia Brownwell Orwell.Reprinted by permission of Harcourt, Inc.

Orwell, George, "A Hanging," from *Such, Such Were the Joys,* by George Orwell. Copyright © 1953 by Sonia Brownwell Orwell and renewed 1982 by Mrs. George K. Perutz, Mrs. Miriam Gross, and Dr. Michael Dickson, Executors of the Estate of Sonia Brownwell Orwell. Reprinted by permission of Harcourt Brace & Company. This material is also Copyright © The Estate of the late Sonia Brownwell Orwell and Martin Secker and Warburg, Ltd.

Orwell, George, "Shooting an Elephant," from *Such, Such Were the Joys,* by George Orwell. Copyright © 1953 by Sonia Brownwell Orwell and renewed 1982 by Mrs. George K. Perutz, Mrs. Miriam Gross, and Dr. Michael Dickson, Executors of the Estate of Sonia Brownwell Orwell.Reprinted by permission of Harcourt Brace & Company. This material is also Copyright © The Estate of the late Sonia Brownwell Orwell and Martin Secker and Warburg, Ltd.

Ozick, Cynthia, "The Seam of the Snail," from *Metaphor and Memory.* Copyright © 1989 by Cynthia Ozick. Reprinted by permission of Alfred A. Knopf, Inc.

Pickering, Sam, "Patterns," from *May Days,* by Samuel F. Pickering, Jr. Copyright © 1988 by The University of Iowa Press. Reprinted by permission of The University of Iowa Press.

Reed, Roy, "Spring Comes to Hogeye," from *Looking for Hogeye.* Reprinted by permission of the University of Arkansas Press. Copyright © 1986 by Roy Reed.

Rodriguez, Richard, "Late Victorians," from *Harper's Magazine.* Copyright ©1991. Reprinted by permission of Georges Borchardt, Inc. for the author.

Rose, Phyllis, "Tools of Torture: An Essay on Beauty and Pain," Copyright ©1984 by Phyllis Rose. Reprinted by permission of The Wylie Agency, Inc.

Russell, Sharman Apt, "Homebirth," from *Songs of the Flute Player: Seasons of Life in the Southwest,* © 1991 Sharman Apt Russell. Reprinted by permission of Addison-Wesley Publishing Company, Inc.

Sanders, Scott Russell, "Wayland," from *Staying Put* by Scott Russell Sanders. Copyright © 1993 by Scott Russell Sanders. Reprinted by permission of Beacon Press, Boston.

Selzer, Richard, "A Mask on the Face of Death." Copyright © 1987 by Richard Selzer. Reprinted by permission of Georges Borchardt, Inc. for the author.

Shilts, Randy, "Talking AIDS to Death." this essay originally appeared in *Esquire*. Reprinted by permission of Fred Hill.

Silko, Leslie Marmon, "Landscape, History, and the Pueblo Imagination." Copyright © 1987 by Leslie Marmon Silko. Reprinted by permission of Wylie, Aitken & Stone, Inc.

Sontag, Susan, "AIDS and Its Metaphors," excerpts from *Aids and Its Metaphors* by Susan Sontag. Copyright © 1988, 1989 by Susan Sontag. Reprinted by permission of Farrar, Straus & Giroux.

Staples, Brent, "Just Walk on By: A Black Man Ponders His Power to Alter Public Space." Reprinted by permission of the author.

Strand, Mark, "Crossing the Tracks to Hopper's World," from *Antaeus*. Copyright © 1990. Reprinted by permission of the author.

Talbot, Margaret, "Les Tres Riches Heures de Martha Stewart," from *The New Republic*, May 13, 1996. Reprinted by permission of The New Republic, Inc.

Tan, Amy, "Mother Tongue," Copyright © 1990 by Amy Tan. First appeared in *The Three-Penny Review*. Reprinted by permission of the author and the Sandra Dijkstra Literary Agency.

Walker, Alice, "Beauty: When the Other Dancer Is the Self," from *In Search of Our Mothers' Gardens: Womanist Prose*. Copyright © 1983 by Alice Walker. Reprinted by permission of Harcourt Brace & Company.

West, Cornel, "Race Matters," from *Race Matters*, by Cornel West. Copyright © 1993, by Cornel West. Reprinted by permission of Beacon Press.

White, E.B., "Once More to the Lake," from *One Man's Meat*. Copyright © 1941 by E.B. White. Reprinted by permission of Tilbury House Publishers, Gardiner, Maine.

White, E.B., "The Ring of Time," from *The Points of My Compass* by E.B. White. Copyright © 1956 by E.B. White. Originally appeared in *The New Yorker*. Reprinted by permission of HarperCollins Publishers, Inc.

White, E.B., "The Geese," from *Essays of E.B. White* by E.B. White. Copyright © 1971 by E.B. White. Originally appeared in *The New Yorker*. Reprinted by permission of HarperCollins Publishers, Inc.

Wolfe, Tom, "The Right Stuff," from *The Right Stuff*, by Tom Wolfe. Copyright © 1979 by Tom Wolfe. Reprinted by permission of Farrar, Straus & Giroux.

Woolf, Virginia, "Old Mrs. Grey," from *The Death of the Moth and Other Essays* by Virginia Woolf. Copyright © 1942 by Harcourt, Inc. and renewed 1970 by Marjorie T. Parsons, Executrix. Reprinted by permission of the publisher.

INDEX